T0337941

Print ISSN 0020-6598, Online ISSN 1468-2354

INTERNATIONAL ECONOMIC REVIEW

Blackwell Publishing, Inc.
350 Main Street
Malden, MA 02148

Blackwell Publishing, Ltd.
108 Cowley Road
Oxford OX4 1JF
United Kingdom

Library of Congress Cataloging-in-Publication Data

Economics to econometrics : contributions in honor of Daniel L. McFadden/Randall Wright, editor; Charles F. Manski and Whitney Newey, special guest editors.
    p. cm.
Includes bibliographical references.
ISBN 978-1-4051-8033-7
    1. Econometrics. 2. Economics. 3. McFadden, Daniel. I. McFadden, Daniel. II. Wright, Randall. III. Manski, Charles F. IV. Newey, Whitney K.
    HB139.E345 2007
    330.01'5195–dc22

                                                                    2007050332

ISBN: 978-1-4051-8033-7

ECONOMICS TO ECONOMETRICS:
Contributions in Honor of
Daniel L. McFadden

Randall Wright, Editor
Charles F. Manski and Whitney Newey,
Special Guest Editors

Pictured, left to right – top row: Jerry Hausman, Tom Stoker, Joel Horowitz, Rosa Matzkin, Jim Heckman, Ken Wolpin, Arthur Lewbel; second row: Steve Cosslett, Mike Keane, Hide Ichimura; third row: Tulin Erdem, Ariel Pakes; fourth row: Whitney Newey, Chuck Manski, Guido Imbens, Jim Powell; fifth row: Dan McFadden, Paul Ruud, Li Gan, Richard Blundell; bottom row: Christine Pinto, Paul Chen, Kostantinos Hatzitasksos, Byung-hill Jun, Richard Crump

INTERNATIONAL
ECONOMIC
REVIEW

November 2007

Vol. 48, No. 4

ECONOMICS TO ECONOMETRICS: IN HONOR
OF DANIEL L. McFADDEN*

BY CHARLES F. MANSKI AND WHITNEY K. NEWEY

Northwestern University, U.S.A.; Massachusetts Institute of Technology, U.S.A.

In 1968 Daniel McFadden circulated a working paper on "Revealed Preferences of a Government Bureaucracy." In this empirical study of the decision making of the California Highway Commission, Dan first put forward the set of ideas that developed into the modern econometric analysis of discrete choice. In the early 1970s, Dan deepened and refined his ideas as he performed an influential empirical study of household travel decisions, eventually published as the book *Urban Travel Demand: A Behavioral Analysis*. At the same time, he abstracted from particular empirical questions to consider in generality the problem of econometric inference on individual behavior. The result was his classic contribution to econometric theory "Conditional Logit Analysis of Qualitative Choice Behavior," published in 1974.

Discrete choice analysis has become so much a part of the fabric of modern economics that it may be difficult now to recall how revolutionary Dan's ideas were at the time. The economic conceptualization of decision making as maximization of utility subject to constraints has exceedingly broad potential application. However, empirical economic research prior to Dan's work was largely concerned with the limited class of decision problems envisioned in classical consumer demand theory, where the objects of choice are bundles of homogeneous and infinitely divisible goods available to consumers at given prices per unit. To the extent that choice problems with other characteristics were examined, the prevailing practice was to shoehorn them into the classical framework. Thus one would find studies of "travel demand" or the "demand for education" or the "demand for consumer durables."

The econometric analysis of discrete choice developed by Dan provided an appropriate framework for the empirical analysis of choice among finite sets of alternatives, each alternative being characterized as a bundle of attributes. The close coordination between development of econometric theory in the "Conditional Logit" article and its application to empirical problems of substantive importance has been emblematic of Dan's research throughout his career. Theoretical

---

* Manuscript received May 2007.

development and empirical application nurture each other, yielding contributions of greater significance than would each in isolation.

From the early 1970s onward, discrete choice analysis has deepened and broadened as econometricians and empirical researchers have joined Dan in generalizing the theory and applying it to a wide range of applications. An important objective of Dan's methodological research has been to loosen the behavioral restrictions of the conditional logit model while maintaining computational tractability. One stream of this work culminated in his development in the late 1970s of the *generalized extreme value* model. Another began in the 1970s with early research on random-coefficients discrete choice models and eventually led in the 1990s to his research with Ken Train on models of the *mixed logit* form. Computation of estimates of such models has been eased through Dan's development in the mid-1980s of the *method of simulated moments*.

Throughout his career, Dan's research has emphasized the application of discrete choice analysis. His research in the first half of the 1980s focused on residential energy choices and then shifted to the demand for residential telephone service and the housing choices of the elderly. The work on energy choices yielded an important methodological contribution on the analysis of choice problems having both discrete and continuous components. The resulting article, co-authored with Jeff Dubin, was awarded the Econometric Society's Frisch Medal in 1986. Dan' work has, of course, been honored in other ways as well, from his receipt of the John Bates Clark Medal in 1975 and his election to the National Academy of Sciences in 1981 through his receipt of the Nemmers Prize in Economics and the Nobel Memorial Prize in Economics, both in 2000.

The original research articles collected in this issue continue the development of discrete choice analysis, of related structural models for analysis of choice behavior, and of the statistical theory used in inference on these models. Most articles in the issue are revised versions of ones presented at a conference in Dan's honor at the University of California, Berkeley on May 6–7, 2005. We think that the best way to honor Dan, more than any prize, is to make new contributions that build on his insights. This is the aim of the research reported here.

INTERNATIONAL ECONOMIC REVIEW
Vol. 48, No. 4, November 2007

SEMINONPARAMETRIC MAXIMUM LIKELIHOOD ESTIMATION OF CONDITIONAL MOMENT RESTRICTION MODELS*

By Chunrong Ai[1]

University of Florida, U.S.A., and Shanghai University of Finance and Economics, China

This article studies estimation of a conditional moment restriction model with the seminonparametric maximum likelihood approach proposed by Gallant and Nychka (*Econometrica* 55 (March 1987), 363–90). Under some sufficient conditions, we show that the estimator of the finite dimensional parameter θ is asymptotically normally distributed and attains the semiparametric efficiency bound and that the estimator of the density function is consistent under L_2 norm. Some results on the convergence rate of the estimated density function are derived. An easy to compute covariance matrix for the asymptotic covariance of the θ estimator is presented.

1. INTRODUCTION

The moment restriction model is often the model of choice for analyzing economic data. And the Generalized Method of Moment estimation (hereafter GMM) proposed by Hansen (1982) is often the method of choice for estimating the moment restriction model. Under some sufficient conditions, Hansen (1982) shows that the GMM estimator is asymptotically normally distributed and that the optimally weighted GMM estimator is efficient for the unconditional moment restriction model. Newey (1990) extends Hansen's work to the conditional moment restriction model by showing that some optimally weighted version of the GMM estimator attains the semiparametric efficiency bound derived by Chamberlain (1992). Despite of its popularity and desirable large sample properties, it has been documented that the optimally weighted GMM estimator for the unconditional moment restriction model has poor finite sample performance (see Altonji and Segal, 1996, for an example). Although no formal arguments have been made, it is widely expected that Newey's weighted version of GMM estimator for the conditional moment restriction model may also have poor finite sample performance. Thus, it is imperative to find alternative estimators that are asymptotically as efficient as the optimally weighted GMM estimators but have better finite sample performance. Recently, the empirical likelihood estimation has been suggested as such an alternative. Owen (1990, 1991), Kitamura and Stutzer (1997), Qin and

* Manuscript received August 2005; revised August 2006.

[1] I am grateful to two anonymous referees and Whitney Newey for useful comments that improve the article substantially. Please address correspondence to: Chunrong Ai, Department of Economics, University of Florida, Gainesville, FL 32611, USA. Phone: 352-392-7895. Fax: 352-392-7880. E-mail: *chunrong.ai@cba.ufl.edu*.

Lawless (1994), Imbens (1997), Imbens et al. (1998), and Newey and Smith (2004) propose empirical likelihood estimation for the unconditional moment restriction model, whereas Kitamura et al. (2004) and Donald et al. (2003) study the empirical likelihood estimation of the conditional moment restriction model. Indeed, Newey and Smith (2004) show that, for the unconditional moment restriction model, the empirical likelihood estimator has better second order properties than the optimally weighted GMM estimator. It remains to be seen whether the same result holds for the conditional moment restriction model.

Another alternative to the GMM estimation is the seminonparametric maximum likelihood (hereafter SNP) estimation proposed by Gallant and Nychka (1987) and Gallant and Tauchen (1989).[2] Surprisingly, this alternative has received little attention from the literature. One possible explanation for the lack of attention is that the large sample properties of the SNP estimator have not been completely established.[3] Gallant and Nychka (1987), Fenton and Gallant (1996a, 1996b), and Coppejans and Gallant (2002) only prove consistency of the SNP density estimator. The asymptotic distribution of the SNP estimator of the finite dimensional parameter, for example, has not been derived. The main objective of this article is to derive the asymptotic distribution of the SNP estimator of the finite dimensional parameter.

There are several reasons to suspect that the SNP estimator may have better higher order properties than the empirical likelihood estimator. To elaborate, consider the following conditional moment restriction model

$$(1) \qquad E\{\rho(Y, X, \theta_o) \mid X\} = 0,$$

where $Z = (Y, X) \in \mathcal{Y} \times \mathcal{X} = \mathcal{Z}$ denotes data and ρ is a vector of functions known up to a finite dimensional unknown parameter θ_0. Throughout the article, we will always use capital letters to denote random variables and lowercase letters to denote their realizations. Let $f_0(y \mid x)$ denote the true conditional density of Y given X, and let $f(y \mid x)$ denote any density function that satisfies the moment restriction for arbitrary θ:

$$(2) \qquad \int \rho(y, x, \theta) f(y \mid x) \, dy = 0, \quad f(y \mid x) > 0, \quad \int f(y \mid x) \, dy = 1.$$

Then the true value $(\theta_0, f_0(y \mid x))$ solves

$$(3) \qquad \max_{f(.) \in \mathcal{F}, \theta \in \Theta} E\{\ln(f(Y \mid X))\} \text{ subject to}$$

$$\int \rho(y, x, \theta) f(y \mid x) \, dy = 0, \quad f(y \mid x) > 0, \quad \int f(y \mid x) \, dy = 1,$$

---

[2] Hall and Horowitz (1996) suggest using bootstrapped distribution instead of the asymptotic distribution of the GMM estimator. For applications of SNP estimator, see Hall (1990), Brunner (1992), Davidian and Gallant (1993), Gallant et al. (1992), Ai (1997), and Gabler et al. (1993).

[3] Other explanations are (i) the SNP estimator is difficult to compute and (ii) the SNP estimator is sensitive to the number of the approximating terms in the density approximation. See Gallant and Tauchen (1996) for further discussion on this issue and Eastwood and Gallant (1991) for discussion on order selection in the SNP estimation.

where Θ denotes the parameter space of θ and $\mathcal{F}$ denotes the density function space that contains the true density $f_0(y \mid x)$. The model is identified if and only if the true value is the unique solution to the above optimization problem. The SNP procedure proposed in Gallant and Nychka (1987) and Gallant and Tauchen (1989) is to use a parametric approximation, say $f_k(y \mid x, \theta, \beta_k)$, that always satisfies the restrictions (2) and converges to some density function in $\mathcal{F}$ as k goes to infinity, and then to estimate the parameters by maximizing the sample log likelihood function:

$$(\hat{\theta}, \hat{\beta}_K) = \arg\max_{\theta, \beta_K} \sum_{i=1}^n \ln \left[f_k(y_i \mid x_i, \theta, \beta_k) \right],$$

where $\{(y_i, x_i), i = 1, 2, \ldots, n\}$ denotes a random sample.

Now, consider the following less restrictive problem:

(4) $$\max_{f(.) \in \mathcal{F}, \theta \in \Theta} E\{\ln(f(Y \mid X))\} \text{ subject to}$$

$$\int \rho(y, x, \theta) f(y \mid x) \, dy = 0, \quad \int f(y \mid x) \, dy = 1.$$

Problem (4) is same as problem (3) except that the positive restriction on density function is dropped. Let $\lambda(x)$ denote the Lagrange multiplier associated with the moment restriction and let $\mu(x)$ denote the multiplier associated with the density restriction. Then, the Lagrangian for problem (4) is

$L(\theta, f, \lambda, \mu)$

$$= E\left\{ \int (\ln(f(y \mid X)) f_0(y \mid X) - \lambda(X)' \rho(y, X, \theta) f(y \mid X) - \mu(X) f(y \mid X)) \, dy \right\},$$

where the expectation is taken with respect to the true density of X. The true value $(\theta_0, f_0(y \mid x), \lambda_0(x), \mu_0(x))$ solves

$$(\theta_0, f_0(y \mid x), \lambda_0(x), \mu_0(x)) = \arg \min_{\lambda(.), \mu(.)} \max_{f(.) \in \mathcal{F}, \theta \in \Theta} L(\theta, f, \lambda, \mu).$$

For arbitrary θ, $\lambda(.)$ and $\mu(.)$, let $f(y \mid x, \theta, \lambda, \mu)$ denote the solution to

$$f(y \mid x, \theta, \lambda, \mu) = \arg \max_{f(.) \in \mathcal{F}} L(\theta, f, \lambda, \mu).$$

Applying calculus of variation, we obtain

$$f(y \mid x, \theta, \lambda, \mu) = \frac{f_0(y \mid x)}{\mu(x) + \lambda(x)' \rho(y, x, \theta)}.$$

Applying the constraints $\int f(y\,|\,x)\,dy = 1$ and $\int \rho(y, x, \theta)f(y\,|\,x)\,dy = 0$, we obtain $\mu(x) = 1$ and

$$(5) \qquad\qquad f(y\,|\,x, \theta, \lambda, 1) = \frac{f_0(y\,|\,x)}{1 + \lambda(x)'\rho(y, x, \theta)}.$$

Substituting the solution back into the log likelihood function we obtain

$$E\{\ln(f(Y\,|\,X, \theta, \lambda, 1))\} = E\left\{\ln\left(\frac{1}{1 + \lambda(X)'\rho(Y, X, \theta)}\right)\right\} - E\{\ln(f_0(Y\,|\,X))\}.$$

Note that the second term on the right-hand side is a constant independent of the parameters. The true value $(\theta_0, \lambda_0(x))$ solves

$$(\theta_0, \lambda_0(x)) = \arg\min_{\lambda(.)}\max_{\theta\in\Theta} E\left\{\ln\left(\frac{1}{1 + \lambda(X)'\rho(Y, X, \theta)}\right)\right\}.$$

The empirical likelihood procedure implements the sample version of the above optimization problem with $\lambda(.)$ replaced by some parametric approximation such as sieve approximation $\lambda_k(x, \beta_k)$:

$$(\hat{\theta}, \hat{\beta}_k) = \arg\min_{\beta_k}\max_{\theta\in\Theta} \sum_{i=1}^{n} \ln\left(\frac{1}{1 + \lambda_k(x_i, \beta_k)'\rho(y_i, x_i, \theta)}\right).$$

Clearly, the empirical likelihood procedure can be interpreted as the profile Lagrangian approach, where the unknown density function is concentrated out.

There are at least four differences between the SNP and the empirical likelihood procedure. The first and the most obvious difference is that problem (4) does not impose the restriction $f(y\,|\,x) > 0$. As a result, the solution $f(y\,|\,x, \theta, \lambda, 1)$ is not guaranteed to be positive everywhere. For example, when $\rho(y, x, \theta)$ is unbounded, ranging from $-\infty$ to $+\infty$, $f(y\,|\,x, \theta, \lambda, 1)$ takes negative values for some large y unless $\lambda(x) = 0$. But if we set $\lambda(x) = 0$, the parameter θ disappears from the criterion function and consequently cannot be estimated by the empirical likelihood approach. The second difference is that, for arbitrary θ and $\lambda(.)$, $f(y\,|\,x, \theta, \lambda, 1)$ does not necessarily satisfy the density restriction $\int f(y\,|\,x, \theta, \lambda, 1)\,dy = 1$ and the moment restriction $\int \rho(y, x, \theta)f(y\,|\,x, \theta, \lambda, 1)\,dy = 0$ except for when

$$\lambda(x) = \lambda(x, \theta) = \arg\min_{\lambda(.)} E\left\{\ln\left(\frac{1}{1 + \lambda(X)'\rho(Y, X, \theta)}\right)\right\}.$$

Hence, $f(y\,|\,x, \theta, \lambda, 1)$ is not necessarily a density function and does not necessarily satisfy the moment restriction. In contrast, the SNP procedure always imposes the density and the moment restriction. One would expect that imposition of these restrictions may help (at least not hurt) the finite sample performance of the SNP estimator. The third difference is that the empirical likelihood procedure does not estimate the density function, whereas the SNP procedure estimates the density function directly. The density estimator allows us to compute other interesting estimates such as quantiles. The fourth and the last difference is that, in some applications, the empirical likelihood function is not differentiable whereas the SNP likelihood function is differentiable. To see this difference, consider a simple example of quantile regression with $x = 1$ and $\rho(y, x, \theta) = 1\{y < \theta\} - 1\{y > \theta\}$. $\rho(y, x, \theta)$ is obviously not differentiable at $\theta = y$. Hence, the empirical likelihood function $\ln(\frac{1}{1+\lambda(x)'\rho(y,x,\theta)})$ is not differentiable at $\theta = y$. On the other hand, the SNP estimation smoothes the moment function by integration:

$$\int \rho(y, x, \theta)\, dy = \int^{\theta} f(y)\, dy - \int_{\theta} f(y)\, dy = 0,$$

where $f(y)$ denotes the density function of Y. The left-hand side of the above moment restriction is differentiable everywhere. The differentiability is a desirable property that should help both estimation and finite sample performance of the estimator.

Despite these advantages, there are at least two criticisms that can be raised against the SNP estimation. The first is that the analytical expressions for the integrations $\int \rho(y, x, \theta) f(y \mid x)\, dy$ and $\int f(y \mid x)\, dy$ in most applications do not exist. Although in many applications these integrations can be computed with numerical methods, they may require high dimensional integration that is beyond the capacity of the current computing technology. This criticism is addressed here with simulation technique. The simulation technique replaces the numerical integration with a simulated integration. The simulated integration undoubtedly is going to have an effect on the second order properties of the SNP estimator. But the effect can be kept small and negligible by using a large number of simulation draws. The second criticism is that, since the unknown density function is approximated by sieve, the approximation error may have an effect on the SNP estimator of θ. Although the sufficient conditions we present below ensure that the approximation error does not affect the first order properties of the SNP estimator, the approximation error may affect the higher order properties of the SNP estimator. Exactly how the higher order properties are affected, however, is not investigated here and will be pursued in a separate paper.

The outline of the article is as follows: Section 2 formally introduces the SNP procedure, Section 3 proves the consistency of the SNP estimator, Section 4 derives the asymptotic distribution of the SNP estimator of θ, Section 5 provides a consistent covariance estimator for the θ estimator, and Section 6 concludes. Technical derivations are relegated to an Appendix.

2. SNP ESTIMATOR

Throughout the article, we assume that $\{z_i = (y_i, x_i), i = 1, 2, \ldots, n\}$ is a sample of observations on $Z = (Y, X)$, drawn from the joint density $f_0(y \mid x) f_0(x)$, where $f_0(x)$ is the marginal density of X. The joint density is unknown but satisfies the moment restriction (1) for some true value θ_0. Our primary interest is the estimation of $(\theta_0, f_0(y \mid x))$ through empirically implementing (3).

There are two difficulties with implementation of (3). The first is that the unknown density function is infinite dimensional and it is impossible to estimate it from finite data points. The second is that the density and moment restriction on the infinite dimensional parameter (i.e., density function) are highly nonlinear and difficult to impose. To overcome these difficulties, Gallant and Nychka (1987) propose a series approximation to the unknown density function. To describe their approach, let $g(y \mid x)$ denote some known conditional density function with unbounded support and let $q(u)$ denote some known and positive transformation function that is monotone over $[0, +\infty)$. The density function $g(y \mid x)$ is practitioner's initial guess of the true density function. $g(y \mid x)$ also plays the role of weighting function, ensuring that integration of some unbounded functions such as power functions over unbounded support exists. Obviously, $g(y \mid x)$ should be chosen as close to the true density as possible. But, given that the true density is unknown, this may be an impossible task. We suggest that one should choose $g(y \mid x)$ so that $\frac{f_0(y \mid x)}{g(y \mid x)}$ is bounded, if not constant. The primary reason for this suggestion is that it is easier to approximate a bounded function than an unbounded function. The function $g(y \mid x)$ may depend on some other parameters. Gallant and Nychka (1987), for example, choose $g(y \mid x)$ to be the normal density function with unknown mean and variance. Adding additional parameters to $g(y \mid x)$ only complicates notation with no additional insight. So, to simplify exposition, we assume that $g(y \mid x)$ is known. The transformation function q is introduced to ensure that the density function is positive everywhere. In addition, q is chosen so that $q^{-1}\left(\frac{f_0(y \mid x)}{g(y \mid x)}\right)$ has a series expansion:

$$q^{-1}\left(\frac{f_0(y \mid x)}{g(y \mid x)}\right) = p(y)' \pi_0(x),$$

where $p(y) = (p_1(y), p_2(y), \ldots)'$ denote the known series basis functions and $\pi_0(x) = (\pi_{01}(x), \pi_{02}(x), \ldots)'$ denote the expansion coefficients which are obviously functions of x. The true conditional density is now expressed as

$$f_0(y \mid x) = q\big(p(y)' \pi_0(x)\big) g(y \mid x).$$

Common choice of q includes the power function $q(u) = u^2 + c_n$ with c_n a known and small constant possibly depending on the sample size, the exponential function $q(u) = \exp(u)$, and any other positive function that is invertible over $[0, +\infty)$. Common choice of series basis functions includes power functions, wavelets, and B-splines.

Write $p(y) = (p^1(y)', p^2(y)')'$ and write $\pi_0(x) = (\pi_0^1(x), \pi_0^2(x))'$ accordingly. For arbitrary coefficients $\pi(x) = (\pi_1(x), \pi_2(x), \ldots)'$, decompose $\pi(x)$ accordingly and write

$$p(y)' \pi(x) = p^1(y)' \pi^1(x) + p^2(y)' \pi^2(x) = p^1(y)' \pi^1(x) + h(y, x).$$

Then the true values of $\pi^1(x)$ and $\pi^2(x)$ are $\pi_0^1(x)$ and $\pi_0^2(x)$, respectively, and the true value of $h(y, x)$ is $h_0(y, x) = p^2(y)'\pi_0^2(x)$. Denote

$$f(y \mid x) = q(p^1(y)'\pi^1(x) + h(y, x))g(y \mid x).$$

Let $\Lambda^\gamma(\mathcal{Z})$ denote a Hölder space (see Ai and Chen, 2003, for an exact definition of the Hölder space). The Hölder space is a space of functions with up to γth derivatives. Suppose that $h(\cdot)$ is restricted to

$$\mathcal{H} = \left\{ \begin{array}{c} p^2(y)'\pi^2(x) : p^2(y)'\pi^2(x) \in \Lambda^\gamma(\mathcal{Z}) \text{ and} \\ \|p^2(y)'\pi^2(x)\|_{\infty,\mu} = \sup_{y,x}\{|p^2(y)'\pi^2(x)| \times \mu(y, x)\} \le C \end{array} \right\},$$

where $\mu(y, x)$ is a known weighting function. Denote

$$\mathcal{F} = \{q(p^1(y)'\pi^1(x) + h(y, x))g(y \mid x) : h \in \mathcal{H}\}.$$

For arbitrary $h(y, x)$ and θ, let $\pi^1(x, \theta, h)$ denote the unique solution to

(6) $$\int \rho(y, x, \theta)q(p^1(y)'\pi^1(x) + h(y, x))g(y \mid x) \, dy = 0,$$

(7) $$\int q(p^1(y)'\pi^1(x) + h(y, x))g(y \mid x) \, dy = 1.$$

Then $q(p^1(y)'\pi^1(x, \theta, h) + h(y, x))g(y \mid x)$ satisfies the moment and density restriction for arbitrary θ and h. The constrained optimization problem (3) can now be rewritten as the following unconstrained problem:

(8) $$\max_{h \in \mathcal{H}, \theta \in \Theta} E\{\ln[q(p^1(Y)'\pi^1(X, \theta, h) + h(Z))]\}.$$

Let $\{a_1(x), a_2(x), \ldots\}$ denote the known series functions that can approximate any square-integrable function of x arbitrarily well. For some integers K_1 and K_2, denote

$$B^K(y, x) = (b_1(y, x), b_2(y, x), \ldots, b_K(y, x))'$$
$$= (a_1(x), a_2(x), \ldots, a_{K_1}(x))' \otimes (p_1^2(y), \ldots, p_{K_2}^2(y))',$$

where $\otimes$ is the Kronecker product. $B^K(y, x)$ is a vector of known series functions that can approximate any function $h \in \mathcal{H}$ arbitrarily well in the sense that $\|h(y, x) - B^K(y, x)'\beta_K\|_\infty \to 0$ as $K \to +\infty$ for some coefficients β_K. Denote $h_K(y, x) = B^K(y, x)'\beta_K$. Then the parametric approximation to the density function is

$$f_k(y \mid x, \theta, \beta_k) = q(p^1(y)'\pi^1(x, \theta, B^K(y, x)'\beta_K) + B^K(y, x)'\beta_K)g(y \mid x)$$

and the SNP estimator is

$$(\hat{\theta}, \hat{\beta}_K) = \arg\max_{\theta, \beta_K} \sum_{i=1}^{n} \ln\left[f_k(y_i \mid x_i, \theta, \beta_k) \right].$$

The SNP estimator for the density function is $f_k(y \mid x, \hat{\theta}, \hat{\beta}_k)$. Our main objective is to derive the asymptotic distribution of $\hat{\theta}$ and prove consistency of $f_k(y \mid x, \hat{\theta}, \hat{\beta}_k)$.

Notice that the SNP estimation requires integration with respect to the endogenous variables y. In many applications, y has low dimension. In those applications, the integration can be computed with a numerical method (see, e.g., Gallant and Nychka, 1987; Gallant and Tauchen, 1989). In some other applications, the SNP estimation requires high dimensional integration that cannot be computed accurately with a numerical method. In those applications, we replace the analytical integration by simulated integration with simulation draws from the density $g(y \mid x)$. Specifically, let $\{y^{ir}, r = 1, 2, \ldots, R\}$ denote independent simulation draws from the conditional density $g(y \mid x_i)$ for each x_i. The moment and density restrictions are now replaced by

$$\frac{1}{R} \sum_{r=1}^{R} p(y^{ir}, x_i, \theta) q\left(p(y^{ir})' \tilde{\pi}^1(x_i, \theta, h) + h(y^{ir}, x_i)\right) = 0,$$

$$\frac{1}{R} \sum_{r=1}^{R} q\left(p(y^{ir})' \tilde{\pi}^1(x_i, \theta, h) + h(y^{ir}, x_i)\right) = 1,$$

where $\tilde{\pi}^1(x_i, \theta, h)$ denotes the unique solution to the above equations system. The simulated density approximation is

$$\tilde{f}_k(y \mid x, \theta, \beta_k) = q\left(p^1(y)' \tilde{\pi}^1(x, \theta, B^K(y, x)' \beta_K) + B^K(y, x)' \beta_K\right) g(y \mid x).$$

The simulated SNP estimator is defined as

$$(\tilde{\theta}, \tilde{\beta}_K) = \arg\max_{\theta, \beta_K} \sum_{i=1}^{n} \ln[\tilde{f}_k(y_i \mid x_i, \theta, \beta_k)].$$

The simulated SNP estimator for the density function is $\tilde{f}_k(y \mid x, \tilde{\theta}, \tilde{\beta}_k)$.

It is worth noting that the above simulation approach requires $R * n$ simulation draws, which can be very large even for a moderate sample size and require large memory space to store them. To reduce the number of simulations and consequently to conserve memory usage, one can replace $g(y \mid x)$ with unconditional density function $g(y)$. With the unconditional density $g(y)$, we only need to generate a fixed simulation draws $\{y^r, r = 1, 2, \ldots, R\}$ from the density $g(y)$ for all of the observations and solve $\tilde{\pi}^1(x, \theta, h)$ from the following equations:

(9)
$$\frac{1}{R}\sum_{r=1}^{R}\rho(y^r, x, \theta)q(p(y^r)'\tilde{\pi}^1(x, \theta, h) + h(y^r, x)) = 0,$$

(10)
$$\frac{1}{R}\sum_{r=1}^{R}q(p(y^r)'\tilde{\pi}^1(x_i, \theta, h) + h(y^r, x)) = 1.$$

Asymptotically, both the conditional and the unconditional simulations have no effects on the proposed estimator as long as the number of simulations R is sufficiently large.

In the following sections, we derive the asymptotic distribution of $\hat{\theta}$ for the case $q(u) = \exp(u)$ and of $\tilde{\theta}$ for cases (9) and (10). Our main results are

$$\sup_{x,y}\{|f_k(y \mid x, \hat{\theta}, \hat{\beta}_k) - f_0(y \mid x)|\} = o_p(n^{-1/4}),$$

$$\sup_{x,y}\{|\tilde{f}_k(y \mid x, \tilde{\theta}, \tilde{\beta}_k) - f_0(y \mid x)|\} = o_p(n^{-1/4}),$$

$$\sqrt{n}(\hat{\theta}_n - \theta_0) \Longrightarrow N(0, V_0^{-1}),$$

$$\sqrt{n}(\tilde{\theta}_n - \theta_0) \Longrightarrow N(0, V_0^{-1}),$$

where V_0^{-1} is the semiparametric efficiency bound of θ_0, derived by Chamberlain (1992).

3. CONSISTENCY

For the remainder of the article, we will use $E\{\cdot\}$ to denote the expectation taken with respect to the true density and use $E_f\{\cdot\}$ to denote the expectation taken with respect to the density f. Denote $\mathcal{A} = \Theta \times \mathcal{H}$ and denote $\alpha = (\theta, h)$ with $\alpha_0 = (\theta_0, h_0)$. Let $\|\cdot\|_s$ denote the pseudo metric given by

$$\|\alpha - \alpha_0\|_s = \max_{1 \le j \le d_\theta} |\theta_j - \theta_{j0}| + \sup_{y,x} |h(y, x) - h_0(y, x)|,$$

where d_θ denotes the dimension of θ. First, we present sufficient conditions and prove consistency of the proposed estimator under the pseudo metric. The first condition is on the manner the sample is generated.

ASSUMPTION 1. $\{(y_i, x_i), i = 1, 2, \ldots, n\}$ *is an independent sample drawn from the joint density* $f_0(y \mid x) f_0(x)$. *The joint density* $f_0(y \mid x) f_0(x)$ *is unknown but satisfies (1).*

This condition is clearly restrictive since it rules out dependent data. However, our main results can be easily extended to weakly dependent data using the technique developed in Chen and Shen (1998). The next set of conditions identify the true value of the model parameters θ_0 and $h_0(y, x)$.

ASSUMPTION 2. *The true value θ_0 is the only value that satisfies (1). The true density $f_0(y \mid x)$ is the only solution to* $\sup_{f(\cdot) \in \mathcal{F}} E\{\ln(f(Y \mid X))\}$.

ASSUMPTION 3. *The series basis functions $p(y)$ are chosen such that*

$$p(y)'\pi(x) = p(y)'\pi_0(x)$$

for all y, x if and only if $\pi(x) = \pi_0(x)$.

Assumption 2 identifies the true values θ_0 and $f_0(y \mid x)$. This condition together with Assumption 3 identifies θ_0 and $h_0(y, x)$. Assumption 3 requires that the approximating functions $p(y)$ are linearly independent. This condition is satisfied, for example, if the approximating functions are orthonormal conditional on X. If the approximating functions are not orthonormal, it is common practice to require that the minimum eigenvalue of $E\{p_{KK}(Y)p_{KK}(Y)' \mid X = x\}$ is bounded away from zero for all K and x, where $p_{KK}(y) = (p_1(y), p_2(y), \ldots, p_K(y))'$ (see Newey, 1997, for an example). Hence, it is always possible to transform the basis functions $p(y)$ so that $p(y)'\pi(x) = \bar{p}(y, x)'\bar{\pi}(x)$ and $E\{\bar{p}^1(Y, x)\bar{p}^2(Y, x)' \mid X = x\} = 0$ hold, where $\bar{p}(y, x)' = (\bar{p}^1(y, x), \bar{p}^2(y, x))$. We notice that the transformed basis functions $\bar{p}(y, x)$ may depend on x. But adding the x argument to the basis functions will not change any of our proofs. Thus, to keep exposition simple and without loss of generality, we will assume $E\{p^1(Y)p^2(Y)' \mid X\} = 0$ holds for the remainder of the article.

Denote $\mathcal{A}_k = \Theta \times \mathcal{H}_k$ with $\mathcal{H}_k = \{h_K(y, x) = B^K(y, x)'\beta_K : h_K(y, x) \in \mathcal{H}\}$ as the sieve space. Obviously, the sieve spaces satisfy: $\mathcal{H}_1 \subset \mathcal{H}_2 \subset \cdots$. Denote $\tilde{\rho}(z, \theta) = (\rho(z, \theta)', 1)'$. Let $N(\varepsilon, \mathcal{A}_k, \|\cdot\|_s)$ denote the number of covering balls with radius ε that cover the sieve space $\mathcal{A}_k$. The number of covering ball measures the size of $\mathcal{A}_k$.

ASSUMPTION 4. *The closure of $\mathcal{A}$ with respect to $\|\alpha\|_s$ is compact in the relative topology generated by $\|\alpha\|_s$.*

ASSUMPTION 5. *$\mathcal{X}$ is compact and the density function of X is bounded and bounded away from zero.*

ASSUMPTION 6. *(i) For any $x \in \mathcal{X}, \theta \in \Theta$, and $h \in \mathcal{H}, \pi^1(x, \theta, h)$ is the unique solution to (6) and (7); (ii) the largest and the smallest eigenvalues of*

$$E_f\{p^1(Y)\tilde{\rho}(Z, \theta)' \mid X = x\} \times E_f\{\tilde{\rho}(Z, \theta)p^1(Y)' \mid X = x\}$$

are uniformly bounded and bounded away from zero over $x \in \mathcal{X}, \theta \in \Theta$, and $f \in \mathcal{F}$; (iii) $E_f\{\rho(Z, \theta) \mid X = x\}$ is continuously differentiable with respect to θ; and (iv) $E_f\{\rho(Z, \theta) \mid X = x\}$ and $E_f\{\rho(Z, \theta)'\rho(Z, \theta) \mid X = x\}$ are continuous in (x, θ).

ASSUMPTION 7. $E\{|p^1(Y)|^\gamma\} < +\infty$ and $E\{\mu(Z)^{-\gamma}\} < +\infty$ for some $\gamma > 2$.

ASSUMPTION 8. $\ln(N(\varepsilon, \mathcal{A}_k, \|\cdot\|_s) \le const \times K \times \ln(K/\varepsilon)$.

ASSUMPTION 9. (i) $\cup_{k=1}^\infty \mathcal{A}_k$ is dense in the closure of $\mathcal{A}$ with respect to $\|\alpha\|_s$; (ii) $K = O(n^\nu)$ for some $0 < \nu < 1$.

The compact condition of Assumption 4 is commonly imposed in the literature (e.g., Gallant and Nychka, 1987). This condition is needed to prove consistency. Assumption 5 is made for convenience. This condition can always be satisfied by discarding large values of the regressors. Assumption 6(i) basically requires that $p^1(y)$ is highly correlated with $\rho(z, \theta)$ for any $\theta \in \Theta$ so that the solution $\pi^1(x, \theta, h)$ always exists and is unique. This condition must hold for the proposed procedure to work. Assumption 6(ii) and (iii) ensure that $\pi^1(x, \theta, h)$ is continuous in (x, θ, h) and have first directional derivative with respect to (θ, h). Moreover, this condition together with Assumptions 4 and 5 imply that $\pi^1(x, \alpha)$ is bounded and that $|\pi^1(x, \alpha) - \pi^1(x, \alpha')| \le c * \|\alpha - \alpha'\|_s$ for some constant c. These implications and Assumption 7 ensure that the log likelihood function

$$l(z, \alpha) = p^1(y)'\pi^1(x, \alpha) + h(z)$$

satisfies conditions (i) and (ii) of Lemma A.1 of Ai and Chen (2003). Assumption 8 restricts the size of the sieve space, whereas Assumption 9 requires the sieve spaces to approximate the parameter space. Condition (iii) of Lemma A.1 of Ai and Chen (2003) is satisfied by Assumptions 8 and 9. Applying Part A of Lemma A.1 of Ai and Chen (2003), we obtain

$$\frac{1}{n}\sum_{i=1}^n l(z_i, \alpha) - E\{l(Z, \alpha)\} = o_p\left(\sqrt{n^{-(1-\nu)}\ln(n)}\right)$$

uniformly over $\alpha \in \mathcal{A}_k$. The continuity of $E\{l(Z, \alpha)\}$ in α and Assumption 9 ensure that

$$\frac{1}{n}\sum_{i=1}^n l(z_i, \alpha) \to E\{l(Z, \alpha)\}$$

uniformly over $\alpha \in \mathcal{A}$. With $\hat{h}_k = B^K(y, x)'\hat{\beta}_K$ and $\hat{\alpha} = (\hat{\theta}, \hat{h}_k)$, applying Theorem 0 of Gallant and Nychka (1987), we obtain

THEOREM 1. Under Assumptions 1–9, we have $\|\hat{\alpha} - \alpha_o\|_s \to 0$ in probability.

To show consistency of the SNP estimator $\tilde{\alpha} = (\tilde{\theta}, \tilde{h}_k)$ with $\tilde{h}_k = B^K(y, x)'\tilde{\beta}_K$, we need to strengthen Assumptions 6 and 7 so that the simulated solution $\tilde{\pi}^1(x, \theta, h)$

converges to $\pi^1(x, \theta, h)$ in probability uniformly over (x, θ, h). The following conditions are sufficient.

ASSUMPTION 10. *(i) For any $x \in \mathcal{X}, \theta \in \Theta$, and $h \in \mathcal{H}, \tilde{\pi}^1(x, \theta, h)$ is the unique solution to (9) and (10); (ii) there exists a measurable function $C(y)$ satisfying $E\{C(Y)^\gamma\} < +\infty$ for some $\gamma > 2$ such that $|\tilde{\rho}(y, x, \theta)f(y \mid x)/g(y)| \leq C(y)$ for all $x \in \mathcal{X}, \theta \in \Theta$, and $f \in \mathcal{F}$; (iii) $\rho(y, x, \theta)\}$ is continuously differentiable with respect to (x, θ); and (iv) there exists a measurable function $C(y)$ satisfying $E\{C(Y)^2\} < +\infty$ such that the derivatives of $\tilde{\rho}(y, x, \theta)f(y \mid x)/g(y)$ with respect to x, θ, and f are all bounded by $C(y)$.*

ASSUMPTION 11. *$R = n^\varsigma \ln(n)$ for some $\varsigma > \nu$.*

Assumption 10 requires that the summands in (9) and (10) satisfy the stochastic dominance and Lipschitz condition of Lemma A.1 of Ai and Chen (2003). Applying that lemma, we obtain

$$\frac{1}{R}\sum_{r=1}^{R}\tilde{\rho}(y^r, x, \theta)f(y^r \mid x)/g(y^r) - E\{\tilde{\rho}(Y, x, \theta)f(Y \mid x)/g(Y)\} = o_p\big(n^{-(\varsigma-\nu)/2}\big)$$

uniformly over $x \in \mathcal{X}, \theta \in \Theta$, and $f \in \mathcal{F}$. Under Assumption 6(ii), it follows immediately that

$$\tilde{\pi}^1(x, \alpha) = \pi^1(x, \alpha) + o_p\big(n^{-(\varsigma-\nu)/2}\big)$$

uniformly over $x \in \mathcal{X}, \theta \in \Theta$. Invoking Theorem 0 of Gallant and Nychka (1987), we obtain

THEOREM 2. *Under Assumptions 1–11, we have $\|\tilde{\alpha} - \alpha_0\|_s \to 0$ in probability.*

To show consistency of $f_k(y \mid x, \hat{\theta}, \hat{\beta}_k)$ and $\tilde{f}_k(y \mid x, \tilde{\theta}, \tilde{\beta}_k)$, notice that

$$f_k(y \mid x, \hat{\theta}, \hat{\beta}_k) - f_0(y \mid x) = \exp(\bar{l}(z))g(y \mid x) \times (l(z, \hat{\alpha}) - l(z, \alpha_0)),$$

$$\tilde{f}_k(y \mid x, \tilde{\theta}, \tilde{\beta}_k) - f_0(y \mid x) = \exp(\tilde{l}(z))g(y \mid x)$$
$$\times \big(p^1(y)'(\tilde{\pi}^1(x, \tilde{\alpha}) - \pi^1(x, \tilde{\alpha}) + \pi^1(x, \tilde{\alpha})$$
$$- \pi^1(x, \alpha_0)) + \tilde{h}(z) - h_0(z)\big),$$

where $\bar{l}(z)$ and $\tilde{l}(z)$ are between $l(z, \hat{\alpha})$ and $l(z, \alpha_0)$ and between $p^1(y)'(\tilde{\pi}^1(x, \tilde{\alpha}) + \tilde{h}_h(y, x)$ and $l(z, \alpha_0)$, respectively. The consistency of the estimated density now follows from the following condition:

ASSUMPTION 12. *$\exp(p^1(y)'\pi^1(x) + h(y, x))g(y \mid x) \times p^1(y)$ is bounded for all (x, y) and for all $(\pi^1(x), h(y, x))$ in the neighborhood of $(\pi_0^1(x), h_0(y, x))$ defined by $\|\cdot\|_{\infty, \mu}$.*

LEMMA 1. *Under Assumptions 1–9 and 12, we obtain*

$$\sup_{x, y}\{|f_k(y \mid x, \hat{\theta}, \hat{\beta}_k) - f_0(y \mid x)|\} = o_p(1).$$

Under additional Assumptions 10 and 11, we have

$$\sup_{x,y}\{|\tilde{f}_k(y\,|\,x,\tilde{\theta},\tilde{\beta}_k) - f_0(y\,|\,x)|\} = o_p(1).$$

The above consistency results are useful but not enough for deriving the asymptotic distribution of $\hat{\theta}$ and $\tilde{\theta}$. To derive the asymptotic distribution, we also need the convergence rate of the estimator. The convergence rate is closely related to the curvature of the criterion function. Write

$$E\{l(Z,\alpha)\} = E\{l(Z,\alpha_0)\} + \frac{1}{2}\frac{\partial^2 E\{l(Z,\alpha_0 + t(\alpha - \alpha_0))\}}{\partial t^2}\Big|_{t=0} + r(\alpha,\alpha_0),$$

where $r(\alpha,\alpha_0)$ is the remainder term. We now show that the remainder term has smaller order than the second term when α is sufficiently close to α_0. Notice that the equality

$$\frac{\partial^2 E\{l(Z,\alpha_0 + t(\alpha - \alpha_0))\}}{\partial t^2}\Big|_{t=0} + E\left\{\left[\frac{\partial l(Z,\alpha_0 + t(\alpha - \alpha_0))}{\partial t}\Big|_{t=0}\right]^2\right\} = 0$$

holds for any t and α. Define

$$\|\alpha - \alpha_o\|^2 = E\left\{\left[\frac{\partial l(Z,\alpha_0 + t(\alpha - \alpha_0))}{\partial t}\Big|_{t=0}\right]^2\right\}.$$

Applying $E\{p^1(y)p^2(y)'\,|\,x\} = 0$, we obtain

$$\|\alpha - \alpha_o\|^2 = E\left\{\left[p^1(Y)' \times \frac{\partial \pi^1(X,\alpha_0 + t(\alpha - \alpha_0))}{\partial t}\Big|_{t=0}\right]^2 + (h(Z) - h_0(Z))^2\right\}.$$

Notice that the eigenvalues of $E\{p^1(Y)p^1(Y)'\,|\,X=x\}$ are bounded and bounded away from zero. This and the fact that

$$\left|\frac{\partial \pi^1(X,\alpha_0 + t(\alpha - \alpha_0))}{\partial t}\Big|_{t=0}\right| \le c \times \|\alpha - \alpha_0\|_2,$$

where

$$\|\alpha - \alpha_0\|_2^2 = (\theta - \theta_0)'(\theta - \theta_0) + E\{(h(Z) - h_0(Z))^2\},$$

imply $\|\cdot\|$ and $\|\cdot\|_2$ are equivalent. Notice that $r(\alpha,\alpha_0)$ is in the order of $\|\cdot\|_2^3$. This shows that $\|\cdot\|^2$ is a local approximation to the average Kullback-Leibler information $E\{l(Z,\alpha_0)\} - E\{l(Z,\alpha)\}$.

We now present additional conditions and compute the convergence rates under the metric $\|\cdot\|$ (and $\|\cdot\|_2$).

ASSUMPTION 13. *For any $\alpha \in \mathcal{A}$, there exists $\alpha_k \in \mathcal{A}_K$ satisfying*

$$\|\alpha - \alpha_K\|_s = o(K^{-\zeta}) = o(n^{-\zeta\nu}).$$

ASSUMPTION 14. *$\rho(z, \theta)$ has up to third derivatives with respect to θ almost everywhere and the derivatives are dominated by some measurable function with finite second moment.*

Assumption 13 quantifies the approximation error by the sieve space $\mathcal{A}_K$. This condition is satisfied for a variety of parameter spaces and commonly used basis functions. For example, it is satisfied by Sobolev, Besov, and Hölder space when the basis functions are power series, B-splines, or wavelet series. Under this condition, we have $E\{l(Z, \alpha)\} - E\{l(Z, \alpha_K)\} = o(n^{-\zeta\nu})$ and hence

$$\frac{1}{n}\sum_{i=1}^{n} l(z_i, \alpha) - E\{l(Z, \alpha)\} = o_p\big(\max\{n^{-(1-\nu)/2}\ln(n), n^{-\zeta\nu}\}\big)$$

uniformly over $\alpha \in \mathcal{A}$. The following lemma is proved in the Appendix.

LEMMA 2. *Under Assumptions 1–9 and 12–14, we obtain*

$$\|\hat{\alpha} - \alpha_o\|_2 = o_p\big(\max\{n^{-(1-\nu)/2}\ln(n), n^{-\zeta\nu}\}\big).$$

Similarly, we can show

LEMMA 3. *Under Assumptions 1–14, we have*

$$\|\tilde{\alpha} - \alpha_o\|_2 = o_p\big(\max\{n^{-(\varsigma-\nu)/2}, n^{-(1-\nu)/2}\ln(n), n^{-\zeta\nu}\}\big).$$

Clearly, the simulation has an effect on the convergence rate of the estimator unless $\varsigma \geq 1$. Given the above results, it is straightforward to compute the convergence rate of the estimated density:

$$\sup_{x,y}\{|f_k(y\,|\,x, \hat{\theta}, \hat{\beta}_k) - f_0(y\,|\,x)|\} = o_p\big(\max\{n^{-(1-\nu)/2}\ln(n), n^{-\zeta\nu}\}\big),$$

$$\sup_{x,y}\{|\tilde{f}_k(y\,|\,x, \tilde{\theta}, \tilde{\beta}_k) - f_0(y\,|\,x)|\} = o_p\big(\max\{n^{-(\varsigma-\nu)/2}, n^{-(1-\nu)/2}\ln(n), n^{-\zeta\nu}\}\big).$$

4.   ASYMPTOTIC DISTRIBUTION

Having computed the convergence rate of the proposed estimator under the L_2 norm, we now derive the asymptotic distribution of $\hat{\theta}$ and $\tilde{\theta}$. Denote $f(\alpha) \equiv \lambda'\theta$ for any fixed and nonzero $\lambda \in \mathcal{R}^{d_\theta}$. Let $\bar{\mathbf{V}}$ denote the closure of the linear span of $\mathcal{A} - \{\alpha_0\}$ under the metric $\|\cdot\|$. Then $(\bar{\mathbf{V}}, \|\cdot\|)$ is a Hilbert space with the inner product

$$\langle \alpha, \bar{\alpha} \rangle = E \left\{ \begin{array}{l} \left(\dfrac{\partial l(Z, \alpha_0)}{\partial \theta'} \theta + \dfrac{dl(Z, \alpha_0)}{dh}[h] \right) * \\ \left(\dfrac{\partial l(Z, \alpha_0)}{\partial \theta'} \bar{\theta} + \dfrac{dl(Z, \alpha_0)}{dh}[\bar{h}] \right) \end{array} \right\},$$

where

$$\frac{dl(Z, \alpha_0)}{dh}[\Delta h] = \frac{dl(Z, \theta_0, h_0 + t \Delta h)}{dt}\Big|_{t=0}.$$

By the results in Van der Vaart (1991) and Shen (1997), the linear functional $f(\alpha) = \lambda'\theta$ must be *bounded* (i.e., $\sup_{0 \neq \alpha - \alpha_0 \in \bar{\mathbf{V}}} \frac{|f(\alpha) - f(\alpha_0)|}{\|\alpha - \alpha_0\|} < \infty$) in order for it to be estimated at the $\sqrt{n}-$ rate. Also, the Riesz representation exists if and only if $f(\alpha)$ is bounded. Thus, our immediate task is to show that the linear functional is bounded.

Write $\bar{\mathbf{V}} = \mathcal{R}^{d_\theta} \times \bar{\mathcal{W}}$ with $\bar{\mathcal{W}} \equiv \bar{\mathcal{H}} - \{h_0\}$. For each component θ_j of θ, let $w_j^* \in \bar{\mathcal{W}}$ denote the solution to

(11) $$\min_{w_j \in \bar{\mathcal{W}}} E \left\{ \left(\frac{\partial l(Z, \alpha_0)}{\partial \theta_j} - \frac{dl(Z, \alpha_0)}{dh}[w_j] \right)^2 \right\}.$$

Define $w^* = (w_1^*, \ldots, w_{d_\theta}^*)$, $\frac{dl(z, \alpha_0)}{dh}[w^*] = (\frac{dl(z, \alpha_0)}{dh}[w_1^*], \ldots, \frac{dl(z, \alpha_0)}{dh}[w_{d_\theta}^*])$, and

$$D_{w^*}(z) \equiv \frac{\partial l(z, \alpha_0)}{\partial \theta'} - \frac{dl(z, \alpha_0)}{dh}[w^*].$$

It is easy to show that

$$\sup_{0 \neq \alpha - \alpha_0 \in \bar{\mathbf{V}}} \frac{|f(\alpha) - f(\alpha_0)|^2}{\|\alpha - \alpha_0\|^2} = \lambda' \left(E\{D_{w^*}(Z)' D_{w^*}(Z)\} \right)^{-1} \lambda.$$

Suppose that $E\{D_{w^*}(Z)' D_{w^*}(Z)\}$ is finite positive-definite. Then $f(\alpha) = \lambda'\theta$ is bounded and has the following Riesz representation:

$$f(\alpha) - f(\alpha_0) \equiv \lambda'(\theta - \theta_0) = \langle v^*, \alpha - \alpha_0 \rangle \quad \text{for all } \alpha \in \mathcal{A},$$

where $v^* \equiv (v_\theta^*, v_h^*) \in \bar{\mathbf{V}}$ with $v_\theta^* = (E\{D_{w^*}(Z)' D_{w^*}(Z)\})^{-1}\lambda$, $v_h^* = -w^* \times v_\theta^*$. Hence, the asymptotic distribution of $f(\hat{\alpha}) - f(\alpha_0)$ (and $f(\tilde{\alpha}) - f(\alpha_0)$ in the case of simulation estimation) is the same as the asymptotic distribution of $\langle v^*, \hat{\alpha} - \alpha_0 \rangle$ (and $\langle v^*, \tilde{\alpha} - \alpha_0 \rangle$).

We notice that the moment restriction (1) implies

$$E\left\{\rho(Z,\theta_0)\frac{\partial l(Z,\alpha_0)}{\partial\theta'}\mid X\right\} + E\left\{\frac{\partial\rho(Z,\theta_0)}{\partial\theta'}\mid X=x\right\} = 0.$$

Write

$$\frac{\partial l(z,\alpha_0)}{\partial\theta_j} =$$

$$-\rho(z,\theta_0)' E\left\{\rho(Z,\theta_0)\rho(Z,\theta_0)'\mid X=x\right\}^{-1} E\left\{\frac{\partial\rho(Z,\theta_0)}{\partial\theta_j}\mid X=x\right\} + \upsilon_j(z).$$

It is easy to verify that $E\{\rho(Z,\theta_0)\upsilon_j(Z)\mid X=x\} = 0$. Again, the moment restriction (1) implies

$$E\left\{\rho(Z,\theta_0)\frac{dl(Z,\alpha_0)}{dh}[w]\mid X=x\right\} = 0$$

for any $w \in \bar{\mathcal{W}}$. The tangent space that is the closure of

$$\Gamma = \left\{\frac{dl(z,\alpha_0)}{dh}[w] : E\left\{\rho(Z,\theta_0)\frac{dl(Z,\alpha_0)}{dh}[w]\mid X=x\right\} = 0 \text{ and } w \in \bar{\mathcal{W}}\right\}$$

contains $\upsilon_j(z)$. Hence,

$$D_{w^*}(z) \equiv \frac{\partial l(z,\alpha_0)}{\partial\theta'} - \frac{dl(z,\alpha_0)}{dh}[w^*]$$

$$= -\rho(z,\theta_0)' * E\left\{\rho(Z,\theta_0)\rho(Z,\theta_0)'\mid X=x\right\}^{-1}$$

$$* E\left\{\frac{\partial\rho(Z,\theta_0)}{\partial\theta'}\mid X=x\right\}$$

and

$$E\{D_{w^*}(Z)' D_{w^*}(Z)\} = E\left\{\begin{array}{c} E\left\{\frac{\partial\rho(Z,\theta_0)}{\partial\theta'}\mid X\right\}' \times \\ E\left\{\rho(Z,\theta_0)\rho(Z,\theta_0)'\mid X\right\}^{-1} \times E\left\{\frac{\partial\rho(Z,\theta_0)}{\partial\theta'}\mid X\right\} \end{array}\right\}$$

$$= E\left\{E\left\{\frac{\partial\rho(Z,\theta_0)}{\partial\theta'}\mid X\right\}' \times \Sigma_0^{-1}(X) \times E\left\{\frac{\partial\rho(Z,\theta_0)}{\partial\theta'}\mid X\right\}\right\}$$

$$= V_0,$$

which is exactly the semiparametric efficiency information of θ_0 for model (1) (Chamberlain, 1987). Thus, our estimator is asymptotically efficient if its asymptotic covariance is the inverse of V_0.

The following conditions are sufficient for establishing the $\sqrt{n}$ consistency of the estimators $\hat{\theta}_n$ and $\tilde{\theta}_n$.

ASSUMPTION 15. *(i)* $\Sigma_0(x) = E\{\rho(Z, \theta_0)\rho(Z, \theta_0)' \mid X = x\}$ *is nonsingular for all* x; *(ii)* V_0 *is nonsingular; (iii)* $\theta_0 \in int(\Theta)$.

ASSUMPTION 16. *There is a* $v_n^* = (v_\theta^*, -\Pi_n w^* \times v_\theta^*) \in \mathcal{A}_n - \alpha_0$ *such that* $\|v_n^* - v^*\|_2 = O(n^{-1/4})$.

ASSUMPTION 17. $v \le 1/2$ *and* $\zeta v \ge 1/4$.

ASSUMPTION 18. $\varsigma = 1 + v$.

Assumption 15(i and ii) is a local identification condition for θ_0. This condition must be satisfied for the estimated finite dimensional parameter to be $\sqrt{n}$ consistent. Unfortunately, this condition is difficult to verify in practice since it requires knowing the true value of the model. Assumption 16 is a "bias controlling" condition. This condition is needed due to the presence of the unknown function h_0. Here for simplicity we assume that the same sieve space $\mathcal{H}_n$ approximates the space $\bar{\mathcal{W}} \equiv \bar{\mathcal{H}} - \{h_0\}$ well. Theorem 3 can be proved even if $v_h^* = -w^* v_\theta^*$ is approximated by other sieve spaces. Assumption 17 ensures that the proposed SNP estimators $\hat{\alpha}$ and $\tilde{\alpha}$ converge to the true value under the L_2 norm faster than the rate $n^{-1/4}$. Consequently, we have

$$\sup_{x,y} \{|f_k(y \mid x, \hat{\theta}, \hat{\beta}_k) - f_0(y \mid x)|\} = o_p(n^{-1/4}),$$

$$\sup_{x,y} \{|\tilde{f}_k(y \mid x, \tilde{\theta}, \tilde{\beta}_k) - f_0(y \mid x)|\} = o_p(n^{-1/4}).$$

Assumption 18 is needed to ensure that the simulation has no effect on the asymptotic distribution of $\tilde{\theta}$. The following result is proved in the Appendix.

THEOREM 3. *Under Assumptions 1–9, 12–14, and 15–17, we obtain* $\sqrt{n}(\hat{\theta}_n - \theta_o) \Longrightarrow N(0, V_0^{-1})$. *Under Assumptions 1–14, and 15–18, we obtain* $\sqrt{n}(\tilde{\theta}_n - \theta_o) \Longrightarrow N(0, V_0^{-1})$.

Theorem 3 simply shows that, under some sufficient conditions, the proposed SNP estimator of θ_0 has the same first order properties as do the estimators proposed in Newey (1990), Kitamura et al. (2003), and Donald et al. (2003). It is not clear whether these same sufficient conditions also ensure that the SNP estimator of θ_0 has the same or better second order properties. Our guess is that these sufficient conditions, particularly Assumptions 17 and 18, need to be strengthened in order for the SNP estimator to have better second order properties. For example, Assumption 18 is sufficient for the simulation to have no effect on the first order properties. To ensure that the simulation has no effect on the second order properties, we probably need a larger number of simulation draws such as $R = O(n^2)$. Assumption 17 permits a range of values of K that are all sufficient for the first order efficiency. This range probably needs to be tightened up to obtain the second order superiority.

5. COVARIANCE MATRIX

The asymptotic distribution derived above can be used for statistical inference only if a practical and easy to compute the covariance estimator is available. One way to estimate the asymptotic covariance is to use the estimated conditional density. For example, we can estimate the conditional covariance matrix $\Sigma_0(X)$ by

$$\hat{\Sigma}_0(x) \equiv \int \rho(y, x, \hat{\theta})\rho(y, x, \hat{\theta})' f_k(y \mid x, \hat{\theta}, \hat{\beta}_k) \, dy$$

and V_0 by

$$\hat{V}_0 =$$

$$\frac{1}{n} \sum_{i=1}^{n} \int \frac{\partial \rho(y, x_i, \hat{\theta})'}{\partial \theta} f_k(y \mid x_i, \hat{\theta}, \hat{\beta}_k) \, dy * \hat{\Sigma}_0^{-1}(x_i) \int \frac{\partial \rho(y, x_i, \hat{\theta})}{\partial \theta'} f_k(y \mid x_i, \hat{\theta}, \hat{\beta}_k) \, dy.$$

In the simulation case, we estimate $\Sigma_0(X)$ by

$$\tilde{\Sigma}_0(x_i) \equiv \frac{1}{R} \sum_{r=1}^{R} \rho(y^{ir}, x_i, \tilde{\theta})\rho(y^{ir}, x_i, \tilde{\theta})' \times q(p^1(y^{ir})'\tilde{\pi}^1(x_i, \tilde{\alpha}) + \tilde{h}_K(y^{ir}, x_i))$$

and V_0 by

$$\tilde{V}_0 = \frac{1}{n} \sum_{i=1}^{n} \tilde{A}(x_i) \times \tilde{\Sigma}_0^{-1}(x_i) \times \tilde{A}(x_i)', \quad \text{where}$$

$$\tilde{A}(x_i) = \frac{1}{R} \sum_{r=1}^{R} \frac{\partial \rho(y^{ir}, x_i, \tilde{\theta})'}{\partial \theta} \times q(p^1(y^{ir})'\tilde{\pi}^1(x_i, \tilde{\alpha}) + \tilde{h}_K(y^{ir}, x_i)).$$

The consistency of these covariance matrices require the following conditions.

ASSUMPTION 19. *(i) $\rho(z, \theta)'\rho(z, \theta)$ is differentiable almost everywhere with respect to θ, and the derivative is bounded by a measurable function with a finite second moment.*

ASSUMPTION 20. *(i) $\rho(z, \theta)'\rho(z, \theta) f(y \mid z)/g(y)$ is differentiable almost everywhere with respect to θ, and the derivative is bounded by a measurable function with a finite second moment.*

An alternative approach is to estimate $w^* = (w_1^*, \ldots, w_{d_\theta}^*)$, given by (11), by simple OLS regression. Specifically, for each component θ_j, $j = 1, \ldots, d_\theta$, we approximate w_j^* by $B^K(y, x)'\delta_K$ and estimate δ_K by

$$\text{regressing } \frac{\partial l(z_i, \hat{\alpha})}{\partial \theta_j} \text{ on } \frac{dl(z_i, \hat{\alpha})}{dh}[b_1(z_i)], \ldots, \frac{dl(z_i, \hat{\alpha})}{dh}[b_K(z_i)].$$

Notice that the above regression is the same as

$$\text{regressing } \frac{\partial l(z_i, \hat{\alpha})}{\partial \theta_j} \text{ on } \frac{\partial l(z_i, \hat{\alpha})}{\partial \beta_{1K}}, \ldots, \frac{\partial l(z_i, \hat{\alpha})}{\partial \beta_{KK}}.$$

The regression residuals from the above regression are the estimates of $D_{w^*}(y, x)$. Let $\hat{D}_{ji}$ denote the regression residuals and denote $\hat{D}_i = (\hat{D}_{1i}, \ldots, \hat{D}_{d_\theta i})'$. Then we estimate V_0 by

$$\hat{V}_0 = \frac{1}{n} \sum_{i=1}^{n} \hat{D}_i \hat{D}_i'.$$

Similarly, we can construct the covariance estimator for the simulation case.

$$\text{Regress } \frac{\partial \tilde{l}(z_i, \tilde{\alpha})}{\partial \theta_j} \text{ on } \frac{\partial \tilde{l}(z_i, \tilde{\alpha})}{\partial \beta_{1K}}, \ldots, \frac{\partial \tilde{l}(z_i, \tilde{\alpha})}{\partial \beta_{KK}}.$$

Let $\tilde{D}_{ji}$ denote the regression residuals and denote $\tilde{D}_i = (\tilde{D}_{1i}, \ldots, \tilde{D}_{d_\theta i})'$. Then we estimate V_0 by

$$\tilde{V}_0 = \frac{1}{n} \sum_{i=1}^{n} \tilde{D}_i \tilde{D}_i'.$$

The following theorem is proved in the Appendix.

THEOREM 4. *Under Assumptions 1–14, 15–18, and 19–20, we have:* $\hat{V}_0 = V_0 + o_p(1)$ *and* $\tilde{V}_0 = V_0 + o_p(1)$.

It follows from Theorems 3 and 4 that the usual t-statistics, computed as the ratio of the parameter estimate $\hat{\theta}(\tilde{\theta})$ divided by its estimated standard error, have standard normal distribution, and hence the standard t-test for significance is still valid. To test a joint restriction on θ_0, the usual Wald and Hausman tests are still valid. The likelihood ratio test should also work here. To test the restriction on the density function, in principle the likelihood ratio test still applies, but the asymptotic distribution of the test statistic needs to be worked out.

It is worth pointing out that the covariance matrices of $\hat{\theta}$ and $\tilde{\theta}$ computed in the second approach are the same as the covariance matrices of the ML estimators of $\hat{\theta}$ and $\tilde{\theta}$ if $B^K(y, x)'\beta_K$ is treated as the parametric specification of $h(y, x)$ and K is fixed. Thus, the covariance matrices can be computed from any standard maximum likelihood estimation statistical package.

6.   CONCLUSION

In this article, we study the seminonparametric maximum likelihood estimation of the conditional moment restriction model. We present some sufficient conditions, under which we show that the estimated finite dimensional parameter is $\sqrt{n}$ consistent and asymptotically normally distributed and the estimated density function is consistent. We provide an easy to compute and consistent covariance matrix and show that the covariance matrix is same as the covariance matrix of the maximum likelihood estimator if the sieve approximation is treated as the correct parametric specification, and hence can be computed from any standard statistical package that computes the maximum likelihood estimation. We argue that it is possible that the seminonparametric maximum likelihood estimator may have potential advantages over the empirical maximum likelihood estimator. It is unclear however whether those advantages truly exist in finite samples. Moreover, we are not certain that the seminonparametric maximum likelihood estimator has better second order properties than the empirical maximum likelihood estimator since we have to approximate the true density function and the number of approximating terms is undetermined. The proposed estimator will be sensitive to the selection of the approximating basis functions. The higher order properties of the proposed estimator will be explored in a future study. The issue of testing restrictions on the density function also is important and will be dealt with in a separate paper.

In our moment restriction model, we only permit the finite dimensional parameter θ. In some applications, the conditional moment restriction may contain unknown functions. Thus, it is necessary to extend the results here to a model similar to the one studied by Ai and Chen (2003). Ai and Chen proposed a minimum distance estimator that is very similar to Newey's weighted version of the GMM formulation and hence may suffer from the same finite sample problems. The extension of the seminonparametric maximum likelihood estimation to that model would be useful addition to the literature. This extension will be pursued in a separate paper.

APPENDIX: PROOFS

PROOF (THEOREM 1).   First, we derive the Lipschitz condition

$$|\pi^1(x, \alpha) - \pi^1(x, \bar{\alpha})| \le c * \|\alpha - \bar{\alpha}\|_s.$$

Define

$$\phi(t) = \pi^1(x, \bar{\alpha} + t(\alpha - \bar{\alpha})).$$

Then

$$\pi^1(x, \alpha) - \pi^1(x, \bar{\alpha}) = \phi(1) - \phi(0) = \frac{d\phi(\bar{t})}{dt},$$

with $\bar{t}$ between 0 and 1. Notice that

$$\int \rho(y, x, \bar{\theta} + t(\theta - \bar{\theta})) \exp\left(\frac{p^1(y)'\phi(t) +}{\bar{h}(y, x) + t(h(y, x) - \bar{h}(y, x))}\right) g(y \mid x)\, dy = 0,$$

$$\int \exp\left(\frac{p^1(y)'\phi(t) +}{\bar{h}(y, x) + t(h(y, x) - \bar{h}(y, x))}\right) g(y \mid x)\, dy = 1,$$

hold for all t. Differentiating both sides with respect to t gives

$$E_f\left\{\frac{\partial \tilde{\rho}(Z, \bar{\theta} + t(\theta - \bar{\theta}))}{\partial \theta'} \mid X = x\right\}(\theta - \bar{\theta})$$

$$+ E_f\left\{\tilde{\rho}(Z, \bar{\theta} + t(\theta - \bar{\theta}))(h(Z) - \bar{h}(Z)) \mid X = x\right\}$$

$$= -E_f\left\{\tilde{\rho}(Z, \bar{\theta} + t(\theta - \bar{\theta}))p^1(Y) \mid X = x\right\} \times \frac{d\phi(t)}{dt}.$$

Solving the above equation, we obtain

$$\frac{d\phi(t)}{dt} = -E_f\left\{\tilde{\rho}(Z, \bar{\theta} + t(\theta - \bar{\theta}))p^1(Y) \mid X = x\right\}^{-1}$$

$$\times \frac{\partial E_f\{\tilde{\rho}(Z, \bar{\theta} + t(\theta - \bar{\theta})) \mid X = x\}}{\partial \theta'}(\theta - \bar{\theta})$$

$$- E_f\{\tilde{\rho}(Z, \bar{\theta} + t(\theta - \bar{\theta}))p^1(Y) \mid X = x\}^{-1}$$

$$\times E_f\{\tilde{\rho}(Z, \bar{\theta} + t(\theta - \bar{\theta}))(h(Z) - \bar{h}(Z)) \mid X = x\}.$$

Applying Assumption 5, we have that

$$\frac{d\phi(t)'}{dt}\frac{d\phi(t)}{dt} \leq c \times \|\alpha - \bar{\alpha}\|_s^2$$

holds for some constant c and for all t. The theorem now follows from application of Part A of Lemma A.1 of Ai and Chen (2003). ∎

PROOF (THEOREM 2). To prove this theorem, let $\pi^1(x, \alpha, s, \Delta)$ denote the unique solution to

$$\int \rho(y, x, \theta) \exp(p^1(y)'\pi^1(x, \alpha, s, \Delta) + h(y, x))g(y \mid x)\, dy = 0 + s\Delta,$$

$$\int \exp p^1(y)'\pi^1(x, \alpha, s, \Delta) + h(y, x))g(y \mid x)\, dy = 1 + s\Delta.$$

Then $\pi^1(x,\alpha) = \pi^1(x,\alpha,0,\Delta)$. For small s, differentiating both sides with respect to s, we obtain

$$\frac{\partial \pi^1(x,\alpha,s,\Delta)}{\partial s} = -E_f\{\tilde{\rho}(Z, \bar{\theta} + t(\theta - \bar{\theta}))p^1(Y) \mid X = x\}^{-1}\Delta.$$

Hence

$$\frac{\partial \pi^1(x,\alpha,s,\Delta)'}{\partial s} \frac{\partial \pi^1(x,\alpha,s,\Delta)}{\partial s} \le c \times \Delta^2.$$

Notice that, applying Lemma A.1 of Ai and Chen, equation system (9)–(10) can be rewritten as

$$\int \rho(y,x,\theta)\exp\left(p^1(y)'\pi^1(x,\alpha,s) + h(y,x)\right)g(y\mid x)\,dy$$
$$= 0 + s \times o_p\left(n^{-(\varsigma-v)/(2\varsigma)}\ln(n)\right),$$
$$\int \exp\,p^1(y)'\pi^1(x,\alpha,s) + h(y,x))g(y\mid x)\,dy$$
$$= 1 + s \times o_p\left(n^{-(\varsigma-v)/(2\varsigma)}\ln(n)\right).$$

Hence, $\tilde{\pi}^1(x,\alpha) = \pi^1(x,\alpha,1,o_p(n^{-(\varsigma-v)/2}))$ and

$$\left|\tilde{\pi}^1(x,\alpha) - \pi^1(x,\alpha)\right| = \left|\pi^1(x,\alpha,1,o_p(n^{-(\varsigma-v)/2})) - \pi^1(x,\alpha,0,o_p(n^{-(\varsigma-v)/2}))\right|$$
$$\le o_p(n^{-(\varsigma-v)/2}).$$

It follows immediately that

$$\frac{1}{n}\sum_{i=1}^n p^1(y_i)'\tilde{\pi}^1(x_i,\theta,h) + h(y_i,x_i)$$
$$= \frac{1}{n}\sum_{i=1}^n l(z_i,\alpha) + o_p(n^{-(\varsigma-v)/2})$$
$$= E\{l(Z,\alpha)\} + o_p\left(\max\left\{n^{-(\varsigma-v)/2}, n^{-(1-v)/2}\ln(n)\right\}\right).$$

The theorem now follows from Theorem 0 of Gallant and Nychka (1987). ∎

PROOF (LEMMA 2). From the proof of Theorem 1, applying the Cauchy-Schwartz inequality, we obtain

$$\frac{d\phi(t)'}{dt}\frac{d\phi(t)}{dt} \le c \times \|\alpha - \bar{\alpha}\|_2^2.$$

Hence, the Fisher-like metric $\|\cdot\|$ and the L_2 norm $\|\cdot\|_2$ are equivalent. The lemma is proved by applying the same arguments that are used to prove Theorem 3.1 in Ai and Chen (2003). ∎

PROOF (THEOREM 3). Denote

$$\varphi(t) = \frac{1}{n} \sum_{i=1}^{n} l(z_i, \hat{\alpha} + t \upsilon_n^*).$$

The fact that $\hat{\alpha}$ is the maximizer implies that $\varphi(t)$ is maximized at $t = 0$. The following first order condition must be satisfied:

$$\varphi'(0) = \frac{1}{n} \sum_{i=1}^{n} \frac{\partial l(z_i, \hat{\alpha} + t \upsilon_n^*)}{\partial t} \Big|_{t=0} = 0.$$

Since $\hat{\alpha}$ converges to α_0 in probability, applying the empirical process theorem yields

$$\frac{1}{n} \sum_{i=1}^{n} \left(\frac{\partial l(z_i, \hat{\alpha} + t \upsilon_n^*)}{\partial t} \Big|_{t=0} - \frac{\partial l(z_i, \alpha_0 + t \upsilon_n^*)}{\partial t} \Big|_{t=0} \right)$$
$$- E\left\{ \frac{\partial l(Z, \hat{\alpha} + t \upsilon_n^*)}{\partial t} \Big|_{t=0} - \frac{\partial l(Z, \alpha_0 + t \upsilon_n^*)}{\partial t} \Big|_{t=0} \right\} = o_p(n^{-1/2}).$$

Hence

$$E\left\{ \frac{\partial l(Z, \hat{\alpha} + t \upsilon_n^*)}{\partial t} \Big|_{t=0} - \frac{\partial l(Z, \alpha_0 + t \upsilon_n^*)}{\partial t} \Big|_{t=0} \right\}$$
$$= -\frac{1}{n} \sum_{i=1}^{n} \frac{\partial l(z_i, \alpha_0 + t \upsilon_n^*)}{\partial t} \Big|_{t=0} + o_p(n^{-1/2}).$$

By linearizing $E\{\frac{\partial l(Z, \alpha + t \upsilon_n^*)}{\partial t} |_{t=0}\}$ around $\alpha = \alpha_0$ and noting that the second order term is dominated by $\|\hat{\alpha} - \alpha_0\|_2^2$, we have

$$E\left\{ \frac{\partial l(Z, \hat{\alpha} + t \upsilon_n^*)}{\partial t} \Big|_{t=0} - \frac{\partial l(Z, \alpha_0 + t \upsilon_n^*)}{\partial t} \Big|_{t=0} \right\}$$
$$= E\left\{ \frac{\partial^2 l(Z, \alpha_0 + s(\hat{\alpha} - \alpha_0) + t \upsilon_n^*)}{\partial t \partial s} \Big|_{t=0, s=0} \right\} + o_p(n^{-1/2})$$
$$= -\langle \hat{\alpha} - \alpha_0, \upsilon_n^* \rangle + o_p(n^{-1/2})$$
$$= -\langle \hat{\alpha} - \alpha_0, \upsilon^* \rangle + o_p(n^{-1/2}),$$

where the last equality follows from Assumption 16. Notice that

$$E\left\{\frac{\partial l(Z, \alpha_0 + tv_n^*)}{\partial t}|_{t=0}\right\} = E\left\{\frac{\partial l(Z, \alpha_0 + tv^*)}{\partial t}|_{t=0}\right\} = 0.$$

Applying the Chebyshev inequality, we obtain

$$\frac{1}{n}\sum_{i=1}^{n}\frac{\partial l(z_i, \alpha_0 + tv_n^*)}{\partial t}|_{t=0} = \frac{1}{n}\sum_{i=1}^{n}\frac{\partial l(z_i, \alpha_0 + tv^*)}{\partial t}|_{t=0} + o_p(n^{-1/2}).$$

Combining the results, we have

$$\langle \hat{\alpha} - \alpha_0, v^* \rangle = \frac{1}{n}\sum_{i=1}^{n}\frac{\partial l(z_i, \alpha_0 + tv^*)}{\partial t}|_{t=0} + o_p(n^{-1/2}).$$

Part (i) of the theorem now follows from applying a central limit theorem. Denote $\tilde{l}(z, \alpha) = p^1(y)'\tilde{\pi}^1(x, \alpha) + h(z)$. We now have

$$\frac{1}{n}\sum_{i=1}^{n}\frac{\partial \tilde{l}(z_i, \tilde{\alpha} + tv_n^*)}{\partial t}|_{t=0} = 0.$$

Notice that

$$\left|\frac{1}{n}\sum_{i=1}^{n}\frac{\partial \tilde{l}(z_i, \tilde{\alpha} + tv_n^*)}{\partial t}|_{t=0} - \frac{1}{n}\sum_{i=1}^{n}\frac{\partial l(z_i, \tilde{\alpha} + tv_n^*)}{\partial t}|_{t=0}\right|$$

$$= \left|\frac{1}{n}\sum_{i=1}^{n}p^1(y_i)'\left(\frac{\partial \tilde{\pi}^1(z_i, \tilde{\alpha} + tv_n^*)}{\partial t}|_{t=0} - \frac{\partial \pi^1(z_i, \tilde{\alpha} + tv_n^*)}{\partial t}|_{t=0}\right)\right|$$

$$\leq \sqrt{\frac{1}{n}\sum_{i=1}^{n}p^1(y_i)'p^1(y_i)} \times o_p(n^{-1/2}),$$

where the last inequality follows from

$$\frac{\partial \tilde{\pi}^1(z_i, \tilde{\alpha} + tv_n^*)}{\partial t}|_{t=0} - \frac{\partial \pi^1(z_i, \tilde{\alpha} + tv_n^*)}{\partial t}|_{t=0} = o_p(n^{-1/2})$$

by Assumption 18. Hence, we have

$$\frac{1}{n}\sum_{i=1}^{n}\frac{\partial l(z_i, \tilde{\alpha} + tv_n^*)}{\partial t}|_{t=0} = o_p(n^{-1/2}).$$

Applying the same line of arguments as in the proof of part (i), we have

$$\langle \tilde{\alpha} - \alpha_0, \upsilon^* \rangle = \frac{1}{n} \sum_{i=1}^{n} \frac{\partial l(z_i, \alpha_0 + t\upsilon^*)}{\partial t}\Big|_{t=0} + o_p(n^{-1/2}).$$

Part (ii) of the theorem now follows from applying a central limit theorem. ∎

PROOF (THEOREM 4). The consistency of the covariance matrix in the first approach follows directly from the fact that $\hat{\alpha}$ and $\tilde{\alpha}$ converge to the true value under the L_2 norm at the rate $o_p(n^{-1/4})$ and the conditions that both $\rho(z, \theta)'\rho(z, \theta)$ is differentiable with respect to θ almost everywhere and the derivative satisfies a stochastic dominance condition.

To prove consistency of the covariance matrix in the alternative approach, we notice that, using the fact that $\hat{\alpha}$ converges to the true value under the L_2 norm at the rate $o_p(n^{-1/4})$, we can show that

$$\frac{1}{n} \sum_{i=1}^{n} \left(\frac{\partial l(z_i, \hat{\alpha})}{\partial \theta_j} - \frac{\partial l(z_i, \hat{\alpha})}{\partial h}[w] \right)^2$$

converges in probability to

$$E\left\{ \left(\frac{\partial l(zZ, \alpha_0)}{\partial \theta_j} - \frac{\partial l(Z, \alpha_0)}{\partial h}[w] \right)^2 \right\}$$

uniformly over $w \in \bar{\mathcal{W}}$. Applying the same arguments that are used to prove Theorem 1, we can show that the estimator $\hat{w}_j = B^K(z)'\hat{\delta}$, where $\hat{\delta}$ is the least square estimator of regressing $\frac{\partial l(z_i, \hat{\alpha})}{\partial \theta_j}$ on $\frac{\partial l(z_i, \hat{\alpha})}{\partial \beta_j}$, converges to w_j^* in probability under the metric $\|\cdot\|_s$. The consistency of $\hat{V}_0$ now follows immediately. The consistency of $\tilde{V}_0$ can be proved similarly. ∎

REFERENCES

AI, C., "A Semiparametric Maximum Likelihood Estimator," *Econometrica* 65 (1997), 933–64.

———, AND X. CHEN, "Efficient Estimation of Conditional Moment Restrictions Models Containing Unknown Functions," *Econometrica* 71 (2003), 1795–843.

ALTONJI, J. G., AND L. M. SEGAL, "Small Sample Bias in GMM Estimation of Covariance Structures," *Journal of Economics and Business Statistics* 14 (1996), 353–66.

BRUNNER, A. D., "Conditional Asymmetries in Real GNP: A Seminonparametric Approach," *Journal of Business & Economic Statistics* 10 (1992), 65–72.

CHAMBERLAIN, G., "Asymptotic Efficiency in Estimation with Conditional Moment Restrictions," *Journal of Econometrics* 34 (1987), 305–34.

———, "Efficiency Bounds for Semiparametric Regression," *Econometrica* 60 (1992), 567–96.

CHEN, X., AND X. SHEN, "Sieve Extremum Estimates for Weakly Dependent Data," *Econometrica* 66 (1998), 289–314.

COPPEJANS, M., AND A. R. GALLANT, "Cross-Validated SNP Density Estimates," *Journal of Econometrics* 110 (2002), 27–65.

DAVIDIAN, M., AND A. R. GALLANT, "The Nonlinear Mixed Effects Model with a Smooth Random Effects Density," *Biometrika* 80 (1993), 475–88.

DONALD, S., G. IMBENS, AND W. NEWEY, "Empirical Likelihood Estimation and Consistent Tests with Conditional Moment Restrictions," *Journal of Econometrics* 117 (2003), 55–93.

EASTWOOD, B. J., AND A. R. GALLANT, "Adaptive Rules for Seminonparametric Estimators that Achieve Asymptotic Normality," *Econometric Theory* 7 (1991), 307–40.

FENTON, V., AND A. R. GALLANT, "Convergence Rates of SNP Density Estimators," *Econometrica* 64 (1996), 719–27.

———, AND ———, "Qualitative and Asymptotic Performance of SNP Density Estimators," *Journal of Econometrics* 74 (1996), 77–118.

GABLER, S., F. LAISNEY, AND M. LECHNER, "Seminonparametric Estimation of Binary-Choice Models with an Application to Labor-Force Participation," *Journal of Economics and Business Statistics* 11 (1993), 61–80.

GALLANT, A. R., AND D. W. NYCHKA, "Semi-Nonparametric Maximum Likelihood Estimation," *Econometrica* 55 (1987), 363–90.

———, AND G. TAUCHEN, "Seminonparametric Estimation of Conditionally Constrained Heterogeneous Processes: Asset Pricing Applications," *Econometrica* 57 (1989), 1091–120.

———, P. ROSSI, AND G. TAUCHEN, "Stock Prices and Volume," *The Review of Financial Studies* 5 (1992), 199–242.

HALL, A., "Lagrange Multiplier Tests for Normality against Seminonparametric Alternatives," *Journal of Economics and Business Statistics* 8 (1990), 417–26.

HALL, P., AND J. HOROWITZ, "Bootstrap Critical Values for Tests Based on Generalized Method of Moments Estimators," *Econometrica* 64 (1996), 891–916.

HANSEN, L. P., "Large Sample Properties of Generalized Method of Moments Estimators," *Econometrica* 50 (1982), 1029–54.

IMBENS, G. W., "One-Step Estimators for Over-identified Generalized Method of Moments Models," *Review of Economic Studies* 64 (1997), 359–83.

———, R. H. SPADY, AND P. JOHNSON, "Information Theoretic Approaches to Inference in Moment Conditions Models," *Econometrica* 66 (1998), 333–57.

KITAMURA, Y., AND M. STUTZER, "An Information-Theoretic Alternative to Generalized Method of Moments Estimation," *Econometrica* 65 (1997), 861–74.

———, G. TRIPATHI, AND H. AHN, "Empirical Likelihood-Based Inference in Conditional Moment Restriction Models," *Econometrica* 72 (2004), 1667–714.

NEWEY, W. K., "Efficient Instrumental Variables Estimation of Nonlinear Models," *Econometrica* 58 (1990), 809–37.

———, "Convergence Rates and Asymptotic Normality for Series Estimators," *Journal of Econometrics* 79 (1997), 147–68.

———, AND R. SMITH, "Higher Order Properties of GMM and Generalized Empirical Likelihood Estimators," *Econometrica* 72 (2004), 219–55.

OWEN, A., "Empirical Likelihood Ratio Confidence Regions," *The Annals of Statistics* 18 (1990), 90–120.

———, "Empirical Likelihood for Linear Models," *The Annals of Statistics* 19 (1991), 1725–47.

QIN, J., AND J. LAWLESS, "Empirical Likelihood and General Estimating Equations," *The Annals of Statistics* 22 (1994), 300–25.

SHEN, X., "On Methods of Sieves and Penalization," *The Annals of Statistics* 25 (1997), 2555–91.

VAN DER VAART, A., "On Differentiable Functionals," *The Annals of Statistics* 19 (1991), 178–204.

INTERNATIONAL ECONOMIC REVIEW
Vol. 48, No. 4, November 2007

PAIRWISE DIFFERENCE ESTIMATION WITH NONPARAMETRIC CONTROL VARIABLES*

By Andres Aradillas-Lopez, Bo E. Honoré, and James L. Powell[1]

Princeton University, U.S.A.; Princeton University, U.S.A.; University of California, Berkeley, U.S.A.

This article extends the pairwise difference estimators for various semilinear limited dependent variable models proposed by Honoré and Powell (*Identification and Inference in Econometric Models. Essays in Honor of Thomas Rothenberg* Cambridge: Cambridge University Press, 2005) to permit the regressor appearing in the nonparametric component to itself depend upon a conditional expectation that is nonparametrically estimated. This permits the estimation approach to be applied to nonlinear models with sample selectivity and/or endogeneity, in which a "control variable" for selectivity or endogeneity is nonparametrically estimated. We develop the relevant asymptotic theory for the proposed estimators and we illustrate the theory to derive the asymptotic distribution of the estimator for the partially linear logit model.

1. INTRODUCTION

Using an analogy between the partially linear regression model (Engle et al., 1986; Robinson, 1988) and linear panel data models with fixed effects, Honoré and Powell (2005) showed how partially linear versions of several limited dependent variable models (e.g., logit, censored, and Poisson regression models) could be constructed using the corresponding estimators for panel data versions of these models with individual fixed effects. The resulting estimation method involved "pairwise differences" of observations for which the regressors in the nonparametric component of the regression function are approximately equal, in an analogy of first-differencing to eliminate fixed effects in panel data models. Assuming the regressors in the nonparametric component were either known or linear in parametrically estimated coefficients, the paper derived conditions under which the proposed estimators of the parameters of interest were root-n consistent and asymptotically normal.

Recent work on semiparametric and nonparametric "control function" estimation of nonlinear models with selectivity or endogenous regressors has shown how such models can often be recast as partially linear regression models with

* Manuscript received December 2005; revised February 2007.

[1] The authors are grateful to three anonymous referees for their valuable comments and suggestions. This research is supported by The Gregory C. Chow Econometric Research Program at Princeton University (Aradillas-Lopez and Honoré), the NSF grant No. SES-0417895 and the Danish National Research Foundation, through CAM at The University of Copenhagen (Honoré). Please address correspondence to: Andres Aradillas-Lopez, Department of Economics, Princeton University, Princeton, NJ 08544. E-mail: *aaradill@princeton.edu*.

"control variables" for selection or endogeneity in the nonparametric component of the regression function; these "control variables" are either conditional expectations (e.g., the conditional probability of selection, or "propensity score", as in Ahn and Powell, 1993, to control for selection bias) or residuals from conditional expectations (e.g., first-stage residuals to control for endogenous regressors, as in Newey et al., 1999; Blundell and Powell, 2004) or both (Das et al., 2003). Thus, an obvious approach to estimation of these models would extend the "pairwise difference" estimation method of Honoré and Powell (2005) to accommodate nonparametric estimation methods of the "control variables" appearing in the nonparametric component. This article makes this extension and illustrates how the approach would specialize to a logit model with endogenous regressors.

2. MOTIVATION AND EXAMPLES

Before describing the econometric model of interest, let us denote the vector of observable covariates for the ith observation by $z_i \equiv (v_i, w_i)$, where $v_i \in \mathbb{R}^M$ and $w_i \in \mathbb{R}^L$ may have some elements in common. The rationale behind this partition will become clear below. We will assume throughout that we have an i.i.d. sample $(z_i)_{i=1}^n$ from the population to be described below. The type of econometric models we study have two general features. The first feature is that there is a finite-dimensional parameter of interest $\beta \in \mathbb{R}^K$ and two nuisance parameters: a finite-dimensional vector $\gamma \in \mathbb{R}^D$ and an unknown function $\mu(w_i, \gamma)$, effectively an infinite-dimensional nuisance parameter. The parameter γ is either known or can be estimated by the econometrician. We refer to μ as the "control function," which can be real or vector-valued. We will let β_0 and γ_0 denote the true parameter values. The second feature of the models of interest here is the existence of a function $s(v_i, v_j; \beta)$—which is either known or estimable by the econometrician—such that β_0 is identified as the unique solution to the following problem:

$$\underset{\beta}{\text{Min}}\ E[s(v_i, v_j; \beta) \mid \mu(w_i, \gamma_0) - \mu(w_j, \gamma_0) = 0].$$

The specific features of $s(\cdot)$ depend on the model in question. Honoré and Powell (2005) studied the case in which $\mu(w_i, \gamma) = \mu(w_i'\gamma)$. This article relaxes this assumption and studies the general case. We now present a series of examples that fit this general framework. As we shall see, the control function μ may arise naturally in very different contexts including (not necessarily known) transformations of partially linear index models, nonlinear models with endogeneity, as well as some game-theoretic models.

2.1. *Partially Linear Model.*   One of the most basic examples of the family of models studied here is a partially linear model, described by $y_i = \beta'x_i + g(w_i) + u_i$, where $g(\cdot)$ is an unknown function and u_i is unobserved but satisfies $E[u_i \mid x_i, w_i] = 0$ almost surely. This yields $y_i - E[y_i \mid w_i] = \beta'(x_i - E[x_i \mid w_i]) + u_i$ a.s. If x_i has full rank and is not deterministic conditional on w_i, it is a well-known result (e.g., Robinson, 1988) that β can be $\sqrt{n}$-consistently estimated by

(1)
$$\tilde{\beta} = \left[\sum_{i=1}^{n} (x_i - \hat{E}[x_i \mid w_i])(x_i - \hat{E}[x_i \mid w_i])' \mathbb{I}(w_i) \right]^{-1}$$
$$\times \sum_{i=1}^{n} (x_i - \hat{E}[x_i \mid w_i])(y_i - \hat{E}[y_i \mid w_i]) \mathbb{I}(w_i),$$

where $\hat{E}[x_i \mid w_i]$ is a nonparametric estimator and $\mathbb{I}(w_i)$ is a trimming function, introduced to make the bias of $\hat{E}[x_i \mid w_i]$ disappear uniformly at the same rate. Alternatively, we could reformulate this problem by noting that under the same set of identifying restrictions, with probability one $w_i = w_j$ implies $y_i - y_j = \beta'(x_i - x_j) + u_i - u_j$ and therefore $E[(y_i - y_j - \beta'(x_i - x_j))^2 \mid w_i - w_j = 0]$ is uniquely minimized at $\beta = \beta_0$. This calls for an estimator of the form

(2)
$$\hat{\beta} = \underset{b}{\operatorname{argmin}} \sum_{i<j} K\left(\frac{w_i - w_j}{h}\right) \left[(y_i - y_j) - b'(x_i - x_j)\right]^2,$$

for an appropriately chosen kernel k and bandwidth h. This yields a convenient closed-form estimator,

(3)
$$\hat{\beta} = \left[\sum_{i<j} K\left(\frac{w_i - w_j}{h}\right) \Delta x_{ij} \Delta x_{ij}' \right]^{-1} \sum_{i<j} K\left(\frac{w_i - w_j}{h}\right) \Delta x_{ij} \Delta y_{ij},$$

where $\Delta \xi_{ij} = \xi_i - \xi_j$.

Note that, unlike (1), the estimator proposed requires no trimming function. This is because in this particular example, the control function used (w_i) has a trivial functional form.[2] We will study situations in which the control function used in the procedure analogous to (1) must be estimated in a first stage and w_i is replaced with its estimate $\hat{w}_i$ in a generalized version of (2). For example, the role of w_i could be played by a nonparametric conditional expectation or residual that is not observed but can be uniformly consistently estimated semi or nonparametrically.

2.2. Other Partially Linear Models.

We now discuss briefly some extensions to the model in Section 2.1. These examples were considered in a more restrictive setting in Honoré and Powell (2005). For illustrative purposes we include here only the partially linear logit and Tobit models. We stress that all the examples mentioned in Section 2 of Honoré and Powell are amenable to the methodology described here. These include the partially linear Poisson regression model and partially linear duration models.

2.2.1. Partially linear logit model.

The partially linear logit model is given by $y_i = \mathbb{1}\{x_i'\beta + g(w_i) + \varepsilon_i \geq 0\}$, where ε_i is unobserved, independent of $z_i \equiv (x_i, w_i)$ with logistic distribution. We have

---

[2] If we knew the true functional form for μ, we could reduce the "curse of dimensionality" issues that are present in (3)

(4) $\Pr(y_i = 1 \mid z_i, z_j, y_i + y_j = 1, w_i - w_j = 0) = \dfrac{\exp\{(x_j - x_i)'\beta_0\}}{1 + \exp\{(x_j - x_i)'\beta_0\}}$,

which calls for an estimator of the form

(5) $\hat{\beta} = \underset{b}{\mathrm{argmin}} \sum_{\substack{i < j \\ y_i \neq y_j}} K\left(\dfrac{w_i - w_j}{h}\right) [y_i \ln(1 + \exp\{(x_j - x_i)'b\})$

$$+ y_j \ln(1 + \exp\{(x_i - x_j)'b\})].$$

As we mentioned above, we shall focus on the case in which w_i is not observed and must be estimated semi or nonparametrically prior to the estimation described in (5).

2.2.2. *Partially linear Tobit model.*   The partially linear Tobit model is given by $y_i = \max\{x_i'\beta + g(w_i) + \varepsilon_i\}$. Using the identification insight and results from Honoré (1992) in the context of panel data Tobit models with fixed effects, the framework in Honoré and Powell (2005) suggests an estimator of the form

(6) $\hat{\beta} = \underset{b}{\mathrm{argmin}} \sum_{i < j} K\left(\dfrac{w_i - w_j}{h}\right) q(y_i, y_j, (x_i - x_j)'b)$,

where $q(\cdot)$ is based on a convex-loss function of the type described in Honoré (1992).

2.3. *Rational Expectations and Interaction-based Models.*   Examples of models amenable to our methods also arise in the context of some structural models involving rational expectations with or without strategic interaction across economic agents. We present two examples here.

2.3.1. *Incomplete information games.*   Aradillas-Lopez (2006) studies a 2×2 simultaneous game with incomplete information where two players labeled $p = 1, 2$ can choose two actions, labeled $y_p \in \{1, 0\}$. Take $x_1 \in \mathbb{R}^{L_1}, x_2 \in \mathbb{R}^{L_2}$ and denote $x = x_1 \cup x_2$. Players' expected payoffs of choosing $y_p = 1$ are given by $E[U_1 \mid y_1 = 1] = x_1'\delta_1 + \alpha_1 \Pr[Y_2 = 1 \mid x] - \varepsilon_1$ and $E[U_2 \mid y_2 = 1] = x_2'\delta_2 + \alpha_2 \Pr[Y_1 = 1 \mid x] - \varepsilon_2$, where ε_p is independent of (x_1, x_2) with an unknown, but everywhere strictly increasing cdf given by $F_p(\cdot)$. Let $F_p(x) = \Pr(y_p = 1 \mid x)$. Players' beliefs are assumed unobserved to the econometrician. However, if players are expected utility maximizers, Bayesian–Nash equilibrium choice probabilities are[3]

(7) $\mu_1(x) = F_1(x_1'\delta_1 + \alpha_1\mu_2(x));$ $\mu_2(x) = F_2(x_2'\delta_2 + \alpha_2\mu_1(x)).$

Lack of knowledge of $F_p(\cdot)$ requires further parameter normalization. First, we will only be able to estimate (δ_p, α_p) up to a proportionality constant. In addition,

---

[3] Multiple equilibria concerns are addressed in the paper. We will ignore them here.

an intercept would not be identified. The following normalization will be convenient here. For $p = 1, 2$ we will split $x_p = (w_p, v_p)$, where the coefficient of w_p will be normalized to one. Let $\beta_p = (\delta_p, \alpha_p)$, $z_1 = (v'_1, \mu_2(x))$ and $z_2 = (v'_2, \mu_1(x))$. We can rewrite (7) as

$$(8) \qquad \mu_1(x) = F_1(w_1 + z'_1\beta_1); \quad \mu_2(x) = F_2(w_2 + z'_2\beta_2).$$

Denote $\mu_{p,i} = \mu_p(x_i)$. Using the invertibility properties of the unknown cdf $F_p(\cdot)$, Aradillas-Lopez provides additional conditions on x_p such that $E[((x_{p,i} - x_{p,j})'\delta_p)^2 \mid \mu_{p,i} = \mu_{p,j}]$ is uniquely minimized at $\delta_p = \delta_{p_0} = (1, \beta_{p_0})$. Such conditions involve a simple exclusion restriction and the existence of a continuously distributed covariate with nonzero coefficient. This model has the peculiarity that both the control function $\mu_{p,i}$ and the linear index $x'_{p,i}\delta_p$ involve unknown functions (recall that $x'_p\delta_p = w_p + z'_p\beta_p$, where z_p includes a nonparametric conditional probability). Let $\hat{\mu}_p(x_i) \equiv \hat{\mu}_{1,i}$ denote a nonparametrically estimator of $\mu_{p,i}$ and denote $\hat{\mu}_2(X_i) \equiv \hat{\mu}_{2,i}$ and let $\hat{z}_{1,i} \equiv (v'_{1,i}, \hat{\mu}_{2,i})$ and $\hat{z}_{2,i} \equiv (v'_{2,i}, \hat{\mu}_{1,i})$. Based on the identification condition stated above, the proposed estimator is

$$(9) \quad \hat{\beta}_p = \underset{b}{\operatorname{argmin}} \sum_{i<j} K\left(\frac{\hat{\mu}_{p,i} - \hat{\mu}_{p,j}}{h}\right) [(w_{p,i} - w_{p,j}) + (\hat{z}_{p,i} - \hat{z}_{p,j})'b]^2 \phi(x_i)\phi(x_j),$$

where $\phi(\cdot)$ is a trimming function. Note that the control function arises naturally in this model as a consequence of invertibility conditions of $F_p(\cdot)$, the otherwise unknown transformation of the partially linear index $w_p + z'_p\beta_p$. Notice also that the control functions used in (9) are one-dimensional, regardless of the dimension of x. This estimation procedure can be extended to general index models, whose identification conditions are essentially perfectly compatible with the assumptions used in this model.

2.3.2. Dynamic optimization models.

Consider a model in which agent i solves a dynamic optimization problem of the form

$$(10) \quad \underset{\{q_{it}\}_t}{\operatorname{Max}} E\left[\sum_{t=0}^{\infty} \delta^t U(x_{it}, s_{it}, q_{it}; \theta) \mid \{q_{it}\}_t\right] \quad \text{subject to } x_{it+1} = \mu(x_{it}, q_{it}) + \xi_{it+1}.$$

Using the terminology of dynamic programming models, q_{it} is agent i's control (not to be confused with the "control function") and x_{it} is the stock. $U(\cdot, \cdot, \cdot; \theta)$ is agent i's per-period utility function and s_{it} is an idiosyncratic shock unobserved by the econometrician, i.i.d. across time and agents, with cdf $F_s(\cdot; \gamma)$ assumed to be known up to the finite-dimensional parameter γ. The agent must choose q_{it} before knowing the realization of s_{it}. The accumulation equation $x_{it+1} = \mu(x_{it}, q_{it}) + \xi_{it+1}$ describes the evolution of the stock variable, with $\mu(\cdot)$ being an unspecified (for the moment) function, increasing in both arguments. ξ_{it+1} is a shock that is i.i.d. across time and individuals and is unobserved at time t. We will assume here that ξ_{it+1} is independent of all other covariates in the model. This model was analyzed in detail by Hong and Shum (2004), who assume a deterministic accumulation equation of the form $x_{it+1} = x_{it} + q_{it}$. Our assumptions imply

(11) $x_{it+1} \mid x_{it}, q_{it} \sim x_{it+1} \mid \mu(x_{it}, q_{it})$,

conditional on $\mu(x_{it}, q_{it})$, x_{it+1} is independent of x_{it}, q_{it}. Note that the evolution shock ξ_{it} does not enter the per-period utility function $U(\cdot, \cdot, \cdot; \theta)$. In a stationary setting, agents' optimal policy functions solve the following Bellman equation for $t = 1, 2, 3, \ldots$:

(12)

$$\underset{q}{\text{Max}}\ U(x_{it}, s_{it}, q; \theta) + \delta \cdot E[V(x_{t+1}, s_{t+1}; \theta, \gamma) \mid x_{it}, s_{it}, \xi_{it}, q], \quad \text{where}$$

$$V(x_{t+1}, s_{t+1}; \theta, \gamma) = \underset{\{q_{i\tau}\}_\tau}{\text{Max}}\ E\left[\sum_{\tau=t+1}^{\infty} \delta^{\tau-t-1} U(x_{i,\tau}, s_{i,\tau}, q_\tau; \theta) \,\Big|\, \{q_{i\tau}\}_\tau, x_{t+1}, s_{t+1}\right].$$

Note that this function does not depend on ξ_{t+1} because $E[U(x_{i\tau}, s_{i\tau}, q_\tau; \theta) \mid \{q_{i\tau}\}_\tau, x_{t+1}, s_{t+1}, \xi_{t+1}] = E[U(x_{i\tau}, s_{i\tau}, q_\tau; \theta) \mid \{q_{i\tau}\}_\tau, x_{t+1}, s_{t+1}]$ for all $\tau \geq t + 1$. We have

(13) $E[V(x_{t+1}, s_{t+1}; \theta, \gamma) \mid x_t, s_t, \xi_t, q] = E[V(x_{t+1}, s_{t+1}; \theta, \gamma) \mid x_t, s_t, q]$

$$= E\left[\int V(x_{t+1}, s; \theta, \gamma)\, dF_s(s)\, ds \mid x_t, q\right]$$

$$= E\left[\int V(x_{t+1}, s; \theta, \gamma)\, dF_s(s)\, ds \mid \mu(x_t, q)\right]$$

$$\equiv \bar{V}(\mu(x_t, q); \theta, \gamma),$$

so agent i's optimal policy can be expressed compactly as

(14) $q(x_{it}, s_{it}; \theta, \gamma) = \underset{q}{\text{argmax}}\ U(x_{it}, s_{it}, q; \theta) + \delta \bar{V}(\mu(x_{it}, q); \theta, \gamma).$

As in Hong and Shum (2004), the optimal policy function $q(x_t, s_t; \theta, \gamma)$ will be nondecreasing in s_t conditional on x_t if $U(x, s, q; \theta)$ is supermodular in (q, s) given x. This is a useful result because it enables us to recover s_{it} by inverting conditional quantiles of q_{it} given x_{it}. More precisely, for every quantile $\tau \in [0, 1]$ we have $(q \mid x)_\tau = s_\tau$. Therefore, we can estimate s_{it} by $\hat{s}_{it}(\gamma) = F_s^{-1}(\hat{F}(q_{it} \mid x_{it}); \gamma)$, where $\hat{F}(q \mid x)$ is a nonparametric estimator of the conditional cdf of q_t given x_t. Interior solutions to (12) (i.e., those with $q > 0$) satisfy

(15) $U_{(3)}(x_{it}, s_{it}, q; \theta) + \delta \bar{V}_{(1)}(\mu(x_{it}, q); \theta, \gamma)\mu_{(2)}(x_{it}, q) = 0,$

where $f_{(k)}$ denotes the partial derivative of f with respect to its kth argument. Now let us define $g(x, q) = (\mu(x, q), \mu_{(2)}(x, q))$. Notice from (15) that if $q_{it} > 0$

and $q_{jt} > 0$, then $g(x_{it}, q_{it}) = g(x_{jt}, q_{jt})$ implies $U_{(3)}(x_{it}, s_{it}, q_{it}; \theta) - U_{(3)}(x_{jt}, s_{jt}, q_{jt}; \theta) = 0$ when $\theta = \theta_0$. The (vector-valued) control function $g(x, q)$ can be estimated nonparametrically by noting that, given our assumptions,

(16)

$$\mu(x, q) = E[x_{it+1} \mid x_{it} = x, q_{it} = q], \text{ and } \mu_{(2)}(x, q) = \frac{\partial E[x_{it+1} \mid x_{it} = x, q_{it} = q]}{\partial q}.$$

Both objects can be estimated nonparametrically. Following the notation in Hong and Shum, let θ_1 denote the subvector of θ that "survives" after we take the difference $U_{(3)}(x_{it}, s_{it}, q_{it}; \theta) - U_{(3)}(x_{jt}, s_{jt}, q_{jt}; \theta)$ for two observations such that $g(x_{it}, q_{it}) = g(x_{jt}, q_{jt})$. We have a problem now: Both x and q are scalars. If μ is left completely unspecified, then in general x and q could be deterministic conditional on $\mu(x, q)$ and $\mu_{(2)}(x, q)$. Consequently, s would be deterministic too. Whenever $g(x_{it}, q_{it}) = g(x_{jt}, q_{jt})$, we would have $U_{(3)}(x_{it}, s_{it}, q_{it}; \theta) - U_{(3)}(x_{jt}, s_{jt}, q_{jt}; \theta) = 0$ for any θ. For this reason we need to add structure to μ. We will assume that $\mu(x, q) = \alpha_1 x + \alpha_2 q$, with $\hat{\mu}(x, q) = \hat{\alpha}_1 x + \hat{\alpha}_2 q$ being the estimated control function, which can be estimated based on (16) (note that $\mu_{(2)}(x, q)$ is simply a constant now). Letting $\beta = (\theta_1, \gamma)$, the above discussion calls for an estimator of the form[4]

(17) $$\hat{\beta} = \operatorname*{argmin}_{\gamma, \theta_1} \sum_{t=1}^{T} \sum_{\substack{i < j \\ q_{it} > 0 \\ q_{jt} > 0}} K\left(\frac{\hat{\mu}(x_{it}, q_{it}) - \hat{\mu}(x_{jt}, q_{jt})}{h}\right)$$

$$\times [U_{(3)}(x_{it}, \hat{s}_{it}(\gamma), q_{it}; \theta_1) - U_{(3)}(x_{jt}, \hat{s}_{jt}(\gamma), q_{jt}; \theta_1)]^2.$$

Pairwise-differencing allows us to estimate (at least a subset of) θ and γ without having to estimate the value function $\bar{V}$, which is usually a complex computational task. One would have to undertake this in a second step in order to estimate any parameters that might be in $\theta \setminus \theta_1$ (if there are any such parameters). Hong and Shum describe procedures to do this.

2.4. *The Effect of Pairwise Differencing on Identification.* The discussion at the end of Section 2.3.2 highlights an important issue in pairwise-difference estimation procedures. This is the fact that conditioning on the control variable might effectively "wipe out" some of the parameters of interest from the moment condition used for estimation. This is particularly clear in closed-form estimators like the ones described in Sections 2.1. and 2.3.1. In both cases, simple exclusion restrictions will salvage identification of the entire parameter vector of interest. As we noted above, this issue also arises in nonlinear models and might destroy identification of the entire parameter vector of interest. Conditions that would prevent this from happening are specific to the model at hand, and would go from conditions on the structure of the control function itself (as in Section 2.3.2 to

---

[4] We may still have $\theta_1 \subset \theta$ if taking the difference $U_{(3)}(x_{it}, s_{it}, q_{it}; \theta) - U_{(3)}(x_{jt}, s_{jt}, q_{jt}; \theta)$ always eliminates a subset of parameters.

exclusion restrictions). In general, the effect of pairwise differencing on identification is analogous to panel data fixed effects models, where differencing for a particular individual across time eliminates the unobserved fixed effect but it also wipes out any covariate that is fixed over time. As in our framework, only a subset of parameters would be identified.

2.5. On the Presence of Semi or Nonparametric Control Functions in Econometric Models.

The control functions described in Section 2.3 showed up naturally as a result of the primitive assumptions of the underlying economic models. Without further structure, the presence of control functions in Sections 2.1. and 2.2 appears to be artificially introduced into the models described there. We will argue here that these control functions would appear naturally in the econometric model as propensity scores—in models with some selection mechanism—or in cases where endogeneity is modeled in a particular way.

2.5.1. Control functions in models with selection.

This general notion was studied in a semi or nonparametric context for example in Ahn and Powell (1993) and Honoré and Powell (1994). Suppose $y_i^* = x_i'\beta + \varepsilon_i$, $d_i = 1\{w_i'\gamma + \eta_i > 0\}$ and $y_i = d_i y_i^*$. If (ε_i, v_i) are independent of (x_i, w_i), Then we can express $y_i = x_i'\beta + g(w_i'\gamma) + v_i$, where $g(w_i'\gamma) = E[\varepsilon_i \mid w_i'\gamma + \eta_i > 0]$ and $E[v_i \mid x_i, w_i] = 0$. The parameter vector γ could be estimated using index-model methods without having to assume a particular functional form for the distribution of v_i—as long as it has unbounded support and an everywhere-increasing distribution function. Alternatively, we could assume $d_i = 1\{\phi(w_i) + \eta_i > 0\}$, where $\phi(w_i)$ is an unknown function. This yields $E[d_i \mid w_i] = F_\eta(-\phi(w_i))$, where $\eta_i \sim F_\eta$ is only assumed to be everywhere increasing. Let $g(\phi(w_i)) = E[\varepsilon_i \mid \phi(w_i) + \eta_i > 0]$; invertibility of F_η implies that we can express the model as $y_i = x_i'\beta + \tilde{g}(E[d_i \mid w_i]) + v_i$, where $\tilde{g}(z) = g(-F_\eta^{-1}(z))$. An intermediate case is one where $d_i = 1\{\phi(w_i'\gamma) + \eta_i > 0\}$. Under appropriate assumptions about the otherwise unknown function $\phi(\cdot)$, the linear index $\gamma'x_i$ can be consistently estimated. If the econometrician observes only y_i, x_i, and w_i, all these cases yield special cases of the partially linear model described in Section 2.1. A control function also arises naturally in the context of a Tobit model with selection. Let $y_i^* = \max\{0, x_i'\beta + \varepsilon_i\}$, $d_i = 1\{\phi(w_i) + \eta_i > 0\}$ and $y_i = d_i y_i^*$. Suppose we can express[5] $\varepsilon_i = E[\varepsilon_i \mid d_i, w_i] + v_i \equiv g_1(\phi(w_i), d_i) + v_i$, where $E[v_i \mid w_i, x_i, d_i] = 0$, and obtain $y_i^* = \max\{0, x_i'\beta + g(\phi(w_i), d_i) + v_i\}$. If d_i is observed by the econometrician, then we can use the condition $E[\Delta y_{ij} - \Delta x_{ij}'\beta_0 \mid z_i, z_j \phi(w_i) - \phi(w_j) = 0] = 0$. The control function $\phi(w_i)$ can be estimated nonparametrically from $E[d_i \mid w_i] = F_\eta(-\phi(w_i))$ if we assume that F_η is invertible everywhere. We can show that if d_i is observed only when $y_i > 0$, we would have to proceed by using the entire vector w_i as the control function.

2.5.2. Control function and endogeneity.

Consider the model $y_i = 1\{x_i'\beta + \varepsilon_i \geq 0\}$ and partition $x_i = (x_{1i}, x_{2i})$, where x_{1i} is suspicious of endogeneity. Let $w_i = (x_{1i}, w_{2i})$, where x_{2i} is included in w_{2i}. In the spirit of Blundell and Powell

---

[5] Note that $E[\varepsilon_i \mid d_i, w_i]$ depends on w_i only through $\phi(w_i)$.

(2004), suppose the "reduced form" of the model can be described as follows[6]:
$x_{1i} = \phi(w_{2i}'\gamma) + v_i$, with $E[v_i \mid w_{2i}] = 0$, and $\varepsilon_i = E[\varepsilon_i \mid v_i] + \zeta_i \equiv g(v_i) + \zeta_i$, where
ζ_i is independent[7] of w_i, x_i. The model becomes $y_i = \mathbb{1}\{x_i'\beta + g(v_i) + \zeta_i \geq 0\}$. If
$\zeta_i \sim$ logistic, we obtain the partially linear logit model of Section 2.2.1. Under
appropriate Index-model assumptions, the control function v_i can be estimated
semiparametrically (e.g., Ichimura and Lee, 1991) as a residual. Let $\mu_i \equiv E[y_i \mid x_i,$
$w_i]$. If F_η is only assumed to be strictly increasing with unknown functional
form, the model could be approached by noting that $\mu_i = \mu_j$ and $v_i = v_j$ imply
$E[(x_i - x_j)'\delta_0 \mid \mu_i - \mu_j = 0, v_i - v_j = 0] = 0$, where δ is the vector of identified
parameters in this case. Following the discussion in Section 2.4, identification
would be completely destroyed in this case if $\mu_i = \mu_j$ and $v_i = v_j$ implies $x_i = x_j$.
This immediately imposes a dimensionality constraint on the vector of covariates
x_i. Using these same arguments it is easy to see how the partially linear Tobit
model from Section 2.2.2 could arise in the context of endogeneity. Further
examples where control functions have been used to control for endogeneity
include Newey et al. (1999) and Das et al. (2003), where control functions also
appear as propensity scores in the context of selection.

3. LARGE SAMPLE THEORY FOR THE PROPOSED ESTIMATION PROCEDURE

3.1. *Setup.*   We will assume throughout that we have an i.i.d. sample $\{s_i\}_{i=1}^n$
of size n on an observable vector z_i; letting $w_i \equiv (w_{1i}, w_{2i})' \in \mathbb{R}^{L_1} \times \mathbb{R}^{L_2}$ be a given
subvector of z_i, and $\gamma_0 \in \mathbb{R}^D$ be a vector of nuisance parameters, our "nonparamet-
ric control variable" is defined to be a vector-valued function $\mu : \mathbb{R}^{L_2} \times \mathbb{R}^D \longrightarrow \mathbb{R}^L$
of the form

$$\mu(w_i, \gamma_0) = \tau(w_i, \gamma_0) - E[\eta(w_i, \gamma_0) \mid w_{2i}],$$

where the functional forms for $\tau(\cdot)$ and $\eta(\cdot)$ are known, but the exact expression
for $\mu(\cdot)$ is unknown due to lack of knowledge about the conditional distribution of
w_i given w_{2i}. For example, for censored selection models with a binary indicator
variable d_i for the uncensored observations, the control variable $\zeta_i = \zeta(w_i, \gamma_0)$
might be the propensity score $\zeta_i = E[d_i \mid w_{2i}]$, with w_{2i} being a vector of regressors
in the selection equation, as in Ahn and Powell (1993); for this application, we
would have $w_i \equiv (d_i, w_{2i})$, $\tau(w_i, \gamma_0) \equiv 0$, and $\eta(w_i, \gamma_0) \equiv -d_i$. Alternatively,
in applications with endogenous regressors, μ_i might be the difference between
the endogenous regressor x_i and its conditional mean given some instrumental
variables w_{2i}, as in Blundell and Powell (2004) and the application discussed in
Section 4 below (with $\tau(w_i, \gamma_0) \equiv x_i \equiv \eta(w_i, \gamma_0)$). The nuisance parameter γ_0 might
appear in applications in which some semiparametric structure (e.g., a single index
restriction) is imposed on the control variable.
   Now let $v_i = (y_i, x_i)$ be another subvector of z_i; denoting the vector of parameters
of interest by β_0, suppose there exists a function $s(v_i, v_j; \beta)$ with the property that
the function

---

[6] As before, a linear index model is not required. We can have in general $x_{1i} = \phi(w_{2i}) + v_i$.
[7] More generally, we could simply assume that $\varepsilon_i \mid x_i, v_i \sim \varepsilon_i \mid v_i$.

$$T(\gamma_0, \beta) \equiv E[s(v_i, v_j; \beta) \mid \mu(w_i, \gamma_0) - \mu(w_j, \gamma_0) = 0]$$

is uniquely minimized at $\beta = \beta_0$. In terms of identification, the parameter vector β_0 includes only those that "survive" the pairwise-differencing procedure (see Section 2.4, above). For simplicity, we will focus here on the case where $s(v_i, v_j; \beta)$ is known up to β. We stress however that our methods can be extended to cases where $s(v_i, v_j; \beta)$ includes unknown functions (as in the examples in Section 2.3) or "generated regressors"; for details, see, for example, Aradillas-Lopez (2006). As we illustrated in Section 2 and further examples analyzed in Honoré and Powell (2005), such criterion functions $s(\cdot)$ are available for a number of different nonlinear models, including the partially linear logit, censored regression, and Poisson regression models and the censored regression model with selectivity, in which the control function appears in the nonparametric component of the partially linear regression function. We also showed in Section 2 that further examples have been found in the context of rational expectations and interactions-based models. Following Honoré and Powell (2005), we study the properties of estimators of β_0 defined by minimizing an estimator of $T(\gamma_0, \beta)$ of the form

(18) $$T_n(\hat{\gamma}, b) = \binom{n}{2}^{-1} \sum_{i<j} r_n(z_i, z_j; \hat{\gamma}, b), \quad \text{with}$$

$$r_n(z_i, z_j; \hat{\gamma}, b) = \frac{1}{h_n^L} K\left(\frac{\hat{\mu}_n(w_{2i}, \hat{\gamma}) - \hat{\mu}_n(w_{2j}, \hat{\gamma})}{h_n}\right) s(v_i, v_j; b),$$

where $K(\cdot)$ is a kernel function and $\hat{\mu}_n(\cdot)$ is a nonparametric estimator of $\mu(\cdot)$.

In the following sections, we will provide conditions under which the resulting estimator $\hat{\beta}$ is consistent and asymptotically normal. We assume that the conditioning vector w_{2i} is continuously distributed, and, in our estimation method, realizations near the boundary of its support will be trimmed out in order to avoid the resulting bias on $\hat{\mu}_n(\cdot)$, the nonparametric estimator of $\mu(\cdot)$. We study carefully the implications of trimming on the consistency of our estimators and provide a set of sufficient conditions that ensure the appropriate rate of uniform convergence of the estimator $\hat{\mu}_n(\cdot)$ to achieve $\sqrt{n}$-consistency of $\hat{\beta}$. We also provide conditions under which trimming may disappear asymptotically. Following Honoré and Powell (2005), we propose the use of a simple jackknife procedure as an alternative to the use of a bias-reducing kernel $K(\cdot)$ in (18), which would render the objective function nonconvex and require compactness of the parameter space for uniform consistency. Bias-reducing kernels will be used only in the estimation of $\hat{\mu}_n(\cdot)$, the control function.

3.2. *Some Preliminary Results.*   Suppose $w_i \equiv (w_{1i}, w_{2i})' \in \mathbb{R}^{L_1} \times \mathbb{R}^{L_2}$ is a random vector and let $f_{w_2}(w_2)$ denote the marginal density of w_2. Given two constant vectors $\gamma \in \mathbb{R}^D$ and $\omega = (\omega_1, \omega_2) \in \mathbb{R}^{L_1} \times \mathbb{R}^{L_2}$, the function $\eta : \mathbb{R}^{L_1} \times \mathbb{R}^{L_2} \times \mathbb{R}^D \to \mathbb{R}^L$, a kernel $H : \mathbb{R}^{L_2} \to \mathbb{R}$, and a bandwidth sequence $b_n : \mathbb{N} \to \mathbb{R}_{++}$, let $H_{b_n}(t) = H(t/b_n)$ and define

$$R_n(\omega_2, \gamma) = \frac{1}{nh_n^{L_2}} \sum_{i=1}^{n} \eta(w_{1i}, \omega_2, \gamma) H_{b_n}(w_{2i} - \omega_2),$$

$$\hat{f}_{w_{2n}}(\omega_2) = \frac{1}{nh_n^{L_2}} \sum_{i=1}^{n} H_{b_n}(w_{2i} - \omega_2).$$

Let $\mu(\omega, \gamma) = \tau(\omega, \gamma) - E[\eta(w_i, \gamma) \mid w_{2i} = \omega_2]$ and $\hat{\mu}_n(\omega, \gamma) = \tau(\omega, \gamma) - [R_n(\omega_2, \gamma)/\hat{f}_{w_{2n}}(\omega_2)]$. Denote $M = L + L_2 + 3$, and let $\mathbb{S}(\omega)$ denote the support of a random variable ω. Consider the following assumptions:

ASSUMPTION 1.

    i. w_{2i} is absolutely continuous with respect to Lebesgue measure;

    ii. The density $f_{w_2}(w_2)$ is bounded, M times differentiable with respect to w_2 with bounded Mth derivative everywhere in $\mathbb{S}(w)$.

ASSUMPTION 2. There exists $W_2 \subset \text{interior}\{\mathbb{S}(w_2)\}$ with $\inf_{w_2 \in W_2} f_{w_2}(w_2) > 0$, and $\Gamma \subset \mathbb{R}^D$ where the following conditions hold:

    i. $\mu(\omega, \gamma)$ is M times differentiable with respect to ω and γ with bounded Mth derivatives for every $\omega \in \mathbb{S}(\omega)$ and $\gamma \in \Gamma$;

    ii. There exists a function $\bar{\eta} : \mathbb{R}^{L_1} \to \mathbb{R}_+$ such that $\|\eta(w_{1i}, w_2, \gamma)\| \le \bar{\eta}(w_{1i})$ w.p.1 for all $w_{1i} \in \mathbb{S}(w_1)$, $w_2 \in W_2$, and $\gamma \in \Gamma$ that satisfies the following: $E[\bar{\eta}(w_{1i})^2 \mid w_{2i} = w_2]$ exists and is a continuous function of w_2 for all $w_2 \in \mathbb{S}(w_2)$, and $E[\bar{\eta}(w_{1i})^4] < \infty$;

    iii. There exists a function $\bar{\eta}_1 : \mathbb{R}^{L_1} \to \mathbb{R}_+$ and φ_1 such that $\|\eta(w_{1i}, u, \gamma) - \eta(w_{1i}, u', \gamma)\| \le \bar{\eta}_1(w_{1i})\|u - u'\|^{\varphi_1}$ w.p.1 for all $w_{1i} \in \mathbb{S}(w_1), u, u' \in W_2, \gamma \in \Gamma$, with $E[\bar{\eta}_1(w_{1i})] < \infty$;

    iv. There exists a function $\bar{\eta}_2 : \mathbb{R}^{L_1} \to \mathbb{R}_+$ and φ_2 such that $\|\eta(w_1, u, \gamma) - \eta(w_1, u, \gamma')\| \le \bar{\eta}_2(w_1)\|\gamma - \gamma'\|^{\varphi_2}$ w.p.1 for all $w_1 \in \mathbb{S}(w_1), u \in W_2, \gamma, \gamma' \in \Gamma$, and $E[\bar{\eta}_2(w_1)] < \infty$.

Assumption 1 can be relaxed to permit discrete components of w_{2i}, in which case L_2 would be the number of continuously distributed components. Assumptions 2(iii) and 2(iv) can be seen as "in probability" Lipschitz conditions—see, for example, lemma 2.9 in Newey and McFadden (1994). They would be immediately satisfied, for example, if $\eta(w_1, u, \gamma)$ is assumed to be differentiable with respect to u and γ with bounded derivatives in W_2 and Γ.

ASSUMPTION 3.

    i. Define $\mathcal{H} \equiv \{t \in \mathbb{R}^{L_2} : H(t) \ne 0\}$; then $\mathcal{H} \subset \mathbb{R}^{L_2}$ is compact. $H(\cdot)$ is bounded and symmetric about zero, with $\int H(t)\, dt = 1$. Denote $t = (t_1, \ldots, t_{L_2})'$; then $\int \|t\|^M |H(t)|\, dt < \infty$ and $\int (t_1^{q_1} \cdots t_{L_2}^{q_{L_2}}) H(t)\, dt_1 \ldots dt_{L_2} = 0$ for all $0 < q_1 + \cdots + q_{L_2} < M$. There exist $\varphi \in (0, M)$ and $c_H < \infty$ such that $|H(t) - H(t')| \le c_H \|t - t'\|^{\varphi}\, \forall t, t'$.

    ii. b_n satisfies $b_n = o(1)$, $\ln n b_n^{-2L_2} = o(n)$, $b_n^{2M} = o(n^{-1})$ and $b_n^{-L_2-2\varphi} = o(n^{1-\sigma})$ for some $\sigma > 0$.

iii. *The sets W_2 and H, and the bandwidth b_n are such that $b_n t + w_2 \in$ interior $\{S(w_2)\} \forall t \in H, w_2 \in W_2, n \in \mathbb{N}$.*

The following result will be useful.

THEOREM 1. *If Assumptions (1)–(3) are satisfied, then*

(a) $\sup_{\substack{\omega \in W_2 \\ \gamma \in \Gamma}} (n^{1-\delta} b_n^{L_2})^{1/2} \|\hat{\mu}_n(\omega, \gamma) - \mu(\omega, \gamma)\| = O_p(1)$ *for any $\delta > 0$.*

(b) $\hat{\mu}_n(\omega, \gamma) - \mu(\omega, \gamma) = \frac{1}{f_{w_2}(\omega)} \frac{1}{n b_n^{L_2}} \sum_{i=1}^{n} [\tau(\omega, \gamma) - \eta(w_{1i}, \omega_2, \gamma) - \mu(\omega, \gamma)] \times H_{b_n}(w_{2i} - \omega) + \xi_n(\omega, \gamma)$,

where $\sup_{\substack{\omega \in W_2 \\ \gamma \in \Gamma}} \|\xi_n(\omega, \gamma)\| = O_p(n^{\delta-1} b_n^{-L_2})$ *for any $\delta > 0$.*

Note that $\tau(\omega, \gamma) - \mu(\omega, \gamma) = E[\eta(w_{1i}, \omega_2, \gamma) \mid w_{2i} = \omega_2]$, so the linear representation in part (b) of Theorem 1 depends only on $\eta(w_i, \gamma) - E[\eta(w_i, \gamma) \mid w_{2i} = \omega_2]$. Theorem 1 is a special case of a more general result shown in Aradillas-Lopez (2005). It will be crucial for the main results presented below. The next result is an immediate consequence:

COROLLARY 1. *Suppose we strengthen the condition $\ln n b_n^{-L_2} = o(n)$ to $n^{1-\delta} b_n^{-2L_2} = o(1)$ for some $\delta > 0$. Let $\xi_n(\omega, \gamma)$ be as defined in Theorem 1; then* $\sup_{\substack{\omega \in W_2 \\ \gamma \in \Gamma}} \|\xi_n(\omega, \gamma)\| = o_p(N^{-1/2})$.

3.3. *Estimation.* We will examine the case in which the pairwise difference estimator depends on the unknown function $\mu(\omega, \gamma)$, which was defined in Section 3.2. Because this function is unknown, we will use its nonparametric estimator $\hat{\mu}_n(\omega, \gamma)$, which was also defined above. We assume w_{2i} to be continuously distributed. Thus, in order to avoid the influence of points in the boundary of $S(w_2)$—which would introduce a bias on $\hat{\mu}_n(w_2, \gamma)$, we will analyze a trimmed version of the objective function in Equation (18). We will denote $z_i = (y_i, x_i, w_i)$ and $v_i = (y_i, x_i)$, where $w_i = (w_{1i}, w_{2i})$, and w_i is as described in Section 3.2. We will use W_2 as the trimming set, where W_2 satisfies Assumptions (1) and (2). Let

$$r_n(z_i, z_j; \gamma, b) = \frac{1}{h_n^L} K\left(\frac{\hat{\mu}_n(w_i, \gamma) - \hat{\mu}_n(w_j, \gamma)}{h_n}\right) s(v_i, v_j; b) \cdot a(w_{2i})a(w_{2j}),$$

where $a(\cdot)$ is the trimming function described as

$$a(w_2) = \begin{cases} \phi(w_2) > 0 & \text{if } w_2 \in W_2, \\ 0 & \text{otherwise.} \end{cases}$$

The function $\phi(u)$ is bounded, continuous, and strictly positive for all $u \in \mathbb{R}^{L_2}$. We will describe the properties of the function $s(v_i, v_j; b)$ below. Define

$$(19) \qquad T_n(\gamma, b) = \binom{n}{2}^{-1} \sum_{i<j} r_n(z_i, z_j; \gamma, b),$$

where $\hat{\mu}_n(\omega, \gamma)$ is as defined in Section 3.2.

ASSUMPTION 4.

    i. $E[s(v_i, v_j; b)^2] < \infty$;

    ii. $E[\|\mu(w_i, \gamma) - \mu(w_j, \gamma)\|^2] < \infty$;

    iii. $\mu(w_i, \gamma_0)$ is continuously distributed with bounded density, $f_{\mu(w, \gamma_0)}(\cdot)$, which is a continuous function;

    iv. Denote $\kappa_s(a_1, a_2, b) = E[s(v_i, v_j; b) | z_i = a_1, \mu(w_j, \gamma_0) = a_2]$; then $\kappa_s(\cdot)$ exists and is a continuous function of each of its arguments;

    v. Let $\rho(\mu(w_i, \gamma_0)) = E[a(w_{2i}) | \mu(w_i, \gamma_0)]$. Then $\rho(\mu(w_i, \gamma_0))$ is continuous and strictly positive for all $\mu(w_i, \gamma_0)$ such that $w_{2i} \in \mathcal{W}_2$. Denote $\ell_s(a_1, a_2, b) = \kappa_s(a_1, a_2, b)\rho(a_2) f_{\mu(w, \gamma_0)}(a_2)$; then $|\ell_s(a_1, a_2, b)| \leq c_1(a_1, a_2, b)$ with $E[c_1(v_i, \mu(w_i, \gamma_0), b)] < \infty$ for all b;

    vi. $\{z_i, i = 1, \ldots, n\}$ is an i.i.d. sample.

The use of trimming in the objective function could have an adverse effect on the consistency of $\hat{\beta}$ if the value of β that maximizes $E[a(w_{2i})a(w_{2j})s(v_i, v_j; \beta) | \mu(w_i, \gamma_0) - \mu(w_j, \gamma_0) = 0]$ differs from the one that corresponds to $E[s(v_i, v_j; \beta) | \mu(w_i, \gamma_0) - \mu(w_j, \gamma_0) = 0]$. Typically, this issue would be addressed by introducing some form of exclusion restriction. Suppose all we know is that $E[s(v_i, v_j; \beta) | \mu(w_i, \gamma_0) - \mu(w_j, \gamma_0) = 0]$ is uniquely minimized when $\beta = \beta_0$. The next assumption describes an exclusion restriction that would eliminate any potential trimming bias.

ASSUMPTION 5. $E[s(v_i, v_j; b) | v_i, w_{2j}, \mu(w_j, \gamma_0)] = E[s(v_i, v_j; b) | v_i, \mu(w_j, \gamma_0)]$.

In essence, what we require is that, conditional on v_i, $s(v_i, v_j; b)$ is mean-independent of w_{2j} conditional on $\mu(w_j, \gamma_0)$. The worst-case scenario would be one in which all we have to work with is the assumption that $E[s(v_i, v_j; \beta) | \mu(w_i, \gamma_0) - \mu(w_j, \gamma_0) = 0]$ is uniquely minimized when $\beta = \beta_0$, and Assumption 5 does not hold. In Section 3.9, we present a solution to that case. There, we describe an alternative trimming methodology based on a sequence of trimming functions $a_n(\cdot)$ and a sequence of trimming sets $\mathcal{W}_{2n}$ and we describe conditions under which $E[a_n(w_{2i})a_n(w_{2j})s(v_i, v_j; \beta) | \mu(w_i, \gamma_0) = \mu(w_j, \gamma_0)] \xrightarrow{P} E[s(v_i, v_j; \beta) | \mu(w_i, \gamma_0) = \mu(w_j, \gamma_0)]$ uniformly in B. If such conditions are satisfied, and the alternative trimming methodology is used, then consistency of the resulting estimator $\hat{\beta}$ would rely exclusively on the assumption that $E[s(v_i, v_j; \beta) | \mu(w_i, \gamma_0) - \mu(w_j, \gamma_0) = 0]$ is uniquely minimized when $\beta = \beta_0$ regardless of whether or not Assumption 5 is satisfied. Basically, what we would need is for the properties of $\mathcal{W}_2$ in Assumptions 1 and 2 to be satisfied by any arbitrary compact set in the interior of $\mathbb{S}(w_2)$, the sequence of trimming functions $a_n(w_2)$ to converge to a positive constant c with probability one, and the tails of $f_{w_2}(\cdot)$ to converge to zero at an appropriate rate relative to the one at which W_{2_n} converges to $\mathbb{S}(w_2)$. We will describe the set of conditions in detail in Section 3.9.

ASSUMPTION 6. *We have $h_n = o(1)$. Let b_n be the bandwidth used in the estimation of $\mu(\cdot)$. We will strengthen Assumption 3(ii) and assume that $n^{1-2\delta}b_n^{L_2}h_n^{2(L+2)} \to \infty$ for some $\delta > 0$ and $nb_n^{2M}h_n^{-2(L+1)} \to 0$.*

ASSUMPTION 7. *K is bounded and symmetric about zero with $\int K(u)\,du = 1$ and $\|u\| \cdot |K(u)| \to 0$ as $\|u\| \to \infty$. $K(\cdot)$ is twice differentiable with bounded derivatives. Denote its gradient by $K^{(1)}(\cdot) \in \mathbb{R}^L$; then $K^{(1)}(t) = -K^{(1)}(-t)$ for all t.*

ASSUMPTION 8. *We assume $\gamma_0 \in \Gamma$, which is described in Theorem 1. We allow the use of an estimator $\hat{\gamma}$ of γ_0 if necessary. Then, either*

   i. *$\hat{\gamma} = \gamma_0 \in \Gamma$ or*
   ii. *$\|\hat{\gamma} - \gamma_0\| = O_p(n^{-1/2})$, and $\hat{\gamma} \in \Gamma$ for all n.*

ASSUMPTION 9. *$|s(v_i, v_j; b_1) - s(v_i, v_j; b_2)| \le B_{ij}\|b_1 - b_2\|^\alpha$ for some $\alpha > 0$, where $E[B_{ij}^2] < \infty$.*

Our estimator $\hat{\beta}$ is defined as

(20) $$\hat{\beta} = \operatorname*{argmin}_b T_n(\hat{\gamma}, b).$$

We first analyze the limiting objective function.

3.3.1. *Pointwise convergence to limiting objective function.*   Define

$$T(\gamma_0, b) = E[a(w_{2i})\ell_s(v_i, \mu(w_i, \gamma_0), b)],$$

where $\kappa_s(\cdot)$ and $g(\cdot)$ are described in Assumptions 4(iv) and 4(vi)—above. Then, if Assumptions 1–8 hold, $T_n(\hat{\gamma}, b) \to T(\gamma_0, b)$.

PROOF. Define

$$T_n(\gamma_0, b) = \binom{n}{2}^{-1} \sum_{i<j} \frac{1}{h_n^L} K\left(\frac{\mu(w_i, \gamma_0) - \mu(w_j, \gamma_0)}{h_n}\right) s(v_i, v_j; b)a(w_{2i})a(w_{2j}).$$

First we show that $T_n(\gamma_0, b) \to T(\gamma_0, b)$. Note that if Assumption 7 is satisfied, then

$E[\mathcal{T}_n(\gamma_0, b)]$

$$= E\left[\frac{1}{h_n^L}K\left(\frac{\mu(w_i, \gamma_0) - \mu(w_j, \gamma_0)}{h_n}\right)s(v_i, v_j; b)a(w_{2i})a(w_{2j})\right]$$

$$= E\left[\frac{1}{h_n^L}K\left(\frac{\mu(w_i, \gamma_0) - \mu(w_j, \gamma_0)}{h_n}\right)a(w_{2i})\rho(\mu(w_j, \gamma_0))\kappa_s(v_i, \mu(w_j, \gamma_0); b)\right]$$

$$= E\left[a(w_{2i})\int K(\psi)\rho(h_n\psi + \mu(w_i, \gamma_0))\kappa_s(v_i, h_n\psi + \mu(w_i, \gamma_0); b)\right.$$
$$\left. \times f_\mu(h_n\psi + \mu(w_i, \gamma_0))\, d\psi\right]$$

$$\to E[a(w_{2i})\rho(\mu(w_i, \gamma_0))\kappa_s(v_i, \mu(w_i, \gamma_0), b)f_\mu(\mu(w_i, \gamma_0))]$$

$$= E[f_\mu(\mu(w_i, \gamma_0))\rho(\mu(w_i, \gamma_0))^2 E[\kappa_s(v_i, \mu(w_i, \gamma_0), b)\,|\,\mu(w_i, \gamma_0)]],$$

where the next-to-last line follows from Assumptions 4(iv)–4(vi), 5, and 6, and the last line follows once again from Assumption 5. Using Assumptions 4(i), 6, 7, and the properties of $a(\cdot)$, we have

$$E\left[\left\{\frac{1}{h_n^L}K\left(\frac{\mu(w_i, \gamma_0) - \mu(w_j, \gamma_0)}{h_n}\right)s(v_i, v_j; b)a(w_{2i})a(w_{2j})\right\}^2\right] = O(n),$$

which satisfies lemma A.3 of Ahn and Powell (1993). Consequently, $\mathcal{T}_n(\gamma_0, b) \to E[\mathcal{T}_n(\gamma_0, b)] \to T(\gamma_0, b)$. Next we show that $\mathcal{T}_n(\hat{\gamma}, b) \to \mathcal{T}_n(\gamma_0, b)$:

$|\mathcal{T}_n(\hat{\gamma}, b) - \mathcal{T}_n(\gamma_0, b)|$

$$\leq \binom{n}{2}^{-1}\sum_{i<j}\frac{1}{h_n^L}\left|K\left(\frac{\hat{\mu}_n(w_i, \hat{\gamma}) - \hat{\mu}_n(w_j, \hat{\gamma})}{h_n}\right) - K\left(\frac{\hat{\mu}_n(w_i, \gamma_0) - \hat{\mu}_n(w_j, \gamma_0)}{h_n}\right)\right|$$

$$\times |s(v_i, v_j; b)|a(w_{2i})a(w_{2j}).$$

We have

$$\left|K\left(\frac{\hat{\mu}_n(w_i, \hat{\gamma}) - \hat{\mu}_n(w_j, \hat{\gamma})}{h_n}\right) - K\left(\frac{\hat{\mu}_n(w_i, \gamma_0) - \hat{\mu}_n(w_j, \gamma_0)}{h_n}\right)\right|$$

$$\leq \frac{2L}{h_n}\|K^{(1)}(d_{ij}^*)\| \cdot \left[\max_i\|\hat{\mu}_n(w_i, \hat{\gamma}) - \mu(w_i, \hat{\gamma})\| + \max_i\|\hat{\mu}_n(w_i, \gamma_0) - \mu(w_i, \gamma_0)\|\right.$$

$$\left. + \max_i\|\mu(w_i, \hat{\gamma}) - \mu(w_i, \gamma_0)\|\right]|s(v_i, v_j; b)|a(w_{2i})a(w_{2j}).$$

By Theorem 1, $a(\cdot)$, and Assumption 8, we have $\max_i\|\hat{\mu}_n(w_i, \hat{\gamma}) - \mu(w_i, \hat{\gamma})\| = O_p(n^{1-\delta}b_n^{L_2})^{-1/2}$ for every $\delta > 0$. The same result holds for $\max_i\|\hat{\mu}_n(w_i, \gamma_0) - \mu(w_i, \gamma_0)\|$. By Assumption 2(i), there exists a $C_1 > 0$ such that $\max_i\|\mu(w_i, \hat{\gamma}) - \mu(w_i, \gamma_0)\| \leq C_1\|\hat{\gamma} - \gamma_0\| = O_p(n^{-1/2})$—using Assumption 8. From Assumption 7, there exists $C_2 > 0$ such that $\|K^{(1)}(t)\| \leq C_2$ for all t. Combining all this and letting $C = 2LC_1C_2$, we have

$$|T_n(\hat{\gamma}, b) - T_n(\gamma_0, b)| \leq \frac{C}{h_n^{L+1}} \Big[O_p(n^{1-\delta}b_n^{L_2})^{-1/2} + O_p(n^{-1/2}) \Big] \binom{n}{2}^{-1}$$
$$\times \sum_{i<j} |s(v_i, v_j; b)| a(w_{2i}) a(w_{2j})$$

for all $\delta > 0$. Therefore, Assumption 6 yields $h_n^{-L-1} O_p(n^{1-\delta}b_n^{L_2})^{-1/2} = o_p(1)$ and $h_n^{-L-1} O_p(n^{-1/2}) = o_p(1)$. Combining this with Assumptions 4(i), 6, and the properties of $a(\cdot)$, we have $|T_n(\hat{\gamma}, b) - T_n(\gamma_0, b)| = o_p(1)$, and therefore $T_n(\hat{\gamma}, b) \to T(\gamma_0, b)$, which proves the claim. ∎

Suppose that the following modified version of Assumption 5 holds:

ASSUMPTION   5′. $E[s(v_i, v_j; b) \mid v_i, x_j, w_{2j}, \mu(w_j, \gamma_0)] = E[s(v_i, v_j; b) \mid v_i, x_j, \mu(w_j, \gamma_0)]$.

Based on this condition, we can modify Assumption 4 accordingly:

ASSUMPTION   4′.   *Maintain 4(i), 4(ii), and 4(vi) but modify 4(iii)–4(v) to assume that*

   iii.   *Let* $f_{\mu|x}(\mu; x)$ *be the conditional density of* $\mu(w_j, \gamma_0)$ *given* $x_j = x$. *Then* $f_{\mu|x}(\mu; x)$ *is a continuous function of its first argument.*
   iv.   *Define* $\bar{\kappa}_s(a_1, a_2, a_3) = E[s(v_i, v_j; b) \mid z_i = a_1, x_j = a_2, \mu(w_j, \gamma_0) = a_3]$. *Then* $\bar{\kappa}_s(a_1, a_2, a_3)$ *exists and is a continuous function of each of its arguments;*
   v.   *Let* $\bar{\rho}(a_2, a_3) = E[a(w_{2j}) \mid x_j = a_2, \mu(w_j, \gamma_0) = a_3]$. *Then* $\bar{\rho}(a_2, a_3)$ *is a continuous function of its second argument and is strictly positive for all* $\mu(w_j, \gamma_0)$ *such that* $w_{2j} \in W_2$. *Define* $\bar{\ell}_s(a_1, a_2, a_3, b) = \bar{\rho}(a_2, a_3)\bar{\kappa}_s(a_1, a_2, a_3) f_{\mu|x}(a_3; a_2)$; *then* $|\ell_s(a_1, a_2, a_3, b)| < \bar{c}_1(a_1, a_2, a_3, b)$, *with* $E[\bar{c}_1(a_1, a_2, a_3, b)] < \infty$ *for all* b.

Define

$$\bar{T}(\gamma_0, b) = E[a(w_{2i})\bar{\ell}_s(v_i, x_j, \mu(w_i, \gamma_0))].$$

Then, if Assumptions 1–3, 4′, 5′, and 6–8 hold, $T_n(\hat{\gamma}, b) \to \bar{T}(\gamma_0, b)$. The proof follows the same steps as above, replacing Assumptions 4 and 5 with 4′ and 5′, respectively.

3.4.   *Uniform Convergence to Limiting Objective Function.*   Let B be the parameter space for β. If B is compact, then $\sup_{b \in B} |T_n(\hat{\gamma}, b) - T(\gamma_0, b)| = o_p(1)$.

PROOF.   Using Assumption 9 and following steps parallel to those used to show that $\sup_{b \in B} |T_n(\gamma_0, b) - T(\gamma_0, b)| = o_p(1)$. Take $b_1, b_2 \in B$. Using the same steps as the ones used in the pointwise convergence proof, we can show that

$|T_n(\hat{\gamma}, b_1) - T_n(\gamma_0, b_2)|$

$$\leq \frac{C}{h_n^{L+1}} \left[O_p(n^{1-\delta} b_n^{L_2})^{-1/2} + O_p(n^{-1/2}) \right] \binom{n}{2}^{-1}$$

$$\times \sum_{i<j} |s(v_i, v_j; b_1) - s(v_i, v_j; b_1)| a(w_{2i}) a(w_{2j})$$

$$\leq \frac{C}{h_n^{L+1}} \left[O_p(n^{1-\delta} b_n^{L_2})^{-1/2} + O_p(n^{-1/2}) \right] \binom{n}{2}^{-1} \sum_{i<j} B_{ij} a(w_{2i}) a(w_{2j}) \|b_1 - b_2\|^{\alpha},$$

for all $\delta > 0$, and using Assumptions 6, 9, and the compactness of B, we get $\sup_{b \in B} |T_n(\hat{\gamma}, b) - T_n(\gamma_0, b)| = o_p(1)$, and consequently $\sup_{b \in B} |T_n(\hat{\gamma}, b) - Q(\gamma_0, b)| = o_p(1)$, which establishes uniform convergence. ∎

As with pointwise convergence, a parallel result holds if we replace Assumptions 4 and 5 with 4' and 5', respectively. In this case, we have $\sup_{b \in B} |T_n(\gamma_0, b) - \bar{T}(\gamma_0, b)| = o_p(1)$.

3.5. *Identification.*   As we mentioned above, trimming is done to avoid bias of $\hat{\mu}_n(\cdot)$ that would be caused by points on the boundary of $\mathbb{S}(w_2)$. Given this need, we chose $\mathcal{W}_2$ as the trimming set to take advantage of the results of Theorem 1. Without additional assumptions, trimming may cause bias of $\hat{\beta}$ in this setting. The purpose of Assumptions 4(vi), 4(vii), and 5 is to avoid the presence of such bias. As we stated above, if Assumptions 1–3 hold for any compact set in the interior of $\mathbb{S}(w_2)$ and if $f_{w_2}(\cdot)$ satisfies some additional assumptions (see Assumption 18, below), we could make the trimming disappear asymptotically and leave the rate of convergence of our estimator unchanged. This would allow us to relax Assumptions 4(vi), 4(vii), and 7. Below, we will present conditions under which this can be done.

If Assumption 5 is satisfied, the limiting objective function $T(\gamma_0, b)$ is given by

$$T(\gamma_0, b) = E[a(w_{2i}) \ell_s(v_i, \mu(w_i, \gamma_0), b)]$$
$$= E[f_\mu(\mu(w_i, \gamma_0)) \rho(\mu(w_i, \gamma_0))^2 E[s(v_i, v_j, b) \mid \mu(w_j, \gamma_0) = \mu(w_i, \gamma_0)]],$$

where the last equality comes from Assumption 5. $T(\gamma_0, b)$ is uniquely minimized at β_0 if the following condition holds:

ASSUMPTION 10. $E[s(v_i, v_j; b) \mid \mu(w_j, \gamma_0) = \mu(w_i, \gamma_0)]$ *is uniquely minimized at* $b = \beta_0$.

If Assumption 5' is satisfied, the limiting objective function $\bar{T}(\gamma_0, b)$ is

$$\bar{T}(\gamma_0, b) = E[a(w_{2i}) \bar{\ell}_s(v_i, x_j, \mu(w_i, \gamma_0))]$$
$$= E[a(w_{2i}) \bar{\rho}(x_j, \mu(w_i, \gamma_0)) f_{\mu|x}(\mu(w_i, \gamma_0); x_j)$$
$$\times E[s(v_i, v_j, b) \mid x_i, x_j, \mu(w_j, \gamma_0) = \mu(w_i, \gamma_0)]]$$

The last equality being a consequence of Assumption 5'. $\bar{T}(\gamma_0, b)$ is uniquely minimized at β_0 if the following condition holds:

ASSUMPTION 10'. $E[s(v_i, v_j; b) \mid x_i, x_j, \mu(w_i, \gamma_0) - \mu(w_j, \gamma_0) = 0]$ is uniquely minimized at $b = \beta_0$.

As it is the case with extremum estimators, Assumption 10 (or 10') yields identification and, along with the convergence results of Sections 3.3.1 and 3.4, it will also yield consistency of $\hat{\beta}$. We present the results now.

3.5.1. Consistency theorem.

Let $\hat{\beta}$ be the minimizer of $T_n(\hat{\gamma}, b)$ over the parameter space of β, denoted by B. We have the following results:

THEOREM 2.   Let $K_{h_n}(t) \equiv K(t/h_n)$. If $K_{h_n}(\mu(w_i, \gamma) - \mu(w_j, \gamma))s(v_i, v_j, b) \times a(w_{2i})a(w_{2j})$ is a continuous and convex function of b and B is a convex set with the true value β_0 in its interior, then $\hat{\beta} \xrightarrow{p} \beta_0$ under Assumptions 1–8 and 10. This result remains true if we replace Assumptions 4, 5, and 10 with 4', 5', and 10', respectively.

PROOF.   Follows from the result in Section 3.3.1 and theorem 2.7 in Newey and McFadden (1994). ∎

THEOREM 3.   Let $K_{h_n}(t) \equiv K(t/h_n)$. If $K_{h_n}(\mu(w_i, \gamma) - \mu(w_j, \gamma))s(v_i, v_j, b) \times a(w_{2i})a(w_{2j})$ is a continuous function of b, and B is a compact set that includes the true value β_0 as an interior point; then $\hat{\beta} \xrightarrow{p} \beta_0$ under Assumptions 1–10. This result remains true if we replace Assumptions 4, 5, and 10 with 4', 5', and 10', respectively.

PROOF.   Follows from the result in Section 3.4 and Theorem 2.1 along with lemma 2.9 in Newey and McFadden (1994). ∎

3.6. Asymptotic Normality.

Let β_h be the minimizer of $E[h_n^{-L}K_{h_n}(\mu(w_i, \gamma) - \mu(w_j, \gamma))s(v_i, v_j, b)a(w_{2i})a(w_{2j})]$. The same arguments that lead to the consistency of $\hat{\beta}$ imply that $\beta_h \xrightarrow{p} \beta_0$. Also note that β_h is nonstochastic. In this section we will derive the limiting distribution of $\sqrt{n}(\hat{\beta} - \beta_h)$, where $\hat{\beta}$ is the minimizer of $T_n(\hat{\gamma}, b)$. In all the applications considered in this article, the function $s(v_i, v_j; \beta)$ is left and right differentiable with respect to each component of β. Let

$$v_n(z_i, z_j; \gamma, \beta) = \frac{1}{h_n^L} K\left(\frac{\hat{\mu}_n(w_i, \gamma) - \hat{\mu}_n(w_j, \gamma)}{h_n}\right) t(v_i, v_j, \beta)a(w_{2i})a(w_{2j})$$

$$p_n(z_i, z_j; \gamma, \beta) = \frac{1}{h_n^L} K\left(\frac{\mu(w_i, \gamma) - \mu(w_j, \gamma)}{h_n}\right) t(v_i, v_j, \beta)a(w_{2i})a(w_{2j})$$

and define

$$\hat{G}_n(\gamma, \beta) = \binom{n}{2}^{-1} \sum_{i<j} v_n(z_i, z_j; \gamma, \beta) \text{ and } G_n(\gamma, \beta) = \binom{n}{2}^{-1} \sum_{i<j} p_n(z_i, z_j; \gamma, \beta),$$

where $t(v_i, v_j, \beta)$ is a convex combination of the left and right derivatives of $s(v_i, v_j; \beta)$ with respect to each component of β. Since $\hat{\beta}$ is the minimizer of $T_n(\hat{\gamma}, b)$, the object of interest is $\hat{G}_n(\hat{\gamma}, \beta)$. Below, we will characterize the relationship between $\hat{G}_n(\hat{\gamma}, \beta)$ and $G_n(\hat{\gamma}, \beta)$, which will determine the asymptotic distribution of $\sqrt{n}(\hat{\beta} - \beta_h)$. We will add the following assumptions:

ASSUMPTION 11. *The derivative function $\{t(\cdot, \cdot; \beta) : \beta \in B\}$ is Euclidean for an envelope F, i.e.*,

$$\sup_{n, \beta} |t(z_i, z_j; \beta)| \le F(z_i, z_j),$$

satisfying

$$E[F(z_i, z_j)^2] < \infty \text{ and } \sup_{\gamma \in \Gamma} E[\|F(z_i, z_j)[\tau(w_i, \gamma) - \eta(w_i, \gamma) - \mu(w_j, \gamma)]\|^2] < \infty.$$

The set B need not be the whole parameter space, but could be some other set with β_0 in its interior.

ASSUMPTION 12. *The function $\phi(\cdot)$, in the definition of the trimming function $a(\cdot)$, is M times differentiable with bounded derivatives.*

ASSUMPTION 13. *Define*

$$B_n(w_{2i}; \gamma, \beta) = E\left[\frac{1}{h_n^{L+1}} K^{(1)}\left(\frac{\mu(w_i, \gamma) - \mu(w_j, \gamma)}{h_n}\right) t(v_i, v_j, \beta) a(w_{2j}) \,\Big|\, w_{2i}\right];$$

then $B_n(w_{2i}; \gamma, \beta)$ is M times differentiable with respect to w_{2i} with bounded derivatives everywhere in Γ, B.

Note that if Assumption 7 is satisfied, then $\int K^{(1)}(t)\, dt = 0$. We will now strengthen Assumption 2(iii), one of the "in probability" Lipschitz conditions for $\eta(\cdot)$:

ASSUMPTION 14. *With probability one in $\mathbb{S}(w_1)$, the function $\eta(w, \gamma)$ is M times differentiable with respect to w_2 with bounded Mth derivatives for all $w_2 \in W_2$ and $\gamma \in \Gamma$.*

ASSUMPTION 15. *The true parameter β_0 is in the interior of the parameter space.*

Define the projection functions

$$p_{1n}(z_i; \gamma, \beta) = E[p_n(z_i, z_j; \gamma, \beta) \,|\, z_i] - E[p_n(z_i, z_j; \gamma, \beta)],$$

$$p_{0n}(\gamma, \beta) = E[p_n(z_i, z_j; \gamma, \beta)],$$

and let $\tilde{p}_n(z_i, \gamma, \beta) = p_{0n}(\gamma, \beta) + 2p_{1n}(z_i; \gamma, \beta)$.

Assumption 16.

i. $\tilde{p}_n(z_i, \gamma, \beta)$ satisfies the following:

(a) $\tilde{p}_n(z_i, \gamma, \beta)$ is continuously differentiable in (γ, β) with a derivative $\Delta \tilde{p}_n(z_i, \gamma, \beta)$ with the property that for any sequence (γ^*, β^*) that converges in probability to (γ_0, β_0), $\Delta \tilde{p}_n(z_i, \gamma^*, \beta^*)$ converges to a matrix $\Delta \tilde{p}_0(\gamma_0, \beta_0)$. Let $\Delta \tilde{p}_0^\beta(\gamma_0, \beta_0)$ and $\Delta \tilde{p}_0^\gamma(\gamma_0, \beta_0)$ denote the parts that correspond to the differentiation with respect to β and γ, respectively. Then $\Delta \tilde{p}_0^\beta(z_i, \gamma_0, \beta_0)$ is nonsingular.

(b) There exists a function $p_1(z_i; \gamma_0, \beta_0)$ with $E[\|p_1(z_i; \gamma_0, \beta_0)\|^2] < \infty$ such that

$$\frac{1}{\sqrt{n}} \sum_{i=1}^n \tilde{p}_n(z_i; \gamma_0, \beta_h) - \frac{1}{\sqrt{n}} \sum_{i=1}^n p_1(z_i; \gamma_0, \beta_0) = o_p(1).$$

ii. $\eta(w_i, \gamma)$ and $B_n(w_{2i}; \gamma, \beta)$ are continuously differentiable in γ and (γ, β), respectively, with derivatives $\Delta^\gamma \eta(w_i, \gamma)$ and $\Delta B_n(w_{2i}; \gamma, \beta)$ respectively— the first assumption strengthens the "in probability" Lipschitz condition 2(iv).

iii. Let $\tilde{D}_n(w_i; \gamma, \beta) = B_n(w_{2i}; \gamma, \beta)[\tau(w_i, \gamma) - \eta(w_i, \gamma) - \mu(w_i, \gamma)]a(w_{2i})$. The previous condition, along with Assumption 2(i) imply that $\tilde{D}_n(w_i; \gamma, \beta)$ is continuously differentiable in (γ, β); denote this derivative by $\Delta \tilde{D}_n(w_i; \gamma, \beta)$. We assume that $\Delta \tilde{D}_n(w_i; \gamma, \beta)$ has the property that for any sequence (γ^*, β^*) that converges in probability to (γ_0, β_0), $\Delta \tilde{D}_n(w_i; \gamma^*, \beta^*)$ converges in probability to a matrix $\Delta \tilde{D}_0(\gamma_0, \beta_0)$. Let $\Delta \tilde{D}_0^\beta(\gamma_0, \beta_0)$ and $\Delta \tilde{D}_0^\gamma(\gamma_0, \beta_0)$ be the parts that corresponds to β and γ, respectively.

iv. For some function $D(w_i; \gamma_0, \beta_0)$ with $E[\|D(w_i; \gamma_0, \beta_0)\|^2] < \infty$,

$$\frac{1}{\sqrt{n}} \sum_{i=1}^n \tilde{D}_n(w_i; \gamma_0, \beta_h) - \frac{1}{\sqrt{n}} \sum_{i=1}^n D(w_i; \gamma_0, \beta_0) = o_p(1).$$

Note that $E[\tilde{D}_n(w_i; \gamma, \beta)] = 0$ and $\Delta D_n(w_i; \gamma, \beta) = 0$ for any γ and β. Thus, we must have $E[D(w_i; \gamma_0, \beta_0)] = 0$ and $\Delta \tilde{D}_0^\beta(\gamma_0, \beta_0) = 0$. Let $\Delta \tilde{p}_0^\gamma(\gamma_0, \beta_0)$, $\Delta \tilde{p}_0^\beta(\gamma_0, \beta_0)$, and $p_1(z_i; \gamma_0, \beta_0)$ be as defined in Assumption 16(i). The following is the main asymptotic normality theorem in this section.

THEOREM 4.   Suppose $\hat{\beta}$ is a consistent estimator of β, $\sqrt{n}(\hat{\gamma} - \gamma_0) = n^{-1/2} \sum_{i=1}^n v_i + o_p(1)$ and $\hat{G}_n(\hat{\gamma}, \hat{\beta}) = o_p(n^{-1/2})$. If Assumptions 1–3, 6, 7, and 11–16 are satisfied, then

$$\sqrt{n}(\hat{\beta} - \beta_h) = \frac{1}{\sqrt{n}} \sum_{i=1}^n \psi_i + o_p(1),$$

where

$$\psi_i = -\Delta \tilde{p}_0^\beta(\gamma_0, \beta_0)^{-1} \times \left[(\Delta \tilde{D}_0^\gamma(\gamma_0, \beta_0) + \Delta \tilde{p}_0^\gamma(\gamma_0, \beta_0)) v_i + 2 p_1(z_i; \gamma_0, \beta_0) \right.$$
$$\left. + 2 D(w_i; \gamma_0, \beta_0) \right].$$

Furthermore, assuming v_i, $p_1(z_i; \gamma_0, \beta_0)$, *and* $D(w_i; \gamma_0, \beta_0)$ *are jointly i.i.d. with* $E[v_i] = 0$ *and* $E[\|v_i\|^2] < \infty$,

$$\sqrt{n}(\hat{\beta} - \beta_h) \xrightarrow{d} \mathcal{N}(0, E[\psi_i \psi_i']).$$

PROOF. In the Appendix, we show that if Assumptions 1–3, 6, 7, and 11–14 are satisfied and $\{z_i, i = 1, \ldots, n\}$ is an i.i.d. sample,

$$\hat{G}_n(\gamma, \beta)$$

$$= G_n(\gamma, \beta) + \frac{2(n-2)}{n} \frac{1}{n} \sum_{i=1}^{n} B_n(w_{2i}; \gamma, \beta) [\tau(w_i, \gamma) - \eta(w_i, \gamma) - \mu(w_i, \gamma)] a(w_{2i})$$

$$+ \tilde{e}_n(z_i, z_j; \gamma, \beta)$$

$$\equiv G_n(\gamma, \beta) + \frac{2(n-2)}{n} \frac{1}{n} \sum_{i=1}^{n} \tilde{D}_n(w_i; \gamma, \beta) + \tilde{e}_n(z_i, z_j; \gamma, \beta),$$

where $\sup_{B,\Gamma} |\tilde{e}_n(z_i, z_j; \gamma, \beta)| = o_p(n^{-1/2})$. Note that $E[\tilde{D}_n(w_i; \gamma, \beta)] = 0$ for any γ and β. Therefore, $\sup_{B,\Gamma} |E[\hat{G}_n(\gamma, \beta)] - E[G_n(\gamma, \beta)]| = o_p(n^{-1/2})$. This shows that the additional bias on $\hat{\beta}$ introduced by having to estimate the unknown function $\mu(\cdot)$ nonparametrically is at most of order $o_p(n^{-1/2})$, a consequence of using bias-reducing kernels in the construction of $\hat{\mu}_n(\cdot)$. This allows us to center the distribution of $\hat{\beta}$ around β_h. By the usual projection–decomposition, we have

$$G_n(\gamma, \beta) \equiv \binom{n}{2}^{-1} \sum_{i<j} p_n(z_i, z_j; \gamma, \beta)$$

$$= p_{0n}(\gamma, \beta) + \frac{2}{n} \sum_i p_{1n}(z_i; \gamma, \beta) + \binom{n}{2}^{-1} \sum_{i<j} p_{2n}(z_i, z_j; \gamma, \beta),$$

where p_{2n} is defined implicitly above. By Assumptions 11 and 16, $\{p_{2n}(z_i, z_j; \gamma, \beta)\}$ is Euclidean in a set of the form $\Theta_c \equiv \{(\gamma, \beta) : \|(\gamma - \gamma_0, \beta - \beta_0)\| \leq c\}$ for some constant c, and satisfies $E[\sup_{\Theta_c} p_{2n}(z_i, z_j; \gamma, \beta)^2] < \infty$. Applying theorem 3 of Sherman (1994) to the function $h^L p_{2n}(z_i, z_j; \gamma, \beta)$ we obtain

$$\sup_{\Theta_c} \binom{n}{2}^{-1} \sum_{i<j} h_n^L p_{2n}(z_i, z_j; \gamma, \beta) = O_p\left(\frac{1}{n}\right).$$

Consequently,

$$\hat{G}_n(\gamma, \beta)$$

$$= p_{0n}(\gamma, \beta) + \frac{2}{n} \sum_i p_{1n}(z_i; \gamma, \beta) + \frac{2(n-2)}{n} \frac{1}{n} \sum_{i=1}^n \tilde{D}_n(w_i; \gamma, \beta) + \tilde{e}_n(z_i, z_j; \gamma, \beta)$$

$$\equiv \frac{1}{n} \sum_i \tilde{p}_n(z_i; \gamma, \beta) + \frac{2(n-2)}{n} \frac{1}{n} \sum_{i=1}^n \tilde{D}_n(w_i; \gamma, \beta) + O_p\left(\frac{1}{nh_n^L}\right) + o_p(n^{-1/2}),$$

where the last equality follows from Assumption 6 and the Euclidean property. Denote $\theta \equiv (\beta, \gamma)'$. A first-order approximation yields

$$\sqrt{n}(\hat{\beta} - \beta_h) = -\left(\frac{1}{n} \sum_i \Delta \tilde{p}_n^\beta(z_i; \theta^*) + \frac{1}{n} \sum_i \Delta \tilde{D}_n^\beta(z_i; \theta^{**})\right)^{-1}$$

$$\times \left[\left(\frac{1}{n} \sum_i \Delta \tilde{p}_n^\gamma(z_i; \theta^*) + \frac{1}{n} \sum_i \Delta \tilde{D}_n^\gamma(z_i; \theta^{**})\right) \sqrt{n}(\hat{\gamma} - \gamma_0)\right.$$

$$+ \frac{2}{\sqrt{n}} \sum_i p_{1n}(z_i, \gamma_0, \beta_h) + \frac{2(n-2)}{n} \frac{1}{\sqrt{n}} \sum_{i=1}^n \tilde{D}_n(w_i; \gamma_0, \beta_h)$$

$$\left. + o_p(1) - \sqrt{n}\hat{G}_n(\hat{\gamma}, \hat{\beta})\right].$$

Note that $p_{0n}(z_i, \gamma_0, \beta_h) = 0$ by definition of β_h. Given this, the result follows by noting that $\frac{1}{n} \sum_i \Delta \tilde{D}_n^\beta(z_i; \theta^{**}) \xrightarrow{P} \Delta \tilde{D}_0^\beta(\gamma_0, \beta_0) = 0$. ∎

Under additional assumptions, Lemma 3—below—provides more precise expressions for the asymptotic variance described above. In a number of applications the true value of γ is known. If this is the case, the following result follows immediately from Theorem 4.

COROLLARY 2. *If the true value of γ is known—e.g., if $\mu(w, \gamma) = \tau(w) - E[\eta(w) \mid w_2]$, with $\tau(\cdot)$ and $\eta(\cdot)$ known, then if $\hat{\beta}$ is a consistent estimator of β, $G_n(\hat{\beta}) = o_p(n^{-1/2})$ and Assumptions 1–3, 6, 7, and 11–16 are satisfied, we have*

$$\sqrt{n}(\hat{\beta} - \beta_h) \xrightarrow{d} \mathcal{N}(0, E[\psi_i \psi_i']),$$

where $\psi_i = -2\Delta \tilde{p}_0^\beta(\beta_0)^{-1} p_1(z_i; \beta_0) - 2\Delta \tilde{p}_0^\beta(\beta_0)^{-1} D(w_i; \beta_0)$.

3.7. *Verifying Some of the Conditions.* Theorem 4 makes some high level assumptions. In this section, we present some results that are useful in verifying these assumptions. The following lemma, which follows immediately from lemma 1 in Honoré and Powell (1994), is useful for verifying that $\hat{G}_n(\hat{\gamma}, \hat{\beta}) = o_p(n^{-1/2})$.

LEMMA 1. *If the true parameter value $\beta_0 \in \mathbb{R}^K$ is an interior point in the parameter space, and*

    i. *$S(v_i, v_j, \beta)$ is left-and-right differentiable in each component of β in some open neighborhood of the true parameter β_0,*

    ii. *in an open neighborhood B_0 of β_0,*

$$\sup_{\beta \in B_0} \sum_{i<j} \mathbb{1}\left\{ \frac{\partial^- s(v_i, v_j, \beta)}{\partial \beta_\ell} \neq \frac{\partial^+ s(v_i, v_j, \beta)}{\partial \beta_\ell} \right\} = O_p(1); \quad \ell = 1, \ldots, K,$$

    iii. *in an open neighborhood of β_0,*

$$\left| \frac{\partial^- s(v_i, v_j, \beta)}{\partial \beta_\ell} - \frac{\partial^+ s(v_i, v_j, \beta)}{\partial \beta_\ell} \right| \leq h(v_i, v_j); \quad \ell = 1, \ldots, K,$$

    for some function h with $E[h(v_i, v_j)^{1+\delta}] < \infty$ for some δ; and
    iv. *K is bounded, then*

$$\hat{G}_n(\hat{\gamma}, \hat{\beta}) = o_p\big(n^{-2+2/(1+\delta)} h_n^{-L}\big).$$

Next we provide some sufficient conditions under which Assumption 16 is satisfied. We will employ the usual dominance conditions. Define

$$\ell_t(z_i, a, b) = E[t(v_i, v_j, b) \mid z_i, \mu(w_j, \gamma_0) = a]\rho(a) f_\mu(a)$$

$$\bar{\ell}_t(z_i, a_1, a_2, b) = E[t(v_i, v_j, b) \mid z_i, x_j = a_1, \mu(w_j, \gamma_0) = a_2]\bar{\rho}(a_1, a_2) f_{\mu|x}(a_2; a_1)$$

$$\ell_{t_1}(z_i, a, b) = E\left[\frac{\partial(\mu(w_i, \gamma_0) - \mu(w_j, \gamma_0))}{\partial \gamma} t(v_i, v_j, b) \mid z_i, \mu(w_j, \gamma_0) = a \right]$$
$$\times \rho(a) f_\mu(a)$$

$$\bar{\ell}_{t_1}(z_i, a_1, a_2, b) = E\left[\frac{\partial(\mu(w_i, \gamma_0) - \mu(w_j, \gamma_0))}{\partial \gamma} t(v_i, v_j, b) \mid z_i, x_j = a_1, \right.$$
$$\left. \mu(w_j, \gamma_0) = a_2 \right] \bar{\rho}(a_1, a_2) f_{\mu|x}(a_2; a_1).$$

The following condition will correspond to the case in which the exclusion restriction in Assumption 5 holds:

ASSUMPTION 17. *ℓ_t is differentiable with respect to its second and third argument, ℓ_{t_1} is differentiable with respect to its second argument, and there exists a function g with $E[g(z_i)^2] < \infty$ such that*

$$\text{Max}\left\{\left|\ell_t^{(2)}(z_i, \mu(w_i, \gamma_0) - h_n\psi, \beta_0)\right|, \left|\ell_t^{(3)}(z_i, \mu(w_i, \gamma_0) - h_n\psi, \beta_0)\right|,\right.$$

$$\left.\left|\ell_{t_1}^{(2)}(z_i, \mu(w_i, \gamma_0) - h_n\psi, \beta_0)\right|\right\}$$

$$\leq g(z_i), \quad \text{and} \quad \lim_{\|\psi\|\to\infty} K(\psi) \cdot \ell_t^{(2)}(v_i, \mu(w_i, \gamma_0) - h_n\psi, \beta_0) = 0.$$

If Assumption 5' holds, we modify Assumption 17 in the following way:

ASSUMPTION 17'. $\bar{\ell}_t$ *is differentiable with respect to its third and fourth arguments,* $\bar{\ell}_{t_1}$ *is differentiable with respect to its third argument, and there exists a function $\bar{g}$ with $E[\bar{g}(z_i)^2] < \infty$ such that*

$$\text{Max}\left\{\left|\bar{\ell}_t^{(2)}(z_i, x_j, \mu(w_i, \gamma_0) - h_n\psi, \beta_0)\right|, \left|\bar{\ell}_t^{(3)}(z_i, x_j, \mu(w_i, \gamma_0) - h_n\psi, \beta_0)\right|,\right.$$

$$\left.\left|\bar{\ell}_{t_1}^{(2)}(z_i, x_j, \mu(w_i, \gamma_0) - h_n\psi, \beta_0)\right|\right\}$$

$$\leq g(z_i), \quad \lim_{\|\psi\|\to\infty} K(\psi) \cdot \bar{\ell}_t^{(2)}(z_i, x_j, \mu(w_i, \gamma_0) - h_n\psi, \beta_0) = 0.$$

We have the following result.

LEMMA 2. *Let*

$$p_0^\beta(\gamma_0, \beta_0)$$
$$= E[\ell_t^{(3)}(z_i, \mu(w_i, \gamma_0), \beta_0)], \quad p_0^\gamma(\gamma_0, \beta_0) = -E[\ell_{t_1}^{(2)}(z_i, \mu(w_i, \gamma_0), \beta_0)]$$
$$\bar{p}_0^\beta(\gamma_0, \beta_0)$$
$$= E[\bar{\ell}_t^{(3)}(z_i, x_j, \mu(w_i, \gamma_0), \beta_0)], \quad \bar{p}_0^\gamma(\gamma_0, \beta_0) = -E[\bar{\ell}_{t_1}^{(2)}(z_i, x_j, \mu(w_i, \gamma_0), \beta_0)].$$

Then,

    i. *Under Assumptions 4, 5, 6, 7, and 17, $p_{0n}^\beta(\gamma_0, \beta_0) \to p_0^\beta(\gamma_0, \beta_0)$ and $p_{0n}^\gamma(\gamma_0, \beta_0) \to p_0^\gamma(\gamma_0, \beta_0)$;*

    ii. *Under Assumptions 4', 5', 6, 7, and 17', $p_{0n}^\beta(\gamma_0, \beta_0) \to \bar{p}_0^\beta(\gamma_0, \beta_0)$ and $p_{0n}^\gamma(\gamma_0, \beta_0) \to \bar{p}_0^\gamma(\gamma_0, \beta_0)$.*

The previous result implies that Assumption 16(i.a) is satisfied. The next lemma provides sufficient conditions for Assumptions 16(i.b) and 16(iv) to hold.

LEMMA 3. *Let $\check{D}_n$ and $\Delta^\beta \check{D}_n$ be as defined in Assumption 16(iii). Suppose that $p_{1n}(z_i, \gamma_0, \cdot)$ is continuously differentiable in a neighborhood $N(\beta_0)$ of β_0, and that there exists a function $h(z_i)$ with $E[\|h(z_i)\|^2] < \infty$ such that*

$$\text{Max}\left\{\left\|\Delta^\beta p_{1n}(z_i, \gamma_0, b)\right\|, \left\|\Delta^\beta \check{D}_n(w_{2i}; \gamma_0, b)\right\|\right\} \leq h(z_i) \,\forall b \in N(\beta_0).$$

Then,

$$\frac{1}{\sqrt{n}} \sum_{i=1}^{n} \tilde{p}_n(z_i; \gamma_0, \beta_h) - \frac{1}{\sqrt{n}} \sum_{i=1}^{n} p_{1n}(z_i; \gamma_0, \beta_0) = o_p(1)$$

$$\frac{1}{\sqrt{n}} \sum_{i=1}^{n} \tilde{D}_n(w_i; \gamma_0, \beta_h) - \frac{1}{\sqrt{n}} \sum_{i=1}^{n} \tilde{D}_n(w_i; \gamma_0, \beta_0) = o_p(1).$$

For the first result, note that $p_{0n}(\gamma_0, \beta_h) = 0$ by definition of β_h. Therefore, under Assumptions 4–7 and 17,

$$\frac{1}{\sqrt{n}} \sum_{i=1}^{n} [\tilde{p}_n(z_i; \gamma_0, \beta_h) - \ell_t(z_i, \mu(w_i, \gamma_0), \beta_0)] = o_p(1)$$

$$\frac{1}{\sqrt{n}} \sum_{i=1}^{n} \big[\tilde{D}_n(w_i; \gamma_0, \beta_h) - E\big[\ell_t^{(2)}(zi, \mu(w_i, \gamma_0), \beta_0) \,\big|\, w_{2i} \big]$$

$$\cdot (\mu(w_i, \gamma_0) - \tau(w_i, \gamma_0) - \eta(w_i, \gamma_0)) \big] = o_p(1),$$

and under Assumptions 4′, 5′, 6, 7, and 17′,

$$\frac{1}{\sqrt{n}} \sum_{i=1}^{n} [\tilde{p}_n(z_i; \gamma_0, \beta_h) - E[\bar{\ell}_t(z_i, x_j, \mu(w_i, \gamma_0), \beta_0) \,|\, z_i]] = o_p(1)$$

$$\frac{1}{\sqrt{n}} \sum_{i=1}^{n} \big[\tilde{D}_n(w_i; \gamma_0, \beta_h) - E\big[\bar{\ell}_t^{(2)}(zi, x_j, \mu(w_i, \gamma_0), \beta_0) \,\big|\, w_{2i} \big]$$

$$\cdot (\mu(w_i, \gamma_0) - \tau(w_i, \gamma_0) - \eta(w_i, \gamma_0)) \big] = o_p(1).$$

The previous result provides more precise expressions for the asymptotic distribution results in Theorem 4 and Corollary 2. They are also helpful in showing how to estimate the corresponding standard errors.

3.8. *Bias Reduction.* The asymptotic normality result for $\hat{\beta}$ in Theorem 4 centers the asymptotic distribution of $\hat{\beta}$ at the pseudo-true value β_h. As the proof of Theorem 4 shows, the "contribution" to the bias of $\hat{\beta}$ derived from the need to estimate the unknown function $\mu(\cdot)$ nonparametrically is at most of order $o_p(n^{-1/2})$. This is a result of using a higher-order bias reducing kernel $H(\cdot)$ in the construction of $\hat{\mu}_n(\cdot)$, along with the results of Theorem 1. Nevertheless, the pseudo-true value β_h need not converge to the true value β_0 at a rate faster than $\sqrt{n}$, because of the interaction of the bandwidth sequence h_n and the kernel $K(\cdot)$ in the estimation criterion $T_n(\cdot)$; as in Honoré and Powell (2005), this would be the case even if the control variable $\mu(w_i, \gamma_0)$ were observable. The usual approach to ensuring that $\sqrt{n}(\beta_h - \beta_0) = o(1)$ would use a higher-order bias reducing kernel $K(\cdot)$ to ensure $\sqrt{n}$-consistency, but such a requirement would be unattractive for the kind of estimators proposed here.[8] The resulting negativity of the kernel function for some data points could compromise the convexity of the corresponding minimand, complicating both the asymptotic theory (through an additional compactness restriction) and computation of the estimator. An alternative to the use of higher-order kernels was proposed by Honoré and Powell (2005), which was based upon the familiar jackknife approach. Specifically, assuming the pseudo-true value β_h is a sufficiently smooth function of the bandwidth h_n, it is possible to construct a linear combination $\hat{\beta}$ of different estimators $\hat{\beta}$ of β_0 (involving different choices of the bandwidth h_n, each of which satisfies our assumptions) for which the corresponding linear combination β_n^* of pseudo-true values satisfies $\sqrt{n}(\beta_n^* - \beta_0) = o(1)$; furthermore, since the different estimators have the same linear representation (to order $o(n^{-1/2})$), the "jackknifed" estimator $\hat{\beta}$ will have the same asymptotic distribution as each $\hat{\beta}$, i.e., $\sqrt{n}(\hat{\beta} - \beta_n^*) = \sqrt{n}(\hat{\beta} - \beta_h) + o_p(1)$. It follows that

$$\sqrt{n}(\hat{\beta} - \beta_0) = \sqrt{n}(\hat{\beta} - \beta_n^*) + \sqrt{n}(\beta_n^* - \beta_0) = \sqrt{n}(\hat{\beta} - \beta_h) + o_p(1) + o(1)$$
$$= \sqrt{n}(\hat{\beta} - \beta_h) + o_p(1),$$

so the jackknifed estimator $\hat{\beta}$ will be $\sqrt{n}$-consistent and asymptotically normal, with the same asymptotic distribution as given in Theorem 4. Algebraic details of the construction of the jackknifed estimator $\hat{\beta}$ can be found in Honoré and Powell (2005), Section 3.3.

3.9. *Consistency and Asymptotic Normality without Exclusion Restrictions.* We now present conditions under which we can replicate the previous results without Assumptions 5 (or 5'), which were introduced in order to preserve consistency of $\hat{\beta}$ in the presence of trimming. Take a sequence of trimming sets W_{2_n}. Basically, we could drop the exclusion restrictions if we were able to make the trimming set converge asymptotically to $\mathbb{S}(w_2)$ while preserving the results of Theorem 1 for the entire sequence W_{2_n}. We now outline a set of conditions under which this is possible.

Take a sequence $\varsigma_n \to 0$. Assume that the trimming function is given by

$$a_n(w_2) = \begin{cases} \phi_n(w_2) > 0 & \text{if } \hat{f}_{w_{2_n}}(w_2) > \varsigma_n, \\ 0 & \text{otherwise}, \end{cases}$$

where $\hat{f}_{w_{2_n}}(\cdot)$ is the nonparametric estimator of $f_{w_2}(\cdot)$ used in the construction of $\hat{\mu}_n(\cdot)$. Assume that $\phi_n(\cdot)$ is bounded, strictly positive, and M times differentiable with bounded derivatives for all n, and $\phi_n(\cdot) \to c$ for some $c > 0$. Define $W_{2n} = \{u \in \mathbb{R}^{L_2} : f_{w_2}(u) \geq \varsigma_n\}$ and $\bar{w}_n = \sup_{W_{2n}} \|u\|$.

---

[8] Using higher-order kernels to achieve $\sqrt{n}$-consistency would be an attractive option if the pairwise-difference estimator has a closed form expression. See, for example, Aradillas-Lopez (2006).

ASSUMPTION 18.

i. *All the properties stated for the set W_2 in Assumptions 1 and 2 are satisfied by any compact subset in the interior of $\mathbb{S}(w_2)$.*

ii. *Strengthen Assumption 6 and assume that $n^{1-2\varepsilon}b_n^{L_2}h_n^{2(L+2)}\varsigma_n^2 \to \infty$ for some $\varepsilon > 0$.*

iii. *We will modify Assumption 3(iii) and assume that ς_n converges to zero sufficiently slow relative to b_n such that $b_n t + w_2 \in \text{interior}\{\mathbb{S}(w_2)\}\forall t \in \mathcal{H}, w_2 \in W_{2n}, n \in \mathbb{N}$. Let $\rho_n(\mu(w_i, \gamma_0)) = E[a_n(w_{2i})\,|\,\mu(w_i, \gamma_0)]$. We will generalize Assumption 4(v) and assume that $\rho_n(\mu(w_i, \gamma_0))$ is continuous and strictly positive for all $w_{2i} \in W_{2n}$. We also assume that the tails of $f_{w_2}(\cdot)$ are such that $\ln(\bar{w}_n) = o_p(n^\varepsilon)$, where ε is defined in the previous assumption.*

The next result establishes consistency of $\hat{\beta}$ without Assumption 5 and it also shows that the asymptotic normality results still hold.

THEOREM 5. *Suppose we use the sequence of trimming functions $a_n(\cdot)$ described above. We have the following results:*

i. *If Assumptions 1–4, 6–10, and 18 are satisfied, then $\hat{\beta}$ satisfies the consistency results of Theorems 2 and 3.*

ii. *Suppose Assumption 14 is satisfied for any compact set in the interior of $\mathbb{S}(w_2)$. Then, if Assumptions 1–3, 6–7, 11–13, and 15–16, and 18 are satisfied, the conclusions of Theorem 4 are true with $v_n(z_i, z_j; \gamma, \beta)$ and $p_n(z_i, z_j; \gamma, \beta)$ replaced by*

$$\bar{v}_n(z_i, z_j; \gamma, \beta) = c * \frac{1}{h_n^L} K\left(\frac{\hat{\mu}_n(w_i, \gamma) - \hat{\mu}_n(w_j, \gamma)}{h_n}\right) t(v_i, v_j, \beta)$$

$$\bar{p}_n(z_i, z_j; \gamma, \beta) = c * \frac{1}{h_n^L} K\left(\frac{\mu(w_i, \gamma) - \mu(w_j, \gamma)}{h_n}\right) t(v_i, v_j, \beta)$$

with $c > 0$ being the limit of the sequence of functions $a_n(\cdot)$.

The main steps of the proof are included in the Appendix.

4. EXAMPLE: DISCRETE CHOICE MODEL WITH ENDOGENEITY

Let us revisit more formally the example briefly described in Section 2.5.2. Suppose we have

$$y_i = \mathbb{1}\{x_i'\beta_0 + \varepsilon_i \geq 0\},$$

and let $x_i = (x_{1i}', x_{2i}')'$, $\beta = (\beta_1', \beta_2')'$, and $w_i = (x_{1i}', w_{2i}')'$, where x_{2i} is a subvector of w_{2i}. The subvector $w_{1i} \equiv x_{1i}$ of regressors is assumed to be endogenous, and can be characterized by a (partially known) reduced form

$$x_{1i} = E[x_{1i}\,|\,w_{2i}] + \mu_i,$$

where $E[x_{1i} \mid w_{2i}]$ is of unknown functional form. Using the notation from Section 3, we have $\mu_i \equiv \mu(w_i) = x_{1i} - E[x_{1i} \mid w_{2i}]$ and $\tau(w_i, \gamma) \equiv x_{1i} \equiv \eta(w_i, \gamma)$ for this example. Following Blundell and Powell (2004), suppose we model endogeneity in this model by assuming that the dependence between the structural error term ε_i on the vector of regressors x_i and the "instrumental variables" w_{2i} is completely characterized by the reduced-form residuals μ_i; specifically, suppose we model the structural error term ε_i as additively separable in the reduced-form error term μ_i and a logistic error term ζ_i,

$$\varepsilon_i = g(\mu_i) + \zeta_i,$$

as in Blundell and Smith (1989, which also takes $g(\cdot)$ to be linear). Assuming ζ_i is independent of w_i, so that

$$\varepsilon_i \mid x_i, w_i \sim \varepsilon_i \mid \mu_i,$$

the structural model for the binary variable y_i can be rewritten as

$$y_i = \mathbb{1}\{x_i'\beta_0 + g(\mu_i) + \zeta_i \geq 0\},$$

which reduces to the partially linear logit model discussed in Section 2.2 and analyzed in Ai and McFadden (1997) and Honoré and Powell (2005), albeit with an unknown regressor μ_i in the nonparametric component. Suppose w_{2i} is a continuously distributed random vector with dimension L_2, and let $H(\cdot)$ be the kernel function described in Section 3.2. Define

$$R_n(\omega_2) = \frac{1}{nh_n^{L_2}} \sum_{j=1}^{n} x_{1j} H_{b_n}(w_{2j} - \omega_2), \quad \hat{f}_{w_{2n}}(\omega_2) = \frac{1}{nh_n^{L_2}} \sum_{j=1}^{n} H_{b_n}(w_{2j} - \omega_2), \quad \text{and}$$

$$\hat{\mu}_n(w_i) = x_{1i} - \frac{R_n(w_{2i})}{\hat{f}_{w_{2n}}(w_{2i})};$$

the estimator $\hat{\mu}_n(w_i)$ fits the description of Section 3.2 with $\tau(w_i; \gamma) = w_{1i} \equiv x_{1i} = \eta(w_{1i}, w_{2i}, \gamma)$. The conditions of Assumption 2 will be satisfied if $\mu(w_i)$ is M times differentiable with bounded derivatives, $E[w_{1i}^2 \mid w_{2i}]$ exists and is a continuous function of w_{2i}, and $E[w_{1i}^4] < \infty$. In addition, if the smoothness conditions of Assumption 1 concerning the density of w_{2i} are satisfied, along with the kernel and bandwidth properties of Assumption 3, then $\hat{\mu}_n(w_i)$ will satisfy the results of Theorem 1. Define

$$L_n(b) = \binom{n}{2}^{-1} \frac{1}{h_n^L} \sum_{\substack{i<j \\ y_i \neq y_j}} K\left(\frac{\hat{\mu}_i - \hat{\mu}_j}{h}\right)$$

$$\times [y_i \ln(1 + \exp\{(x_j - x_i)'b\}) + y_j \ln(1 + \exp\{(x_i - x_j)'b\})]a(w_{2i})a(w_{2j}).$$

Following the discussion in Section 2.2.1 and Equations (4) and (5), we propose to estimate β by minimizing $L_n(b)$. The need to add a trimming function to (5) follows from the detailed discussion in Section 3. The problem

$\hat{\beta} = \text{argmin}_b L_n(b)$ fits the framework analyzed in Section 3 with $s(v_i, v_j, b) =$ $\mathbb{1}\{y_i \neq y_j\} \cdot [y_i \ln(1 + \exp\{(x_j - x_i)'b\}) + y_j \ln(1 + \exp\{(x_i - x_j)'b\})]$; in this set-ting, it is important to verity if the model fits the exclusion restrictions 5 or 5'. Since $y_i = \mathbb{1}\{x_i'\beta_0 + g(\mu_i) + \zeta_i \geq 0\}$, where $\zeta_i \sim$ i.i.d. logistic and independent of w_i, it follows that $y_j \mid x_j, \mu(w_j), w_{2j} \sim y_j \mid x_j, \mu(w_j)$ and thus if $v_i \equiv (y_i, x_i')'$, we have $E[s(v_i, v_j, b) \mid v_i, x_j, \mu(w_j), w_{2j}] = E[s(v_i, v_j, b) \mid v_i, x_j, \mu(w_j)]$ and the ex-clusion restriction in Assumption 5' is satisfied. Assumption 4' will be satisfied if the density of μ_i conditional on x_i is a continuous function of ζ_i. Assumption 10' will be satisfied if $E[s_i(v_i, v_j; b) \mid x_i, x_j, \mu_i = \mu_j]$ is uniquely minimized at $b = \beta_0$; given our previous assumptions, this will hold if x_i has full rank. Provided that Assumptions 6, 7, and 9 hold, this would yield consistency of our estimator, and if Assumptions 11–13, 15, and 16 hold, then $\hat{\beta}$ would have the asymptotic distribution described in Corollary 2.[9]

4.1. A Monte Carlo Study.

Having described the large sample properties of the proposed estimator in Section 3, we devote this subsection to evaluate the performance of a simple implementation of our estimation procedure for the case of a discrete choice model with endogeneity. Using the same notation as above, we have $x_{2i} \sim \mathcal{N}(0, 1)$, $w_{2i} \sim U[-1, 1]$, $\mu_i \sim \sqrt{2}\mathcal{N}(0, 1)$, and $\zeta_i \sim$ logistic; all these variables are independent of each other. x_{1i} and ε_i are given by

$$x_{1i} = \underbrace{\frac{(w_{2i} - 1)^2}{2} - \frac{w_{2i}^3}{4} + \frac{w_{2i}^4}{10} - \frac{\exp(w_{2i})}{(1 + \exp(w_{2i}))} + \sin(4w_{2i})}_{= E[x_{1i} \mid w_{2i}]} + \mu_i,$$

$$\varepsilon_i = \underbrace{\frac{2\mu_i}{\pi} \arctan(\mu_i)}_{= g(\mu_i)} + \zeta_i.$$

The functions chosen are smooth but clearly nonlinear in nature. We have

$$y_i = \mathbb{1}\{-1 + x_{1i} + x_{2i} + \varepsilon_i \geq 0\},$$

so $\beta_{1_0} = 1$ and $\beta_{2_0} = 1$. We focus only on the slope coefficients β_1, β_2 because the intercept is not involved in the identifying moment conditions.[10] We are interested in the properties of a quick, simple implementation of our methods. We estimate $E[x_{1i} \mid w_{2i}]$ simply by using a local polynomial of order six and we choose the stan-dard normal density as the kernel $K(\cdot)$. Our focus here is on the bandwidth h_n. Let R_n denote the interquartile range of $(\hat{E}[x_1 \mid w_{2i}])_{i=1}^n$, let $\hat{\sigma}_{E[x_1 \mid w_2]}$ denote the sample standard deviation of $(\hat{E}[x_1 \mid w_{2i}])_{i=1}^n$, and define $A_n = \min\{\hat{\sigma}_{E[x_1 \mid w_2]}, R_n/1.34\}$. Fix a scalar $c \in \mathbb{R}$ and define $\hat{\beta}(c)$ as the estimator obtained by using $h_n = cA_n n^{-1/5}$. Silverman's "rule of thumb" density estimation bandwidth when the reference

---

[9] In this model, $\eta(\cdot)$ is not a function of w_{2i} and γ_0 is trivially known. This makes a number of the conditions studied in Section 3 (e.g., Assumptions 8 and 14) irrelevant.

[10] Recall that the function $g(\cdot)$ is assumed to be unknown.

TABLE 1

SIMULATION RESULTS FOR $\hat{\beta}_1$ (TRUE VALUE IS $\beta_{1_0} = 1$). NUMBER OF SIMULATIONS $= 1000$

	$n = 150$				$n = 450$			
	$|\text{Bias}(\hat{\beta}_1)|$	$\widehat{MSE}(\hat{\beta}_1)$	$\hat{\beta}_{1_{(0.025)}}$	$\hat{\beta}_{1_{(0.975)}}$	$|\text{Bias}(\hat{\beta}_1)|$	$\widehat{MSE}(\hat{\beta}_1)$	$\hat{\beta}_{1_{(0.025)}}$	$\hat{\beta}_{1_{(0.975)}}$
$\hat{\beta}_1^I$	0.10326	0.37230	0.04832	2.41428	0.02729	0.07156	0.53087	1.58677
$\hat{\beta}_1^{II}$	0.03594	0.10319	0.52705	1.78713	0.00576	0.02136	0.72904	1.29874
$\hat{\beta}_1^{III}$	0.06242	0.16345	0.36515	1.98202	0.01182	0.03691	0.65136	1.42428
	$n = 700$				$n = 1000$			
	$|\text{Bias}(\hat{\beta}_1)|$	$\widehat{MSE}(\hat{\beta}_1)$	$\hat{\beta}_{1_{(0.025)}}$	$\hat{\beta}_{1_{(0.975)}}$	$|\text{Bias}(\hat{\beta}_1)|$	$\widehat{MSE}(\hat{\beta}_1)$	$\hat{\beta}_{1_{(0.025)}}$	$\hat{\beta}_{1_{(0.975)}}$
$\hat{\beta}_1^I$	0.00626	0.04195	0.59200	1.42109	0.00992	0.02735	0.69016	1.33034
$\hat{\beta}_1^{II}$	0.00631	0.01288	0.77812	1.22448	0.00852	0.00975	0.80565	1.19510
$\hat{\beta}_1^{III}$	0.00244	0.02276	0.71927	1.30665	0.00293	0.01622	0.75708	1.25162

population is a standard normal is a special case, with $c = 0.90$ (see equation 3.31, p. 48 in Silverman, 1986).

One of our goals in this section is to evaluate the sensitivity of our estimator to the actual bandwidth chosen; we proceed as follows. Let $c_1 = 0.4$ and $c_j = c_{j-1} + 0.5$ for $j \geq 2$. We use a grid of scalar values $(c_1, \ldots, c_M)$ with $M = 5$ (i.e., $c_M = 2.4$). We estimate $\hat{\beta}$ in three different ways, all of which would have the same asymptotic linear representation and $\sqrt{N}$-distribution.[11]

$$(21) \qquad \hat{\beta}^I = \hat{\beta}(c_1), \quad \hat{\beta}^{II} = \hat{\beta}(c_M), \quad \hat{\beta}^{III} = \frac{1}{M}\sum_{\ell=1}^{M}\hat{\beta}(c_\ell),$$

so $\hat{\beta}^I$ chooses the small bandwidth, $\hat{\beta}^{II}$ chooses the large bandwidth, and $\hat{\beta}^{III}$ takes a simple average over the bandwidths in our grid. We trimmed out the observations with the highest 5% of values for $|\hat{E}[x_1 \mid w_{2i}]|$. Tables 1 and 2 present the results of 1000 simulations for each one of the estimators described above.

As we should expect, our simulation results show that the actual choice of bandwidth has a relatively more important effect on smaller samples. In this particular case, using the larger bandwidth in our arbitrary grid yielded better results than those of the smaller bandwidth. The difference became less relevant for larger sample sizes. The results also illustrate that taking a simple average of the estimators in the bandwidth grid is a good "rule of thumb" to safeguard against the problem of finding the "correct bandwidth" to commit to. In fact, the absolute bias of $\hat{\beta}^{III}$ was smaller than those of $\hat{\beta}^I$ and $\hat{\beta}^{II}$ for sample sizes $N = 700$ and 1000.

The individual mean squared errors decreased steadily with the sample size in all cases, and their magnitudes also became closer across the three estimators

---

[11] Any weighted average of the resulting estimators would have the same Bahadur representation as any individual estimator (see Theorem 1), as long as the weights add up to one.

TABLE 2

SIMULATION RESULTS FOR $\hat{\beta}_2$ (TRUE VALUE IS $\beta_{2_0} = 1$). NUMBER OF SIMULATIONS $= 1000$

	$n = 150$				$n = 450$			
	$|\text{Bias}(\hat{\beta}_2)|$	$\widehat{MSE}(\hat{\beta}_2)$	$\hat{\beta}_{2(0.025)}$	$\hat{\beta}_{2(0.975)}$	$|\text{Bias}(\hat{\beta}_2)|$	$\widehat{MSE}(\hat{\beta}_2)$	$\hat{\beta}_{2(0.025)}$	$\hat{\beta}_{2(0.975)}$
$\hat{\beta}_2^I$	0.09622	0.20209	0.43348	2.04395	0.01974	0.02944	0.71601	1.37653
$\hat{\beta}_2^{II}$	0.04243	0.12874	0.45047	1.79982	0.00587	0.02497	0.70021	1.31226
$\hat{\beta}_2^{III}$	0.06454	0.14804	0.43502	1.89152	0.00696	0.02667	0.71132	1.32944
	$n = 700$				$n = 1000$			
	$|\text{Bias}(\hat{\beta}_2)|$	$\widehat{MSE}(\hat{\beta}_2)$	$\hat{\beta}_{2(0.025)}$	$\hat{\beta}_{2(0.975)}$	$|\text{Bias}(\hat{\beta}_2)|$	$M\widehat{S}E(\hat{\beta}_2)$	$\hat{\beta}_{2(0.025)}$	$\hat{\beta}_{2(0.975)}$
$\hat{\beta}_2^I$	0.00360	0.01573	0.76393	1.26773	0.01001	0.01085	0.82532	1.22939
$\hat{\beta}_2^{II}$	0.01445	0.01395	0.75836	1.22905	0.00293	0.00989	0.81105	1.20510
$\hat{\beta}_2^{III}$	0.00452	0.01462	0.76070	1.24420	0.00159	0.01021	0.81711	1.22166

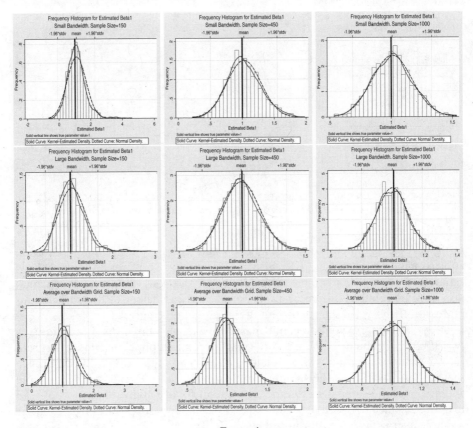

FIGURE 1

HISTOGRAM AND DENSITIES FOR SIMULATED ESTIMATES OF β_1. ROWS SUMMARIZE RESULTS FOR $\hat{\beta}_1^I$, $\hat{\beta}_1^{II}$, AND $\hat{\beta}_1^{III}$, RESPECTIVELY. COLUMNS SUMMARIZE RESULTS FOR $N = 150, 450$, AND 1000, RESPECTIVELY

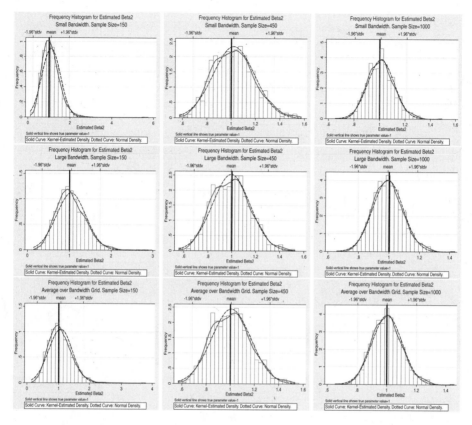

FIGURE 2

HISTOGRAM AND DENSITIES FOR SIMULATED ESTIMATES OF β_2. ROWS SUMMARIZE RESULTS FOR $\hat{\beta}_2^I$, $\hat{\beta}_2^{II}$, AND $\hat{\beta}_2^{III}$, RESPECTIVELY. COLUMNS SUMMARIZE RESULTS FOR $N = 150$, 450, AND 1000, RESPECTIVELY

as the sample size increased. As Figures 1 and 2 show, the asymptotic Normal approximation becomes more precise as the sample size increases for our three estimators. For smaller sample sizes ($N = 150$ and 450), a normal approximation appears relatively more accurate for $\hat{\beta}_1$, the coefficient of the endogenous regressor, than for $\hat{\beta}_2$, the coefficient of the exogenous regressor.[12]

The normal approximation in both cases appears indistinguishably accurate for $N = 1000$. In the majority of cases, a normal approximation seemed more accurate for $\hat{\beta}^{III}$ than for the other two estimators. As with all other results, the difference seemed less obvious as the sample size was increased. Overall, taking a simple average over the estimators that result from a grid of bandwidths seems to lead to a nice balance between bias and dispersion. In our case, this was true even for a simple average using uniform weights.

[12] Note however that the absolute bias and the MSE of $\hat{\beta}_1$ were slightly larger than those of $\hat{\beta}_2$ in the majority of cases.

5. CONCLUDING REMARKS

Econometric models amenable to pairwise-differencing estimation arise in a variety of contexts ranging from sample selection and/or endogeneity to microeconomic models with rational expectations with or without strategic interactions. As this article showed, even if the control function involved in the identifying moment restriction is of unknown functional form, $\sqrt{N}$-consistent estimation is possible. As we argued at length, special care must be placed on the issues of trimming and its implications on identification. As it is always the case in semi or nonparametric estimation procedures, the choice of bias-reducing techniques is up to the researcher. Bias reduction could be done through the density estimator (using bias-reducing kernels) or through the bandwidth (taking advantage of the fact that any estimator that uses a valid bandwidth sequence will have the same asymptotic linear representation). We advocate the latter approach here. A simple Monte Carlo study showed that even using a naive, simple average of estimators over a grid of bandwidths could serve as a simple way of achieving a good balance between bias and dispersion without the need to search to the "correct" finite sample bandwidth. The asymptotic standard errors we found would be valid for such an estimator. As the sample size grows, the actual bandwidth chosen becomes relatively less important.

APPENDIX

A.1. *Steps to Prove Theorem 4.*   Define

$$S_{1n}(z_i, z_j; \gamma, \beta) = \frac{1}{h_n^{L+1}} K^{(1)} \left(\frac{\mu(w_i, \gamma) - \mu(w_j, \gamma)}{h_n} \right) t(v_i, v_j, \beta) a(w_{2i}) a(w_{2j})$$

$$S_{2n}(z_i, z_j; \gamma) = \frac{[\tau(w_i, \gamma) - \eta(w_i, \gamma) - \mu(w_j, \gamma)]}{b_n^{L_2} f_{w_2}(w_{2j})} H_{b_n}(w_{2i} - w_{2j}).$$

and let

$$T_{1n}(z_i, z_j; \gamma, \beta)$$
$$= S_{1n}(z_i, z_j; \gamma, \beta)'[S_{2n}(z_i, z_i; \gamma, \beta) - S_{2n}(z_i, z_j; \gamma, \beta) + S_{2n}(z_j, z_i; \gamma, \beta)$$
$$\qquad - S_{2n}(z_j, z_j; \gamma, \beta)]$$

$$T_{2n}(z_i, z_j, z_k; \gamma, \beta)$$
$$= S_{1n}(z_i, z_j; \gamma, \beta)'[S_{2n}(z_k, z_i; \gamma, \beta) - S_{2n}(z_k, z_j; \gamma, \beta)] + S_{1n}(z_i, z_k; \gamma, \beta)'$$
$$\qquad \times [S_{2n}(z_j, z_i; \gamma, \beta) - S_{2n}(z_j, z_k; \gamma, \beta)] + S_{1n}(z_j, z_k; \gamma, \beta)'$$
$$\qquad \times [S_{2n}(z_i, z_j; \gamma, \beta) - S_{2n}(z_i, z_k; \gamma, \beta)].$$

Note that $T_{1n}(z_i, z_j; \gamma, \beta)$ and $T_{2n}(z_i, z_j, z_k; \gamma, \beta)$ are symmetric in i, j and in i, j, k, respectively. We have the following result.

CLAIM 1. *If Assumptions 1–3, 6, 7, and 11 are satisfied and $\{z_i, i = 1, \ldots, n\}$ is an i.i.d. sample, then*

$$\hat{G}_n(\gamma, \beta)$$

$$= G_n(\gamma, \beta) + \binom{n}{2}^{-1} \frac{1}{n} \sum_{i<j} T_{1n}(z_i, z_j; \gamma, \beta) + \binom{n}{2}^{-1} \frac{1}{n} \sum_{i<j<k} T_{2n}(z_i, z_j, z_k; \gamma, \beta)$$

$$+ c_n(z_i, z_j; \gamma, \beta),$$

where $\sup_{\substack{i,j \\ B,\Gamma}} |c_n(z_i, z_j; \gamma, \beta)| = o_p(n^{-1/2})$.

PROOF. Using Assumption 7, we have

$$\frac{1}{h_n^L} \left[K\left(\frac{\hat{\mu}_n(w_i, \gamma) - \hat{\mu}_n(w_j, \gamma)}{h_n} \right) - K\left(\frac{\hat{\mu}_n(w_i, \gamma) - \hat{\mu}_n(w_j, \gamma)}{h_n} \right) \right]$$

$$\leq \frac{1}{h_n^{L+1}} K^{(1)} \left(\frac{\mu(w_i, \gamma) - \mu(w_j, \gamma)}{h_n} \right)'$$

$$\times ([\hat{\mu}_n(w_i, \gamma) - \mu(w_i, \gamma)] - [\hat{\mu}_n(w_i, \gamma) - \mu(w_i, \gamma)])$$

$$+ \frac{2L}{h_n^{L+2}} \| K^{(2)}(d_{ij}^*) \| \cdot [\|\hat{\mu}_n(w_i, \gamma) - \mu(w_i, \gamma)\|^2 + \|\hat{\mu}_n(w_j, \gamma) - \mu(w_j, \gamma)\|^2].$$

Assumptions 1–3, 6, 7, and 11 and the nature of the trimming function $a(\cdot)$ imply that

$$\sup_{\substack{i,j \\ B,\Gamma}} \frac{\| K^{(2)}(d_{ij}^*) \|}{h_n^{L+2}} \cdot [\|\hat{\mu}_n(w_i, \gamma) - \mu(w_i, \gamma)\|^2] \cdot |t(v_i, v_j, \beta)| \cdot a(w_{2i}) a(w_{2j})$$

$$\leq \frac{C}{nh_n^{L+2}} O_p(n^{1-\delta} b_n^{L_2})^{-1} |F(z_i, z_j)| a(w_{2i}) a(w_{2j})$$

for any $\delta > 0$ and some $C > 0$. Using Assumption 6, there exists a $\delta > 0$ such that $(n^{1-\delta} h_n^{L+2} b_n^{L_2})^{-1} = o(n^{-1/2})$. From Assumption 11 and the properties of $a(\cdot)$, we have $E[\{|F(z_i, z_j) a(w_{2i}) a(w_{2j})\}^2] = O(n)$. Using lemma A.3 in Ahn and Powell, we have

$$c_{1n}(z_i, z_j) \equiv \frac{C}{nh_n^{L+2}} O_p(n^{1-\delta} b_n^{L_2})^{-1} \binom{n}{2}^{-1} \sum_{i<j} |F(z_i, z_j)| a(w_{2i}) a(w_{2j})$$

$$= \frac{1}{n^{1-\delta} h_n^{L+2} b_n^{L_2}} O_p(1)$$

for all $\delta > 0$. Choosing the value of δ in Assumption 6, we obtain $c_{1n}(z_i, z_j) = o_p(n^{-1/2})$. If Assumptions 1–3 hold, Theorem 1 yields

$$\frac{1}{h_n^{L+1}} K^{(1)} \left(\frac{\mu(w_i, \gamma) - \mu(w_j, \gamma)}{h_n} \right)' (\hat{\mu}_n(w_i, \gamma) - \mu(w_i, \gamma)) t(v_i, v_j, \beta) \cdot a(w_{2i}) a(w_{2j})$$

$$= \frac{1}{h_n^{L+1}} K^{(1)} \left(\frac{\mu(w_i, \gamma) - \mu(w_j, \gamma)}{h_n} \right)' t(v_i, v_j, \beta) \cdot a(w_{2i}) a(w_{2j})$$

$$\times \left\{ \sum_{k=1}^{n} \frac{[\tau(w_i, \gamma) - \eta(w_{1k}, w_{2i}, \gamma) - \mu(w_i, \gamma)]}{f_{w_2}(w_{2i}) n b_n^{L_2}} H_{b_n}(w_{2k} - w_{2i}) + \xi_n(w_{2i}, \gamma) \right\},$$

where $\sup_{\substack{v \in W_2 \\ \gamma \in \Gamma}} \|\xi_n(\omega, \gamma)\| = O_p(n^{\delta - 1} b_n^{-L_2})$ for any $\delta > 0$. We have

$$\frac{1}{h_n^{L+1}} \binom{n}{2}^{-1} \sum_{i<j} \sup_{\substack{i,j \\ B,\Gamma}} \left\| K^{(1)} \left(\frac{\mu(w_i, \gamma) - \mu(w_j, \gamma)}{h_n} \right) \right\| |t(v_i, v_j, \beta)|$$

$$\cdot a(w_{2i}) a(w_{2j}) \|\xi_n(w_{2i}, \gamma)\|$$

$$\leq \frac{C}{n h_n^{L+1}} O_p(n^{1-\delta} b_n^{L_2})^{-1} \binom{n}{2}^{-1} \sum_{i<j} |F(z_i, z_j)| a(w_{2i}) a(w_{2j}) \equiv c_{2n}(z_i, z_j)$$

for any $\delta > 0$. By Assumption 6 and the same argument used above, we have $c_{2n}(z_i, z_j) = o_p(n^{-1/2})$. Grouping the terms in the sum, we obtain the result of the claim, with $\sup_{\substack{i,j \\ B,\Gamma}} |c_n(z_i, z_j; \gamma, \beta)\| = D \cdot (c_{1n}(z_i, z_j) + c_{2n}(z_i, z_j))$ for some constant $D > 0$. ∎

CLAIM 2. *If Assumptions 1–3, 6, 7, and 11–14 hold and* $\{z_i, i = 1, \ldots, n\}$ *is an i.i.d. sample, then*

$$\binom{n}{2}^{-1} \frac{1}{n} \sum_{i<j<k} T_{2n}(z_i, z_j, z_k; \gamma, \beta)$$

$$= \frac{2(n-2)}{n} \frac{1}{n} \sum_{i=1}^{n} B_n(w_{2i}; \gamma, \beta)[\tau(w_i, \gamma) - \eta(w_i, \gamma) - \mu(w_i, \gamma)] a(w_{2i}),$$

$$+ \tilde{c}_n(z_i, z_j; \gamma, \beta),$$

where $\sup_{B,\Gamma} |\tilde{c}_n(z_i, z_j; \gamma, \beta)| = o_p(n^{-1/2})$.

PROOF. Recall from Assumption 1 that $f_w(w_1, w_2)$ denotes the joint density of w_{1i} and w_{2i}. Using iterated expectations, we have

$$E[S_{1n}(z_i, z_j; \gamma, \beta)' S_{2n}(z_k, z_i; \gamma, \beta) | z_i]$$

$$= E\left[\frac{1}{h_n^{L+1}} K^{(1)} \left(\frac{\mu(w_i, \gamma) - \mu(w_j, \gamma)}{h_n} \right)' t(v_i, v_j, \beta) a(w_{2i}) a(w_{2j}) \right.$$

$$\left. \times \frac{1}{b_n^{L_2}} \iint \frac{[\tau(w_i, \gamma) - \eta(u, w_{2i}, \gamma) - \mu(w_i, \gamma)]}{f_{w_2}(w_{2i})} H\left(\frac{v - w_{2i}}{b_n} \right) f_w(u, v) \, du \, dv \right].$$

Define $Q_\ell \equiv \{(q_1, \ldots, q_L) \in \mathbb{N}^{L_2} : q_1 + \cdots + q_{L_2} = \ell\}$ and $\Upsilon_\ell(u, v) = \sum_{Q_\ell} \times \frac{\partial^\ell f_w(u,v)}{\partial w_{2_1} \cdots \partial w_{2_{L_2}}^{q_{L_2}}}$. From Assumption 2(i), there exists $C > 0$ such that $\Upsilon_\ell(u, v) < C$ for all u, v and $\ell = 1, \ldots, M$. From Assumptions 1(ii) and 3(i), the following approximation is valid:

$$\int H(\psi) f_w(u, b_n \psi + w_{2i}) d\psi$$

$$= f_w(u, w_{2i}) + b_n^M \frac{(-1)^M}{M!} \int \sum_{Q_M} (\psi_1^{q_1} \cdots \psi_{L_2}^{q_{L_2}}) \Upsilon(u, w_{2i} + b_n^* \psi) H(\psi) \, d\psi,$$

with $b_n^* \in (0, b_n)$. Assumptions 1(ii) and 3(i) imply that $\sup_u \int |\sum_{Q_M} \times (\psi_1^{q_1} \cdots \psi_{L_2}^{q_{L_2}}) \Upsilon(u, w_{2i} + b_n^* \psi) H(\psi)| d\psi < D$ for some $D > 0$. Therefore, we have

$$\sup_{B, \Gamma} E[S_{1n}(z_i, z_j; \gamma, \beta)' S_{2n}(z_k, z_i; \gamma, \beta) | z_i] \le C \frac{b_n^M}{h_n^{L+1}} E[F(z_i, z_j) a(w_{2i}) a(w_{2j})]$$

for some $C > 0$. Using Assumptions 6 and 11, $\sup_{B, \Gamma} E[S_{1n}(z_i, z_j; \gamma, \beta)' \times S_{2n}(z_k, z_i; \gamma, \beta) | z_i] = o_p(n^{-1/2})$. Using iterated expectations and steps parallel to those used above, we obtain the same result for $E[S_{1n}(z_i, z_j; \gamma, \beta)' \times S_{2n}(z_k, z_j; \gamma, \beta) | z_i]$, $E[S_{1n}(z_i, z_k; \gamma, \beta)' S_{2n}(z_j, z_i; \gamma, \beta) | z_i]$, and $E[S_{1n}(z_i, z_k; \gamma, \beta)' \times S_{2n}(z_j, z_k; \gamma, \beta) | z_i]$. Define

$$\tilde{D}_n(v, u; \gamma, \beta) = B_n(v; \gamma, \beta) [\tau(u, v, \gamma) - \eta(u, v, \gamma) - \mu(v, \gamma)] a(v).$$

Using iterated expectations, we have

$$E[S_{1n}(z_j, z_k; \gamma, \beta)' S_{2n}(z_i, z_j; \gamma, \beta) | z_i]$$

$$= E\left[B_n(w_{2j}; \gamma, \beta) \frac{[\tau(w_i) - \eta(w_i, \gamma) - \mu(w_j, \gamma)]}{b_n^{L_2} f_{w_2}(w_{2j})} a(w_{2j}) H_{b_n}(w_{2j} - w_{2i}) | z_i \right]$$

$$= \int \tilde{D}_n(w_{1i}, b_n \psi + w_{2i}; \gamma, \beta) H(\psi) d\psi.$$

From Assumption 12, $a(\cdot)$ is M times differentiable almost everywhere—the boundary of W_2 is a set of Lebesgue-measure zero in $\mathbb{R}^{L_2}$. Therefore, Assumptions 2(i), 12, and 14 imply that with probability one, $\tilde{D}_n(u, v; \gamma, \beta)$ is M times differentiable with respect to v with bounded derivatives for all $\gamma \in \Gamma$ and $\beta \in B$. Let the set Q_ℓ be as defined above and denote $\Lambda_\ell(u, v; \gamma, \beta) = \sum_{Q_\ell} \frac{\partial^\ell \tilde{D}_n(u,v;\gamma,\beta)}{\partial v_1^{q_1} \cdots \partial v_{L_2}^{q_{L_2}}}$. An Mth order approximation yields

$$E[S_{1n}(z_j, z_k; \gamma, \beta)' S_{2n}(z_i, z_j; \gamma, \beta) \mid z_i]$$

$$= \tilde{D}_n(w_{1i}, w_{2i}; \gamma, \beta) + b_n^M \frac{(-1)^M}{M!} \int \sum_{Q_M} (\psi_1^{q_1} \cdots \psi_{L_2}^{q_2}) \Lambda(w_{1i}, w_{2i} + b_n^* \psi; \gamma, \beta) \, d\psi.$$

Assumptions 2(i), 3(i), 12, and 14 yield $\sup_{B,\Gamma} | \int \sum_{Q_M} (\psi_1^{q_1} \cdots \psi_{L_2}^{q_2}) \Lambda(w_{1i}, w_{2i} + b_n^* \psi; \gamma, \beta) \, d\psi| < C$ for some $C > 0$. Therefore, for some $D > 0$,

$$\sup_{B,\Gamma} | E[S_{1n}(z_j, z_k; \gamma, \beta)' S_{2n}(z_i, z_j; \gamma, \beta) \mid z_i] - B_n(w_{2i}; \gamma, \beta)$$

$$\times [\tau(w_i, \gamma) - \eta(w_i, \gamma) - \mu(w_i, \gamma)] a(w_{2i}) | \le D b_n^M = o(n^{-1/2}),$$

where the last equality follows from Assumption 6—or its weaker version, Assumption 3(ii). Using iterated expectations and following parallel steps, we have

$$\sup_{B,\Gamma} | E[S_{1n}(z_j, z_k; \gamma, \beta)' S_{2n}(z_i, z_k; \gamma, \beta) \mid z_i] + B_n(w_{2i}; \gamma, \beta)$$

$$\times [\tau(w_i, \gamma) - \eta(w_i, \gamma) - \mu(w_i, \gamma)] a(w_{2i}) | = o(n^{-1/2}).$$

The change in sign with respect to the previous result is a direct consequence of the properties of $K^{(1)}(\cdot)$ stated in Assumption 7. Combining all these results together, we get

$$E[T_{2n}(z_i, z_k, z_k; \gamma, \beta) \mid z_i]$$

$$= 2 B_n(w_{2i}; \gamma, \beta)[\tau(w_i, \gamma) - \eta(w_i, \gamma) - \mu(w_i, \gamma)] a(w_{2i}) + \tilde{c}_n(z_i, z_j; \gamma, \beta),$$

where $\sup_{B,\Gamma} |\tilde{c}_n(z_i, z_j; \gamma, \beta)| = o_p(n^{-1/2})$. Note that

$$E[B_n(w_{2i}; \gamma, \beta)[\tau(w_i, \gamma) - \eta(w_i, \gamma) - \mu(w_i, \gamma)] a(w_{2i})] = 0.$$

Using Assumptions 3(i), 6, 7, and 11, the properties of the trimming set, we have

$$\sup_{B,\Gamma} E[\| S_{1n}(z_i, z_j; \gamma, \beta)' S_{2n}(z_i, z_j; \gamma, \beta)\|^2] \le \frac{C}{h_n^{2(L+1)} b_n^{2L_2}}$$

$$\times \sup_\Gamma E\left[\| F(z_i, z_j)[\tau(w_i, \gamma) - \eta(w_{1i}, w_{2j}, \gamma) - \mu(w_j, \gamma)]\|^2 \left(\frac{a(w_{2i})a(w_{2j})}{f_{w_2}(w_{2j})} \right)^2 \right].$$

Using Assumptions 11 and 6, the right-hand side is $O(n)$. This result also holds for all the remaining components of $T_{2n}(z_i, z_j, z_k; \gamma, \beta)$. Therefore, we obtain

$$\sup_{B,\Gamma} E[\| T_{2n}(z_i, z_j, z_k; \gamma, \beta)\|^2] = O(n),$$

and lemma A.3 in Ahn and Powell yields

$$\binom{n}{3} \sum_{i<j<k} T_{2n}(z_i, z_j, z_k; \gamma, \beta) = \frac{3}{n} \sum_{i=1}^{n} E[T_{2n}(z_i, z_k, z_k; \gamma, \beta) \mid z_i] + \tilde{d}_n(z_i, z_j; \gamma, \beta)$$

$$= \frac{6}{n} \sum_{i=1}^{n} B_n(w_{2i}; \gamma, \beta)[\tau(w_i, \gamma) - \eta(w_i, \gamma) - \mu(w_i, \gamma)]a(w_{2i}) + \tilde{d}_n(z_i, z_j; \gamma, \beta)$$

$$+ o_p(n^{-1/2}),$$

where $\sup_{B,\Gamma} |\tilde{d}_n(z_i, z_j; \gamma, \beta)| = o_p(n^{-1/2})$. The result from the Claim follows immediately by noting that $\frac{1}{n}\binom{n}{2}^{-1} = \frac{1}{3}\frac{n-2}{n}\binom{n}{3}^{-1}$. ∎

CLAIM 3. *If Assumptions 1–3, 6, 7, and 11–14 are satisfied and $\{z_i, i = 1, \dots, n\}$ is an i.i.d. sample, then*

$$\hat{G}_n(\gamma, \beta) = G_n(\gamma, \beta) + \frac{2(n-2)}{n}\frac{1}{n}\sum_{i=1}^{n} B_n(w_{2i}; \gamma, \beta)$$

$$\times [\tau(w_i, \gamma) - \eta(w_i, \gamma) - \mu(w_i, \gamma)]a(w_{2i}) + \tilde{e}_n(z_i, z_j; \gamma, \beta),$$

where $\sup_{B,\Gamma} |\tilde{e}_n(z_i, z_j; \gamma, \beta)| = o_p(n^{-1/2})$.

PROOF. The same argument we used to show that $\sup_{B,\Gamma} E[\|T_{2n}(z_i, z_j, z_k; \gamma, \beta)\|^2] = O(n)$ also yields $\sup_{B,\Gamma} E[\|T_{1n}(z_i, z_j; \gamma, \beta)\|^2] = O(n)$. Consequently, $\sup_{B,\Gamma}\binom{n}{2}\sum_{i<j}\|T_{1n}(z_i, z_j; \gamma, \beta)\| = O_p(1)$ and therefore $\sup_{B,\Gamma} \times \frac{1}{n}\binom{n}{2}\sum_{i<j}T_{1n}(z_i, z_j; \gamma, \beta) = o_p(n^{-1/2})$. Given this, the result follows from Claims 1 and 2. ∎

PROOF OF THEOREM 5. We will outline the general steps of the proof. We begin by noting that our assumptions are consistent with lemma 25 in Ichimura (2004), which implies that

$$\Pr\left(\mathbb{1}\{f_{w_{2n}}(w_{2i})\} - \mathbb{1}\{f_{w_2}(w_{2i})\} \neq 0 \text{ for at least one } w_{2i}\right) \longrightarrow 0.$$

This result is very useful since our trimming set $\mathcal{W}_{2n}$ is defined in terms of $f_{w_{2n}}(w_{2i})$. Given this, we now present the key components that lead to consistency. As we did previously, define

$$T_n(\gamma_0, b) = \binom{n}{2}^{-1} \sum_{i<j} \frac{1}{h_n^L} K\left(\frac{\mu(w_{2i}, \gamma_0) - \mu(w_j, \gamma_0)}{h_n}\right) s(v_i, v_j; b)a_n(w_{2i})a_n(w_{2j}).$$

Using Assumptions 4(i), 6, 7, 18(iii), the properties of $a_n(\cdot)$, and Lebesgue's Dominated Convergence Theorem, we obtain

$$E[T_n(\gamma_0, b)] \to E[f_{\mu(w_2, \gamma_0)}(\mu(w_i, \gamma_0))\kappa_s(v_i, \mu(w_i, \gamma_0); b)] \equiv T_0(\gamma_0, b),$$

which depends on w_{2i} only through $\mu(w_i, \gamma_0)$. Therefore, consistency will rely exclusively on Assumption 10, namely that $E[s(v_i, v_j; b) \mid \mu(w_j, \gamma_0) = \mu(w_i, \gamma_0)]$ is uniquely minimized at $b = \beta_0$, without the need of Assumption 5.

If Assumptions 1 and 2 are satisfied for any compact subset in the interior of $\mathbb{S}(w_2)$ and if the condition $\log(\bar{w}_n) = o_p(n^\varepsilon)$ holds, we can extend Theorem 1 to show that

(a) $\sup_{\substack{v \in \mathcal{W}_{2n} \\ \gamma \in \Gamma}} (n^{1-\delta} b_n^{L_2})^{1/2} \| \hat{\mu}_n(v, \gamma) - \mu(v, \gamma) \| = O_p(1)$ for any $\delta > 0$.

(b) $\hat{\mu}_n(v, \gamma) - \mu(v, \gamma) = \frac{1}{f_{w_2}(v)} \frac{1}{n b_n^2} \sum_{i=1}^n [\tau(w_i, \gamma) - \eta(w_{1i}, v, \gamma) - \mu(v, \gamma)] \times H_{b_n}(w_{2i} - v) + \xi_n(\omega, \gamma),$

where $\sup_{\substack{v \in \mathcal{W}_{2n} \\ \gamma \in \Gamma}} \| \xi_n(\omega, \gamma) \| = O_p(n^{\delta-1} b_n^{-L_2})$ for any $\delta > 0$. Following the same steps as in Sections 3.3.1 and 3.4, we use this result to establish pointwise and uniform convergence of $T_n(\hat{\gamma}, b)$ to $T_0(\gamma_0, b)$ and thus establish consistency of $\hat{\beta}$.

To establish asymptotic normality, we rely once again on the extension of Theorem 1 to the set $\mathcal{W}_{2n}$. The remaining key step is to note that

$$\sup_{B, \Gamma} E\left[\| S_{1n}(z_i, z_j; \gamma, \beta)' S_{2n}(z_i, z_j; \gamma, \beta) \|^2 \right] \leq \frac{C}{h_n^{2(L+1)} b_n^{2L_2} \varsigma_n^2}$$

$$\times \sup_\Gamma E\left[\| F(z_i, z_j) [\tau(w_i, \gamma) - \eta(w_{1i}, w_{2j}, \gamma) - \mu(w_j, \gamma)] \|^2 \left(\frac{a(w_{2i}) a(w_{2j})}{f_{w_2}(w_{2j})} \right)^2 \right].$$

Using Assumptions 3(i), 7, 11, and 18(ii), the right-hand side is $O(n)$. Using the same steps as we did in Claim 3, this result leads to the conclusion that

$$\hat{G}_n(\gamma, \beta) = G_n(\gamma, \beta) + \frac{2(n-2)}{n} \frac{1}{n} \sum_{i=1}^n B_n(w_{2i}; \gamma, \beta)$$

$$\times [\tau(w_i, \gamma) - \eta(w_i, \gamma) - \mu(w_i, \gamma)] a(w_{2i}) + \tilde{e}_n(z_i, z_j; \gamma, \beta)$$

$$\equiv G_n(\gamma, \beta) + \frac{2(n-2)}{n} \frac{1}{n} \sum_{i=1}^n \tilde{D}_n(w_i; \gamma, \beta) + \tilde{e}_n(z_i, z_j; \gamma, \beta).$$

The final result follows from the exact same steps used to prove Theorem 4, and the fact that $a_n(\cdot) \to c$. ∎

REFERENCES

AHN, H., AND J. L. POWELL, "Semiparametric Estimation of Censored Selection Models with a Nonparametric Selection Mechanism," *Journal of Econometrics* 58 (1993), 3–29.

AI, C., AND D. L. McFADDEN, "Estimation of Some Partially Specified Nonlinear Models," *Journal of Econometrics* 76 (1997), 1–37.

ARADILLAS-LOPEZ, A., "Semiparametric Estimation of a Simultaneous Game with Incomplete Information," Mimeo, Princeton University, 2005.

——, "Pairwise Difference Estimation of Incomplete Information Games," Mimeo, Princeton University, 2006.

BLUNDELL, R., AND J. L. POWELL, "Endogeneity in Semiparametric Binary Response Models," *Review of Economic Studies* 71 (2004), 581–913.

——, AND R. J. SMITH, "Estimation in a Class of Simultaneous Equation Limited Dependent Variable Models," *Review of Economic Studies* 56 (1989), 37–58.

DAS, M., W. K. NEWEY, AND F. VELLA, "Nonparametric Estimation of Sample Selection Models," *Review of Economic Studies* 70 (2003), 33–58.

ENGLE, R. F., C. W. J. GRANGER, J. RICE, AND A. WEISS, "Semiparametric Estimates of the Relation between Weather and Electricity Sales," *Journal of the American Statistical Association* 81 (1986), 310–20.

HONG, H., AND M. SHUM, "Pairwise Difference Estimator of a Dynamic Optimization Model," Mimeo, Duke University, 2004.

HONORÉ, B. E., "Trimmed LAD and Least Squares Estimation of Truncated and Censored Regression Models with Fixed Effects," *Econometrica* 60 (1992), 533–65.

——, AND J. L. POWELL, "Pairwise Difference Estimators of Censored and Truncated Regression Models," *Journal of Econometrics* 64 (1994), 241–78.

——, AND ——, "Pairwise Difference Estimation of Nonlinear Models," in D. W. K. Andrews and J. H. Stock, eds., *Identification and Inference in Econometric Models. Essays in Honor of Thomas Rothenberg* (Cambridge: Cambridge University Press, 2005), 520–53.

ICHIMURA, H., "Computation of Asymptotic Distribution for Semiparametric GMM Estimators," Mimeo, University College London, 2004.

——, AND L. F. LEE, "Semiparametric Estimation of Multiple Index Models," in W. A. Barnett, J. L. Powell, and G. Tauchen, eds., *Nonparametric and Semiparametric Methods in Econometrics and Statistics. Proceedings of the Fifth International Symposium in Economic Theory and Econometrics* (Cambridge: Cambridge University Press, 1991).

NEWEY, W. K. AND D. L. MCFADDEN, "Large Sample Estimation and Hypothesis Testing," in R. F. Engle and D. L. McFadden eds., *Handbook of Econometrics, Vol. IV* (Amsterdam: Elsevier, 1994).

——, J. L. POWELL, AND F. VELLA, "Nonparametric Estimation of Triangular Simultaneous Equations Models," *Econometrica* 67 (1999), 565–603.

ROBINSON, P., "Root-N Consistent Semiparametric Regression," *Econometrica* 56 (1988), 931–54.

SHERMAN, R., "U-Processes in the Analysis of a Generalized Semiparametric Regression Estimator," *Econometric Theory* 10 (1994), 372–95.

SILVERMAN, B. W., *Density Estimation for Statistics and Data Analysis* (London: Chapman and Hall, 1986).

INTERNATIONAL ECONOMIC REVIEW
Vol. 48, No. 4, November 2007

DISCRETE CHOICE MODELS WITH MULTIPLE UNOBSERVED CHOICE CHARACTERISTICS*

BY SUSAN ATHEY AND GUIDO W. IMBENS[1]

Harvard University, U.S.A.

Since the pioneering work by Daniel McFadden, utility-maximization-based multinomial response models have become important tools of empirical researchers. Various generalizations of these models have been developed to allow for unobserved heterogeneity in taste parameters and choice characteristics. Here we investigate how rich a specification of the unobserved components is needed to rationalize arbitrary choice patterns in settings with many individual decision makers, multiple markets, and large choice sets. We find that if one restricts the utility function to be monotone in the unobserved choice characteristics, then up to two unobserved choice characteristics may be needed to rationalize the choices.

1. INTRODUCTION

Since the pioneering work by Daniel McFadden in the 1970s and 1980s (1973, 1981, 1982, 1984; Hausman and McFadden, 1984) discrete (multinomial) response models have become an important tool of empirical researchers. McFadden's early work focused on the application of logit-based choice models to transportation choices. Since then these models have been applied in many areas of economics, including labor economics, public finance, development, finance, and others. Currently, one of the most active areas of application of these methods is to demand analysis for differentiated products in industrial organization. A common feature of these applications is the presence of many choices.

The application of McFadden's methods to industrial organization has inspired numerous extensions and generalizations of the basic multinomial logit model. As pointed out by McFadden, multinomial logit models have the Independence of Irrelevant Alternatives (IIA) property, so that, for example, an increase in the price for one good implies a redistribution of part of the demand for that good to the other goods in proportions equal to their original market shares. This places strong restrictions on the substitution patterns (cross-price elasticities) of products: Elasticities are proportional to market shares. McFadden proposed various extensions to the standard model in order to relax the IIA property and

* Manuscript received January 2006; revised May 2007.
[1] We are grateful to Gary Chamberlain, Dan McFadden, Charles Manski, other conference participants, and an anonymous reviewer for comments. Financial support for this research was generously provided through NSF grants SES 0351500 (Athey) and SES 0452590 (Imbens). Please address correspondence to: Guido W. Imbens, Department of Economics, Harvard University, Cambridge, MA 02138. E-mail: *imbens@harvard.edu*.

generate more realistic substitution patterns, including "nested logit" models and "mixed logit" models. The subsequent literature has explored extensions to and implementations of these ideas. The nested logit model allows for layers of choices, grouped into a tree structure, where the IIA property is imposed within a nest, but not across nests (McFadden, 1982; Goldberg, 1995; Bresnahan et al., 1997). The random coefficients or mixed logit approach was generalized in an influential pair of papers by Berry et al. (1995, 2004; BLP from here on) and applied to settings with a large number of choices. BLP developed methods for estimating models with random coefficients on product attributes (mixed logit models) as well as unobserved choice characteristics in settings with aggregate data. Exploiting the logistic structure of the model, Berry (1994) proposed a method to relate market shares to a scalar unobserved choice characteristic. Their methods have found widespread application.

One strand of this literature has focused on hedonic models, where the utility is modeled as a parametric function of a finite number of choice characteristics and a finite number of individual characteristics. Researchers have considered hedonic models both with and without individual-choice specific error terms (Berry and Pakes, 2007; Bajari and Benkard, 2004). These models have some attractive properties, especially in settings with many choices, because the number of parameters does not increase with the number of choices. Unlike the nested and random coefficient logit models, hedonic models can potentially predict zero market share for some choices. On the other hand, simple forms of those models rule out particular choices for individuals with specific characteristics, making them very sensitive to misspecification. To make these models more flexible, researchers have typically allowed for unobserved choice and individual characteristics. To maintain computational feasibility, the number of unobserved choice characteristics is typically limited to one.

This article explores a version of the multinomial choice model that has received less attention in the literature. We consider a random coefficients model of individual utility that includes observed individual and product characteristics, as well as multiple unobserved product characteristics and unobserved individual preferences for both observed and unobserved product characteristics. The idea of specifying such a model goes back at least to McFadden (1981), but only a few papers have followed this approach (e.g., Elrod and Keane, 1995; Keane, 1997, 2004; Harris and Keane, 1999; Goettler and Shachar, 2001). This model has several desirable features. For example, the model nests both models based on unobserved product characteristics (BLP) as well as unrestricted multinomial probit models (e.g., McCulloch et al., 2000; hereafter MPR). In addition, by describing products as combinations of attributes, it is possible to consider questions about the introduction of new products in particular parts of the product space.

In many cases researchers applying this class of models have employed restrictions on the number of unobserved choice characteristics. In other cases (e.g., Goettler and Shachar, 2001) authors have allowed for a large number of choice characteristics, with the data determining the number of unobserved characteristics that enter the utility function. However, the literature has not directly considered the question of what restrictions are implied by limiting the number of choice characteristics, nor is it clear whether, in the absence of parametric restrictions, the data can provide evidence for the existence of multiple unobserved product characteristics. Understanding the answers to these questions is important for empirical researchers who may not always be aware of the implications of the modeling choices. Although researchers may still find it useful to apply a model that cannot rationalize all patterns of choice data, we argue that the researcher should be aware of any limitations the model imposes in this regard. Similarly, if only functional form restrictions enable the researcher to infer the existence of multiple unobservable choice characteristics, the researcher should highlight clearly the role of the functional form.

In this article, we provide formal results to address these questions. We begin by asking how flexible a model is required—that is, how many and what kind of unobserved variables must be included in the specification of consumer utility— to rationalize choice data. We are interested in whether any pattern of market shares that might be consistent with utility maximization can be rationalized. We discuss settings and data configurations where one can establish that the utility function must depend on multiple unobserved choice characteristics instead of a single unobserved product characteristic. We also discuss the extent to which models with no unobserved individual characteristics can rationalize observed data.

We explore the implications of these models in an application to demand for yogurt. We consider models with up to two unobserved choice characteristics, and assess the implied price elasticities. In order to implement these models we employ Bayesian methods. Such methods have been used extensively in multinomial choice settings by Rossi et al. (1996; hereafter RMA), MPR, McCulloch and Rossi (1994), Allenby et al. (2003), Rossi et al. (2005), Bajari and Benkard (2003), Chib and Greenberg (1998), Geweke and Keane (2002), Romeo (2003), Osborne (2005), and others. These authors have demonstrated that Bayesian methods are very convenient for latent index discrete choice models with large numbers of choices, using modern computational methods for Bayesian inference, in particular data augmentation and Markov Chain Monte Carlo (MCMC) methods (Tanner and Wong, 1987; Geweke, 1997; Chib, 2003; Gelman et al. 2004; Rossi et al. 2005). See Train (2003) for a comparison with frequentist simulation methods.

2. THE MODEL

Consider a model with M "markets," where markets might be distinguished by variation in time as well as location. In market m there are N_m consumers, each choosing one product from a set of J products.[2] In this market product j has two sets of characteristics, a set of observed characteristics, denoted by X_{jm}, and a set of unobserved characteristics, denoted by ξ_j. The observed product characteristics may vary by market, though they need not do so. The vector of unobserved

---

[2] In the implementation we allow for the possibility that in some markets only a subset of the products is available. In order to keep the notation simple we do not make this explicit in the discussion in this section. Similarly, we allow for multiple purchases by the same individual, although the notation does not make this explicit at this point.

product characteristics does not vary by market.[3] The vector of observed product characteristics X_{jm} is of dimension K, and the vector of unobserved product characteristics ξ_j is of dimension P. Individual i has a vector of observed characteristics Z_i (which for notational convenience includes a constant term) of dimension L, and a vector of unobserved characteristics ν_i of dimension $K + P$.[4]

The utility associated with choice j for individual i in market m is U_{ijm}, for $i = 1, \ldots, N_m$, $j = 1, \ldots, J$, and $m = 1, \ldots, M$. Individuals choose product j if the associated utility is higher than that associated with any of the alternatives.[5] Hence the probability that an individual in market m with characteristics z chooses product j is

(1) $s_{jm}(z) = \Pr(U_{ijm} > U_{ikm} \text{ for all } k \neq j \,|\, X_{1m}, \ldots, X_{Jm}, Z_i = z).$

We assume there is a continuum of consumers in each market so that this probability is equal to the market share for product j in market m among the subpopulation with characteristics z.

We consider the following model for U_{ijm}:

$$U_{ijm} = g(X_{jm}, \xi_j, Z_i, \nu_i) + \epsilon_{ijm},$$

where g is unrestricted, and the additional component ϵ_{ijm} is assumed to be independent of observed and unobserved product characteristics and observed and unobserved individual characteristics. It is also assumed to be independent across choices, markets, and individuals and have a logistic distribution. This idiosyncratic error term is interpreted as incorporating individual-specific preferences for a product that are unrelated to all other product features.

Let us briefly consider a parametric version of this model in order to relate it more closely to models used in the empirical literature. Suppose the systematic part of the utility has the form

$$g(X_{jm}, \xi_j, Z_i, \nu_i) = X'_{jm}\beta_i + \xi'_j\gamma_i,$$

[3] We make the assumption that unobserved product characteristics do not vary by market, a defining characteristic of multiple markets with the same goods (conditional on observables): If products vary across markets in unobservable ways, there is little value to having observations from multiple markets absent additional assumptions about the way in which these unobservables vary across markets. One common approach to deal with unobservable characteristics that vary by market is to specify a model with a single unobserved characteristic, specify a model of competition, and assume equilibrium price setting, so that observed prices are in one-to-one correspondence with the unobservable. Equilibrium pricing assumptions are clearly more appropriate in some settings than in others (e.g., regulated markets). We do not pursue that approach here.

[4] We assume that the dimension of the unobserved individual component is equal to the sum of the number of observed and unobserved choice characteristics, allowing each choice characteristic to have its own individual-specific effect on utility. Although we do establish the importance of allowing for unobserved individual heterogeneity, we do not explore the extent of this need. It may not be necessary to allow the dimension of the unobserved individual heterogeneity to be as large as $K + P$.

[5] We ignore the possibility of ties in the latent utilities. In the specific models we consider such ties would occur with probability zero.

where the individual specific marginal utilities β_i and γ_i relate to the observed and unobserved individual characteristics through the equation

$$\begin{pmatrix} \beta_i \\ \gamma_i \end{pmatrix} = \begin{pmatrix} \Delta_o \\ \Delta_u \end{pmatrix} Z_i + \begin{pmatrix} v_{oi} \\ v_{ui} \end{pmatrix} = \Delta Z_i + v_i.$$

In this representation β_i is a K-dimensional column vector, γ_i is an P-dimensional column vector, Δ is a $(K + P) \times L$-dimensional matrix of coefficients that do not vary across individuals, and v_i is a $(K + P)$-dimensional column vector. The unobserved components of the individual characteristics are assumed to have a normal distribution:

$$v_i \mid \mathbf{X}_m, Z_i \sim \mathcal{N}(0, \Omega),$$

where $\mathbf{X}_m$ is the $J \times K$ matrix with jth row equal to X'_{jm}, and Ω is a $(K + P) \times (K + P)$-dimensional matrix. Now we can write the utility as

(2) $$U_{ijm} = X'_{jm} \Delta_o Z_i + \xi'_j \Delta_u Z_i + X'_{jm} v_{oi} + \xi'_j v_{ui} + \epsilon_{ijm}.$$

We contrast this model with three models that have been discussed and used more widely in the literature. The first is the special case with no unobserved product or individual characteristics:

$$U_{ijm} = X'_{jm} \Delta_o Z_i + \epsilon_{ijm}.$$

This is the standard multinomial logit model (McFadden, 1973). It has the IIA property that the conditional probablity of making choice j instead of k, given that one of the two is chosen, does not depend on characteristics of other choices. This in turn implies severe restrictions on cross-elasticities and thus on substitution patterns. For a general discussion, see McFadden (1982, 1984).

A second alternative model features a single unobserved product characteristic ($P = 1$) and unobserved individual characteristics:

$$U_{ijm} = X'_{jm} \beta_i + \xi_j + \varepsilon_{ij} = X'_{jm} \Delta_o Z_i + \xi_j + X'_{jm} v_{oi} + \epsilon_{ijm}.$$

This is a special case of the model used in BLP (who allow for endogeneity of some of the observed product characteristics, which for simplicity we do not consider here). This model allows for much richer patterns of substitution, while remaining computationally tractable even in settings with many choices. This model, with the generalization to allow for endogeneity of some choice characteristics, has become very popular in the applied literature. See Ackerberg et al. (2006) for a recent survey.

The third alternative model is typically set up in a different way, specifying

(3) $$U_{ijm} = X'_{jm} \Delta_o Z_i + \eta_{ijm},$$

with unrestricted dependence between the unobserved components for different choices. Thus,

$$
\begin{pmatrix} \eta_{i1m} \\ \eta_{i2m} \\ \vdots \\ \eta_{iJm} \end{pmatrix} \sim \mathcal{N}(0, \Omega),
$$

where $\eta_{i \cdot m}$ is the J vector with all η_{ijm} for individual i in market m, with the $J \times J$ matrix Ω not restricted (beyond some normalizations). This is the type of model studied in MPR and McCulloch and Rossi (1994).

The latter model can be nested in the model in (2). To see this, simplify (2) to eliminate the idiosyncratic error ϵ_{ijm} as well as random coefficients on observable individual and choice characteristics, leaving the following specification:

$$
U_{ijm} = X'_{jm} \Delta_o Z_i + \xi'_j v_{ui},
$$

where the dimension of the vector of unobserved choice characteristics ξ_j and the dimension of the vector of unobserved individual characteristics v_{ui} are both equal to J. Moreover, suppose that all elements of the J-vector ξ_j are equal to zero other than the jth element, which is equal to one. Then if we assume that $v_{ui} \sim \mathcal{N}(0, \Omega)$ and define $\eta_{ijm} \equiv \xi'_j v_{ui} = v_{uij}$, it follows that the two models are equivalent:

$$
\begin{pmatrix} \eta_{i1m} \\ \eta_{i2m} \\ \vdots \\ \eta_{iJm} \end{pmatrix} = (\xi_1 \ \xi_2 \ \ldots \ \xi_J)' v_{ui} = v_{ui} \sim \mathcal{N}(0, \Omega).
$$

The insight from this representation is that we can view the MPR set up as equivalent to (2) by allowing for as many unobserved choice characteristics as there are choices. The view underlying this approach is that choices are fundamentally different in ways that cannot be captured by a few characteristics.

Our discussion below will focus largely on the need for unobserved choice characteristics in order to explain data on choices arising from utility maximizing individuals. We will argue that in the absence of functional form restrictions a single unobserved product characteristic as in the BLP set up may not suffice to rationalize all choice data, but that the MPR approach allows for more unobserved choice characteristics than the data can ever reveal the existence of: A model with as many multiple unobserved choice characteristics as there are choices is non-parametrically not identified. We show that two unobserved choice characteristics are sufficient, even in the case with many choices, to rationalize choice data arising from utility maximizing behavior. By providing formal support for the ability of characteristic-based models to rationalize choice data, this discussion complements the substantive discussion in, among others, Ackerberg et al. (2006), who argue in favor of characteristics-based approaches, and the contrasting arguments in Kim et al. (2007), who argue in favor of the view that generally choices cannot be captured by a low-dimensional set of characteristics.

2.1. *The Motivation for the Idiosyncratic Error Term.* In this subsection, we briefly state our arguments for including the additive, choice, and individual specific extreme value error term ϵ_{ij} in the model. Such an error term is the only source of stochastic variation in the original multinomial choice models with only observed choice and individual characteristics, but in models with unobserved choice and individual characteristics their presence needs more motivation. Following Berry and Pakes (2002) we refer to models without such an ϵ_{ij} as pure characteristics models. We discuss two arguments in favor of the models with the additive error term. The first centers on the lack of robustness of the pure characteristics models to measurement error. The second argument concerns the ability of the model with the additive ϵ_{ij} to approximate arbitrarily closely the model without such an error term. Hence in large samples the inclusion of this error term does not affect the ability to explain choices arising from a pure characteristics model.

Let us examine these arguments in more detail. First, consider the fact that the pure characteristics model may have stark predictions: It can predict zero market shares for some products. An implication of this feature is that such models are very sensitive to measurement error. For example, consider a case where choices are generated by a pure characteristics model with utility $g(x, v, z, \xi)$, and suppose that this model implies that choice j, with observed and unobserved characteristics equal to Z_j and ξ_j, has zero market share. Now suppose that there is a single unit i for whom we observe, due to measurement error, the choice $Y_i = j$. Irrespective of the number of correctly measured observations available that were generated by the pure characteristics model, the estimates of the parameters will not be close to the true values corresponding to the pure characteristics model due to the single mismeasured observation. Such extreme sensitivity puts a lot of emphasis on the correct specification of the model and the absence of measurement error and is undesirable in most settings.

Thus, one might wish to generalize the model to be robust against small amounts of measurement error of this type. One possibility is to define the optimal choice Y_i^* as the choice that maximizes the utility and assume that the observed choice Y_i is equal to the optimal choice Y_i^* with probability $1 - \delta$, and with probability $\delta/(J - 1)$ any of the other choices is observed:

$$\Pr\left(Y_i = y \mid Y_i^*, X_i, v_i, Z_1, \ldots, Z_J, \xi_1, \ldots, \xi_J\right) = \begin{cases} 1 - \delta & \text{if } Y = Y_i^*, \\ \delta/(J - 1) & \text{if } Y \neq Y_i^*. \end{cases}$$

This nests the pure characteristics model (by setting $\delta = 0$), without having the disadvantages of extreme sensitivity to mismeasured choices that the pure characteristics model has. If the true choices are generated by the utility function $g(x, v, z, \xi)$, the presence of a single mismeasured observation will not prevent the true values of the parameters from maximizing the expected log likelihood function. However, this specific generalization of the pure characteristics model has an unattractive feature: If the optimal choice Y_i^* is not observed, all of the remaining choices are equally likely. One might expect that choices with utilities closer to the optimal one are more likely to be observed conditional on the optimal choice not being observed.

An alternative modification of the pure characteristics model is based on adding an idiosyncratic error term to the utility function. This model will have the feature that, conditional on the optimal choice not being observed, a close-to-optimal choice is more likely than a far-from-optimal choice. Suppose the true utility is

$$U_{ij}^* = g(X_i, v_i, Z_j, \xi_j),$$

but individuals base their choice on the maximum of mismeasured version of this utility:

$$U_{ij} = U_{ij}^* + \epsilon_{ij} = g(X_i, v_i, Z_j, \xi_j) + \epsilon_{ij},$$

with an extreme value ϵ_{ij}, independent across choices and individuals. The ϵ_{ij} here can be interpreted as an error in the calculation of the utility associated with a particular choice. This model does not directly nest the pure characteristics model, since the idiosyncratic error term has a fixed variance. However, it approximately nests it in the following sense. If the data are generated by the pure characteristics model with the utility function $g(x, v, z, \xi)$, then the model with the utility function $\lambda \cdot g(x, v, z, \xi) + \epsilon_{ij}$ leads, for sufficiently large λ, to choice probabilities that are arbitrarily close to the true choice probabilities (e.g., Berry and Pakes, 2007).[6]

Hence, even if the data were generated by a pure characteristics model, one does not lose much by using a model with an additive idiosyncratic error term, and one gains a substantial amount of robustness to measurement or optimization error.

3.　SOME RESULTS ON RATIONALIZABILITY OF CHOICE DATA

In Section 2, we introduced a general nonparametric model. In this section, we consider the ability of this model to rationalize data arising from choices based on utility maximizing behavior, as well as the question of whether the primitives of this model can be identified.

Our model decomposes individual-product unobservables into individual observed and unobserved preferences (random coefficients) for observed and unobserved product characteristics, where individual- and product-level unobservables interact. An initial question concerns how different types of variation that might be present in a data set potentially shed light on the importance of various elements of the model. In particular, we ask whether the data can in principle reject restricted versions of the model, such as a model with a single unobserved

---

[6] This closeness is not uniform, because for individuals who are indifferent between two alternatives the two models will predict different choice probabilities irrespective of the value of λ, but the proportion of such individuals is assumed to be zero.

product characteristic or a model with homogeneous individuals conditional on observables.

A model is said to be testable if it cannot rationalize all hypothetical data sets that might be observed. Questions about identification and testability are generally considered in the context of hypothetical data sets that are large in some dimension. Typically we consider settings with independent draws from a common distribution, and the limit is based on the number of draws going to infinity. In the current setting, there are several different dimensions where the data set may be large. Specifically, we will consider settings with a large number of individuals facing the same choice set (large N_m), when each choice corresponds to a vector of characteristics. Some of our results will apply to settings where the number of choices or products itself is large (large J), so that for each product there is a nearby product (in terms of observed product characteristics). Such settings have been the motivation for BLP and literature that follows them (e.g., Nevo, 2000, 2001; Ackerberg and Rysman, 2002; Petrin, 2002; Bajari and Benkard, 2003). Finally, some of our results will consider a large number of markets (large M), where some observed choice characteristics may vary between markets (but all unobserved choice characteristics are constant within markets).

We shall see that a data set with a large number of choices can be used to distinguish between the absence or presence of unobserved choice characteristics, and that a data set with a large number of markets and sufficient variation in observed product characteristics can be used to establish the presence of unobserved individual heterogeneity.

3.1. *Rationalizability in a Single Market.* In this subsection, we set $M = 1$ and suppress the subscript indicating the market in our notation. First, consider the case with a finite number of choices J and an infinite number of individuals. We can summarize what we can learn from the data in terms of the conditional probability of choice j given individual characteristics $Z_i = z$. We denote this probability, equal to the market share because we have a large number of individuals in each market, by $s_j(z)$. Note that utility maximization does not place restrictions on how the functions $s_j(\cdot)$ vary with z; any pattern of market share variation is possible. We proceed to ask how rich a model is necessary to rationalize all possible patterns of market shares, starting with the case of a finite number of products and then proceeding to the case where the number of products grows large enough so that there are multiple products with very similar characteristics.

To begin, we show that a model with no unobserved individual and no unobserved choice characteristics cannot rationalize all choice data. Let the utility associated with choice j for individual i be $U_{ij} = g(X_j, Z_i)$, without functional form assumptions. Consider the subpopulation with characteristics $Z_i = z$. Within this subpopulation all individuals face the same decision problem,

$$\max_{j \in \{1,\dots,J\}} g(X_j, z).$$

Since we have no randomness in this simplified model, the market shares $s_j(z)$ implied by this model are degenerate: If individual i with characteristics $Z_i = z$ prefers product j, then $g(X_j, z) > g(X_k, z)$ for all $k \neq j$, so that any other individual i' with $Z_{i'} = z$ would make the same choice. Hence, under this model we would expect to see a degenerate distribution of choices conditional on the individual characteristics. Specifically, all individuals would choose j, where $j = \arg\max_{j'=1,\dots,J} g(X_{j'}, z)$, so that for this j we have $s_j(z) = 1$, and for all other choices $k \neq j$ we would see $s_k(z) = 0$. Hence, as soon as we see two individuals with the same observed individual characteristics making different chocies, we can reject such a model with certainty.

Next, consider a slightly more general model, where in addition to the observed choice and individual characteristics there is an additive idiosyncratic error term ϵ_{ij}, independent across choices and individuals. We argue that this model has *no* testable restrictions, so long as there is a finite number of choices. The utility associated with individual i and choice j is then $g(X_j, Z_i) + \epsilon_{ij}$. In that case we would see a distribution of choices even within a subpopulation homogenous in terms of the observed individual characteristics, and we would see $s_j(z) > 0$ for all $j = 1, \dots, J$ given large enough support for ϵ_{ij}.

For purposes of exposition, suppose that the ϵ_{ij} have an extreme value distribution (although for computational reasons we will consider normally distributed ϵ_{ij} when implementing the model from Section 5.1). Then the probabilities $s_j(z)$ have a logit form:

$$s_j(z) = \frac{\exp(g(x_j, z))}{\sum_{k=1}^{J} \exp(g(x_k, z))}.$$

This in turn implies that the log of the ratio of the probability of choice j versus choice k has the form

$$\ln\left(\frac{s_j(z)}{s_k(z)}\right) = g(X_j, z) - g(X_k, z).$$

We can normalize the functions $g(x, z)$ by setting $g(X_1, z) = 0$. For a finite number of choices, all with unique characteristics, we can always find a continuous function $g(x, z)$ that satisfies this restriction for all pairs (j, k) and all z. Hence in this setting we cannot reject the semiparametric version of the conditional logit model, nor its implication of independence of irrelevant alternatives.

One reason we cannot reject this simple model is that we never see individuals choosing among products that appear similar. In other words, there need not be choices with similar observable characteristics. We now turn to consider a setting with a large number of choices, so that some choices are similar in observable characteristics. We show that in this setting, the simple model does have testable restrictions.

Following Berry et al. (2004), consider a model where for all choices j and for all individual characteristics z the choice probabilities, normalized by the number of choices J, are bounded away from zero and one, so that $0 < \underline{c} \leq J \cdot s_j(z) \leq \bar{c} < 1$.

Suppose that we observe $J \cdot s_j(z)$ for a large number of choices and all $z \in \mathbb{Z}$. With the choice characteristics in a compact subset of $\mathbb{R}^K$, it follows that eventually we will see choices with very similar observed characteristics. Now suppose we have two choices j and k with X_j equal to X_k. In that case, we should see identical choice probabilities within a given subpopulation, or $s_j(z) = s_k(z)$. Thus, the model will be rejected if in fact we find that the choice probabilities differ.

One possible source of misspecification is an unobserved choice characteristic. Note that the finding $s_j(z) \neq s_k(z)$ can *not* be explained by (unobserved) heterogeneity in individual preferences: If the two products are identical in all characteristics, their market shares within the same market should be identical (given that the idiosyncratic error ϵ_{ij} is independent across products).

Now let us consider whether, and under what conditions, it is sufficient to have a single unobserved product characteristic. Much of the existing literature (e.g., BLP) assumes that the utility function is strictly monotone in the unobserved choice characteristics for each individual and that there is a single unobserved product characteristic. We now argue that this combination of assumptions can be rejected by the data. Without loss of generality assume that $g(x, z, \xi)$ is nondecreasing in the scalar unobserved component ξ. Consider two choices j and k with the same values for the observed choice characteristics, $X_j = X_k$. Suppose that for a given subpopulation with observed characteristics $Z_i = z$ we find that $s_j(z) > s_k(z)$. We can infer that the unobserved choice characteristic for product j is larger than that for product k: $\xi_j > \xi_k$. Now suppose we have a second subpopulation with different individual characteristics $Z_i = z'$. The assumption of monotonicity of the utility function in ξ implies that the same ordering of the choice probabilities must hold for this second subpopulation: $s_j(z') > s_k(z')$. If we find that $s_j(z') < s_k(z')$, we can reject the original model with a single unobserved choice characteristic.

A natural source of misspecification is that the model ruled out multiple unobserved choice characteristics. If we relax the model to allow for two unobserved choice characteristics ξ_{j1} and ξ_{j2}, it could be that individuals with $Z_i = z$ put more weight in the utility function on the first characteristic $\xi_{.1}$, and as a result prefer product j to product k because $\xi_{j1} > \xi_{k1}$, although individuals with $Z_i = z'$ put more weight on the second characteristic $\xi_{.2}$ and prefer product k to j because $\xi_{j2} < \xi_{k2}$. This argument shows that in settings with a single market and no variation in product characteristics, the presence of multiple choices with similar observed choice characteristics can imply the presence of at least two choice characteristics, under monotonicity of the utility function in the unobserved choice characteristic. Again, the presence of unobserved individual heterogeneity cannot explain the pattern of the probabilities described above.

An alternative way to generalize the model has been considered in an interesting study of the demand for television shows by Goettler and Shachar (2001). They allow for the presence of multiple unobserved characteristics that enter the utility function in a nonmonotone manner (in their application consumers have a bliss point in each unobserved choice characteristics, and utility is quadratic; each consumer's bliss point is unrestricted). Models with multiple unobserved product characteristics have been considered in an interesting series of papers by Keane and coauthors (Elrod and Keane, 1995; Harris and Keane, 1997; Keane, 1997, 2004) and in work by Poole and Rosenthal (1985).

Here, we argue that with a flexible specification of utility and a countable number of products, a single dimension of unobserved product characteristics can rationalize the data. However, it is necessary that utility be nonmonotone in this unobservable characteristic. With a restriction to utility that is monotone in the unobservable, it is not sufficient to have a single unobserved product characteristic. However, one can say more. In the example it was possible to rationalize the data with two unobserved choice characteristics that enter the utility function monotonically. We show that this is true in general, as formalized in the following theorem.

The setting is one with a countable number of products with identical observed product characteristics, and a compact set of observed individual characteristics. There are many individuals, so the market shares $s_j(z)$ are known for all $z \in \mathbb{Z}$ and for all $j = 1, \ldots, J$. We show that irrespective of the number of products J we can rationalize the pattern of market shares with a utility function that is increasing in two unobserved product characteristics.

THEOREM 1. *Suppose that for each subpopulation indexed by characteristics $z \in \mathbb{Z}$, and for all $J = 1, \ldots, \infty$, there exist J products with identical observed characteristics and an observable vector of market shares $s_{jJ}(z)$, $j = 1, \ldots, J$, such that $\sum_{j=0}^{J} s_{jJ}(z) = 1$. Then we can rationalize these market shares with a utility function*

$$U_{ij} = g(Z_i, \xi_j) + \epsilon_{ij},$$

where ξ_j is a scalar, ϵ_{ij} has an extreme value distribution and is independent of ξ_j, and where $g(z, \xi)$ is continuous in ξ. Moreover we can also rationalize these market shares with a utility function

$$U_{ij} = h(Z_i, \xi_{1j}, \xi_{2j}) + \epsilon_{ij},$$

where ξ_{1j}, ξ_{2j} are scalars, ϵ_{ij} has an extreme value distribution and is independent of ξ_{1j}, ξ_{2j}, and where $h(z, \xi_1, \xi_2)$ is continuous and monotone in ξ_1 and ξ_2.

PROOF. The proof is constructive. Under the assumptions in the theorem we can infer the market shares $s_j(z)$ for all choices and all values of z. The form of the utility function implies that the market shares have the form

$$s_j(z) = \frac{\exp(g(z, \xi_j))}{\sum_{k=1}^{J} \exp(g(z, \xi_k))}.$$

Define $r_j(z) = \ln(s_j(z)/s_1(z))$ (so that $r_1(z) = 0$). The proof of the first part of the theorem amounts to constructing a function $g(z, \xi)$ and a sequence $\xi_1, \ldots, \xi_J$ such that $r_j(z) = g(z, \xi_j)$ for all z and j. First, let

(4) $$\xi_j = 1 - 2^{-j}, \text{ for } j = 1, \ldots, J.$$

Next, for $\xi \in [0, 1]$

(5) $g(z, \xi) = \begin{cases} r_j(z) & \text{if } \xi = 1 - 2^{-j}, j = 1, \ldots, J \\ 0 & \text{if } 0 \le \xi < 2^{-1} \\ r_j(z) + \frac{\xi - (1 - 2^{-j})}{2^{-j} - 2^{-(j+1)}} \cdot (r_{j+1}(z) - r_j(z)) & \text{if } 1 - 2^{-j} < \xi < 1 - 2^{-(j+1)} \\ r_J(z) & \text{if } 1 - 2^{-J} < \xi \le 1. \end{cases}$

This function $g(z, \xi)$ is continuous in ξ on $[0, 1]$ for all z, and piece-wise linear with knots at $1 - 2^{-j}$. Thus, the function is of bounded variation.

To construct the function $h(z, \xi_1, \xi_2)$ we use the fact that a continuous function $k(\xi)$ of bounded variation on a compact set can be written as the sum of a nondecreasing continuous function $k_1(\xi)$ and a nonincreasing function $k_2(\xi)$. We apply this to the function $g(z, \xi)$ in (5) for each value of z so that $g(z, \xi) = h_1(z, \xi) + h_2(z, \xi)$ with $h_1(z, \xi)$ nondecreasing and $h_2(z, \xi)$ nonincreasing, and both continuous. Then define

(6) $$h(z, \xi_1, \xi_2) = h_1(z, \xi_1) + h_2(z, 1 - \xi_2),$$

which is by construction nondecreasing and continuous in both ξ_1 and ξ_2. Then choose $\xi_{1j} = \xi_j$ and $\xi_{2j} = 1 - \xi_j$, where ξ_j is as defined in equation (4), and the function satisfies

(7) $\quad h(z, \xi_{1j}, \xi_{2j}) = h(z, \xi_j, 1 - \xi_j) = h_1(z, \xi_j) + h_2(z, \xi_j) = g(z, \xi_j) = r_j(z).$

∎

In both cases, utility will potentially be highly nonlinear in the unobservable, and so with a restriction to linear and monotone effects of the unobservables, a particular functional form might fit better with multiple dimensions of unobservables, to capture nonlinearities in the true model. However, to conclude that the true model has multiple dimensions of unobserved characteristics, one must rely crucially on the functional form assumption. Thus, the researcher should emphasize that a finding that a model with a particular number of unobserved characteristics fits the data well can be meaningfully interpreted only relative to the given functional form.

The restriction in the theorem that all products have the same observed characteristics is imposed only to simplify the notation. We can allow for a finite set of different values for the observed product characteristics. More generally, we interpet this theorem as demonstrating that unless one allows for utility functions that are highly nonlinear, with derivatives large in absolute value, one may need two unobserved product characteristics (or one if one allows for nonmonotonicity in this unobserved product characteristic), in order to rationalize arbitrary patterns of market shares.

The construction in the theorem implies that neither of the two models considered there (the model with one unobservable and the model with two unobservables and monotonicity restrictions) are uniquely identified, even after making location and scale normalizations. By reordering the products in the construction of g, one obtains a function with a different shape. This is a substantive problem because there will typically be no "natural" ordering of the products, and even the ranking of the magnitudes of market shares will typically vary with z. Thus, establishing what additional assumptions and normalizations are required for identification, particularly for models that also include unobserved individual heterogeneity, remains an open problem.

3.2. *Rationalizability in Multiple Markets.* In this subsection, we consider the evidence for the presence of unobserved heterogeneity at the individual level. We show that when there is a large number of markets and sufficient variation in observable choice characteristics across markets, a model without unobserved individual heterogeneity can be rejected.

To some extent allowing for unobserved individual heterogeneity substitutes for heterogeneity in unobserved choice characteristics. It was argued before that in the case with no unobserved choice or individual characteristics one would expect to see the choice probabilities be equal to zero or one. Introducing unobserved individual characteristics will generate a distribution of choices in that case. More importantly, however, unobserved individual characteristics generate substitution patterns that are more realistic. Consider again a situation with a large number of individuals and a finite number of choices J. We have already argued that such a model fits the data arbitrary well. However, suppose that we have data from multiple markets. Markets may be distinguished by geography or time. These markets have different populations, and thus potentially different distributions of individual characteristics. We assume that the choice set is the same in all markets, but the observed choice characteristics of the products may differ between markets. Key examples of such choice characteristics that vary by market include prices and marketing variables.

In order to discuss this setting we need to return to the general notation of Section 2. Let $m = 1, \ldots, M$ index the markets. In market m there are N_m individuals. They choose between J products, where product j has observed characteristics X_{jm} and unobserved characteristics ξ_j. The general form for the utility for individual i in market m associated with product j is

$$U_{ijm} = g(X_{jm}, \xi_j, Z_i, v_i) + \epsilon_{ijm},$$

for $i = 1, \ldots, N_m$, $j = 1, \ldots, J$, and $m = 1, \ldots, M$. The idiosyncratic error ϵ_{ijm} is independent of $\epsilon_{i'j'm'}$ unless $(i, j, m) = (i', j', m')$, and has an extreme value distribution.

First consider a model with no unobserved individual characteristics, so that

$$U_{ijm} = g(X_{jm}, \xi_j, Z_i) + \epsilon_{ijm}.$$

Recall that the unobserved choice characteristics do not vary by market. Consider a subpopulation of individuals with observed characteristics $Z_i = z$. Consider two markets m and m', and three choices, j, k, and l, where for two of the choices, j and

k, the characteristics do not differ between markets, and for the third choice, l, the observed characteristics do differ between markets, so that $X_{jm} = X_{jm'}$, $X_{km} = X_{km'}$, and $X_{lm} \neq X_{lm'}$. In this case the market share of choice j in markets m and m' is

$$s_{jm}(z) = \frac{\exp(g(X_{jm}, \xi_j, z))}{\exp(g(X_{jm}, \xi_j, z)) + \exp(g(X_{km}, \xi_k, z)) + \exp(g(X_{lm}, \xi_l, z))}$$

and

$$s_{jm'}(z) = \frac{\exp(g(X_{jm'}, \xi_j, z))}{\exp(g(X_{jm'}, \xi_j, z)) + \exp(g(X_{km'}, \xi_k, z)) + \exp(g(X_{lm'}, \xi_l, z))}.$$

The ratio of the market shares for choices j and k in the two markets are

$$\frac{s_{jm}(z)}{s_{km}(z)} = \frac{\exp(g(X_{jm}, \xi_j, z))}{\exp(g(X_{km}, \xi_k, z))} \quad \text{and} \quad \frac{s_{jm'}(z)}{s_{km'}(z)} = \frac{\exp(g(X_{jm'}, \xi_j, z))}{\exp(g(X_{km'}, \xi_k, z))}.$$

These relative market shares are identical in both markets because $X_{jm} = X_{jm'}$ and $X_{km} = X_{km'}$, and by assumption the unobserved choice characteristics do not vary by market. Thus the IIA property of the conditional logit model implies in this case that the ratio of market shares for choices k and j should be the same in the two markets.[7] If the two ratios differ, obviously one possibility is that the unobserved choice characteristics for these choices differ between markets. (Note that a market-invariant choice-specific component would not be able to explain this pattern of choices.) Ruling out changes in unobserved choice characteristics across markets by assumption, another possibility is that there are unobserved individual characteristics that imply that individuals who are homogenous in terms of observed characteristics do in fact have differential preferences for these choices.

Let us assess how unobserved individual heterogeneity can explain differences in market share ratios in such settings. The unobserved individual components are interpreted here as individual preferences for product characteristics, such as a taste for quality. As before, let us denote such components by v_i. We assume the distribution of individual unobserved characteristics is constant across markets. The utility becomes

$$U_{ijm} = U(X_{jm}, Z_i, v_i) + \epsilon_{ijm},$$

still with the ϵ_{ijm} independent across all dimensions. Given the observed and unobserved individual characteristics the market share for product j in market m, given $Z_i = z$ and $v_i = v$, is

---

[7] Although other functional forms for the distribution of ϵ_{ij} do not impose the independence of irrelevant alternatives property, as long as independence of ϵ_{ij} is maintained, other functional forms also impose testable restrictions on how market shares vary when product characteristics change.

$$s_{jm}(z, v) = \frac{\exp(g(X_{jm}, \xi_j, z, v))}{\exp(g(X_{jm}, \xi_j, z, v)) + \exp(g(X_{km}, \xi_k, z, v)) + \exp(g(X_{lm}, \xi_l, z, v))}.$$

Integrating over v the marginal market share becomes

$$s_{jm}(z) =$$

$$\int_v \frac{\exp(g(X_{jm}, \xi_j, z, v))}{\exp(g(X_{jm}, \xi_j, z, v)) + \exp(g(X_{km}, \xi_k, z, v)) + \exp(g(X_{lm}, \xi_l, z, v))} f_v(v)\, dv.$$

If the characteristics of product l varies across markets, the ratio of markets shares for choices j and k are no longer restricted to be identical in two markets even if their observed characteristics are the same in both markets. Thus the IIA property no longer holds in the presence of unobserved individual heterogeneity in tastes. This model still requires that two markets with exactly the same set of products have the same market shares for all products. More generally, the question of whether and under what conditions this model has additional testable restrictions remains open.[8]

So far we have considered a fixed distribution over individual characteristics. If we relax this assumption, it is straightforward to see that a model with unobserved individual heterogeneity can always rationalize observed market shares. To see why, note that in each market, market shares can be rationalized without individual heterogeneity using the analysis of Theorem 1. Let $g^m(X_{jm}, \xi_j, z)$ be the function that rationalizes the data in market m constructed in the proof of Theorem 1. Then given any order over markets, we can let $g(X_{jm}, \xi_j, z, v) = g^m(X_{jm}, \xi_j, z)$ for v in a neighborhood of m, and we can let $f_v(v)$ put all the weight on that neighborhood in market m.

4. PREDICTING THE MARKET SHARE OF NEW PRODUCTS

Suppose we wish to predict the market share of a new product, call it choice 0. In order to make such a prediction, the analyst must provide some information about the product's observed and unobserved characteristics. One possibility is to consider products that lie in some specified quantile of the distribution of characteristics in the population. For example, one could consider a product with the median values of observed and unobserved characteristics. However, that may or may not be an interesting hypothetical product to consider, since products in the population may tend to be outliers in some dimensions and not others.

A second alternative approach might be to make some assumptions about the costs of entry and production at various points in the product space, and to calculate the optimal position for a new product. Although an assumption of

---

[8] In a simple example with two markets and four products, where each market has a different subset of three products, it is straightforward to verify that a model with just two distinct types of individuals with the same distribution in both markets can rationalize any market share patterns. To address the problem more generally, one must specify how the number of products changes with the number of markets.

equilibrium pricing on the part of firms might enable inferences about marginal costs of production for different products, additional assumptions would be required to estimate entry costs at different points.

If there are many products, a third approach would be to model the joint distribution of observed and unobserved product characteristics in the population, and take draws from that joint distribution, thus generating a distribution of predicted market shares. Our estimation routine generates different conditional distributions of unobserved characteristics for each product, and to construct this joint distribution, it would be necessary to combine these estimates with an estimate of the marginal distribution of observed characteristics. Some extrapolation would be required to infer this distribution at values of observed characteristics that are not observed in the population.

Finally, as a fourth approach, in some cases it might be interesting to consider entry of a product with prespecified observed characteristics but unknown unobserved characteristics. For example, a foreign entrant might be planning to introduce an existing product with observable attributes into the markets under study. In that case, the analyst must make some decisions about how to model the unobserved characteristics for this product. One possibility is to use the marginal distribution of unobserved product characteristics in the population. This is the method we use in our empirical application. However, this approach has some important limitations. Most importantly, it does not account for the fact that unobserved characteristics may vary systematically with observed characteristics: For example, prices may vary with unobserved quality. As described in the third approach, it is possible to generate an estimate of the distribution of unobserved characteristics conditional on a particular set of observables, but it requires some extrapolation; since our application has only eight brands, we do not pursue it here.

Following the third or fourth approaches, one immediate implication of the presence of unobserved choice characteristics is that we are unable to predict the market share exactly even in settings with an infinite number of individuals. Instead, a given set of observable characteristics of a new product would be consistent with a range of market shares. We view this as a realistic feature of the model. Of course, the analyst is free to put more structure on the prediction of the unobservable characteristics, along the lines suggested in the second approach.

5.   A BAYESIAN APPROACH TO ESTIMATION

This section presents a proposed approach for estimating a model with multiple unobserved choice characteristics. Although our rationalizability discussion was largely nonparametric, we focus on estimation of parametric models. Our view is that these can be viewed as approximations to the nonparametric models studied in the previous sections, with our results showing that the evidence for, for example, multiple unobserved product characteristics, is not coming solely from the functional form restrictions. We begin by returning to the parametric model introduced in Section 2, after which we describe a Bayesian approach to estimation. A Bayesian approach is in this case attractive from a computational perspective.

5.1. *The Parameterized Model.* Recall the general model for U_{ijm}:

$$U_{ijm} = g(X_{jm}, \xi_j, Z_i, \nu_i) + \epsilon_{ijm},$$

where the additional component ϵ_{ijm} is assumed to be independent of ($X_{jm}, \xi_j, Z_i,$ ν_i). Rather than assume that each ϵ_{ijm} has an extreme value distribution, as we did in some of the discussion above, for the purposes of estimation we assume that it has a standard (mean zero, unit variance) normal distribution, independent of ($X_{jm}, \xi_j, Z_i, \nu_i$), as well as independent across choices, markets, and individuals. We parametrize the systematic part of the utility associated with choice j as

$$g(X_{jm}, \xi_j, Z_i, \nu_i) = X'_{jm}\beta_i + \xi'_j\gamma_i = \begin{pmatrix} X_{jm} \\ \xi_j \end{pmatrix}' \begin{pmatrix} \beta_i \\ \gamma_i \end{pmatrix},$$

where the individual specific coefficients θ_i satisfy

$$\begin{pmatrix} \beta_i \\ \gamma_i \end{pmatrix} = \begin{pmatrix} \Delta_o \\ \Delta_u \end{pmatrix} Z_i + \begin{pmatrix} \nu_{oi} \\ \nu_{ui} \end{pmatrix} = \Delta Z_i + \nu_i.$$

In this representation β_i is a K-dimensional column vector, γ_i is an P-dimensional column vector, Δ is a $(K + P) \times L$-dimensional matrix, and ν_i is a $(K + P)$-dimensional column vector. The unobserved components of the individual characteristics are assumed to have a normal distribution:

$$\nu_i \mid \mathbf{X}_m, Z_i \sim \mathcal{N}(0, \Omega),$$

where $\mathbf{X}_m$ is the $J \times K$ matrix with jth row equal to X'_{jm}, and Ω is a $(K + P) \times (K + P)$-dimensional matrix.

Now we can write U_{ijm} as

$$U_{ijm} = \begin{pmatrix} X_{jm} \\ \xi_j \end{pmatrix}' (\Delta Z_i + \nu_i) + \epsilon_{ijm}$$

$$= X'_{jm}\Delta_o Z_i + \xi'_j\Delta_u Z_i + X'_{jm}\nu_{oi} + \xi'_j\nu_{ui} + \epsilon_{ijm}.$$

Let us consider the vector of latent utilities for all J choices for individual i in market m:

$$(8) \qquad U_{i \cdot m} = \begin{pmatrix} U_{i1m} \\ U_{i2m} \\ \vdots \\ U_{iJm} \end{pmatrix} = (\mathbf{X}_m \xi)\Delta Z_i + (\mathbf{X}_m \xi)\nu_i + \epsilon_{i \cdot m},$$

where ξ is the $J \times P$ matrix with jth row equal to ξ'_j. Conditional on $\mathbf{X}_m$, Z_i, and ξ the joint distribution of the J-vector $U_{i \cdot m}$ is

$$U_{i \cdot m} \mid \mathbf{X}_m, Z_i, \xi \sim \mathcal{N}((\mathbf{X}_m \xi) \Delta Z_i, (\mathbf{X}_m \xi) \Omega (\mathbf{X}_m \xi)' + I_J).$$

This model imposes considerable structure on the correlation between the latent utilities, with the covariance matrix and the mean parameters intricately linked, but at the same time does allow for complex patterns in this correlation structure.

5.2. *Posterior Calculations.* In order to estimate the parameters of interest and carry out inference we use a Bayesian approach. We specify prior distributions for the parameters Δ, Ω, and ξ and use MCMC methods for obtaining draws from the posterior distribution of these parameters and functions thereof. The structure of the model is particularly well suited to such an approach. There are large numbers of parameters that can be treated as unobserved random variables and imputed in the MCMC algorithm. In addition, the likelihood function is likely to have multiple modes, implying that quadratic approximations to its shape are likely to be poor, resulting in poor properties of large sample confidence intervals for the underlying parameters. It should be noted though that these multiple modes need not make the normal approximation to the posterior distribution of the effects of policies of interest (e.g., price changes or the market share of a new product) inaccurate. For example, one problem with frequentist inference in the current setting with at least two unobserved product characteristics is that these are never separately identified. This does not matter for most purposes because many estimands of interest would be invariant to the relabeling of the unobserved product characteristics. However, if an asymptotic approximation is based on a quadratic approximation to the likelihood function in all its arguments, followed by the delta method, the results could be sensitive to such multiple modes. More generally, the numerical problems in locating the maximum or maxima of the likelihood function can be severe.

The implementation of the MCMC algorithm borrows heavily from RMA as well as more indirectly from work by Chib and Greenberg (1998) on Gibbs sampling in latent index models. For a general discussion of MCMC methods see Tanner (1993), Gelman et al. (2004), and Geweke (1997). Here we briefly discuss the general approach we take in this article. The Appendix contains more details on the specific implementation.

The specific model we estimate is given in (8). Let Y_{it} denote the choice, $Y_{it} \in \{1, \ldots, J\}$. We observe T_i choices for individual i, each in a different market. For each of these choices we observe the product chosen, the product characteristics of the all the products in that market, X_{jm}, and the individual characteristics Z_{it}. We assume that conditional on ν_i, ξ_j, Z_{it}, and X_{jm} the idiosyncratic error term ϵ_{ijt} is normally distributed with mean zero and unit variance. Conditional on ξ_j, Z_{it}, and X_{jm} the unobserved individual component ν_i is normally distributed with mean zero and covariance matrix Ω.

In order to calculate the posterior distribution we need to specify prior distributions for common parameters Ω, Δ, and for the unobserved choice characteristics ξ_j. We use proper prior distributions for each parameter. The prior distribution on each element of Δ is normal with mean zero and variance 1/4. The elements of Δ are assumed to be independent a priori. The prior variance of the elemets of

TABLE 1
SUMMARY STATISTICS: INDIVIDUAL CHARACTERISTICS

Characteristic	Mean	SD	Minimum	Maximum
Number of purchases	16.21	24.04	1.00	285.00
Household income	34.47	22.98	2.50	125.00

NOTES: The first row gives summary statistics for the number of purchases for the 1038 households. The second row gives summary statistics for income per household, weighted by the number of purchases per household. Total number of purchases is 16,824.

Δ is chosen so that the prior variance of the effect of an increase of one standard deviation in observed choice and individual characteristics (e.g., $\Delta_{kl} \cdot \text{std}(X_k) \cdot \text{std}(Z_l)$) is of the same magnitude as the variance of the idiosyncratic error term, to ensure that the prior distribution does not impose that one of these two components dominates the other. The prior distribution on Ω is Wishart with parameters 100 and 0.01 times the $K + P$ dimensional identity matrix. This allows for the possibility that the variance of the individual heterogeneity is small. The prior distribution on ξ_j is normal with mean zero and unit variance, allowing the unobserved choice characteristics to have an effect comparable in magnitude to that of the idiosyncratic error term.

6. APPLICATION

6.1. *Data.* To illustrate the methods developed in this article we analyze the demand for yogurt using scanner data from a market research firm (A.C. Nielsen) collected from 1985 through 1988. See Ackerberg (2001, 2003) for more information regarding these data. We focus on data from a single city, Springfield, Illinois. We restrict attention to purchases of a single-serving size. We excluded purchases where more than a single unit of yogurt was purchased.[9] Eight brands of yogurt appear in the remaining data set. We have a total of 16,824 purchases by 1038 households. These are divided over 21 stores during a period of 138 weeks. For each household we use a single observed household characteristic, household income. This is measured in 14 categories, ranging from 0–5000 to more than 100,000. For each category we impute the midpoint of the category as the actual household income, with 125,000 for the highest (over 100,000) income category. Table 1 presents some summary statistics for this variable and for the number of purchases per household. We average the income over the 1038 households, weighted by the number of purchases per household.

---

[9] We lose about one third of the observations due to this restriction. This is clearly a crude approach to dealing with the issues that arise in modeling multiple purchases, which may include multiple purchases of a single brand as well as purchases of more than one brand on a single trip. However, it simplifies the analysis and exposition of the application of the methods.

For each yogurt brand we use two observed characteristics, price measured in cents[10] and a binary indicator for whether the product was featured in advertising that week. In our empirical model, we treat price as exogenous; substantively, this assumption holds if the consumer population that purchases yogurt is stable in terms of its unobservables and unrelated to price variation.[11] For each purchase we directly observe these variables for the brand that was actually purchased. For our analysis we also need to know the values of these variables for the seven brands that were not purchased in that transaction for that particular market. We take the market to be a store in a particular week. We impute the price for the other seven brands by taking the average price for all purchases of each of these seven brands over all transactions for that brand in the same week and in the same store. We impute the feature variable as one if for any purchase of that brand in the same store in the same week the product was featured. Typically there was no recorded purchase for at least some of the eight brands during that week in that store. In that case we remove the brands for which there were no purchases from the choice set of the individual for that purchase. As a result the choice set varies in size across observations. On average there are 2.36 brands in a consumer's choice set on a trip in which the consumer purchased yogurt.

Table 2 reports summary statistics for the eight brands. We report averages over all purchases where the brand was included in the choice set, as well as over purchases of each brand. For example, the second row of Table 2 presents the information for the biggest brand, Dannon. Its market share is 49%. Its average price (averaged over all purchases where Dannon was in the choice set) was 60.13 cents, ranging from 20 to 73 cents. It was featured in the store during 9% of the purchases. It was in 88% of the choice sets. Averaged over all purchases of Dannon its price was 58.36 cents, slightly lower than the average over all purchases. It was more likely to be featured when it was purchased. On average there were 2.25 products in the choice set when Dannon was purchased.

6.2. *Posterior Distribution of Parameters and Elasticities.*   We estimate four versions of the model. These versions are nested, so that it is straightforward to see the biases generated by placing unwarranted restrictions on the model. First we estimate the model with no unobserved product characteristics ($P = 0$), and with no unobserved individual characteristics ($\Omega = 0$). The second model allows for individual unobserved heterogeneity by freeing up Ω. The third model incorporates a single unobserved choice characteristic ($P = 1$). The fourth model allows for two unobserved product characteristics ($P = 2$).

---

[10] We ignore the presence of coupons. Coupons are notoriously difficult to deal with because whether or not a consumer has access to a coupon is unobservable. It is possible to impute whether a coupon was in principle available in a market by checking whether any consumer used one for a particular product in a particular week, but not all consumers are aware of available coupons. Ackerberg (2001) ignores manufacturer coupons within a city, and treats store coupons as a control variable. Our sample from Springfield, Illinois, has negligible use of store coupons. See Osborne (2005) for an innovative way of estimating the propensity to use coupons.

[11] For yogurt, seasonal and holiday effects, which might shift both price and the distribution of consumer tastes for products, are less important than for some other consumer products. Ackerberg (2001) also makes this assumption.

TABLE 2

SUMMARY STATISTICS: CHOICE CHARACTERISTICS

Brand	Market Share		Averaged over All Transactions					Brand Purchases		
		Ave	Price SD	Min	Max	Feature Ave	Incl in Choice Set	Price Ave	Feature Ave	Ave Size Choice Set
Wght Wtch	0.09	62.74	6.79	25.00	73.00	0.04	0.41	61.33	0.09	2.73
Dannon	0.49	60.13	9.84	20.00	73.00	0.09	0.88	58.36	0.13	2.25
Elmgrove	0.04	30.94	3.56	22.00	33.00	0.15	0.11	29.84	0.25	2.77
YAMI	0.04	32.06	9.54	20.00	59.00	0.21	0.11	29.18	0.36	2.56
HWT MDY	0.06	30.72	3.54	25.00	33.00	0.13	0.15	29.33	0.22	2.16
HILAND	0.10	37.20	9.62	20.00	55.00	0.16	0.24	35.49	0.21	2.47
NTRL LE	0.02	32.40	10.39	20.00	55.00	0.11	0.11	32.81	0.09	3.10
CTL BR	0.17	35.65	5.79	20.00	45.00	0.20	0.36	34.47	0.23	2.30

NOTES: Column 2 reports the market share of the brand in this data set. Columns 3–6 report the average price over all store/weeks in which this brand was in the choice set, as well as the standard deviation, minimum, and maximum. Column 7 reports the fraction of the times the brand was featured. Column 8 reports the fraction of the store/week combinations that the brand was in the choice set (had at least one purchase in that market). Columns 7 and 8 report averages for price and feature variable over the all purchases of the brand. Column 9 gives the average size of the choice set during the purchases of that brand.

In Table 3, we report the posterior distribution for selected parameters. First, we report the posterior mean and standard deviation for the average of the price coefficient β_{price}. We also report measures of the variation in this coefficient. We decompose this variation into the part due to variation in the observed individual coefficients and due to variation in the unobserved individual characteristics. We report the standard deviation of both components. We also report the summary statistics for the average and the two standard deviations of the feature coefficient $\beta_{feature}$. Finally, we report summary statistics of the posterior distribution of the effect of income on the price coefficient, $\Delta_{price,income}$, and the effect of income on the feature coefficient, $\Delta_{feature,income}$.

For the model with two unobserved product characteristics we see that on average, a higher price lowers utility (the posterior mean of the average over all individuals of β_{price} is negative), but that there is considerable variation in the price coefficient between individuals. This variation is partly due to variation in the observed individual characteristics (a standard deviation of 0.233) and partly due to variation in the unobserved individual characteristics (a standard deviation of 0.463). On average being featured increases demand for a product. Invididuals with higher income are found to be less price sensitive (the posterior mean of $\Delta_{price,income}$ is positive). With income measured in 10,000s of dollars, the point estimates suggest that individuals with a household income of $60,000 have a price coefficient of approximately zero ($-4.09 + 60 \times 0.069 \approx 0$). (Recall from Table 1 that average household income in this data set is $35,000.) Income does not appear to have much of an effect on the relation between feature and demand.

It is interesting to note that with no unobserved choice characteristics the model estimates a much larger role for the feature variable. This would be consistent with

TABLE 3

SUMMARY STATISTICS POSTERIOR DISTRIBUTION FOR SELECTED PARAMETERS

Parameter	$P = 0, \Omega = 0$		$P = 0$		$P = 1$		$P = 2$	
	Mean	SD	Mean	SD	Mean	SD	Mean	SD
Mean(β_{price})	−0.012	0.004	−0.007	0.007	−0.302	0.020	−0.409	0.020
SD($\Delta_{price,income} \cdot Z_{income}$)	0.253	0.005	0.289	0.041	0.230	0.039	0.233	0.039
$\sqrt{\Omega_{price,price}}$	0	0	0.586	0.022	0.541	0.021	0.463	0.027
Mean($\beta_{feature}$)	0.663	0.026	0.743	0.041	0.449	0.051	0.379	0.047
SD($\Delta_{feature,income} \cdot Z_{income}$)	0.111	0.008	0.379	0.100	0.070	0.034	0.067	0.037
$\sqrt{\Omega_{feature,feature}}$	0	0	0.983	0.070	0.133	0.017	0.153	0.026
$\Delta_{price,income}$	0.048	0.003	0.060	0.010	0.053	0.011	0.069	0.010
$\Delta_{feature,income}$	−0.007	0.013	−0.025	0.032	−0.028	0.017	−0.011	0.024

NOTES: Columns 2–3 report the mean and standard deviation for various parameters for the model with no unobserved choice characteristics ($P = 0$) and no unobserved individual heterogeneity ($\Omega = 0$). Columns 4–5 report the mean and standard deviation for the same parameters for the model with no unobserved choice characteristics ($P = 0$) allowing for unobserved individual heterogeneity ($\Omega \neq 0$). Columns 6–7 report the mean and standard deviation for the same parameters for the model with a single unobserved choice characteristics ($P = 1$) allowing for unobserved individual hetero-geneity ($\Omega \neq 0$). Columns 8–9 report the mean and standard deviation for the same parameters for the model with two unobserved choice characteristics ($P = 2$) allowing for unobserved individual het-erogeneity. The parameters reported on include the average effect of price on the utility, the standard deviation of the component of that effect corresponding to the observed individual characteristics, and the standard deviation of the component of that effect corresponding to the unobserved individual characteristics, the same three parameters for the feature variable, and the effect of the interactions of income and price and income and feature on utility. The price is measured in dollars.

the feature variable being a noisy measure for the unobserved product character-istics that actually matter for utility.

A potentially important difference between the estimates from the model with two unobserved choice characteristics and the model with only one is that the estimated standard deviation of the price coefficient is larger in the model with one unobserved choice characteristic (.541 versus .463, with the standard deviations of these parameters equal to 0.021 and 0.027, respectively). This suggests that using a model that is too restrictive in terms of unobservable product characteristics can force estimates that imply too much heterogeneity in price sensitivity. For some counterfactuals, these differences might lead to inaccurate predictions. For example, using a model with only one unobserved product characteristic, the entry of a low-price, low-quality brand or a high-price, high-quality brand might lead to predictions of market shares for the new product that are too large.

Next we report own- and cross-price elasticities for the eight brands. To estimate the elasticities, we first estimate them for each individual conditional on the choice sets and the unobserved individual and choice characteristics. Then we average over all individuals. The results for the four models are in Tables 4–7. For the first two models we see large positive own-price elasticies, as well as numerous (large) negative cross-price elasticities. For the model with one unobserved characteristic the elasticities have a few entries with unexpected signs and magnitudes. For

TABLE 4

ELASTICITIES FOR MODEL WITH NO UNOBSERVED PRODUCT CHARACTERISTICS AND NO UNOBSERVED
INDIVIDUAL HETEROGENEITY $(P = 0, \Omega = 0)$

With Respect to →	Wght W	Dannon	Elmgr	YAMI	HWT	HILA	NTRL	CTL
Wght Wtch	4.94	−5.99	0.93	−0.16	1.18	0.18	−0.04	0.36
Dannon	−5.74	1.22	0.84	0.50	0.73	−0.06	−0.03	0.30
Elmgrove	1.10	1.45	−1.83	0.00	2.67	2.65	2.10	2.10
YAMI	−0.23	0.91	0.00	−1.19	1.86	−0.29	−0.65	1.13
HWT MDY	1.31	1.29	2.69	2.91	−1.29	0.00	0.00	4.37
HILAND	0.28	−0.10	1.98	−0.25	0.00	−1.23	2.46	1.68
NTRL LE	−0.07	−0.05	1.68	−0.63	0.00	3.29	−2.84	1.46
CTL BR	0.49	0.42	2.45	1.24	5.12	1.57	1.34	−0.51

NOTES: Each row reports average elasticities for one product with respect to its own price and with respect to the price of the seven other products. These elasticities are calculated at the individual level for all markets that had both products in the choice set and then averaged over all those markets weighted by the number of transactions per market. A "−" indicates that there were no markets (store/week combinations) with both products.

TABLE 5

ELASTICITIES FOR MODEL WITH NO UNOBSERVED PRODUCT CHARACTERISTICS $(P = 0, \Omega \neq 0)$

With Respect to →	Wght W	Dannon	Elmgr	YAMI	HWT	HILA	NTRL	CTL
Wght Wtch	16.16	−17.93	0.72	−1.32	1.06	0.20	−0.21	0.28
Dannon	−16.12	4.82	0.92	0.28	0.27	−0.51	−0.32	0.10
Elmgrove	0.74	1.70	−3.13	0.00	9.53	5.96	5.34	5.14
YAMI	−2.04	0.52	0.00	−2.20	4.82	4.56	−1.89	2.99
HWT MDY	1.08	0.50	9.60	8.89	−1.94	0.00	0.00	6.92
HILAND	0.31	−0.89	4.71	2.51	0.00	−3.17	7.56	4.60
NTRL LE	−0.34	−0.72	4.28	−1.81	0.00	9.60	−7.97	4.46
CTL BR	0.38	0.14	6.63	3.15	12.71	3.80	3.57	−0.61

the model with two unobserved product characteristics we see all of the own- and cross-price elasticities are of the expected sign, and they are of reasonable magnitudes (all own-price elasiticies are larger than one in absolute value). For the largest brand, Dannon, the own-price elasticity is −5.37, and the cross-price elasticity of Dannon with respect to the second biggest is 2.84. These results suggest an important role for unobserved product characteristics, which could include the propensity to issue coupons (which were excluded from our model for simplicity), quality, flavor mix (also excluded for simplicity), and brand recognition.

6.3. *Predicting Market Shares for New Products.* To compare the counterfactual predictions arising from the different models, we simulate market shares for a new product. The product we introduce has the same observed characteristics in each market, a price equal to the average value of the price in the entire market (47 cents), and is never featured (feature = 0). It is included in every individual's

TABLE 6

ELASTICITIES FOR MODEL WITH A SINGLE UNOBSERVED PRODUCT CHARACTERISTIC $(P = 1, \Omega \neq 0)$

With Respect to →	Wght W	Dannon	Elmgr	YAMI	HWT	HILA	NTRL	CTL
Wght Wtch	1.52	−3.19	0.96	0.34	2.10	0.45	0.11	1.02
Dannon	−1.23	−4.28	2.60	3.66	2.66	3.03	1.15	3.64
Elmgrove	0.68	6.40	−6.09	0.00	9.86	10.78	6.60	7.51
YAMI	0.23	9.99	0.00	−7.32	5.68	10.92	1.90	4.57
HWT MDY	1.37	7.23	9.64	13.93	−5.22	0.00	0.00	8.97
HILAND	0.52	6.68	6.79	3.67	0.00	−7.54	8.77	7.06
NTRL LE	0.13	3.75	5.41	2.18	0.00	13.56	−13.12	6.26
CTL BR	0.84	7.34	12.01	4.78	16.78	5.26	3.72	−4.19

TABLE 7

ELASTICITIES FOR MODEL WITH TWO UNOBSERVED PRODUCT CHARACTERISTICS $(P = 2, \Omega \neq 0)$

With Respect to →	Wght W	Dannon	Elmgr	YAMI	HWT	HILA	NTRL	CTL
Wght Wtch	−6.40	2.92	1.83	3.79	3.02	2.04	1.83	2.84
Dannon	1.17	−5.37	2.34	3.94	2.85	3.60	1.60	3.54
Elmgrove	1.48	5.73	−5.60	0.00	8.78	8.82	4.48	7.42
YAMI	2.21	11.15	0.00	−7.72	5.10	9.12	3.56	3.57
HWT MDY	1.90	7.34	10.16	10.32	−5.10	0.00	0.00	9.34
HILAND	2.58	8.21	7.04	3.81	0.00	−8.49	8.68	8.03
NTRL LE	2.70	5.75	5.01	3.17	0.00	14.39	−14.78	6.29
CTL BR	2.44	7.17	12.63	3.60	21.83	5.59	3.15	−4.51

choice set. For the first two models this information is sufficient to predict the market share. For the models with unobserved product characteristics we also need to specify values for the unobserved characteristics. As discussed in Section 4, we draw the unobserved choice characteristics randomly from the marginal distribution of unobserved choice characteristics estimated from the sample. This has the effect of making the predicted market shares more uncertain, so that even with an infinitely large sample we would not be able to predict the market share for the new product with certainty. Instead, there is a range of possible market shares, depending on the values of the unobserved characteristics.

The results for this exercise are in Table 8, where the additional variation from adding unobservable product characteristics is apparent. Perhaps surprisingly, there is little change in the estimates from including two versus one unobserved product characteristic.

6.4. *Sensitivity to Choices for Prior Distributions.* Here we investigate the sensitivity of the results to the specification of the prior distributions. We focus on the most general model with two unobserved choice characteristics, which is most likely to be sensitive to this specification. For five different specifications

TABLE 8

PREDICTED MARKET SHARE FOR NEW PRODUCT

	$P = 0, \Omega = 0$	$P = 0$	$P = 1$	$P = 2$
Average	0.254	0.201	0.241	0.254
Standard deviation	0.001	0.001	0.110	0.125
0.05 quantile	0.252	0.199	0.117	0.116
0.95 quantile	0.256	0.203	0.360	0.394

NOTES: The first row contains posterior means for the market share for a new product that is available in each market (each store/week), always with a price of 47 cents and not featured. For the models with unobserved product characteristics we draw the unobserved product characteristic(s) from their estimated marginal distribution. The second row gives the posterior standard deviation of this market share, and the third and fourth rows give the 0.05 and 0.95 quantiles of this posterior distribution.

TABLE 9

SENSITIVITY OF POSTERIOR DISTRIBUTIONS TO PRIOR DISTRIBUTION

Parameter	Base Prior		Prior II		Prior III		Prior IV		Prior V	
Mean(β_{price})	−0.40	0.02	−0.39	0.02	−0.42	0.02	−0.41	0.02	−0.40	0.02
SD($\Delta_{price,income} \cdot Z_{income}$)	0.26	0.03	0.25	0.04	0.22	0.08	0.26	0.07	0.26	0.04
$\sqrt{\Omega_{price,price}}$	0.49	0.04	0.46	0.03	0.62	0.05	0.56	0.03	0.48	0.03
Mean($\beta_{feature}$)	0.40	0.05	0.405	0.05	0.37	0.07	0.38	0.06	0.39	0.05
SD($\Delta_{feature,income} \cdot Z_{income}$)	0.07	0.04	0.08	0.04	0.19	0.14	0.23	0.09	0.08	0.04
$\sqrt{\Omega_{feature,feature}}$	0.15	0.03	0.16	0.03	1.00	0.12	0.61	0.08	0.17	0.03
$\Delta_{price,income}$	0.07	0.01	0.06	0.01	0.08	0.02	0.07	0.02	0.06	0.01
$\Delta_{feature,income}$	−0.01	0.03	−0.01	0.03	−0.01	0.04	−0.01	0.03	−0.01	0.03
Cross-elast D wrt CRT BL	3.66	0.27	3.49	0.27	3.61	0.25	3.72	0.27	3.62	0.30
Own elast D	−5.36	0.35	−5.27	0.30	−4.88	0.33	−5.12	0.24	−5.31	0.28
Market share new product	0.25	0.13	0.26	0.12	0.26	0.12	0.25	0.12	0.25	0.12

of the prior distributions we report the same parameter estimates as in Table 3, the own-price for Dannon, and the cross-price elasticity for Dannon with respect to the price of CTL BR, and the summary statistics for the distribution of the predicted market share for a new product.

In the first pair of columns we report the results for the baseline prior distribution. Differences between these columns and the previously reported results for the $P = 2$ model reflect on the lack of accuracy of the MCMC calculations (based on runs of 40,000 iterations). In the second pair of columns we change the prior variance for Δ from an identity matrix multiplied by 0.25 to an identity matrix multiplied by 0.125. In the third pair of columns we change the first parameter of the prior distribution of Σ from 100 to 50. In the fourth pair of columns we change the second parameter of the prior distribution of Σ from 0.01 to 0.1. The results are in Table 9. Generally the specification of the prior distributions changes the posterior distributions somewhat, but it does not change the qualitative conclusions.

7. CONCLUSION

This article explores an issue first raised by McFadden (e.g., 1981), namely, the extent to which discrete choice models should incorporate unobserved product characteristics in order to rationalize choice data in settings with many products and/or multiple markets. We find that in general a model should include at least two unobserved choice characteristics if monotonicity of the utility function in the unobserved choice characteristics is imposed. More than two unobserved characteristics may be needed only if the functional form of the utility function (and in particular, its dependence on unobserved characteristics) is restricted.

We find that MCMC methods enable us to implement such models in a straightforward manner. We illustrate the method using scanner data about yogurt purchases. Our main findings are that the inclusion of two unobserved choice characteristics leads to more reasonable estimates of elasticities. We also argue that our approach leads to more realistic predictions about the heterogeneity in potential market shares that might arise on introduction of a new product. With additional structure, these predictions can be sharpened. In addition, the dependence of predicted market share on the location of a new product in characteristic space (both observable and unobservable characteristics) can be analyzed. We believe that an important advantage of the framework we propose is that the unobservable component of utility has a fair amount of structure, and the interpretability of the resulting estimates help guide the researcher in conducting counterfactual simulations. In applications, it may be possible to analyze and interpret the unobservable product characteristics, in order to gain a sense of how existing products are positioned and to help discover what parts of the product space might be most ripe for entry.

A number of questions are left open for future work. Among these is the question of how much individual heterogeneity is necessary to rationalize choice data in a variety of settings, and how that depends on any functional form or monotonicity restrictions that are imposed in the specification of individual utility.

APPENDIX

A.1. *Implementation of the Markov-Chain-Monte-Carlo Algorithm.* In this appendix, we describe the specific implementation of the Gibbs algorithm we use for obtaining draws from the posterior distribution of the parameters of interest. It relies critically on viewing the latent utitilies as well as the individual specific parameters as unobserved random variables to be imputed given the observed variables. The implementation borrows heavily from RMA, as well as more indirectly from Chib (2003) and Chib and Greenberg (1998). For a general discussion of MCMC methods see Tanner (1993) and Gelman et al. (2004). For notational simplicity we focus on the case with a single market and with only one purchase per household.

We construct an MCMC sequence that imputes the unobserved latent utilities $U_{i,j,t}$, the individual specific parameters β_i and γ_i, and the unobserved product characteristics ξ_j, and delivers draws from the posterior distribution of the common parameters Δ, Ω. We divide the unobserved random variables (including the parameters) into five groups. The first consists of the latent utilities U_{ik} for all individuals and all choices. The second consists of the individual taste parameters $\theta_i = (\beta_i, \gamma_i)$ for all individuals. The third group consists of the (matrix-valued) common taste parameter Δ. The fourth group consists of the unobserved choice characteristics ξ_k. The final group consists of the covariance matrix of the individual taste parameters Ω.

A.2. *Preliminary Result.* Suppose that X and Y are random vectors of dimension M_X and M_Y respectively, with

$$X \mid Y \sim \mathcal{N}(a + BY, \Sigma_{X|Y}),$$
$$Y \sim \mathcal{N}(\mu_Y, \Sigma_Y).$$

Here a is $M_X \times 1$, B is $M_X \times M_Y$, $\Sigma_{X|Y}$ is $M_X \times M_X$, μ_Y is $M_Y \times 1$, and Σ_Y is $M_Y \times M_Y$. Then

(A.1)

$$Y \mid X \sim \mathcal{N}\left(\left(B' \Sigma_{X|Y}^{-1} B + \Sigma_Y^{-1} \right)^{-1} \left(B' \Sigma_{X|Y}^{-1} X + \Sigma_Y^{-1} \mu_Y \right), \left(B' \Sigma_{X|Y}^{-1} B + \Sigma_Y^{-1} \right)^{-1} \right).$$

A.2.1. *Step I: Starting values.* The first step consists of choosing starting values for the individual characteristics β_i and γ_i, for $i = 1, \ldots, N$, for the choice characteristics ξ_k, $k = 1, \ldots, K$, and the latent utilities U_{ij}. If there is only a single unobserved product characteristic the starting values are drawn randomly from a standard normal distribution. With $P > 1$ the starting values for the first set of unobserved choice characteristics are set equal to the posterior mode for the unobserved product characteristic in the $P = 1$ case, which is $\xi_1 = ()$. The starting values for the second unobserved choice characteristic are drawn from a standard normal distribution. Next, we draw the latent utilities in two steps. We first fix the latent utilities at one for the product chosen and at zero for the products not chosen. Then we sequentially draw the latent utilities from a truncated normal distribution with mean zero and unit variance, with the truncation determined by the values of the other latent utilities. Finally, we draw starting values for the individual-specific parameters β_i and γ_i using the latent utilities and the observed and unobserved choice characteristics, as described in more detail in Step III below.

A.2.2. *Step II: Latent utilities U_{ij}.* The second step consists of drawing the latent utilities U_{ij} given the observed choices $\mathbf{Y} = (Y_1, Y_2, \ldots, Y_N)'$, the observed individual characteristics $\mathbf{Z}$, the observed and unobserved choice characteristics $\mathbf{X}$ and ξ, and the individual preference parameters β and γ. Following RMA, we do this sequentially, individual by individual, and choice by choice, each time conditioning on the latent utilities for the other $K - 1$ choices. Thus, for the jth choice, we draw from the conditional distribution of U_{ij} given Y_i, $(U_{ik})_{k=1, \ldots, J, k \neq j}$, $\mathbf{X}$, $\mathbf{Z}$, β, γ, Ω, and Δ.

First note that

$$U_{ij} \mid U_{i1}, \ldots, U_{ij-1}, U_{ij+1}, \ldots, U_{iJ}, U_{1\cdot}, \ldots, U_{i-1\cdot}, U_{i+1\cdot}, \ldots, U_{N\cdot},$$
$$\mathbf{Y}, \mathbf{X}, \mathbf{Z}, \xi, \beta, \gamma, \Delta, \Omega$$
$$\sim U_{ij} \mid U_{i1}, \ldots, U_{ij-1}, U_{ij+1}, \ldots, U_{iJ}, U_{1\cdot}, \ldots, U_{i-1\cdot}, U_{i+1\cdot}, \ldots, U_{N\cdot},$$
$$\mathbf{Y}, \mathbf{X}, \mathbf{Z}, \xi, \beta, \gamma.$$
$$\sim U_{ij} \mid U_{i1}, \ldots, U_{ij-1}, U_{ij+1}, \ldots, U_{iJ}, Y_i, X_j, \xi_j, \beta_i, \gamma_i.$$

Conditioning only on X_j, β_i, ξ_j, and γ_i, we have

$$U_{ij} \sim \mathcal{N}(X'_j\beta_i + \xi'_j\gamma_i, 1).$$

Conditioning also on Y_i and U_{ij} for $k \neq j$ changes this into a truncated normal distribution. Let $\mathcal{N}(c, \mu, \sigma^2)$ denote a normal distribution with mean μ and variance σ^2 truncated from below at c, and $\bar{\mathcal{N}}(c, \mu, \sigma^2)$ a normal distribution with mean μ and variance σ^2 truncated from above at c. If $Y_i = j$, then $U_{ij} \geq \max_{k \neq j} U_{ij}$, and so

$$U_{ij} \mid U_{i1}, \ldots, U_{ij-1}, U_{ij+1}, \ldots, U_{iJ}, Y_i = j, X_j, \beta_i, \xi_j,$$
$$\gamma_i \sim \underline{\mathcal{N}} \left(\max_{k \neq j} U_{ik}, X'_j\beta_i + \xi'_j\gamma_i, 1 \right).$$

Similarly, if $Y_i \neq j$, then $U_{ij} \leq \max_{k \neq j} U_{ik}$, and so

$$U_{ij} \mid U_{i1}, \ldots, U_{ij-1}, U_{ij+1}, \ldots, U_{iJ}, Y_i \neq j, X_j, \beta_i, \xi_j,$$
$$\gamma_i \sim \bar{\mathcal{N}} \left(\max_{k \neq j} U_{ik}, X'_j\beta_i + \xi'_j\gamma_i, 1 \right).$$

The problem of drawing from a normal truncated distribution from below or above can be reduced to that of drawing from a standard (mean zero, unit variance) normal distribution truncated from below by c. Again following RMA we consider three cases. If $c < 0$ we draw v from a standard normal distribution and reject the draw if $w < c$. If $0 \leq c \leq 0.6$ we draw from the distribution of $|v|$ where v has a standard normal distribution, and reject the draw if $|v| < c$. If $c > 0.6$, we use importance sampling. We draw v from a standard exponential distribution, divide by c and add c. We then accept the draw with probability equal to the ratio of the normal density to the density we drew from, divided by the maximum of that ratio over the range of the random variable. This leads to an acceptance probability equal to

$$\frac{\exp(-c^2/2)}{c\sqrt{2\pi}} \cdot \frac{(1/\sqrt{2\pi})\exp(-v^2/2)}{c\exp(-c(v-c))}.$$

A.2.3. *Step III: Individual coefficients β_i and γ_i.* Consider the distribution of the $K + P$-dimensional vector of individual coefficients, $\theta_i = (\beta_i', \gamma_i')'$:

$$\theta_i \mid \{\theta_j\}_{j \neq i}, \mathbf{U}, \mathbf{Y}, \mathbf{X}, \mathbf{Z}, \xi, \Delta, \Omega \sim \theta_i \mid U_i, \mathbf{X}, \xi, Z_i, \Delta, \Omega.$$

Consider the conditional distribution of the latent utilities:

$$U_{ij} \mid \mathbf{X}, Z_i, \theta_i, \xi, \Delta, \Omega \sim \mathcal{N}\left(\begin{pmatrix} X_j \\ \xi_j \end{pmatrix}' \theta_i, 1\right).$$

Define the J-vector $U_{i\cdot} = (U_{i1}\ U_{i2}\ \ldots\ U_{iJ})$, the $K \times J$ matrix $\mathbf{X} = (X_1\ X_2\ \ldots\ X_J)$, and the $P \times J$ matrix $\xi = (\xi_1\ \xi_2 \ldots \xi_J)$, so that

$$U_{i\cdot} \mid \mathbf{X}, Z_i, \theta_i, \xi, \Delta, \Omega \sim \mathcal{N}\left(\begin{pmatrix} \mathbf{X} \\ \xi \end{pmatrix}' \theta_i, I_J\right).$$

Also,

$$\theta_i \mid \mathbf{X}, Z_i, \xi, \Delta, \Omega \sim \mathcal{N}(Z_i\Delta, \Omega).$$

Hence, using (A.1),

$$\theta_i \mid U_{i\cdot}, \mathbf{X}, \xi, Z_i, \Delta, \Omega$$

$$\sim \mathcal{N}\left(\left(\begin{pmatrix} \mathbf{X} \\ \xi \end{pmatrix} \begin{pmatrix} \mathbf{X} \\ \xi \end{pmatrix}' + \Omega^{-1}\right)^{-1} ((\mathbf{X}\,\xi)'U_{i\cdot} + \Omega^{-1}Z_i\Delta)^{-1}, \left(\begin{pmatrix} \mathbf{X} \\ \xi \end{pmatrix} \begin{pmatrix} \mathbf{X} \\ \xi \end{pmatrix}' + \Omega^{-1}\right)^{-1}\right).$$

A.2.4. *Step IV: Common regression coefficients Δ.* Let θ be the $N \times (K + P)$ dimensional matrix with ith row equal to θ_i'. Then

$$\Delta \mid \mathbf{Y}, \mathbf{X}, \mathbf{Z}, \xi, \theta, \Omega \sim \Delta \mid \mathbf{Z}, \theta, \Omega.$$

Moreoever, the N rows of θ are independent of each other conditional on $(\mathbf{Z}, \Delta, \Omega)$ and

$$\theta_i \mid \mathbf{Z}, \Delta, \Omega \sim \mathcal{N}(\Delta'Z_i, \Omega).$$

Let $\delta = (\Delta_{1\cdot}, \Delta_{2\cdot}, \ldots, \Delta_{(K+P)\cdot})'$, so that δ is a $L \cdot (K + P)$-dimensional column vector. Then we can write

$$\theta_i \mid \mathbf{Z}, \Delta, \Omega \sim \mathcal{N}((I_{K+P} \otimes (Z_i'))\delta, \Omega).$$

Stack all the $K + P$ vectors θ_i into a $N \times (K + P)$ dimensional column vector $\tilde{\theta}$, and stack all the matrices $I_{K+P} \otimes (Z_i)$ into the $N \cdot (K + P) \times L \cdot (K + P)$ matrix $\tilde{\mathbf{Z}}$. Then we have the following distribution for $\tilde{\theta}$:

$$\tilde{\theta} \mid \mathbf{Z}, \Delta, \Omega \sim \mathcal{N}(\tilde{\mathbf{Z}}\delta, I_N \otimes \Omega).$$

The prior distibution for δ is normal with mean equal to the $L \cdot (K + P)$-vector of zeros, and as variance σ_δ^2 times the $L \cdot (M + P)$-dimensional identity matrix $I_{L \times (K+P)}$. Thus the posterior distribution for δ given $(\mathbf{Y}, \mathbf{X}, \mathbf{Z}, \xi, \Omega, \tilde{\theta})$ is

$$\delta \mid \mathbf{Y}, \mathbf{X}, \mathbf{Z}, \xi, \Omega, \tilde{\theta} \sim \mathcal{N}\big((\sigma_\delta^{-2} \cdot I_{L \times (M+P)} + \tilde{\mathbf{Z}}'\,(I_N \otimes \Omega^{-1})\,\tilde{\mathbf{Z}})^{-1}\,(\tilde{\mathbf{Z}}'\,(I_N \otimes \Omega^{-1})\,\tilde{\theta}),$$
$$(\sigma_\delta^{-2} \cdot I_{L \times (M+P)} + \tilde{\mathbf{Z}}'\,(I_N \otimes \Omega^{-1})\,\tilde{\mathbf{Z}})^{-1}\big).$$

A.2.5. *Step V: Latent choice characteristics ξ_j.* Consider the conditional distribution of the latent choice characteristics ξ_j:

$$\xi_j \mid \theta, \mathbf{U}, \xi_1, \ldots, \xi_{j-1}, \xi_{j+1}, \ldots, \xi_J, \mathbf{Y}, \mathbf{X}, \mathbf{Z}, \Delta, \Omega \sim \xi \mid U_{\cdot j}, X_j, \theta.$$

First,

$$U_{ij} - \beta_i' X_j \mid U_{1j}, \ldots, U_{i-1,j}, U_{i+1,j}, \ldots, U_{Nj}, \theta, \xi_j \sim \mathcal{N}(\gamma_i' \xi_j, 1),$$

so that

$$U_{\cdot j} - \beta X_j \mid \mathbf{X}, \theta_i, \xi \sim \mathcal{N}(\gamma \xi_j, I_N),$$

where β is the $N \times K$ matrix with ith row equal to β_i', and γ is the $N \times P$ matrix with ith row equal to γ_i'. The prior distribution on ξ_j is normal with the mean equal to the P-vector of zeros, and as variance the $P \times P$ dimensional identity matrix. Hence

$$\xi_j \mid U_{\cdot j}, \mathbf{X}, \theta \sim \mathcal{N}\big((\gamma'\gamma + I_P)^{-1}(\gamma'(U_{\cdot j} - \beta X_j)), (\gamma'\gamma + I_P)^{-1}\big).$$

A.2.6. *Step VI: Covariance matrix of individual taste parameters Ω.* First,

$$\Omega \mid \mathbf{X}, \mathbf{Z}, \mathbf{Y}, \theta \sim \Omega \mid \nu,$$

where ν is the $N \times (K + P)$ matrix with ith row equal to $\theta_i - Z_i'\Delta'$. Next,

$$\nu_i \perp \nu_{i'} \mid \Omega,$$

and

$$\nu_i \mid \Omega \sim \mathcal{N}(0, \Omega).$$

The prior distribution for Ω^{-1} is a Wishart distribution with degrees of freedom 100 and scale matrix I_{K+P}. Hence the posterior distribution of Ω^{-1} given ν is a Wishart distribution with degrees of freedom $100 + N$ and scale matrix $I_{K+P} + \sum_{i=1}^{N} v_i v_i'$, so

$$\Omega^{-1} \mid \mathbf{X}, \mathbf{Z}, \mathbf{Y}, \theta \sim \mathcal{W}\left(100 + N, I_{K+P} + \sum_{i=1}^{N} v_i v_i'\right).$$

A.3. *Calculation of Elasticities.* Here we describe the calculation of the price elasticities reported in Section 6.2. The elasticities vary by price and individual, and depend on unknown parameters. We summarize these by calculating an average elasticity over all individuals and transactions, and by integrating out the unknown parameters using their posterior distribution. First we average over all transactions where products j and k are both in the choice set:

$$(A.2) \qquad \epsilon_{jk} = \frac{\overline{\text{price}_k}}{\frac{1}{N_{jk}} \sum_{j,k \in \mathbb{C}_i} \text{pr}(Y_i = j)} \cdot \frac{1}{N} \sum_{j,k \in \mathbb{C}_i} \frac{\partial \text{pr}(Y_i = j)}{\partial \text{price}_k},$$

where $\mathbb{C}_i$ is the choice set for transaction i, consisting of all brands for which we observe a transaction in the market (store/week combination), and N_{jk} is the number of transactions where both products j and k are in the choice set. We calculate the probability of individual i purchasing product j conditional on the observed and unobserved individual- and choice-specific components. Rather than calculating the exact probability and its derivatives given the unobserved components we approximate them using a the approximate equality of a normal distribution with mean zero and variance three and an extreme value distribution, so that

$$(A.3) \qquad \text{pr}(Y_i = j \mid j \in \mathbb{C}_i, \xi_j, X_{jm}, \beta_i, \gamma_i) = \frac{\exp(\sqrt{3} \cdot (X'_{jm}\beta_i + \xi'_j \gamma_i))}{\sum_{k \in \mathbb{C}_i} \exp(\sqrt{3} \cdot (X'_{km}\beta_i + \xi'_k \gamma_i))}.$$

Substituting (A.3) and its derivative into (A.2) gives us the elasticities as a function of the individual unobserved components β_i and γ_i and the unobserved choice characteristics ξ_j (as well as observed quantities). We then average these conditional elasticities over the posterior distribution of the unknown quantities.

For the average price_k we use the average price for product k over all transactions where product k was in the choice set, that is the average prices in column 2 in Table 2. Note also that in calculating (A.2) we average over all transactions, in each case calculating the choice probabilities as if all eight products are in the choice set.

REFERENCES

ACKERBERG, D., "Empirically Distinguishing Informative and Prestige Effects of Advertising," *RAND Journal of Economics* 32 (2001), 100–18.
——, "Advertising, Learning and Consumer Choice in Experience Good Markets: A Structural Empirical Examination," *International Economic Review* 44 (2003), 1007–40.

——, AND M. RYSMAN, "Unobserved Product Differentiation in Discrete Choice Models: Estimating Price Elasticities and Welfare Effects," Department of Economics, UCLA, 2002.

——, L. BENKARD, S. BERRY, AND A. PAKES, "Econometric Tools for Analyzing Market Outcomes," in J. Heckman and E. Leamer, eds., *Handbook of Econometrics*, Volume 5B (Amsterdam: North Holland, 2006).

ALLENBY, G., Y. CHEN, AND S. YANG, "Bayesian Analysis of Simultaneous Demand and Supply," *Quantitative Marketing and Economics* 1 (2003), 251–75.

BAJARI, P., AND L. BENKARD, "Discrete Choice Models as Structural Models of Demand: Some Economic Implications of Common Approaches," Stanford Business School, 2003.

——, AND ——, "Demand Estimation with Heterogenous Consumers and Unobserved Product Characteristics: A Hedonic Approach," Stanford Business School, 2004.

BERRY, S., "Estimating Discrete-Choice Models of Product Differentiation," *RAND Journal of Economics* 25 (1994), 242–62.

——, AND A. PAKES, "The Pure Characteristics Demand Model," International Economic Review 48 (2007), 1193–1275.

——, J. LEVINSOHN, AND A. PAKES, "Automobile Prices in Market Equilibrium," *Econometrica* 63 (1995), 841–89.

——, ——, AND ——, "Differentiated Products Demand Systems from a Combination of Micro and Macro Data: The New Car Market," *Journal of Political Economy* 112 (2004), 68–105.

——, O. LINTON, AND A. PAKES, "Limit Theorems for Estimating the Parameters of Differentiated Product Demand Systems," *Review of Economic Studies* 71 (2004), 613–54.

BRESNAHAN, T., M. TRAJTENBERG, AND S. STERN, "Market Segmentation and the Sources of Rents from Innovation: Personal Computers in the Late 1980's," *RAND Journal of Economics* 28 (1997), S17–44.

CHIB, S., "Markov Chain Monte Carlo Methods: Computation and Inference," in J. Heckman and E. Leamer, eds., *Handbook of Econometrics* (Amsterdam: North Holland, 2003).

——, AND E. GREENBERG, "Analysis of Multivariate Probit Models," *Biometrika* (1998), 347–61.

ELROD, T., AND M. KEANE, "A Factor-Analytic Probit Model for Representing the Market Structure in Panel Data," *Journal of Marketing Research* XXXII (1995), 1–16.

GELMAN, A., J. CARLIN, H. STERN, AND D. RUBIN, *Bayesian Data Analysis* (London: Chapman and Hall, 2004).

GEWEKE, J., "Posterior Simulators in Econometrics," in D. Kreps and K. Wallis, eds., *Advances in Economics and Econometrics: Theory and Applications* (Cambridge, UK: Cambridge University Press, 1997).

——, AND M. KEANE, "Bayesian Inference for Dynamic Discrete Choice Models without the Need for Dynamic Programming," in R. Mariano, T. Schuermann, and M. Weeks, eds., *Simulation Based Inference and Econometrics: Methods and Applications* (Cambridge, UK: Cambridge University Press, 2002), 100–31.

GOETTLER, J., AND R. SHACHAR, "Spatial Competition in the Network Television Industry," *RAND Journal of Economics* 32 (2001), 624–56.

GOLDBERG, P., "Product Differentiation and Oligopoly in International Markets: The Case of the U.S. Automobile Industry," *Econometrica* 63 (1995), 891–951.

HARRIS, K., AND M. KEANE, "A Model of Health Plan Choice: Inferring Preferences and Perceptions from a Combination of Revealed Preference and Attitudinal Data," *Journal of Econometrics* 89 (1999), 131–57.

HAUSMAN, J., AND D. MCFADDEN, "Specification Tests for the Multinomial Logit Model," *Econometrica* 52 (1984), 1219–40.

KEANE, M., "Modeling Heterogeneity and State Dependence in Consumer Choice Behavior," *Journal of Business and Economic Statistics* 15 (1997), 310–27.

——, "Modeling Health Insurance Choice Using the Heterogenous Logit Model," Unpublished Manuscript, Department of Economics, Yale University, 2004.

KIM, J., G. ALLENBY, AND P. ROSSI, "Product Attributes and Models of Multiple Discreteness," *Journal of Econometrics* 138 (2007), 208–30.

McCULLOCH, R., AND P. ROSSI, "An Exact Likelihood Analysis of the Multinomial Probit Model," *Journal of Econometrics* 64 (1994), 207–40.

——, N. POLSON, AND P. ROSSI, "A Bayesian Analysis of the Multinomial Probit Model with Fully Identified Parameters," *Journal of Econometrics* 99 (2000), 173–93.

McFADDEN, D., "Conditional Logit Analysis of Qualitative Choice Behavior," in P. Zarembka, ed., *Frontiers in Econometrics* (New York: Academic Press, 1973), 105–42.

——, "Econometric Models of Probabilistic Choice," in C. Manski and D. McFadden, eds., *Structural Analysis of Discrete Data with Econometric Applications* (Cambridge, MA: MIT Press, 1981).

——, "Qualitative Response Models," in W. Hildenbrand, ed., *Advances in Econometrics: Invited Papers for the Fourth World Congress of the Econometric Society* (Cambridge, UK: Cambridge University Press, 1982), 1–37.

——, "Econometric Analysis of Qualitative Response Models," in Z. Griliches and M. Intriligator, eds., *Handbook of Econometrics*, Volume 2 (Amsterdam: North Holland, 1984), 1395–1457.

NEVO, A., "A Practitioner's Guide to Estimation of Random-Coefficients Logit Models of Demand," *Journal of Economics and Management Strategy* 9 (2000), 513–48.

——, "Measuring Market Power in the Ready-to-Eat Cereal Industry," *Econometrica* 69 (2001), 307–42.

OSBORNE, M., "Consumer Learning, Habit Formation and Heterogeneity: A Structural Examination," Mimeo, Stanford University, 2005.

PETRIN, A., "Quantifying the Benefits of New Products: The Case of the Minivan," *Journal of Political Economy* 110 (2002), 705–29.

POOLE, K., AND H. ROSENTHAL, "A Spatial Model for Legislative Roll Call Analysis," *American Journal of Political Science* 29 (1985), 357–84.

ROMEO, C., "A Gibbs Sampler for Mixed Logit Analysis of Differentiated Product Markets Using Aggregate Data," Unpublished Manuscript, Economic Analysis Group, US Department of Justice, 2003.

ROSSI, P., G. ALLENBY, AND R. McCULLOCH, *Bayesian Statistics and Marketing* (Chichester, UK: John Wiley and Sons, 2005).

——, R. McCULLOCH, AND G. ALLENBY, "The Value of Purchase History Data in Target Marketing," *Marketing Science* 15 (1996), 321–40.

ROUSSEEUW, P., AND A. LEROY, *Robust Regression and Outlier Detection* (New York, Wiley, 1987).

TANNER, M., *Tools for Statistical Inference: Methods for the Exploration of Posterior Distributions and Likelihood Functions* (Berlin: Springer, 1993).

——, AND W. WONG, "The Calculation of Posterior Distributions by Data Augmentation," *Journal of the American Statistical Association* 82 (1987), 528–40.

TRAIN, K., *Discrete Choice Methods with Simulation* (Cambridge, UK: Cambridge University Press, 2003).

INTERNATIONAL ECONOMIC REVIEW
Vol. 48, No. 4, November 2007

THE PURE CHARACTERISTICS DEMAND MODEL*

By Steven Berry and Ariel Pakes[1]

Yale University and NBER, U.S.A.
Harvard University and NBER, U.S.A.

In this article, we consider a class of discrete choice models in which consumers care about a finite set of product characteristics. These models have been used extensively in the theoretical literature on product differentiation and the goal of this article is to translate them into a form that is useful for empirical work. Most recent econometric applications of discrete choice models implicitly let the dimension of the characteristic space increase with the number of products (they have "tastes for products"). The two models have different theoretical properties, and these, in turn, can have quite pronounced implications for both substitution patterns and for the welfare impacts of changes in the number and characteristics of the goods marketed. After developing those properties, we provide alternative algorithms for estimating the parameters of the pure characteristic model and compare their properties to those of the algorithm for estimating the model with tastes for products. We conclude with a series of Monte Carlo results. These are designed to illustrate: (i) the computational properties of the alternative algorithms for computing the pure characteristic model, and (ii) the differences in the implications of the pure characteristic model from the models with tastes for products.

1. INTRODUCTION

The theory and econometrics of demand models that treat products as bundles of characteristics dates back at least to Lancaster (1971) and McFadden (1974). Early applications of these models used restrictive assumptions and a primary concern of the literature that followed (including many contributions by McFadden himself) was that the structure of the discrete choice model used would in some way restrict the range of possible outcomes, thereby providing misleading empirical results. This article is a continuation of that tradition. In contrast to the empirical models currently available, we consider estimation of a class of discrete choice models in which consumers care about a finite set of product characteristics. These models have been used extensively in the theoretical literature on product differentiation, but have been used much less in empirical work.

Typical discrete choice empirical models (including those in our own work) implicitly assume that the dimension of the product space increases with the number

---

* Manuscript received October 2005; revised June 2007.

[1] We are grateful for the opportunity to publish this article in a volume in honor of Daniel McFadden. The article illustrates just one way in which Dan's path-breaking work on the economics and econometrics of choice theory has impacted Industrial Organization. We would also like to thank two referees and Charles Manski for helpful comments. Please address correspondence to Steven Berry, Department of Economics, Yale and NBER. E-mail: *steven.berry@yale.edu*.

of products. This assumption is often embedded in an otherwise unexplained i.i.d. additive random term in the utility function. One interpretation is that these terms represent variance in the "taste for the product," as opposed to a taste for the characteristics of the products. Though these models can do quite a good job in approximating some aspects of demand, they also have some counterintuitive implications as the number of products increases. As a result, we worry about their ability to analyze substitution patterns when there are a large number of goods and also about their ability to answer questions about changes in the number of goods.

Recent advances in econometric technique, computing power, and data availability have significantly increased the use of characteristic based models with "tastes for products" in analyzing demand in differentiated products markets. If one can condition on the major characteristics that consumers value, the characteristic based demand models have a number of advantages over the more traditional demand models in "product space." One of those advantages concerns the analysis of demand for products not yet marketed.[2] Demand systems estimated purely in product space do not allow us to analyze the demand for potential products. Provided that we are willing to specify the characteristics of the new product and the form of the equilibrium in the product market, the characteristic based models do (see, e.g., Berry et al., 2004a, henceforth MicroBLP.)

An important issue closely related to the demand for new products is the problem of estimating the consumer surplus generated by previously introduced products. This type of retrospective analysis dates back at least to Trajtenberg (1989), and its usefulness is illustrated clearly in Petrin's (2002) investigation of the consumer surplus gains from the (privately funded) research expenditures that lead to the development of a major innovation (the Minivan) and Hausman's (1997) investigation of the consumer surplus losses caused by regulatory delay in the introduction of the cell phone. In addition, measuring the consumer surplus gains from new products is an integral part of constructing ideal price indices (see, e.g., Pakes et al., 1993; Nevo 2000). Moreover, at least according to the Boskin Commission Report (1996), failure to adequately measure the gains from new products is the major source of bias in the Consumer Price Index (see also Pakes, 2003).

The consumer surplus generated by products already introduced can, at least in principle, be analyzed using either product based or characteristic based demand systems. However in either case the results of the analysis are likely to be particularly sensitive to a priori modeling assumptions. This is because we typically do not have data on the demand for new products at prices that are high enough to enable us to nonparametrically estimate the reservation prices of a large fraction of consumers. When using product based demand systems the utility gains for

---

[2] The other major advantage of estimating demand systems in characteristic space is that they typically constrain own and cross price (and characteristic) elasticities to be functions of a small number of parameters describing the distribution of tastes for characteristics. In particular, the number of parameters needed is independent of the number of products. In contrast, if we worked in product space a (log) linear demand system for J products would require the estimation of a number of parameters that grows like J^2.

the inframarginal consumers who purchased the good at all *observed* prices are obtained by extrapolating the demand curve estimated at lower prices to a higher price range, and these extrapolations can be very sensitive to the assumptions built into the model.[3] The characteristic based demand model uses slightly more information in its estimation of consumer surplus gains, since it uses the price variance for products with similar characteristics, but analogous problems can and do arise.[4] As a result, the measurement of gains from product introductions is likely to be particularly sensitive to assumptions like those we discuss extensively below.

The next section introduces our pure characteristics model and provides a more extended discussion of the reason we think it might be useful. There are at least two of these. The model with tastes for products implicitly places a limit on substitution patterns between products and hence on markups, whereas the pure characteristics model does not. As a result, at least in markets with a large number of products, the substitution patterns implied by the estimates from the two models might be expected to differ. Second, the model with tastes for products has the implication that every consumer's utility grows without bound as the number of products are increased, no matter the characteristics of those products. In the pure characteristic model with standard regularity conditions, the increment in each consumer's welfare as the number of products grows must eventually decline to zero (often at an exponential rate). So one might also expect the two models to give different results for consumer welfare gains.

We then develop some of the properties of our model. These properties enable us to build an algorithm for estimating the pure characteristics model from market level data on prices, quantities, and characteristics (Section 3). This section provides an analog to the algorithm developed for the model with "tastes for products" in Berry et al. (1995, henceforth BLP). The article concludes with some Monte Carlo evidence. The Monte Carlo studies are designed to give the reader (i) some indication of the performance of our estimators, (ii) an indication of the computational burden of the pure characteristics model relative to the model with a taste for products, and (iii) an indication of the performance of the pure characteristic model relative to the performance of a model with tastes for products.

The Monte Carlo studies suggest a number of important points for future research. First, we find that the most precise of the computational techniques works well, but can result in time-consuming estimation routines. Simpler and faster techniques that are closer to the original BLP methods sometimes work quite well in providing useful estimates, but not always. In some cases we find that a practical compromise is to use a method very close to the original BLP, but then to compute the predictions of the model using our most precise computational techniques for the pure characteristics model.

---

[3] Hausman (1997), e.g., reports infinite consumer surplus gains from some of his specifications.

[4] See the discussion below or Petrin (2002), who reports large differences in consumer surplus gains from differences in specifications and data sources.

2. DISCRETE CHOICE MODELS AND THEIR IMPLICATIONS

We consider models in which each consumer chooses to buy at most one product from some set of differentiated products. Consumer i's (indirect) utility from the purchase of product j is

$$(1) \qquad\qquad U_{ij} = U(X_j, V_i, \theta),$$

where X_j is a vector of product characteristics (including the price of the good), V_i is a vector of consumer tastes and θ is a vector of parameters to be estimated.

Probably the earliest model of this sort in the economic literature is the Hotelling (1929) model of product differentiation on the line. In that model X is the location of the product and V is the location of the consumer. Other well-known industrial organization models in this class include the vertical model of Mussa and Rosen (1978) (see also Gabszewicz and Thisse, 1979, and the model of competition on a circle by Salop, 1979). For early empirical use of these models see Bresnahan (1987), Feenstra and Levinsohn (1995), Greenstein (1996), and more recently Song (2006).

To obtain the market share of good j (our s_j) implied by the model we simply add up the number of consumers who prefer good j over all other goods. That is

$$(2) \qquad\qquad s_j = \Pr\{V_i : U(X_j, V_i, \theta) \geq U(X_k, V_i, \theta), \forall k \neq j)\}.$$

To ease the transition to empirical work we follow the notation in MicroBLP (2004) and

  (i) partition the vector of consumer attributes, V_i, into z_i, which an econometrician with a micro data set might observe, and v_i, which the econometrician does not observe,
  (ii) and partition product characteristics, X_j, into x_j, which is observed by the econometrician, and ξ_j, which is unobserved to the econometrician (though observed to the agents).[5]

The models taken to data impose more structure. They typically assume that the utility function is additively separable in a deterministic function of the product attributes and the observed consumer data, and a disturbance term, i.e.,

$$(3) \qquad\qquad U_{ij} = f(X_j, z_i; \theta) + \mu_{ij},$$

where θ is a parameter to be estimated. The model is then completed by making alternative assumptions on the joint distribution of the $\{\mu_{ij}, X_j, z_i\}$ tuples.

---

[5] Often, especially in the study of consumer (in contrast to producer) goods, the ξ refer to the aggregate impact of a large number of relatively unimportant characteristics, some or all of which may, in fact, be observed. Even if they are potentially observed, the researcher may not include them in the specification taken to data because of the worry that the data cannot support an investigation of preferences on such a detailed space.

In particular, we require (i) an assumption on the distribution of the μ_{ij} conditional on (X_j, z_i) and (ii) either an assumption on the distribution of the unobserved product characteristic (on ξ) given (x, z) or a procedure that estimates the ξ pointwise.[6] In this section, we focus on the assumption on μ_{ij} conditional on (X_j, z_i) as it is this assumption that differentiates the pure characteristic model from the model with tastes for products.

2.1. Conditional Distributions for μ_{ij} and Their Implications.

Both the pure characteristics model and the model with tastes for products allow the μ_{ij} to contain a set of interactions between the unobserved determinants of consumer tastes (say $v_{i,k}$) and the product characteristics $X_{j,k}$ (both observed and unobserved). As is typical, we will assume these interactions are linear: i.e., given K characteristics, then one component of μ_{ij} is $\sum_k v_{i,k} X_{j,k}$. This component allows each consumer to have a different marginal utility for each characteristic, which ameliorates many of the problems caused by the independence of irrelevant alternatives property of earlier models.[7] The model with tastes for products and the pure characteristic model differ in whether μ_{ij} has an additional component.

The empirical specifications to date typically assume that each μ_{ij} has an additional component whose conditional distribution, conditional on (X_j, z_i) *and* all other $\mu_{ij'}(\forall j' \neq j)$, that has support on the entire real line. Letting that component be $\{\epsilon_{ij}\}_{j=1}^{J}$ and indexing the μ_{ij} from these models with a *tp* superscript (for "tastes for products"), the model is usually written as

$$(4) \qquad \mu_{ij}^{tp} \equiv \sum_{k=1}^{K} v_{ik} X_{jk} + \epsilon_{ij}.$$

Special cases of this assumption include the random coefficient logit model used in BLP and McFadden and Train (2000) and the random coefficient probit discussed in Hausman and Wise (1978) and McFadden (1981).

One way to obtain a model with an additive component with full support (i.e., to obtain Equation (4)) is to make the dimension of the characteristic space, K, be a function of the number of products. Indeed the suggestion of Caplin and Nalebuff (1991) is to think of the additive component as being formed from the interaction of a set of product-specific dummy variables and a set of tastes for each product that are distributed i.i.d. both across products and across individuals for a given product. Thus our labeling of these models as models with "tastes for products."

The pure characteristic model only differs from the model with tastes for products in that it does not contain the $\{\epsilon_{i,j}\}_{j=1}^{J}$. That is if we index the $\mu_{i,j}$ from the pure characteristic model with a superscript of *pc*, the pure characteristic model is written as

---

[6] The choice typically depends on whether micro data, data that matches individuals to the choice they made, is available; for a discussion see MicroBLP (2004).

[7] See McFadden (1981) for a statement of the problem, and BLP and MicroBLP for its implications on estimates of market demand systems used in Industrial Organization.

$$(5) \qquad \mu_{ij}^{pc} \equiv \sum_{k=1}^{K} v_{ik} X_{jk}.$$

One can show that Equation (5) is related to the "ideal point" models that date back to Hotelling and have been used extensively in the theory literature.[8] In the ideal point models consumers care about the distance between their location (v_i) and the products' location (X_j) in $\mathcal{R}^k$, that is

$$(6) \qquad u_{ij} = \| X_j - v_i \| - \alpha_i p_j,$$

where $\|\cdot\|$ is some distance metric. If one assumes that $\|\cdot\|$ refers to Euclidean distance and expands the squares, we get a utility function where the mean utility depends on characteristics and the error term depends on interactions between product and individual characteristics as in Equation (6).

2.2. *Differences in the Implications of the Two Specifications.* The two specifications for μ_{ij} place different a priori restrictions on the implications of the model estimated. If the model with tastes for products is estimated, then the estimated model will imply that

(i) there is a limit on substitution possibilities between products, and
(ii) that as we increase the number of products each individual's utility increases to infinity as the number of new products grows, *regardless* of the observed characteristics of either the products that enter or of the individual.

As is explained below, neither of these implications holds true when the model without tastes for products is estimated.

An implication of the first point is that if we add products whose X characteristic are very similar (indeed they can be identical) to those of product A, the markup of product A will remain bounded away from zero (a similar point is made by Anderson et al., 1992, in the context of the logit model). This follows from the presence of the i.i.d. component, which ensures that there will always be consumers who prefer the new product to the old even if they have to pay a positive price difference, and in virtually all equilibrium pricing models this will imply prices greater than costs.

The fact that markups will not go to zero no matter how much we fill up the "product space" has at least two implications that might be problematic. First, even with a large number of products there will always be a further incentive for product development. Second, market outcomes will not approach a competitive equilibrium as the number of products grows large. One might be particularly worried about using a model that imposes these restrictions when studying markets where there are a large number of products.

The second itemized point, that each consumer's utility must grow without bound as we increase the number of products marketed no matter the

---

[8] See the discussion in Caplin and Nalebuff (1991) and Anderson et al. (1992).

characteristics of the products, is a particular concern for the analysis of prospective and retrospective gains from product introductions. Particularly when we use the model to extrapolate outside of the range of the data, as we must do to measure welfare gains from new products, we may obtain results that are not meaningful.

The finite-dimensional pure characteristics model is very different in both the itemized respects. In that model the agent's utility gain from new product introduction is limited by a smooth (usually linear) function of the distance in characteristic space between the new and previously existing products. As the number of products increases, the products become increasingly good substitutes for one another and oligopolistic competition will approach the competitive case, with prices driven toward marginal cost and no additional incentive for product development. As the product space fills up, the incremental consumer gain from new product introductions will decline to zero.[9] That is, the gains to "variety" will be bounded in the pure characteristics model whereas they grow without bound in models with tastes for products.

On the other hand, models that include a taste for products do have a number of important practical advantages. These models

(a) define all probabilities by integrals with simple limits of integration (see McFadden, 1981),

(b) insure that all the purchase probabilities are nonzero (at every value of the parameter vector) and (provided certain other regularity conditions are satisfied) have smooth derivatives (McFadden, 1981), and

(c) aggregate into market shares that can be easily inverted to solve for the unobservable characteristics (the $\{\xi_j\}$) as a linear function of the parameters and the data, enabling the use of instrumental variable techniques to solve simultaneity problem induced by correlation between the unobserved characteristics and price (see BLP).

2.3. *Nesting the Two Models.* Looking at Equations (4) and (5) one might think it easy to nest the two models and let the data decide which of them is appropriate for the problem at hand. In particular, we could introduce the additional parameter σ_ϵ and then assume

$$(7) \qquad \mu_{ij} \equiv \sum_{k=1}^{K} v_{ik} X_{jk} + \sigma_\epsilon \epsilon_{ij}.$$

The model with tastes for products is the special case of Equation (7) with $\sigma_\epsilon = 1$ whereas the pure characteristic model is the special case with $\sigma_\epsilon = 0$.

To see the problems we run into with specifications like (7) take the familiar case where the $\{\epsilon_{ij}\}$ have extreme value distributions and let the interactions with

---

[9] In cases we have worked out this decline will be at an exponential rate. We note that we are implicitly assuming the "environment" does not change as the number of products grows. That is, we are ruling out both technological changes and changes in competing and/or complimentary products that alter the relative benefits of producing in different parts of the characteristic space.

the observable individual characteristics in the utility function in Equation (3) be $f_{ij}(\theta)$, so

(8) $$u_{ij} = f_{ij}(\theta) + \sum_{k=1}^{K} v_{ik} X_{jk} + \sigma_\epsilon \epsilon_{ij}.$$

Assume $\sigma_\epsilon > 0$ (though perhaps very small) so that we can define $\mu_\epsilon \equiv \sigma_\epsilon^{-1}$ and multiply all utilities by it (this does not change the ordering of utilities and hence does not change the implications of the model; we come back to a fuller discussion of normalizations below). Then if $F(\cdot)$ provides the distribution of $v = [v_1, \ldots, v_K]$, the familiar "logit" formula gives us

(9) $$\Pr(i \text{ chose } j) = \int_v \frac{\exp\left(\left[f_{ij}(\theta) + \sum_{k=1}^{K} v_k X_{jk}\right]\mu_\epsilon\right)}{\sum_q \exp\left(\left[f_{i,q}(\theta) + \sum_{k=1}^{K} v_k X_{qk}\right]\mu_\epsilon\right)} dF(v).$$

Since we needed to assume $\sigma_\epsilon > 0$ to obtain the probabilities in (9) there is no "special case" of this formula that gives us the probabilities from the pure characteristic model. However it is straightforward to show that if we consider any sequence of probabilities obtained by letting $\mu_\epsilon \to \infty$ then, under standard regularity conditions, that sequence converges to the probabilities from the pure characteristic model (indeed we can show that the convergence is uniform in θ).[10] That is, the probabilities from the pure characteristics model are a limiting case of the probabilities in (9).

The question then is: what would happen if the data generating process corresponded to the pure characteristics model and yet we estimated the "modified BLP" model represented by (9)? The hope would be that the resulting estimate of μ_ϵ would be large enough for the probabilities in (9) to approximate the probabilities from the pure characteristics model quite well. Indeed, if this were so, then there would be no need for a separate estimation algorithm for the pure characteristics model.

There are, however, reasons to doubt that the modified BLP model would produce estimates that "mimic" the pure characteristic model. First, when we consider consistency we generally assume the true value of the parameter is in a compact set. So were we to apply standard consistency proofs we would have to prove consistency of $1/\mu_\epsilon = \sigma_\epsilon$ (and not μ_ϵ per se). Once we do that, the model's prediction for the sample shares will not converge to the true shares uniformly in θ (these shares are undefined at $\sigma_\epsilon = 0$). So standard consistency proofs do not apply.

Second, one might think that to get estimated probabilities from the modified BLP model that well approximate those of the pure characteristic model we might

[10] The convergence result follows from the fact that for every v, except for a measure zero set of v's that generate a tie, the integrand in (9) converges to one or zero according as the probability of the pure characteristic model is zero or one, and then applying dominated convergence. A covering argument shows that the convergence is uniform in θ.

need to set σ_ϵ close to zero. However, as a practical matter, we then have to compute the exponent of $\mu_\epsilon = 1/\sigma_\epsilon$, and when μ_ϵ is large enough the computer cannot compute $\exp[\mu_\epsilon]$. Third, there is the usual matter of efficiency, i.e., if we know that σ_ϵ is zero, and we had an estimation algorithm that could utilize this fact, we would expect that algorithm to produce more precise estimators of the remaining parameters. Since demand models are frequently estimated on market level data, this "efficiency" issue can be important. Finally, to investigate whether these issues are important in a given setting we need an estimation routine that does not rely on the modified BLP approximation in Equation (9).

This article first develops that algorithm and then compares Monte Carlo results from it to that from the modified BLP model. The comparison is done in two ways. First, we use the probabilities from (9) and a μ_ϵ exogenously set to be as large as our computer can handle. Second, we use the probabilities from (9) to jointly estimate the parameters of the model and μ_ϵ. We will show that sometimes one obtains acceptable estimators for the pure characteristics model using the modified BLP model in (9), and sometimes we do not. Moreover the difference typically depends on characteristics of the data generating process.

We now proceed to provide an algorithm for estimating a pure characteristics model that does not rely on the approximation in Equation (9). We then generate data from the pure characteristic model and ask whether we can characterize (i) when is it easy to estimate the pure characteristic model and (ii) when would the estimates from the model with tastes for products, possibly adjusted to allow for a μ_ϵ as in the modified BLP model in (9), generate implications that are similar to the implications for the pure-characteristics model. The implications we consider in this context are own and cross-price elasticities and the welfare gains from new goods.

3. ESTIMATING THE PURE-CHARACTERISTIC MODEL

Utility in our model is given by

$$(10) \qquad u_{ij} = x_j\beta_i - \alpha_i p_j + \lambda_i \xi_j,$$

for $j = 0,\ldots,J$, where 0 designates the outside good and $j = 1,\ldots,J$ are the goods competing in the market. Here $\beta_{i,k} = \beta_k + v_{i,k}, \alpha_i = \alpha + v_{i,p}$ and we assume that $\lambda_i > 0$ for all i.[11] That is β_k is the mean of the utility for an increment in x_k and $v_{i,k}$ is the individual specific deviation from that mean.

Two assumptions implicit in Equation (10) are worth emphasizing:

(A1) There is only one unobserved product characteristic; i.e., $X = (x, \xi) \in R^k \times R^1$, and

(A2) That ξ is a "vertical" characteristic in the sense that every individual would prefer more of it.

[11] We note that this would be identical to the model used in Das et al. (1995) were we to *omit* their i.i.d. disturbances with full support. Also if there were consumer level data we would let β_i be a function of those variables as in MicroBLP.

3.1. *Further Constraints and Normalizations.* Since the utility functions of consumers can only be identified up to a monotone (in our case affine) transformation, theory implies that we can take each consumer's utility from every choice and

(i) multiply them by a consumer specific positive constant, and
(ii) add to them a consumer specific constant.

We add $-u_{i,0}$ to the utility of each choice so that the utility of the outside option is zero and the utility of the inside options should be interpreted as their utility relative to that of the outside option. Our second normalization is to divide each u_{ij} by λ_i (so that the coefficient of ξ is one for all consumers). Imposing these normalizations and (for notational simplicity) reinterpreting the characteristic values for option j to be the value of the jth option for that characteristic *minus* the value of the outside option for that characteristic, we have

$$(11) \qquad\qquad u_{ij} = x_j \beta_i - \alpha_i p_j + \xi_j,$$

and

$$u_{i,0} = 0.$$

This is identical to the model in BLP *without* their i.i.d. additive component with full support. Our change of notation implies that the ξ variables represent the difference in the unobserved quality of the inside options from that of the outside option.[12]

We still need to choose units.[13] One useful normalization is to set the mean of $\alpha_i = 1$, so that the units of utility and of ξ are in terms of the mean price coefficient.

Our previous work emphasized the reasons for (and the empirical importance of) allowing for unobserved product characteristics, ξ, in estimating discrete choice demand (see Berry, 1994; BLP; and MicroBLP). The ξ are the analog of the disturbances in the standard demand model, i.e., they account for the factors that are unobserved to the econometrician but affect demand. Without them it will typically be impossible to find parameter values that make the implications of the model consistent with the data. Moreover, if we incorporate them and consider any realistic model of market equilibrium we are led to worry about a simultaneous equations bias resulting from price being a function of the ξ.

Of course in reality there may be more than one unobserved characteristic that is omitted from the empirical specification and, provided consumers varied in their

----

[12] This becomes important when we try to measure welfare gains over time, as we are implicitly doing when we construct a price index. This is because the difference in the average estimated level of ξ across periods can be due either to a change in the average unobserved quality of the products in the market being analyzed or to a change in the average value of the outside alternative. For more details and an attempt to decompose movements in ξ into its components see Pakes et al. (1993) and Song (forthcoming).

[13] Multiply all ξ_j, α_i, and β_i, by the same positive constant and the implications of the model are not changed.

relative preferences for the different unobserved characteristics, the model in (11) is, at least strictly speaking, misspecified. Though allowing for one unobserved factor seems to be particularly important in obtaining realistic implications for own and cross price elasticities, our ability to estimate "multiunobserved factor" discrete choice models with such data seems extremely limited.[14]

As noted above the fact that the model with a single unobserved factor might provide good fits "in sample" does not imply that it delivers meaningful welfare measures. On the other hand, if we allow for as many unobserved factors as there are products, then the pure characteristics model with multiple unobserved characteristics has the traditional models with tastes for products as a special case. In this sense the pure characteristics model with *one* unobserved characteristic is an opposite extreme to the model with tastes for products. We might hope that the two models would bound the impacts of unobserved product heterogeneity.

4. ESTIMATING THE MODEL

The issues that arise when estimating the pure characteristics model are similar to those found in estimating more traditional discrete choice models. As a result we use the techniques in BLP (1995) and MicroBLP (2004), and the vast literature cited therein, as starting points. There are, however, four modifications of those techniques we will need in order develop an estimator for the pure characteristics model. The modifications provide

1. A method of calculating the aggregate market share function conditional on the vectors of characteristics and parameters (θ).
2. An argument that proves existence of a unique ξ vector conditional on any vector of model parameters and observed market shares.
3. An algorithm for computing that ξ vector.
4. A limiting distribution of the estimated parameter vector.

The modifications we use to accomplish these tasks imply different computational trade-offs as opposed to the model with tastes for products—differences that play out differently when using different types of data.

4.1. *Computing Market Shares.* In the model with product-specific tastes, market shares can be calculated by a two-step method. The first step conditions on preferences for the product characteristics (the β_i) and integrates out the product-specific tastes. This provides market shares conditional on the β_i. When the additive product-specific tastes has a "logit" form the market shares conditional on the β_i have an analytic form, so that there is no approximation error in calculating them, and they are a smooth function of the β_i. The second step

---

[14] We note here that this is likely to change when richer data are available. For example, Goettler and Shachar (2001) and a related literature in the field of marketing, successfully estimate multiple unobserved product characteristics from data that observe the same consumers making a repeated set of choices, and Heckman and Snyder (1997) have used multifactor discrete choice models to analyze political choice.

follows Pakes (1986) and uses simulation to provide an approximation to the integral defining the expectation (over β_i) of the conditional market shares (i.e., to the aggregate market share).

When there are no additive product-specific tastes we must compute market shares in a different way. A simple two-step replacement is to use the structure of the vertical model to integrate out one of the dimensions of heterogeneity in the pure characteristics model, thereby producing market shares conditional on the rest of the β_i, and then use the suggestion in Pakes (1986) again to compute the aggregate share. Given an appropriate distribution for the dimension of heterogeneity integrated out in the first step (see below), this produces a smooth objective function.

To see how to do this we first consider the simple vertical model

$$(12) \qquad\qquad\qquad u_{ij} = \delta_j - \alpha_i p_j,$$

for $j =, \ldots, J$, where δ_j is product "quality"

$$(13) \qquad\qquad\qquad \delta_j = x_j \beta + \xi_j,$$

and $u_{i,0} = 0$.

Order the goods in terms of increasing price. Then good j is purchased *iff* $u_{ij} > u_{ik}, \forall k \neq j$, or equivalently

$$(14) \qquad \delta_j - \alpha_i p_j > \delta_k - \alpha_i p_k, \Rightarrow \alpha_i(p_j - p_k) < \delta_j - \delta_k, \quad \forall k \neq j.$$

Recall that $(p_j - p_k)$ is positive if $j > k$ and negative otherwise. So a consumer endowed with α_i will buy product j iff

$$(15) \qquad \begin{aligned} \alpha_i &< \min_{k<j} \frac{\delta_j - \delta_k}{(p_j - p_k)} \equiv \bar{\Delta}_j(\delta, p), \quad \text{and} \\ \alpha_i &> \max_{k>j} \frac{\delta_k - \delta_j}{(p_k - p_j)} \equiv \underline{\Delta}_j(\delta, p). \end{aligned}$$

These formulas assume that $0 < j < J$. However, if we set

$$(16) \qquad\qquad \bar{\Delta}_0 = \infty, \quad \text{and} \quad \underline{\Delta}_J = 0$$

they extend to the $j = 0$ (the outside good) and $j = J$ cases.

If the cdf of α is $F(\cdot)$, then the market share of product j is

$$(17) \qquad s_j(x, p, \xi; \theta, F) \equiv (F(\bar{\Delta}_j(x, p, \xi)) - F(\underline{\Delta}_j(x, p, \xi)))1[\bar{\Delta}_j > \underline{\Delta}_j],$$

where here and below $1[\cdot]$ is the indicator function for the condition in the brackets and θ is a vector containing all unknown parameters.

If $\bar{\Delta}_j \leq \underline{\Delta}_j$, then $s_j(\cdot) = 0$. Since the data have positive market shares, the model should predict positive market shares at the true value of the parameters. Note that the vertical model behaves differently then does the model with tastes for products; the latter *never* predicts zero market shares for any parameter value. In the vertical model any parameter vector that generates an ordering that leaves one product with a higher price but lower quality than some other product predicts a zero market share for that product.

4.1.1. *The extension to K dimensions.* Recall that the difference between the vertical model and the pure characteristics model is that in the pure characteristics model characteristics other than price can have coefficients that vary over consumers (the β_i). However, if $u_{ij} = x_j\beta_i - \alpha_i p_j + \xi_j$ then, conditional on β_i, the model is once again a vertical model with cutoff points in the space of α_i (but now the quality levels in those cutoffs depend on the β_i). So to obtain market shares in this case we do the calculation in (17) conditional on the β_i and then integrate over the β_i distribution.

More precisely we begin as before by ordering the goods by their price. Then for a fixed β we can compute the cutoff points $\bar{\Delta}(x, p, \xi, \beta)_j$ and $\underline{\Delta}(x, p, \xi, \beta)_j$, so the market share function is

$$(18)\, s_j(x, p, \xi; \theta, F, G) \equiv \int (F(\bar{\Delta}_j(\delta, p, X, \beta) \,|\, \beta)$$
$$- F(\underline{\Delta}_j(\delta, p, X, \beta) \,|\, \beta))1[\bar{\Delta}_j(\cdot, \beta) > \underline{\Delta}_j(\cdot, \beta)]\, dG(\beta),$$

where $F(\cdot \,|\, \beta)$ is the cdf of α given β and $G(\cdot)$ is the cdf of β.

That is the pure characteristic model's market share function can be expressed as a mixture of the market share functions of the pure vertical models. The conditioning argument used here avoids the difficult problem of solving for the exact region of the β_i space on which a consumer prefers product j.[15] It does, however, produce an integral that is typically not analytic. So we use a simulation estimator to approximate it. That is, we obtain an unbiased estimator of the integral by taking ns draws from the distribution G of the random coefficients β and then calculating

(19)

$$s_j(x, p, \xi; \theta, F, G_{ns})$$

$$\equiv \frac{1}{ns}\sum_i (F(\bar{\Delta}_j(x, p, \xi, \beta_i) \,|\, \beta_i) - F(\underline{\Delta}_j(x, p, \xi, \beta_i) \,|\, \beta_i))1[\bar{\Delta}_j(\cdot, \beta_i) > \underline{\Delta}_j(\cdot, \beta_i)],$$

where $G_{ns}(\cdot)$ is notation for the empirical distribution of the simulated β_i.[16]

---

[15] Feenstra and Levinsohn (1995) directly calculate the region of integration, $A_j \subset \mathcal{R}^K$ such that if $(\beta, \alpha) \in A_j$ then good j is purchased directly, but this becomes quite complicated.

[16] The calculation of market shares is further simplified by noting that a necessary and sufficient condition for the indicator function's condition for product j to be one conditional on a particular value for β is that $\max_{q<j} \underline{\Delta}_q(\cdot, \beta_i) < \underline{\Delta}_j(\cdot, \beta_i)$ (recall that the j-ordering is the price ordering). As a result for a given value of β our program first computes the $\{\underline{\Delta}_j(\cdot, \beta)\}$, then drops those goods for whom $\underline{\Delta}(\cdot, \beta)$ are "out of order," and then computes the shares.

Note that if $F(\cdot)$ has a density (with respect to Lebesgue measure) that is a differentiable function of the parameter vector, then the market share function is a continuously differentiable function of the parameter vector. Of course, this introduces simulation error into the calculated shares, just as in the original BLP.

4.2. *Existence and Uniqueness of the $\xi(\cdot)$ Function.* Recall that BLP proceed in three steps. First, they show that their model associates a unique $\xi(\cdot)$ with any triple consisting of a vector of parameters, a vector of observed shares, and a distribution over individual characteristics. They then provide a contraction mapping that computes the $\xi(\cdot)$. Finally, they make an identifying assumption on the distribution of ξ and estimate by finding that value of θ that makes the theoretical restrictions implied by the identifying assumption as "close as possible" to being satisfied.

We will mimic those steps. The first task is to show that for every θ and distribution of consumer characteristics there is a unique value of ξ that equates the model's predicted shares to the observed shares, s^o. As in BLP, we assume that s^o, the ($J + 1$-dimensional) vector of observed market shares, is in the interior of the J-dimensional unit simplex (all market shares are strictly between zero and one.) Simplify notation and let $s(\theta, \xi) \equiv s(x, p, \xi; \theta, F, G)$ for any fixed (F, G, x, p).

Consider the system of $J + 1$ equations

$$(20) \qquad\qquad\qquad s(\theta, \xi) = s^o.$$

Our goal is to provide conditions under which, given the normalization $\xi_0 = 0$, this system has exactly one solution, $\xi(\theta, s^o)$.

Let the discrete choice market share, as a function of all unobserved product characteristics (including ξ_0) be

$$(21) \qquad\qquad\qquad s_j(\xi_j, \xi_{-j}, 0),$$

where ξ_j is the own-product characteristic, ξ_{-j} is the vector of rival-product characteristics, and 0 is the (normalized) value of ξ_0.

Now define the "element-by-element" inverse for product j, $r_j(s_j, \xi_{-j})$, as

$$(22) \qquad\qquad\qquad s_j(r_j, \xi_{-j}, 0) = s_j.$$

The vector of element-by-element inverses, say $r(s, \xi)$, when viewed as a function of ξ, takes $R^J \to R^J$. It is more convenient to work with a fixed point defined by the element-by-element inverse than to work directly with the equations defined by (20). In particular, the inverse of the market share function (i.e., $\xi(\cdot)$) exists and is unique if there is a unique solution to the fixed point

$$(23) \qquad\qquad\qquad \xi = r(s, \xi).$$

THEOREM 1. *Suppose the discrete choice market share function has the following properties:*

(i) Monotonicity. s_j is weakly increasing and continuous in ξ_j and weakly decreasing in ξ_{-j}. Also, for all ξ_{-j} there must be values of ξ_j that set s_j arbitrarily close to zero and values of ξ_j that set s_j arbitrarily close to one.

(ii) Linearity of utility in ξ. If the ξ for every good (including the outside good) is increased by an equal amount, then no market share changes.

(iii) Substitutes with Some Other Good. Whenever s is strictly between 0 and 1, every product must be a strict substitute with some other good. In particular, if $\xi' \leq \xi$, with strict inequality holding for at least one component, then there is a product (j) such that

$$(24) \qquad s_j(\xi_j, \xi_{-j}, 0) < s_j(\xi_j, \xi'_{-j}, 0).$$

Similarly, if $\xi' \geq \xi$, with strict inequality holding for at least one component, then there is a product (j) such that

$$(25) \qquad s_j(\xi_j, \xi_{-j}, 0) > s_j(\xi_j, \xi'_{-j}, 0).$$

Then, for any market share vector s that is strictly interior to the unit simplex: (i) an inverse exists, and (ii) this inverse is unique.

COMMENTS.

1. The theorem is true independent of the values of (θ, F, G, x, p) that go into the calculation of $s(\cdot)$ provided those values imply an $s(\cdot)$ function that satisfies conditions (i) and (iii). It is easy to verify that those conditions will be satisfied for any finite θ as long as F has a density that is positive on the real line (a.e. β). In particular, $G(\cdot)$ need not have a density (w.r.t. Lebesgue measure), and indeed the simulated $G_{ns}(\cdot)$ we typically use in computation will not have a density.

2. The *Linearity* assumption is redundant if we stick with the model in (11). That is, a nonlinear model that was linear only in ξ would have exactly the same properties as those developed here provided it satisfied the usual identification conditions.

PROOF. Existence follows from the argument in Berry (1994). Our first step in proving uniqueness is to show that the map $r(\xi, s)$ is a weak contraction (a contraction with modulus ≤ 1), a fact that we use later in computation.

Take any ξ and $\xi' \in R^J$ and let $\|\xi - \xi'\|_{\sup} = d > 0$. From (22) and Linearity

$$(26) \qquad s_j(r_j + d, \xi_{-j} + d, d) = s_j.$$

By Monotonicity

$$(27) \qquad s_j(r_j + d, \xi', 0) \geq s_j,$$

and by (iii) there is at least one good, say good q, for which this inequality is strict (any good that substitutes with the outside good). By Monotonicity, this implies that, for all j,

(28) $$r'_j \leq r_j + d$$

with strict inequality for good q. A symmetric argument shows that the condition

(29) $$s_j(r_j - d, \xi_{-j} - d, -d) = s_j$$

implies that, for all j,

(30) $$r'_j \geq r_j - d$$

with strict inequality for at least one good. Clearly then $\|r(\xi', s) - r(\xi, s)\| \leq d$, which proves that the inverse function is a weak contraction.

Now assume that both ξ and ξ' satisfy (23), and that $\|\xi - \xi'\|_{\sup} = \kappa > 0$, i.e., that there are two distinct solutions to the fixed point. In particular, let $\xi_q - \xi'_q = \kappa$. Without loss of generality assume that q substitutes to the outside good (if this were not the case, then renormalize in terms of the good that substitutes with q and repeat the argument that follows). From above, $s_q(r_q + \kappa, \xi'_{-q}, 0) > s_q$. But this last expression equals $s_q(\xi'_q, \xi'_{-q}, 0)$, which, since ξ' is a fixed point, equals s_q, a contradiction. ∎

4.3. *Computation of $\xi(\cdot)$.* We provide three different methods for computing $\xi(\cdot)$. They are

   (a) use of BLP's contraction mapping for the modified BLP model given in Equation (9) with μ_ϵ set as high as is computationally practical,
   (b) use of the element by element inverse introduced in the proof of uniqueness, and
   (c) a homotopy method similar to those used in the literature on the computation of general equilibrium models.

We introduce all three of these methods because no single method works well in all situations. Each of the methods given above has a limitation that has proven to be problematic in certain Monte Carlo examples. The first method is fast but will be inaccurate if μ_ϵ cannot be set sufficiently high, and there are data designs where good approximations require a μ_ϵ larger than this algorithm appears able to handle. The second method is not guaranteed to converge at any particular speed and, in fact, appears to converge very slowly in some of our Monte Carlo runs. The third method is, at least in principle, guaranteed to be converge, but, as we shall show, can also be fairly slow.

As a result our suggestion is to use the first method when practical and a combination of all three when necessary. As is explained below, the combination begins with the modified BLP model with a large fixed μ_ϵ. It then switches to a homotopy when the rate of change in the sup norm for the contraction used in modified BLP is too small. The homotopy is constructed from the element by element inverse introduced in the proof of uniqueness. Finally when the homotopy is close to the truth and is not progressing quickly enough, we switch to a Newton method.

4.3.1. *BLP's contraction and the modified BLP model.* For a fixed μ_ϵ this method is just the BLP method applied using the normalization of this article. The question that remains is how to chose μ_ϵ. As is explained above if one chooses a value of μ_ϵ that is too small, the approximation will not be adequate whereas if one chooses a value that is too high, the computer will not be able to calculate the needed exponents. Our Monte Carlo results experiment with two ways of setting μ_ϵ. In one we set μ_ϵ as high a value as seems initially practical and then reduce it if necessary. In the second, we estimate μ_ϵ together with the rest of the parameters of the model.

4.3.2. *Element-by-element inverse.* This procedure uses the element-by-element inverse shown to lead to a weak contraction in the proof of the theorem in Section 4.2 (i.e., the $r(s, \xi)$ in the proof of Theorem 1). If the weak contraction had modulus that was strictly less than one, this contraction would be guaranteed to converge to the fixed point at a geometric rate. Unfortunately we have been unable to prove that the modulus is strictly less than one, and in Monte Carlo studies we find that it sometimes contracts so slowly as to become useless.

To implement this procedure we use the simulated pure characteristic share function as given in (19). That is we begin with a candidate ξ vector, hold ξ_{-1} fixed, then find the value of ξ_1 that makes the simulated share for the first product match the actual share for that product, and proceed similarly for $j = 2, \ldots, J$ (always holding the ξ_{-j} vector at its initial value). This provides the new ξ vector, which is then passed through the same algorithm. We continue in this fashion until the predicted shares at the new vector match the observed shares.

In practice, sometimes this method provides large improvements for the first few iterations and then slows nearly to a stop. If the predicted shares at that point are positive, we can try a simple Newton method to look for the solution. If that fails, we then require our third method.

4.3.3. *Homotopy.* Homotopy methods are frequently used with great success to find fixed points in the computable general equilibrium literature.[17] The basic idea is to consider a sequence of objective functions formed as a weighted average of the true fixed point problem and a similar problem with a known solution. We begin with the objective function that places all weight on the fixed point with a known solution, and slowly change the weights to place more weight on the true problem.

Starting with the standard fixed-point homotopy we have

$$(31) \qquad h(\xi, t, \xi_0) = (1 - t) * (\xi - \xi_0) + t * (\xi - r(s, \xi)),$$

where

(a) t is a parameter that takes values between zero and one,
(b) the function $r(\cdot)$ returns the element-by-element inverse of the market share function (see Equation 22), and

[17] See, for example, Whitehead (1993) and Eaves and Schmedders (1999).

(c) ξ_0 is a good initial guess at the true ξ^i; in particular, take it as the output one of the other methods when those have failed to converge.

For each value of t, consider the value of ξ that sets $h(\xi, t, \xi_0)$ to zero. Call this $\xi(t, \xi_0)$. For $t = 0$ the solution is trivially the starting guess of ξ_0. For $t = 1$ the solution is the fixed point that we are looking for. The homotopy methods suggest starting at $t = 0$, where the solution is trivial, and slowly moving t toward one. The series of solutions $\xi(t)$ should then move toward the fixed-point solution $\xi(1)$. If t is moved slowly enough, then by continuity the new solution should be close to the old solution and therefore "easy" to find (say, by a Newton method starting at the prior solution).

In our problem a version of the fixed-point homotopy is a strong contraction when $t < 1$, making it easy to compute the ξ from successive t. That is, the homotopy implies that

$$(32) \qquad \xi(t, \xi_0) = (1 - t) * \xi_0 + t * r\left(s, \xi(t, \xi_0)\right),$$

which, when viewed as an operator which takes $\mathcal{R}^J$ into itself, is a contraction mapping with modulus less than t. This suggests a recursive solution method, taking an initial guess, ξ, for the solution $\xi(t, \xi_0)$ and then placing this guess on the RHS of (32) to create a new guess, ξ':

$$(33) \qquad \xi' = (1 - t) * \xi_0 + t * r(s, \xi).$$

Equation (33) is a recursive method suggested by the logic of the homotopy. We can set t close to one and get a reasonably good approximation to ξ.

Our "homotopy" method involves fixing a value for t and then using Equation (33) to recursively compute a value of ξ that solves the fixed-point implied by that equation. For t sufficiently less than one, this is very fast. As t approaches one, the modulus of contraction for fixed point in (33) also approaches one.

In practice, we can start with a fairly large value for t, say $t = 0.99$, because that still gives us a quick answer. However, as t gets closer and closer to one, it is sometimes necessary to move t very slowly while solving for the next $\xi^*(t_k)$ via Newton's method. However, whereas the element-by-element inverse can slow down fairly far away from the truth, the homotopy method in practice gets us much closer to the correct answer before slowing down.

When we refer to the "homotopy" method in remainder of the article, we actually mean an integrated routine that incorporates all of the methods of this subsection. First, we fix a "high" value of μ_ϵ and use the BLP contraction (switching to a lower value of μ_ϵ if numeric errors arise). This is quite fast. Then, if necessary we switch to the element-by-element inverse, in conjunction with periodic Newton steps when possible, to see if this gives us a quick answer. If not, we only then move to the homotopy method defined by (33). For small problems (like our initial Monte Carlo examples), we look for a very precise answer with t very close to or equal to one and often succeed in solving the original fixed point nearly exactly. For large and difficult problems (like our last Monte Carlo example below), we apply (33) only for a limited set of values of t (say, $t = 0.99, 0.995$, and 0.998) without trying to push t closer to one. These few steps move the computed δ's quite far, and the resulting Monte Carlo estimates seem good, whereas the computational burden is still manageable.

The computational burden in the pure characteristics model also turns out to be related to asymptotic behavior as the number of products increases. The next subsection provides an overview of related results on limit theorems.

4.4. *Limit Theorems and Simulation Error.* Berry et al. (2004b) provides limit theorems for the parameter estimates from differentiated product models both with and without tastes for products. The limit theorems for the different models differ, which leads to a better understanding of the differences in the computational properties of the estimators for these models. Indeed, together with the discussion above, they imply computational trade-offs that will make different models easier to compute in different situations.

In particular, the argument in Berry et al. (2004b) shows that in BLP-style random coefficient logit models, the calculated unobservables, ξ, are very sensitive to simulation error. Therefore, the number of simulation draws has to increase rapidly with the number of products. On the other hand, in pure characteristic models, the calculation of ξ is much less sensitive to simulation error. A practical implication is that we may be able to use many fewer simulation draws to estimate pure characteristics models, as opposed to random coefficient logit models. This advantage can partly offset the otherwise more burdensome computational problem presented by the pure characteristics model.

The difference in the limit properties of the estimators from the two model stems from differences in the mapping from market shares to $\xi(\cdot)$ as the number of products, J, grows large (and therefore at least some of the market shares become small.) Take the logit model as a special case of the original BLP. In the pure logit model, no simulation is necessary, but errors in observed market shares, s_j, might similarly be introduced by sampling error from a finite sample of consumers. Berry et al. (2004b) show that simulation error introduces the same sort of problem in the random coefficients logit model that sampling error introduces in the logit model.

In the pure logit model, it is well known that the solution for ξ is analytic:

$$(34) \qquad \xi_j = \ln(s_j) - \ln(s_0) - x_j\beta,$$

so that

$$(35) \qquad \frac{\partial \xi_j}{\partial s_j} = \frac{1}{s_j}.$$

As J becomes large, by necessity many market shares must become small and so the calculated ξ_j's become very sensitive to any error in s_j, whether from a small sample of consumers or from simulation error.

This effect is natural in logit-style models, where substitution patterns between products are very diffuse. When there are many products in such models, small changes in ξ produce only small changes in observed market shares—i.e., $\partial s_j/\partial \xi$ is small. It may be intuitive, then, that the derivative of the inverse mapping $\partial \xi_j/\partial s_j$, can be correspondingly large under the same circumstances. But when ξ is sensitive to errors in computed market shares, a large number of simulation draws will be necessary to compute accurate ξ's.

Pure characteristics models have different properties. In these models, competition becomes very localized and "fierce" as the number of products increases. That is, $\partial s_j/\partial \xi_j$ becomes very large. It may be intuitive, then, that the derivative of the inverse mapping $\partial \xi_j/\partial s_j$, can be correspondingly small under the same circumstances. So, a relatively small number of simulation draws may be adequate to compute accurate accurate ξ's.

For example, Berry et al. (2004b) formally show that to obtain asymptotically normal estimates of the parameter vector in the vertical model the number of simulation draws has to grow only at rate J, whereas in logit-style models the number of draws has to grow at the much faster rate J^2.

Similarly, in Monte Carlo exercises they show that as a practical matter pure characteristics models can be estimated with many fewer simulation draws than in BLP-style models. The differences between the two models increase in the number of products marketed, but it is clear that they can be large for numbers of products that are relevant for empirical work. For example, for the limiting distribution to provide an accurate description of the Monte Carlo distribution of the vertical model with up to 200 products, 50 simulation draws seem to suffice. In contrast, the logit model with 100 products requires over 2000 simulation draws.

The advantage held by pure characteristics models in controlling simulation error provides a partial offset to their otherwise greater computational complexity. Readers desiring a (much) more formal treatment of simulation error, sample size and limit theorems in these models should consult Berry et al. (2004b).

4.5. *Computational Comparisons.* Gathering the results of prior sections, we have two theoretical reasons for expecting the computational burden of the pure characteristics model to differ from the computational burden of the model with tastes for products, but they have opposite implications:

(a) First, the number of simulation draws needed to get accurate estimates of the moment conditions must grow at rate J^2 in the model with a taste for products, whereas it need only grow at rate J in the pure characteristics model.
(b) Second, the contraction mapping used to compute the inverse is expected to converge at a geometric rate for the model with tastes for products, but we do not have such a rate for the pure characteristics model.

The first argument implies that computation should be easier in the pure characteristics model, the second that computation should be easier in the model with tastes for products. Of course which of the two effects turns out to dominate may well depend on features of the data being analyzed: the number of products, the number of times the inverse must be evaluated in the estimation algorithm (which typically is related to the number of parameters), and so on.

There is a great deal of evidence on the speed and accuracy of BLP's algorithm for estimating the model with tastes for products (and we will provide a bit more below). As a result the next section focuses on the properties of the algorithms available for estimating the pure characteristic model.

5. EVIDENCE FROM SIMULATED DATA

Our goal in this section is to investigate the properties of alternative algorithms for estimating the pure characteristic model. As noted, the computational difficulties that arise in the pure characteristic model are a result of the need to compute the δ that solve the fixed point in Equation (23). We compare algorithms based on the following three different methods for computing this fixed point:

(a) The "homotopy" method outlined in the text. This begins with the weak contraction obtained from the element by element inverse in Equation (23), moves to the homotopy in Equation (32) when the element-by-element inverse fails to improve the objective function, and then moves to a Newton method when the homotopy method gets close enough to the true solution.

(b) The second method sets the μ_ϵ in Equation (9) to some fixed number, and proceeds using BLP's contraction.

(c) The third method only differs from the second in that it estimates μ_ϵ along with the other parameters of the model.

The comparison will be done in terms of both compute times and the precision of various estimates. We consider precision in three steps: first of the estimates of the δ themselves, then of the estimates of the parameters of the underlying model, and finally of the estimates of the implications of interest to applied studies (own and cross price elasticities and welfare).

5.1. *A Model for Simulation.* For most of the results we report, data are drawn from a model with utility function

$$(36) \qquad u_{ij} = \delta_j + \sigma_x v_{ix} x_j - (\alpha_i * p_j),$$

where

$$(37) \qquad \ln(\alpha_i) = \sigma_p v_{ip}$$

and

$$(38) \qquad \delta_j = \beta_0 + \beta_x x_j + \xi_j.$$

The consumer-specific random terms (v_{ix}, v_{ip}) are distributed standard normal (so that α_i is log normal, with a normalized mean.)

The x variable is drawn as twice a uniform $(0,1)$ draw that is firm specific plus 1/2 a uniform $(0,1)$ draw that is common to all firms in a market. This is to allow for within-market correlation across observables. Initially ξ is drawn as a uniform on $(-0.5, 0.5)$. Note that the variance of x is then greater than that of ξ, which is likely to help the Monte Carlo find good parameter estimates with limited data. Later we will increase the variance of ξ and see how this affects the results. Price, p, is set equal to a convex function of δ, $p_j = e^{\delta_j}/20$, and this insures positive shares for all goods (though some of the shares get very small when we consider markets with a large number of products). Note also that p is a function of δ and δ is a function of ξ, so that p and ξ are correlated in the simulated data sets. Finally, the actual consumer choice data is generated from 5000 independent draws on v_i who choose optimally given the true values of the parameter.

5.2. *Calculating δ.*   We begin with the calculation of delta. We can illustrate our results here by looking at a simple example with only five products. The example uses randomly drawn data from the base model of the last subsection. The first column of Table 1 shows the "true" values of the randomly drawn δ.

With five products and our data-creation model our homotopy method can almost always find a δ vector that exactly reproduces the "true" market shares. The first homotopy column uses the same 5000 draws on v used to create the data, so it has no simulation error and it recovers the exact values of the true δ's. The second homotopy column uses only 500 simulation draws and so some error is introduced. Although the homotopy method with simulation error fits the shares to computer precision, it does so with δ's that vary from the originals. On the other hand, even with simulation error the order of the δ's is preserved. The last row of the table gives the computational time relative to using the full homotopy method with 5000 draws. Decreasing the number of draws on v decreases compute time almost in the proportion of the decrease in the number of draws.

The columns labeled "Modified BLP Contraction: Fixed μ_ϵ" use the contraction in BLP with the shares modified as in Equation (9). Recall that this multiplies the variance of the Type II extreme value errors by μ_ϵ^{-1}. In Table 1 we first look at columns that use the same 5000 draws on v with μ_ϵ set at 1, which gives us back

TABLE 1

AN EXAMPLE OF CALCULATING δ USING DIFFERENT METHODS

	True	Homotopy		Modified BLP Contraction; Fixed μ_ϵ			
				5000	5000	5000	500
nsim	5000	5000	500	$\mu_\epsilon = 1$	$\mu_\epsilon = 10$	$\mu_\epsilon = 50$	$\mu_\epsilon = 50$
δ_1	2.99	2.99	3.14	3.08	3.02	3.04	3.25
δ_2	3.21	3.21	3.36	2.09	3.19	3.26	3.51
δ_3	3.56	3.56	3.71	3.13	3.60	3.62	3.94
δ_4	4.04	4.04	4.27	4.13	4.10	4.10	4.61
δ_5	4.10	4.10	4.32	2.68	4.06	4.16	4.65
Rel. Time:		1	0.15	0.02	0.12	0.58	0.03

BLP's contraction, and then μ_ϵ set to 10 and 50, respectively. In the last column, simulation error is again introduced by using only 500 draws with $\mu_\epsilon = 50$.

With $\mu_\epsilon = 1$ there is little correlation between the true δ and those obtained from the contraction. On the other hand the compute time is only (1/50)th of the compute time for the full homotopy. With $\mu_\epsilon = 10$ only one of the δ obtained from the contraction is "out of order." When we get to $\mu_\epsilon = 50$ the order of the δ obtained from the contraction is correct, though they still have a 1% or 2% error in their values. Now however the compute time is 60% of the compute time for the full homotopy. There is also some indication that even at $\mu_\epsilon = 50$ the modified BLP contraction is more sensitive to simulation error.

We note that this is illustrative of the results we got on computing δ with other sample designs. So we conclude that from the point of view of estimating the δ it might be efficient to go to the modified BLP contraction, but only if μ_ϵ is kept very high.

5.3. Sample Designs.

The results for the remainder of the issues we investigated depended somewhat on the sample designs. The major feature of the design that seemed relevant was the number of products marketed. So we focused on two sample designs: one where there are a small number of products marketed but a reasonably large number of markets, and one with a large number of products marketed but a small number of markets.

The sample with a small number of products marketed consists of 20 markets, and for each market the number of products was chosen randomly from a distribution that put equal weight on $[2, \ldots, 10]$. With this design estimation is very fast and we have experimented with a number of alternative assumptions, some of which will be illustrated below. The sample with a large number of products has 100 products per market, but only three markets. The homotopy's compute time is quite large under this sample design, and as a result we have done less experimentation with it. All samples used 5000 simulation draws to construct the model's predictions for market shares (i.e., this is the size of the consumer sample).

5.3.1. Parameter estimates: small number of products.

First, we look at estimates of parameter values in Tables 2 and 3. The instruments used are a constant, x, x^2, the mean x in the market and the minimum distance to the nearest x.[18]

Starting with Table 2 we see that with a small number of products per market, and a small variance on the unobservable, the modified BLP contraction mapping with a μ_ϵ set exogenously to 30 does quite well, not noticeably worse than our full homotopy. However, to get the performance of the two algorithms to be comparable when the distribution of ξ had more variance we needed to push μ_ϵ up to 50. Computational problems made it difficult to push μ_ϵ much higher than this.

---

[18] We also tried an approximation to "optimal instruments" as in Berry et al. (1999) but this had little effect on the results.

TABLE 2

MONTE CARLO RESULTS, SMALL NUMBER OF PRODUCTS (MODIFED BLP CONTRACTION
WITH FIXED μ_ϵ VERSUS HOMOTOPY)

	(1)	(2)	(3)	(4)
Method	Mod. BLP	Homotopy	Mod. BLP	Homotopy
Scale (μ_ϵ):	30	n.r.	50	n.r.
$\xi_j =$	$U(-\frac{1}{2}, \frac{1}{2})$	$U(-\frac{1}{2}, \frac{1}{2})$	$U(-1.5, 1.5)$	$U(-1.5, 1.5)$
$\sigma_x (=1)$	1.04	1.03	1.24	1.26
	(0.04)	(0.03)	(0.06)	(0.06)
$\sigma_p (=1)$	1.00	0.98	1.02	1.02
	(0.01)	(0.01)	(0.03)	(0.03)
$\beta_0 (=2)$	2.06	2.00	2.34	2.33
	(0.05)	(0.05)	(0.10)	(0.09)
$\beta_x (=1)$	0.99	1.00	1.04	1.05
	(0.01)	(0.01)	(0.02)	(0.03)

TABLE 3

SMALL NUMBER OF PRODUCTS, ESTIMATED μ_ϵ

		(1)	(2)
ξ Distribution		$U(-\frac{1}{2}, \frac{1}{2})$	$U(-1.5, 1.5)$
nsim	True	500	500
σ_x	1	1.14	1.64
		(0.04)	(0.08)
σ_p	1	1.03	1.09
		(0.01)	(0.03)
β_0	2	2.19	2.79
		(0.06)	(0.12)
β_x	1	1.00	1.03
		(0.01)	(0.03)
Scale, μ_ϵ	∞	34.08	15.50
		(3.31)	(1.98)
μ_ϵ (Median)	∞	17.81	4.67

NOTES: All estimates are means across 100 simulated data sets. Estimated standard deviations of the mean estimates are given in parentheses. The homotopy estimates took on the order of 10 times as long to compute.

The numbers reported underneath the coefficient estimates are the standard errors of the estimates across different Monte Carlo samples. Since the estimates are a mean across these 100 samples, the standard error of this mean should be about one-10th of the reported standard error. So the asymptotic approximation of the distribution of the estimator is underestimating the estimator's variance by quite a bit with these sample sizes. Also all algorithms do worse when we increase the variance of ξ; i.e., intuitively we need more data to obtain a given level of precision as the unobservable variance increases.

One problem with using the modified BLP contraction with a fixed μ_ϵ is that we would not know how high we needed to set μ_ϵ to get reasonable approximations if we were working with a real data set. Moreover, we experimented some to find the best values for these runs. We rejected any value for the fixed scale that resulted in numeric errors, and in the first experiment $\mu_\epsilon = 30$ worked a bit better than $\mu_\epsilon = 50$ even though there were no obvious numeric errors.[19]

An alternative that avoids the problem of choosing the scale is to let the data try to estimate μ_ϵ. Table 3 presents the results from this exercise. We note that in several cases the scale parameter, which is now set by the search algorithm, increased to the point where numeric errors occurred. In those cases, we fixed μ_ϵ at 50. In one of those cases, even $\mu_\epsilon = 50$ caused problems and so we fixed μ_ϵ at 25.[20]

Table 3 presents both the estimates of the parameter of interest and of the "auxiliary" parameter μ_ϵ. In particular, it provides both the mean and median of the estimates of μ_ϵ across runs. The first column of results uses the base specification for the unobservable, and the second column increases the variance of the unobservable. In both cases this gives us results that are worse than those obtained in Table 2, though probably still acceptable, especially for the sample design with less variance in ξ.

We conclude that with a small number of products, the modified BLP contraction with μ_ϵ fixed at a large value we may do well, especially if the variance of of the unobservable is small. However, at high values of μ_ϵ numeric errors are quite common, and when we estimate μ_ϵ instead of fixing it exogenously, we do seem to do noticeably worse.

5.3.2. *Substitution effects: small number of products.* Table 2 shows that, for the example data-generating process, if we could fix μ_ϵ at a large enough value the modified BLP estimation does about as well as the homotopy. On the other hand if we did not know what value was large enough and consequently decided to estimate μ_ϵ, then Table 3 indicates that how well we do depends on the variance in ξ relative to the variance in x. On the other hand there is an advantage of the modified BLP algorithm that estimates μ_ϵ over the fixed point homotopy; it is much easier to compute. So, just on the basis of parameter estimates, which procedure seems the best one to apply depends on the nature of the problem. Of course parameter estimates are not usually the objects of interest; rather it is their implications we are usually concerned with.

Own and cross-price elasticities are one frequent focus of empirical applications in I.O. If we use a modified BLP contraction to estimate parameters we still have more than one option for computing own and cross-price elasticities. The standard procedure would be to use the parameter estimates obtained from the modified contraction together with its functional forms to compute the elasticities.

---

[19] This could be because of approximation errors in the computer routines that calculate the exponents of large numbers.

[20] We also tried experiments where we imposed the traditional logit scale normalization of one, while dropping our current normalization on the price coefficient. Those runs where much less likely to converge without numeric errors.

TABLE 4

EXAMPLES OF SUBSTITUTION PATTERNS

			Modified BLP		Blp Parms, But $\partial s/\partial p$ via	
Product	True	Homotopy	Fix $\mu_\epsilon = 50$	Estimate μ_ϵ	Homotopy	Mod. BLP
1	−0.6027	−0.6198	−0.7313	−0.4130	−0.5241	−0.6353
		(0.0337)	(0.0220)	(0.0232)	(0.0267)	(0.0226)
2	0.1981	0.2093	0.2531	0.1656	0.1629	0.2034
		(0.0233)	(0.0140)	(0.0139)	(0.0133)	(0.0144)
3	0.1621	0.1624	0.1183	0.0331	0.1461	0.1096
		(0.0106)	(0.0022)	(0.0059)	(0.0129)	(0.0024)
4	0.0000	0.0002	0.0278	0.0348	0.0001	0.0172
		(0.0001)	(0.0038)	(0.0042)	(0.0001)	(0.0031)
5	0.0204	0.0252	0.0292	0.0235	0.0212	0.0296
		(0.0026)	(0.0024)	(0.0023)	(0.0023)	(0.0031)

Alternatively, we could subsitute the parameter estimates from the modified BLP contraction that estimates μ_ϵ into the share equations generated from the pure characteristic models and calculate the own and cross-price elasticities from this "hybrid" model.

There is some intuition for this hybrid model. We know that we could choose a scale parameter large enough to make the predictions of the modified BLP algorithm as close as we like to those of the pure characteristic model that generates our data. The problem is that the BLP estimation algorithm may not be able to pick out a value of μ_ϵ that is large enough for the approximation in Equation (9) to be accurate. However if the only error in the BLP estimates were in the estimate of μ_ϵ, so that the problem in estimating the scale did not "spill over" to other coefficients, we would expect the hybrid model to produce exact estimates of the appropriate elasticities.

Table 4 provides an example of results on how well the methods reproduce the true substitution patterns. The example considers one market from the data-generating process that has more spread in the unobservables and therefore less precise estimates (i.e., the one in the last column of Tables 2 and 3). The column labeled "true" gives the true derivatives of the market share of the first (lowest priced) product in that market with respect to the row product. The first entry is therefore an own-price derivative, the second entry is the cross-price derivative of product one with respect to product two, and so forth.

The last five columns of Table 4 recompute those derivatives using five different methods that differ from one another in either the parameters used or in the functional forms used to compute the derivatives conditional on the parameter estimates. They are (i) estimates from the homotopy and functional forms from the pure characteristic model, (ii) estimates from the modified BLP algorithm with μ_ϵ set to 50 and those functional forms, (iii) estimates from the modified BLP algorithm that estimates μ_ϵ and those functional forms, (iv) estimates from the modified BLP algorithm that estimates μ_ϵ *but* functional forms from the pure charactersitic model, and (v) estimates from the modified BLP algorithm that estimates μ_ϵ but the functional forms from the modified BLP algorithm with μ_ϵ set to 50. We do the computation for each of the parameters generated by a single Monte Carlo run in the earlier tables, and then average across the Monte Carlo sample of parameters. This approximates the answer we would get by averaging over the asymptotic distribution of the parameters as estimated by the appropriate method. We also provide the standard deviation of the calculated sample mean.

Table 4 indicates that use of the homotopy estimates and the functional form from from the pure characteristics model does a much better job of reproducing the true substitution pattern than using either of the modified BLP estimates and their functional forms. This is especially true relative to the model with an estimated μ_ϵ, but even the model that fixed μ_ϵ at a large number, and consequently does not have great computational advantages, misses rather dramatically on the fourth elasticity. The surprising result in this table is how well we do using the parameters of the modified BLP algorithm that estimates μ_ϵ and the functional forms from the pure characteristic model. Indeed even using the functional forms from the modified BLP algorithm that sets μ_ϵ to 50 does fairly well, again except for the fourth elasticity.

Of course this is just one example, and it need not be indicative of what would happen under different data designs. Still this example does have the following implications:

(a) "Good" parameter estimates from a particular model need not imply that use of those parameter estimates and the model's functional forms lead to good predictions for the implications of interest, i.e., in our case the functional form approximation used to compute derivatives matters, and

(b) even if we use the modified BLP contraction for estimation, we may not want to use the functional form in Equation (9) to compute our estimates of the implications of the parameter estimates.

5.4. *A Large Number of Products.*   In this section, we consider a sample with a larger number of products (an average of 100 per market) and a smaller number of markets (three) structured as a time series on a market with improving characteristics. In particular, we use the data on the evolution of megahertz in the computer market from 1995 to 1997, taken from Pakes (2003), to pattern the x's in our sample.

Year:	1	2	3
Min Mhz:	25	25	33
Max Mhz:	133	200	240

The Monte Carlo sample lets the number of products increase across the three years, from 75 to 100 and then to 125, and has x's drawn from uniform on min-max range of megahertz (divided by 10). So that the ξ's scale with x, the ξ's are set equal to the range of the megahertz for the year times $(2u_i - 1)$ where u_i is a draw from uniform on $[0, 1]$.

The δ's are determined as above $(\delta_j = \beta_0 + \beta_1 x_j + \xi_j)$, as are the parameters and the distribution of α_i. To mimic a high tech market we let prices fall over time, t, according to

$$(39) \qquad\qquad \ln(p_j) = (t-1) * \ln(0.7) + 1.1 * \ln(\delta_j).$$

Note that again price is convex in δ_j, thus assuring positive shares. However the shares we generate are sometimes very small, smaller than we typically observe in actual data sets[21] (see below). Price for the same set of characteristics declines at roughly 30% per year. This together with the increase in the number of products and the improvement in the product characteristics over time are consistent with a market that generates "large" increases in welfare over time.

The instruments used here are a constant and x, both interacted with a set of dummies for each market. That these seem to suffice is probably a result of the fact that we are requiring the "same utility model" to fit in each time period and letting the products in the market change rather dramatically over time.

The fact that market shares are so small makes computation of the δ more difficult in this example. Partly as a result, we estimate on only one example data set, and use asymptotic standard errors. We obtain estimates from all three algorithms discussed above. In the homotopy method we begin with the δ outputted by the modified BLP contraction with fixed μ_ϵ, say δ_0, and then iterate only 25 times on the "homotopy" equation:

$$(40) \qquad\qquad \delta' = 0.05\delta + 0.95r(\delta),$$

where $r(\delta)$ is the element-by-element inversion.

We note that even this limited search greatly improves the calculated δ's. In particular, the mean of the calculated δ's are much too small if we stop at the solution to the modified BLP contraction with fixed μ_ϵ. This contrasts with the case with a small number of products: The modified BLP contraction with fixed μ_ϵ did rather well with that sample design. The difference is that the current sample design generates products with small market shares, and though the pure-characteristic model will do that if the characteristics of products are close enough to one another, the model with tastes for products can only generate small shares if the δ's are very small.

In Table 5, we see much bigger differences between the parameter estimates from the different estimation algorithms than we did when we had a small number of products. The estimates from the modified BLP algorithm with estimated μ_ϵ

---

[21] This may well be more of a result of the data not reflecting reality than our simulation not reflecting reality. That is, goods that truly have very small market shares might exist and simply not be included in traditional data sets.

TABLE 5
PARAMETER ESTIMATES (DATA SET WITH A LARGE NUMBER OF PRODUCTS)

Parameter	True	Homotopy	Modified BLP	
			Fix μ_ϵ	Estimate μ_ϵ
σ_x	1	0.833	0.862	0.832
		(0.194)	(0.380)	(6.956)
σ_p	1	1.192	1.188	1.207
		(0.556)	(0.621)	(1.783)
β_0	2	1.956	1.354	−6.455
		(2.013)	(2.066)	(66.864)
β_x	1	0.984	0.986	0.879
		(0.209)	(0.198)	(1.102)
Scale, μ_ϵ		∞	10*	0.934
				(6.680)

NOTES: The scale was initially set to 10, but some combinations of parameter values and markets caused numeric problems and the scale in those cases was halved until the numeric problems went away. In a few cases, a scale as low as 2.5 was necessary. Asymptotic standard errors are in parentheses.

are clearly the worst of the three. The estimated value of the scale parameter μ_ϵ, is relatively small, which implies that the logit error is being assigned a relatively important role. To counteract the effects of the logit and still match the small shares, the constant in δ is driven down to less than −6. The modified BLP contraction with a fixed μ_ϵ does better, but still suffers from a β_0 which is too low.

5.4.1. *Substitution patterns and own price elasticities.* In this example all the models do a good job of capturing the general pattern of substitution across products, although the BLP model is a bit more diffuse, as expected. However, only the homotopy method does a good job of capturing the overall level of elasticities. This is shown in Table 6, which gives, for the first five products in the year 1 data (the lowest price products), actual share and price data and then price elasticities (calculated from a discrete 1% change in price.) The products with a very small share have excellent substitutes in the pure characteristics model, but the modified BLP contraction with estimated μ_ϵ does not capture this effect and even the model with a fixed μ_ϵ has a lot of trouble reproducing this result. Note that for the fourth product, the share is truly tiny and that a 1% increase in price would wipe out all of the sales of that product.[22]

The last column of the table is particularly interesting. This column uses the BLP estimates of σ as given in the last column of Table 5. However, given those σ estimates we now solve for δ via the "homotopy" contraction described above and recalculate the linear β parameters from that new δ. Because the BLP σ's are close to the truth, the recalculated β's are also close to the truth. Finally,

---

[22] Such a product would likely only survive in the market if produced by a multiproduct firm, so that some markup could be sustained and fixed-costs perhaps shared across products.

BERRY AND PAKES

TABLE 6

PREDICTED ELASTICITIES (DATA SET WITH A LARGE NUMBER OF PRODUCTS)

| | | | | % Change in Share from a 1% Price Chg. | | |
| | | | | Modified BLP | | BLP, But $\partial s/\partial p$ via |
% Share	Price	True	Homotopy	Fixed μ_ϵ	Est. μ_ϵ	Homotopy
5.2109	1.26	−11.0	−14.6	−6.8	−1.8	−14.6
4.0180	1.58	−26.8	−24.5	−9.2	−2.3	−24.7
0.1078	2.93	−30.8	−46.3	−11.0	−2.9	−45.3
0.0038	3.85	−100.0	−100.0	−14.8	−3.7	−100.0
0.8855	4.01	−63.4	−58.5	−19.3	−4.9	−57.9

TABLE 7

WELFARE EFFECTS

Method	Gain
True	266.1
Homotopy	265.3
Modified BLP $\mu_\epsilon = 10$	270.0
Modified BLP μ_ϵ estimated	259.0
Mod. BLP, μ_ϵ est., but	
Final homotopy contraction	272.1

we use the BLP σ's and the recalculated β's to compute the price elasticities in the last column of Table 6. These elasticities, unlike the pure BLP elasticities, are quite close to the correct values.

The last column of Table 5 suggests the possibility that BLP might sometimes get the σ's correct even when the scale parameter is badly estimated—i.e., there is information in the data on the relative importance (in determining substitution patterns) of various x's, but there is not a lot of information on exactly how "local" are the substitution patterns. In such a case, the method of the last column of Table 6 may provide a good, and relatively easy to compute, estimate of elasticities. If nothing else, the calculation in that column provides a robustness check in answering the question about what elasticities would be if we held σ fixed and took μ off to infinity.

5.4.2. *Welfare effects.* We now calculate the average per-person welfare gain (in dollars) of moving from the year 1 choice set to the year 3 choice set. Recall that we greatly increase both the number of goods as well as their quality at the same time as lowering prices. As a result there is both a large influx of consumers from the outside good over time, and a "large" true welfare increase (much of it going to the new consumers).

Results on the total welfare gain are given in Table 7. The rows of that table correspond to the last five columns of Table 6.

The surprising result here is that all methods do very well. The homotopy is within 0.5% of the true result, but even the modified BLP algorithm with an estimated μ_ϵ is within 3% of the truth. The modified BLP methods do not do as well on the parameters, or on the elasticities, but the fact that the contraction fits the shares exactly means that the extra gain from the logit errors is offset by lower δ's, and this roughly counteracts the problems generated for welfare measurement by the model with tastes for products.

6. SUMMARY AND CONCLUSION

This article largely focuses on the practical and computational problems of estimating the pure characteristics model. We provide several possible algorithms.

Of these algorithms, the easiest is to simply use the existing BLP method, perhaps using the "units" normalization of this article as opposed to the traditional normalization on the scale of the i.i.d. term. One can hope that even if the pure characteristics model is correct, then the estimated scale parameter, μ_ϵ, will be large enough to closely reproduce the implications of the true model. In Monte Carlo exercises, we did find this result when the data was "high quality" in the sense that the number of products was not large and the relative variance of the unobservable ξ was not too high.

If one prefers to impose the restriction of the pure characteristics model, then one could consider the modified BLP algorithm with the scale parameter μ_ϵ fixed at a large value. This method leads to relatively easy computation using already existing methods and we find in Monte Carlo exercises that it can work quite well. As compared to tradtional BLP, it also gains efficiency by estimating one fewer parameter. However, it is difficult to know a priori what value of μ_ϵ is sufficiently large to provide a good approximation, and in practice there are limits to how large a value of μ_ϵ can be used before numeric errors start to arise.

Our most complicated computation method uses a homotopy argument to compute an accurate but slow value for the mean utility δ. For large numbers of products, it proved difficult to let that algorithm fully converge, but the method still provided good estimates, although at large computational cost.

We also had some success in estimating the model via either traditional or modified BLP methods, and then using the homotopy computation only to compute the implications of the model.

One conclusion, then, is that it would be strictly best to use the homotopy method when that is feasible, but that the other methods may also work well then the data quality is good. However, another practical suggestion is to simply estimate the model via traditional BLP, but then also compute the predictions of the pure characteristics model via the homotopy method. At the least this provides a robustness check, and in some cases may provide a good approximation to the fully estimated pure characteristics model. The exact conditions under which this idea will work well is a good topic for further research.

REFERENCES

ANDERSON, S., A. DePALMA, AND F. THISSE, *Discrete Choice Theory of Product Differentiation* (Cambridge, MA: MIT Press, 1992).

BERRY, S., "Estimating Discrete Choice Models of Product Differentiation," *RAND Journal of Economics* 23 (1994), 242–62.

——, J. LEVINSOHN, AND A. PAKES, "Automobile Prices in Market Equilibrium," *Econometrica* 60 (1995), 889–917.

——, ——, AND ——, "Voluntary Export Restraints on Automobiles: Evaluating a Strategic Trade Policy," *American Economic Review* 89 (1999), 189–211.

——, ——, AND ——, "Differentiated Products Demand Systems from a Combination of Micro and Macro Data: The New Vehicle Market," *Journal of Political Economy* 112 (February 2004a), 68–105.

——, O. LINTON, AND A. PAKES, "Limit Theorems for Differentiated Product Demand Systems," *Review of Economic Studies* 71 (2004b), 613–14.

BOSKIN COMMISSION, *Final Report to the Senate Finance Committee from the Advisory Commission to Study the Consumer Price Index*, Senate Finance Committee, 1996.

BRESNAHAN, T., "Competition and Collusion in the American Automobile Oligopoly: The 1955 Price War," *Journal of Industrial Economics* 35 (1987), 457–82.

CAPLIN, A., AND B. NALEBUFF, "Aggregation and Imperfect Competition: On the Existence of Equilibrium," *Econometrica* 59 (1991), 1–23.

DAS, S., G. S. OLLEY, AND A. PAKES, "The Market for TVs," Technical Report, Yale Univeristy, 1995.

EAVES, B. C., AND K. SCHMEDDERS, "General Equilibrium Models and Homotopy Methods," *Journal of Economic Dynamics and Control* 23 (1999), 1249–79.

FEENSTRA, R., AND J. LEVINSOHN, "Estimating Markups and Market Conduct with Multidimensional Product Attributes," *Review of Economic Studies* 62 (1995), 19–52.

GABSZEWICZ, J. J., AND J.-F. THISSE, "Price Competition, Quality and Income Disparity," *Journal of Economic Theory* 20 (1979), 340–59.

GOETTLER, R. L., AND R. SHACHAR, "Spatial Competition in the Network Television Industry," *RAND Journal of Economics* 32 (2001), 624–56.

GREENSTEIN, S. M., "From Superminis to Supercomputers: Estimating the Surplus in the Computing Market," in T. F. Bresnahan and R. J. Gordon, eds., *The Economics of New Goods* (Chicago: University of Chicago Press, 1996).

HAUSMAN, J., "Valuing the Effect of Regulation on New Services in Telecommunications," *The Brookings Papers on Economic Activity: Microeconomics*, (1997), 1–38.

HAUSMAN, J. A., AND D. WISE, "A Conditional Probit Model for Qualitative Choice: Discrete Decisions Recognizing Interdependence and Heterogeneous Preferences," *Econometrica* 46 (1978), 403–26.

HECKMAN, J., AND J. SNYDER, "Linear Probability Models of the Demand for Attributes with an Empirical Application to Estimating the Preferences of Legislators," *RAND Journal of Economics* 28 (1997), S142–S189.

HOTELLING, H., "Stability in Competition," *Economic Journal* 39 (1929), 41–57.

LANCASTER, K., *Consumer Demand: A New Approach* (New York: Columbia University Press, 1971).

——, "Conditional Logit Analysis of Qualitative Choice Behavior," in P. Zarembka, ed., *Frontiers of Econometrics* (New York: Academic Press, 1974).

——, "Econometric Models of Probabilistic Choice," in C. Manski and D. McFadden, eds., *Structural Analysis of Discrete Data with Econometric Applications* (Cambridge, MA: MIT Press, 1981).

MCFADDEN, D., AND K. TRAIN, "Mixed MNL Models for Discrete Response," *Journal of Applied Econometrics* 15 (2000), 447–70.

MUSSA, M., AND S. ROSEN, "Monopoly and Product Quality," *Journal of Economics Theory* 18 (1978), 301–7.

NEVO, A., "Mergers with Differentiated Products: The Case of the Ready-to-Eat Cereal Industry," *RAND Journal of Economics* 31 (2000), 395–421.

PAKES, A., "Patents as Options: Some Estimates of the Value of Holding European Patent Stocks," *Econometrica* 54 (1986), 755–84.

——, "A Reconsideration of Hedonic Price Indices with an Application to PC's," *American Economic Review* 93 (2003), 1578–96.

——, S. BERRY, AND J. LEVINSOHN, "Some Applications and Limitations of Recent Advances in Empirical Industrial Organization: Price Indexes and the Analysis of Environmental Change," *American Economic Review, Paper and Proceedings* 83 (1993), 240–46.

PETRIN, A., "Quantifying the Benefits of New Products: The Case of the Minivan," *JPE* 110 (2002), 705–29.

SALOP, S., "Monopolistic Competition with Outside Goods," *RAND Journal of Economics* 10 (1979), 141–56.

SONG, M., "Measuring Consumer Welfare in the CPU Market: An Application of the Pure Characteristics Demand Model," Working Paper, Georgia Tech 2006, *RAND Journal of Economics* (forthcoming).

TRAJTENBERG, M., "The Welfare Analysis of Product Innovations: With an Application to Computed Tomography Scanners," *Journal of Political Economy* 97 (1989), 444–79.

WHITEHEAD, G. W., *Elements of Homotopy Theory* (Berlin: Springer-Verlag, 1993).

1226

INTERNATIONAL ECONOMIC REVIEW
Vol. 48, No. 4, November 2007

IMPROVING REVEALED PREFERENCE BOUNDS
ON DEMAND RESPONSES*

By Richard Blundell, Martin Browning, and Ian Crawford[1]

University College London, and IFS, U.K.; University of Oxford, U.K.; and University of Surrey, and IFS, U.K.

There are three key dimensions by which revealed preference bounds on consumer demand responses can be improved. The first relates to the improvements that arise from using expansion paths for given relative prices, E-bounds. The second concerns the addition of new price information. Thirdly, there are improvements due to assuming separability. Our previous research has examined the first two cases. In this article, we show how to impose separability assumptions within a fully nonparametric analysis and distinguish between weak and homothetic separability. We also apply these ideas to the analysis of demand responses using United Kingdom household level data.

1. INTRODUCTION

Measuring the responses of consumers to variation in relative prices and in income is at the center of applied welfare economics: It is a vital ingredient of tax policy reform analysis and is also key to the measurement of market power in modern empirical industrial economics. Parametric models have dominated applications in this field, but this is increasingly seen to be both unwise and unnecessary. To quote Dan McFadden in his presidential address to the Econometric Society: "[Parametric regression] interposes an untidy veil between econometric analysis and the propositions of economic theory." Popular parametric models place strong assumptions on both income and price responses. The objective of the research agenda that underlies this article is to accomplish all that is required from parametric models of consumer behavior using only nonparametric regression and revealed preference theory.

The aim of this research is to combine the inequalities that summarize the axioms of revealed preference (RP) with the nonparametric estimation of consumer

* Manuscript received October 2005; revised March 2007.

[1] Revised version of a paper presented at the Conference to honor Dan McFadden, Berkeley, May 2005. We would like to thank the editor and two annonymous referees for their helpful comments. The research is part of the program of research of the ESRC Centre for the Microeconomic Analysis of Public Policy at IFS. Funding from the ESRC, grant number R000239865, the Leverhulme Trust, and from the Danish National Research Foundation through its grant to CAM is gratefully acknowledged. Material from the FES made available by the ONS through the ESRC Data Archive has been used by permission of the controller of HMSO. Neither the ONS nor the ESRC Data Archive bear responsibility for the analysis or the interpretation of the data reported here. The usual disclaimer applies. Please address correspondence to: Richard Blundell, Department of Economics, University College London. Gower Street, London, WC1E 6BT. Phone: 44(0)2076795863. Fax: 44(0)2073234780. E-mail: *r.blundell@ud.ac.uk*.

expansion paths (Engel curves). The empirical setting we have in mind is one where we have consumer level data on commodity expenditures and incomes across a finite set of *discrete* relative price or tax regimes. In Blundell et al. (2003, 2007) we have shown how to use the RP inequalities of Afriat (1967) and Varian (1982, 1983) in such an empirical setting to generate tight bounds on welfare measures and on consumers demand responses. In this article, we extend these results to examine the impact of nonparametric separability restrictions. These are shown to further tighten the bounds on demand responses. However, without parametric restrictions demand responses remain only set identified in the sense of Manski (2003).

Freeing up the variation in demand responses to relative price changes across the income distribution is one of the key contributions of this research agenda. Historically parametric specifications in the analysis of consumer behavior have been based on the Working-Leser or Piglog form of preferences that underlie the popular Almost Ideal and Translog demand models of Deaton and Muellbauer (1980) and Jorgenson et al. (1982). Even though more recent empirical studies have suggested further nonlinear income terms (see, e.g., Lewbel, 1991; Blundell et al., 1993; Hausman et al., 1991; Banks et al., 1997), responses to relative prices at different incomes for these parametric forms remain unnecessarily constrained.

There are three broad mechanisms for the improvement of revealed preference bounds. The first of these uses nonparametrically estimated Engel curves (or expansion paths) to provide tight bounds on cost of living indices and on demand responses. These 'expansion path based bounds' are labeled *E-bounds*, see Blundell et al. (2003, 2007). The second improvement comes from the use of more price information. Typically consumers are observed choosing demands under a finite set of different relative prices. Relative prices are assumed to be different over time or across different markets as supply costs and production technology changes. Blundell et al. (2007) investigate the value of more relative price variation in improving the bounds on demand responses. In this article, we turn to improvements that can be achieved through grouping goods according to separability. We show how to impose separability restrictions within a fully nonparametric analysis and distinguish between weak, homothetic, and exact index separability. These improvements are first considered theoretically using standard consumer theory arguments and are then applied to the empirical analysis of consumer behavior.

In our empirical analysis relative price variation occurs over time and we consider consumer behavior as it is recorded in standard repeated consumer expenditure surveys such as the U.S. Consumers Expenditure Survey and the U.K. Family Expenditure Survey. The latter is the source for our empirical analysis. We observe samples of consumers, each of a particular household type, at specific points in time. Assuming consumers are price-takers, we can recover expansion paths by estimating Engel curves at each point in time. In this research, we present E-bounds for own and cross-price responses using these expansion paths. We allow for sampling variation in the estimated expansion paths and consider whether perturbations to preferences can be found that allow revealed preference theory to be maintained while lying within standard confidence intervals.

The remainder of the article is as follows: in Section 2, we examine the improvements in RP bounds on demand responses that occur due to the use of expansion paths. We also consider the advantage of adding in more relative price variation. This section draws heavily on Blundell et al. (2007). In Section 3, we consider improvements that can result from different forms of separability. We show how to impose separability restrictions within a fully nonparametric analysis and distinguish between weak, homothetic, and exact index separability. These improvements are first considered theoretically using standard consumer theory arguments and are then applied to the empirical analysis of consumer behavior. In Section 4, we apply these ideas to analyze demand responses using the household level data in the U.K. Family Expenditure Survey. Section 5 concludes.

2. IMPROVING BOUNDS WITH EXPANSION PATHS

Let $\mathbf{p}$ be a J-vector of prices and x total expenditure. We assume that every agent responds to a given budget $(\mathbf{p}, x)$, with a unique, positive demand J-vector, which we denote $\mathbf{q}(\mathbf{p}, x)$. We further assume that these demands satisfy adding-up $(\mathbf{p}'\mathbf{q}(\mathbf{p}, x) = x)$ and normality $(\mathbf{q}(\mathbf{p}, x') \geq \mathbf{q}(\mathbf{p}, x'')$ if $x' > x'')$. We shall only be considering demand functions for a finite number of distinct relative prices; an *expansion path* for for a given price vector $\mathbf{p}_t$ is defined as $\mathbf{q}_t(x) = \mathbf{q}(\mathbf{p}_t, x)$ (with q_t^j denoting the demand for good j in period t). In our empirical analysis below we shall estimate an expansion path for each price regime in our data; we refer to these expansion paths as *observed expansion paths* or *observed demands*.

The goal of our research is to find the set of possible demand responses to a new budget and set of relative prices, such that these are consistent with already observed demands and utility maximization. That is, we take a set of observed prices and expansion paths $\{\mathbf{p}_t, \mathbf{q}_t(x)\}_{t=1,...T}$ and ask what demands that are consistent with utility theory could arise, given a new budget $\{\mathbf{p}_0, x_0\}$. To do this with no appeal to parametric assumptions we use revealed preference conditions. Specifically, we take the Strong Axiom of Revealed Preference (SARP) (see Varian, 1982, for the relationship between SARP and the more usual GARP). To state SARP we need to define what we mean by revealed preference. If at prices $\mathbf{p}_t$ the agent chooses $\mathbf{q}_t$ and we have $\mathbf{p}_t'\mathbf{q}_t \geq \mathbf{p}_t'\mathbf{q}_s$ then we say that $\mathbf{q}_t$ is *directly revealed weakly preferred* to $\mathbf{q}_s$, denoted $\mathbf{q}_t R^0 \mathbf{q}_s$. If we have a chain $\mathbf{q}_t R^0 \mathbf{q}_u$, $\mathbf{q}_u R^0 \mathbf{q}_v, \ldots \mathbf{q}_w R^0 \times \mathbf{q}_s$ then we say that $\mathbf{q}_t$ is *revealed weakly preferred* to $\mathbf{q}_s$ and denote this by $\mathbf{q}_t R \, \mathbf{q}_s$. Given this, SARP is defined by the following:

DEFINITION 1. SARP: $\mathbf{q}_t R \, \mathbf{q}_s$ and $\mathbf{q}_t \neq \mathbf{q}_s$ implies not $\mathbf{q}_s \, R^0 \mathbf{q}_t$ (that is, $\mathbf{p}_s'\mathbf{q}_s < \mathbf{p}_s'\mathbf{q}_t$) for all s, t.

The main features of our analysis can be captured in a simple two good, two period example, as shown in Figure 1.[2] In this figure, the two expansion paths are shown as $\mathbf{q}_1(x)$ and $\mathbf{q}_2(x)$. The hypothetical budget line is given by the budget $\{\mathbf{p}_0, x_0\}$. The points at which the two expansion paths intersect the new budget, at $\mathbf{q}_1(\tilde{x}_1)$

---

[2] This figure reproduces a figure in Blundell et al. (2007).

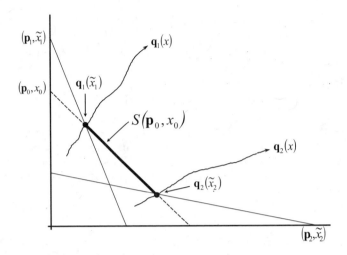

FIGURE 1

DEFINING THE SUPPORT SET

and $\mathbf{q}_2(\tilde{x}_2)$, are termed *intersection demands*.[3] Formally, the $\tilde{x}_t$ at which expansion path $\mathbf{q}_1(x)$ intersects is defined implicitly by the equation

$$(1) \qquad\qquad \mathbf{p}_0'\mathbf{q}_0 = \mathbf{p}_0'\mathbf{q}_t(\tilde{x}_t).$$

Given uniqueness and normality, a unique value of $\tilde{x}_t$ will always exist for every expansion path. The budget lines for the intersection demands are labeled $\{\mathbf{p}_1, \tilde{x}_1\}$ and $\{\mathbf{p}_2, \tilde{x}_2\}$, respectively. Given the budget lines we have drawn, the two intersection demands satisfy SARP since neither is revealed weakly preferred to the other. Given all this, we are now in a position to identify the points on the $\{\mathbf{p}_0, x_0\}$ budget line that are consistent with utility theory and the observed expansion paths. These are simply the points $\mathbf{q}_0$ such that $\{(\mathbf{p}_0, \mathbf{q}_0), (\mathbf{p}_1, \mathbf{q}_1), (\mathbf{p}_2, \mathbf{q}_2)\}$ satisfy SARP. The set of all such points are labeled $S(\mathbf{p}_0, x_0)$; following Varian (1982), we term this the *support set* for $\{\mathbf{p}_0, x_0\}$. It will be clear that any point on the new budget line that is not in $S(\mathbf{p}_0, x_0)$ leads to a violation of SARP. Conversely, any point in $S(\mathbf{p}_0, x_0)$ is weakly revealed preferred to the intersection demands and they are not directly revealed preferred to any point in the interior of $S(\mathbf{p}_0, x_0)$. Extending this insight to many goods and many periods we have the following general definition for the support set for any $(\mathbf{p}_0, x_0)$:

$$(2) \qquad S(\mathbf{p}_0, x_0) = \left\{ \mathbf{q}_0 : \begin{array}{c} \mathbf{q}_0 \geq \mathbf{0},\ \mathbf{p}_0'\mathbf{q}_0 = x_0 \\ \{\mathbf{p}_0, \mathbf{p}_t; \mathbf{q}_0, \mathbf{q}_t(\tilde{x}_t)\}_{t=1,\dots,T} \text{ satisfy SARP} \end{array} \right\},$$

---

[3] We could denote these by $\mathbf{q}_t(\tilde{x}_t(\mathbf{p}_0, x_0))$ to emphasize the dependence of $\tilde{x}_t$ on the hypothetical budget but we prefer to use the clearer notation.

where $\tilde{x}_t$ is defined as in Equation (1). Note that the support set is empty if and only if the observed data set fails SARP and it is a singleton if and only if the hypothetical relative prices are the same as an observed set of relative prices; that is, if $\mathbf{p}_0 = \lambda \mathbf{p}_t$ for some t and $\lambda > 0$. We refer to the boundaries of the support set as *E-bounds* since they are the bounds derived from the expansion paths. The definition of $S(\mathbf{p}_0, x_0)$ as given in (2) is not suited to empirical implementation as it stands; Blundell et al. (2007) show how to calculate E-bounds using standard linear programming techniques.

Blundell et al. (2007) show that the support set as defined here makes the best use of the data in the following sense. Take any points on the expansion paths, $\hat{\mathbf{q}}_t$ for $t = 1, \ldots T$ and construct the pseudo-support set

$$(3) \qquad S'(\mathbf{p}_0, x_0) = \left\{ \mathbf{q}_0 : \begin{array}{c} \mathbf{q}_0 \geq \mathbf{0}, \; \mathbf{p}_0' \mathbf{q}_0 = x_0 \\ \{\mathbf{p}_0, \mathbf{p}_t; \mathbf{q}_0, \hat{\mathbf{q}}_t\}_{t=1,\ldots,T} \text{ satisfy SARP} \end{array} \right\}.$$

Blundell et al. (2007) show that $S'(\mathbf{p}_0, x_0)$ contains $S(\mathbf{p}_0, x_0)$. In general, the set inclusion will be strict if $\hat{\mathbf{q}}_t \neq \mathbf{q}_t(\tilde{x}_t)$ so our E-bounds are strictly smaller than those given by any other choice of observed demands to generate the support set.

With no further structural restrictions and no more information this is the most that we can squeeze out of the data and basic consumer theory to bound demands. Considering more time periods, Blundell et al. (2007) give conditions under which an extra observation $\{\mathbf{p}_{T+1}, \mathbf{q}_{T+1}(x)\}$ leads to tighter bounds. They show that adding more information in the form of a previously unobserved price vector and a corresponding expansion path is not always informative: It will only improve the bound if the new budget plane defined by the new intersection demand cuts through the original support set. The purpose of this article is to consider how far we can improve bounds by imposing structure in the form of separability restrictions.

3. IMPROVING BOUNDS WITH SEPARABILITY AND PRICE AGGREGATION

The aggregation of goods or the incorporation of some form of separability assumption is commonplace in the empirical analysis of consumer behavior. The main benefits are those brought about by the corresponding dimension reduction in the demand system and the consequent easing of the data requirements and the simplification of the estimation procedure. Here we examine the impact on bounds on demand responses that arises from assuming separability of different forms, as well as the effect of aggregating commodities.

Suppose that we are principally interested in the own-price demand curve of a particular good of interest. Partition the set of goods into the good of interest q_t^1 and all other goods, which are labeled $\mathbf{q}_t^2$ for convenience. The utility function $u(.)$ is (weakly) separable with respect to the group $\mathbf{q}_t^2$ if we can write the utility function as

$$(4) \qquad u = u(q_t^1, U^2(\mathbf{q}_t^2)),$$

where $U^2(\cdot)$ is a subutility function and u is strictly increasing in U^2. The RP conditions for separability provided by Matzkin and Richter (1991) and Varian (1983) can be used to define a new, separability-consistent support set that we denote by $S^S(\mathbf{p}_0, x_0)$:

$$S^S(\mathbf{p}_0, x_0) = \left\{ \mathbf{q}_0 : \begin{array}{c} \mathbf{q}_0 \in S(\mathbf{p}_0, x_0) \\ \{p_t^1, 1/\lambda_t; q_t^1, U_t^2\}_{t=0,\dots,T} \text{ satisfies } SARP \\ U_s^2 < U_t^2 + \lambda_t \mathbf{p}_t^{2'}(\mathbf{q}_s^2 - \mathbf{q}_t^2) \text{ for all } s, t = 0, \dots, T; s \neq t \end{array} \right\},$$

(5)

where we note that $1/\lambda_t$ can be interpreted as the price index for U_t^2. The definition of the separability-consistent support set makes clear that the restrictions required by separability (weakly) improve the bound.

Under weak separability the price index for $\mathbf{q}_t^2$ depends on group expenditure $(\mathbf{p}_t^{2'}\mathbf{q}_t^2)$. We can add the requirement that $U^2(\cdot)$ is homothetic and define a homothetic separability-consistent support set that we denote by $S^H(\mathbf{p}_0, x_0)$:

(6) $$S^H(\mathbf{p}_0, x_0) = \left\{ \mathbf{q}_0 : \mathbf{q}_0 \in S^S(\mathbf{p}_0, x_0); U_t^2/\lambda_t = \mathbf{p}_t^{2'}\mathbf{q}_t^2 \right\}.$$

This further restriction weakly improves the separability-consistent bound. As well as potentially improving the bounds, the homothetic separability requirement is also computationally convenient because it reduces the number of "free parameters" (the Afriat Numbers $\{U_t^2, 1/\lambda_t\}_{t=0,\dots,T}$ and the demand vector $\mathbf{q}_0$) in the problem to $J + T + 1$ compared to $J + 2(T + 1)$ in the separable case. Additively separability can also be used[4] to define improved bounds using the restrictions in Varian (1983, theorem 6).

The use of separability restrictions improves bounds by restricting substitution responses and achieving a dimension reduction to a two group demand system (the good of interest and "other goods"). The principal difference from a simple two-good system is that the quantity and price indices for the separable group are not known; they are represented by the Afriat Numbers $\{U_t^2, 1/\lambda_t\}_{t=0,\dots,T}$ and although their values are restricted by the inequalities in (5) and (6), any values that satisfy these requirements are valid. Since the support set will, in general, depend on the selected values for these Afriat Numbers, it needs to be defined over *all* admissible values. If, however, the price and quantities indices were known uniquely, then the support set could be defined for the two-good system using (2) with the price and quantity indices replacing the data for the group.

The impact of utilizing these restrictions can be seen from the Figure 2. This simulation utilizes Cobb–Douglas preferences over three goods with four observed relative price regimes. The simulated data are homothetically separable for any two of the three goods and the true demand curve for the remaining good (the good of interest) is illustrated. We then consider the gains of various improvements to the basic support set. The bounds labeled "RP Bounds" illustrate the maximum and minimum demands for the good of interest within the support set defined in

---

[4] We are grateful to a referee for pointing this out.

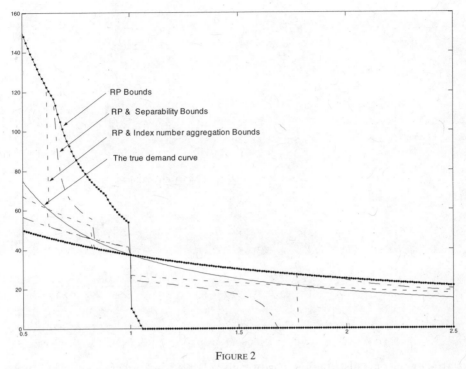

FIGURE 2

IMPROVING E-BOUNDS UNDER SEPARABILITY AND AGGREGATION

(2). As expected, these bounds are the widest. In Figure 2 we first note the improvement from exploiting homothetic separability restrictions (labeled "RP and Separability Bounds") and then the further improvement that can be made if we use the correct Cobb–Douglas price and quantities indices for the separable group (labeled "RP and Index Number Aggregation"), thereby reducing the dimension of the problem to a simple two-good situation.

4. AN EMPIRICAL ANALYSIS OF DEMAND BOUND IMPROVEMENTS

4.1. *Data.* In this empirical analysis we begin by taking three broad consumption goods: food, other nondurables, and services (for precise definitions see the Appendix). These are the same commodity groupings used in Blundell et al. (2007). The empirical analysis also uses the same 25 years of British Family Expenditure Surveys from 1975 to 1999. This choice of goods is made because in many contexts the price responsiveness of food relative to services and to other nondurables is of particular interest. It is a key parameter in the indirect tax debate. Although food is largely free of value added tax (VAT) in the United Kingdom, the discussions over the harmonization of indirect tax rates across Europe and the implications of a flat expenditure tax raised uniformly across all consumption items requires a good understanding of food demand responses across the income distribution. It is also important in general discussions of cost of living changes

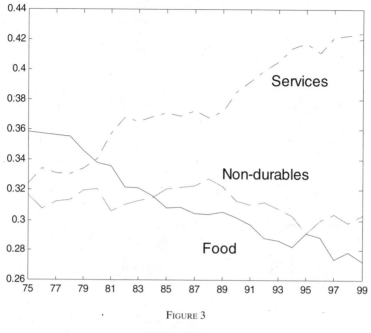

FIGURE 3

MEAN BUDGET SHARES

across the income distribution. Historically relative food prices saw some abrupt rises as the tariff structure and food import quotas were changed in Europe early in the period under study. In our discussion of separability we also examine a higher dimensional system.

The Family Expenditure Survey is a repeated cross-section survey consisting of around 7,000 households in each year. From these data we draw a relatively homogeneous subsample of couples with children. This gives us between 1,421 and 1,906 observations per year and 40,731 observations over the entire period. We use total spending on nondurables to define our total expenditure variable. Figure 3 shows the mean budget shares for these goods over the period.[5] As can be seen, the mean budget share for food exhibits a large fall whereas services are rising steadily over our data period.

The substantial relative price variation can be seen in the dated points in Figure 4. This figure shows the scatter plot of the prices of food and services relative to nondurables. The relative prices show a dramatic change in the mid- to late 1970s. The figure also illustrates the convex hull of the relative price data. The annual price indices for these commodity groups are taken from the annual Retail Prices Index. Nondurables are treated as the numeraire good. We see a steadily rising price for services relative to food and nondurables.

4.2. *Estimating Expansion Paths.* Consumers who are observed in the same time period and location are assumed to face the same relative prices. Under this

[5] Further details are provided in Blundell et al. (2007).

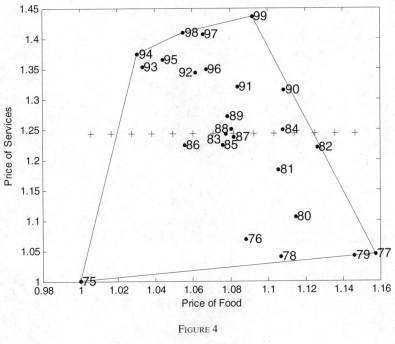

FIGURE 4

RELATIVE PRICES, 1975–99

assumption, Engel curves for each location and period correspond to expansion paths for each price regime. We use a shape invariant specification to pool over different demographic types of households (see, e.g., Blundell et al., 2003), who show that is an effective way of allowing for demographics). We account for the possible endogeneity of total expenditure using the control function approach (see Blundell and Powell, 2003).[6] Let $\mathbf{d}^i$ represent a $(D \times 1)$ vector of household composition variables relating to household i. Our specification takes the form

$$(7) \qquad w_j^i = g_j(\ln x_i - \phi(\mathbf{d}_i'\alpha)) + \mathbf{d}_i'\gamma_j + \varepsilon_j^i,$$

where w_j^i is the expenditure share for household i on good j. To account for the endogeneity of $\ln x$ we specify

$$(8) \qquad \ln x_i = \mathbf{z}_i'\pi + v_i,$$

where $\mathbf{z}$ are a set of variables that include the demographic variables $\mathbf{d}_i$ and earned income as an excluded instrument. The required assumption for the control function approach is

---

[6] This is analyzed in Blundell et al. (forthcoming) and compared to a the fully nonparametric instrument variables (NPIV) case. It is found to account quite well for the endogeneity of total expenditure in comparison to a full NPIV approach.

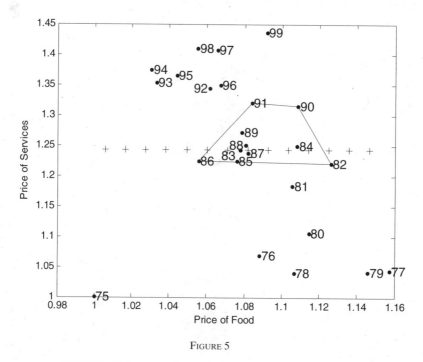

FIGURE 5

PRICE SCATTER PLOT OF THE SARP-CONSISTENT INTERSECTION DEMANDS

$$(9) \qquad\qquad E\big(\varepsilon^i_j \mid \ln x_i,\, \mathbf{d}_i,\, v_i\big) = 0$$

so that semiparametric regression using an augmented Equation (7) that includes functions of v_i will produce consistent estimates of g_j, α and γ (see Newey et al., 1999).

4.3. *E-Bounds on Demand Responses.*   We begin by illustrating the idea of E-bounds using a three-good demand system. Using the estimated expansion paths we recover the intersection demands for each $\{\mathbf{p}_0, x_0\}$ budget and check the revealed preference conditions for the data $\{\mathbf{p}_t, \mathbf{q}_t(\tilde{x}_t)\}$. We find (by searching for chronologically ordered SARP-consistent subperiods) that the periods 1982–91 satisfy SARP. Figure 5 shows the convex hull of the price data corresponding to this subperiod. Comparison of Figures 4 and 5 shows the reduction in the space spanned by the convex hull of the prices once SARP-violating intersection demands have been dropped.

   In Figures 6–8,[7] we present the own and cross-price demand curves for food for the median income individual using the reduced set of SARP-consistent observations. As can be seen from a comparison with Figure 4, the bounds on the food demand curve are particularly tight when the $\mathbf{p}_0$ vector is in the dense part of the observed price data. Outside the convex hull of the price data the E-Bounds widen

---

[7] These figures reproduce figures in Blundell et al. (2007).

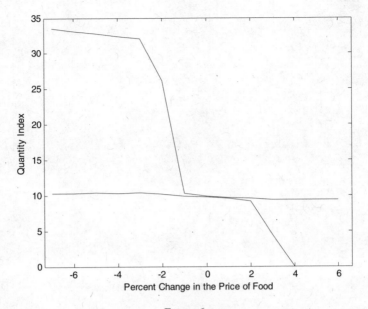

FIGURE 6

THE OWN-PRICE DEMAND BOUNDS FOR FOOD

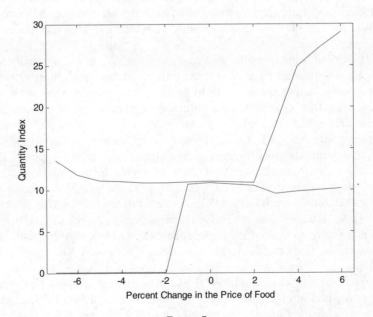

FIGURE 7

THE CROSS-PRICE DEMAND BOUNDS FOR NONDURABLES

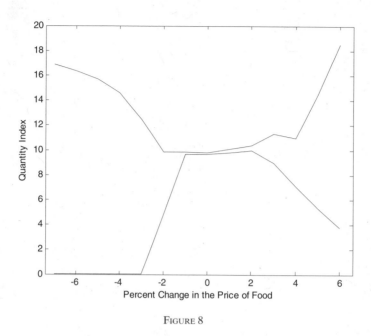

FIGURE 8

THE CROSS-PRICE DEMAND BOUNDS FOR SERVICES

considerably; so much so, indeed, that we cannot rule out that households would stop buying food if the relative price of food rose a little above the price seen in 1982! We now consider whether imposing separability tightens the bounds.

4.4. *E-Bound Improvements with Separability.* We begin the analysis of the improvements afforded by adding separability restrictions to those that just use the intersection demands and SARP by looking at how the bounds on the own demand curve for food change when nondurables and services are grouped together in a separable subgroup. The raw data reject weak separability of services and nondurables with respect to food. We have therefore imposed separability at the intersection demands using the minimum distance criteria developed in Blundell et al. (2007), suitably augmented to account for separability restrictions. The intersection demands have thus been perturbed by the minimum (Euclidean) distance such that they satisfy the RP conditions for separability provided by Matzkin and Richter (1991) and Varian (1983). Using the separability-consistent intersection demands we have computed the support sets (2) and (5), and the resulting own-price and cross-price bounds are illustrated in Figures 9–11. The bounds with the separability restrictions are shown as dashed lines and the bounds without separability are shown by the solid lines (the same as in Figures 6–8). Note that since we use perturbed intersection points, the bounds with separability imposed are not always inside the unrestricted bounds, but they are very close.

The general improvement in the bounds that separability restrictions provide is immediately apparent in the figures. This is particularly so when we consider

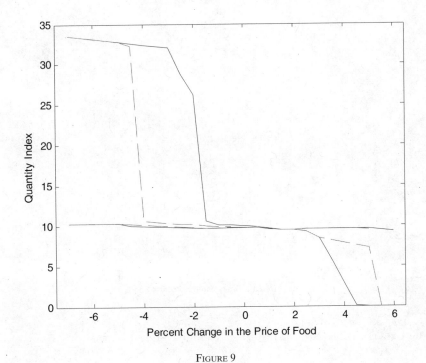

FIGURE 9

THE OWN-PRICE DEMAND BOUNDS FOR FOOD—WITH AND WITHOUT SEPARABILITY RESTRICTIONS

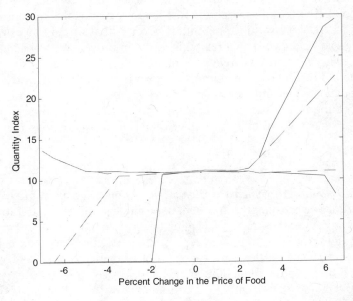

FIGURE 10

THE CROSS-PRICE DEMAND BOUNDS FOR NONDURABLES—WITH AND WITHOUT SEPARABILITY RESTRICTIONS

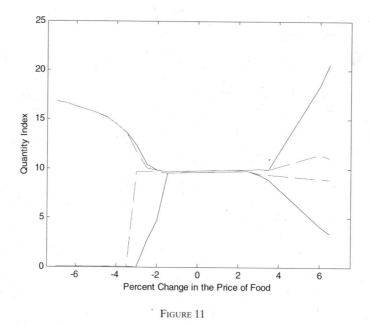

Figure 11

THE CROSS-PRICE DEMAND BOUNDS FOR SERVICES—WITH AND WITHOUT SEPARABILITY RESTRICTIONS

the range of price variation over which it is possible to find tight bounds. Previously we could only be reasonably precise over the range [−1.8% to +2.5%] of the mean price of food. The use of separability restrictions expands this to approximately [−4% to +5%]. What is also apparent, however, is that within ranges where the demand curve bounds where already tight, the improvement brought about by the separability restrictions is relatively modest.

Separability restrictions come into their own in demand systems that need to accommodate a larger number of goods. The greater the level of disaggregation confronting the researcher, the greater the potential benefits of separability. It is to this issue of separability in higher dimensional restrictions that we now turn.

4.5. *E-Bound Improvements in Higher Dimensional Systems with Separability.* In this section, we consider the impact of imposing separability restrictions on the E-bounds on demand responses in a higher dimensional case in which preferences over many goods are constrained by separability restrictions over subsets of these goods. In particular, we take an expanded set of demands over six commodity groups that break up the food, other goods, and services, into six categories, food consumed at home ("Food In"), food consumed away from home ("Food Out"), alcohol and tobacco, other nondurables, services, and travel (see Appendix for the breakdown of the commodity groups). We examine the two food categories and consider separability restrictions on the other goods.

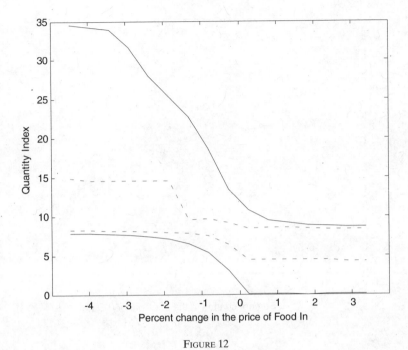

FIGURE 12

SEPARABILITY IN A HIGHER DIMENSION SYSTEM—THE OWN PRICE DEMAND BOUNDS FOR "FOOD IN"

It might be expected that the real improvements in the E-bounds from separability come from reducing a higher dimensional problem. Indeed the gains could be substantial when there are many goods. The changes in VAT rates over the period provide useful variation in the relative price of food consumed inside the home (which is not eligible for VAT) and food consumed outside (which is eligible). In the following examples we continue to use the subperiod 1982 through 1991.

Figure 12 shows the own-price demand curve for food consumed at home (Food In) in the six-good system (outer solid lines). The first notable effect is that of the impact of disaggregation on the bounds: Compared to those in the previous section the demand curve bounds are far wider, reflecting perhaps the more general nature of the substitution possibilities in a six-good system. We then use the separability restriction on the "other goods" (alcohol and tobacco, other nondurables, services, and travel) and recompute the E-bounds focusing on the own price response of Food In and the cross-price effects on the demand for food consumed outside the home. The results are shown by the inner dashed bounds. A large improvement in the bounds is apparent but note that the resulting bounds from this separable system are wider than those for the three-good system. This is because of the flexibility over the choice of Afriat numbers compared to simple aggregation—precisely as one would expect given the discussion around Figure 2. Figure 13 show that the gains are equally large for the cross-price effect on food consumed outside the home.

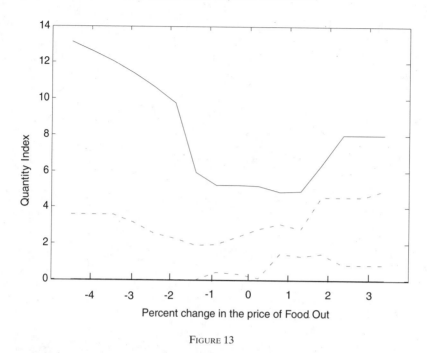

FIGURE 13

SEPARABILITY IN A HIGHER DIMENSION SYSTEM—CROSS-PRICE EFFECT ON FOOD CONSUMED OUTSIDE THE HOME

5. SUMMARY AND CONCLUSIONS

The research reported in this article forms part of a broad agenda examining key dimensions by which revealed preference bounds on consumer demand responses to price variation can be improved. In earlier research we have shown how improvements can arise from using expansion paths for given relative prices, *E-bounds*. We have also documented conditions under which new price information improves these E-bounds. In this article, we have considered the way in which revealed preference bounds on consumer demand responses can be improved using separability assumptions. We have also shown how to impose these separability assumptions within a fully nonparametric analysis and distinguish between weak, homothetic, and exact index separability.

Looking forward, this research will move on naturally to examine the *distribution* of demands across the heterogeneity distribution and not focus on average demands at all; see Brown and Matzkin (1998). If we describe consumer behavior by the share equations $\mathbf{w} = \mathbf{g}$ ($\ln x$, $\ln \mathbf{p}$, $\mathbf{d}$, ε) where ε is a $J - 1$ vector of unobservable heterogeneity, then global invertibility is required to identify the complete distribution of demands (see Brown and Matzkin, 1998; Beckert and Blundell, 2005). In this case generalizations of quantile regression are required for estimation, see Matzkin (2007).

For the more limited case considered here we could ask whether there is a general interpretation of local average demands that is consistent with consumer behavior. For empirical demand analysis a natural assumption is that unobservable preference heterogeneity, conditional on observable demographics, is independent of prices and total outlay: $F(\varepsilon \mid \ln x, \ln \mathbf{p}, \mathbf{d}) = F(\varepsilon \mid \mathbf{d})$. The covariance between budget shares and the responsiveness of these to changes in log total outlay, conditional on the observable determinants of demand, is defined as

$$H(\ln x, \ln \mathbf{p}, \mathbf{d}) = \text{cov}\left(\frac{\partial \mathbf{g}}{\partial \ln x}, \mathbf{g}' \mid \ln x, \ln \mathbf{p}, \mathbf{d}\right).$$

Lewbel (2001) shows that *average* demands of rational consumers satisfy integrability conditions *iff* $H(\cdot)$ is symmetric and positive semidefinite.[8] If H is small relative to the the *Slutsky* matrix for these average demands, then the system will be "close" to integrable. This result extends the usefulness of the local average regression results used in this article in the presence of nonseparable unobserved heterogeneity. However, as stressed above, in future research we will want to describe and predict the complete distribution of demands.

APPENDIX: COMMODITY GROUPS

Six Commodity Group System. "Food In": {bread, cereals, biscuits & cakes, beef, lamb, pork, bacon, poultry, other meats & fish, butter, oil & fats, cheese, eggs, fresh milk, milk products, tea, coffee, soft drinks, sugar & preserves, sweets & chocolate, potatoes, other vegetables, fruit, other foods}.

"Food Out": {canteen meals, other restaurant meals, and snacks}.

"Alcohol & tobacco": {beer, wine & spirits, cigarettes, other tobacco}.

"Other Nondurables": {household consumables, petcare, mens outer clothes, women's outer clothes, children's outer clothes, other clothes, footwear, chemist's goods, audio visual goods, records and toys, book & newspapers, gardening goods}.

"Services": {domestic fuels, postage & telephone, domestic services, fees & subscriptions, personal services}.

"Travel": {maintenance of motor vehicles, petrol and oil, vehicle tax and insurance, travel fares, tv licences, entertainment}.

Three Commodity Group System. "Food" = "Food In" + "Food Out"

"Nondurables" = "Alcohol & tobacco" + "Nondurables"

"Services" = "Services" + "Travel"

---

[8] For example, in the Almost Ideal Demand system (Deaton and Muellbuaer, 1980), heterogeneity in the $a(p)$ parameters would automatically satisfy this condition.

REFERENCES

AFRIAT, S. N., "On a System of Inequalities in Demand Analysis: An Extension of the Classical Method," *International Economic Review* 14 (1967), 460–72.

BANKS, J., R. W. BLUNDELL, AND A. LEWBEL, "Quadratic Engel Curves, Indirect Tax Reform and Welfare Measurement," *Review of Economics and Statistics* LXXIX (1997), 527–39.

BECKERT, W., AND R. W. BLUNDELL, "Invertibility of Nonparametric Stochastic Demand Functions," Cemmap Working Paper CWP09/05, July 2005.

BLUNDELL, R., M. BROWNING, AND I. CRAWFORD, "Nonparametric Engel Curves and Revealed Preference" *Econometrica* 71 (2003), 205–40.

——, ——, AND ——, "Best Nonparametric Bounds on Demand Responses," Walms-Bowley Lecture, Econometric Society IFS Working Paper, 05/20, revised February 2007.

——, X. CHEN, AND D. KRISTENSEN, "Semiparametric Engel Curves with Endogenous Expenditure," *Econometrica* (forthcoming).

——, P. PASHARDES, AND G. WEBER, "What Do We Learn about Consumer Demand Patterns from Micro Data?" *American Economic Review* 83 (1993), 570–97.

——, AND J. POWELL, "Endogeneity in Nonparametric and Semiparametric Regression Models," Chapter 8 in M. Dewatripont, L. Hansen, and S. J. Turnovsky, eds., *Advances in Economics and Econometrics* (Cambridge: Cambridge University Press, ESM 36, 2003), 312–57.

BROWN, D. J., AND R. L. MATZKIN, "Estimation of Simultaneous Equations Models, with an Application to Consumer Demand," Cowles Foundation Discussion Paper, 1998.

DEATON, A. S., AND J. MUELLBAUER, "An Almost Ideal Demand System," *American Economic Review* 70 (1980), 312–36.

HAUSMAN, J. A., W. K. NEWEY, H. ICHIMURA, AND J. L. POWELL, "Identification and Estimation of Polynomial Errors-in-Variables Models," *Journal of Econometrics* 50 (1991), 273–95.

JORGENSON, D. W., L. J. LAU, AND T. M. STOKER, "The Transcendental Logarithmic Model of Aggregate Consumer Behavior," in R. Basmann and G. Rhodes, eds., *Advances in Econometrics,* Volume 1 (Greenwich, Connecticut: JAI Press, 1982).

LEWBEL, A., "The Rank of Demand Systems: Theory and Nonparametric Estimation," *Econometrica* 59 (1991), 711–30.

——, "Demand Systems with and without Errors: Reconciling Econometric, Random Utility and GARP Models," *American Economic Review* 91 (2001) 611–8.

MANSKI, C., *Partial Identification of Probability Distributions* (New York: Springer-Verlag, 2003).

MATZKIN, R., "Heterogeneous Choice," in R.W. Blundell, W. Newey, and T. Persson, eds., *Advance in Econometrics: Proceedings of the 9th World Congress* (Cambridge: Econometric Society Monographs, 2007).

——, AND M. K. RICHTER, "Testing Strictly Concave Rationality," *Journal of Economic Theory* 53 (1991), 287–303.

NEWEY, W., J. POWELL, AND F. VELLA, "Nonparametric Estimation of Triangular Simultaneous Equations Models," *Econometrica* 67 (1999), 565–604.

VARIAN, H., "The Nonparametric Approach to Demand Analysis,"*Econometrica* 50 (1982), 945–74.

——, "Nonparametric Tests of Consumer Behaviour," *Review of Economic Studies* 50 (1983), 99–110.

INTERNATIONAL ECONOMIC REVIEW
Vol. 48, No. 4, November 2007

EFFICIENT ESTIMATION OF SEMIPARAMETRIC MODELS BY SMOOTHED MAXIMUM LIKELIHOOD*

By Stephen R. Cosslett[1]

Ohio State University, U.S.A.

A smoothed likelihood function is used to construct efficient estimators for some semiparametric models that contain unknown density functions together with parametric index functions. Smoothing the likelihood makes maximization with respect to the unknown density functions more tractable. The method is used to show the efficiency gains from knowledge of population shares in three cases: (1) binary choice; (2) binary choice when only one outcome is sampled, supplemented by random sampling of the explanatory variables; and (3) linear regression, where the shares are defined by a threshold value of the dependent variable. Semiparametric efficiency is achieved both for parametric components and for a class of functionals of the error density.

1. INTRODUCTION

This article shows how a smoothed likelihood function can be used to construct efficient estimators for some semiparametric models that contain unknown density functions together with parametric index functions.

The main focus here is on the use of aggregate constraints to improve the efficiency of the estimators. The method is illustrated in two relatively simple cases—linear regression and binary choice—where efficient semiparametric estimators are well known for the standard case (without the constraints). For binary choice, the additional information consists of the population shares of the two choices, whereas for the linear model it consists of the population shares of two strata defined according to whether the dependent variable is above or below a given threshold value.

A second focus of this article is on estimation of a binary choice model from a choice-based sample where only one outcome is sampled but there is a supplementary random sample of observations on the explanatory variables, both with and without knowledge of the population shares. (An example would be a consumer-response survey plus census data, where the census did not ask about the binary response; alternatively, it can be viewed as a contaminated choice-based sample, the random sample being the contaminated stratum.)

These models and sample designs were considered in early work on choice-based sampling, including Manski and McFadden (1981), Cosslett (1981), and McFadden (1979). The estimators derived in those papers are partly

* Manuscript received January 2006; revised May 2007.

[1] I would like to thank two referees for helpful comments. Please address correspondence to: Stephen R. Cosslett, Department of Economics, Ohio State University, Columbus, OH 43210, U.S.A. Phone: 614-292-4106. Fax: 614-292-3906. E-mail: *cosslett.1@osu.edu*.

semiparametric in the sense that, although the distribution of the error terms is assumed to have a specified functional form, the distribution of the explanatory variables remains unspecified. The present article provides one method of extending these to the fully semiparametric case, where both distributions are unspecified, while achieving the semiparametric efficiency bounds. The smoothed likelihood method can also be used to obtain efficient semiparametric estimators for the Tobit model (single-equation censored regression), for truncated regression, for endogenously stratified regression with two strata, and the sample selection model.[2]

The maximum likelihood approach leads to estimators of the unknown error distribution functions (for binary choice) or density functions (for the linear model), as well as the finite-dimensional parameters. Semiparametric efficiency for these functions is considered here in a limited sense, where we consider the asymptotic variances of a class of functionals of the distribution that converge at the parametric rate.

The basic idea here is to use kernel smoothing to make functional maximization of the likelihood more tractable, as opposed to its more usual application as a technique for direct estimation of a density or conditional density from the data. Although the maximum likelihood principle is used to find a suitable candidate for an efficient estimator, the estimators themselves are implemented by solving a set of scorelike moment equations (rather than direct maximization of an objective function), and in that regard they are similar to the semiparametric maximum likelihood estimator of Ai (1997).[3]

In some cases the smoothed likelihood approach just leads to a unified method of deriving estimators that are already known; in other cases, it shows how to construct efficient estimators when solution of the functional maximization problem is relatively complicated (requiring more than an application of Jensen's inequality) but still tractable; in yet other cases, where there is no explicit solution of the maximization problem, it remains to be seen whether any progress can be made by using only numerical solutions.

2.   SMOOTHED MAXIMUM LIKELIHOOD

2.1.   *Likelihood Function.*   Consider a log likelihood function for observation i ($i = 1, \ldots, n$) of the form

$$(1) \qquad \log \ell(x_i, y_i, \theta, f) = \sum_j d_{j,i} \log p_j(v_j(x_i, y_i, \theta), f) + \log h(x_i).$$

The observed data consist of dependent variables y_i, explanatory variables x_i, and indicators $d_{j,i} \in \{0, 1\}$ representing different strata. Let $z = (x, y)$. Each component of the vector $v_j(z, \theta)$ may consist of a residual of the form

---

[2] The Tobit estimator was obtained by a different (but closely related) method involving a smoothed self-consistency equation in Cosslett (2004). Results for the other cases will be presented elsewhere. For efficiency bounds, see Newey (1990) and Cosslett (1985, 1987).

[3] A comparison with that estimator is given in Section A.4 of the Appendix.

$u_{j,k}(z_i, \theta) = y_i - x_{i,k}\theta_k$ or an index function of the form $u_{j,k}(z_i, \theta) = x_{i,k}\theta_k$, where $x_{i,k}$ is a subvector of x_i and θ_k is a subvector of θ. The task is to estimate the unknown finite-dimensional parameter vector θ and one or more unknown density functions represented by f.

The smoothing technique consists of replacing each term of the form $\log p_j(v_j, f)$ by

(2)
$$\int du \, \frac{1}{h_n^{r_j}} K\left(\frac{v_j - u}{h_n}\right) \log p_j(u, f),$$

where r_j is the dimension of v_j, K is an r_j-dimensional kernel function, and the bandwidth h_n shrinks at a suitable rate as $n \to \infty$.

The smoothed log likelihood has the form

(3)
$$n^{-1} \log \tilde{L}(\theta, f) = \sum_j \int du \, \tilde{g}_{\theta,j}(u) \log p_j(u, f),$$

where

(4)
$$\tilde{g}_{\theta,j}(u) = \frac{1}{nh_n^{r_j}} \sum_{i=1}^{n} d_{j,i} K\left(\frac{v_j(z_i, \theta) - u}{h_n}\right).$$

Note that in Equation (3), all dependence on the data is contained in the functions $\tilde{g}_{\theta,j}$, and all dependence on the unknown function f is contained in the functions p_j.

In the cases considered here, f will be the density function of a scalar error term, there will be at most two regimes j, and each component p_j of the likelihood will depend on only a single index or residual. This will allow a conventional univariate kernel to be used for smoothing, with $K(u) \geq 0$, $K(u) = K(-u)$, $\int du \, K(u) = 1$, $\int du \, u^2 K(u) < \infty$, and $\int du [K(u)]^2 < \infty$.

The unknown density $h(x)$, which has to be taken into account when there are aggregate constraints (and, more generally, in the case of endogenous stratification), typically has a high-dimensional argument that makes it unsuitable for kernel estimation. Instead, it is estimated (for given θ and f) by its empirical likelihood subject to the aggregate constraints, as in Cosslett (1981).

2.2. *Variational Equation.* The next step is to maximize the smoothed log likelihood (3) with respect to f (or equivalently with respect to $\sqrt{f}$), subject to the normalization $\int du \, f(u) = 1$ and the condition $f(u) \geq 0$. In some simple examples this can be done directly, using Jensen's inequality. In general, the maximization problem involves solving a variational equation. Define the score operator $s_{f,j}(u, f)$ by

(5)
$$s_{f,j}(u, f)[\varphi] = 2p_j^{-1/2}(u, f) D_f p_j^{1/2}(u, f)[\varphi],$$

where $D_f a(f)[\varphi]$ represents the pathwise (Hadamard) functional derivative of $a(f)$ with respect to $\sqrt{f}$ in the direction φ. Because f is a density function, φ is a function such that

(6)
$$\int dv \sqrt{f(v)}\varphi(v) = 0, \quad \int dv \, \varphi(v)^2 < \infty.$$

The variational equation for f is

(7)
$$\sum_j \int du \, \tilde{g}_{\theta,j}(u) s_{f,j}(u, f)[\varphi] = 0$$

for all φ satisfying (6). Considering (7) as a linear operator on φ, and provided that it is mean-square continuous, (7) has a representation of the form $\int du \, A(u, \theta, f)\sqrt{f(u)}\varphi(u) = 0$, so that the equation determining f becomes $A(u, \theta, f) = c$.

The transformation $(u, f) \mapsto p_j$ in typical semiparametric models should involve nothing worse than differentiable functions, integration, and possibly also differentiation. In that case, the functional derivative can be constructed by straightforward functional differentiation based on $\delta f(u)/\delta f(v) = \delta(u - v)$, which is a legitimate operation as long as u is an integration variable and the rest of the integrand is continuous. (A Lagrange multiplier will take care of the restriction $\int du \, f(u) = 1$.) This is of course the motivation for bringing in the smoothing operation (2) before attempting the functional maximization.

Let the solution of (7), when it exists, be $\tilde{f}_\theta(v) = f(v \mid \tilde{g}_\theta)$, where $\tilde{g}_\theta$ is a vector with components $\tilde{g}_{\theta,j}$. The concentrated log likelihood is then

(8)
$$n^{-1} \log \tilde{L}(\theta) = \sum_j \int du \, \tilde{g}_{\theta,j}(u) \log p_j(u, \tilde{f}_\theta).$$

2.3. *Score Function.* The semiparametric estimator $\hat{\theta}$ could in principle be defined as the maximum likelihood estimator corresponding to (8). In practice, however, it will be the solution of a suitably trimmed version of the corresponding score equation. (This is because, except in a few special cases, existing techniques for deriving asymptotic properties rely on convergence of a trimmed score function rather than on convergence of the log likelihood itself.) Before constructing the score function, we take a step back: Substitute the expression (4) for $\tilde{g}_{\theta,j}(u)$ in (8) and change the integration variable to $\eta = (v_j(z_i, \theta) - u)/h_n$, which gives

(9)
$$\log \tilde{L}(\theta) = \sum_{i=1}^{n} \sum_j \int d\eta \, K(\eta) \log p_j(v_j(z_i, \theta) - h_n\eta, \tilde{f}_\theta).$$

The score function is $\tilde{S}(\theta) = \partial \log \tilde{L}(\theta)/\partial\theta$. However, the smoothing over η does not play any substantive role in the asymptotic properties of the score function and can be dropped without loss. We can therefore avoid an additional layer of computational complexity by instead working with the simplified score function

(10)
$$\tilde{S}(\theta) = \sum_{i=1}^{n} \sum_{j} \frac{d}{d\theta} \log p_j(v_j(z_i, \theta), \tilde{f}_\theta).$$

The derivative has been written as $d/d\theta$ to emphasize that it operates on all occurrences of θ, both in the index function v and in the estimated density $\tilde{f}_\theta$, which depends on θ indirectly through its dependence on the functions $\tilde{g}_\theta$.

2.4. *Trimming Correction.* As is well known, a complication of kernel-based estimators is the need for trimming. A typical term in the score function is $\partial \log \tilde{g}/\partial\theta = \tilde{g}^{-1}\partial\tilde{g}/\partial\theta$. Because the denominator $\tilde{g}$ is not bounded away from zero, it has to be trimmed in order to get the uniform convergence in y_i, x_i, and θ that is needed to derive asymptotic properties. Define a general trimming function t such that $t(u) = 1$ for $u \geq 1$ and $t(u) = 0$ for $u \leq 0$, with a smooth polynomial interpolation for $0 \leq u \leq 1$ such that the second derivative is continuous (see, for example, Ai, 1997). Then define the trimming function for $\tilde{g}$ by

$$\tau(\tilde{g}) = t([\tilde{g} - b_n]/b_n),$$

where b_n is a shrinking lower bound on $\tilde{g}$, with the understanding that $g^{-1}\tau(g)$ is zero if $g = 0$. (The dependence of τ on b_n will not be shown explicitly.) A trimmed version of $\partial \log \tilde{g}/\partial\theta$ is then $\tau(\tilde{g})\partial \log \tilde{g}/\partial\theta$. More generally, if the score function contains several denominator terms, an overall trimming factor of the form $\tau(\tilde{g}_1\tilde{g}_2)$ can be used to trim the common denominator.

The existing literature is somewhat unclear about how the argument for asymptotic efficiency of the semiparametric maximum likelihood estimator, as given by Newey (1994), survives this type of trimming. A useful property of the efficient score is

(11)
$$E[D_f s(Z, \theta_0)] = 0,$$

where D_f denotes the functional derivative with respect to f (see Newey, 1994, in particular equations (3.12)–(3.16) and the associated discussion). In effect, this says that variations in the likelihood due to $\tilde{f}$ are asymptotically orthogonal to variations due to $\hat{\theta}$. Since $f_\theta(\varepsilon) = f(\varepsilon \mid g_\theta)$ depends on g_θ, and in general the components of g_θ can vary independently, we can replace (11) by the equivalent condition

(12)
$$E[D_g s(Z, \theta_0)] = 0.$$

However, Equation (12) does not necessarily hold for the trimmed score $s^*(z, \theta_0, f_0)$, and to overcome the resulting asymptotic bias one may have to use higher-order (bias-reducing) kernels or a more complex trimming scheme.

This asymptotic bias can sometimes be corrected by recentering, using the following method. It is applicable if the efficient score (or, more specifically, the part of it that requires trimming) satisfies $E[s(\theta_0) \mid y_d, v(\theta_0)] = 0$ and $E[s(\theta_0) \mid x] = 0$ (where y_d represents the discrete dependent variables, if any), while the corresponding trimmed score satisfies $E[s^*(\theta_0) \mid y_d, v(\theta_0)] = 0$. These conditions hold for the models considered in this article. The recentered or "corrected" trimmed score function in the regression context, where $v(\theta_0) = \varepsilon$ (the error term in the regression), is

$$\tilde{s}^{**}(z, \theta) = \tilde{s}^*(z, \theta) - \tilde{s}^c(x, \theta)$$

with the correction term

(13)
$$\tilde{s}^c(x, \theta) = \int dy\, \tilde{f}_\theta(y - x\theta)\tilde{s}^*(x, y, \theta).$$

In the case of discrete dependent variables, $\tilde{f}_\theta(y - x\theta)$ is replaced by the estimated discrete probability $\tilde{P}(y_d \mid v(\theta), \tilde{f}_\theta)$ and the integral is replaced by a sum over y_d. In fact, (13) can be extended in a straightforward way to models with both discrete and continuous variables. As shown in Lemmas A.1 and A.2 (in the Appendix), the corrected trimmed score then satisfies the required orthogonality property, $E[D_g s^{**}(Z, \theta_0)] = 0$, while also maintaining the properties $E[s^{**}(\theta_0)] = 0$ and $s^{**}(\theta) \to s(\theta)$.

2.5. *Asymptotic Properties.*   Why would we expect the solution of the score equations (or a suitably trimmed version of them) to result in efficient estimators? Under some standard regularity conditions, the kernel estimators $\tilde{g}_{\theta,j}(u)$ converge, uniformly in u and θ, to asymptotic limits $g_{\theta,j}(u)$ at a rate depending on the rate at which $h_n \to 0$, and similarly for derivatives of $\tilde{g}_{\theta,j}(u)$ (see Appendix A.2 for further details). The limiting functions $g_{\theta,j}(u)$ involve the conditional expectations of the functions $p_j(u, f)$, and it follows that

(14) $n^{-1} \log \bar{L}(\theta, f) \equiv \sum_j \int du\, g_{\theta,j}(u) \log p_j(u, f) = E[\log \ell(z, \theta, f)].$

The function $f_\theta = f_\theta(\varepsilon) = f(\varepsilon \mid g_\theta)$ therefore maximizes $E[\log \ell(z, \theta, f)]$. It follows (see Newey, 1994) that the score function

$$s(z, \theta, f_\theta) = \frac{d}{d\theta}\ell(z, \theta, f_\theta)$$

is the (semiparametric) efficient score. This implies that $\bar{\theta}$, the infeasible estimator obtained from the moment conditions $\sum_i s(z_i, \theta, f_\theta) = 0$ (infeasible because the function f_θ is unknown), meets the semiparametric efficiency bound.

The essential step is then to show that uniform convergence of $\tilde{g}$ to g implies uniform convergence of a suitably trimmed version of the score function when expressed in terms of the solution of (7), i.e.,

(15) $$s(z, \theta, f(\cdot \mid \tilde{g}_\theta)) \to s(z, \theta, f(\cdot \mid g_\theta)).$$

Specifically, if we denote the score functions corresponding to the left- and right-hand sides of (15) by $\tilde{S}(\theta) = \sum_i \tilde{s}_i(\theta)$ and $S(\theta) = \sum_i s_i(\theta)$, then a standard classical argument shows that $\hat{\theta}$ will have the same asymptotic distribution as $\bar{\theta}$ (and so will be asymptotically efficient) if (i) $n^{-1}\tilde{S}(\theta)$ and $n^{-1}\partial \tilde{S}(\theta)/\partial \theta$ converge to $n^{-1}S(\theta)$ and $n^{-1}\partial S(\theta)/\partial \theta$ in probability uniformly in θ and (ii) $n^{-1/2}\tilde{S}(\theta_0)$ converges in probability to $n^{-1/2}S(\theta_0)$.

It is difficult to find general conditions on the likelihood function such that these convergence conditions hold. Instead, we proceed by first deriving an explicit expression for the estimated score function and then verifying that it does indeed converge to the efficient score. The convergence rate of the trimmed score and its derivative can be found by methods developed in the literature on kernel-based semiparametric estimators by, among others, Ichimura and Lee (1991), Klein and Spady (1993), and Ai (1997). A summary is given in Appendix A.2: Under standard regularity conditions, there is a range of convergence rates for the window width h_n and the trimming parameter b_n that is sufficient for asymptotic efficiency of $\hat{\theta}$. These rates depend only on the convergence rates of $\tilde{g}$ and its derivatives and are the same for each of the single-index models considered in this article.

2.6. Estimated Distribution Function.

Semiparametric maximum likelihood also delivers an estimator $\tilde{F}$ of the distribution function, and this may improve when there is additional information such as knowledge of aggregate shares. For binary choice models, we consider efficiency of $\tilde{F}$ in the limited sense of efficient estimation of the functional $\psi(a) = \int du\, a(u)F(u)$, for a suitable class of bounded integrable functions $a(u)$. Estimates of $\psi(a)$ converge at the parametric rate $n^{-1/2}$, so its asymptotic variance can be compared with a conventional semiparametric efficiency bound. One can also estimate functionals of the form $\psi(a) = \int du\, a(u)f(u)$ in regression models, although this is probably less useful.

The estimator of $\psi(a)$ is $\hat{\psi}(a) = \int du\, a(u)\tilde{F}(u \mid \hat{\theta})$, where now $\tilde{F}(\cdot \mid \theta)$ is re-estimated using a faster-shrinking bandwidth h_n in order to control asymptotic bias. This is an easier strategy than maximizing $\log \tilde{L}(\theta, F)$ with respect to F subject to $\int du\, a(u)F(u) = \psi$ and then maximizing the concentrated log likelihood with respect to the parameters θ and ψ. The derivation of the asymptotic variance is summarized in Appendix A.7, and with some restrictions on $a(u)$ we find that $\hat{\psi}(a)$ achieves the efficiency bound.

3. BINARY CHOICE

This provides a relatively simple example to illustrate the basic approach, without having to solve a variational equation or to estimate the density of the explanatory variables. Not surprisingly, the resulting estimator in this case is essentially the same as the efficient semiparametric estimator of Klein and Spady (1993). The present approach allows the use of standard (as opposed to bias-reducing) kernels, although it is based on the solution of the score equations rather than maximization of a bona fide objective function (the estimated log likelihood in the Klein–Spady estimator). In the following, F is unrestricted, so there is no intercept in the index function $x\theta$ and there is an (unspecified) scale normalization for θ.

For the standard binary choice model (with random sampling and unknown aggregate shares) the log likelihood is

$$\log L(\theta, F) = \sum_{i=1}^{n} \{1(y_i = 1) \log F(x_i\theta) + 1(y_i = 0) \log[1 - F(x_i\theta)]\},$$

and the smoothed version is

$$(16) \quad n^{-1} \log \tilde{L}(\theta, F) = \int du \, \{\tilde{g}_{\theta,1}(u) \log F(u) + \tilde{g}_{\theta,0}(u) \log[1 - F(u)]\},$$

where

$$\tilde{g}_{\theta,j}(u) = \frac{1}{nh_n} \sum_{i=1}^{n} 1(y_i = j) K\left(\frac{x_i\theta - u}{h_n}\right).$$

By Jensen's inequality, (16) is maximized with respect to F at

$$(17) \quad \tilde{F}_\theta(u) = \tilde{g}_{\theta,1}(u)/\tilde{g}_\theta(u),$$

where $\tilde{g}_\theta(u) = \tilde{g}_{\theta,1}(u) + \tilde{g}_{\theta,0}(u)$, and the concentrated likelihood is

$$n^{-1} \log \tilde{L}(\theta) = \int du \, \{\tilde{g}_{\theta,1}(u) \log \tilde{g}_{\theta,1}(u) + \tilde{g}_{\theta,0}(u) \log \tilde{g}_{\theta,0}(u) - \tilde{g}_\theta(u) \log \tilde{g}_\theta(u)\}.$$

The score function corresponding to (10) (after dropping the "outer" smoothing, as discussed in Section 2.3) is then

$$(18)$$

$$\tilde{S}(\theta) = \sum_{i=1}^{n} \tilde{s}_i(\theta) = \sum_{i=1}^{n} \left\{ 1(y_i = 1) \frac{d}{d\theta} \log \frac{\tilde{g}_{\theta,1}(x_i\theta)}{\tilde{g}_\theta(x_i\theta)} + 1(y_i = 0) \frac{d}{d\theta} \log \frac{\tilde{g}_{\theta,0}(x_i\theta)}{\tilde{g}_\theta(x_i\theta)} \right\},$$

which is the same as the score for the Klein and Spady (1993) estimator.

One way of ensuring that $E[D_g s^*(\theta_0)] = 0$ is to multiply all terms in $\tilde{s}_i(\theta)$ by a common trimming factor $\tilde{\tau}_i(\theta)$:

$$(19) \quad \tilde{s}_i^*(\theta) = 1(y_i = 1)\tilde{\tau}_i(\theta) \frac{d}{d\theta} \log \frac{\tilde{g}_{\theta,1}(x_i\theta)}{\tilde{g}_\theta(x_i\theta)} + 1(y_i = 0)\tilde{\tau}_i(\theta) \frac{d}{d\theta} \log \frac{\tilde{g}_{\theta,0}(x_i\theta)}{\tilde{g}_\theta(x_i\theta)}.$$

A suitable term is $\tilde{\tau}_i(\theta) = \tau[\tilde{g}_{\theta,1}(x_i\theta)] \cdot \tau[\tilde{g}_{\theta,0}(x_i\theta)]$. (There is no need to trim $\tilde{g}$ separately because $\tilde{g} \geq \max\{\tilde{g}_0, \tilde{g}_1\}$, with nonnegative kernels.) The asymptotic limit of (19) at θ_0 is

(20) $s_i^*(\theta_0) = -(x_i - E[X \mid X\theta_0 = x_i\theta_0])$

$$\times \tau_i(\theta_0) \left\{ 1(y_i = 1)\frac{f(x_i\theta_0)}{F(x_i\theta_0)} - 1(y_i = 0)\frac{f(x_i\theta_0)}{1 - F(x_i\theta_0)} \right\},$$

where $\tau_i(\theta_0) = \tau[h_*(x_i\theta_0)F(x_i\theta_0)] \cdot \tau[h_*(x_i\theta_0)(1 - F(x_i\theta_0))]$ and $h_*(\cdot)$ is the marginal density of $x\theta_0$. Then $E[s^*(\theta_0) \mid y, x\theta_0] = 0$ and $E[s(\theta_0) \mid x] = 0$, so Lemma A.2 is applicable. Substituting (19) in Equation (A.3) gives $\tilde{s}^c(\theta) = 0$, and therefore no trimming correction is needed when a common trimming factor is used. The trimmed score function $\tilde{S}^*(\theta)$ is then defined by substituting $\tilde{s}_i^*(\theta)$ for $\tilde{s}_i(\theta)$ in (18).

Finally, $\hat{\theta}$ is computed by solving the trimmed score equation $\tilde{S}^*(\theta) = 0$. Asymptotic efficiency can be demonstrated by the method discussed in Section 2.5, and the rate-of-convergence calculations are summarized in Appendix A.2. We note that efficiency of $\hat{\theta}$ can be achieved using a standard kernel function if the bandwidth shrinks at a rate between $n^{-1/5}$ and $n^{-1/8}$. The asymptotic variance of $\hat{\theta}$ is then given by the efficiency bound

(21) $$V_\theta^{-1} = \int du\, h_*(u) \frac{f(u)^2}{F(u)[1 - F(u)]} \mathrm{var}[X \mid X\theta_0 = u].$$

To estimate the functional $\psi(a) = \int du\, a(u)F(u)$, we have to trim the denominator in $\tilde{F}$:

(22) $$\hat{\psi}(a) = \int du\, a(u)\tau[\tilde{g}_{\hat{\theta}}(u)]\tilde{F}_{\hat{\theta}}(u).$$

The kernel bandwidth used to compute (22) has to shrink at a faster rate, between $n^{-1/2}$ and $n^{-1/4}$, to avoid asymptotic bias in $\sqrt{n}(\hat{\psi} - \psi)$. There is no practical way (within the present approach) to avoid trimming bias in the tails of the integrand, so we require $a(u)$ to have bounded support and that $h_*(u) > 0$. The derivation of the asymptotic variance is summarized in Appendix A.7. It is again equal to the semiparametric efficiency bound, which in this case is

(23) $$V_\psi = V_1 + V_2' V_\theta V_2,$$

where

(24) $$V_1 = \int du\, \frac{a(u)^2}{h_*(u)} F(u)[1 - F(u)]$$

(25) $$V_2 = \int du\, a(u)\, f(u)\, E[x \mid x\theta_0 = u]$$

provided the integral in (24) exists.

4. BINARY CHOICE WITH KNOWN SHARES

Let the population shares of the two outcomes be Q_0 and Q_1, and let the sample shares be $H_0 = n_0/n$ and $H_1 = n_1/n$. The new information is given by the constraint equation

$$(26) \qquad \int dx\, h(x) F(x\theta) = Q_1,$$

where Q_1, the population share of outcome 1, is known. This shows that the unknown density $h(x)$ of the explanatory variables cannot be ignored in maximizing the likelihood

$$\log L(\theta, F, h) = \sum_{i=1}^{n} \{1(y_i = 1) \log F(x_i\theta) + 1(y_i = 0) \log[1 - F(x_i\theta)] + \log h(x_i)\},$$

i.e., the constraint will affect the estimates of both F and $h(x)$. This leads to a three-step estimator: (i) estimate h by empirical likelihood, subject to the constraint, for given F and θ; (ii) estimate F by solving the variational equation for the smoothed (partially concentrated) likelihood, for given θ; and (iii) estimate θ from the resulting score equation.

As in the case of endogenously stratified sampling (Cosslett, 1981, 1993), construct the nonparametric maximum likelihood estimator of $h(x)$ subject to (26) for given F and θ. This assigns a mass point w_i to each observation,

$$w_i = w_i(\theta, F) = \frac{1}{n} \frac{1}{1 + \lambda[Q_1 - F(x_i\theta)]},$$

where the Lagrange multiplier $\lambda = \lambda(\theta, F)$ is determined by the aggregate share constraint,

$$(27) \qquad \frac{1}{n} \sum_{i=1}^{n} \frac{F(x_i\theta)}{1 + \lambda[Q_1 - F(x_i\theta)]} = Q_1.$$

(This equation has a spurious solution at $\lambda = -1/Q_1$, but this will not be a problem because $\lambda \to 1$ in the asymptotic limit.) Substituting back in $L(\theta, F, h)$ gives the partially concentrated log likelihood

$$\log L(\theta, F) = \sum_{i=1}^{n} \{1(d_i = 1) \log F(x_i\theta) + 1(d_i = 0) \log[1 - F(x_i\theta)]$$
$$- \log(1 + \lambda[Q_1 - F(x_i\theta)])\}$$

(apart from constants). Smoothing over $x_i\theta$ then gives

$$n^{-1} \log \tilde{L}(\theta, F) = \int du \{\tilde{g}_{\theta,1}(u) \log F(u) + \tilde{g}_{\theta,0}(u) \log[1 - F(u)]$$
$$- \tilde{g}_\theta(u) \log(1 + \tilde{\lambda}[Q_1 - F(u)])\}$$

with $\tilde{\lambda} = \tilde{\lambda}(\theta, F)$ determined by the smoothed version of (27),

$$(28) \qquad \int du \, \tilde{g}_\theta(u) \frac{F(u)}{1 + \tilde{\lambda}[Q_1 - F(u)]} = Q_1,$$

and $\tilde{g}_{\theta,1}(u)$, $\tilde{g}_{\theta,0}(u)$, and $\tilde{g}_\theta(u)$ defined as in the previous section.

Let $\tilde{F}_\theta(u)$ be the distribution function that maximizes $\log \tilde{L}(\theta, F)$. The variational equation (first-order condition for F) gives

$$(29) \qquad \frac{\tilde{g}_{\theta,1}(u)}{\tilde{F}_\theta(u)} - \frac{\tilde{g}_{\theta,0}(u)}{1 - \tilde{F}_\theta(u)} + \tilde{\lambda} \frac{\tilde{g}_\theta(u)}{1 + \tilde{\lambda}[Q_1 - \tilde{F}_\theta(u)]} = 0.$$

Note that (28) is the implicit definition of $\tilde{\lambda}(\theta, F)$, not a constraint equation, and that $\partial \log \tilde{L}/\partial \tilde{\lambda} = 0$. From (29), the solution is

$$\tilde{F}_\theta(u) = \frac{(1 + \tilde{\lambda} Q_1)\tilde{g}_{\theta,1}(u)}{(1 + \tilde{\lambda} Q_1)\tilde{g}_{\theta,1}(u) + (1 - \tilde{\lambda} Q_0)\tilde{g}_{\theta,0}(u)},$$

although it is not guaranteed to be a proper distribution function. Substituting $F(u) = \tilde{F}_\theta(u)$ in (28) gives

$$\int du \, \tilde{g}_{\theta,1}(u)/[1 - \tilde{\lambda} Q_0] = Q_1.$$

But $\int du \, \tilde{g}_{\theta,1}(u) = H_1$, and therefore $\tilde{\lambda}(\theta, \tilde{F}_\theta)$ does not depend on θ:

$$\tilde{\lambda} = (H_0/Q_0) - (H_1/Q_1).$$

Note that $H_1 \to Q_1$ and $H_0 \to Q_0$ (under random sampling) as $n \to \infty$ and therefore $\tilde{\lambda} \to 0$. The solution of the maximization problem can now be written as

$$(30) \qquad \tilde{F}_\theta(u) = \frac{Q_1}{H_1}\tilde{g}_{\theta,1}(u) \left(\frac{Q_1}{H_1}\tilde{g}_{\theta,1}(u) + \frac{Q_0}{H_0}\tilde{g}_{\theta,0}(u) \right)^{-1}.$$

Substituting for F and $\tilde{\lambda}$ in $\log \tilde{L}(\theta, F)$, and using the identities $\int du \, \tilde{g}_{\theta,1}(u) = H_1$ and $\int du \, \tilde{g}_{\theta,0}(u) = H_0$ to eliminate constant terms, the concentrated log likelihood can be written as

$$n^{-1} \log \tilde{L}(\theta) = \int du \left\{ \tilde{g}_{\theta,1}(u) \log \frac{\tilde{g}_{\theta,1}(u)}{\tilde{g}_\theta(u)} + \tilde{g}_{\theta,0}(u) \log \frac{\tilde{g}_{\theta,0}(u)}{\tilde{g}_\theta(u)} \right\}.$$

This is the same as in the case of unknown aggregate shares, so knowledge of the aggregate shares does not affect estimation of θ (which is not surprising because the semiparametric efficiency bounds are the same in the two cases).

The additional information is, however, responsible for the improved estimator (30) of the distribution function. Let $\tilde{g}_{\theta,d}(u)$ denote the denominator term in (30). Then the analog of (22) is

(31) $$\hat{\psi}(a) = \int du\, a(u)\tau[\tilde{g}_{\hat{\theta},d}(u)]\tilde{F}_{\hat{\theta}}(u)$$

with $\tilde{F}_{\hat{\theta}}(u)$ now given by (30). The asymptotic variance again has the form $V_\psi = V_1 + V_2'V_\theta V_2$, with V_2 given by (25) and V_θ by (21), but with an extra term in V_1,

(32) $$V_1 = \int du\, \frac{a(u)^2}{h_*(u)} F(u)[1 - F(u)] - \frac{1}{Q_1 Q_0}\left(\int du\, a(u)F(u)[1 - F(u)]\right)^2,$$

where the second integral represents the improvement due to knowledge of Q.

5. BINARY CHOICE WITH A "CONTAMINATED" CHOICE-BASED SAMPLE

In this case the data consist of two samples of x, one drawn from the stratum with $y = 1$ and the other from the whole population. In the context of endogenous stratification, this can be viewed as a truncated sample, where only one of the strata is sampled and a supplementary random sample of x is then needed to identify the model. Alternatively, it can be viewed as a contaminated choice-based sample, where the random sample is "contaminated" by cases with $y = 1$ instead of being drawn entirely from the stratum with $y = 0$. There do not seem to be any previous results on fully semiparametric estimation of this model, where $F(\varepsilon)$ is unknown as well as $h(x)$.

Define stratum indicators by $s = 1$ for the n_1 choice-based observations with $y = 1$, and $s = 2$ for the n_2 observations from a random sample on x. Let $H_1 = n_1/n$ and $H_2 = n_2/n$, where $n = n_1 + n_2$. Note that the likelihood for an observation with $s = 1$ is $\Pr\{x \mid y = 1\}$. The overall log likelihood is then

(33) $$n^{-1}\log L(\theta, F, h) = \frac{1}{n}\sum_{i=1}^{n}\{1(s_i = 1)\log[F(x_i\theta)/Q_1] + \log h(x_i)\},$$

where, as before,

(34) $$Q_1 = \int dx\, h(x)F(x\theta).$$

If Q_1 is unknown, then (34) defines Q_1 in (33) as a function of θ and F. If Q_1 is known, then (34) is a constraint to be taken into account when maximizing the likelihood. In either case we have to deal with the unknown function $h(x)$.

5.1. *Unknown Shares.*   The first step is nonparametric maximum likelihood estimation of $h(x)$ for given θ and F. This is the same as in the case of a parametric distribution function F (Cosslett, 1981). The discrete weights are

$$w_i = \frac{1}{n} \frac{1}{(H_1/q_1)F(x_i\theta) + H_2},$$

where q_1 is defined as the solution of

$$(35) \qquad \frac{1}{n} \sum_{i=1}^{n} \frac{1}{(H_1/q_1)F(x_i\theta) + H_2} = 1.$$

The partially concentrated likelihood is

$$\log L(\theta, f) = \sum_{i=1}^{n} \{1(s_i = 1) \log F(x_i\theta) - \log[(H_1/q_1)F(x_i\theta) + H_2]\} - H_1 \log q_1.$$

The smoothed version is

$$n^{-1} \log \tilde{L}(\theta, f) = \int du \{\tilde{g}_{\theta,1}(u) \log F(u) - \tilde{g}_\theta(u) \log[(H_1/\tilde{q}_1)F(u) + H_2]\}$$
$$- H_1 \log \tilde{q}_1,$$

where

$$(36) \qquad \tilde{g}_{\theta,s}(u) = \frac{1}{nh_n} \sum_{i=1}^{n} 1(s_i = s) K\left(\frac{x_i\theta - u}{h_n}\right), \quad s = 1, 2$$

$$\tilde{g}_\theta(u) = \tilde{g}_{\theta,1}(u) + \tilde{g}_{\theta,2}(u)$$

and $\tilde{q}_1$ is the solution of the smoothed version of (35),

$$(37) \qquad \int du\, \tilde{g}_\theta(u) \frac{1}{(H_1/\tilde{q}_1)F(u) + H_2} = 1.$$

The variational equation for maximization of $\tilde{L}(\theta, F)$ with respect to F is

$$\frac{\tilde{g}_{\theta,1}(u)}{\tilde{F}_\theta(u)} - \frac{H_1}{\tilde{q}_1} \frac{\tilde{g}_\theta(u)}{(H_1/\tilde{q}_1)\tilde{F}_\theta(u) + H_2} = 0$$

(the derivative of $\tilde{L}(\theta, F)$ with respect to $\tilde{q}_1$ is zero, so the functional derivative of $\tilde{q}_1$ with respect to F is not needed), and therefore

$$(38) \qquad \tilde{F}_\theta(u) = \tilde{q}_1 \frac{H_2}{H_1} \frac{\tilde{g}_{\theta,1}(u)}{\tilde{g}_{\theta,2}(u)}.$$

Substituting into $\tilde{L}(\theta, F)$ finally gives the concentrated smoothed log likelihood,

$$(39) \qquad n^{-1} \log \tilde{L}(\theta) = \int du \left\{ \tilde{g}_{\theta,1}(u) \log \frac{\tilde{g}_{\theta,1}(u)}{\tilde{g}_\theta(u)} + \tilde{g}_{\theta,2}(u) \log \frac{\tilde{g}_{\theta,2}(u)}{\tilde{g}_\theta(u)} \right\}.$$

This has the same form as binary choice between the two strata—we can just assign $y = 0$ to all cases in the supplementary (or contaminated) sample and proceed as if the pooled data had been randomly sampled.

The same trimmed score can be used as in Section 3—Lemma A.2 is still valid if $\Pr\{y \mid x\theta_0\}$ is replaced by $\Pr\{s \mid x\theta_0\}$, the probability that a randomly drawn observation from the pooled sample is in stratum s conditional on the value of $x\theta_0$. Although the score has the same functional form as for conventional binary choice, its asymptotic limit is different:

$$s(\theta_0) = -(x - E[X \mid x\theta_0]) f(x\theta_0) \left\{ 1(s = 1) \frac{1}{F(x\theta_0)} - \frac{H_1}{Q_1} \left(\frac{H_1}{Q_1} F(x\theta_0) + H_2 \right)^{-1} \right\}$$

is the same as the efficient score, and the asymptotic variance for $\hat{\theta}$ is equal to the semiparametric efficiency bound

$$(40) \quad V_\theta^{-1} = \frac{H_1 H_2}{Q_1} \int du\, h_0(u) \frac{f(u)^2}{F(u)[(H_1/Q_1)F(u) + H_2]} \text{var}[X \mid X\theta_0 = u].$$

Substituting $F(u) = \tilde{F}_\theta(u)$ in (37) results in an identity, so $\tilde{q}_1$ is not identified, and (38) determines $\tilde{F}_\theta(u)$ only up to a constant factor. One could attempt "identification at infinity" by setting $\tilde{F}_{\hat{\theta}}(x\hat{\theta}) = 1$ at the largest observed value of $x\hat{\theta}$, but the information bound for $\psi(a)$ is zero and thus there is no $\sqrt{n}$-consistent estimator of $\psi(a)$.

5.2. *Known Shares.* The first step, nonparametric estimation of $h(x)$, is the same as for standard binary choice with known shares, in Section 4. The partially concentrated smoothed log likelihood is

$$(41) \quad n^{-1} \log \tilde{L}(\theta, F) = \int du\, \{\tilde{g}_{\theta,1}(u) \log F(u) - \tilde{g}_\theta(u) \log(1 + \tilde{\lambda}[Q_1 - F(u)])\},$$

where $\tilde{g}_{\theta,1}$ and $\tilde{g}_\theta$ are defined by (36) and $\tilde{\lambda} = \tilde{\lambda}(\theta, F)$ is determined as the solution of (28). The solution of the variational problem for maximizing $\tilde{L}(\theta, F)$ with respect to F is

$$(42) \quad \tilde{F}_\theta(u) = -[(1 + \tilde{\lambda} Q_1)/\tilde{\lambda}] \cdot \tilde{g}_{\theta,1}(u)/\tilde{g}_{\theta,2}(u).$$

Substituting for F in (28) gives

$$\int du\, \tilde{g}_{\theta,2}(u)/[1 + \tilde{\lambda} Q_1] = H_2/[1 + \tilde{\lambda} Q_1] = 1,$$

and therefore $\tilde{\lambda} = \tilde{\lambda}(\theta, \tilde{F}) = -H_1/Q_1$.

The resulting expressions for $\tilde{F}_\theta(u)$ and $\tilde{L}(\theta)$ are the same as for the case of unknown shares, (38) and (39), except that $\tilde{q}_1$ is replaced by Q_1. The estimator of θ is unchanged, which again is not surprising because the semiparametric efficiency bound is also the same. On the other hand, $\tilde{F}_\theta(u)$ is now properly identified because Q_1 is known.

The functional $\psi(a) = \int du\, a(u)F(u)$ can be estimated by the analog of (22), which is

$$(43) \qquad \hat{\psi}(a) = \int du\, a(u)\tau[\tilde{g}_{\hat\theta,2}(u)]\tilde{F}_{\hat\theta}(u).$$

The asymptotic variance again has the form $V_\psi = V_1 + V_2'V_\theta V_2$, with V_2 given by (25), but now V_θ is given by (40) and there is a new expression for V_1,

$$(44) \quad V_1 = \int du\, \frac{a(u)^2}{h_*(u)}F(u)\left(\frac{1}{H_2}F(u)+\frac{Q_1}{H_1}\right) - \frac{1}{H_1 H_2}\left(\int du\, a(u)F(u)\right)^2.$$

6.   LINEAR REGRESSION

The adaptive estimator for linear regression (Bickel, 1982) is by now a classic example of efficient semiparametric estimation. All the same, linear regression provides a nice illustration of smoothed maximum likelihood and trimming bias correction, before considering the more complicated case of known population shares. In the following, f is unrestricted, so there is no intercept in the regression. The smoothed log likelihood is

$$(45) \qquad n^{-1}\log \tilde{L}(\theta, f) = \int du\, \tilde{g}_\theta(u)\log f(u)$$

with

$$(46) \qquad \tilde{g}_\theta(u) = \frac{1}{nh_n}\sum_{i=1}^{n} K\left(\frac{y_i - x_i\theta - u}{h_n}\right).$$

By Jensen's inequality, (45) is maximized at $f = \tilde{f}_\theta(u) = \tilde{g}_\theta(u)$. The concentrated log likelihood function is

$$n^{-1}\log \tilde{L}(\theta) = \int du\, \tilde{g}_\theta(u)\log \tilde{g}_\theta(u)$$

and the trimmed score function corresponding to (10) is

$$(47) \qquad \tilde{S}^*(\theta) = \sum_{i=1}^{n}\tilde{s}_i^*(\theta) = \sum_{i=1}^{n}\tau[\tilde{g}_\theta(y_i - x_i\theta)]\frac{d}{d\theta}\log \tilde{g}_\theta(y_i - x_i\theta).$$

This converges at $\theta = \theta_0$ to

$$s_i^*(\theta_0) = -(x_i - E[X])\tau[f(\varepsilon_i)]f'(\varepsilon_i)/f(\varepsilon_i),$$

(where $\varepsilon_i = y_i - x_i\theta_0$), which is a trimmed version of the efficient score. The conditions for Lemma A.1 hold, and the trimming bias correction is given by (A.1). The final expression for the trimmed, bias-corrected score is[4]

(48)

$$\tilde{s}_i^*(\theta) = \tau[\tilde{g}_\theta(y_i - x_i\theta)]\frac{d}{d\theta}\log\tilde{g}_\theta(y_i - x_i\theta) - \int dy\,\tau[\tilde{g}_\theta(y - x_i\theta)]\frac{d}{d\theta}\tilde{g}_\theta(y - x_i\theta).$$

Then $\hat{\theta}$ is the solution of $\tilde{S}^*(\theta) = 0$ (or if there are multiple solutions, the one closest to the least squares estimator).

As in the case of binary choice, asymptotic efficiency can be demonstrated by the method discussed in Section 2.5, and the rate-of-convergence calculations summarized in Appendix A.2 also apply here, with h_n shrinking at a rate between $n^{-1/5}$ and $n^{-1/8}$. Convergence of the second term in (48) is discussed in Appendix A.6 and can be achieved without trimming of the range of integration. The asymptotic variance of $\hat{\theta}$ is equal to the usual semiparametric efficiency bound, $V_\theta^{-1} = \text{var}[X]\int d\varepsilon\, f'(\varepsilon)^2/f(\varepsilon)$.

7. LINEAR REGRESSION WITH KNOWN STRATUM SHARES

Without loss, let the two strata be $\{y < 0\}$ and $\{y \geq 0\}$. The known shares are Q_0 and $Q_1 = 1 - Q_0$, where

$$Q_0 = \Pr\{y_i < 0\} = \int dx\,h(x)F(-x\theta).$$

As in the other cases of known shares (Sections 4 and 5.2), we start by nonparametric maximum likelihood estimation of the density $h(x)$. The only difference is that, according to the usual conventions, the labeling of the strata is reversed and the sign of the argument of F is changed. The resulting smoothed log likelihood is given by

(49) $$n^{-1}\log\tilde{L}(\theta, f) = \int du\,\{\tilde{g}_{\theta,1}(u)\log f(u) - \tilde{g}_{\theta,2}(u)\log\bar{F}(-u, \lambda)\},$$

where

$$\tilde{g}_{\theta,1}(u) = \frac{1}{nh_n}\sum_{i=1}^{n}K\left(\frac{y_i - x_i\theta - u}{h_n}\right), \quad \tilde{g}_{\theta,2}(u) = \frac{1}{nh_n}\sum_{i=1}^{n}K\left(\frac{x_i\theta - u}{h_n}\right),$$

$$\bar{F}(u, \lambda) \equiv 1 + \lambda[Q_0 - F(u)],$$

---

[4] The integral does increase the computational complexity—it has to be evaluated numerically over the range where $0 < \tau[\tilde{g}(y - x\theta)] < 1$, although this should be small and not require great precision.

and $\lambda = \lambda\,(\theta, f)$ is the solution of

$$(50) \qquad \int du\, \tilde{g}_{\theta,2}(u) \frac{F(-u)}{\bar{F}(-u, \lambda)} = Q_0.$$

7.1. *Optimization.* Maximize $\tilde{L}(\theta, f)$ subject to $\int du\, f(u) = 1$. Let $f = \tilde{f}_\theta(u)$ be the solution, with distribution function $\tilde{F}_\theta(u)$, and let $\bar{\tilde{F}}_\theta(u, \lambda)$ be the corresponding solution for $\bar{F}(u, \lambda)$. The first-order condition is

$$(51) \qquad \frac{\tilde{g}_{\theta,1}(v)}{\tilde{f}_\theta(v)} + \int_{-\infty}^{-v} du\, \tilde{g}_{\theta,2}(u) \frac{\lambda}{\bar{\tilde{F}}_\theta(-u, \lambda)} + \mu = 0,$$

where μ is a Lagrange multiplier. This can be rewritten as

$$\tilde{g}_{\theta,1}(v) - \tilde{g}_{\theta,2}(-v) - \frac{d}{dv}\left\{ \bar{\tilde{F}}_\theta(v, \lambda) \int_{-\infty}^{-v} du\, \tilde{g}_{\theta,2}(u) \frac{1}{\bar{\tilde{F}}_\theta(-u, \lambda)} \right\} + \mu \tilde{f}_\theta(v) = 0.$$

Integrate from $-\infty$ to v:

$$\tilde{G}_\theta(v) - \frac{1}{\lambda}(1 + \lambda Q_0)(1 - \lambda Q_1)$$

$$- \bar{\tilde{F}}_\theta(v, \lambda)\left\{ \int_{-\infty}^{-v} du\, \tilde{g}_{\theta,2}(u) \frac{1}{\bar{\tilde{F}}_\theta(-u, \lambda)} - \frac{1}{\lambda}(1 + \lambda Q_0) \right\} = 0,$$

where we define

$$(52) \qquad \tilde{G}_\theta(v) = \int_{-\infty}^{v} du\, \{\tilde{g}_{\theta,1}(u) - \tilde{g}_{\theta,2}(-u)\}$$

and use the boundary condition $\tilde{G}_\theta(\infty) = 0$ to eliminate the Lagrange multiplier μ. Finally, after dividing by $\bar{\tilde{F}}_\theta(v, \lambda)$ and differentiating with respect to v, the first-order condition becomes a linear differential equation

$$\frac{d\bar{\tilde{F}}_\theta(v, \lambda)}{dv}\{\tilde{G}_\theta(v) - \lambda^{-1}(1 + \lambda Q_0)(1 - \lambda Q_1)\} - \bar{\tilde{F}}_\theta(v, \lambda)\tilde{g}_{\theta,1}(v) = 0.$$

Taking into account the boundary condition $\bar{F}(-\infty, \lambda) = 1 + \lambda Q_0$, and defining

$$(53) \qquad \tilde{m}_{\theta,1}(v, \lambda) = \frac{\tilde{g}_{\theta,1}(v)}{(1 + \lambda Q_0)(1 - \lambda Q_1) - \lambda \tilde{G}_\theta(v)},$$

the solution is

$$(54) \qquad \bar{\tilde{F}}_\theta(u, \lambda) = (1 + \lambda Q_0)\exp\left\{ -\lambda \int_{-\infty}^{u} dv\, \tilde{m}_{\theta,1}(v, \lambda) \right\}.$$

The upper boundary condition $\bar{F}(\infty, \lambda) = 1 - \lambda Q_1$ then gives the restriction

(55) $$\lambda \int dv\, \tilde{m}_{\theta,1}(v, \lambda) - \log \frac{1 + \lambda Q_0}{1 - \lambda Q_1} = 0.$$

Given (54), the restrictions (50) and (55) are equivalent.

The resulting concentrated log likelihood is

(56) $$\log \tilde{L}(\theta) = \sum_{i=1}^{n} \log \tilde{m}_{\theta,1}(y_i - x_i\theta, \lambda) - \sum_{i=1}^{n} \lambda \int_0^{y_i} dv\, \tilde{m}_{\theta,1}(v - x_i\theta, \lambda)$$

with the understanding that $\int_0^y dv$ is to be interpreted as $-\int_y^0 dv$ when $y < 0$.

7.2. *Score Function.* Note that the Lagrange multiplier λ is not a free parameter, but is determined implicitly as a function of θ by the subsidiary condition (55). Since $\lambda \to 0$ in the asymptotic limit, we can simplify the restriction. The expansion of (55) in powers of λ has the form $\tilde{r}_1(\theta)\lambda^2 + \tilde{r}_2(\theta)\lambda^3 + \cdots$, and without loss we can use the asymptotic approximation[5]

(57) $$d\lambda/d\theta = -\tilde{r}_1'(\theta)/\tilde{r}_2(\theta).$$

The score function is

(58) $$\tilde{S}(\theta) = \sum_{i=1}^{n} \{\tilde{s}_{i,\theta}(\theta) - [\tilde{r}_1'(\theta)/\tilde{r}_2(\theta)]\tilde{s}_{i,\lambda}(\theta)\},$$

where

$$\tilde{s}_{i,\theta}(\theta) = \frac{d}{d\theta}\left(\log \tilde{m}_{\theta,1}(y_i - x_i\theta, \lambda)\right) - \lambda \int_0^{y_i} dv\, \frac{d}{d\theta}\tilde{m}_{\theta,1}(v - x_i\theta, \lambda)$$

$$\tilde{s}_{i,\lambda}(\theta) = \frac{\partial}{\partial\lambda}\left(\log \tilde{m}_{\theta,1}(y_i - x_i\theta, \lambda)\right) - \int_0^{y_i} dv\, \frac{\partial}{\partial\lambda}\left(\lambda\tilde{m}_{\theta,1}(v - x_i\theta, \lambda)\right).$$

7.3. *Trimming.* Because $|\tilde{G}(u \mid \theta)| \le 1$, the denominator term $(1 + \lambda Q_0)(1 - \lambda Q_1) - \lambda\tilde{G}(u \mid \theta)$ is bounded away from zero, provided that $|\lambda| < \frac{1}{2}$. (That is not a substantive restriction because the known asymptotic limit of λ is 0.) The term $\tilde{r}_2(\theta)$ is not necessarily positive in finite samples, but it converges in probability to a strictly positive limit. It follows that the only term in the score function that needs to be trimmed (in order to derive asymptotic results) is the same as the score for the unrestricted linear model:

---

[5] From (61) below, $E[s_\lambda(\theta_0)] = 0$; otherwise, we would need to expand $d\lambda/d\theta$ to first order in λ in order to get the correct expression for the asymptotic Hessian matrix $dS(\theta_0)/d\theta$.

$$\tilde{s}_U(\theta) \equiv \frac{d}{d\theta} \log \tilde{g}_{\theta,1}(y_i - x_i\theta).$$

Apply the same trimming scheme as in (48), with the correction term, and leave the rest of the score function unchanged.[6] Then $s^{**}(\theta) - s(\theta) = s_U^{**}(\theta) - s_U(\theta)$. Because the untrimmed scores satisfy the orthogonality condition (12), and because $E[D_g s_U^{**}(\theta_0)] = 0$ by Lemma A.1, it follows that the orthogonality condition $E[D_g s^{**}(\theta_0)] = 0$ also holds for the restricted model.

7.4. *Asymptotics.* The asymptotic score function at $\theta = \theta_0$ is now more complicated:

(59) $$s_i(\theta_0) = s_{i,\theta}(\theta_0) - [r_1'(\theta_0)/r_2(\theta_0)]s_{i,\lambda}(\theta_0),$$

with the following components:

(60) $$s_{i,\theta}(\theta_0) = (E[X] - x_i)f'(\varepsilon_i)/f(\varepsilon_i)$$

(61) $$s_{i,\lambda}(\theta_0) = F(-x_i\theta) + H_0(-\varepsilon_i) - 2Q_0$$

(62) $$r_1'(\theta_0) = \int dv \, f(v)h_0(-v)\,(E[X] - E[X|\,X\theta_0 = -v])$$

(63) $$r_2(\theta_0) = \int dv \left[h_0(-v)F(v)^2 + f(v)H_0(-v)^2\right] - 2Q_0^2.$$

Asymptotic efficiency can again be demonstrated by the method discussed in Section 2.5, using the rate-of-convergence calculations summarized in Appendix A.2. The only new feature to be taken into account is that, conditional on θ, (55) defines an implicit functional dependence of λ on $\tilde{g}_{\theta,1}$ and $\tilde{G}_\theta$. The analog of (57) is

$$D_g\lambda = -D_g[\tilde{r}_1(\theta)]/\tilde{r}_2(\theta),$$

which is then used in carrying out the linear expansion of the score in $(\tilde{g}_1 - g)$ and $(\tilde{G} - G)$.

The asymptotic variance of $\hat{\theta}$ is given by

(64) $$V_\theta^{-1} = \int d\varepsilon \, \frac{f'(\varepsilon)^2}{f(\varepsilon)} \text{var}[X] + \frac{r_1'(\theta_0)r_1'(\theta_0)^T}{r_2(\theta_0)}.$$

---

[6] A simplification is to use $\tilde{g}(u\,|\,\theta)$ instead of $\tilde{f}(u\,|\,\theta)$ in the correction term. Both converge to $f(u)$ at the same rate, and there is no need for efficiency in estimating the bias.

The second term represents the improvement due to knowledge of the population shares. As expected, (59) is the efficient score and (64) the semiparametric
efficiency bound.

8. CONCLUSION

Smoothing the log likelihood makes maximization with respect to unknown
functions tractable in a number of cases, without compromising the efficiency of
estimation from the concentrated likelihood. In some cases, the method provides
a unifying perspective on existing efficient semiparametric estimators, whereas in
other cases it can lead to new and reasonably tractable efficient estimators both
for the parametric component and for functionals of the unknown distribution
function.

APPENDIX

A.1. *Estimation of the Probability Density Function.* For each of the estimators
considered here, the asymptotic properties can be derived by essentially the same
method as in Ai (1997); for a presentation more closely aligned with the present
setup, see also Cosslett (2004). The basic approach, using methods developed
in the semiparametric literature by Ichimura and Lee (1991), Klein and Spady
(1993), and others, is to show the asymptotic equivalence between the estimator
$\hat{\theta}$ and the infeasible estimator $\bar{\theta}$ based on the efficient score.

This and the following section outline the derivation of the asymptotic properties of the estimator, and in doing so present a set of sufficient conditions for
asymptotic efficiency of the estimator. They are not, however, suitable for characterizing the set of models for which the method can be used; in particular, the
requirement that the solution of the variational problem can be regularized (Condition 4) warrants further investigation.

As before, denote the likelihood function for a single observation by $\ell(z, \theta, f)$,
$\theta \in \Theta$, $f \in \mathcal{F}$. For simplicity, we suppose that auxiliary parameters arising from
external constraints or from endogenous stratification have been concentrated
out (although that might not be the best way to proceed in practice). Let $f_\theta \in \mathcal{F}$
maximize $E[\log \ell(Z, \theta, f)]$. When the likelihood has the form given in (1), then
(in an abbreviated notation) $E[\log (Z, \theta, f)] = \int dv\, g_\theta(v) p(v, f)$, where $g_\theta(v)$
represents the marginal densities of the index functions $v(z_i, \theta)$. Let $\mathcal{G}$ be the set
of all densities of this form (for example, if g_1 is the density of (v_1, v_2) and g_2 is the
density of v_2, then $g \in \mathcal{G}$ would satisfy $\int dv_1 g_1(v_1, v_2) = g_2(v_2)$ and $\int dv_2 g_2(v_2) = 1$,
but not any further constraints that might be imposed on $g(v \mid \theta)$ by the structure
of the likelihood), such that the integral

$$q(f \mid g) = \int dv\, g(v) \log p(v, f)$$

exists. Suppose that $f = f(\cdot \mid g)$ solves the variational problem $D_f q(f \mid g)[\phi] =
0$ for all $\phi \in \Phi$, where $D_f a(f)[\varphi]$ is the pathwise derivative of $a(f)$ with respect
to $\sqrt{f}$ in the direction φ, and Φ represents the relevant tangent space (i.e., the
set of square-integrable functions ϕ that are orthogonal to $\sqrt{f}$ and satisfy any

other restrictions that follow from $f \in \mathcal{F}$). Then $f_\theta = f(\cdot \mid g_\theta)$. Denote the score function for the concentrated likelihood by $S_n(\theta) = \sum_i s(z_i, \theta)$, where $s(z, \theta) = (d/d\theta)\log \ell(z, \theta, f_\theta)$. Then, under appropriate regularity conditions, the (infeasible) estimator $\bar{\theta}$ defined by $S_n(\bar{\theta}) = 0$ achieves the semiparametric efficiency bound (see Newey, 1994).

The following summarizes a suitable set of conditions for the argument so far; some are not specific to the estimation method in this article and are not given in detail. The preliminary estimator is needed because the method is based on the score function rather than the log likelihood.

CONDITION 1. (i) The likelihood $\ell(z, \theta, f)$, $\theta \in \Theta$, $f \in \mathcal{F}$ satisfies conditions for consistency of the maximum likelihood estimator of (θ, f). (ii) The moment equation $S_n(\theta) = 0$ satisfies a set of classical conditions for consistency and asymptotic normality of the estimator $\bar{\theta}$. (iii) A preliminary consistent estimator of θ is available.

CONDITION 2. The function $q(f \mid g)$ is pathwise differentiable with respect to $\sqrt{f}$ for $g \in \mathcal{G}$, and the corresponding linear operator $D_f q(f \mid g)$ is mean square continuous.

Let $\tilde{g}_\theta$ be the kernel estimator of g_θ, and let $\tilde{f}_\theta = f(\cdot \mid \tilde{g}_\theta)$. Let $D_g f(u \mid g)$ denote the linear operator corresponding to the pathwise derivative of $f(u \mid g)$ with respect to g. The essential problem is that $D_g f(u \mid g)$ is generally not bounded, so we cannot derive uniform convergence of $f(\cdot \mid \tilde{g}_\theta)$ to $f(\cdot \mid g_\theta)$. In specific examples, with an explicit expression for $f(u \mid g)$, this problem can usually be solved by inspection—for example, if a term of the form a/g_1 appears, it could be replaced by the trimmed term $\tau(g_1)a/g_1$ (with the trimming function τ defined as in Section 2.4). In general, however, the feasibility of regularization remains as a condition to be verified.

CONDITION 3. The kernel K is such that $\tilde{g}_\theta \in \mathcal{G}$ for all θ in a neighborhood of θ_0.

CONDITION 4. There is a regularized version $f^*(\cdot \mid g, b)$ of the function $f(\cdot \mid g)$, with trimming parameter b, such that (i) $D_g f^*(u \mid g, b) = O(b^{-1})$ and (ii) $f^*(\cdot \mid g, b) \to f(\cdot \mid g)$ as $b \to 0$.

CONDITION 5. For θ in a neighborhood of θ_0, there is a uniform convergence bound for $(D_g f^*) \cdot [\tilde{g}_\theta - g_\theta]$ in terms of n and h_n as $n \to \infty$ and $h_n \to 0$, and similarly for the derivatives $\partial f^*/\partial\theta$ and $\partial^2 f^*/\partial\theta\partial\theta'$.

For a given choice of kernel K, Condition 3 does place a restriction on how fast $p(v, \theta)$ can decrease with v. With regard to Condition 5, uniform convergence bounds on kernel estimators of density functions and their derivatives have been given by Bierens (1983), Andrews (1995), Ai (1997), and others. Specific examples of such bounds are given in Section A.2. Section A.6 illustrates how these uniform convergence results can be applied to a more complicated linear transformation, specifically the case where the kernel appears in an integrand. Derivatives such as $\partial f^*/\partial\theta$ are evaluated by the chain rule as $D_g f^*[\partial g_\theta/\partial\theta]$.

As discussed in Section A.2, we also require a second-order expansion of the score in g at $\theta = \theta_0$, so Conditions 4 and 5 need to be extended:

CONDITION 6. At $\theta = \theta_0$, (i) $D_g^2 f^*(u \mid g, b) = O(b^{-2})$, and (ii) there is a uniform convergence bound for $(D_g^2 f^*) \cdot [\tilde{g}_\theta - g_\theta]$, and similarly for $\partial f^* / \partial \theta$.

Finally, f^* is substituted into the score $s(z, \theta) = (d/d\theta) \log p(v(z, \theta), f)$ and its derivative $ds(z, \theta)/d\theta$, so we need:

CONDITION 7. $(d/d\theta) p(v(z, \theta), f)$ and $(d^2/d\theta d\theta') p(v(z, \theta), f)$ are uniformly continuous in f and its first two derivatives.

The explicit denominator terms in the score also need to be trimmed, as in Ai (1997), but this does not present any further difficulty. The resulting regularized score is denoted $s^*(z, \theta)$. Note that in the examples presented in this article, explicit expressions for $p(v, f(\cdot \mid g))$ in terms of g allowed the regularization of f and the trimming of s to be done in a single step.

A.2. *Convergence of the Score Function.* The convergence rate of the trimmed score and its derivative can be found by methods developed in the semiparametric literature by Ichimura and Lee (1991), Klein and Spady (1993), Ai (1997), and others. A detailed account is given in Ai (1997); for a discussion more closely aligned with the present setup, see also Cosslett (2004). Essentially the same proofs hold here with minor variations. We summarize the procedure, including also an explanation of the role of the orthogonality condition $E[D_g s^*(Z, \theta_0)] = 0$.

As discussed in Section 2.5, one needs to show that $n^{-1}[\tilde{S}^*(\theta) - S(\theta)] \to 0$ and $n^{-1}[\partial \tilde{S}^*(\theta)/\partial \theta - \partial S(\theta)/\partial \theta] \to 0$ in probability uniformly in θ, and that $n^{-1/2}[\tilde{S}^*(\theta_0) - S(\theta_0)] \to 0$ converges in probability. Each of these is done in two steps, for example $n^{-1}[\tilde{S}^*(\theta) - S^*(\theta)] \to 0$ and $n^{-1}[S^*(\theta) - S(\theta)]$, where $S^*(\theta)$ denotes the trimmed version of $S(\theta)$. The first step is the critical one; the second step requires $E[S^*(\theta_0)] = 0$, but then just depends on $b_n \to 0$ at a rate that can be made as slow as needed to accommodate the first step. However, uniform convergence of $E[S^*(\theta)]$ requires one more condition on the regularization scheme:

CONDITION 8. The trimmed score $s^*(z, \theta)$ is bounded by a function with finite expectation for all θ in a neighborhood of θ_0 and all sufficiently small b (the trimming parameter).

The following discussion assumes that the dominant terms involved in the convergence rates of $n^{-1} \tilde{S}^*(\theta)$ and $n^{-1} \partial \tilde{S}^*(\theta)/\partial \theta$ are $d\tilde{g}_\theta/d\theta$ and $d^2\tilde{g}_\theta/d\theta^2$ respectively, as in the examples considered here.

(i) Under some standard regularity conditions, there are uniform bounds for the convergence of kernel estimators $\tilde{g}_{\theta, j}(u)$ and their derivatives to their limiting values. Specifically,[7]

---

[7] The notation n^{p+} means any power of n greater than p; logarithmic terms have been dropped.

$$\left| d^r \tilde{g}_\theta(u - x\theta)/d\theta^r - d^r g_\theta(u - x\theta)/d\theta^r \right|$$
$$= (c + |x|^r)\{O(h_n^{-r-1/2})o_p(n^{-1/2+}) + O(h_n^2)\}$$

(where the first bound comes from uniform convergence and the second is the kernel bias). For definiteness, consider the regression estimator. In showing that $n^{-1}[\tilde{S}^*(\theta) - S^*(\theta)] \to 0$ and $n^{-1}[\partial \tilde{S}^*(\theta)/\partial \theta - \partial \tilde{S}(\theta)/\partial \theta] \to 0$, the critical term (i.e., with the slowest rate of convergence) is

$$\tau(\tilde{g})\tilde{g}^{-1}(d^2\tilde{g}/d\theta^2) - \tau(g)g^{-1}(d^2g/d\theta^2)$$
$$= (c + |x|^2)O(b_n^{-1}h_n^{-5/2})o_p(n^{-1/2+})$$

(anticipating that b_n will shrink more slowly than h_n), so we must have $b_n^{-1}h_n^{-5/2}n^{-1/2+} \to 0$.

(ii) A different technique is needed to show that $n^{-1/2}(\tilde{S}^*(\theta_0) - S^*(\theta_0)) \to 0$, because the kernel estimates necessarily converge at a slower rate than $n^{-1/2}$. Instead, expand the difference in powers of $(\tilde{g} - g)$ and $(d\tilde{g}/d\theta - dg/d\theta)$ and then deal separately with the linear terms and the higher-order terms. The second-order terms are quite complicated: The worst-case terms are $\tau(g)g^{-2}(\tilde{g} - g)(d\tilde{g}/d\theta - dg/d\theta)$ and $\tau'(g)g^{-1}(\tilde{g} - g)(d\tilde{g}/d\theta - dg/d\theta)$ with rate $b_n^{-2}h_n^{1/2}n^{-1/2+}$, and $\tau''(g)g^{-1}(\tilde{g} - g)^2(dg/d\theta)$ with rate $b_n^{-3}h_n^4$. We therefore need $b_n^{-2}h_n^{1/2} \to 0$ and $b_n^{-3}h_n^4 n^{1/2} \to 0$.

(iii) Finally, the linear terms are disposed of by combining the sum over observations i contributing to the score function with the sums over observations j in the kernel estimates, resulting in a double sum of the form $n^{-3/2}\sum_{i,j}\psi_{i,j}$ with $\psi_{i,j} = \psi(\varepsilon_i, \varepsilon_j, x_i, x_j)$ and $E[\psi_{i,j}] = 0$. This can be symmetrized to form a U-statistic, and the projection theorem of Powell et al. (1989) can be applied to show that this term is of order $E[\psi_{i,j} | \varepsilon_i, x_i] + E[\psi_{i,j} | \varepsilon_j, x_j]$. The first of these conditional expectations contains the bias in the kernel estimates and is $O(b_n^{-2}h_n^2)$, which is not a limiting factor, and the second term is zero. This is where the orthogonality condition $E[D_g s(Z, \theta_0)] = 0$ comes into play—it is the reason for $E[\psi_{i,j} | \varepsilon_j, x_j] = 0$, whereas otherwise the convergence rate would depend on the tail structure of the density f as well as on b_n and would be difficult to control.

Putting all the rate requirements together, the bandwidth h_n for a scalar index function can shrink at a rate $n^{-\alpha}$ with $\frac{1}{8} < \alpha < \frac{1}{5}$ (as far as asymptotic theory is concerned).[8,9]

---

[8] The trimming factor b_n can then converge at a rate $n^{-\beta}$, where β is the smallest of $\alpha/4, (1 - 5\alpha)/2$, and $(8\alpha - 1)/6$. As with other kernel-based semiparametric estimators, these rates are very slow and are admittedly of little practical significance. Some previous simulation studies of kernel-based estimators for regression and binary choice suggest that the trimming parameter can in fact shrink faster than the rates that have been proved sufficient.

[9] For a bivariate index function, a similar calculation shows that a bias-reducing kernel is needed. In that case we can no longer start from a smoothed log likelihood ($\tilde{\ell}$ is not a likelihood), but it should still be possible to show asymptotic equivalence of $\hat{\theta}$ and $\bar{\theta}$.

A.3. *Unrestricted Density of Index Functions.* A special case of the variational problem occurs when the functions $g \in G$ are "unrestricted," in following sense. Suppose that for any $g \in G$ there are densities f_1 and h_1, depending on g but not depending on θ, such that $g(v)$ is the density of $v(z, \theta)$ under $\ell(z, \theta, f_1, h_1)$. (The density h_1 need not be unique, but f_1 must be unique for identification.) It follows immediately that $q(f \mid g)$ is maximized at $f(\cdot \mid g) = f_1$. In some cases, solving for f_1 in terms of g might be easier than solving the variational problem.

An example in which the density of the index functions is unrestricted is the Tobit model (Cosslett, 2004). Let g_1 be the joint probability density of $y - x\theta$ and $d = 1$ (where d is the censoring indicator) and let g_2 be the joint probability density of $-x\theta$ and $d = 0$. Then under $\ell(z, \theta, f, h)$, $g_{\theta,1}(u) = f(u)[1 - H_*(-u)]$ and $g_{\theta,2}(u) = F(u)h_*(-u)$, where f is the density of the error term, h_* is the marginal density of $x\theta$, and F and H_* are the corresponding distribution functions. This represents a pair of integral equations for f and h_*. Noting that $g_1 + g_2$ is an exact differential, we can readily find the solution

$$F(u \mid g) = \exp\left\{-\int_u^\infty dv\, g_1(v)/G(v)\right\},$$

where G is the distribution function corresponding to $g_1 + g_2$.

A.4. *Semiparametric Maximum Likelihood Estimator.* A closely related estimator is the semiparametric maximum likelihood estimator of Ai (1997). In a large class of semiparametric models, the likelihood can be expressed as the conditional density of an index function, conditional on a second index function. This can be expressed in a form analogous to (1),

$$\log \ell(y \mid x, \theta, f) = \log p_1(v(z, \theta), f) - \log p_2(v_2(x, \theta), f) - \log p_3(v_3(z, \theta)),$$

where $p_1(v, f) = g(v \mid \theta)$, the density of $v(z, \theta) = (v_1(z, \theta), v_2(x, \theta))$, $p_2(v_2(x, \theta), f) = g_2(v_2 \mid \theta)$, the density of $v_2(x, \theta)$, and $p_3(v_3) = v_3$, where $v_3(z, \theta)$ is the Jacobian term. The estimator is constructed by substituting $\tilde{g}_\theta$ for g_θ. There is, however, no optimization with respect to f.

The unrestricted case occurs when any conditional density $g(v_1, v_2)/g_2(v_2)$ can be represented as the conditional density of $v_1(z, \theta)$ given $v_2(x, \theta)$ under $\ell(y \mid x, \theta, f_1)$ for some f_1. In that case the two estimators are the same: The optimal f is $f_\theta = f_1$, but there is no need to solve for f_1 because the likelihood is already expressed in terms of g_θ.[10] The set of such models is now smaller, because the conditional density does not depend on h, and it does not include the example in the previous section.

As noted by Ai (1997), when the structure of the likelihood does restrict the space of conditional densities of the index functions, the semiparametric maximum likelihood estimator is still consistent and asymptotically normal with an

---

[10] This also implies that regularization of f is not needed here.

asymptotic variance that can be estimated, but it generally does not meet the efficiency bound.

A.5. *Trimming Bias Correction.* The following results were used in re-centering the trimmed score functions so as to restore the orthogonality condition $E[D_g s^*(Z, \theta_0)] = 0$.

LEMMA A.1. *In the case where $y = x\theta_0 + \varepsilon$, with ε and x independent, suppose that $E[s^*(Z, \theta_0) \mid \varepsilon] = 0$ and $E[s(x, Y, \theta_0) \mid x] = 0$. Let*

$$(A.1) \qquad \tilde{s}^c(x, \theta) = \int dy \, \tilde{f}_\theta(y - x\theta) \tilde{s}^*(x, y, \theta)$$

and let $\tilde{s}^{**}(z, \theta) = \tilde{s}^*(z, \theta) - s^c(x, \theta)$ be the corrected trimmed score. Then (i) $E[D_g s^{**}(Z, \theta_0)] = 0$; (ii) $s^{**}(z, \theta_0) \to s(z, \theta_0)$ as $b_n \to 0$, where b_n is the trimming parameter; and (iii) $E[s^{**}(Z, \theta_0)] = 0$.

PROOF. To verify (i), consider the functional derivative

$$D_g s^c(x, \theta_0) = \int dy \, f_0(y - x\theta_0) D_g s^*(x, y, \theta_0) + \int dy \, (D_g \, f_0(y - x\theta_0)) s^*(x, y, \theta_0)$$

$$= E[D_g s^*(x, Y, \theta_0) \mid x] + \int d\varepsilon (D_g \, f_0(\varepsilon)) s^*(x, x\theta_0 + \varepsilon, \theta_0)$$

with expected value

$$E[D_g s^c(X, \theta_0)] = E[D_g s^*(Z, \theta_0)] + \int d\varepsilon (D_g \, f_0(\varepsilon)) E[s^*(Z, \theta_0) \mid \varepsilon].$$

By assumption the last term is zero and therefore

$$E[D_g s^*(X, Y, \theta_0)] - E[D_g s^c(X, \theta_0)] = 0$$

as required. To verify (ii), consider the asymptotic limit of (A.1) at $\theta = \theta_0$:

$$(A.2) \qquad s^c(x, \theta_0) = \int d\varepsilon \, f_0(\varepsilon) s^*(x, x\theta_0 + \varepsilon, \theta_0) = E[s^*(x, Y, \theta_0) \mid x].$$

As $b_n \to 0$, $E[s^*(x, Y, \theta_0) \mid x] \to E[s(x, Y, \theta_0) \mid x]$, which is zero by assumption. Therefore $s^c(x, \theta_0) \to 0$, which is the same as $s^{**}(z, \theta_0) \to s(z, \theta_0)$. To verify (iii), note that (A.2) implies $E[s^{**}(x, Y, \theta_0) \mid x] = 0$, and the result follows. ∎

LEMMA A.2. *In the case where y is discrete, with $p(y \mid x, \theta) = p(y \mid x\theta)$, suppose that $E[s^*(X, y, \theta_0) \mid y, x\theta_0] = 0$ and $E[s(x, Y, \theta_0) \mid x] = 0$. Then the results of Lemma A.1 hold if we replace the correction term (A.1) by*

$$(A.3) \qquad \tilde{s}^c(x, \theta) = \sum_y \tilde{p}(y \mid x\theta, \theta) \tilde{s}^*(x, y, \theta).$$

The proofs of Lemmas A.1 and A.2 are essentially the same. An obvious corollary is that, under the stated conditions, $E[D_g s^*(Z, \theta_0)] = 0$ if (A.1) or (A.3) is zero.

A.6. *Integrals of Trimmed Kernel Estimates.* These convergence results can be extended to the case where a kernel estimate is integrated over an infinite range, such as the bias correction term in (48) or the constraint equation (55). This avoids the need to trim the range of integration, which would introduce a whole new layer of complexity. For definiteness, consider the example

$$\Delta \tilde{M}(\theta) = \tilde{M}(\theta) - M(\theta) = \int du \, \frac{\partial \tilde{g}_\theta(u)}{\partial \theta} \tau(\tilde{g}_\theta(u)) - \int du \, \frac{\partial g_\theta(u)}{\partial \theta} \tau(g_\theta(u)),$$

where $\tilde{g}_\theta(u)$ is given by (46). Rewrite as $\tilde{M}(\theta) = \tilde{M}_1(\theta) + \tilde{M}_2(\theta)$, where

$$\tilde{M}_1(\theta) = \int du \, \frac{\partial \tilde{g}_\theta(u)}{\partial \theta} \tau(g_\theta(u)), \quad \tilde{M}_2(\theta) = \int du \, \frac{\partial \tilde{g}_\theta(u)}{\partial \theta} [\tau(\tilde{g}_\theta(u)) - \tau(g_\theta(u))].$$

Change the order of summation and integration,

$$\tilde{M}_1(\theta) = -\frac{1}{n} \sum_{i=1}^{n} x_i \int du \, \frac{1}{h_n^2} K'\left(\frac{e_i - u}{h_n}\right) \tau(g_\theta(u)),$$

where $e_i = y_i - x_i \theta$, and then integrate by parts and change the integration variable,

$$\tilde{M}_1(\theta) = -\frac{1}{n} \sum_{i=1}^{n} x_i \int d\eta \, K(\eta) \tau'(g_\theta(e_i - h_n\eta)) \frac{\partial g_\theta(e_i - h_n\eta)}{\partial \theta}.$$

This is a sum of independent terms, and $\tilde{M}_1(\theta) - E[\tilde{M}_1(\theta)]$ is uniformly bounded (under conventional regularity conditions) by $o_p(n^{-1/2}) O(b_n^{-1})$. Similarly,

$$\tilde{M}_2(\theta) = -\frac{1}{n} \sum_{i=1}^{n} x_i \int d\eta \, K(\eta) \left(\tau'(\tilde{g}_\theta(e_i - h_n\eta)) \frac{\partial \tilde{g}_\theta(e_i - h_n\eta)}{\partial \theta} \right.$$

$$\left. - \tau'(g_\theta(e_i - h_n\eta)) \frac{\partial g_\theta(e_i - h_n\eta)}{\partial \theta} \right).$$

Applying the uniform bounds $\partial \tilde{g}/\partial \theta - \partial g/\partial \theta = o_p(n^{-1/2+}) O(h_n^{-3/2})$ and $\tau'(\tilde{g}) - \tau'(g) = O(h_n^2 b_n^{-2})$, we find that $\tilde{M}_2(\theta)$ is bounded by $o_p(n^{-1/2+}) O(h_n^{-3/2} b_n^{-1}) + O(h_n^2 b_n^{-2})$. The remaining term is the kernel bias $M_1(\theta) - E[\tilde{M}_1(\theta)] = O(h_n^2)$. Collecting terms, the bound on $\Delta \tilde{M}(\theta)$ is $o_p(n^{-1/2+}) O(h_n^{-3/2} b_n^{-1}) + O(h_n^2 b_n^{-2})$. This is the same as the rate of convergence of the integrand apart from a factor $O(b_n^{-1})$, which is an adequate bound for present purposes.

If the integrand does not need to be trimmed, as in (55), the additional factor $O(b_n^{-1})$ does not arise.

A.7. Estimating a Weighted Integral of the Distribution Function.

The rates of convergence associated with a weighted integral of the distribution function are different from those associated with the score function. For definiteness, consider binary choice with $\hat{\psi} = \hat{\psi}(a)$ defined by (22). The assumption that $A = \{u \mid a(u) > 0\}$ is bounded and that $h_*(u)$ is bounded away from zero for $u \in A$ means that eventually $\psi^* = \psi$, where ψ^* is the trimmed version of ψ, $\psi^* = \int du\, a(u) F(u) \tau[h_*(u)]$. Expand $\sqrt{n}(\hat{\psi} - \psi)$ to first order in $\tilde{G}_{\theta_0,1}(u) - G_{\theta_0,1}(u)$, $\tilde{G}_{\theta_0}(u) - G_{\theta_0}(u)$, and $\hat{\theta} - \theta_0$, noting that $G_{\theta_0,1}(u) = F(u) h_*(u)$ and $G_{\theta_0}(u) = h_*(u)$:

$$\frac{1}{\sqrt{n}} \sum_{i=1}^{n} \int du\, \frac{a(u)}{h_*(u)} \frac{1}{h_n} K\left(\frac{x_i\theta_0 - u}{h_n}\right) [d_{1,i} - F(u)]$$

$$+ \frac{1}{n} \sum_{i=1}^{n} \int du\, \frac{a(u)}{h_*(u)} \frac{1}{h_n^2} K'\left(\frac{x_i\theta_0 - u}{h_n}\right) x_i [d_{1,i} - F(u)]$$

$$\cdot \sqrt{n}(\hat{\theta} - \theta_0) + o_p(n^{-1/2+}) O(h_n^{-1} b_n^{-3}),$$

where the remainder term comes from the uniform convergence rate for $\tilde{G}_{\theta,1}(u)$ and $\tilde{G}_\theta(u)$ and from expansion of the trimming factor. Under conventional regularity conditions, the sample mean in the second sum converges in probability to $-V_2 + O(h_n^2)$, where V_2 is given by (25). Substitute for $\hat{\theta} - \theta_0$,

$$n^{1/2}(\hat{\theta} - \theta_0) = n^{-1/2} V_\theta \sum_{i=1}^{n} s_i(\theta_0) + o_p(1),$$

where V_θ is the asymptotic variance of $\hat{\theta}$ and $s_i(\theta_0)$ is the efficient score for the binary choice model. Suppose that $h_n = o(n^{-1/4})$, so that the asymptotic bias is negligible. Then the remaining sum

$$\frac{1}{\sqrt{n}} \sum_{i=1}^{n} \left\{ \int du\, \frac{a(u)}{h_*(u)} \frac{1}{h_n} K\left(\frac{x_i\theta_0 - u}{h_n}\right) [d_{1,i} - F(u)] - V_2 V_\theta s_i(\theta_0) \right\}$$

converges in distribution with asymptotic variance

$$V_\psi = \int du\, \frac{a(u)^2}{h_*(u)} F(u)[1 - F(u)] + V_2' V_\theta V_2$$

as required. Examining the bounds on the bias and remainder terms shows that we need $h_n \sim n^{-\alpha}$ with $\frac{1}{4} < \alpha < \frac{1}{2}$. (This is, of course, a different bandwidth from the one used in estimating θ.) A drawback of this approach is that slow convergence rate of the trimming parameter b_n generally does not allow $\psi^* - \psi$ to converge at the parametric rate, which is why we had to restrict $a(u)$ to functions with bounded support.[11]

REFERENCES

AI, C., "A Semiparametric Maximum Likelihood Estimator," *Econometrica* 65 (1997), 933–63.

ANDREWS, D. W. K., "Nonparametric Kernel Estimation for Semiparametric Models," *Econometric Theory* 11 (1995), 560–96.

BICKEL, P. J., "On Adaptive Estimation," *Annals of Statistics* 10 (1982), 647–71.

BIERENS, H. J., "Uniform Consistency of Kernel Estimators of a Regression Function under Generalized Conditions," *Journal of the American Statistical Association* 77 (1983), 699–707.

COSSLETT, S. R., "Efficient Estimation of Discrete Choice Models," in C. F. Manski and D. McFadden, eds., *Structural Analysis of Discrete Data with Econometric Applications* (Cambridge, MA: MIT Press, 1981).

———, "Efficiency Bounds for Distribution-Free Estimators from Endogenously Stratified Samples," paper presented at the World Congress of the Econometric Society, 1985.

———, "Efficiency Bounds for Distribution-Free Estimators of the Binary Choice and the Censored Regression Models," *Econometrica* 55 (1987), 559–85.

———, "Estimation from Endogenously Stratified Samples," in *Handbook of Statistics, Volume 11: Econometrics* (Amsterdam: North Holland, 1993).

———, "Efficient Semiparametric Estimation of Censored and Truncated Regressions via a Smoothed Self-Consistency Equation," *Econometrica* 72 (2004), 1277–93.

ICHIMURA, H., AND L.-F. LEE, "Semiparametric Least Squares Estimation of Multiple Index Models: Single Equation Estimation," in W. A. Barnett, J. Powell, and G. E. Tauchen, eds., *Nonparametric and Semiparametric Methods in Econometrics and Statistics* (Cambridge: Cambridge University Press, 1991), 3–49.

KLEIN, R. W., AND R. H. SPADY, "An Efficient Semiparametric Estimator of Binary Response Models," *Econometrica* 61 (1993), 387–421.

MANSKI, C., AND D. McFADDEN, "Alternative Estimators and Sample Designs for Discrete Choice Analysis," in C. F. Manski and D. McFadden, eds., *Structural Analysis of Discrete Data with Econometric Applications* (Cambridge, MA: MIT Press, 1981).

McFADDEN, D., "Econometric Analysis of Discrete Data," *Fisher-Schultz Lecture*, Athens, 1979.

NEWEY, W. K., "Semiparametric Efficiency Bounds," *Journal of Applied Econometrics* 5 (1990), 99–135.

———, "The Asymptotic Variance of Semiparametric Estimators," *Econometrica* 62 (1994), 1349–82.

POWELL, J. L., J. H. STOCK, AND T. M. STOKER, "Semiparametric Estimation of Index Coefficients," *Econometrica* 57 (1989), 1403–30.

---

[11] Even with higher-order kernels, $\tilde{G}$ necessarily converges more slowly than $n^{-1/2}$, and therefore convergence of the remainder term requires b_n to converge more slowly than $n^{-1/6}$.

INTERNATIONAL ECONOMIC REVIEW
Vol. 48, No. 4, November 2007

THE IDENTIFICATION AND ECONOMIC CONTENT OF ORDERED CHOICE MODELS WITH STOCHASTIC THRESHOLDS*

BY FLAVIO CUNHA, JAMES J. HECKMAN, AND SALVADOR NAVARRO[1]

University of Pennsylvania, U.S.A.; University of Chicago, U.S.A., American Bar Foundation and University College, Dublin; and University of Wisconsin, U.S.A.

This article extends the widely used ordered choice model by introducing stochastic thresholds and interval-specific outcomes. The model can be interpreted as a generalization of the GAFT (MPH) framework for discrete duration data that jointly models durations and outcomes associated with different stopping times. We establish conditions for nonparametric identification. We interpret the ordered choice model as a special case of a general discrete choice model and as a special case of a dynamic discrete choice model.

1. INTRODUCTION

Throughout his career, Daniel McFadden (1974, 1981) has stressed the importance of economic theory in formulating and interpreting econometric models. He has also stressed the value of stating the exact conditions under which an econometric model is identified. The best-known example of his approach is his analysis of discrete choice, but there are other examples (e.g., Fuss and McFadden, 1978). In some of his earliest work (1963), he exposited the implicit economic assumptions used by Theil in the Rotterdam model of consumer demand. [2]

This article continues the McFadden tradition by examining the economic foundations of the widely used ordered discrete choice model. We extend this model to allow for thresholds that depend on observables and unobservables to jointly

* Manuscript received May 2007; revised June 2007.

[1] Earlier versions of this article circulated as part of "Dynamic Treatment Effects" (Heckman and Navarro, 2004) and "Dynamic Discrete Choice and Dynamic Treatment Effects" (Heckman and Navarro, 2007). This research was supported by NIH R01-HD043411 and NSF SES-0241858. Cunha acknowledges support from the Claudio Haddad Dissertation Fund at the University of Chicago. The views expressed in this article are those of the authors and not necessarily those of the funders listed here. Versions of this article were presented at the UCLA Conference on Panel Data in April 2004; at the Econometrics Study Group, UCL, in London in June 2004; at econometrics seminars at the University of Toulouse in November 2004 and at Northwestern University in April 2005; and at the Festschrift in honor of Daniel McFadden at the University of California at Berkeley in May 2005. Jeremy Fox, Han Hong, Rosa Matzkin, and Aureo de Paula provided useful comments on previous versions. We benefited from comments received at the University of Chicago econometrics workshop in May 2007, especially those from Victor Chernozhukov and Lars Hansen. We also thank two anonymous referees who made helpful comments on the penultimate draft as well as Fei He, John Trujillo, and Jordan Weil, who checked the notation. Please address correspondence to: James Heckman, University of Chicago, Department of Economics, 1126 East 59th Street, Chicago, IL 60637, USA. Phone: +1-773-702-0634. Fax: +1-773-702-8490. E-mail: *jjh@uchicago.edu.*

[2] Theil's work is summarized in his collected papers on consumer demand (1975, 1976).

analyze discrete choices and associated choice outcomes and to accommodate uncertainty at the agent level.

Ordered choice models arise in many areas of economics. Goods can sometimes be defined in terms of their quality as measured along a one-dimensional spectrum. In this case, consumer choice of a good can be modeled as the choice of an interval of the quality spectrum (Prescott and Visscher, 1977; Shaked and Sutton, 1982; Bresnahan, 1987). Schooling choices are often modeled using an ordered choice model (see, e.g., Machin and Vignoles, 2005). Cameron and Heckman (1998) present an economic analysis that justifies the application of the ordered choice model to schooling choices and a proof of the semiparametric identification of their model.[3]

In the analysis of taxation and labor supply with kinked convex constraints, choices of intervals of hours of work and segments of the consumer's budget set are often modeled using ordered choice models (Heckman and MaCurdy, 1981). Ordered choice models encompass a widely used class of duration models. Ridder (1990) established the equivalence of the conventional ordered choice model and Generalized Accelerated Failure Time (GAFT) models for discrete time duration data that include the Mixed Proportional Hazard (MPH) model as a special case.

The conventional ordered choice model is assumed to be additively separable in observables (Z) and in unobservables (U_I) and is generated by an index

$$(1) \qquad\qquad I = \varphi(Z) + U_I,$$

where the observed–unobserved distinction is made from the point of view of the econometrician. U_I is a mean zero scalar random variable that is assumed to be independent of Z. It is traditionally assumed that I is separable in Z and U_I.[4] Individuals select a state $s \in \{1, \ldots, \bar{S}\}$ if the index lies between certain threshold or cutoff values c_s, which are assumed to be constants. We let $D(s) = 1$ if the agent chooses $S = s$. Cutoffs c_s are ordered so that $c_s \le c_{s+1}, s = 1, \ldots, \bar{S} - 1$. In this notation, the ordered choice model can be written as

$$(2) \qquad D(1) = \mathbf{1}(I \le c_1), \ldots, D(s) = \mathbf{1}(c_{s-1} < I \le c_s), \ldots, D(\bar{S}) = \mathbf{1}(c_{\bar{S}-1} < I),$$

where $c_{\bar{S}} = \infty$ and $c_0 = -\infty$. The defining feature of the classical ordered choice model is that choices are generated by ordered sections of the support of a scalar latent continuous random variable I (e.g., durations or hours of work).[5] Throughout we assume that I is a continuous random variable, so that for any $a \in \mathcal{R}$, $\Pr(I \le a) = \Pr(I < a)$.

In a number of contexts, it is plausible that the cutoff values differ among persons depending on variables that cannot be observed by the econometrician. In an analysis of taxation and labor supply, the locations of the kink points of the

---

[3] Our model generalizes Cameron and Heckman (1998) by allowing the cutoffs or thresholds that define the ordered choice model to depend on regressors and unobservables. We also establish that the ordered choice model can represent forward looking economic models, contrary to claims made by those authors.

[4] If $I^* = g(Z, U_I)$, there may exist one or more monotonic transformations h, such that $h(I^*) = I = \varphi(Z) + U_I$. The conventional approach works with this representation.

[5] Separability of the index in Z and U_I as in (1) is a secondary requirement, but is a part of the specification of the classical ordered choice model.

budget set, $c_s, s = 1, \ldots, \bar{S} - 1$, depend on assets and exemptions to which the agent is entitled. These may not be fully observable, especially if wages or assets are imputed.[6] In an analysis of schooling, there may be grade-specific subsidies and genuine grade-specific uncertainty at the agent level arising from learning about abilities and labor market shocks. Uncertainty is an essential feature of job search models.

To capture these possibilities, Carneiro et al. (2003) generalize the ordered choice model by allowing the cutoffs c_s to depend on (a) state-s-specific regressors (Q_s) and (b) variables unobserved by the econometrician (η_s).[7] The thresholds are written as $c_s(Q_s, \eta_s)$. To preserve the separability of the classical ordered choice model, we assume that $c_s(Q_s, \eta_s) = c_s(Q_s) + \eta_s, s = 1, \ldots, \bar{S}$. We array the Q_s into a vector $Q = (Q_1, \ldots, Q_{\bar{S}})$. Carneiro et al. (2003) adjoin systems of both discrete and continuous outcomes associated with the choice of each state, $s = 1, \ldots, \bar{S}$.

This article builds on their analysis. We develop conditions for nonparametric identification of ordered choice models with stochastic thresholds and associated outcomes that are applicable to a variety of economic problems. We consider classes of economic models that can be represented by the ordered choice model. We also develop the restrictions on information processing and the arrival of new information that are required to produce a separable-in-observables-and-unobservables ordered choice duration model with stochastic thresholds that can be used to analyze dynamic discrete choices and associated outcomes.

We generate the ordered choice model from an index of marginal returns. The marginal returns must be monotone across the ordered states to preserve the structure of the ordered choice model. The unobservables must satisfy a stochastic monotonicity property. More formally, we define the generalized ordered choice model by extending (2), in weak inequality form, to

$$(3) \quad D(s) = \mathbf{1}(c_{s-1}(Q_{s-1}) + \eta_{s-1} \le \varphi(Z) + U_I \le c_s(Q_s) + \eta_s), \quad s = 1, \ldots, \bar{S},$$

where $c_0(Q_0) = -\infty, c_{\bar{S}}(Q_{\bar{S}}) = \infty$, and $\eta_0 = \eta_{\bar{S}} = 0$. When the $\eta_s, s = 1, \ldots, \bar{S}$, are nondegenerate, they can absorb U_I (i.e., setting $U_I = 0$ is innocuous). The model is separable in terms of observables (functions of $Q_s, s = 1, \ldots, \bar{S} - 1$) and the unobservables ($U_I, \eta_s, s = 1, \ldots, \bar{S} - 1$). For this representation to be probabilistically meaningful, it is required that the upper and lower limits on $\varphi(Z) + U_I$ be ordered across all choices. We call this property *stochastic monotonicity* and we define it in Assumption 1, where we condition on $Q = q$ and $Z = z$:

ASSUMPTION 1. $\Pr(c_s(q_{s-1}) + \eta_{s-1} - \varphi(z) - U_I \le c_s(q_s) + \eta_s - \varphi(z) - U_I \mid$
$$Q = q, Z = z) = 1, \text{for all } s = 1, \ldots, \bar{S}.[8]$$

---

[6] This problem is discussed by Heckman and MaCurdy (1981) and Heckman (1983).

[7] See Carneiro et al. (2003, footnote 23). This model is also discussed in Heckman et al. (1999). For a recent analysis of this model and its relationship to the treatment effect literature, see Vytlacil (2006).

[8] An alternative and equivalent formulation is Assumption (1)': $\Pr(c_s(q_{s-1}) + \eta_{s-1} \le c_s(q_s) + \eta_s \mid Q = q, Z = z) = 1$ for all $s = 1, \ldots, \bar{S}$, where the conditioning on Z is redundant for this condition, but we maintain it to unify the notation in this article.

Assumption 1 defines ordered stochastic intervals that replace the non-stochastic intervals assumed in (2). Assumption 1 ensures that probabilities associated with the events characterized by (3) sum to one and are nonnegative. Assumption 1 is a coherency condition for ordered choice models. This article analyzes an array of well defined economic models that can be characterized by (3) and Assumption 1.

The plan of this article is as follows. Section 2 presents four ordered choice models to demonstrate the range of economic phenomena that the ordered choice model can capture. The first is a model under perfect certainty for the choice of goods when qualities are heterogeneous. A version of this model can be used to analyze labor supply in the presence of discontinuous tax schedules. The second is a prototypical model of discrete choice under perfect certainty. The third and fourth are models of agent decision making under uncertainty with sequential revision of information. Section 3 establishes conditions for nonparametric identification of the generalized ordered choice model. Section 4 discusses identification of ordered choice models with adjoined state-specific outcomes. Section 5 concludes.

2.   ORDERED CHOICE MODELS

Let "s" denote a state generated by some latent variable falling in an interval. The latent variable can be an index associated with different lengths of durations as it falls into different segments of an underlying continuum as in the GAFT model of Ridder (1990). "s" can be a stage in a process or a quality interval that defines a good as in Prescott and Visscher (1977), Shaked and Sutton (1982), and Bresnahan (1987). It can also represent intervals of hours of work as in Heckman (1974) and Heckman and MaCurdy (1981). Schooling with $\bar{S}$ stages is another example where the latent index is a marginal return function. The framework is general and can be used to model the choice of the time at which a drug is taken or the date (stage) at which a machine is installed. We present four examples. One is a model for the choice of differentiated goods. The second is a version of the deterministic Wicksell (1934) capital model applied to the cutting of a tree. The third is a stochastic tree cutting problem. The fourth is an optimal schooling model that captures the essential features of the model of Keane and Wolpin (1997).

2.1.   *Choice of Differentiated Goods.*   Following the analysis of Prescott and Visscher (1977), let τ_i be consumer i's marginal valuation of quality X. Goods come in discrete packages with quality X_g and price P_g, $g = 1, \ldots, G$. A quality-price bundle (X_g, P_g) defines a good. Consumers can buy at most one unit of the good. Bundles are ordered so that $X_{g+1} > X_g$ and $P_{g+1} > P_g$. Assume that all of the goods are purchased in equilibrium. Consumer preferences are over X and the rest of consumption M:

$$U(X_g, M) = \tau_i X_g + M.$$

For income Y, if a person buys good g at price P_g, $M = Y - P_g$.
Consumer i is indifferent between two goods $g + 1$ and g if

$$X_{g+1} \tau_i - P_{g+1} = X_g \tau_i - P_g.$$

Thus, persons are indifferent between goods $g + 1$ and g if their value of $\tau_i = c_g$, where

$$c_g = \frac{P_{g+1} - P_g}{X_{g+1} - X_g}.$$

The "cutoff value" c_g has the interpretation of the marginal price per unit quality. If $c_g < \tau_i \leq c_{g+1}$, the consumer buys good $g + 1$. As an equilibrium condition, the marginal price of quality must be nondecreasing in the level of quality. If there are some agents at each margin of indifference, an ordered choice model is generated with these threshold values. In the notation of the ordered choice model, $I_i = \tau_i$, $c_s = \frac{P_{s+1} - P_s}{X_{s+1} - X_s}$, $s = 1, \ldots, \bar{S} - 1$, and the goods are ordered by their price per unit quality. The demand function in terms of τ is generated as the envelope of $\tau X_g - P_g$, $g = 1, \ldots, G$.[9] The cutoffs may depend on both observed and unobserved variables. Prices may depend on the characteristics of the buyer. Quality may be measured with error so the thresholds may be stochastic.

In the analysis of taxes and labor supply (Heckman, 1974; Heckman and MaCurdy, 1981), the ordered choice model arises as the natural econometric framework for analyzing labor supply in the presence of progressive taxation associated with different tax brackets at different levels of earnings. Cutoffs correspond to points of discontinuity of the tax schedule that are determined by exemptions and asset levels, and that may be only partially observed by the econometrician. We next develop a stopping time example that is a vehicle for introducing uncertainty into the framework of the ordered choice model, thereby extending it. We begin by developing the case of perfect certainty. This is a version of a tree cutting problem, originally analyzed by Wicksell (1934) and applied to the analysis of human capital by Rosen (1977).

2.2. An Optimal Stopping Model Under Perfect Certainty.

Let $S = s$ denote an individual's choice of stopping time, where $s \in \{1, \ldots, \bar{S}\}$. Let $R(s, X)$ denote the discounted net lifetime reward associated with stopping at stage s, where the discounting is done at the end of period s. An example would be a model of the choice of schooling s where each schooling level is assumed to take one year and the opportunity cost of schooling is the foregone earnings.[10]

In an environment of perfect certainty, the agent solves the problem $\max_{s \in \{1, \ldots, \bar{S}\}} \{\frac{R(s, X)}{(1+r)^s}\}$, where r is the interest rate and $R(s, X)$ is the reward from stopping at stage s. The value function at stage $S - 1$ is $V(S - 1, X) = \max\{R(S - 1, X), \frac{V(S, X)}{1+r}\}$, where the agent's value function at $\bar{S} - 1$, $V(\bar{S} - 1, X)$, is $V(\bar{S} - 1, X) = \max\{R(\bar{S} - 1, X), \frac{R(\bar{S}, X)}{1+r}\}$. In the general case, an individual will stop at stage s if $R(s, X) \geq \frac{V(s+1, X)}{1+r}$. For the agent to reach stage s, it is required that $R(s - 1, X) < \frac{V(s, X)}{1+r}$. This rule produces the global optimum.

---

[9] One good might have zero price at zero quality.

[10] Agents pay a fixed cost $C(s, X)$ after completing each grade of school, and $R(s, X)$ is the reward to schooling net of these costs. When $C(s, X) = 0$, the agent's only costs are forgone earnings. This model includes both Card's (1999) and Rosen's (1977) versions of Becker's Woytinsky Lecture (1967). We work with present values of earnings associated with schooling states and Card works with annualized returns.

An ordered choice model representation of the general choice problem can be written when pairwise comparisons of returns $R(s, X)$ across adjacent states characterize the optimum and additional separability assumptions are invoked. This model is based on the *marginal return function*

$$f(s, X) = \frac{R(s, X)}{1 + r} - R(s - 1, X).$$

We make the following assumption.

ASSUMPTION 2. *The marginal return function $f(s, X)$ is nonincreasing in s for all X.*

This assumption is satisfied if the reward function $R(s, X)$ is concave in s. The optimum for the general problem is characterized by $s = s^*$ if and only if $f(s^* + 1, X) \leq 0 \leq f(s^*, X)$. The optimum is unique if the weak inequalities are replaced by strict inequalities.

The general rule for locating the optimum s^* is

$$\frac{V(s^* + 1, X)}{1 + r} - R(s^*, X) \leq 0 \leq \frac{V(s^*, X)}{1 + r} - R(s^* - 1, X).$$

Because of the concavity assumed in Assumption 2, one can replace $V(s^*, X)$ and $V(s^* - 1, X)$ in these expressions with $R(s^*, X)$ and $R(s^* - 1, X)$, respectively. We now introduce unobservables into the model. With additional separability assumptions about the unobservables, Assumptions 1 and 2 produce the conventional ordered choice model.

2.2.1. *Introducing unobservables into the model.* Unobservables are introduced into the model in two distinct ways. Both preserve additive-separability-in-unobservables that is a defining feature of the conventional ordered choice model. First, we introduce a scalar random variable U_I representing an invariant individual-specific shifter of the net gain function that is observed and acted on by the individual but is not observed by the econometrician.[11] Second, there may be transition-specific regressors that determine the net return (e.g., tuition in a schooling model), some of which are unobserved.

For the optimal stopping model defined in the preceding section to be represented by separable ordered choice model (3), we need to invoke separability in the marginal return function $f(s, X)$ in addition to monotonicity in s.

ASSUMPTION 3. *Assume that the marginal return depends on individual characteristics where $f(s + 1, X) = \frac{R(s + 1, X)}{1 + r} - R(s, X) = -(c_s(Q_s) + \eta_s) + \varphi(Z) + U_I, s \in \{1, \ldots, \bar{S}\}$, where $X = (Q_1, \ldots, Q_{\bar{S}-1}, Z)$, and $E(U_I) = 0$. The Z variables are common across all states, $s = 1, \ldots, \bar{S}$. The Q_s are the state-specific arguments of*

---

[11] Such invariant random variables are sometimes called components of "heterogeneity" in the literature.

$R(s + 1, X)$ and $R(s, X)$, and components of X are observed. The η_s are unobservables from the point of view of the econometrician.

The η_s and the $c_s(Q_s)$ can be interpreted as cost shocks. Under Assumption 3, the choice of schooling level s is characterized by (3). The cutoffs must satisfy the stochastic monotonicity assumption. This restriction imposes constraints on the model that are not present in standard discrete choice models. The traditional ordered choice model treats the $c_s(Q_s)$ as constants and sets $\eta_j \equiv 0$, $j = 1, \ldots, \bar{S}$.

It is fruitful to compare this model with a general discrete choice model with net rewards for choice s written as

$$R(s, X) = \mu_R(s, X) - \varepsilon(s), \ s = 1, \ldots, \bar{S},$$

where preference shocks satisfy $\varepsilon(s) \perp\!\!\!\perp X$ for all s, where "$\perp\!\!\!\perp$" denotes independence. The optimal s, defined as s^*, is

$$s^* = \underset{j}{\mathrm{argmax}}\{R(j)\}_{j=1}^{\bar{S}}.$$

In the general model, the states are unordered. In the ordered choice specialization of this model,

$$f(s, X) = R(s, X) - R(s - 1, X) = \mu_R(s, X) - \mu_R(s - 1, X) - (\varepsilon(s) - \varepsilon(s - 1)),$$

$$s = 1, \ldots, \bar{S} - 1,$$

where $\varphi(Z)$ in Equation (3) consists of components of $\mu_R(s, X) - \mu_R(s - 1, X)$ that are functionally independent of s, and $- c_s(Q_s)$ are the components of $\mu_R(s, X) - \mu_R(s - 1, X)$ that are $(s - 1, s)$-specific and $\eta_s - U_I = \varepsilon(s) - \varepsilon(s - 1)$. These shocks can be interpreted as either negative marginal return shocks or as marginal cost shocks added to gross returns. Assumption 1 restricts the admissible shocks in a general discrete choice model to satisfy the *ordered discrete choice condition* for $X = x$:

(OD) $\Pr(c_{j+1}(q_{j+1}) - c_j(q_j) \geq 2\varepsilon(j) - \varepsilon(j - 1) - \varepsilon(j + 1) \mid X = x) = 1.$[12]

This condition is testable because Matzkin (1994) shows that the general multinomial choice model is nonparametrically identified, so that it is possible to identify the joint distribution of the $\varepsilon(s), s = 1, \ldots, \bar{S}$ up to pairwise contrasts, and the $c_j(q_j), j = 1, \ldots, \bar{S}$ up to pairwise contrasts.[13]

In this specification, agents are assumed to be making choices in an atemporal setting. They draw shocks $\varepsilon(s)$ across all states, $s = 1, \ldots, \bar{S}$, subject to condition

---

[12] Recall that X contains both Q and Z components.

[13] Crawford et al. (1998) analyze restrictions on the derivatives of ordered logit and general logit choice models for an ordered logit model with nonstochastic thresholds that do not depend on the regressors.

(**OD**) and maximize their utility. In Section 3, we establish conditions under which this model is nonparametrically identified.

The ordered choice model is a version of the mixed proportional hazards for discrete durations (Ridder, 1990), which is widely used in applied work on unemployment and other dynamic outcomes. It is thus of interest to examine whether the ordered choice model can be modified to capture the sequential arrival of information under uncertainty. We generalize the analysis of this section to account for uncertainty and agent information updating. Additional assumptions are required to justify the ordered choice framework of this section as a well-defined economic model for the analysis of uncertain environments in which agents update their information about their future choices.

2.3. *Adding Sequential Revelation of Information.* This section extends the ordered choice model under certainty to a model with period-specific shocks that are not known by the agents in advance. We consider a prototypical tree-cutting problem that motivates economically richer models. We give conditions under which the ordered choice framework accurately captures the economic model. In Section 2.4, we generalize our analysis to a model that is a version of the general framework of Keane and Wolpin (1997).

Let L_t denote the length of a tree t periods after it is planted. $L_{t+1} = (1 - \rho)\bar{L} + \rho L_t + \varepsilon_{t+1}$, where $E(\varepsilon_{t+1} \mid L_t) = 0$, $-1 < \rho < 1$, and $\bar{L}$ is the steady state mean.[14] Assume that the agent has to decide when to cut the tree. The agent has a finite number of periods to make this decision. Thus, if the agent does not cut the tree by the end of period T, he loses the right to cut the tree and his payoff is zero. If the individual cuts the tree in period $t(\leq T)$, he collects L_t, where we assume that the price of one foot of lumber is unity in each period. The individual may decide not to cut the tree and keep the option of selling it tomorrow when it may be a little longer. As in Wicksell's (1934) model, the opportunity cost of not cutting the tree is generated by the forgone interest, which accumulates at a deterministic rate r. We may write the value function of the individual at stage t as

$$(4) \qquad V(L_t) = \max\left\{ L_t, \frac{1}{1+r} E[V(L_{t+1}) \mid L_t] \right\} \qquad \text{if } t = 1, \ldots, T-1$$

$$V(L_T) = L_T.$$

The agent will always cut the tree. If by the last period he has not yet cut the tree, it is always preferable to cut the tree instead of forgoing the right to do so. Assume that the growth process of the tree satisfies the condition that

$$(5) \qquad \frac{1}{1+r} E[L_{t+1} \mid L_t] - L_t \leq \frac{1}{1+r} E[L_t \mid L_{t-1}] - L_{t-1}.$$

Condition (5) guarantees that the stochastic monotonicity Assumption 1 is satisfied. Thus, this problem can be econometrically formulated as an ordered choice model with stochastic thresholds.

---

[14] Our version of the tree-cutting problem is closely related to the case discussed by Brock et al. (1989), who analyze a model with a random walk error term. Our model is stationary in tree lengths and their model is nonstationary in tree lengths, but stationary in present values.

Consider an agent who at the beginning of period $t = 1, \ldots, T - 1$ is contemplating whether to cut the tree or not. If $\frac{1}{1+r} E[L_{t+1} \mid L_t] - L_t > 0$ he should not cut the tree. To see why, note that $L_{t+1} \leq V(L_{t+1}) = \max\{L_{t+1}, \frac{E[L_{t+2} \mid L_{t+1}]}{1+r}\}$. Consequently, $E[L_{t+1} \mid L_t] \leq E[V(L_{t+1}) \mid L_t]$ so that $L_t \leq \frac{1}{1+r} E[L_{t+1} \mid L_t] \leq \frac{1}{1+r} E[V(L_{t+1}) \mid L_t]$ and thus $V(L_t) = \max\{L_t, \frac{1}{1+r} E[V(L_{t+1}) \mid L_t]\} = \frac{1}{1+r} E[V(L_{t+1}) \mid L_t]$. If, on the other hand, $\frac{1}{1+r} E[L_{t+1} \mid L_t] - L_t \leq 0$, the agent should cut the tree. To see why, consider the value function in the next to last period. By definition,

$$V(L_{T-1}) = \max\left\{ L_{T-1}, \frac{1}{1+r} E[L_T \mid L_{T-1}] \right\} = L_{T-1}.$$

The first equality arises because in the last period, $V(L_T) = L_T$. The second equality arises because if $t < T - 1$ and $\frac{1}{1+r} E[L_{t+1} \mid L_t] - L_t \leq 0$, then $\frac{1}{1+r} E[L_T \mid L_{T-1}] - L_T \leq 0$ is implied by (5). Proceeding by backward induction, at period t we have

$$V(L_t) = \max\left\{ L_t, \frac{1}{1+r} E[V(L_{t+1}) \mid L_t] \right\} = \max\left\{ L_t, \frac{1}{1+r} E[L_{t+1} \mid L_t] \right\} = L_t.$$

The second equality shows that we can write the problem of the agent using a one stage look ahead rule substituting the conditional expectation of the value function $E[V(L_{t+1}) \mid L_t]$ by the conditional expectation of the length of the tree, $E[L_{t+1} \mid L_t]$.[15]

The agent cuts the tree at the period $t = 1, \ldots, T - 1$ that satisfies

$$\frac{1}{1+r} E[L_{t+1} \mid L_t] - L_t \leq 0 \quad \text{and} \quad \frac{1}{1+r} E[L_t \mid L_{t-1}] - L_{t-1} \geq 0.$$

If we define

$$\frac{1}{1+r} E[L_{t+1} \mid L_t] - L_t = \varphi(Z) + U_I - c_t(Q_t) - \eta_t,$$

it follows from (5) that

$$\Pr(c_t(Q_t) + \eta_t - (\varphi(Z) + U_I)$$
$$\geq c_{t-1}(Q_{t-1}) + \eta_{t-1} - (\varphi(Z) + U_I) \mid Q = q, Z = z) = 1,$$

which is *stochastic monotonicity* Assumption 1. Consequently, the tree-cutting problem can be formulated as a generalized ordered choice model, and the tree is cut in period t if $c_{t-1}(Q_t) + \eta_{t-1} \leq \varphi(Z) + U_I \leq c_t(Q_t) + \eta_t$. We next consider a more general model of dynamic discrete choice under uncertainty.

---

[15] Ferguson (2003) shows that the one step ahead rule is only optimal in monotone optimal stopping problems.

2.4. *A Dynamic Schooling Choice Model.* We next consider a richer dynamic model where individuals decide between two choices that are stochastically updated. This is a two sector version of the general model estimated by Keane and Wolpin (1997).[16]

Consider a model in which an individual with ability a at each period t decides whether to enroll in school or not, where $t = 1, \ldots, T$. Instead of schooling, we can analyze other types of discrete states in which agents decide to remain in the state 0 and then drop out (e.g., a spell of training or a physical therapy program). We denote the current schooling level of the individual by s_t, $s_t = 1, \ldots, \bar{S}$. Let $d_t = 0$ if the agent decides not to enroll in school in period t and $d_t = 1$ otherwise. If an agent with schooling level s does not enroll in school, he works full time and increases his schooling-sector-s specific experience by one unit. If the same agent decides to enroll in school, he works part time, but does not accumulate experience. In each period t and at each schooling level s, let $x_{s,t} \in \mathfrak{R}_+$ denote the accumulated experience of the individual in schooling sector s. Let $x_t = (x_{1,t}, \ldots, x_{\bar{S},t}) \in \mathfrak{R}_+^{\bar{S}}$ denote the vector of accumulated experience in all schooling sectors $s = 1, \ldots, \bar{S}$. It simplifies notation to define the vector $e_{s,t} \in \mathfrak{R}_+^{\bar{S}}$ and vector $\bar{x}_{s,t} \in \mathfrak{R}_+^{\bar{S}}$ as $e_{s,t} = (0, \ldots, 1, \ldots, 0)$ and $\bar{x}_{s,t} = (0, \ldots, x_{s,t}, \ldots, 0) = x_{s,t}e_{s,t}$, respectively.

If the individual decides not to enroll in school in period t, he works full time and has earnings $r_0(t, s, x_{s,t}, a)$, which depends on schooling level s, accumulated experience by period t in sector s, $x_{s,t}$, and ability a. If the individual decides to enroll in school in period t his earnings are $r_1(t, s, x_{s,t}, a)$. We assume that the earnings functions $r_k(t, s, x_{s,t}, a)$, $k = 0, 1$, satisfy the following conditions.

ASSUMPTION 4.

(a) $r_0(t, s, x_{s,t}, a) = \alpha(s, a) + \gamma x_{s,t} + \Delta r_0(t, s, x_{s,t})$, where $\Delta r_0(t, s, x_{s,t})$ is unknown from the point of view of the agent at all periods $\tau < t$. We assume that $\gamma \geq 0$.

(b) $r_1(t, s, x_{s,t}, a) = \delta(s, a) + \Delta r_1(t, s, x_{s,t})$, where $\Delta r_1(t, s, x_{s,t})$ is unknown from the point of view of the agent at all periods $\tau < t$.

(c) For every $s, a: \alpha(s + 1, a) \geq \alpha(s, a)$.

(d) For every $s, a: \alpha(s + 1, a) - \alpha(s, a) \leq \alpha(s, a) - \alpha(s - 1, a)$;

(e) For every $s, a: \alpha(s, a) \geq 0$. If $a' \geq a$ then $\alpha(s, a') \geq \alpha(s, a)$;

(f) For every $a, \alpha(\bar{S} + 1, a) - \alpha(\bar{S}, a) \leq 0$;

(g) For every $s, a: \alpha(s, a) - \delta(s, a) \geq 0$;

(h) For every $t, s, x_t, a:$
$\Pr[\Delta r_0(t, s, x_{s,t}) - \Delta r_1(t, s, x_{s,t}) \leq \delta(s, a) - \alpha(s, a)] = 0$.

(i) Let $\Delta r(t) = (\Delta r_0(t, 1, x_{1,t}), \ldots, \Delta r_0(t, \bar{S}, x_{\bar{S},t}), \Delta r_1(t, 1, x_{s,t}), \ldots, \Delta r_1(t, \bar{S}, x_{\bar{S},t}))$. We assume that $\Delta r(t)$ is independent of $\Delta r(t')$ for $t \neq t'$.

---

[16] Keane and Wolpin do not consider nonparametric identification of their model.

Conditions (a) and (b) state that the earnings functions $r_k(t, s, x_{s,t}, a)$, $k = 0, 1$, are linear and separable in schooling and experience. This specification is commonly invoked in labor economics (see, e.g., Keane and Wolpin, 1997, or Heckman et al., 2006a). The stochastic components are also assumed to be separable from the deterministic components. However, we do not require s and a to be separable. To maintain mathematical tractability and to simplify the argument, we assume the "Mincer" model that assumes that the experience profiles are parallel—that is, that $\gamma_s = \gamma$ for all s. For simplicity, we also assume that the earnings of the agents enrolled in school do not depend on their work experience. The Mincer assumptions can be relaxed at the cost of greater notational complexity.

Condition (c) states that $\alpha(s, a)$ is increasing in schooling s for all ability levels a. From Condition (d), the marginal returns to schooling, $\alpha(s + 1, a) - \alpha(s, a)$ are decreasing in schooling for all ability levels a. Condition (e) says that $\alpha(s, a)$ is increasing in ability a for all schooling levels s. Condition (f) states that the returns to school above maximum schooling level $\bar{S}$ are nonpositive for all levels of ability a. Conditions (g) and (h) impose the requirement that the current opportunity costs of attending school are nonnegative.

Assuming that the agent starts with schooling level s_0 and accumulated experience x_0, the individual is assumed to maximize the following criterion:

$$V(1, s_0, x_0, a)$$

$$= \max_{\{d_t\}_{t=1}^T} E\left\{ \sum_{t=1}^T \beta^{t-1}[d_t r_1(t, s_t, x_{s_t,t}, a) + (1 - d_t)r_0(t, s_t, x_{s_t,t}, a)] \,\middle|\, s_0, x_0, a \right\}$$

subject to

$$s_0 = 0, x_0 = 0;$$

$$s_{t+1} = s_t + d_t;$$

$$x_{s_{t+1},t+1} = x_{s_{t+1},t+1} + 1 \text{ if } d_t = 0;$$

$$x_{s_{t+1},t+1} = x_{s_t,t} \text{ if } d_t = 1.$$

Consider an agent in period t who has accumulated a total of s years of schooling and experience vector x_t. Let $z_t = (x_{1,t}, \ldots, x_{s,t} + 1, \ldots, x_{\bar{S},t})$. We can write the problem of the agent recursively as

(6) $V(t, s, x_t, a)$

$$= \max \left\{ \begin{array}{l} \alpha(s, a) + \gamma x_{s,t} + \Delta r_0(t, s, x_{s,t}) + \beta E[V(t + 1, s, z_t, a) \,|\, s, x_t, a], \\ \delta(s, a) + \Delta r_1(t, s) + \beta E[V(t + 1, s + 1, x_t, a) \,|\, s, x_t, a] \end{array} \right\}.$$

The agent decides to enroll in school, $d_t = 1$, if and only if

$$\{\alpha(s, a) + \gamma x_{s,t} - \delta(s, a) + \Delta r_0(t, s, x_{s,t}) - \Delta r_1(t, s)\}$$

$$+ \{\beta E[V(t + 1, s, z_t, a) - V(t + 1, s, x_t, a) \mid s, x_t, a]\}$$

$$\leq \beta E[V(t + 1, s + 1, x_t, a) - V(t + 1, s, x_t, a) \mid s, x_t, a].$$

The left-hand side of the inequality has two components in braces that represent the costs of enrolling in school. The first is the forgone earnings of being enrolled in school, which is nonnegative according to Conditions (g) and (h) of Assumption 4. The second term in braces arises from returns to investment. If the agent decides to enroll in school today he will not collect the higher pay associated with work experience he would accumulate if he had decided not to enroll in school. The opportunity cost of enrolling in school is the current earnings forgone plus the future return to current work experience. The future benefits, which appear on the right-hand side, arise from higher levels of education. The agent decides to enroll in school if the net benefit is positive.

In general, the solution to the dynamic schooling choice model may involve dropping out of school for some periods to take advantage of favorable labor market conditions. Note that if there are T periods, there are a total of 2^T possible paths. Denote by $\mathcal{I}_t$ the information set of the agent at time t. The solution of the model is obtained by generating a set of decision rules $\{d_t^*(s_t, \mathcal{I}_t)\}_{t=1}^T$ by backward induction.

2.4.1. *Sufficient conditions for the ordered choice model of schooling to represent the stochastic dynamic schooling choice model.* As shown in our analysis of the tree-cutting problem, the ordered choice model can sometimes represent an optimal stopping problem. This is not always true in a general stochastic dynamic schooling choice model, where agents may drop out of school and return at a later date. The first step required to justify an ordered choice model in this more general setup is to obtain conditions that guarantee that if the agent finds it optimal not to enroll in school at date t, i.e., $d_t = 0$, then he will also find it optimal not to return, so that $d_\tau = 0$ for any $\tau > t$. We establish a series of propositions that justify application of the ordered choice model.

PROPOSITION 1.   *Under conditions (d) and (f) of Assumption 4, for each ability level a there exists a schooling level $s^*(a)$ such that:*

$$\alpha(s^*(a) + 1, a) - \alpha(s^*(a), a) \leq \gamma.$$

PROOF. This is a consequence of the assumption that $\alpha(s, a)$ is concave in s and that for all a, $\alpha(\bar{S} + 1, a) - \alpha(\bar{S}, a) \leq 0$. ∎

PROPOSITION 2. *Under Assumption 4, for any ability level a, schooling level $s \geq s^*(a)$, experience vector $\bar{x}_{s,t}$, and period $t \geq s^*(a)$* :

(7)

$$V(t, s, \bar{x}_{s,t}, a) = E\left[\sum_{\tau=t}^{T} \beta^{\tau-t} r_0(\tau, s, x_{s,t} + \tau - t, a) \,\middle|\, s, \bar{x}_{s,t}, a\right] + \Delta r_0(t, s, x_{s,t})$$

$$= \sum_{\tau=t}^{T} \beta^{\tau-t}[\alpha(s, a) + \gamma(x_{s,t} + \tau - t)] + \Delta r_0(t, s, x_{s,t}).$$

PROOF. See Appendix A.

From this proposition it follows that the value of the program after $s^*(a)$ is just the present value of earnings in the no schooling state. This proposition implies the following useful corollary.

COROLLARY 1 *(to Proposition 2). Under Assumption 4, if the agent reaches school level $s^*(a)$ at some period $t < T$, then at period t, he drops out of school with $s^*(a)$ years of education and he never returns to school at any period $\tau = t + 1, \ldots, T$.*

We next analyze the behavior of an agent with schooling level $s < s^*(a)$. To do so, we impose the following additional assumption that guarantees that the returns to experience grow faster than the returns to education.

ASSUMPTION 5 *(Entrapment). For any school level $s = 1, \ldots, \bar{S}$ and ability level a,*

$$\alpha(s + k, a) - \alpha(s, a) \leq (k + 1)\gamma,$$

where k is a nonnegative integer.

This condition, joined with Assumption 4, allows us to simplify the value function, as we record in the next proposition.

PROPOSITION 3. *Under Assumptions 4 and 5, at every period t, schooling level s such that $s^*(a) = s + k(a)$, $k(a) \geq 0$, for persons with experience vector $x_t = 0$ (no* *work experience up to t), and ability level a,*

(8)

$V(t, s, 0, a)$

$$
= \max \left\{ \begin{array}{c} \Delta r_0(t, s, 0) + \sum_{\tau=t}^{T} \beta^{\tau-t}[\alpha(s, a) + \gamma(\tau - t)], \\ \delta(s, a) + \Delta r_1(t, s) + \beta \sum_{\tau=t+1}^{T} \beta^{\tau-t-1}[\alpha(s+1, a) + \gamma(\tau - t - 1)], \\ \vdots \\ \sum_{l=1}^{k(a)-1} \beta^{l-1} \delta(s+l, a) + \Delta r_1(t, s) + \beta^{k(a)} \sum_{\tau=t+k(a)}^{T} \beta^{\tau-t-k(a)} \\ \times [\alpha(s^*(a), a) + \gamma(\tau - t - k(a))] \end{array} \right\}.
$$

Proof. See Appendix A.

From Proposition 3, we obtain the following corollary.

Corollary 2 *(to Proposition 3). Under Assumptions 4 and 5, at every period t, schooling level s such that $s^*(a) = s + k(a)$, $k(a) \geq 0$, experience vector $x_t = 0$, and ability level a, if the agent decides to drop out of school at period t with schooling level s, he/she never returns to school.*

Define the expected reward to permanently dropping out at schooling level s at time t as

$$
R(t, s, 0, a) = \alpha(s, a) + \Delta r_0(t, s, 0) + \sum_{\tau=t+1}^{T} \beta^{\tau-t}[\alpha(s, a) + \gamma(\tau - t)].
$$

Under Assumptions 4 and 5, we can rewrite the value function in this notation as

$$
V(t, s, 0, a) = \max\{R(t, s, 0, a), \delta(s, a) + \Delta r_1(t, s, 0) + \beta E_t[V(t+1, s+1, 0, a)]\}.
$$

We have just shown that under our assumptions, for any period t, schooling level s, experience x_t, and ability level a, once the agent leaves school he never returns. The optimal schooling problem is an optimal stopping problem. Note that if $R(t, s, 0, a) \leq \delta(s, a) + \Delta r_1(t, s, 0) + \beta E_t[R(t+1, s+1, 0, a)]$, then the agent would not leave school. This is a straightforward consequence of Proposition 2, which establishes that $E_t[R(t+1, s+1, 0, a)] \leq E_t[V(t+1, s+1, 0, a)]$. Note that if we normalize the variables in a way that the first period is "1" and the first schooling level is also "1," then an agent who never drops out of school and advances one grade per period will reach schooling level "s" at period "s."

Assumptions 4 and 5 guarantee that the dynamic discrete choice model is an optimal stopping model. They are not enough to deliver an ordered choice model representation. Additional conditions are required. We invoke the additional assumption:

ASSUMPTION 6.   *For any schooling level s and ability a,*

$$\alpha(s+k,a) - \delta(s+k,a) \geq \frac{1 - \beta^{T-s-k}}{1 - \beta^{T-s}}(\alpha(s,a) - \delta(s,a))$$

and

$$\Pr\left(\Delta r_0(s+k,s+k,0) - \Delta r_1(s+k,s+k,0)\right.$$

$$\left.\geq \frac{1 - \beta^{T-s-k}}{1 - \beta^{T-s}}[\Delta r_0(s,s,0) - \Delta r_1(s,s,0)]\right) = 1.$$

These conditions ensure that the schooling problem is a monotone optimal stopping problem as defined in Ferguson (2003). In a monotone optimal stopping problem, local comparisons of returns generate globally optimal choices. We establish the following claim:

PROPOSITION 4.   *Under Assumptions 4–6, dynamic discrete schooling choice model is a monotone optimal stopping problem.*

PROOF.   See Appendix A.

Under Assumptions 4–6 we can solve the global optimization problem by making local or one stage ahead comparisons.

PROPOSITION 5.   *Under Assumptions 4–6, we can write the value function of the dynamic discrete schooling choice model as*

$$V(t,s,0,a) = \max\{R(t,s,0,a), \delta(s,a) + \Delta r_1(t,s,0) + \beta E_t[R(t+1,s+1,0,a)]\}.$$

PROOF.   This is true because for monotone optimal stopping problems, the one stage look ahead rule is optimal. For a proof, see Ferguson (2003).   ∎

We now collect the results established in this section on conditions on a general dynamic discrete choice model that justify the ordered choice model.

THEOREM 1.   *Under Assumptions 4–6, the dynamic discrete schooling choice model can be represented by an ordered choice model with stochastic thresholds that satisfies stochastic monotonicity Assumption 1.*

PROOF. Define

$$\varphi(Z, U_I) = -\gamma$$

$$C_s(Q_s) = \beta \left(\frac{1 - \beta^{T-s}}{1 - \beta} \right) [\alpha(s, a) - \delta(s, a)]$$

$$- [\alpha(s + 1, a) - \alpha(s, a)]$$

$$\eta_s = \beta \left(\frac{1 - \beta^{T-s}}{1 - \beta} \right) [\Delta r_0(s, s, 0) - \Delta r_1(s, s, 0)].$$

To show that it satisfies stochastic monotonicity, by the definition of $C_s(Q_s)$ and η_s, together with Assumption 6, we have, for any $s = 1, \ldots, \bar{S}$,

$$C_s(Q_s) + \eta_s \leq C_{s+1}(Q_{s+1}) + \eta_{s+1}$$

and hence Assumption 1 is satisfied.[17]   ∎

We next consider some simple examples to illustrate the various economic models analyzed in this article.

2.5. *A Three Period Example.* A three period (schooling level) example helps to fix ideas developed for different models. Suppose that the reward function associated with each schooling level can be written as

$$R(1) = \mu_1(X) - \varepsilon(1), \quad R(2) = \mu_2(X) - \varepsilon(2), \quad R(3) = \mu_3(X) - \varepsilon(3).$$

Assume no discounting. A standard discrete choice model postulates that the agent draws $\varepsilon = (\varepsilon(1), \varepsilon(2), \varepsilon(3))$ and $s = \text{argmax}_j \{R(j)\}_{j=1}^3$. There is no restriction on the $\varepsilon(j)$, $j = 1, 2, 3$. The ordered choice model applied to this setting imposes the restriction (**OD**) given in Section 2.2.1.

Next, we take the same reward functions but use them in a simple version of the sequential dynamic discrete choice model with information updating developed in Section 2.4. Agents are assumed to choose among states, and states and periods are the same. Assume that agents know X. The only uncertainty at the agent level is about the $\varepsilon(j)$. Let $\mathcal{I}_j$ denote the agent's period j information set. In period i, the agent knows $\varepsilon(i)$ but not $\varepsilon(i')$, $i' > i$. The agent stops at stage 1 if

(9a)

$$\mu_1(X) - \varepsilon(1)$$

$$> E[(\mu_2(X) - \varepsilon(2)) \mathbf{1}[\mu_2(X) - \varepsilon(2) > \mu_3(X) - E(\varepsilon(3) \mid \mathcal{I}_2)]$$

$$+ (\mu_3(X) - E(\varepsilon(3) \mid \mathcal{I}_2)) \mathbf{1}[\mu_2(X) - \varepsilon(2) \leq \mu_3(X) - E(\varepsilon(3) \mid \mathcal{I}_2)] \mid \mathcal{I}_1].$$

---

[17] In addition to the shocks associated with uncertainty at the agent level, we can add components of heterogeneity known to the agent but not observed by the econometrician. U_I can be interpreted as such a component. Cameron and Heckman (1998) and Carneiro et al. (2003) analyze mixture versions of the ordered choice model. See the analysis in Section 3 below.

The agent stops at stage 2 if the inequality is reversed in the previous expression and

(9b) $$\mu_2(X) - \varepsilon(2) > \mu_3(X) - E(\varepsilon(3) \mid \mathcal{I}_2).$$

The agent stops at stage 3 if the inequality is reversed in both previous expressions.

Observe that if the $\varepsilon(i)$ are independently distributed, as is assumed in Keane and Wolpin (1997), the expression on the right-hand side of inequality (9a) can be written as

$$(\mu_2(X) - E[\varepsilon(2) \mid \mu_2(X) - \varepsilon(2) > \mu_3(X)]) \Pr(\mu_2(X) - \varepsilon(2) > \mu_3(X))$$
$$+ \mu_3(X)\Pr(\mu_2(X) - \varepsilon(2) \le \mu_3(X)).$$

The right-hand side of (9a) in this case does not depend on $\varepsilon(1)$ and is clearly separable in X and $\varepsilon(1)$. Thus it is possible to represent this version of the dynamic discrete choice model under uncertainty using the ordered choice model. However, the independence of the shocks is crucial to this example. Suppose instead that $\varepsilon(2)$ and $\varepsilon(1)$ are dependent. Learning about $\varepsilon(1)$ changes the expression on the right-hand side of Equation (9a). In general, $\varepsilon(1)$ is in the conditioning set on the right-hand side interacted with X (via $\mu_2(X)$ and $\mu_3(X)$) and is clearly on the left-hand side of the expression. This modification generates a fundamental nonseparability in the unobservables of the model. A key requirement of the classical ordered choice model is violated. If $\varepsilon(j)$ is a random walk

$$\varepsilon(2) = \omega(2) + \varepsilon(1), \quad \omega(2) \perp\!\!\!\perp \varepsilon(1)$$
$$\varepsilon(3) = \omega(3) + \varepsilon(2), \quad \omega(3) \perp\!\!\!\perp \varepsilon(2),$$

the expression on the right-hand side of (9a) simplifies, since $E(\varepsilon(3) \mid \mathcal{I}_2) = \varepsilon(2)$, so it can be written as

$$(\mu_2(X) - \varepsilon(1))\mathbf{1}(\mu_2(X) > \mu_3(X)) + (\mu_3(X) - \varepsilon(1))\mathbf{1}(\mu_2(X) > \mu_3(X)),$$

which is clearly nonseparable in $\varepsilon(1)$, X. However, the optimal decision does not depend on $\varepsilon(2)$ and $\varepsilon(3)$.

These examples illustrate the sensitivity of the stochastic structure of the choice model to the specification of agent information sets and learning rules. As developed in Section 2.4, the requirement built into decision rules (9a) and (9b) that a person who drops out cannot return to a state is sometimes artificial. For example, if at the end of period 3, suppose that the agent who had dropped out in a previous period gets a very favorable draw of $\varepsilon(3)$. Suppose that there is recall. Since $\varepsilon(1)$, $\varepsilon(2)$, $\varepsilon(3)$ are known at the end of the period, the agent will be back in a static decision world. He could optimally return to school. This possibility is ruled out in the ordered choice model, but it arises in a variety of dynamic discrete choice models in economics.[18]

However, there are many events where reentry is not possible, e.g., a person can die only once, a company can only be founded once. For these and other examples, the ordered choice model is a useful framework. Even for events that are not irreversible, after a stage, irreversibility may characterize the generating process and the ordered choice model may adequately characterize it.

2.6. *Summary of the Results of This Section.* The ordered choice model (3) with stochastic thresholds that satisfy the stochastic monotonicity condition of Assumption 1, can be used to represent a variety of interesting economic choice models. An essential feature of these models is that decisions about the choice of a state can be made by comparing (expected) returns in the adjacent ordered states. In a model with sequential information updating, this requires that one stage look ahead rules be optimal. We next present conditions for the nonparametric identification of our generalization of the ordered choice model.

3.   NONPARAMETRIC IDENTIFICATION OF THE GENERALIZED
ORDERED CHOICE MODEL

Assumption 1 is essential for the definition of a coherent discrete choice model. In general, Assumption 1 imposes restrictions on the dependence between the η_j and the Q_j for $j > 1$. One cannot freely specify the c_j, Q_j, and η_j without violating the assumption. The dependence induced by Assumption 1 must be addressed in any proof of identification of the ordered choice model.

It is easy to satisfy Assumption 1 in a variety of leading cases. Thus in the conventional ordered choice model with $\eta_j \equiv 0$, $j = 1, \ldots, \bar{S} - 1$ and with $c_j(Q_j) = \bar{c}_j$, the same constant for all Q_j, Assumption 1 is satisfied if the $\bar{c}_j$ are properly ordered. Even if $c_j(Q_j)$ is a nontrivial function of Q_j, Assumption 1 is satisfied, and the model is coherent if the restriction is imposed in estimation. When $c_j(Q_j) = \bar{c}_j$, a constant, and η_j is general, Assumption 1 requires that $\eta_{j+1} + \bar{c}_{j+1} \geq \eta_j + \bar{c}_j$ for all $j = 1, \ldots, \bar{S} - 1$. When $c_j(Q_j)$ is a nondegenerate function of Q_j and the η_j are nondegenerate, establishing nonparametric identifiability becomes more difficult, but is still possible. One case where Assumption 1 is satisfied and η_j, η_{j+1} are independent of Q_j, Q_{j+1} occurs when $\eta_{j+1} \geq \eta_j$, $j = 1, \ldots, \bar{S} - 1$, almost everywhere and $c_{j+1}(Q_{j+1}) > c_j(Q_j)$ almost everywhere. This case is a strong form of a "no news is good news" assumption.

We first prove nonparametric identification under assumptions that cover all of these cases. We denote the support of a variable as "Supp." We collect all of these cases into Assumption 7.

ASSUMPTION 7. *For all $j = 1, \ldots, \bar{S} - 1$, one of the following holds*
(i) $\eta_j \equiv 0, c_j(Q_j) = \bar{c}_j, \bar{c}_{j+1} \geq \bar{c}_j$; *or*
(ii) $\eta_j \equiv 0, c_{j+1}(Q_{j+1}) \geq c_j(Q_j)$; *or*

---

[18] See the survey in Abbring and Heckman (2007).

(iii) $\Pr(\eta_{j+1} \geq \eta_j) = 1, c_j(Q_j) = \bar{c}_j, \bar{c}_{j+1} \geq \bar{c}_j;$ or
(iv) $\Pr(\eta_{j+1} + \bar{c}_{j+1} \geq \eta_j + \bar{c}_j) = 1, \bar{c}_{j+1} \geq \bar{c}_j;$ or
(v) $\Pr(\eta_{j+1} \geq \eta_j) = 1, c_{j+1}(Q_{j+1}) \geq c_j(Q_j).$

The first three cases are special versions of (iv) and (v). We distinguish them because these simpler cases are likely to be used in applied work. For any of these cases, we prove the following theorem.

THEOREM 2. *Assume that one of the conditions in Assumption 7 holds, and in addition,*

(i) *The $\{\eta_s\}_{s=1}^{\bar{S}-1}$ are absolutely continuous with respect to Lebesgue measure and have finite means, $E(\eta_1) = 0$ (alternatively, the median or mode is zero), $\eta_{\bar{S}} \equiv 0$; $\text{Supp}(\eta_s) \subseteq [\underline{\eta}_s, \bar{\eta}_s]$ and $\text{Supp}(\eta) = \text{Supp}(\eta_1, \ldots, \eta_{\bar{S}-1}) = \text{Supp}(\eta_1) \times \cdots \times \text{Supp}(\eta_{\bar{S}-1})$;*

(ii) *$\eta_j \perp\!\!\!\perp (Z, Q)$;*

(iii) *$\text{Supp}(\eta_s) \subseteq \text{Supp}(\varphi(Z) - c_s(Q_s)), s = 1, \ldots, \bar{S} - 1$;*

(iv) *Assumption 1, where $c_0(Q_0) = -\infty$; and $c_{\bar{S}}(Q_{\bar{S}}) = \infty$ for all Q_0 and $Q_{\bar{S}}$ and $\eta_{\bar{S}} = 0$;*

(v) *$\text{Supp}(Q, Z) = \text{Supp}(Q_1) \times \cdots \times \text{Supp}(Q_{\bar{S}-1}) \times \text{Supp}(Z)$; $\text{Supp}(\varphi(Z), c_1(Q_1), \ldots, c_{\bar{S}-1}(Q_{\bar{S}-1})) = \text{Supp}(\varphi(Z)) \times \text{Supp}(c_1(Q_1)) \cdots \times \text{Supp}(c_{\bar{S}-1}(Q_{\bar{S}-1}))$;*

(vi) *$c_s(Q_s) = 0$ at known $Q_s = \bar{q}_s, s = 1, \ldots, \bar{S} - 1; \bar{q}_s$ is in the support of $c_s(Q_s)$;*

(vii) *$\varphi(Z), c_s(Q_s), s = 1, \ldots, \bar{S} - 1$, are members of the Matzkin class of functions (1992) defined in Appendix B (i.e., they satisfy one of the conditions 1–4 in that Appendix). If $\varphi(Z)$ satisfies her conditions, the $c_s(Q_s)$, $s = 1, \ldots, \bar{S} - 1$, need not. If $\varphi(Z)$ fails her conditions, the $c_s(Q_s)$, $s = 1, \ldots, \bar{S} - 1$ satisfy her conditions;*

(viii) *$U_I \equiv 0$ (normalization).*

(ix) *For the configurations of $\varphi(Z)$ and/or $c_1(Q_1), \ldots, c_{\bar{S}-1}(Q_{\bar{S}-1})$ specified in (vii), every open neighborhood of z and/or $q_s, s = 1, \ldots, \bar{S} - 1$, in the intersection of the support of $[Z, Q_1], [Z, Q_2], \ldots, [Z, Q_{\bar{S}-1}]$ and the domain of definition of the $[\varphi(Z), c_1(Q_1)], [\varphi(Z), c_2(Q_2)], \ldots, [\varphi(Z), c_{\bar{S}-1}(Q_{\bar{S}-1})]$ respectively, as specified in (vii), has positive probability with respect to the joint density of $(Z, Q_1, \ldots, Q_{\bar{S}-1})$ or Z or $(Q_1, \ldots, Q_{\bar{S}-1})$ respectively, depending on the specific conditions in (vii) that are satisfied. If absolute continuity (i) is relaxed, we require that each configuration of $[\varphi(Z), c_1(Q_1)], [\varphi(Z), c_2(Q_2)], \ldots, [\varphi(Z), c_{\bar{S}-1}(Q_{\bar{S}-1})]$ possesses at least one coordinate with Lebesgue density conditional on the other coordinates for each configuration $[Z, Q_1], [Z, Q_2], \ldots, [Z, Q_{\bar{S}-1}]$ respectively and that one coordinate in the pairs $[\varphi(Z), c_1(Q_1)], [\varphi(Z), c_2(Q_2)], \ldots, [\varphi(Z), c_{\bar{S}-1}(Q_{\bar{S}-1})]$ be strictly increasing in its argument.*

Then the $\varphi(Z), c_s(Q_s), s = 1, \ldots, \bar{S} - 1$, are identified over their supports and the distributions of the $\eta_j, F_{\eta_j}, j = 1, \ldots, \bar{S} - 1$ are identified up to an unknown mean.

PROOF. See Appendix A.

Matzkin's assumptions set the scale of the functions. One can weaken her assumptions and obtain identification up to scale. If we relax (v), we can still identify components of $\varphi(Z)$ and the $c_j(Q_j), j = 1, \ldots, \bar{S} - 1$, or the combined functions $\varphi(Z) - c_j(Q_j)$, without identifying the individual components. Assumption (vi) and the normalization of the mean of η_1 set the location parameters. The classical ordered choice model $c_j(Q_j) = \bar{c}_j, \eta_j = 0, j = 1, \ldots, \bar{S} - 1$, follows as a trivial case of Theorem 2. The case of deterministic thresholds ($\eta_j = 0$ but $c_j(Q_j)$ nontrivial functions of the Q_j) follows as a separate case of the theorem. So does a model with $c_j(Q_j) = 0, j = 1, \ldots, \bar{S} - 1$, and stochastic thresholds. (The η_j are nondegenerate random variables with $\eta_{j+1} \geq \eta_j, j = 1, \ldots, \bar{S} - 1$.) The theorem also applies when $\eta_{j+1} \geq \eta_j$ and $c_{j+1}(Q_{j+1}) \geq c_j(Q_j), j = 1, \ldots, \bar{S} - 1$, independently of each other. Under the alternative set of assumptions embodied in Assumption 7, there is no contradiction between condition (ii) and Assumption 1.

The model can be nonparametrically identified for more general cases that satisfy Assumption 1. We now produce a model where η_j and Q_j are dependent and hence fail Assumption (ii) in Theorem 2, but the ordered choice model is nonparametrically identified. It constructs the η_j from a hyperpopulation of latent random variables that in general do not satisfy Assumption 1, but are sampled by a known rule to generate a population that satisfies Assumption 1. The population so generated represents an economic environment where cost shocks increase at progressive stages. This could be associated with deteriorating skills or marketability or rising direct and psychic costs of schooling with age. Since the sampling rule is known, it is possible to account for it and establish identification.

Assume a hyperpopulation of latent random variables $(\eta_j^*, Q_j^*), j = 1, \ldots, \bar{S} - 1$, where the population of observed (η_j, Q_j) is generated by a recursive sampling rule from the hyperpopulation that generates random variables that satisfy Assumption 1. We call this model $(\mathbf{S})$.

$(\mathbf{S})$

$$\begin{cases} (\eta_1, Q_1) = (\eta_1^*, Q_1^*) \\ (\eta_j, Q_j) = (\eta_j^*, Q_j^*) \text{ if } \eta_{j-1}^* + c_{j-1}(Q_{j-1}^*) \leq \eta_j^* + c_j(Q_j^*) \quad j = 2, \ldots, \bar{S} - 1. \end{cases}$$

No restrictions are imposed on (η_1^*, Q_1^*) by the sampling rule.

We assume that $\eta^* = (\eta_1^*, \ldots, \eta_{\bar{S}-1}^*)$ has mutually independent components and is independent of $Q^* = (Q_1^*, \ldots, Q_{\bar{S}-1}^*)$ and Z.[19] We make the following assumption for the hyperpopulation:

[19] It is possible to relax the independence assumption, but it simplifies the analysis to maintain it. Sampled η are dependent.

ASSUMPTION 8. $\eta^* \perp\!\!\!\perp (Q^*, Z)$.

As a consequence of **(S)** and Assumption 8, the density of η_2 given $Q_2 = q_2$ and $Q_1 = q_1$ is

(10) $$g(\eta_2 \mid Q_2 = q_2, Q_1 = q_1) = \frac{f_{\eta_2^*}(\eta_2) \int_{-\infty}^{\eta_2 + c_2(q_2) - c_1(q_1)} f_{\eta_1^*}(\tau)\, d\tau}{K(q_2, q_1)},$$

where

$$K(q_2, q_1) = \int_{-\infty}^{\infty} f_{\eta_2^*}(\eta_2) \int_{-\infty}^{\eta_2 + c_2(q_2) - c_1(q_1)} f_{\eta_1^*}(\tau)\, d\tau\, d\eta_2.$$

The dependence among the η_j and the Q arises from the sampling process **(S)**.

The $Q_s, s = 1, \ldots, \bar{S} - 1$, are assumed to be observed by the econometrician. As before, we can absorb U_I into the η_j; alternatively, we set $U_I \equiv 0$. We now establish nonparametric identification of this model. As in the proof of Theorem 2, we use many standard assumptions from the discrete choice literature. We prove the following theorem under assumption **(S)**.

THEOREM 3. *Assume that*

  (i) *The $\{\eta_s^*\}_{s=1}^{\bar{S}-1}$ are mutually independent, absolutely continuous, random variables and have finite means. Assume $E(\eta_1^*) = 0$. (Alternatively, the median or mode of η_1 is known.) $\eta_{\bar{S}}^* \equiv 0; \eta_s^* \in [\underline{\eta}_s^*, \bar{\eta}_s^*]$ for $s = 1, \ldots, \bar{S} - 1$;*
 (ii) *Assumption 8;*
(iii) *$\mathrm{Supp}(\eta_s^*) \subseteq \mathrm{Supp}(\varphi(Z) - c_s(Q_s^*))$ for $s = 1, \ldots, \bar{S} - 1$ for each $Q_s^* = q_s$;*
 (iv) *Selection rule **(S)** holds;*
  (v) *$\varphi(Z), c_s(Q_s^*), s = 1, \ldots, \bar{S} - 1$, are members of the Matzkin class of functions (1992) defined in Appendix B (i.e., they satisfy one of the conditions 1–4 in that Appendix);*
 (vi) *$\mathrm{Supp}(Q^*, Z) = \mathrm{Supp}(Q_1^*) \times \cdots \times \mathrm{Supp}(Q_{\bar{S}-1}^*) \times \mathrm{Supp}(Z)$,*
        $s = 1, \ldots, \bar{S} - 1; \mathrm{Supp}(\varphi(Z), c_1(Q_1^*), \ldots, c_{\bar{S}-1}(Q_{\bar{S}-1}^*)) = \mathrm{Supp}(\varphi(Z)) \times$
        $\mathrm{Supp}(c_1(Q_1^*)) \times \cdots \times \mathrm{Supp}(c_{\bar{S}-1}(Q_{\bar{S}-1}^*));$
(vii) *$c_s(Q_s^*) = 0$ at known $Q_s^* = \bar{q}_s, s = 1, \ldots, \bar{S} - 1; \bar{q}_s$ is in the support of $c_s(Q_s);$*
(viii) *$U_I \equiv 0$ (normalization).*
 (ix) *Every open neighborhood of z and q_s^* in the intersection of the support of $Z, Q_1^*, \ldots, Q_{\bar{S}-1}^*$ and the domain of definition of the $\varphi(Z), c_1(Q_1^*), \ldots,$ $c_{\bar{S}-1}(Q_{\bar{S}-1}^*)$ functions, $s = 1, \ldots, \bar{S} - 1$ possesses positive probability with respect to the joint density of $(Z, Q_1^*, \ldots, Q_{\bar{S}-1}^*)$. If the absolute continuity condition (i) is relaxed, then the $Z, Q_1^*, \ldots, Q_{\bar{S}-1}^*$ each have at least one coordinate with Lebesgue density conditional on the other coordinates and each nontrivial function $\varphi(Z), c_1(Q_1^*), \ldots, c_{\bar{S}-1}(Q_{\bar{S}-1}^*)$ is increasing in one coordinate.*

Then the $\varphi(Z)$, $c_s(Q_s^*)$, $s = 1, \ldots, \bar{S} - 1$ are identified, over their supports and the distributions of the η_j, F_{η_j}, $j = 1, \ldots, \bar{S} - 1$ are identified, as are the distributions $F_{\eta_j^*}$, $j = 1, \ldots, \bar{S} - 1$.

PROOF. See Appendix A.

Notice that from the mutual independence of η_j^*, we trivially identify the joint distribution of η_j^*, $j = 1, \ldots, \bar{S} - 1$. Other assumptions about the arrival of new information rationalize the ordered choice model and produce a model that can be nonparametrically identified. These assumptions allow for some news to be good news, but not too good. One can generate the η_j from the process

(11) $\eta_j = -c_j(Q_j) + \eta_{j-1} + \omega_j$, $\eta_0 = 0$, $c_0(Q_0) = 0$ and $j > 1$,

where $\omega_j \geq 0$, $j = 1, \ldots, \bar{S} - 1$ is a nonnegative random variable assumed to be independent of Q and η_{j-1} and $c_j(Q_j) \geq c_{j-1}(Q_{j-1})$, $j = 2, \ldots, \bar{S} - 1$. Array the ω_j into a vector ω. Assume the following for this process.

ASSUMPTION 9.

(a) $\omega \perp\!\!\!\perp (Q, Z)$ and
(b) $\omega_j \perp\!\!\!\perp \omega_{j'}$ $\forall j \neq j'$, $j, j' = 1, \ldots, \bar{S} - 1$.

It is straightforward to establish identification of the model using the argument in Theorem 2. Effectively, this model replaces η_j with $\sum_{\ell=1}^{j} \omega_\ell$ and eliminates the $c_j(Q_j)$ so that it is a version of case (iii) of Assumption 7. Generating the η_j in this fashion essentially removes transition-specific regressors from the model and hence we lose identifiability of $c_j(Q_j)$. We can identify the marginal distributions of the ω_j, $j = 1, \ldots, \bar{S} - 1$ by applying deconvolution to specification (11) applied to the successive marginal distributions of the η_j.

4.   ADJOINING S-SPECIFIC OUTCOMES

Associated with each choice s is an associated outcome vector $Y(s, W)$. The outcomes could be binary (e.g., employment indicators), continuous variables (present values), durations, or any combination of such variables. This includes the case where the $Y(s, W)$ are, for example, the net present values associated with each completed schooling level, $Y(s, W) = R(s, W)$ in the notation of Section 2. To simplify the analysis, we focus on the continuous outcome case.[20] Write

$$Y(s, W) = \mu(s, W) + U(s), s = 1, \ldots, \bar{S},$$

---

[20] We can develop the analysis for discrete components of outcomes using the analysis of Carneiro et al. (2003). They use latent variables crossing thresholds to generate the discrete variables and identify the latent variables and their distribution up to an unknown scale. Abbring and Heckman (2007) present conditions for identifying discrete and continuous outcomes in related models.

where $U(s) \in [\underline{U}(s), \bar{U}(s)]$. In addition to choice-specific outcomes, we may have access to a vector of measurements $M(W)$ that do not depend on s. We write

$$M(W) = \mu_M(W) + U_M,$$

where $U_M \in [\underline{U}_M, \bar{U}_M]$. We assume that $E(U(s)) = 0, s = 1, \ldots, \bar{S}, E(U_M) = 0$ and make the following assumption.

ASSUMPTION 10. $(Z, Q, W) \perp\!\!\!\perp (U(s), U_M), s = 1, \ldots, \bar{S}.$

In this section, we allow for the possibility that W contains variables distinct from (Z, Q).

The analysis of Section 3 presents conditions for identifying the marginal distribution of each $\eta_s, s = 1, \ldots, \bar{S} - 1$, up to scale. We can identify the marginal distribution of the $U(s)$ using an extension of the limit set arguments developed in Carneiro et al. (2003, Theorem 3). Thus we can identify $\mu(s, W), s = 1, \ldots, \bar{S}$, the marginal distributions of $U(s)$, $\mu_M(W)$, the marginal distribution of U_M, and the joint distribution of $(U(s), U_M, \eta_s), s = 1, \ldots, \bar{S} - 1$, and $U(\bar{S}), U_M, \eta_{\bar{S}-1})$ using the analysis in their Theorem 3. They assume that it is possible to vary (Z, Q) freely and attain a limit set that produces $\Pr(S = s | Z, Q) = 1$, for all $W = w$.

To sketch their proof structure, note that from information on $D(s) = 1, W, Y(s, W), Z, Q$, we can construct $\Pr(D(s) = 1 | W, Z, Q)$ and $\Pr(Y(s, W) \leq y(s, W), M(W) \leq m(w) | D(s) = 1, W = w, Z = z)$. In this notation, the joint distribution of $Y(s, W), M(W), D(s) = 1, s = 1, \ldots, \bar{S} - 1$, given $W = w, Z = z$, and $Q = q$ multiplied by the probability that $D(s) = 1$ can be written as

$$\Pr \left(\begin{array}{c|c} Y(s, W) \leq y(s, W), & D(s) = 1, W = w, \\ M(W) \leq m(w) & Q = q, Z = z \end{array} \right)$$

$$\cdot \Pr(D(s) = 1 \mid W = w, Q = q, Z = z)$$

$$= \int_{\underline{U}(s)}^{y(s,w)-\mu(s,w)} \int_{\underline{U}_M}^{m(w)-\mu_M(w)}$$

$$\cdots \int_{(\eta_1,\ldots,\eta_s)\in\Gamma} f_{U(s),U_M,\eta}(u(s), u_M, \eta_1, \ldots, \eta_s) \, d\eta_s \cdots d\eta_1 \, du_M \, du_s,$$

where $\Gamma = \{(\eta_1, \ldots, \eta_s) \mid \eta_1 + c_1(q_1) - \varphi(z) < \eta_2 + c_2(q_2) - \varphi(z) < \cdots < \eta_s + c_s(q_s) - \varphi(z)\}$. We assume either Assumption 7 characterizes the model or condition $(\mathbf{S})$, in which case we interpret the η_j as η_j^* in this section.

Assume that we can freely vary the arguments of this expression in the following sense. We assume continuous outcomes and measures.

ASSUMPTION 11. $\text{Supp}(\varphi(Z) - c_1(Q_1), \ldots, \varphi(Z) - c_{\bar{S}-1}(Q_{\bar{S}-1})) = \text{Supp}(\varphi(Z) - c_1(Q_1)) \times \cdots \times \text{Supp}(\varphi(Z) - c_{\bar{S}-1}(Q_{\bar{S}-1}))$ and $\text{Supp}(Z, Q) = \text{Supp}(Z) \times \text{Supp}(Q_1) \times \ldots \times \text{Supp}(Q_{\bar{S}-1}).$

Also assume that the supports of the latent random variables in the underlying hyperpopulation are not restricted.

ASSUMPTION 12. $\text{Supp}(U(1), \ldots, U(\bar{S}), U_M, \eta_1, \ldots, \eta_{\bar{S}-1}) = \text{Supp}(U(1)) \times \ldots \times \text{Supp}(U(\bar{S})) \times \text{Supp}(U_M) \times \text{Supp}(\eta_1) \times \ldots \times \text{Supp}(\eta_{\bar{S}-1})$, *where this condition applies to all components.*

Assumptions 10, 11, and 12, coupled with the assumptions used in either Theorem 2 or 3, suitably extended to the arguments of the discrete outcome equations in a more general analysis in order to satisfy the Matzkin conditions, so that all open neighborhoods of variables in the arguments of the outcome equations conditioned on the remaining variables have positive probabilities, along with the requirement that there are no restrictions on the support of the components of $M(W)$ and $Y(s, W)$, produce identification of the means, the joint distributions of the $(U(s), U_M, \eta_s), s = 1, \ldots, \bar{S} - 1$, and $(U(\bar{S}), U_M, \eta_{\bar{S}-1})$. The proof is a straightforward extension of proofs in the published literature.[21] For the sake of brevity, it is deleted.

From the limit sets that drive $\Pr(D(s) = 1 \mid Z = z, Q = q)$ to $1, s = 1, \ldots, \bar{S}$, one can identify the average treatment effects across different outcome states $E(Y(s) - Y(s') \mid W)$. The marginal treatment effects for transitions $(s, s + 1), s = 1, \ldots, \bar{S} - 1$ can be identified by applying the local instrumental variable method following Heckman et al. (2006b), or Heckman and Vytlacil (2007) or directly by using the argument of Carneiro et al. (2003). The parameters Treatment on the Treated or Treatment on the Untreated require information on the joint distributions of random variables like $(U(\ell), \eta_1, \ldots, \eta_{\bar{S}-1})$.[22]

If we use the model based on independent latent censored variables as described in condition (S), we can identify the joint density of the $\eta = (\eta_1, \ldots, \eta_{\bar{S}-1})$ under the conditions of Theorem 3. We can identify the scales and all of the marginal densities, given the normalizations for the η, using the limit set argument. The joint distributions do not contain the information required to identify the full joint distribution of $(U(s), \eta_1, \ldots, \eta_s)$ without additional assumptions such as those invoked in Theorem 3 or to identify the joint distribution $(U(1), \ldots, U(\bar{S}), \eta_1, \ldots, \eta_{\bar{S}-1})$.[23]

[21] See Carneiro et al. (2003) and Abbring and Heckman (2007).

[22] See the discussion in Abbring and Heckman (2007).

[23] Under a factor structure assumption and under conditions specified in Carneiro et al. (2003), Heckman and Navarro (2007) and Abbring and Heckman (2007), we can identify the factor loadings as well as distribution of the factors and uniquenesses from data on $Y(s, W)$, for each $s = 1, \ldots, \bar{S}$, and any associated measurements $M(W)$. If we assume a factor model for the choice process and a corresponding structure for measurements and outcomes, then we can identify the covariances between $U(s)$ and $(\eta_1, \ldots, \eta_s)$. This requires a restriction on the dimension of the admissible factors. Under the factor structure assumption and with suitable restrictions on the dimension of the model, we can identify the joint distribution of $(U(1), \ldots, U(\bar{S}), U_M, \eta_1, \ldots \eta_{\bar{S}-1})$. From this information, and the parameters previously identified, we can form all of the desired counterfactuals, applying the analysis of Carneiro et al. (2003) and Abbring and Heckman (2007).

5. SUMMARY AND CONCLUSIONS

This article examines the economic foundations of ordered discrete choice models. The classical ordered discrete choice model is generalized to accommodate stochastic thresholds and associated outcome variables. We develop conditions for nonparametric identification. We discuss classes of interesting economic models that can be represented by the generalized ordered choice model. We also develop restrictions on information processing and the arrival of new information that are required to justify the application of the generalized ordered choice model to adequately represent dynamic discrete choice models.

There are two key requirements for the model. The first is that local comparisons between the rewards of adjacent states locate the global optimum. In a deterministic setting, this is justified by global concavity, where the unobservables respect a stochastic monotonicity condition. In an environment of uncertainty, assumptions that produce a monotone optimal stopping condition justify a naive one-step-ahead forecasting rule as a way of characterizing optimal policies. The local comparisons used in the ordered choice model contrast with more general choice frameworks, which rely on global comparisons. A second requirement is separability between observables and unobservables. We conjecture that it is possible to relax separability, but we leave the analysis for another occasion.[24] Separability is a hallmark feature of the classical ordered choice model and we maintain it for the sake of familiarity and ease of analysis.

APPENDIX A: PROOFS OF THEOREMS AND PROPOSITIONS

PROOF OF PROPOSITION 2   We show that this is true by backward induction. Consider an individual with ability level a. We want to calculate the value function when the schooling level is $s > s^*(a)$. We first derive the value functions for the last period $t = T$. Note that

(A.1)
$$V(T, s, \bar{x}_{s,T}, a) = \max\{\alpha(s, a) + \gamma x_{s,T} + \Delta r_0(T, s, x_{s,T}), \delta(s, a) + \Delta r_1(T, s)\}$$

$$= \alpha(s, a) + \gamma x_{s,T} + \Delta r_0(T, s, x_{s,T}).$$

So the proposition is true for $t = T$. Note that the value function at period T of a person who is working, with schooling s, until period $T - 1$ and decides to return to school at period $T - 1$ is

(A.2)
$$V(T, s + 1, \bar{x}_{s,T}, a) = \max\{\alpha(s + 1, a) + \Delta r_0(T, s, x_{s,T}), \delta(s, a) + \Delta r_1(T, s)\}$$

$$= \alpha(s + 1, a) + \Delta r_0(T, s, x_{s,T}).$$

---

[24] Cameron and Heckman (1998) relax separability in one version of the ordered choice model. See also Carneiro et al. (2003).

Next we show that the proposition is also true for period $T - 1$. Note that $x_{s,T} = x_{s,T-1} + 1$ if the agent decides to work in period $T - 1$. In period $T - 1$, the problem of the agent is

(A.3)
$$V(T - 1, s, \bar{x}_{s,T-1}, a)$$
$$= \max\left\{\begin{array}{c} \alpha(s, a) + \gamma x_{s,T-1} + \Delta r_0(T - 1, s, x_{s,T-1}) + \beta E_{T-1}[V(T, s, \bar{x}_{s,T}, a)], \\ \delta(s, a) + \Delta r_1(T - 1, s) + \beta E_{T-1}[V(T, s + 1, \bar{x}_{s,T-1}, a)] \end{array}\right\},$$

where we use shorthand $E_T(Y)$ for the expectation of the random variable conditional on the information available at T: $E_T(Y) = E(Y|\mathcal{I}_T)$. If we substitute (A.1) and (A.2) into (A.3), we conclude that the agent decides not to enroll in school in period $T - 1$ if and only if

$$\alpha(s, a) + \gamma(1 + \beta)x_{s,T-1} + \Delta r_0(T - 1, s, x_{s,T-1}) + \beta\alpha(s, a) + \beta\gamma$$
$$\geq \delta(s, a) + \Delta r_1(T - 1, s) + \beta\alpha(s + 1, a),$$

which is guaranteed by Proposition 1 for any schooling level $s > s^*(a)$. Consequently,

$$V(T - 1, s, \bar{x}_{s,T-1}, a) = \sum_{\tau=T-1}^{T} \beta^{\tau-T+1} E[r_0(\tau, s, x_{s,T-1} + \tau - T + 1, a) \mid s, x_\tau, a]$$
$$+ \Delta r_0(T - 1, s, x_{s,T-1}).$$

We now show that the proposition also holds for the value function $V(T - 1, s + 1, \bar{x}_{s,T-2}, a)$. This is the value function of an agent who until period $T - 2$ was working at school level s, but at the beginning of period $T - 2$ decides to go back to school. Define z_T as the vector of length $\bar{S}$ that describes the experience of this agent, who works at period $T - 1$ with schooling $s + 1$:

$$z_T = (0, \ldots, x_{s,T-2}, 1, \ldots, 0).$$

The value function $V(T - 1, s + 1, \bar{x}_{s,T-2}, a)$ satisfies

$$V(T - 1, s + 1, \bar{x}_{s,T-2}, a)$$
$$= \max\left\{\begin{array}{c} \alpha(s + 1, a) + \Delta r_0(T - 1, s + 1, 0) + \beta E_{T-1}[V(T, s + 1, z_T, a)], \\ \delta(s + 1, a) + \Delta r_1(T - 1, s) + \beta E_{T-1}[V(T, s + 2, \bar{x}_{s,T-2}, a)] \end{array}\right\}.$$

Now, it can be shown that

$$E_{T-1}[V(T, s + 1, z_T, a)] = \alpha(s + 1, a) + \gamma$$

and

$$E_{T-1}[V(T, s+2, \bar{x}_{s,T-2}, a)] = \alpha(s+2, a).$$

Consequently, the agent does not enroll in school if and only if

$$\alpha(s+1, a) + \Delta r_0(T-1, s+1, 0) + \beta\alpha(s+1, a) + \beta\gamma$$

$$\geq \delta(s+1, a) + \Delta r_1(T-1, s) + \beta\alpha(s+2, a).$$

Note that by Proposition 1, this inequality is always true for any schooling level $s \geq s^*(a)$. Therefore (7) is true for $V(T-1, s+1, \bar{x}_{s,T-2}, a)$.

We seek to prove that the proposition is true for a generic period t, schooling level s, and experience x_t. Before we proceed, we define the jth component of the experience vector x_{t+1} as

$$x_{j,t+1} = \begin{cases} x_{j,t} & \text{if } j < s \\ x_{j,t} + 1 & \text{if } j = s \\ 0 & \text{if } j > s \end{cases}.$$

Note that if the agent decides to work, his next period experience will be denoted by x_{t+1}. If he decides not to work, then his experience vector is summarized by x_t.

To continue with the proof by backward induction, we assume that the claim is true for the value functions $V(t+1, s, x_{t+1}, a)$ and $V(t+1, s+1, x_t, a)$. From the definition of the Bellman equation,

$$V(t, s, x_t, a) = \max \left\{ \begin{array}{l} \alpha(s, a) + \Delta r_0(t, s, x_{s,t}) + \beta E[V(t+1, s, x_{t+1}, a) \mid s, x_t, a], \\ \delta(s, a) + \Delta r_1(t, s) + \beta E[V(t+1, s+1, x_t, a) \mid s, x_t, a] \end{array} \right\}.$$

But recall that

$$V(t, s, x_t, a) = \max \left\{ \begin{array}{l} \alpha(s, a) + \Delta r_0(t, s, x_{s,t}) + \beta \sum_{\tau=t+1}^{T} \beta^{\tau-t-1} \\ \quad \times [\alpha(s, a) + \gamma(\tau - (t+1) + x_{s,t} + 1)], \\ \delta(s, a) + \Delta r_1(t, s) + \beta \sum_{\tau=t+1}^{T} \beta^{\tau-t-1} \\ \quad \times [\alpha(s+1, a) + \gamma(\tau - t - 1)] \end{array} \right\}.$$

Note that the agent decides not to enroll if and only if

$$\alpha(s, a) + \Delta r_0(t, s, x_{s,t}) + \beta \sum_{\tau=t+1}^{T} \beta^{\tau-t-1}[\alpha(s, a) + \gamma(\tau - (t+1) + x_{s,t} + 1)]$$

$$\geq \delta(s, a) + \Delta r_1(t, s) + \beta \sum_{\tau=t+1}^{T} \beta^{\tau-t-1}[\alpha(s+1, a) + \gamma(\tau - t - 1)].$$

This inequality reduces to

$$\alpha(s, a) + \Delta r_0(t, s, x_{s,t}) - \delta(s, a) - \Delta r_1(t, s) + \frac{1 - \beta^{T-t}}{1 - \beta} x_{s,t} + \frac{1 - \beta^{T-t}}{1 - \beta} \gamma$$

$$\geq \frac{1 - \beta^{T-t}}{1 - \beta}[\alpha(s + 1, a) - \alpha(s, a)],$$

which is true for any $s > s^*(a)$. Consequently,

$$V(t, s, x_t, a) = \sum_{\tau=t}^{T} \beta^{\tau-t}[\alpha(s, a) + \gamma(x_{s,t} + \tau - t)] + \Delta r_0(t, s, 0). \qquad \blacksquare$$

PROOF OF PROPOSITION 3   Again, by backward induction. Note that from Proposition 2, we conclude that Corollary 1 of Proposition 2, is also true for $V(t, s^*(a), 0, a)$. Next, we assume that (8) is true in period $t' + 1$ with schooling level $s + 1$, such that $s^*(a) = s + k(a) - 1$, where $k(a)$ is a nonnegative integer, experience vector $x_{t'+1} = 0$, and ability level is a and show that it is also valid for period t', schooling level s, experience $x_t = 0$, and ability a. By definition,

$$V(t', s, 0, a) = \max \left\{ \begin{array}{l} \alpha(s, a) + \Delta r_0(t', s, 0) + \beta E_{t'}[V(t' + 1, s, x_{t'+1}, a)], \\ \delta(s, a) + \Delta r_1(t', s) + \beta E_{t'}[V(t' + 1, s + 1, 0, a)], \end{array} \right\}$$

where

$$x_{j,t'+1} = \begin{cases} 0 & \text{if } j \neq s \\ 1 & \text{if } j = s \end{cases}.$$

Again, suppose that the agent does not enroll in school at period t' and starts working with schooling s. We next investigate whether he ever returns to school again, perhaps at period $t' + p$, for $p = 1, \ldots, T - t'$. We show that, under our assumptions, this cannot happen. Let

$$x_{j,t'+p} = \begin{cases} 0 & \text{if } j \neq s \\ p & \text{if } j = s, \text{ for } p = 1, \ldots, T - t' \end{cases}$$

Note that at period $t' + p$, the problem of the agent is

$$V(t' + p, s, x_{t'+p}, a)$$
$$= \max \left\{ \begin{array}{l} \alpha(s, a) + \gamma p + \Delta r_0(t' + p, s, x_{s,t'+p}). \\ + \beta E_{t'+p}[V(t' + p + 1, s, x_{t'+p+1}, a)], \\ \delta(s, a) + \Delta r_1(t', s) + \beta E_{t'+p}[V(t' + p + 1, s + 1, x_{t'+p}, a)] \end{array} \right\}.$$

Note that the agent has accumulated experience only at schooling level s. Because s-specific experience is not useful in sector $s' \neq s$,

$$V(t' + p + 1, s + 1, x_{t'+p}, a) = V(t' + p + 1, s + 1, 0, a).$$

The agent does not enroll in school again at period $t' + p$ if and only if

(A.4) $\alpha(s, a) + \gamma p - \delta(s, a) + \Delta r_0(t' + p, s, x_{s,t'+p}) - \Delta r_1(t' + p, s)$

$$\geq \beta E_{t'+p}[V(t' + p + 1, s + 1, 0, a) - V(t' + p + 1, s, x_{t'+p+1}, a)].$$

Note that the right-hand side of this equation is the expectation of the difference of two value functions. We assume that the proposition is true for the first value function, $V(t' + p + 1, s + 1, 0, a)$, propose a lower bound for the second value function, $V(t' + p + 1, s, x_{t'+p+1}, a)$, and show that it is not optimal to return to school at period $t' + p$.

Define n^* as the optimal date of dropping out of school:

$$n^* = \underset{n}{\operatorname{argmax}} \left\{ \begin{array}{l} \sum_{l=1}^{n-1} \beta^{l-1} \delta(s + l, a) + \Delta r_1(t' + p, s) + \beta^n \\ + \sum_{\tau=t'+p+n}^{T} \beta^{\tau-t'-p-n}[\alpha(s + n, a) + \gamma(\tau - t' - p - n)] \end{array} \right\}.$$

Assuming that the proposition is true for period $t' + p + 1$ and schooling level $s + 1$, we can write

$V(t' + p + 1, s + 1, 0, a)$

$$= \max \left\{ \begin{array}{l} \Delta r_0(t' + p + 1, s + 1, 0) + \sum_{\tau=t'+p+1}^{T} \beta^{\tau-t'-p-1} \\ \times [\alpha(s + 1, a) + \gamma(\tau - t' - p - 1)], \\ \sum_{l=1}^{n^*-1} \beta^{l-1} \delta(s + l, a) + \Delta r_1(t' + p, s) \\ + \beta^{n^*} \sum_{\tau=t'+p+n^*}^{T} \beta^{\tau-t'-p-n^*}[\alpha(s + n^*, a) + \gamma(\tau - t' - p - n^*)] \end{array} \right\}.$$

Suppose that

(A.5)
$V(t' + p + 1, s + 1, 0, a) = \Delta r_0(t' + p + 1, s + 1, 0)$

$$+ \sum_{\tau=t+p+1}^{T} \beta^{\tau-t'-p-1}[\alpha(s + 1, a) + \gamma(\tau - t' - p - 1)].$$

Then the agent does not enroll in school in period $t' + p$. To see why, note that we have the following bound:

$$(A.6) \quad E_{t'+p}[V(t' + p + 1, s, x_{t'+p+1}, a)] \geq \sum_{\tau=t'+p+1}^{T} \beta^{\tau-t'-p-1}[\alpha(s, a) + \gamma(\tau - t)].$$

Now, if (A.5) is true, we can bound the difference:

$$E_{t'+p}[V(t' + p + 1, s + 1, 0, a) - V(t' + p + 1, s, x_{t'+1}, a)]$$

$$\leq \sum_{\tau=t+p+1}^{T} \beta^{\tau-t'-p-1}[\alpha(s + 1, a) - \alpha(s, a) + \gamma(\tau - t)] \leq 0,$$

where the last inequality is guaranteed by Assumption 5. Because of Condition (g) of Assumption 4, we can also bound the difference:

$$\alpha(s, a) + \gamma p - \delta(s, a) + \Delta r_0(t' + p, s, 0) - \Delta r_1(t' + p, s) \geq 0.$$

Thus, under (A.5), inequality (A.4) holds and it is not optimal to return to school. Now, suppose that

$$V(t' + p + 1, s + 1, 0, a)$$

$$= \sum_{l=1}^{n^*-1} \beta^{l-1}\delta(s + l, a) + \Delta r_1(t' + p, s)$$

$$+ \beta^{n^*} \sum_{\tau=t'+p+n^*}^{T} \beta^{\tau-t'-p-n^*}[\alpha(s + n^*, a) + \gamma(\tau - t' - p - n^*)].$$

Again, we can use (A.6) to claim that

$$E_{t'+p}[V(t' + p + 1, s, x_{t'+p+1}, a)]$$

$$\geq \sum_{\tau=t+p+1}^{t+p+n^*-1} \beta^{\tau-t'-p-1}[\alpha(s, a) + \gamma(\tau - t)]$$

$$+ \beta^{n^*} \sum_{\tau=t+p+n^*}^{T} \beta^{\tau-t'-p-n^*}[\alpha(s, a) + \gamma(\tau - t)].$$

Consequently, because of Assumption 5 the following difference can be bounded above by zero

$$
\left\{ \sum_{\tau=t'+p+n^*}^{T} \beta^{\tau-t'-p-n^*}[\alpha(s+n^*,a)+\gamma(\tau-t'-p-n^*)] \right.
$$

$$
\left. - \sum_{\tau=t+p+n^*}^{T} \beta^{\tau-t'-p-n^*}[\alpha(s,a)+\gamma(\tau-t)] \right\}
$$

$$
= \sum_{\tau=t'+p+n^*}^{T} \beta^{\tau-t'-p-n^*}[\alpha(s+n^*,a)-\alpha(s,a)-\gamma(p+n^*)]
$$

$$
= \frac{1-\beta^{T-t'-p-n^*+1}}{1-\beta}[\alpha(s+n^*,a)-\alpha(s,a)-\gamma(p+n^*)] \leq 0.
$$

So the gross returns to going back to school are negative. On the other hand, note that the gross costs are positive:

$$
\alpha(s,a)-\delta(s,a)+\gamma p+\Delta r_0(t'+p,s,0)-\Delta r_1(t'+p,s)
$$

$$
+\beta^{n^*}\sum_{l=1}^{n^*-1}\beta^{l-1}[\alpha(s,a)+\gamma(\tau-t)-\delta(s+l,a)]
$$

$$
= \{\alpha(s,a)-\delta(s,a)+\gamma p+\Delta r_0(t'+p,s,0)-\Delta r_1(t',s)\}
$$

$$
+\left\{\beta^{n^*}\sum_{l=1}^{n^*-1}\beta^{l-1}[\alpha(s+l,a)-\delta(s+l,a)]\right\}
$$

$$
+\left\{\beta^{n^*}\sum_{l=1}^{n^*-1}\beta^{l-1}[\alpha(s,a)+\gamma(\tau-t)-\alpha(s+l,a)]\right\} \geq 0.
$$

Note that because of Condition (g) of Assumption 4, the first term (in braces) in the final expression before the inequality is nonnegative. The second term is nonnegative because of Condition (f) of Assumption 4. The third part is nonnegative because of Assumption 5. Consequently, if the agent drops out of school at period t' with school level s, he will never return. This implies that for any period $t'+p$, schooling level s, and experience vector $x_{t'+p} \neq 0$ that satisfies

$$
x_{j,t'+p} = \begin{cases} 0 & \text{if } j \neq s \\ p & \text{if } j = s \end{cases} \quad \text{for } p=1,\ldots,T-t'.
$$

The value function $V(t' + p, s, x_{t'+p}, a)$ satisfies

$$V(t' + p, s, x_{t'+p}, a) = \alpha(s, a) + \gamma p + \Delta r_0(t' + p, s, x_{s,t'+p})$$

$$+ \beta \sum_{\tau=t'+p+1}^{T} \beta^{\tau-t'-p-1}[\alpha(s, a) + \gamma(\tau - t')].$$

In particular, note that

(A.7) $V(t' + 1, s, x_{t'+1}, a) = \alpha(s, a) + \gamma + \Delta r_0(t' + 1, s, x_{s,t'+1})$

$$+ \beta \sum_{\tau=t'+1}^{T} \beta^{\tau-t'-1}[\alpha(s, a) + \gamma(\tau - t' + 1)].$$

This is important because by definition of the Bellman equation,

$V(t' + 1, s + 1, 0, a)$

$$= \max \left\{ \begin{array}{l} \alpha(s + 1, a) + \Delta r_0(t' + 1, s + 1, 0) + \beta E_{t'}[V(t' + 2, s, x_{t'+2}, a)], \\ \delta(s + 1, a) + \Delta r_1(t' + 1, s + 1) + \beta E_{t'}[V(t' + 2, s + 2, 0, a)] \end{array} \right\}.$$

Thus, we can write

$V(t' + 1, s + 1, 0, a)$

$$= \max \left\{ \begin{array}{l} \alpha(s, a) + \Delta r_0(t' + 1, s, x_{s,t'+1}) + \beta \sum_{\tau=t'+2}^{T} \beta^{\tau-t'-2} \\ \times [\alpha(s, a) + \gamma(\tau - t' - 1)], \\ \delta(s + 1, a) + \Delta r_1(t' + 1, s + 1) + \beta E_{t'}[V(t' + 2, s + 2, 0, a)] \end{array} \right\},$$

and by substituting the equality (A.7) sequentially, we conclude that (8) is true for all $s \leq s^*(a)$ as we sought to prove. ∎

PROOF OF PROPOSITION 5   To prove the claim we must show that an agent who decides to drop out at period t with schooling level s would also choose to remain out of school at school level $s + k, k \in \mathbb{Z}^+$. To see why, consider the one stage look ahead rule

$$\max\{R(t, s, 0, a), \delta(s, a) + \Delta r_1(t, s, 0) + \beta E_t[R(t + 1, s + 1, 0, a)]\}.$$

Suppose that the agent decides to drop out of school. Then, it must be true that

$$\alpha(s, a) + \Delta r_0(s, s, 0) - \delta(s, a) - \Delta r_1(s, s, 0)$$

$$\geq \beta \frac{1 - \beta^{T-s}}{1 - \beta}[\alpha(s + 1, a) - \alpha(s, a) - \gamma].$$

Now, suppose that the agent faces the same choice at some school level $s + k$, $k \geq 1$. Then, the agent would still drop out of school if and only if

$$\alpha(s + k, a) + \Delta r_0(s + k, s, 0) - \delta(s + k, a) - \Delta r_1(s, s, 0)$$

$$\geq \beta \frac{1 - \beta^{T-s-k}}{1 - \beta} [\alpha(s + 1, a) - \alpha(s, a) - \gamma].$$

Note that it is always true that, for all nonnegative integers k,

$$[\alpha(s + k, a) - \alpha(s, a) - \gamma] \geq [\alpha(s + k, a) - \alpha(s, a) - \gamma].$$

So, if we know that

$$\alpha(s + k, a) - \delta(s + k, a) \geq \frac{1 - \beta^{T-s-k}}{1 - \beta^{T-s}} (\alpha(s, a) - \delta(s, a))$$

and

$$\Delta r_0(s + k, s + k, 0) - \Delta r_1(s + k, s + k, 0) \geq \frac{1 - \beta^{T-s-k}}{1 - \beta^{T-s}} \Delta r_0(s, s, 0) - \Delta r_1(s, s, 0),$$

then we know that the agent would still decide to drop out of school. But these inequalities are guaranteed by Condition 8.   ∎

PROOF OF THEOREM 2   Normalize $U_I = 0$ (alternatively absorb it into the η_j). From the assumptions,

$$\Pr(D(1) = 1 \mid Z = z, Q = q) = \Pr(\varphi(z) - c_1(q_1) \leq \eta_1).$$

Using Matzkin's (1992) extension of Manski (1988), for the class of functions for $\varphi(Z)$ and $c_1(Q_1)$ defined by Matzkin (1992), we invoke assumptions (i), (ii), and (iii) to identify F_{η_1} up to an unknown mean and $\varphi(Z) - c_1(Q_1)$ over its support. Following Matzkin's argument as summarized in Appendix B, invoking (vii) and (ix) ensures us that identification is on nonnegligible sets. From (v) and (vii) we can separately identify $\varphi(Z)$ and $c_1(Q_1)$ up to constants. From (i) and (vi) we can pin down the constants in $\varphi(Z)$ given that $\bar{q}_1$ is in Supp (Q_1) by assumption (vi) since we fix the location of η_1 by (i). Next consider the event $D(1) + D(2) = 1$ given $Q = q$, $Z = z$. This can be written as $\Pr(D(1) + D(2) = 1 \mid Z = z, Q = q) = \Pr(\varphi(z) - c_2(q_2) \leq \eta_2)$. We can repeat the argument made for $\Pr(D(1) = 1 \mid Z, Q)$ for this probability. Alternatively, we can vary $\varphi(Z)$ and identify the distribution of $\eta_2 + c_2(q_2)$. $\bar{q}_2$ is in Supp (Q_2) from assumption (vi). We can identify the distribution of η_2 up to an unknown location parameter. We can identify the location parameter since we know the constant in $\varphi(Z)$. Proceeding in this fashion for $\Pr(D(1) + D(2) + D(3) = 1 \mid Z = z, Q = q)$ and successive probabilities of this type, we establish identifiability of the model on non-negligible sets.   ∎

PROOF OF THEOREM 3   Instead of normalizing $U_I = 0$, we can absorb it into the definition of η_j. From the assumptions,

$$\Pr(D(1) = 1 \mid Z = z, Q_1 = q_1) = \Pr(\varphi(z) - c_1(q_1) \leq \eta_1).$$

Assumption 1 and sampling rule (**S**) impose no restriction on (Q_1^*, η_1^*). Using Matzkin's extension of Manski (1988) and the Matzkin class of functions, we invoke conditions (i), (ii), (iii), (v), (vi) and (ix), we identify $F_{\eta_1^*}$ up to its mean (=0), the $\varphi(Z)$, and the $c_1(Q_1)$. The constants in $\varphi(Z)$ and $c_1(Q_1)$ cannot be separated without the information provided by assumption (vii).

Proceeding sequentially, consider the event $D(1) + D(2) = 1$, given $Z = z$, $Q_2 = q_2$, $Q_1 = q_1$. Its probability can be written as $\Pr(D(1) + D(2) = 1 \mid Z = z, Q_2 = q_2, Q_1 = q_1) = \Pr(\varphi(z) - c_2(q_2) \leq \eta_2 \mid Q_2 = q_2, Q_1 = q_1)$. Absorb $c_2(q_2)$ into η_2: $\tilde{\eta}_2 = \eta_2 + c_2(q_2)$. Since we know $\varphi(Z)$ from the first step of the proof, under (vi), we can identify $F_{\tilde{\eta}_2}$. At the point of evaluation $q_2 = \bar{q}_2$, $c_2(q_2) = 0$. We thus obtain the distribution of η_2 and its density as a consequence of (i).

Using $c_2(\bar{q}_2) = 0$ for $Q_2 = \bar{q}_2$, and (10), we obtain for each value of η_2,

$$\frac{f_{\eta_2^*}(\eta_2)}{K(\bar{q}_2, q_1)} = \frac{g(\eta_2 \mid Q_2 = \bar{q}_2, Q_1 = q_1)}{\int_{-\infty}^{\eta_2 - c_1(q_1)} f_{\eta_1^*}(\tau) \, d\tau},$$

where the right-hand side is known for each value of q_1 and η_2. Since $\int_{-\infty}^{\infty} f_{\eta_2^*}(\eta_2) \, d\eta_2 = 1$, we can identify $K(\bar{q}_2, q_1)$ for each q_1 and hence we can identify $f_{\eta_2^*}(\eta_2)$ over the full support of η_2.

To recover $c_2(q_2)$, invoke (iii) and (vi). There exists a limit set $S(\lim Q_1)$ such that

$$\Pr(D(1) + D(2) = 1 \mid Z = z, Q_1 = q_1, Q_2 = q_2, Q_1 \in S(\lim Q_1))$$

$$= \Pr(D(2) = 1 \mid Z = z, Q_1 = q_1, Q_2 = q_2, Q_1 \in S(\lim Q_1))$$

$$= \Pr(\varphi(Z) - c_2(q_2) \leq \eta_2).$$

This limit set drives $c_1(q_1)$ small enough that sampling rule (**S**) for $j = 2$ is satisfied almost everywhere and

$$\lim_{c_1(q_1) \to S(\lim Q_1)} \Pr(D(1) = 1 \mid Z = z, Q_1 = q_1, Q_2 = q_2, Q_1 \in S(\lim Q_1)) = 0.$$

Under (ix) we obtain identifiability on nonnegligible sets. Proceeding sequentially, we establish the claim in Theorem 3.   ∎

APPENDIX B: THE MATZKIN CLASS OF FUNCTIONS

Consider a binary choice model, $D = 1$ $(\varphi(Z) > V)$, where Z is observed and V is unobserved. $\varphi \in \Phi$, a class of real valued continuous functions with domain T_t. The support of Z is $\mathcal{Z}$. Let φ^* denote the true φ and let F_V^* denote the true cdf of V. Matzkin (1992) establishes conditions for identifiability of $\varphi(Z) \in T$, where $T = T_t \cap \mathcal{Z}$. There exists a subset $\bar{T} \subseteq T$ such that (i) for all $\varphi, \varphi' \in \Phi$ and all $z \in \bar{T}, \varphi(z) = \varphi'(z)$ and (ii) for all $\varphi \in \Phi$ and all t in the domain of the true value of $\varphi, \varphi^* \in \Phi$, there exists $z \in \bar{T}$ such that $\varphi(z) = t$. φ^* is strictly increasing in the Kth coordinate of Z. Instead of assuming absolute continuity for V, she assumes a set of distributions Γ with the properties: Γ is the set of monotone increasing functions on $\mathfrak{R}$ with values in $[0, 1]$; and the true distribution, F_V^*, is in $\Gamma, F_V^* \in \Gamma; F_V^*$ is strictly increasing over $\varphi^*(T)$. Finally, she assumes that for any $z \in T$ and any $\delta > 0$, using G as the distribution of the Z, $G[B(z, \delta) \cap T] > 0$, where $B(z, \delta) = \{z' \in Z \mid \|z - z'\| < \delta\}$ and K^{th} coordinate of Z possesses on T a Lebesgue density conditional on the other components of Z.

She notes that if the V are assumed to be absolutely continuous, it is not necessary to assume that there is a coordinate of the φ^* that is strictly increasing in its argument or that the Kth coordinate of Z has a Lebesgue density conditional on the other components of Z. She shows that the following alternative representations of functional forms satisfy the conditions for exact identification for $\varphi(Z)$. We refer to these as the Matzkin class of functions in the text.

(1) $\varphi(Z) = Z\gamma$, $\|\gamma\| = 1$ or $\gamma_1 = 1$, or
(2) $\varphi(Z)$ is homogeneous of degree one and attains a given value α, at $Z = z^*$ (e.g., cost functions where $\alpha = 0$ when $Z = 0$), or
(3) the $\varphi(Z)$ is a member of a class of least-concave function that attains common values at two points in their domain, or
(4) additively separable function, for $\varphi(Z)$:

    (a) functions additively separable into a continuous and monotone increasing function and a continuous monotone increasing, concave and homogeneous of degree one function;

    (b) functions additively separable into the value of one variable and a continuous, monotone increasing function of the remaining variables;

    (c) a set of additively separable functions in each argument (see Matzkin, 1992, example 5, p. 255).

REFERENCES

ABBRING, J. H., AND J. J. HECKMAN, "Econometric Evaluation of Social Programs, Part III: Distributional Treatment Effects, Dynamic Treatment Effects, Dynamic Discrete Choice, and General Equilibrium Policy Evaluation," in J. Heckman and E. Leamer, eds., *Handbook of Econometrics*, Volume 6B (Amsterdam: Elsevier, 2007), 5145–5303.

BECKER, G. S., "Human Capital and the Personal Distribution of Income: An Analytical Approach," Woytinsky Lecture no. 1. Ann Arbor: University of Michigan, Institute of Public Administration (1967).

BRESNAHAN, T. F., "Competition and Collusion in the American Automobile Industry: The 1955 Price War," *Journal of Industrial Economics* 35 (1987), 457–82.

BROCK, W. A., M. ROTHSCHILD, AND J. E. STIGLITZ, "Stochastic Capital Theory," in G. R. Feiwel, ed., *Joan Robinson and Modern Economic Theory* (New York: New York University Press, 1989), 591–622.

CAMERON, S. V., AND J. J. HECKMAN, "Life Cycle Schooling and Dynamic Selection Bias: Models and Evidence for Five Cohorts of American Males," *Journal of Political Economy* 106 (1998), 262–333.

CARD, D., "The Causal Effect of Education on Earnings," in O. Ashenfelter and D. Card, eds., *Handbook of Labor Economics*, Volume 5 (New York: North-Holland, 1999), 1801–63.

CARNEIRO, P., K. HANSEN, AND J. J. HECKMAN, "Estimating Distributions of Treatment Effects with an Application to the Returns to Schooling and Measurement of the Effects of Uncertainty on College Choice," *International Economic Review* 44 (2003), 361–422.

CRAWFORD, D., R. POLLAK, AND F. VELLA, "Simple Inference in Multinomial and Ordered Logit," *Econometric Reviews* 17 (1998), 289–99.

FERGUSON, T. S., "Optimal Stopping and Applications," Electronic text, available at: http://www.math.ucla.edu/tom/Stopping/Contents.html (2003).

FUSS, M. A., AND D. MCFADDEN, *Production Economics: A Dual Approach to Theory and Applications* (New York: North-Holland Publishing Company, 1978).

HECKMAN, J. J., "Effects of Child-Care Programs on Women's Work Effort," *Journal of Political Economy* 82 (1974), S136–63.

——, "Comment," in M. Feldstein, ed., *Behavioral Simulation Methods in Tax Policy Analysis* (Chicago: University of Chicago Press, 1983), 70–82.

——, AND T. E. MACURDY, "New Methods for Estimating Labor Supply Functions," in R. Ehrenberg, ed., *Research in Labor Economics* (Greenwich, CT: JAI Press, 1981), 65–102.

——, AND S. NAVARRO, "Dynamic Discrete Choice and Dynamic Treatment Effects," *Journal of Econometrics* 136 (2007), 341–96.

——, S. URZUA, AND E. J. VYTLACIL, "Understanding Instrumental Variables in Models with Essential Heterogeneity," *Review of Economics and Statistics* 88 (2006b), 389–432.

——, AND E. J. VYTLACIL, "Econometric Evaluation of Social Programs, Part I: Causal Models, Structural Models and Econometric Policy Evaluation," in J. Heckman and E. Leamer, eds., *Handbook of Econometrics*, Volume 6B (Amsterdam: Elsevier, 2007), 4779–4874.

——, R. J. LALONDE, AND J. A. SMITH, "The Economics and Econometrics of Active Labor Market Programs," in O. Ashenfelter and D. Card, eds., *Handbook of Labor Economics* (New York: North-Holland, 1999), 1865–2097.

——, L. J. LOCHNER, AND P. E. TODD, "Earnings Equations and Rates of Return: The Mincer Equation and Beyond," in E. A. Hanushek and F. Welch, eds., *Handbook of the Economics of Education* (Amsterdam: North-Holland, 2006a), 307–458.

KEANE, M. P., AND K. I. WOLPIN, "The Career Decisions of Young Men," *Journal of Political Economy* 105 (1997), 473–522.

MACHIN, S., AND A. VIGNOLES, *What's the Good of Education?* The Economics of Education in the UK (Princeton, N.J.: Princeton University Press, 2005).

MANSKI, C. F., "Identification of Binary Response Models," *Journal of the American Statistical Association* 83 (1988), 729–38.

MATZKIN, R. L., "Nonparametric and Distribution-Free Estimation of the Binary Threshold Crossing and the Binary Choice Models," *Econometrica* 60 (1992), 239–70.

——, "Restrictions of Economic Theory in Nonparametric Methods," in R. Engle and D. McFadden, eds., *Handbook of Econometrics* (New York: North-Holland, 1994), 2523–58.

McFADDEN, D., "Existence Conditions for Theil-Type Preferences," Unpublished Manuscript, Center for Mathematical Economics, University of Chicago, June 1963.

——, "Conditional Logit Analysis of Qualitative Choice Behavior," in P. Zarembka, ed., *Frontiers in Econometrics* (New York: Academic Press, 1974).

——,"Econometric Models of Probabilistic Choice," in C. Manski and D. McFadden, eds., *Structural Analysis of Discrete Data with Econometric Applications* (Cambridge, MA: MIT Press, 1981).

PRESCOTT, E. C., AND M. VISSCHER, "Sequential Location among Firms with Foresight," *Bell Journal of Economics* 8 (1977), 378–893.

RIDDER, G., "The Non-parametric Identification of Generalized Accelerated Failure-Time Models," *Review of Economic Studies* 57 (1990), 167–81.

ROSEN, S., "Human Capital: A Survey of Empirical Research," in R. Ehrenberg, ed., *Research in Labor Economics* (Greenwich, CT: JAI Press, 1977), 3–40.

SHAKED, A., AND J. SUTTON, "Relaxing Price Competition through Product Differentiation," *Review of Economic Studies* 49 (1982), 3–13.

THEIL, H., *Theory and Measurement of Consumer Demand Volume 1* (New York: American Elsevier Publishing Company, 1975).

——, *Theory and Measurement of Consumer Demand Volume 2* (New York: American Elsevier Publishing Company, 1976).

VYTLACIL, E. J. "Ordered Discrete-Choice Selection Models and Local Average Treatment Effect Assumptions: Equivalence, Nonequivalence, and Representation Results," *Review of Economics and Statistics* 88 (2006), 578–81.

WICKSELL, K., *Lectures on Political Economy* (New York: Macmillan Company, 1934).

INTERNATIONAL ECONOMIC REVIEW
Vol. 48, No. 4, November 2007

USING A LAPLACE APPROXIMATION TO ESTIMATE THE RANDOM COEFFICIENTS LOGIT MODEL BY NONLINEAR LEAST SQUARES*

By   Matthew C. Harding and Jerry Hausman[1]

Stanford University, U.S.A.; MIT, U.S.A.

Current methods of estimating the random coefficients logit model employ simulations of the distribution of the taste parameters through pseudo-random sequences. These methods suffer from difficulties in estimating correlations between parameters and computational limitations such as the curse of dimensionality. This article provides a solution to these problems by approximating the integral expression of the expected choice probability using a multivariate extension of the Laplace approximation. Simulation results reveal that our method performs very well, in terms of both accuracy and computational time.

1.   INTRODUCTION

Understanding discrete economic choices is an important aspect of modern economics. McFadden (1974) introduced the *multinomial logit* model as a model of choice behavior derived from a random utility framework. An individual i faces the choice between K different goods $i = 1, \ldots, K$. The utility to individual i from consuming good j is given by $U_{ij} = x'_{ij}\beta + \epsilon_{ij}$, where x'_{ij} corresponds to a set of choice relevant characteristics specific to the consumer-good pair (i, j). The error component ϵ_{ij} is assumed to be independently identically distributed with an extreme value distribution $f(\epsilon_{ij}) = \exp(-\epsilon_{ij})\exp(-\exp(-\epsilon_{ij}))$.

If individual i is constrained to choose a single good within the available set, utility maximization implies that some good j will be chosen over all other goods $l \neq j$ such that $U_{ij} > U_{il}$, for all $l \neq j$. We are interested in deriving the probability that consumer i chooses good j, which is

$$(1) \qquad P_{ij} = \Pr[x'_{ij}\beta + \epsilon_{ij} > x'_{il}\beta + \epsilon_{il}, \text{ for all } l \neq j].$$

McFadden (1974) shows that the resulting integral can be solved in closed form, implying the familiar expression

$$(2) \qquad P_{ij} = \frac{\exp(x'_{ij}\beta)}{\sum_{k=1}^{K} \exp(x'_{ik}\beta)}(=s_{ij}).$$

* Manuscript received December 2005; revised September 2006.

[1] We thank Ketan Patel for excellent research assistance. We thank Ronald Butler, Kenneth Train, Joan Walker, and participants at the MIT Econometrics Lunch Seminar and at the Harvard Applied Statistics Workshop for comments. Please address correspondence to: Jerry Hausman, Department of Economics, MIT. 50 Memorial Drive, Cambridge, MA 02142, U.S.A. E-mail: *Jhausman@MIT.edu*.

In some analyses it is also useful to think of the market shares of different firms. Without loss of generality we can also consider the choice probability described above to be the share of the total market demand that goes to good j in market i, and we will denote this by s_{ij}. All the results derived in this article will be valid for either interpretation. For convenience we shall focus on the market shares interpretation of the above equation.

The vector of coefficients β can be thought of as a representation of the individual tastes and determines the choice, conditional on the observable consumer-good characteristics. Although an extremely useful model, the multinomial model suffers from an important limitation: It is built around the assumption of independence of irrelevant alternatives (IIA), that implies equal cross price elasticities across all choices, as demonstrated by Hausman (1975). Additionally, it does not allow for correlations between the random components of utility, thus limiting the complexity of individual choice that can be modeled (Hausman and Wise, 1978).

Although a number of more flexible specifications have been proposed, few proved to be computationally tractable. The addition of a random coefficients framework to the logit model provides an attractive alternative (Cardell and Dunbar, 1980). In many applications however it is important to think of tastes as varying in the population of consumers according to a distribution $F(\beta)$. It is particularly important not to assume the taste parameters to be independent. The estimation of correlations between the components of the vector β is of major interest. The resulting correlations describe patterns of substitution between different product characteristics.

In practice, we often assume that the distribution $F(\beta)$ is Normal with mean b and covariance Σ. The purpose of random coefficients models is to estimate the unknown parameters b and Σ from the available sample. From a computational point of view, the aim is to obtain the expected share of good j in market i from the evaluation of the following expectation:

$$
(3) \qquad E_\beta(s_{ij}) = \int_{-\infty}^{+\infty} \frac{\exp(x_{ij}'\beta)}{\sum_{k=1}^{K} \exp(x_{ik}'\beta)} \, dF(\beta).
$$

We denote this model to be the random coefficients logit model. The above expression corresponds to a multivariate integral over the dimension of the space of the taste parameters. Since the integral does not have a known analytic solution, the use of simulation methods currently plays an important part in the implementation of these models (Lerman and Manski, 1981) with recent applications employing pseudo-random Halton sequences (Train, 2003; Small et al., 2005).

The random coefficients logit model is an extremely versatile tool for the analysis of discrete choices since it can be thought of as an arbitrarily close approximate representation of any random utility model consistent with choice probabilities (McFadden and Train, 2000). This has prompted researchers to think of this model as "one of the most promising state of the art discrete choice models" (Hensher and Green, 2003). Applications of the random coefficients logit model abound, not only within economics, but also in related disciplines such as marketing or transportation research (Hess and Polak, 2005). The random coefficients model is also an important building block for more complex models. Thus, Berry et al. (1995) employ the random coefficients logit model to analyze demand based on market-level price and quantity data. Bajari et al. (2005) incorporate it into an econometric model of discrete games with perfect information, where it selects the probability of different equilibria.

The implementation of the random coefficients model remains a challenging application of the method of simulated moments. In particular, the estimation of a full covariance matrix of the taste parameters, which fully incorporates all the possible correlations between parameters, seems to elude most researchers and appears to be a serious limitation of the simulation approach. In Section 2 of this article we will derive an analytic approximation of the integral expression in Equation (3) which can be incorporated into an extremely convenient nonlinear least squares framework for the estimation of all mean and variance–covariance parameters of the taste distribution. Section 3 shows the superior performance of the new method based on the Laplace method compared to the simulation alternative in cases where the model is specified with nonzero correlations.

2.   A LAPLACE APPROXIMATION OF THE EXPECTED SHARE

Consider the expected share of product j in market i under the random coefficients logit model introduced above.

$$(4) \qquad E_\beta(s_{ij}) = E_\beta \left\{ \frac{\exp(x'_{ij}\beta)}{\sum_{k=1}^{K} \exp(x'_{ik}\beta)} \right\} = E_\beta \left\{ \left(\sum_{k=1}^{K} \exp(x'_{ijk}\beta) \right)^{-1} \right\},$$

where $x_{ijk} = x_{ik} - x_{ij}$ for all k. Assume that the taste parameters β are drawn from a normal multivariate distribution with mean b and covariance matrix Σ,

$$(5) \qquad f(\beta) = (2\pi)^{-p/2}|\Sigma|^{-1/2} \exp\left\{ -\frac{1}{2} (\beta - b)' \Sigma^{-1} (\beta - b) \right\}.$$

For simplicity we focus in our derivations on the case where all coefficients are random. More generally, we may wish to allow for mixture of fixed and random coefficients. The results in this article will continue to hold in this case too and we restate the main result of this paper in terms of both random and fixed coefficients in Appendix B.

Then the expected share is given by the following multivariate integral:

$$(6) \qquad E_\beta(s_{ij}) = (2\pi)^{-p/2}|\Sigma|^{-1/2} \int_{-\infty}^{+\infty} \exp[-g(\beta)]\, d\beta,$$

where

$$(7) \qquad g(\beta) = \frac{1}{2}(\beta - b)'\Sigma^{-1}(\beta - b) + \log\left(\sum_{k=1}^{K} \exp(x'_{ijk}\beta) \right).$$

In this section, we provide an approximation to the integral expression above using the asymptotic method of Laplace. Although univariate applications of this method are common to mathematics and physics, where they are routinely applied to the complex functions in order to derive "saddle-point approximations," few applications to econometrics or statistics have been attempted. The extension of the method to multivariate settings was developed by Hsu (1948) and Glynn (1980). A statement of the main theorem is given in Appendix A together with the technical conditions required for the approximation to exist. Statistical applications of the Laplace approximation were developed by Daniels (1954) and Barndorff-Nielsen and Cox (1979), who employ the Laplace approximation to derive the *indirect Edgeworth expansion*, a generalization of the Edgeworth expansion method for distributions to exponential families. The Laplace method was also applied in Bayesian statistics to derive approximations to posterior moments and distributions (Tierney and Kadane, 1986; Efstathiou et al., 1998). More recently, Butler and Wood (2002) noticed that the Laplace approximation often produces accurate results in subasymptotic situations that are not covered by the traditional setting. It is this insight that we will use below.

Now perform a Taylor expansion of the function $g(\beta)$ around the point $\tilde{\beta}_{ij}$, such that $g(\tilde{\beta}_{ij}) < g(\beta)$ for all $\beta \neq \tilde{\beta}$. This expansion is given by

$$(8) \qquad g(\beta) \cong g(\tilde{\beta}_{ij}) + (\beta - \tilde{\beta}_{ij})' \left[\frac{\partial g}{\partial \beta} \bigg|_{\beta = \tilde{\beta}_{ij}} \right]$$

$$+ \frac{1}{2}(\beta - \tilde{\beta}_{ij})' \left[\left(\frac{\partial^2 g(\beta)}{\partial \beta \partial \beta'} \right)_{\beta = \tilde{\beta}_{ij}} \right] (\beta - \tilde{\beta}_{ij}) + O((\beta - \tilde{\beta}_{ij})^3).$$

Substituting in the integral expression above we obtain

$$(9) \qquad E_\beta(s_{ij}) \cong |\Sigma|^{-1/2} \exp(-g(\tilde{\beta}_{ij}))$$

$$\times \int_{-\infty}^{+\infty} (2\pi)^{-p/2} \exp\left\{ -\frac{1}{2}(\beta - \tilde{\beta}_{ij})' \left[\left(\frac{\partial^2 g(\beta)}{\partial \beta \partial \beta'} \right)_{\beta = \tilde{\beta}_{ij}} \right] (\beta - \tilde{\beta}_{ij}) \right.$$

$$\left. + O((\beta - \tilde{\beta}_{ij})^3) \right\} d\beta.$$

The intuition for this approach is given by the fact that if $g(\beta)$ has a minimum at the point $\tilde{\beta}_{ij}$, then the contribution of the function $g(\beta)$ to the exponential integral will be dominated by a small region around the point $\tilde{\beta}_{ij}$. Furthermore, by using a second order Taylor expansion around $\tilde{\beta}_{ij}$, we make the further assumption that the higher order terms of the expansion may be safely ignored. Let $\tilde{\Sigma}_{ij}$ be the inverse of the Hessian of $g(\beta)$ evaluated at $\tilde{\beta}_{ij}$, i.e., $\tilde{\Sigma}_{ij}^{-1} = (\frac{\partial^2 g(\beta)}{\partial \beta \partial \beta'})_{\beta = \tilde{\beta}_{ij}}$. Note that both $\tilde{\beta}_{ij}$ and $\tilde{\Sigma}_{ij}$ are indexed by i and j to remind us that these values depend on the covariates of product j in market i explicitly and in general will not be constant across products or markets.

Then, we can rewrite the integral above as

$$(10) \qquad E_\beta(s_{ij}) \cong |\Sigma|^{-1/2} \exp(-g(\tilde{\beta}_{ij}))|\tilde{\Sigma}_{ij}|^{1/2}(2\pi)^{-p/2}|\tilde{\Sigma}_{ij}|^{-1/2}$$
$$\times \int_{-\infty}^{+\infty} \exp\left\{-\frac{1}{2}(\beta - \tilde{\beta}_{ij})'\tilde{\Sigma}_{ij}^{-1}(\beta - \tilde{\beta}_{ij})\right\} d\beta.$$

We recognize the right-hand side of this expression to be the Gaussian integral, that is, the integral over the probability density of a Normal variable β with mean $\tilde{\beta}_{ij}$ and covariance $\tilde{\Sigma}_{ij}$. Since this area integrates to 1 we have

$$(11) \qquad (2\pi)^{-p/2}|\tilde{\Sigma}_{ij}|^{-1/2}\left[\int_{-\infty}^{+\infty} \exp\left\{-\frac{1}{2}(\beta - \tilde{\beta}_{ij})'\tilde{\Sigma}_{ij}^{-1}(\beta - \tilde{\beta}_{ij})\right\} d\beta\right] = 1$$

and we can write the expected share of product i in market j as

$$(12) \qquad E_\beta(s_{ij}) \cong \sqrt{\frac{|\tilde{\Sigma}_{ij}|}{|\Sigma|}} \exp(-g(\tilde{\beta}_{ij})).$$

The expansion point $\tilde{\beta}_{ij}$ has to be chosen optimally for each share, that is, $\tilde{\beta}_{ij}$ solves the equation $g'(\beta)|_{\beta=\tilde{\beta}_{ij}} = 0$, that is,

$$(13) \qquad (\tilde{\beta}_{ij} - b)'\Sigma^{-1} + \sum_{k=1}^{K}\left\{x_{ijk}' \frac{\exp(x_{ijk}'\tilde{\beta}_{ij})}{\sum_{k=1}^{K}\exp(x_{ijk}'\tilde{\beta}_{ij})}\right\} = 0.$$

In Appendix B, we show that $-g(\beta)$ is the sum of two strictly concave functions and thus it is also concave. Hence, the function $g(\beta)$ attains a unique minimum at the point $\tilde{\beta}_{ij}$. We can also think of the optimal expansion point $\tilde{\beta}_{ij}$ as solving a fixed-point equation, $\tilde{\beta}_{ij} = B(\tilde{\beta}_{ij})$, where

$$(14) \qquad B(\tilde{\beta}_{ij}) = b' - \left[\sum_{k=1}^{K}\left\{x_{ijk}' \frac{\exp(x_{ijk}'\tilde{\beta}_{ij})}{\sum_{k=1}^{K}\exp(x_{ijk}'\tilde{\beta}_{ij})}\right\}\right]\Sigma.$$

Additionally, the Hessian of $g(\beta)$ is given by

$$(15) \qquad \frac{\partial^2 g(\beta)}{\partial\beta\partial\beta'} = \Sigma^{-1} + \frac{\sum_{k=1}^{K} x_{ijk}x_{ijk}' \exp(x_{ijk}'\tilde{\beta}_{ij})}{\sum_{k=1}^{K} \exp(x_{ijk}'\tilde{\beta}_{ij})}$$
$$- \frac{\left[\sum_{k=1}^{K} x_{ijk}\exp(x_{ijk}'\tilde{\beta}_{ij})\right]\left[\sum_{k=1}^{K} x_{ijk}'\exp(x_{ijk}'\tilde{\beta}_{ij})\right]}{\left[\sum_{k=1}^{K}\exp(x_{ijk}'\tilde{\beta}_{ij})\right]^2}.$$

The following proposition summarizes the main result of this article by approximating the Gaussian integral corresponding to the expected share of product i in market j using a Laplace approximation.

PROPOSITION 1.   *If β has a Normal distribution with mean b and covariance Σ, we can approximate $E_\beta(s_{ij}) = E_\beta\{(\sum_{k=1}^{K} \exp(x_{ijk}'\beta))^{-1}\}$ by*

$$(16) \quad E_\beta(s_{ij}) \cong \sqrt{\frac{|\tilde{\Sigma}_{ij}|}{|\Sigma|}} \exp\left\{-\frac{1}{2}(\tilde{\beta}_{ij} - b)'\Sigma^{-1}(\tilde{\beta}_{ij} - b)\right\} \left(\sum_{k=1}^{K} \exp(x_{ijk}'\tilde{\beta}_{ij})\right)^{-1},$$

where

$$(17) \quad \tilde{\Sigma}_{ij} = \left\{\Sigma^{-1} + \frac{\sum_{k=1}^{K} x_{ijk} x_{ijk}' \exp(x_{ijk}'\tilde{\beta}_{ij})}{\sum_{k=1}^{K} \exp(x_{ijk}'\tilde{\beta}_{ij})}\right.$$

$$\left. - \frac{\left[\sum_{k=1}^{K} x_{ijk} \exp(x_{ijk}'\tilde{\beta}_{ij})\right]\left[\sum_{k=1}^{K} x_{ijk}' \exp(x_{ijk}'\tilde{\beta}_{ij})\right]}{\left[\sum_{k=1}^{K} \exp(x_{ijk}'\tilde{\beta}_{ij})\right]^2}\right\}^{-1},$$

and $\tilde{\beta}_{ij}$ solves the fixed-point equation $\tilde{\beta}_{ij} = B(\tilde{\beta}_{ij})$ for

$$(18) \quad B(\tilde{\beta}_{ij}) = b' - \left[\sum_{k=1}^{K}\left\{x_{ijk}'\frac{\exp(x_{ijk}'\tilde{\beta}_{ij})}{\sum_{k=1}^{K} \exp(x_{ijk}'\tilde{\beta}_{ij})}\right\}\right]\Sigma.$$

In the next section, we present detailed simulation results that show the performance of the approximation in estimating the unknown parameters b and Σ of the model. Figure 1 shows the remarkably good fit between of the Laplace approximation of the true market share at fixed values of b and Σ for two covariates.

The exact expected share obtained by numerical integration coincides with the expected share obtained by the Laplace approximation almost everywhere. The only noticeable deviation occurs for values of the expected share close to 1. Fortunately, this case is relatively infrequent in economic applications, where in multibrand competition models we may expect to have many small shares in any given market, but it is unlikely to have more than a few very large shares in the entire sample. The Laplace approximation introduced in this section has the peculiar property of being an asymmetrical approximation to a symmetrical function. This feature however proves to be extremely useful for economic applications since it provides a very close approximation to small shares that are much more likely to occur in economic data than shares close to 1, where the approximation tends to underestimate the true expected share.

The optimal expansion point $\tilde{\beta}_{ij}$ used in Proposition 1 can be computed by standard iterative methods that solve the fixed-point equation $\tilde{\beta}_{ij} = B(\tilde{\beta}_{ij})$. Although such methods are widely available in commercial software packages and tend to be extremely fast, the optimal expansion point $\tilde{\beta}_{ij}$ needs to be computed for each

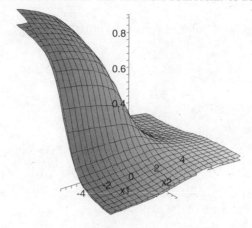

FIGURE 1

COMPARISON OF EXPECTED SHARE OBTAINED BY NUMERICAL INTEGRATION AND THE CORRESPONDING
LAPLACE APPROXIMATION FOR A MODEL WITH 2 COVARIATES AT FIXED VALUES OF b AND Σ

firm in each market separately, which may potentially slow down numerical optimization routines if large data sets are used. To improve computational efficiency we can further derive an approximate solution to the fixed point equation, which, as we will show in the next section, performs very well.

Let $h(\beta) = \log(\sum_{k=1}^{K} \exp(x'_{ijk}\beta))$ and perform a quadratic Taylor approximation of $g(\beta)$ around the constant parameter vector b. Then,

$$(19) \quad h(\beta) \cong h_{ij}(b) + (\beta - b)' J_{ij}(b) + \frac{1}{2}(\beta - b)' H_{ij}(b)(\beta - b) + O((\beta - b)^3),$$

where the Jacobian and Hessian terms are given by

$$(20) \qquad J_{ij}(b) = \sum_{k=1}^{K} \left\{ x'_{ijk} \frac{\exp(x'_{ijk}b)}{\sum_{k=1}^{K} \exp(x'_{ijk}b)} \right\}$$

and

$$(21)$$
$$H_{ij}(b) = \frac{\sum_{k=1}^{K} x_{ijk} x'_{ijk} \exp(x'_{ijk}b)}{\sum_{k=1}^{K} \exp(x'_{ijk}b)} - \frac{\left[\sum_{k=1}^{K} x_{ijk} \exp(x'_{ijk}b)\right]\left[\sum_{k=1}^{K} x'_{ijk} \exp(x'_{ijk}b)\right]}{\left[\sum_{k=1}^{K} \exp(x'_{ijk}b)\right]^2}.$$

Thus, we can rewrite the expression for $g(\beta)$ as

$$(22)$$
$$g(\beta) = \frac{1}{2}(\beta - b)' \Sigma^{-1}(\beta - b) + h_{ij}(b) + (\beta - b)' J_{ij}(b) + \frac{1}{2}(\beta - b)' H_{ij}(b)(\beta - b).$$

The optimal expansion point $\tilde{\beta}_{ij}$ solves the equation $\partial g(\beta)/\partial \beta = 0$. Hence,

$$(23) \qquad \frac{\partial g(\beta)}{\partial \beta} = (\beta - b)'\Sigma^{-1} + J_{ij}(b) + (\beta - b)'H_{ij}(b) = 0.$$

Since this expression is now linear we can easily solve for the optimal expansion point $\tilde{\beta}_{ij}$,

$$(24) \qquad \tilde{\beta}_{ij} = b - \left[\Sigma^{-1} + H_{ij}(b)\right]^{-1} J'_{ij}(b).$$

We can now rewrite Proposition 1 to obtain an easily implementable version of the Laplace approximation of the expected share.

PROPOSITION 2. *If β has a Normal distribution with mean β and covariance Σ, we can approximate $E_\beta(s_{ij}) = E_\beta\{(\sum_{k=1}^{K} \exp(x'_{ijk}\beta))^{-1}\}$ by*

$$(25) \qquad E_\beta(s_{ij}) \cong \sqrt{\frac{|\tilde{\Sigma}_{ij}|}{|\Sigma|}} \exp\left\{-\frac{1}{2}(\tilde{\beta}_{ij} - b)'\Sigma^{-1}(\tilde{\beta}_{ij} - b)\right\} \left(\sum_{k=1}^{K} \exp(x'_{ijk}\tilde{\beta}_{ij})\right)^{-1},$$

where

$$(26) \qquad \tilde{\beta}_{ij} = b - \left[\Sigma^{-1} + H_{ij}(b^*)_{b^*=b}\right]^{-1} J'_{ij}(b)$$

$$(27) \qquad \tilde{\Sigma}_{ij}^{-1} = \Sigma^{-1} + H_{ij}(b^*)_{b^*=\tilde{b}_{ij}},$$

and

$$(28) \qquad J_{ij}(b) = \sum_{k=1}^{K} \left\{ x'_{ijk} \frac{\exp(x'_{ijk}b)}{\sum_{k=1}^{K} \exp(x'_{ijk}b)} \right\}$$

$$(29) \qquad H_{ij}(b^*) = \frac{\sum_{k=1}^{K} x_{ijk}x'_{ijk} \exp(x'_{ijk}b^*)}{\sum_{k=1}^{K} \exp(x'_{ijk}b^*)}$$
$$\qquad - \frac{\left[\sum_{k=1}^{K} x_{ijk} \exp(x'_{ijk}b^*)\right]\left[\sum_{k=1}^{K} x'_{ijk} \exp(x'_{ijk}b^*)\right]}{\left[\sum_{k=1}^{K} \exp(x'_{ijk}b^*)\right]^2}.$$

Notice that the Hessian expression $H_{ij}(b^*)$ is evaluated at different points b^* in the computation of the values of $\tilde{\beta}_{ij}$ and $\tilde{\Sigma}_{ij}$. Proposition 2 is also insightful in that it explains why a simple Taylor expansion of the Gaussian integral around the mean b will fail. Consider the expression for $\tilde{\beta}_{ij}$, which is the optimal expansion point in the Laplace approximation. Notice that $\tilde{\beta}_{ij} = b$ only if $J_{ij}(b) = 0$. But this expression can only be zero if the vectors of covariates x_{ijk} are zero for all k. Hence a Taylor approximation of the same problem will fail since it expands each expected share around a constant value when in fact it ought to perform the expansion around an optimal value that will differ from share to share depending on the covariates. The Laplace approximation developed above performs this optimal expansion.

3.   MONTE CARLO SIMULATIONS

In this section, we discuss the estimation of the random coefficients model by nonlinear least squares after applying the Laplace approximation derived in the previous section to each expected market share. We will also compare its performance in Monte Carlo simulations to that of alternative methods used for the estimation of these models in the econometric literature.

Since the model was introduced over 30 years ago, several estimation methods have been proposed that try to circumvent the problem that the integral expression for the expected shares does not have a closed form solution for most distributions of the taste parameters. Although numerical integration by quadrature is implemented in numerous software packages, it is also extremely time consuming. In practice it is not possible to use numerical integration to solve such problems if the number of regressors is greater than two or three. We have found that even for the case of a single regressor this method is extremely slow and not always reliable.

The main attempt to estimate random coefficients models is based on the method of simulated moments (McFadden, 1989; Pakes and Pollard, 1989), where the expectation is replaced by an average over repeated draws from the distribution of taste parameters:

$$(30) \qquad E_\beta(s_{ij}) = \int \frac{\exp(x'_{ij}\beta)}{\sum_{k=1}^{K} \exp(x'_{ik}\beta)} \, dF(\beta) \cong \frac{1}{R} \sum_{r=1}^{R} \frac{\exp(x'_{ij}\overline{\beta_r})}{\sum_{k=1}^{K} \exp(x'_{ik}\overline{\beta_r})},$$

where $\overline{\beta_r}$ is drawn from the distribution $F(\beta)$. Random sampling from a distribution may nevertheless provide poor coverage of the domain of integration. There is no guarantee that in a particular set of draws the obtained sequence will uniformly cover the domain of integration and may in fact exhibit random clusters that will distort the approximation. To achieve a good approximation the number of draws R will have to be very large.

More recently the use of variance reduction techniques has been advocated in an attempt to improve the properties of simulated estimation (Train, 2003). Negatively correlated pseudo-random sequences may lead to a lower variance of the resulting estimator than traditional independent sampling methods. The method currently employed in econometrics uses *Halton sequences* (Small et al., 2005). ·

Halton sequences can be constructed as follows. For each dimension r of the vector β and some prime number k construct the sequence

$$(31) \qquad s_{t+1} = \left\{ s_t, s_t + \frac{1}{k}, \ldots, s_t + \frac{(k-1)}{k^t} \right\}, \qquad \text{for } s_0 = 0.$$

This sequence is then randomized by drawing μ uniform (0,1) and for each element s, letting $s^* = \text{mod}(s + \mu)$.

This method provides coverage of the unit hypercube by associating each dimension with a different prime number k. In order to transform these points into draws from the relevant distribution, an inversion in then applied, e.g., if the desired distribution is Normal one would turn these points on the unit hypercube into values of β, by letting $\overline{\beta}_r = \Phi^{-1}(s_r^*)$, which corresponds to the inverse of the normal distribution.

The use of Halton sequences improves performance over the use of independent draws and yet nevertheless it suffers from the curse of dimensionality. Many thousand draws are required for each observation and the application of this method is extremely problematic for the estimation of even a small number of parameters since it is so time consuming.

The mathematical properties of Halton sequences are not sufficiently well understood and may represent a liability in some applications. Train (2003) reports that in estimating a random coefficients logit model for households' choice of electricity supplier repeatedly, most runs provided similar estimates of the coefficients, yet some runs provided significantly different coefficients even though the algorithm was unchanged and applied to the same data set. Similarly, Chiou and Walker (2005) report that simulation based methods may falsely identify models if the number of draws is not sufficiently large. The algorithm may produce spurious results that "look" reasonable yet are not supported by the underlying data.

Additionally, to our knowledge, it was not possible so far to reliably estimate the full covariance matrix using simulation based methods. Researchers focus exclusively on the estimation of the mean and variance parameters thereby assuming a diagonal structure to the covariance matrix Σ of the taste parameters. We will show how this problem can be easily overcome by the use of the Laplace approximation method we propose in this article. Later on in this section we will also show how ignoring the covariances may lead to biased results and unreliable policy analysis if the taste parameters in the true data generating process are correlated.

We propose estimating the model parameters (b, Σ) by nonlinear least squares. Let s_{ij} be the observed market share of firm j in market i. We can construct the approximation of the expected share using the Laplace approximation as described in Section 2, $\hat{s}_{ij}(b, \Sigma) = E_\beta(s_{ij})$. This will be a nonlinear function in the model parameters b and Σ and can be implemented using either Proposition 1 or Proposition 2. The implementation of Proposition 2 is immediate and only involves the use of matrix functions. We can then proceed to estimate the model parameters by least squares or weighted least squares which can improve efficiency:

$$(32) \qquad (\hat{\beta}, \hat{\Sigma}) = \underset{\beta, \Sigma}{\text{argmin}} \sum_{i=1}^{N} \sum_{j=1}^{K} (s_{ij} - \hat{s}_{ij}(b, \Sigma))^2.$$

TABLE 1

ESTIMATION OF THE ONE VARIABLE RANDOM COEFFICIENTS MODEL. $N = 1000$, $K = 6$

Mean Bias	Quadrature	Fixed Point Laplace	Laplace	Halton
b	0.00778	0.00492	0.00555	0.00269
σ^2	0.04957	0.02348	0.00634	−0.02011
MSE	Quadrature	Fixed Point Laplace	Laplace	Halton
b	0.01003	0.00297	0.00281	0.00301
σ^2	0.09833	0.06641	0.08357	0.07381

The optimization can be achieved using a Newton type constrained optimization routine. Some parameters may require linear constraints (e.g., if the optimization is performed over variance parameters, then $(\sigma^2)_p > 0$ for all taste parameters β_p). The optimization needs to ensure that the estimated covariance matrix is positive definite at each step, for example, by employing an appropriate reparameterization or the Cholesky decomposition.

This can be achieved by an appropriate penalization at the edges of the allowable domain. The model can also be estimated by minimum chi-square techniques or by maximum likelihood given our evaluation of the expected shares. Simulation results suggest no significant performance differences between these different methods of implementation.

In Table 1, we estimate a random coefficients model with a single taste parameter using the methods discussed above. The covariate is drawn from a mixture distribution of a normal and a uniform random variable. This particular construction is performed in order to correct for unreliable estimates that have been reported when only normal covariates are being used. Since the model only requires univariate integration we can also perform numerical integration. We use a second order Newton–Coates algorithm to perform the integration by quadrature for each expected share. Additionally, we compute estimates using the two versions of the Laplace approximation of the expected share as described in Section 2 in Propositions 1 and 2, respectively. The results labeled as "Fixed Point Laplace" compute the optimal expansion points $\tilde{\beta}_{ij}$ using iterative fixed point techniques. The results labeled "Laplace" approximate this fixed point calculation using the analytic expression of Proposition 2. We also compute estimates using Halton sequences as implemented by Small et al. (2005). We perform 500 draws for each observation.

The results in Table 1 show that all four methods produce comparable results. Interestingly though, numerical integration tends to be outperformed by either of the approximation methods presented here. In particular the Laplace approximation we proposed performs very similarly to the simulated estimation based on Halton sequences both in terms of mean bias and mean squared error. This result was confirmed in additional simulations were the number of taste parameters was increased. The Laplace approximation introduced in this article outperforms the method of simulated moments in terms of computational time. Even in this simple one dimensional example the Laplace method runs about three times faster than the corresponding estimation using Halton sequences.

We have found no significantly different performance results between the
Laplace approximation using the fixed point calculation and that using the approximation to the optimal expansion point. The Laplace approximation of Proposition 2 nevertheless outperformed all other methods in terms of computational
time, being three to five times faster than the simulation approach.

Once we allow for multiple taste parameters we can ask the question whether
these taste parameters are correlated with each other. Consider a model with
three taste parameters, drawn from a distribution with mean $(b_1, b_2, b_3)'$ and
variances $(\sigma_1^2, \sigma_2^2, \sigma_3^2)$. In many cases of interest there is no a priori reason to
constrain the covariance matrix of this distribution to be diagonal. We can allow
for correlations between taste parameters by setting the off-diagonal elements of
the covariance matrix equal to $\sigma_{ij} = \rho_{ij}\sigma_i\sigma_j$ for $-1 < \rho_{ij} < 1$. The parameter ρ_{ij}
measures the strength of the correlation between the different taste parameters.
The full covariance matrix that needs to be estimated in this case is

$$
(33) \qquad \Sigma = \begin{pmatrix} \sigma_1^2 & \rho_{12}\sigma_1\sigma_2 & \rho_{13}\sigma_1\sigma_3 \\ \rho_{12}\sigma_1\sigma_2 & \sigma_2^2 & \rho_{23}\sigma_2\sigma_3 \\ \rho_{13}\sigma_1\sigma_3 & \rho_{23}\sigma_2\sigma_3 & \sigma_3^2 \end{pmatrix}.
$$

We use the Laplace approximation method to estimate all nine parameters and
report results for mean bias and MSE in Table 2. We were not able to estimate the
same parameters using the method of simulated moments with Halton sequences.
The algorithm failed to converge for Halton sequences under different model
parameters and different starting values.

Computational issues involving the use of simulated moments seem to have
prevented empirical work involving the estimation of the full covariance matrix.
We now wish to explore to what extent this may bias the results. To this purpose
we estimate the same model as in the above example but ignore the covariances.
Thus the true model has $\rho_{ij} \neq 0$ but we only estimate the restricted model where
we assume $\rho_{ij} = 0$ for all $i, j, i \neq j$.

TABLE 2

ESTIMATION OF THE THREE VARIABLE RANDOM COEFFICIENTS
MODEL WITH COVARIANCES. $N = 2000$, $K = 6$

Laplace	Mean Bias	MSE
b_1	0.01167	0.00233
b_2	0.00679	0.00201
b_3	−0.00371	0.00298
σ_1^2	−0.06889	0.09499
σ_2^2	−0.08245	0.07016
σ_3^2	0.03880	0.03180
ρ_{12}	0.04918	0.00774
ρ_{13}	0.04317	0.00350
ρ_{23}	−0.00702	0.00551

TABLE 3

ESTIMATION OF THE THREE VARIABLE RANDOM COEFFICIENTS MODEL WITHOUT COVARIANCES. THE TRUE MODEL CONTAINS COVARIANCES BUT THESE ARE NOT ESTIMATED. $N = 2000$, $K = 6$

	Mean Bias Laplace	Mean Bias Halton	MSE Laplace	MSE Halton
b_1	0.02037	0.01003	0.00321	0.00256
b_2	0.01582	0.00778	0.00201	0.00258
b_3	0.00651	0.00212	0.00122	0.00197
σ_1^2	−0.01032	−0.21102	0.10192	0.18226
σ_2^2	−0.50883	−0.43340	0.32381	0.27094
σ_3^2	−0.12991	−0.14967	0.03900	0.09577

The results are presented in Table 3. We were able to obtain estimates of the restricted model using both the new Laplace approximation we propose and by using the simulation approach involving Halton sequences. Once again both methods produce comparable results. While the estimates of the mean parameters (b_1, b_2, b_3)' seem to be sufficiently robust to the misspecification of the covariance matrix, the estimates of the variance parameters ($\sigma_1^2, \sigma_2^2, \sigma_3^2$) seem to be strongly affected by the noninclusion of the covariance terms in the optimization. The size of the bias is model dependent and we have found an absolute value of the bias between 30% and 60% in most simulations. Additionally, it seems that negative correlations that are falsely excluded bias the results much more than positive ones.

The failure to include the correlations between taste parameters may also lead to incorrect policy recommendations. Thus, consider the three variable described above, where the true data generating process has nonzero correlation terms and a full covariance matrix. We can interpret the model as follows.

We label the first variable as "price" and consider the policy experiment whereby the government has to decide whether to impose a 10% tax on a specific good. The tax is fully passed on to the consumers in the form of a 10% price increase. There are $K = 6$ competing firms in each market producing differentiated brands of the good on which the tax was imposed. We wish to simulate the ex post effect of the tax on the market shares of each firm. In order to do so we collect a sample of observations consisting of the market shares of each firm in different markets and the product characteristics of the differentiated good produced by brand and market. We estimate the random coefficients model with a full covariance matrix that allows for correlations between taste parameters. We also estimate the same model but limit ourselves to estimating a diagonal covariance, thus restricting the correlations to be zero and also derive the logit estimates of the means corresponding to the case where the taste parameters are assumed to be constant in the population. We can use these estimates to simulate the distribution of market shares of each firm across the markets and compare them to the initial distribution of market shares before the tax was implemented. We present the resulting distributions in Figure 2.

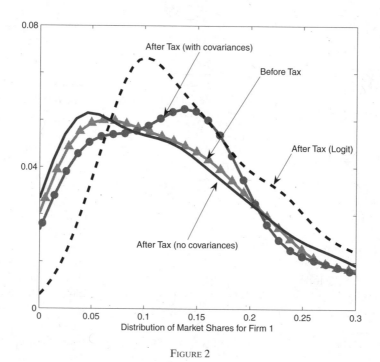

FIGURE 2

MARKET SHARES OF FIRM 1 BEFORE AND AFTER TAX

If we estimate any of the misspecified models by using either the logit estimates of Equation (2) or the random coefficients logit estimates of Equation (3) under the assumption of no correlation we would reach very different conclusions from the case when we take into account the full covariance matrix between taste parameters. Thus we can see how ignoring the correlations may lead to incorrect policy recommendations when the random coefficients model is used to estimate the distribution of taste parameters.

4.   CONCLUSION

In this article, we have introduced a new analytic approximation to the choice probability in a random coefficients logit model. The approximation was derived using a multivariate extension of the Laplace approximation for subasymptotic domains. The expression results in a nonlinear function of the data and parameters that can be conveniently estimated using nonlinear least squares.

This new method of estimating random coefficients logit models allows for the estimation of correlations between taste parameters. The estimation of a full covariance matrix seems to have eluded many previous implementations of the random coefficients logit model employing simulations of the underlying taste distributions.

Simulation results show that our new method performs extremely well, in terms of both numerical accuracy and computational time. We also provide an example of the importance of estimating correlations between taste parameters through a tax simulation where very different policy implications would be reached if the estimated model is misspecified by restricting the correlations to be zero.

In this article, we have focused on the case of Normal preferences. Harding and Hausman (2007) show how the Laplace approximation procedure described in this article can also be applied to more general preference specifications that allow for skewness or multimodality in addition to correlations between taste parameters.

APPENDIX

A. Multivariate Laplace Approximation Theorem.

For additional discussions of the theorem and applications to statistics see Muirhead (2005) and Jensen (1995). A proof is given in Hsu (1948).

LAPLACE APPROXIMATION THEOREM. Let D be a subset of R^p and let f and g be real-valued functions on D and T a real parameter. Consider the integral

$$(A.1) \qquad I = \int_{\beta \in D} f(\beta) \exp(-Tg(\beta)) \, d\beta$$

(a) g has an absolute minimum at an interior point $\tilde{\beta}$ of D;
(b) there exists $T \geq 0$ such that $f(\beta)\exp(-Tg(\beta))$ is absolutely integrable over the domain D;
(c) all first and second order partial derivatives of $g(x)$, $\frac{\partial g}{\partial \beta_i}$, $\frac{\partial^2 g}{\partial \beta_i \partial \beta_j}$, for $i = 1,\ldots,p$ and $j = 1,\ldots,p$ exist and are continuous in the neighborhood $N(\tilde{\beta})$ of $\tilde{\beta}$.
(d) there is a constant $\gamma < 1$ such that $|\frac{\exp(-g(\beta))}{\exp(-g(\tilde{\beta}))}| < \gamma$ for all $x \in D\backslash N(\tilde{\beta})$.
(e) f is continuous in a neighborhood $N(\tilde{\beta})$ of $\tilde{\beta}$.

Then for large T, we have

$$(A.2) \quad \tilde{I} = \left(\frac{2\pi}{T}\right)^{p/2} [\det(H(\tilde{\beta}))]^{-1/2} f(\tilde{\beta}) \exp(-Tg(\tilde{\beta})), \quad \text{where } H(\tilde{\beta}) = \frac{\partial^2 g(\tilde{\beta})}{\partial\tilde{\beta}\partial\tilde{\beta}'}$$

and

$$(A.3) \qquad I = \tilde{I}(1 + O(T^{-1})) \text{ as } T \to \infty.$$

In Section 2, we let $f(\beta) = 1$ and $g(\beta) = \frac{1}{2}(\beta - b)'\Sigma^{-1}(\beta - b) + \log(\sum_{k=1}^{K} \exp(x'_{ijk}\beta))$. This is sometimes referred to as an *exponential form Laplace approximation*.

Moreover we use the observation of Butler and Wood (2002) that in many cases of interest this approximation performs very well even in subasymptotic cases where T remains small. In our case $T = 1$.

B. Restatement of Results.

In some applications we may wish to allow for a mixture of fixed and random coefficients. We can partition the $p \times 1$ dimensional vector of taste parameters into two subvectors b^0 and β^1 of lengths p_0 and p_1, respectively, where $p_0 + p_1 = p$. The vector b^0 contains the fixed (unknown) parameters corresponding to the nonrandom coefficients of the model, and the vector β^1 captures the random coefficients. Furthermore, we can assume that β^1 is Normally distributed with mean b^1 and variance Σ. The results derived in this article extend to the case of a model specification with both random and fixed coefficients by performing the integration over the random coefficients while treating the fixed coefficients as constant for the purpose of deriving the Laplace approximation.

We now restate Proposition 2 for the case with both fixed and random coefficients, $\beta = (b^0, \beta^1)$. The unknown parameters to be estimated are (b^0, b^1, Σ), where b^1 is the vector of mean parameters of the random coefficients β^1 and Σ is the corresponding covariance matrix of β^1.

PROPOSITION 3. *We can approximate* $E_\beta(s_{ij}) = E_\beta\{(\sum_{k=1}^{K} \exp(x'_{ijk}\beta))^{-1}\}$ *by*

$$(\text{B.1}) \quad E_\beta(s_{ij}) \cong \sqrt{\frac{|\tilde{\Sigma}_{ij}|}{|\Sigma|}} \exp\left\{-\frac{1}{2}(\tilde{\beta}_{ij}^1 - b^1)'\tilde{\Sigma}_{ij}^{-1}(\tilde{\beta}_{ij}^1 - b^1)\right\} \left(\sum_{k=1}^{K} \exp(x'_{ijk}\tilde{\beta}_{ij})\right)^{-1},$$

where $\tilde{\beta}_{ij} = (b^0, \tilde{\beta}_{ij}^1)$ *and* $\check{\beta} = (b^0, b^1)$ *and*

$$(\text{B.2}) \qquad\qquad \tilde{\beta}_{ij}^1 = b^1 - [\Sigma^{-1} + H_{ij}(b^*)_{b^*=b}]^{-1} J'_{ij}(\check{b})$$

$$(\text{B.3}) \qquad\qquad \tilde{\Sigma}_{ij}^{-1} = \Sigma^{-1} + H_{ij}(b^*)_{b^*=\tilde{b}_{ij}},$$

and

$$(\text{B.4}) \qquad\qquad J_{ij}(b^*) = \sum_{k=1}^{K}\left\{x'_{ijk}\frac{\exp(x'_{ijk}b^*)}{\sum_{k=1}^{K}\exp(x'_{ijk}b^*)}\right\}$$

$$(\text{B.5}) \qquad H_{ij}(b^*) = \frac{\sum_{k=1}^{K} x_{ijk}x'_{ijk}\exp(x'_{ijk}b^*)}{\sum_{k=1}^{K}\exp(x'_{ijk}b^*)}$$

$$- \frac{\left[\sum_{k=1}^{K} x_{ijk}\exp(x'_{ijk}b^*)\right]\left[\sum_{k=1}^{K} x'_{ijk}\exp(x'_{ijk}b^*)\right]}{\left[\sum_{k=1}^{K}\exp(x'_{ijk}b^*)\right]^2}.$$

In Section 2, we assert one of the conditions required for the existence of a Laplace approximation with a unique expansion point, the concavity of the function $-g(\beta)$. The lemma below proves this result.

LEMMA 1.   *The function $g(\beta)$ is convex, where*

(B.6) $$g(\beta) = \frac{1}{2}(\beta - b)'\Sigma^{-1}(\beta - b) + \log\left(\sum_{k=1}^{K}\exp(x'_{ijk}\beta)\right).$$

PROOF. $g(\beta)$ is the sum of two convex functions, a quadratic form in β and the function $g_1(\beta) = \log(\sum_{k=1}^{K}\exp(x'_{ijk}\beta))$. The Hessian of this function is given by $H_{ij}(\beta)$ defined in Equation (21) above. In order to see that $H_{ij}(\beta) \geq 0$ notice that

(B.7) $$\left[\sum_{k=1}^{K}\exp(x'_{ijk}b)\right]^2 H_{ij}(b) = \sum_{k=1}^{K}\exp(x'_{ijk}b)\sum_{k=1}^{K}x_{ijk}x'_{ijk}\exp(x'_{ijk}b)$$

(B.8) $$-\left[\sum_{k=1}^{K}x_{ijk}\exp(x'_{ijk}b)\right]\left[\sum_{k=1}^{K}x'_{ijk}\exp(x'_{ijk}b)\right].$$

If we expand the right-hand side of Equation (48) and cancel the terms in $x_{ijk}\,x'_{ijk}(\exp(x'_{ijk}b))^2$ we can rearrange this expression as

(B.9) $$\left[\sum_{k=1}^{K}\exp(x'_{ijk}b)\right]^2 H_{ij}(b)$$

$$= \sum_{r=1}^{K-1}\sum_{s=r+1}^{K}(x_{ijr} - x_{ijs})(x_{ijr} - x_{ijs})'\exp(x'_{ijr}b)\exp(x'_{ijs}b) \geq 0. \quad\blacksquare$$

REFERENCES

BAJARI, P., H. HONG, AND S. RYAN, "Identification and Estimation of Discrete Games of Complete Information," Mimeo, MIT, 2005.

BARNDORFF-NIELSEN, O., AND D. R. COX, "Edgeworth and Saddle-point Approximations with Statistical Applications," *Journal of the Royal Statistical Society B* 41 (1979), 179–312.

BERRY, S., J. LEVINSOHN, AND A. PAKES, "Automobile Prices in Market Equilibrium," *Econometrica* 63(1995), 841–90.

BUTLER, R. W., AND A. T. A. WOOD, "Laplace Approximation for Hypergeometric Functions of Matrix Argument," *The Annals of Statistics* 30 (2002), 1155–77.

CARDELL, S., AND F. DUNBAR, "Measuring the Societal Impacts of Automobile Downsizing," *Transportation Research A* 14 (1980), 423–34.

CHIOU, L., AND J. WALKER, "Identification and Estimation of Mixed Logit Models under Simulation Methods," Mimeo, MIT, 2005.

DANIELS, H. E., "Saddlepoint Approximations in Statistics," *The Annals of Mathematical Statistics* 25 (1954), 631–50.

EFSTATHIOU, M., E. GUTIERREZ-PENA, AND A. F. M. SMITH, "Laplace Approximations for Natural Exponential Families with Cuts," *Scandinavian Journal of Statistics* 25 (1998).

GLYNN, W. J., "Asymptotic Representations of the Densities of Canonical Correlations and Latent Roots in Manova When the Population Parameters Have Arbitrary Multiplicity," *The Annals of Statistics* 8 (1980), 958–76.

HARDING, M. C., AND J. A. HAUSMAN, "Flexible Parametric Estimation of the Taste Distribution in Random Coefficients Logit Models," Mimeo, MIT, 2007.

HAUSMAN, J. A., "Project Independence Report: A Review of U.S. Energy Needs up to 1985," *Bell Journal of Economics* (1975).

——, AND D. A. WISE, "A Conditional Probit Model for Qualitative Choice-Discrete Decisions Recognizing Interdependence and Heterogeneous Preferences," *Econometrica* (1978), 403–26.

HENSHER, D., AND W. GREENE, "The Mixed Logit Model: The State of Practice," *Transportation* (2003), 133–76.

HESS, J., AND J. POLAK, "Mixed Logit Modelling of Airport Choice in Multi-Airport Regions," *Journal of Air Transport Management* (2005), 59–68.

HSU, L. C., "A Theorem on the Asymptotic Behavior of a Multiple Integral," *Duke Mathematical Journal* (1948), 623–32.

JENSEN, J. L., *Saddlepoint Approximations* (Oxford: Clarendon Press, 1995).

LERMAN, S., AND C. MANSKI, "On the Use of Simulated Frequencies to Approximate Choice Probabilities," in C. Manski and D. McFadden, eds., *Structural Analysis of Discrete Data with Econometric* (Cambridge: MIT Press, 1981), 305–20.

MCFADDEN, D., "Conditional Logit Analysis of Qualitative Choice Behavior," in A. Karlqvist, L. Lundqvist, F. Snickars, and J. Weibull, eds., *Frontiers in Econometrics* (Amsterdam: Academic Press, 1974), 75–96.

——, "A Method of Simulated Moments for Estimation of Discrete Response Models Without Numerical Integration," *Econometrica* (1989), 995–1026.

——, AND K. TRAIN, "Mixed MNL Models for Discrete Response," *Journal of Applied Econometrics* (2000), 447–70.

MUIRHEAD, R. J., ED., *Aspects of Multivariate Statistical Theory* (New York: Wiley, 2005).

PAKES, A., AND D. POLLARD, "Simulation and the Asymptotics of Optimization Estimators," *Econometrica* (1989), 1027–57.

SMALL, K. A., C. WINSTON, AND J. YAN, "Uncovering the Distribution of Motorists' Preferences for Travel Time and Reliability," *Econometrica* (2005), 1367–82.

TIERNEY, L., AND J. KADANE, "Accurate Approximations for Posterior Moments and Marginal Densities," *Journal of the Americal Statistical Association* (1986), 82–6.

TRAIN, E. K., *Discrete Choice Methods with Simulation* (Cambridge: Cambridge University Press, 2003).

INTERNATIONAL ECONOMIC REVIEW
Vol. 48, No. 4, November 2007

ASYMPTOTIC NORMALITY OF A NONPARAMETRIC
INSTRUMENTAL VARIABLES ESTIMATOR*

By Joel L. Horowitz[1]

Northwestern University, U.S.A.

This article gives conditions under which the nonparametric instrumental variables estimator of Hall and Horowitz (*Annals of Statistics* 33 (December 2005), 2904–2929) is asymptotically normally distributed. With sufficiently large samples, the asymptotic normality result can be used to form confidence intervals for the unknown function that is estimated by the Hall–Horowitz procedure. The article reports the results of a Monte Carlo investigation of the finite-sample coverage probabilities of the confidence intervals.

1. INTRODUCTION

This article is concerned with statistical inference about the unknown function g in the model

$$(1) \qquad Y = g(X) + U; \quad E(U \mid W) = 0,$$

where Y is a scalar dependent variable, X is a scalar explanatory variable, W is a scalar instrument for X, U is an unobserved random variable, and the random pair (X, W) is continuously distributed. The function g is nonparametric. It satisfies regularity conditions but does not belong to a known, finite-dimensional parametric family. It is not assumed that $E(U \mid X)$ vanishes. Therefore, Equation (1) is not a mean regression, and the instrumental variable W is used to identify and estimate g. The data, denoted by $\{Y_i, X_i, W_i : i = 1, \ldots, n\}$, are a simple random sample of (Y, X, W). The article gives conditions under which a certain nonparametric estimator of g is asymptotically normally distributed. With a sufficiently large sample, the asymptotic normality result can be used to obtain confidence intervals for g. The article reports the results of a Monte Carlo investigation of the finite-sample coverage probabilities of these confidence intervals.

If g is known up to a finite-dimensional parameter, the parameter and g can be estimated by using the generalized method of moments. The resulting estimator converges in probability at the rate $n^{-1/2}$ under mild regularity conditions. Nonparametric estimation of g is more difficult because, as is explained in Section 2,

*Manuscript received August 2005; revised September 2006.

[1] I thank Whitney Newey and Rosa Matzkin for helpful comments. Research supported in part by NSF grant SES 0352675. Please address correspondence to: Joel L. Horowitz, Department of Economics, Northwestern University, 2001 Sheridan Road, Evanston, IL 60208, U.S.A. Phone: 847-491-8253. Fax: 847-491-7001. E-mail: *joel-horowitz@northwestern.edu*.

the relation that identifies g is a Fredholm equation of the first kind, which leads to an ill-posed inverse problem (O'Sullivan, 1986; Kress, 1999). Consequently, the rate of convergence in probability of a nonparametric estimator of g is typically very slow. Depending on the details of the probability distribution of (Y, X, W), the rate may be slower than $O_p(n^{-\varepsilon})$ for any $\varepsilon > 0$ (Hall and Horowitz, 2005, hereinafter HH). Nonparametric estimators of g have been developed by Newey and Powell (2003), Darolles et al. (2002), Blundell et al. (2007), HH, and (under assumptions that are quite different from those here or in the other papers) Newey et al. (1999). Darolles et al. (2002) showed that scalar products of their estimator are asymptotically normal. Horowitz (2006) used the kernel estimator of HH to form a test of the hypothesis that g belongs to a specified finite-dimensional parametric family (that is, $g(x) = G(x, \theta)$ for almost every x, some finite-dimensional θ, and a known function G). Blundell and Horowitz (2007) used the HH estimator to form a test of the hypothesis that $E(U \mid X) = 0$.

This article gives conditions under which the kernel estimator of HH is asymptotically normally distributed. This estimator is easy to compute and has the fastest possible L_2 rate of convergence under the assumptions of HH. The asymptotic distribution can be used to form a confidence interval for $g(z)$ or test a hypothesis about the value of $g(z)$ if the asymptotic normal approximation is sufficiently accurate in samples of the sizes encountered in applications.

Section 2 of this article summarizes the HH estimator. Section 3 gives conditions under which the estimator is asymptotically normally distributed. Section 4 presents the results of the Monte Carlo investigation of the finite-sample coverage probabilities of confidence intervals for g. Section 5 presents conclusions. The proofs of theorems are in the Appendix.

2.   DESCRIPTION OF THE ESTIMATOR

This section summarizes the HH estimator of g in model (1).

2.1.   *The Estimator.*   Let f_X, f_W, and f_{XW}, respectively, denote the marginal probability density functions of X and W and the joint density function of (X, W). Assume without loss of generality that the support of (X, W) is the unit square. Define the operator T on the space of functions that are square integrable on L_2 $[0, 1]$ by

$$T\psi(z) = \int t(x, z)\psi(x)\,dx,$$

where

$$t(x, z) = \int f_{XW}(x, w)\,f_{XW}(z, w)\,dw.$$

Assume that T is nonsingular. HH show that

$$E_W[E(Y \mid W)\,f_{XW}(z, W)] = Tg(z)$$

for each $z \in [0, 1]$. Therefore, g is identified by the relation

$$(2) \qquad g(z) = E_W\big[E(Y \mid W)(T^{-1} f_{XW})(z, W)\big].$$

Equation (2) is a Fredholm equation of the first kind. It generates an ill-posed inverse problem if, as happens when f_{XW} is a "well behaved" density function, zero is a limit point of the eigenvalues of T. In that case, T^{-1} is not a bounded operator, and g cannot be estimated consistently by replacing unknown population quantities on the right-hand side of (2) with consistent estimators.[2] This problem is well known in the theory of integral equations and is dealt with by "regularizing" (that is, modifying) T^{-1} to make it a continuous operator. HH use Tikhonov regularization, which consists of replacing T^{-1} for estimation purposes with $(T + a_n I)^{-1}$, where I is the identity operator and $\{a_n\}$ is a sequence of positive constants that converges to 0 as $n \to \infty$.

To describe the HH estimator, let $K_h(\cdot, \cdot)$ denote a boundary kernel function with the property that for all $\xi \in [0, 1]$ and some integer $r \geq 2$

$$(3) \qquad h^{-(j+1)} \int_{\xi}^{\xi+1} u^j K_h(u, \xi)\, du = \begin{cases} 1 & \text{if } j = 0 \\ 0 & \text{if } 1 \leq j \leq r - 1. \end{cases}$$

Here $h > 0$ denotes a bandwidth, and the kernel is defined in a way that overcomes edge effects. In particular, if h is small and ξ is not close to 0 or 1, then we can set $K_h(u, \xi) = K(u/h)$, where K is an "ordinary" order r kernel. If ξ is close to 1, then we can set $K_h(u, \xi) = \bar{K}(u/h)$, where $\bar{K}$ is a bounded, compactly supported function satisfying

$$\int_0^\infty u^j \bar{K}(u)\, du = \begin{cases} 1 & \text{if } j = 0 \\ 0 & \text{if } 1 \leq j \leq r - 1. \end{cases}$$

If ξ is close to 0, we can set $K_h(u, \xi) = \bar{K}(-u/h)$. Assumption 5 in Section 2.2 gives a more precise characterization of the kernel. There are, of course, other ways of overcoming the edge-effect problem, but the boundary kernel approach used here works satisfactorily and is simple analytically.

Now define the kernel density estimators

$$\hat{f}_{XW}(x, w) = \frac{1}{nh^2} \sum_{j=1}^n K_h(x - X_j, x) K_h(w - W_j, w)$$

<hr />

[2] Let $\|\cdot\|$ denote the $L_2[0, 1]$ norm, and let $\{\lambda_j, \phi_j : j = 1, 2, \ldots\}$ denote the eigenvalues and orthonormal eigenvectors of T ordered so that $\lambda_1 \geq \lambda_2 \geq \cdots > 0$. Under the assumptions of HH, $\{\phi_j\}$ is a basis for $L_2[0, 1]$, and $\lim_{j \to \infty} \lambda_j = 0$. A function $\psi \in L_2$ has the representation $\psi(z) = \sum_{j=1}^\infty c_j \phi_j(z)$, where the coefficients c_j satisfy $\sum_{j=1}^\infty c_j^2 = \|\psi\|^2 < \infty$. $T\psi$ and $T^{-1}\psi$, respectively, have the representations $(T\psi)(z) = \sum_{j=1}^\infty \lambda_j c_j \phi_j(z)$, and $(T^{-1}\psi)(z) = \sum_{j=1}^\infty (c_j/\lambda_j)\phi_j(z)$. Since $\lambda_j \to 0$, $\|T^{-1}\psi\| = [\sum_{j=1}^\infty (c_j/\lambda_j)^2]^{1/2}$ can be arbitrarily large even if $\|\psi\|$ is close to 0.

and

$$\hat{f}_{XW}^{(-i)}(x, w) = \frac{1}{(n-1)h^2} \sum_{\substack{j=1 \\ j \neq i}}^{n} K_h(x - X_j, x) K_h(w - W_j, w).$$

Define the following estimators of $t(x, z)$ and T:

$$\hat{t}(x, z) = \int \hat{f}_{XW}(x, w)\, \hat{f}_{XW}(z, w)\, dw$$

and

$$\hat{T}\psi(z) = \int \hat{t}(x, z)\psi(x)\, dx.$$

Define $\hat{T}^{+} = (\hat{T} + a_n I)^{-1}$ for some constant $a_n > 0$. The HH estimator of g is

$$(4) \qquad \hat{g}(z) = n^{-1} \sum_{i=1}^{n} Y_i \left(\hat{T}^{+} \hat{f}_{XW}^{(-i)} \right)(z, W_i).$$

2.2. *Regularity Conditions.* This section presents the conditions under which HH prove that $\hat{g}$ converges to g at the fastest possible L_2 rate. A strengthened form of these conditions is used in Section 3 to obtain the asymptotic normality result. The following notation is used. Let $\{\lambda_j, \phi_j : j = 1, 2, \ldots\}$ denote the eigenvalues and orthonormal eigenfunctions of T ordered so that $\lambda_1 \geq \lambda_2 \geq \cdots > 0$. Under the assumptions of HH, the eigenfunctions form a complete, orthonormal basis for $L_2[0, 1]$. Therefore, we may write

$$t(x, z) = \sum_{j=1}^{\infty} \lambda_j \phi_j(x)\phi_j(z),$$

$$f_{XW}(x, w) = \sum_{j=1}^{\infty} \sum_{k=1}^{\infty} d_{jk}\phi_j(x)\phi_k(w),$$

and

$$g(x) = \sum_{j=1}^{\infty} b_j \phi_j(x),$$

where d_{jk} and b_j are Fourier coefficients that satisfy

$$d_{jk} = \int_0^1 \int_0^1 f_{XW}(x, w)\phi_j(x)\phi_k(w)\, dx\, dw,$$

$$b_j = \int_0^1 g(x)\phi_j(x)\,dx,$$

$\sum_{k=1}^{\infty} d_{jk}d_{\ell k} = \lambda_j$ if $j = \ell$, and $\sum_{k=1}^{\infty} d_{jk}d_{\ell k} = 0$ otherwise. In addition, let $r, \alpha, \beta > 0$ be constants for which

$$r \geq A_1 \equiv \max\left(\frac{2\alpha + 2\beta - 1}{2\beta - \alpha}, \frac{5}{2}\frac{2\alpha + 2\beta - 1}{4\beta - \alpha + 1}, 2\right)$$

and

$$0 < A_2 \equiv \frac{1}{2r}\frac{2\alpha + 2\beta - 1}{2\beta + \alpha} \leq A_3 \equiv \min\left[\frac{1}{2}\frac{2\beta - \alpha}{2\beta + \alpha}, \frac{4\beta - \alpha + 1}{5(2\beta + \alpha)}\right].$$

Let $C > 0$ be a finite constant, and let $\mathcal{G}(C, r, \alpha, \beta)$ denote the class of distributions of (Y, X, W) that satisfy Assumptions 1–3 below.

The regularity conditions are as follows.

ASSUMPTION 1. *The data $\{Y_i, X_i, W_i\}$ are independently and identically distributed as (Y, X, W), where (X, W) is supported on $[0, 1]^2$ and $E[Y - g(X) \mid W] = 0$.*

ASSUMPTION 2. *The distribution of (X, W) has a density f_{XW} with respect to Lebesgue measure. Moreover, f_{XW} is r times differentiable with respect to any combination of its arguments, where derivatives at the boundary of $[0, 1]^2$ are defined as one sided. The derivatives are bounded in absolute value by C. In addition, $E(Y^2 \mid W) \leq C$ and $E(Y^2 \mid X, W) \leq C$.*

ASSUMPTION 3. *The constants α and β satisfy $\alpha > 1$, $\beta > 1/2$, and $\beta - 1/2 \leq \alpha < 2\beta$. Moreover, $b_j \leq Cj^{-\beta}$, $j^{-\alpha} \leq C\lambda_j$, and $\sum_{k=1}^{\infty} |d_{jk}| \leq Cj^{-\alpha/2}$ for all $j \geq 1$.*

ASSUMPTION 4. *The tuning parameters a_n and h satisfy $a_n \asymp n^{-\alpha/(2\beta+\alpha)}$ and $h \asymp n^{-\gamma}$, where $\gamma \in [A_2, A_3]$, and $c_n \asymp d_n$ for positive constants c_n and d_n means that c_n/d_n is bounded away from 0 and ∞.*

ASSUMPTION 5. *K_h satisfies (3). For each $\xi \in [0, 1]$, $K_h(h, \xi)$ is supported on $[(\xi - 1)/h, \xi/h] \cap \mathcal{K}$, where $\mathcal{K}$ is a compact interval not depending on ξ. Moreover,*

$$\sup_{h > 0, \xi \in [0,1], u \in \mathcal{K}} |K_h(hu, \xi)| < \infty.$$

Assumption 1 specifies the model and the data. Assumption 2 is mildly restrictive because it requires boundedness of the derivatives of f_{XW}. Assumption 3 restricts the rates at which the Fourier coefficients of g and eigenvalues of T converge to 0. The ill-posed inverse problem is due to the convergence of the eigenvalues to 0. Its severity increases and the rate of convergence of $\hat{g}$ in (4) decreases as α increases. In contrast, the importance of Fourier coefficients b_j for large values of j decreases as β increases. Large values of β decrease the number of b_j's that must be estimated accurately to estimate g accurately and increase the rate of convergence of $\hat{g}$. Assumptions 2 and 3 together imply that T is a bounded Hilbert–Schmidt operator and, therefore, compact. HH provide further discussion of the foregoing assumptions and their role in establishing the rate of convergence and optimality of $\hat{g}$ in (4).

2.3. *Properties of the HH Estimator.* Let E_G denote the expectation with respect to the distribution $G \in \mathcal{G}$ of (Y, X, W). Let Assumptions 1–5 hold. HH prove the following two theorems.

THEOREM 1. *As* $n \to \infty$

$$\sup_{G \in \mathcal{G}} \int_0^1 E_G[\hat{g}(z) - g(z)]^2 dz = O\left(n^{-(2\beta-1)/(2\beta+\alpha)}\right).$$

THEOREM 2. $\tilde{g}$ *denote any estimator of* g. *Then*

$$\liminf_{n \to \infty} n^{(2\beta-1)/(2\beta+\alpha)} \inf_{\tilde{g}} \sup_{G \in \mathcal{G}} \int_0^1 E_G[\tilde{g}(z) - g(z)]^2 dz > 0.$$

Theorem 1 gives the L_2 rate of convergence of $\hat{g}$. Theorem 2 shows that this rate is the fastest possible in a minimax sense. Theorem 1 implies that $\hat{g}(z) \to^p g(z)$ for almost every $z \in [0, 1]$.

3.   ASYMPTOTIC NORMALITY OF THE ESTIMATOR

This section gives conditions under which a Studentized version of the HH estimator is asymptotically distributed as $N(0, 1)$. The following additional notation is used. Define $U_i = Y_i - g(X_i)$,

$$S_{n1}(z) = n^{-1} \sum_{i=1}^n U_i \hat{T}^+ \hat{f}_{XW}^{(-i)}(z, W_i),$$

and

$$S_{n2}(z) = n^{-1} \sum_{i=1}^n g(X_i) \hat{T}^+ \hat{f}_{XW}^{(-i)}(z, W_i).$$

Then,

(5) $\hat{g}(z) = S_{n1}(z) + S_{n2}(z).$

Observe that $ES_{n1}(z) = 0$, but $ES_{n2}(z) - g(z) \neq 0$ in finite samples except, possibly, in special cases. Therefore, $S_{n2}(z)$ is a source of bias in $\hat{g}(z)$. This section presents conditions under which $S_{n2}(z) - g(z)$ and the bias of $\hat{g}$ are asymptotically negligible, but these quantities are not necessarily small in finite samples. We return to the issue of finite-sample bias of $\hat{g}$ in Section 4.

We now outline the argument leading to the asymptotic normality result. Define $T^+ = (T + a_n I)^{-1}$. Write

$$S_{n1}(z) = n^{-1} \sum_{i=1}^{n} U_i (T^+ f_{XW})(z, W_i) + n^{-1} \sum_{i=1}^{n} U_i (\hat{T}^+ \hat{f}_{XW}^{(-i)} - T^+ f_{XW})(z, W_i)$$

$$= S_{n11}(z) + S_{n12}(z).$$

Define

$$V_n(z) = n^{-1} \mathrm{Var}[U(T^+ f_{XW})(z, W)].$$

It follows from a triangular array version of the Lindeberg–Levy central limit theorem that

$$S_{n11}(z) / \sqrt{V_n(z)} \to^d N(0, 1)$$

as $n \to \infty$. Therefore,

(6) $$[\hat{g}(z) - g(z)] / \sqrt{V_n(z)} \to^d N(0, 1)$$

if

(7) $$[S_{n12}(z) + S_{n2}(z) - g(z)] / \sqrt{V_n(z)} = o_p(1).$$

We ensure that (7) holds for almost every $z \in [0, 1]$ by requiring a_n to converge to 0 at a rate that is faster than the asymptotically optimal rate in Assumption 4 and restricting the bandwidth h to a range that is narrower than that in Assumption 4. The faster than optimal convergence of a_n results in an estimator of g whose rate of convergence is slower than optimal. As often happens in nonparametric estimation, a slower than optimal convergence rate appears to be an unavoidable price that must be paid to obtain a normal limiting distribution that is centered at 0. We also require g to be sufficiently smooth and rule out a form of superconvergence of $\hat{g}(z)$.

We now state the result formally. Let $\|\cdot\|$ denote the $L_2 [0, 1]$ norm. Let ρ be a constant satisfying $1 < \rho < (2\beta + \alpha)/(\alpha + 1)$. Define

$$A_2' = \max \left[\frac{1}{2r - 1} \frac{2\rho\alpha}{2\beta + \alpha}, \frac{1}{4r - 1} \frac{\rho(\alpha - 1)}{2\beta + \alpha}, \frac{1}{2r} \frac{(\rho + 1)\alpha + 2\beta - \rho}{2\beta + \alpha} \right]$$

and

$$A'_3 = \min\left[\frac{1}{2}\frac{2\beta + \alpha(\rho + 1) - \rho}{2\beta + \alpha}, \frac{1}{5}\frac{4\beta - (3\rho - 2)\alpha + 1}{2\beta + \alpha}\right].$$

Make the following new assumptions.

ASSUMPTION 2'. *The distribution of (X, W) has a density f_{XW} with respect to Lebesgue measure. Moreover, f_{XW} is r times differentiable with respect to any combination of its arguments, where derivatives at the boundary of $[0, 1]^2$ are defined as one sided. The derivatives are bounded in absolute value by C. In addition, g is r times differentiable on $[0, 1]$ with derivatives at 0 and 1 defined as one sided. The derivatives of g are bounded in absolute value by C. In addition, $E(Y^2 | W) \leq C$, $E(Y^2 | X, W) \leq C$, and $E(U^2 | W) \geq C_U$ for some finite constant $C_U > 0$.*

ASSUMPTION 3'. *The constants α and β satisfy $\alpha > 1$, $\beta > 1/2$, and $\beta - 1/2 \leq \alpha < 2\beta$. Moreover, $b_j \leq Cj^{-\beta}$ and $\sum_{k=1}^{\infty} |d_{jk}| \leq Cj^{-\alpha/2}$ for all $j \geq 1$. In addition, there are finite, strictly positive constants, $C_{\lambda 1}$ and $C_{\lambda 2}$, such that $C_{\lambda 1}j^{-\alpha} \leq \lambda_j \leq C_{\lambda 2}j^{-\alpha}$ for all $j \geq 1$.*

ASSUMPTION 4'. *The tuning parameters a_n and h satisfy $a_n \asymp n^{-\rho\alpha/(2\beta+\alpha)}$ and $h \asymp n^{-\gamma}$, where $\gamma \in [A'_2, A'_3]$.*

ASSUMPTION 6. $E_W[T^+ f_{XW}(z, W)]^2 \asymp E_W\|T^+ f_{XW}(\cdot, W)\|^2$ and $E_W\|T^+ f_{XW}(\cdot, W)\|^2 \asymp \int_0^1 \|T^+ f_{XW}(\cdot, w)\|^2 \, dw$.

Assumption 2' strengthens Assumption 2 by requiring differentiability of g and $E(U^2 | W) \geq C_U$. Assumption 3' specifies the rate of convergence of the eigenvalues λ_j. This assumption and Assumption 6 make it possible to obtain the precise rate of convergence of $V_n(z)$, whereas Assumption 3 yields only a bound on this rate. A bound is not sufficient to ensure that (7) holds. Assumption 4' requires a_n to converge at a rate that is faster than the asymptotically optimal one. This and the assumption about h make the bias of $\hat{g}$ asymptotically negligible. The first part of Assumption 6 implies that

$$V_n(z) \asymp \int_0^1 V_n(\zeta) \, d\zeta.$$

This rules out a form of superconvergence in which $\hat{g}(z) - g(z)$ converges to 0 more rapidly than $\|\hat{g} - g\|$. This can happen, for example, if $\phi_j(z) = 0$ for too many values of j. Such superconvergence can cause $S_{n11}(z)$ to converge to 0 more rapidly than $S_{n12}(z) + S_{n2}(z) - g(z)$, in which case (6) does not hold. The second part of Assumption 6 restricts f_{XW} so as to prevent a form of superconvergence that occurs if the distribution of W is concentrated on points w for which $\phi_j(w)$ is close to 0 for too many values of j. The second part of Assumption 6 always holds if $W \sim U[0, 1]$.

The main result of this article is the following.

THEOREM 3. *Let Assumptions 1, 2', 3',4', 5, and 6 hold. Then (6) holds except, possibly, on a set of z values whose Lebesgue measure is* 0.

Result (6) continues to hold if $V_n(z)$ is replaced with the consistent estimator

$$(8) \qquad \hat{V}_n(z) = n^{-2} \sum_{i=1}^{n} \hat{U}_i^2 [(\hat{T}^+ f_{XW}^{(-i)})(z, W_i)]^2,$$

where $\hat{U}_i = Y_i - \hat{g}(X_i)$. This yields the Studentized statistic $[\hat{g}(z) - g(z)]/\sqrt{\hat{V}(z)}$.

COROLLARY 1. *Let Assumptions 1, 2', 3', 4', 5, and 6 hold. Then*

$$[\hat{g}(z) - g(z)]/\sqrt{\hat{V}_n(z)} \to^d N(0, 1)$$

except, possibly, on a set of z values whose Lebesgue measure is 0.

Corollary 1 can be used to form an asymptotic confidence interval for $g(z)$. Let $z_{\tau/2}$ denote the $1 - \tau/2$ quantile of the standard normal distribution. Then a symmetrical, asymptotic $1 - \tau$ confidence interval for $g(z)$ is

$$(9) \qquad \hat{g}(z) - z_{\tau/2}\sqrt{\hat{V}_n(z)} \le g(z) \le \hat{g}(z) + z_{\tau/2}\sqrt{\hat{V}_n(z)}.$$

One-sided confidence intervals can be formed similarly. In addition, (9) can be modified to accommodate the possibility that z is in a set of Lebesgue measure 0 to which the asymptotic normality result does not apply. To do this, let $z \in (0, 1)$. For some small $\varepsilon > 0$ such that $0 < z - \varepsilon < z < z + \varepsilon < 1$, let z_0 be sampled from the $U[z - \varepsilon, z + \varepsilon]$ distribution. Then (9) with z replaced by z_0 is a $1 - \tau$ confidence interval for $g(z_0)$ because z_0 has 0 probability of being in an exceptional set of Corollary 1. Moreover, Assumption 2' implies that $|g(z) - g(z_0)| \le C\varepsilon$. Therefore,

$$g(z_0) - C\varepsilon - z_{\tau/2}\sqrt{\hat{V}_n(z_0)} \le g(z) \le g(z_0) + C\varepsilon + z_{\tau/2}\sqrt{\hat{V}_n(z_0)}$$

is a confidence interval for $g(z)$ whose asymptotic coverage probability is at least $1 - \tau$ for any $z \in (0, 1)$ and converges to $1 - \tau$ as $\varepsilon \to 0$. C is not known in applications, but this does not matter because ε and, therefore, $C\varepsilon$ can be chosen to be arbitrarily small.

4.   MONTE CARLO EXPERIMENTS

This section reports the results of a Monte Carlo investigation of the finite-sample coverage probability of the confidence interval (9) for $g(z)$. Realizations of (Y, X, W) were generated from the model

$$f_{XW}(x, w) = C_f \sum_{j=1}^{\infty} (-1)^{j+1} j^{-\alpha/2} \sin(j\pi x) \sin(j\pi w)$$

$$g(x) = 2.2x,$$

$$Y = E[g(X) \mid W] + V,$$

where C_f is a normalization constant chosen so that $\int f_{XW} \, dx \, dw = 1$, and $V \sim N(0, 0.01)$. For computational purposes, the infinite series were truncated at $j = 50$. The kernel function is $K(x) = 0.75(1 - x^2)$ for $|x| \le 1$. The sample size is $n = 500$.

The specification of g gives $\int_0^1 g(x) \sin(j\pi x) \, dx \propto j^{-1}$, so $\beta = 1$. Experiments were carried out with $\alpha = 1.2$ and 10. With $\alpha = 1.2$, it follows from Theorem 2 that the fastest possible rate of convergence of $\hat{g}$ is $n^{-1/6.4}$. With $\alpha = 10$, the fastest possible rate is $n^{-1/24}$, so $\hat{g}$ is likely to be a very imprecise estimator of g in this case. The case $\alpha = 10$, $\beta = 1$ does not satisfy Assumption 3, but the HH estimator is consistent, nonetheless, and $[\hat{g}(z) - g(z)]/\sqrt{V_n(z)}$ is asymptotically normal, though not necessarily with a mean of 0.

The computed estimate of g is a truncated Fourier approximation to $\hat{g}$. To obtain this, $h^{-1} K_h(x - X_i)$ and $h^{-1} K_h(w - W_i)$ were approximated by the truncated Fourier series

$$h^{-1} K_h(x - X_i) \approx 2^{1/2} \sum_{j=1}^{50} r_{ij} \sin(j\pi x)$$

and

$$h^{-1} K_h(w - W_i) \approx 2^{1/2} \sum_{j=1}^{50} q_{ij} \sin(j\pi w),$$

where $r_{ij} = 2^{1/2} h^{-1} \int_0^1 K_h(x - X_i) \sin(j\pi x) \, dx$ and q_{ij} is defined similarly. Let R and Q, respectively, denote the $n \times 50$ matrices whose (i, j) components are r_{ij} and q_{ij}. Replacing $h^{-1} K_h(x - X_i)$ and $h^{-1} K_h(w - W_i)$ with the truncated Fourier series in the formulae for $\hat{f}_{XW}$ and $\hat{\imath}$ yields truncated Fourier representations of the latter quantities. The Fourier coefficients are the elements of the matrices $R'Q/n$ and $R'QQ'R/n^2$ for $\hat{f}_{XW}$ and $\hat{\imath}$, respectively. Therefore, the matrix of Fourier coefficients of the approximation to $\hat{T}^+ \hat{f}_{XW}$ is $D \equiv (R'QQ'R/n^2 + a_n I)^{-1} R'Q/n$. Let D_{jk} denote the (j, k) component of D. Then the truncated Fourier approximation to $\hat{g}$ is

$$(10) \qquad \hat{g}(z) \approx 2 \sum_{i=1}^{n} \sum_{j,k=1}^{50} Y_i D_{jk} \sin(j\pi z) \sin(k\pi W_i).$$

The results reported in this section are based on the approximation (10). Increasing the number of Fourier coefficients beyond 50 yielded no change in the results.

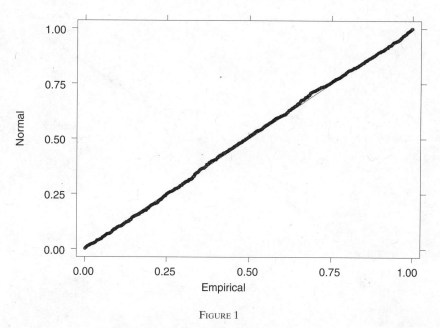

FIGURE 1

NORMAL PROBABILITY PLOT FOR $\hat{g}(0.5)$ WITH $\alpha = 1.2$

The values of the tuning parameters are $h = 0.05$, $a_n = 0.05$ if $\alpha = 1.2$, and $h = 0.025$, $a_n = 0.10$ if $\alpha = 10$. These values were selected through Monte Carlo simulation to roughly minimize the differences between the empirical and nominal coverage probabilities of confidence intervals for $g(z)$. Data-based methods for selecting h and a_n in applications are not yet available.

The results of the experiments are shown in Figures 1 and 2 and Table 1. Figures 1 and 2 show normal probability plots for $\hat{g}(0.5)$ with $\alpha = 1.2$ and 10, respectively. Plots for other values of z are similar. The plots deviate only slightly from 45-degree lines, indicating that the empirical distributions of $\hat{g}(0.5)$ are very close to normal.

Columns 2–4 of Table 1 show the empirical coverage probabilities of nominal 90%, 95%, and 99% confidence intervals for $\hat{g}(z)$. The differences between the empirical and nominal coverage probabilities (hereinafter errors in coverage probabilities or ECPs) are large when $\alpha = 10$ and when $\alpha = 1.2$ and $x = 0.10$ or 0.90. The ECPs are almost entirely due to finite sample bias of $\hat{g}$. This can be seen from the plots of ECP versus bias in Figures 3 and 4. Finite-sample bias causes a confidence interval to be centered at $E\hat{g}(z)$ instead of $g(z)$, and it causes $\hat{V}_n(z)$ to be an inaccurate estimator of $V_n(z)$.

4.1. *Bias Reduction.* The finite-sample bias of $\hat{g}(z)$ is $B_n(z) = E[S_{n2}(z) - g(z)]$. One possible way of reducing the bias is to subtract an estimator of $B_n(z)$ from $\hat{g}(z)$, thereby creating a new estimator

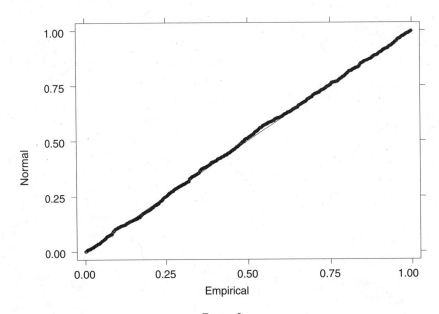

FIGURE 2

NORMAL PROBABILITY PLOT FOR $\hat{g}(0.5)$ WITH $\alpha = 10$

TABLE 1

COVERAGE PROBABILITIES OF CONFIDENCE INTERVALS FOR $g(z)$

	Nominal Probabilities					
z	Asymp. 0.90	Crit. 0.95	Value 0.99	Boot. 0.90	Crit. 0.95	Value 0.99
			$\alpha = 1.2$			
0.10	0.84	0.90	0.97	0.92	0.96	0.99
0.25	0.93	0.96	0.99	0.93	0.96	0.99
0.50	0.94	0.97	0.99	0.94	0.97	0.99
0.75	0.92	0.95	0.99	0.92	0.97	0.99
0.90	0.78	0.86	0.94	0.86	0.93	0.97
			$\alpha = 10$			
0.10	0.46	0.60	0.82	0.68	0.85	0.97
0.25	0.33	0.46	0.69	0.41	0.57	0.81
0.50	0.85	0.93	0.98	0.92	0.96	0.99
0.75	0.05	0.09	0.21	0.09	0.16	0.31
0.90	0.0	0.0	0.0	0	0	0.01

$$\tilde{g}(z) = \hat{g}(z) - \hat{B}_n(z),$$

where $\hat{B}_n(z)$ is the estimator of $B_n(z)$. An obvious estimator of $B_n(z)$ is

$$(11) \qquad \hat{B}_n(z) = n^{-1} \sum_{i=1}^{n} \hat{g}^{(-i)}(X_i) \hat{T}^+ \hat{f}_{XW}^{(-i)}(z, W_i) - \hat{g}(z),$$

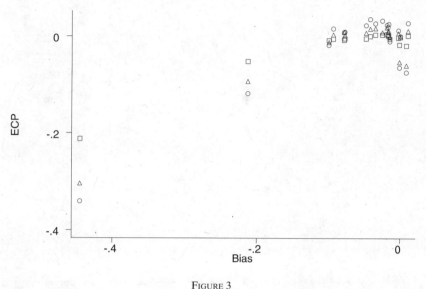

FIGURE 3

ECP VERSUS BIAS FOR $\alpha = 1.2$

where $\hat{g}^{(-i)}$ is the estimator of g that is obtained by omitting observation i from (4). The resulting bias of $\tilde{g}(z)$ is

$$\tilde{B}_n(z) \equiv E[\tilde{g}(z) - g(z)]$$

$$= E\left\{[\hat{g}(z) - g(z)] - n^{-1} \sum_{i=1}^{n} [\hat{g}^{(-i)}(X_i) - g(X_i)\left(\hat{T}^+ \, \hat{f}_{XW}^{(-i)}\right)(z, W_i)\right\}.$$

Calculations like those used to prove Theorem 3 show that $B_n(z)$, $\tilde{B}_n(z) = O(h^r/a_n)$. Thus, "bias correction" using (11) does not accelerate the convergence of the bias of the resulting estimator of $g(z)$. This is because the leading component of the bias is caused by regularization (that is, replacing T^{-1} with $(T + a_n)^{-1}$ in (2)). Regularization affects S_{n2} only through $\hat{T}^+ \hat{f}_{XW}^{(-i)}$, but it affects $\hat{B}_n$ through $\hat{g}^{(-i)}$ as well. Therefore, $\hat{g}$ and $\tilde{g}$ have different regularization biases. I conjecture that this problem will be present in any plug-in type approach to bias correction.

Another possibility is to use the bootstrap to obtain critical values for either $\hat{g}(z) - g(z)$ or the Studentized statistic $[\hat{g}(z) - g(z)]/\sqrt{\hat{V}_n(z)}$. Let $\hat{c}_{\tau/2}$ and $\hat{z}_{\tau/2}$, respectively, denote the bootstrap estimates of the $1 - \tau/2$ quantiles of $|\hat{g}(z) - g(z)|$ and $|\hat{g}(z) - g(z)|/\sqrt{\hat{V}_n(z)}$. Then the resulting $1 - \tau$ confidence intervals for $g(z)$ are

(12)
$$\hat{g}(z) - \hat{c}_{\tau/2} \leq g(z) \leq \hat{g}(z) + \hat{c}_{\tau/2}$$

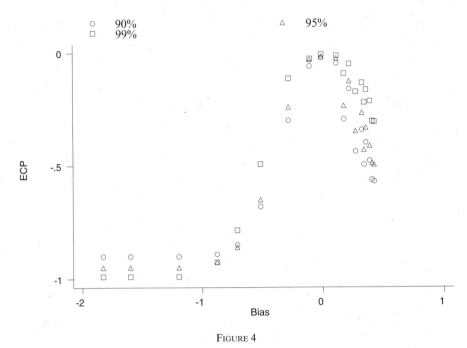

FIGURE 4

ECP VERSUS BIAS FOR $\alpha = 10$

without Studentization and

(13) $$\hat{g}(z) - \hat{z}_{\tau/2}\sqrt{\hat{V}_n(z)} \leq g(z) \leq \hat{g}(z) + \hat{z}_{\tau/2}\sqrt{\hat{V}_n(z)}$$

with Studentization. Proving that the bootstrap is consistent, if it is possible, is a difficult task that is beyond the scope of this article. Here, we report the results of a Monte Carlo investigation of the coverage probability of the bootstrap-based confidence interval (13). Bootstrap samples were generated by sampling (Y, X, W) from the data randomly with replacement. Columns 5–7 of Table 1 show the empirical coverage probabilities. The coverage probabilities of the interval (12) are similar and are not shown. The use of bootstrap critical values greatly reduces the ECPs when $\alpha = 1.2$ and $z = 0.1$ or 0.9 and when $\alpha = 10$. However, the ECPs with $\alpha = 10$ remain large. This is not surprising, because Assumption 3 is violated when $\alpha = 10$. These results illustrate the importance of bias reduction for achieving practical methods for inference with nonparametric IV estimators, especially with large α values that violate the assumptions of HH.

5. CONCLUSIONS

This article has given conditions under which the nonparametric instrumental variables estimator of Hall and Horowitz (2005) is asymptotically normally distributed. The limited Monte Carlo evidence that is presented in Section 4 suggests that the distribution of $\hat{g}$ in a sample of practical size is well approximated by a normal distribution. However, the errors in the coverage probabilities of confidence intervals based on the asymptotic normality result can be quite large, especially when α is large. The errors are caused mainly by finite-sample bias of $\hat{g}$, and development of methods for reducing finite-sample bias is an important topic for future research. Development of methods for selecting the tuning parameters a_n and h in applications is another important research topic. Development of asymptotically efficient estimation methods is also a natural, though difficult, area for future research.

APPENDIX

PROOF OF THEOREM 3. Theorem 3 follows from proving that $S_{n1}(z)/\sqrt{V_n(z)} \to^d N(0, 1)$ and $[S_{n2}(z) - g(z)]/\sqrt{V_n(z)} = o_p(1)$ except, possibly, if z belongs to a set of Lebesgue measure 0. The first result is established in Lemma 1, and the second is established in Lemma 2. The proofs of the lemmas are slightly modified versions of HH's proof of Theorem 1. The proofs are presented in abbreviated form to save space and avoid repeating arguments that are presented in detail in HH. Throughout this appendix, "for almost every z" means "for every $z \in [0, 1]$ except, possibly, a set of Lebesgue measure 0." We make repeated use of the fact that if $E \|\psi\|^2 = o(n^{-s})$ for some $s > 0$, then $\psi(z) = o_p(n^{-s})$ for almost every z.

LEMMA 1 (*Asymptotic normality of* $S_{n1}(z)/\sqrt{V_n(z)}$). *Let Assumptions 1, 2′, 3′, 4′, 5, and 6 hold. Then* $S_{n1}(z)/\sqrt{V_n(z)} \to^d N(0, 1)$ *for almost every* z.

PROOF. Define

$$S_{n11}(z) = n^{-1} \sum_{i=1}^{n} U_i (T^+ f_{XW})(z, W_i),$$

$$A_{n2}(z) = n^{-1} \sum_{i=1}^{n} U_i [T^+ (\hat{f}_{XW}^{(-i)} - f_{XW})](z, W_i),$$

$$A_{n3}(z) = n^{-1} \sum_{i=1}^{n} U_i [(\hat{T}^+ - T^+) f_{XW}](z, W_i),$$

and

$$A_{n4}(z) = n^{-1} \sum_{i=1}^{n} U_i [(\hat{T}^+ - T^+)(\hat{f}_{XW}^{(-i)} - f_{XW})](z, W_i).$$

Then $S_{n1}(z) = S_{n11}(z) + A_{n2}(z) + A_{n3}(z) + A_{n4}(z)$. $S_{n11}(z)/\sqrt{V_n(z)} \to^d N(0, 1)$ by a triangular array version of the Lindeberg–Levy central limit theorem. The proof of the triangular-array version of the theorem is identical to the proof of the ordinary Lindeberg–Levy theorem. The lemma follows if we can prove that $A_{nj}(z)/\sqrt{V_n(z)} = o_p(1)$ for $j = 2, 3, 4$ and almost every $z \in [0, 1]$.

Assumption 6 and arguments like those leading to Equation (6.2) of HH show that

$$\int_0^1 V_n(z)\,dz \asymp n^{-[2\beta+\alpha-\rho(\alpha+1)]/(2\beta+\alpha)}.$$

It follows from the Cauchy–Schwartz inequality, $E(\hat{f}_{XW}^{(-i)} - f_{XW}) = O(h^r)$, and $\mathrm{Var}(\hat{f}_{XW}^{(-i)}) = O[1/(nh^2)]$ that

$$E\|A_{n2}\|^2 = O\left(\frac{1}{n^2 h^2 a_n^2} + \frac{h^{2r}}{n a_n^2}\right).$$

Therefore, it follows from Assumptions 4′ and 6 that $A_{n2}(z)/\sqrt{V_n(z)} = o_p(1)$ for almost every z.

Now consider $A_{n3}(z)$. Define the operator $\Delta = \hat{T} - T$. Then

$$A_{n3}(z) = -(\hat{T} + a_n I)\Delta A_{n1}(z).$$

Therefore, the Cauchy–Schwartz inequality gives

$$E\|A_{n3}\|^2 \le E\left\|(\hat{T} + a_n I)\Delta\right\|^2 E\|S_{n11}\|^2$$

$$= E\left\|(\hat{T} + a_n I)\Delta\right\|^2 \int_0^1 V_n(z)\,dz.$$

HH show that

(A.1) $$E\left\|(\hat{T} + a_n I)\Delta\right\|^2 = O\left(\frac{1}{n h a_n^2} + \frac{h^{2r}}{a_n^2}\right).$$

Therefore, it follows from Assumptions 4′ and 6 that $A_{n3}(z)/\sqrt{V_n(z)} = o_p(1)$ for almost every z.

Finally, some algebra shows that

$$A_{n4}(z) = -(\hat{T} + a_n I)^{-1}\Delta A_{n2}(z).$$

Therefore, $A_{n4}(z)/\sqrt{V_n(z)} = o_p(1)$ for almost every z follows from (A.1) and $A_{n2}(z)/\sqrt{V_n(z)} = o_p(1)$. ∎

LEMMA 2 (*Asymptotic negligibility of $S_{n2}(z) - g(z)$*). *Let Assumptions 1, 2', 3', 4', 5, and 6 hold. Then $[S_{n2}(z) - g(z)]/\sqrt{V_n(z)} = o_p(1)$ for almost every z.*

PROOF. Define

$$D_n(z) = \int_0^1 \int_0^1 g(x) f_{XW}(x, w) T^+ (\hat{f}_{XW} - f_{XW})(z, w) \, dx \, dw$$

and

$$A_{n1}(z) = n^{-1} \sum_{i=1}^n g(X_i)(T^+ f_{XW})(z, W_i).$$

Redefine

$$A_{n2}(z) = n^{-1} \sum_{i=1}^n g(X_i)\big[T^+\big(\hat{f}_{XW}^{(-i)} - f_{XW}\big)\big](z, W_i) - D_n(z),$$

$$A_{n3}(z) = n^{-1} \sum_{i=1}^n g(X_i)[(\hat{T}^+ - T^+) f_{XW}](z, W_i) + D_n(z),$$

and

$$A_{n4}(z) = n^{-1} \sum_{i=1}^n g(X_i)\big[(\hat{T}^+ - T^+)\big(\hat{f}_{XW}^{(-i)} - f_{XW}\big)\big](z, W_i).$$

Then $S_{n2}(z) = \sum_{j=1}^4 A_{nj}(z)$.

Arguments identical to those used to derive Equations (6.2) and (6.3) of HH show that $\|EA_{n1} - g\|^2 = O[n^{-\rho(2\beta-1)/(2\beta+\alpha)}]$ and

$$\int_0^1 \text{Var}[A_{n1}(z)] \, dz = O\big\{n^{-[2\beta+\alpha-\rho(\alpha+1)]/(2\beta+\alpha)}\big\}.$$

Therefore, it follows from Assumptions 4' and 6 that

(A.2) $$[EA_{n1}(z) - g(z)]/\sqrt{V_n(z)} = o(1)$$

and

(A.3) $$V_n^{-1}(z) \int_0^1 \text{Var}[A_{n1}(z)] \, dz = O(1)$$

for almost every z.

Now consider $A_{n2}(z)$. Define

$$D_{ni}(z) = \int_0^1 \int_0^1 g(x) f_{XW}(x, w) T^+ (\hat{f}_{XW}^{(-i)} - f_{XW})(z, w)\, dx\, dw,$$

$$A_{n21}(z) = n^{-1} \sum_{i=1}^n g(X_i)[T^+(\hat{f}_{XW}^{(-i)} - f_{XW})](z, W_i) - D_{ni}(z),$$

and

$$A_{n22}(z) = n^{-1} \sum_{i=1}^n [D_{ni}(z) - D_n(z)].$$

HH show that

$$E\|A_{n21}\|^2 = O\left(\frac{h^{2r}}{na_n^2} + \frac{1}{n^2 h^2 a_n^2}\right)$$

and

$$E\|A_{n22}\|^2 = O\left(\frac{1}{n^2 a_n^2}\right).$$

Therefore, it follows from Assumptions 4' and 6 that

(A.4) $$A_{n2}(z)/\sqrt{V_n(z)} = o_p(1)$$

for almost every z.

Now consider $A_{n3}(z)$. Write

$$A_{n3}(z) = A_{n31}(z) + A_{n32}(z),$$

where

$$A_{n31}(z) = -(I + T^+\Delta)^{-1} T^+ \Delta g(z) + D_n(z)$$

and

(A.5) $$A_{n32}(z) = -(\hat{T} + a_n I)^{-1} \Delta (A_{n1} - g)(z).$$

It follows from (A.1)–(A.3) and (A.5) that

(A.6) $$A_{n32}(z)/\sqrt{V_n(z)} = o_p(1)$$

for almost every z.

To analyze A_{n31}, define

$$B_{n1}(z) = \int_0^1 \int_0^1 [\hat{f}_{XW}(x, w) - f_{XW}(x, w)] f_{XW}(z, w) g(x) \, dx \, dw,$$

$$B_{n2}(z) = \int_0^1 \int_0^1 [\hat{f}_{XW}(z, w) - f_{XW}(z, w)] f_{XW}(x, w) g(x) \, dx \, dw,$$

$$B_{n3}(z) = \int_0^1 \int_0^1 [\hat{f}_{XW}(x, w) - f_{XW}(x, w)][\hat{f}_{XW}(z, w) - f_{XW}(z, w)] g(x) \, dx \, dw,$$

$$B_{n11}(z) = \int_0^1 \int_0^1 [E\hat{f}_{XW}(x, w) - f_{XW}(x, w)] f_{XW}(z, w) g(x) \, dx \, dw,$$

$$B_{n12}(z) = \int_0^1 \int_0^1 [\hat{f}_{XW}(x, w) - E\hat{f}_{XW}(x, w)] f_{XW}(z, w) g(x) \, dx \, dw,$$

$$B_{n21}(z) = \int_0^1 \int_0^1 [E\hat{f}_{XW}(z, w) - f_{XW}(z, w)] f_{XW}(x, w) g(x) \, dx \, dw,$$

and

$$B_{n22}(z) = \int_0^1 \int_0^1 [\hat{f}_{XW}(z, w) - E\hat{f}_{XW}(z, w)] f_{XW}(x, w) g(x) \, dx \, dw.$$

Define $\delta = h^{2r} + (nh)^{-1}$. HH show that

$$A_{n31}(z) = -(I + T^+ \Delta)^{-1} T^+ (B_{n11} + B_{n12} + B_{n3})(z)$$
$$+ (I + T^+ \Delta)^{-1} T^+ \Delta T^+ (B_{n21} + B_{n22})(z).$$

Define

$$\tilde{A}_{n31}(z) = -(I + T^+ \Delta)^{-1} T^+ (B_{n11} + B_{n12} + B_{n3})(z) + (I + T^+ \Delta)^{-1} T^+ \Delta T^+ B_{n21}.$$

Then

(A.7) $$E\|A_{n31}\|^2 \le \text{const.} \left[E\|\tilde{A}_{n31}\|^2 + E\|(I + T\Delta)^{-1} T^+ \Delta T^+ B_{n22}\|^2 \right]$$

and

(A.8) $$E\|\tilde{A}_{n31}\|^2 \le \text{const.} \big(\|T^+ B_{n11}\|^4 + E\|T^+ B_{n12}\|^4 + E\|T^+ \Delta T^+ B_{n21}\|^4$$
$$+ E\|T^+ B_{n3}\|^4 \big)^{1/2}.$$

HH show that

(A.9) $$\|T^+ B_{n11}\| = O(h^r / a_n),$$

(A.10) $$\left(E \, \| T^+ \Delta T^+ B_{n21} \|^4 \right)^{1/2} = O\left(\frac{\delta h^{2r}}{a_n} \right),$$

and

(A.11) $$\left(E \, \| T^+ B_{n3} \|^4 \right)^{1/2} = O(\delta^2 / a_n^2).$$

See Equations (6.11), (6.13), (6.14), and (6.15) of HH. Moreover,

(A.12) $$E \, \| (I + T\Delta)^{-1} T^+ \Delta T^+ B_{n22} \|^2 = O\left(\frac{h^{2r-1}}{n a_n^{2+(\alpha+1)/\alpha}} + \frac{1}{n^3 h^5 a_n^4} + \frac{h^{4r}}{n h a_n^2} \right).$$

See the arguments leading to Equation (6.24) in HH and the analogous result for their quantity $E \, \| H_{n2} \|^2$. Combining (A.7)–(A.12) with Assumptions 4′ and 6 yields the result that

(A.13) $$A_{n31}(z)/\sqrt{V_n(z)} = -(I + T^+ \Delta)^{-1} T^+ B_{n12}/\sqrt{V_n(z)} + o_p(1).$$

Now consider $-(I + T^+ \Delta)^{-1} T^+ B_{n12}$. Standard calculations for kernel estimators show that

$$\int_0^1 \int_0^1 \hat{f}_{XW}(z, w) f_{XW}(z, w) g(x) \, dx \, dw = n^{-1} \sum_{i=1}^n f_{XW}(z, W_i) g(X_i) + O(h^r).$$

Therefore,

$$T^+ \int_0^1 \int_0^1 \hat{f}_{XW}(z, w) f_{XW}(z, w) g(x) \, dx \, dw = A_{n1}(z) + O(h^r / a_n),$$

and

(A.14) $$T^+ B_{n12}(z) = A_{n1}(z) - E A_{n1}(z) + o(h^r / a_n).$$

But

$$(I + T^+ \Delta)^{-1} T^+ B_{n12} = T^+ B_{n12} + [(I + T^+ \Delta)^{-1} - I] T^+ B_{n12}$$
$$= T^+ B_{n12} + (\hat{T} + a_n I)^{-1} \Delta T^+ B_{n12}.$$

Therefore, it follows by combining Assumption 6, Equations (A.1), (A.3), and (A.14) that

$$(I + T^+ \Delta)^{-1} T^+ B_{n12}(z) = A_{n1}(z) - E A_{n1}(z) + r_n,$$

where $E \|r_n\|^2 / V_n(z) = o(1)$ for almost every z. Combining this result with (A.6) and (A.13) gives

$$(A.15) \qquad A_{n3}(z)/\sqrt{V_n(z)} = -[A_{n1}(z) - EA_{n1}(z)]/\sqrt{V_n(z)} + o_p(1)$$

for almost every z.

Now consider $A_{n4}(z)$. HH show that

$$A_{n4}(z) = -(I + T^+\Delta)^{-1} T^+ \Delta (A_{n2} - T^+ B_{n2})(z).$$

Therefore, it follows from (A.4) and (A.12) that

$$(A.16) \qquad\qquad A_{n4}(z)/\sqrt{V_n(z)} = o_p(1)$$

for almost every z.

Now combine (A.4), (A.15), and (A.16) to obtain

$$S_{n2}(z)/\sqrt{V_n(z)} = \sum_{j=1}^{4} A_{nj}(z)/\sqrt{V_n(z)}$$

$$= EA_{n1}(z)/\sqrt{V_n(z)} + o_p(1)$$

for almost every z. The lemma follows by combining this result with (A.2). ∎

REFERENCES

BLUNDELL, R., AND J. L. HOROWITZ, "A Nonparametric Test of Exogeneity," *Review of Economic Studies*, 2007, forthcoming.

———, X. CHEN, AND D. KRISTENSEN, "Semi-Nonparametric IV Estimation of Shape Invariant Engle Curves," *Econometrica*, 2007, forthcoming.

DAROLLES, S., J.-P. FLORENS, AND E. RENAULT, "Nonparametric Instrumental Regression," Working Paper, GREMAQ, University of Social Science, Toulouse, 2002.

HALL, P., AND J. L. HOROWITZ, "Nonparametric Methods for Inference in the Presence of Instrumental Variables," *Annals of Statistics* 33 (2005), 2904–29.

HOROWITZ, J. L, "Testing a Parametric Model against a Nonparametric Alternative with Identification through Instrumental Variables," *Econometrica* 74 (2006), 521–38.

KRESS, R, *Linear Integral Equations*, 2nd ed. (New York: Springer, 1999).

NEWEY, W. K., AND J. L. POWELL, "Instrumental Variable Estimation of Nonparametric Models," *Econometrica* 71 (2003), 1565–78.

———, ———, AND F. VELLA, "Nonparametric Estimation of Triangular Simultaneous Equations Models," *Econometrica* 67 (1999), 565–603.

O'SULLIVAN, F., "A Statistical Perspective on Ill Posed Problems," *Statistical Science* 1 (1986), 502–27.

INTERNATIONAL ECONOMIC REVIEW
Vol. 48, No. 4, November 2007

EXPLORING THE USEFULNESS OF A NONRANDOM HOLDOUT SAMPLE FOR MODEL VALIDATION: WELFARE EFFECTS ON FEMALE BEHAVIOR*

BY MICHAEL P. KEANE AND KENNETH I. WOLPIN[1]

*University of Technology Sydney, Australia, and Arizona State University, U.S.A.;
University of Pennsylvania, U.S.A.*

A particularly challenging use of decision-theoretic models in economics is to forecast the impact of large changes in the environment. The problem we explore in this article is how to gain confidence in a model's ability to predict the impact of such large changes. We show that an approach to validation and model selection that includes the choice of a "nonrandom holdout sample," a sample that differs significantly from the estimation sample along the policy dimension that the model is meant to forecast, can be fruitful.

1. INTRODUCTION

An important goal of empirical research in economics is to provide evidence on the validity of decision-theoretic models that describe the behavior of economic agents. There are two approaches to this endeavor that stem from different epistemological perspectives. The first stems from a view that knowledge is absolute, that is, there exists a "true" decision-theoretic model from which observed data are generated. This leads naturally to a model validation strategy based on testing the validity of the behavioral implications of the model and/or testing the fit of the model to the data. A model is not deemed invalid if it is not rejected in such tests, according to some statistical criterion. Rejected models are deemed invalid and discarded.

The second approach stems from a pragmatic epistemological view, in which it is assumed that all models are necessarily simplifications of agents' actual decision-making behavior. Hypothesis testing as a means of model validation or selection is eschewed because, given enough data, all models would be rejected as true models. In this pragmatic view, there is no true decision-theoretic model, only models that perform well or poorly, or better or worse, in addressing particular questions. Models should be chosen that are "best" for some specific purpose, and alternative models may coexist or be valid for different purposes.

* Manuscript received July 2005; revised May 2006.
[1] The authors are grateful for support from NICHD under grant HD-34019 and from several grants from the Minnesota Supercomputer Institute. Part of Keane's work on this project was completed while he was visiting Arizona State University as the Goldwater Chair in American Institutions. We thank two anonymous referees and a guest editor for helpful comments. Please address correspondence to: Kenneth I. Wolpin, Department of Economics, University of Pennsylvania, 3718 Locust Walk, Philadelphia, PA 19104, U.S.A. Phone: 215-898-7709. Fax: 215-746-2947. E-mail: *wolpink@ssc.upenn.edu*.

Decision-theoretic models are typically designed and estimated with the goal of predicting the impact on economic agents of changes in the economic environment. Thus, one criterion for model validation/selection that fits within the "pragmatic" view is to examine a model's predictive accuracy, namely, how successful the model is at predicting outcomes of interest within the particular context for which the model was designed. In contrast, in the absolutist view, a model would be considered useful for prediction only if it were not rejected, despite the fact that nonrejection does not necessarily imply predicted effects will be close to actual effects. Nor will nonrejected models necessarily outperform rejected models in terms of their (context-specific) predictive accuracy.

A particularly challenging use of decision-theoretic models in economics is to forecast the impact of large changes in the environment. Often, these changes are related to policy interventions that are outside of the scope of current policies, such as the recent 1996 welfare reform or the new expansion of Medicare to cover prescription drugs. A "good" in-sample fit of a model is unlikely, in itself, to give us much confidence in its forecasting ability in such contexts. This problem arises in large part because of the common practice of using the same data both for estimation and for model development.[2] The problem we explore in this article is how to gain confidence in a model's ability to predict the impact of such large changes.

Below, we show that an approach to validation and model selection that includes the choice of a "nonrandom holdout sample," a sample that differs significantly from the estimation sample along the policy dimension that the model is meant to forecast, can be fruitful. The idea is that if a model can provide a good forecast for a holdout sample that faces a policy regime well outside the support of the data (and that is not used in model formulation), then we gain confidence that it can provide a good forecast of impacts of other policy changes along that same dimension.[3] We explore the usefulness of this external validation approach, as a component of an overall validation strategy, using the model of female life-cycle behavior in Keane and Wolpin (2006). We choose a holdout sample that faced very different welfare policy rules from the estimation sample.[4]

---

[2] This practice is ubiquitous in both structural and nonstructural estimation.

[3] It is useful to contrast the nonrandom holdout sample with cross-validation (CV), which relies on random holdout samples. A typical cross validation procedure is to split the data into K mutually exclusive, randomly chosen subsets of (approximately) equal size, estimate the model on each possible group of $K-1$ subsets, and assess the model's predictive accuracy based on each left out set. By design, cross validation methods are based on predicted outcomes that, although out of sample, are always within the support of the current regime. Thus, we would argue they do not, by themselves, create confidence in a model's ability to predict effects of large regime changes.

[4] The deliberate choice of a nonrandom holdout sample for the purpose of model validation is commonplace in time-series analysis. We are, however, unaware of its use in cross section or panel data settings in economics. The idea seems to be a rather old one in psychology. Mosier (1951) suggested the procedure, naming it "validity generalization," that is, validation by generalizing beyond the sample. Recently, Busemeyer and Wang (2000) have argued for its more widespread adoption in psychology and provide Monte Carlo evidence on its performance in model selection. The use of models to forecast out-of-sample behavior is also common in the marketing literature, where considerable effort has been devoted to forecasting demand for new products. Few of the papers in that literature, however, compare predictions to subsequent demand after the product is introduced.

The most convincing examples in economics of external validations of decision-theoretic models have been based on randomized social experiments or on large regime shifts (that can be treated as experiments for the purpose of model validation), but such opportunities are rare. Among the earliest examples in which such a large regime shift is exploited is work by McFadden (1977) on forecasting the demand for rail rapid transport in the San Francisco Bay area. McFadden estimated a random utility model (RUM) of travel demand before the introduction of the Bay Area Rapid Transit (BART) system, obtained a forecast of the level of patronage that would ensue, and then compared the forecast to actual usage after BART's introduction.[5] Since that work, there have been, to our knowledge, only a handful of papers in the economics literature that have pursued a similar method of model validation.

McFadden's model validation treats pre-BART observations as the estimation sample and post-BART observations as the validation sample. A similar opportunity was exploited by Lumsdaine et al. (1992). They estimated a model of retirement behavior of workers in a single firm who were observed before and after the introduction of a temporary one-year pension window. They estimated several models on data before the window was introduced and compared the forecast of the impact of the pension window on retirement based on each estimated model to the actual impact as a means of model validation and selection. Keane and Moffitt (1998) estimated a model of labor supply and welfare program participation using data after federal legislation (OBRA 1981) that significantly changed the program rules. They used the model to predict behavior prior to that policy change. Keane (1995) used the same model to predict the impact of planned expansions of the Earned Income Tax Credit in 1994–96.

Randomized social experiments have also provided opportunities for model validation and selection. Wise (1985) exploited a housing subsidy experiment to evaluate a model of housing demand. In the experiment, families that met an income eligibility criterion were randomly assigned to control and treatment groups. The latter were offered a rent subsidy. The model was estimated using only control group data and was used to forecast the impact of the program on the treatment group. The forecast was compared to its actual impact. More recently, Todd and Wolpin (2006) used data from a large-scale school subsidy experiment in Mexico, where villages were randomly assigned to control and treatment groups. Using only the control villages, they estimated a behavioral model of parental decisions about child schooling and work, as well as family fertility. The validity of the model was then assessed according to how well it could forecast (predict) the behavior of households in the treatment villages.[6] Similarly, Lise et al. (2005)

---

[5] A regime shift, as opposed to a randomized experiment, is generally characterized by a time lapse between observations on the estimation sample (the control group) and those on the validation sample (the treatment group). Over that period, changes may have occurred that would affect behavior in ways not captured in the estimation. In addition, whatever assumption is made about the exogeneity of a regime shift becomes part of the validation exercise.

[6] When the model provides sufficient structure, and assuming that the model is deemed "valid," it is possible to simulate the impact of regime shifts other than the one used for validation. For example, Wise (1985) and Todd and Wolpin (2006) contrasted the effect of the policies evaluated in the experiments to several alternative policies.

used data from a Canadian experiment designed to move people off of welfare
and into work to validate a calibrated search-matching model of labor market
behavior.[7]

All of these papers made use of what was, from the researcher's perspective, a
fortuitous event. The common and essential element is the existence of some form
of a regime change radical enough to provide a degree of distance between the
estimation and validation samples. The more different the regimes, the less likely
are forecasted and actual behaviors in the validation sample to be close purely by
chance. However, waiting for such regime shifts to arise, given their rarity, does
not lead to a viable research approach to model validation and selection. Our
alternative approach attempts to mimic the essential element of regime change
by nonrandomly holding out from estimation a portion of the sample that faces
a significantly different policy regime. This "nonrandom holdout sample" is then
used for model validation/selection.

We illustrate the nonrandom holdout sample approach to model validation in
the context of a model of welfare program participation. The policy heterogeneity that we exploit to generate the hold-out sample takes advantage of the wide
variation across U.S. states that has existed in welfare policy. Specifically, we for-
mulate and estimate a dynamic programming (DP) model of the joint schooling,
welfare take-up, work, fertility, and marriage decisions of women using data from
one group of U.S. states (the estimation or "control" sample) and forecast these
same decisions on another state (the validation or "treatment" sample) that differs
dramatically in the generosity of its welfare program. Notably, our model extends
the literature on welfare participation in several dimensions.[8] We augment the
choice set to include schooling and fertility in addition to work, marriage, and
welfare participation and allow for a richer modeling framework within which
those choices are made.

We implement the model using 15 years of information from the 1979 youth
cohort of the National Longitudinal Surveys of Labor Market Experience
(NLSY79), supplemented with state-level welfare benefit rules that we have collected for each state over a 24-year period prior to the new welfare reform.
The model is estimated on five of the largest states represented in the NLSY79
(California, Michigan, New York, North Carolina, and Ohio) and validated on
data from Texas. In terms of generosity, California, Michigan, and New York are
high benefit states, North Carolina and Ohio are medium benefit states, and Texas
is a low benefit state.

Both to establish a performance metric and to provide potential alternatives
to the DP model, we also estimate four multinomial logit (MNL) specifications,
differentiated by whether they include state fixed-effects and by the complexity of
the specification of welfare rules (i.e., whether the rules are characterized by one
parameter or five parameters). These MNL models are consistent with a myopic
random utility model or a flexible approximation to a DP model.

---

[7]The use of laboratory experiments to validate economic models has, of course, a long tradition.
Bajari and Hortacsu (2005) provide a recent example of evaluating a structurally estimated auction
model by comparing the estimated valuations to those randomly assigned in an experimental setting.

[8] See Moffitt (1992) for a review of the early literature based on static models. Previous DP models
of welfare participation include Sanders (1993) and Swann (2005).

To highlight the results, we find that the nonrandom holdout sample approach provides useful information for model validation and selection. But, we also find that it can be quite misleading when relied on exclusively. Specifically, as expected, it is difficult to distinguish among the DP model and the four logits in terms of within-sample fit, applying a root mean squared error (RMSE) criterion to the five states used in estimation (the models have a similar number of parameters). On the other hand, using the same RMSE criterion, the holdout sample does differentiate among models. In particular, one of the two logit models without state fixed-effects clearly gives unreasonable forecasts for Texas. The other logit without state fixed-effects performs better for minorities than the DP model but worse for white women. The two logits with state-fixed effects perform better than both the DP model and the logits without state effects.[9] Based on these external validation results alone, one might well favor the logit specifications with state fixed-effects, and conclude they would provide more reliable forecasts of other counterfactual experiments related to welfare generosity than would the DP model.

However, based on our earlier work (see Keane and Wolpin, 2001a), it seemed implausible that the state fixed-effects logit specifications would provide the best forecast of Texas. In that paper, we note that, in models with state fixed-effects, estimates are based only on within-state over-time variation in welfare benefits. Thus, such models provide estimates of the impact of transitory changes in welfare rules. Yet, the external validation performed by forecasting behavior under Texas' rules requires prediction of behavior under a permanently different welfare regime, one with both a change in the "long-run" level of benefits and their transitory fluctuations over time. Why were fixed-effects models successful in such an exercise? As noted earlier, in carrying out the external validation, we estimated the state fixed-effects for Texas, thus effectively fitting mean behaviors. To see if the estimation of Texas dummies was critical to the superior performance of the state fixed-effect specifications, we performed a further exercise, a counterfactual experiment in which we gave the five estimation states the same welfare rules as Texas, maintaining the previous estimates of the state fixed-effects for the five states.

Of course, our expectation was that welfare participation would decline; no reasonable behavioral model would predict otherwise. But, consistent with our concern, the logit models with state fixed-effects predicted a substantial increase. Moreover, the one logit model without state fixed-effects that performed about equally to the DP model in our previous validation also produced unexpected results, forecasting that the decline in welfare participation would be considerably less than the increase in employment, a result that also seems inconsistent with a reasonable behavioral model.[10] The DP model, which imposes restrictions on

---

[9] The Texas state fixed-effects were estimated while all of the other parameters were fixed at the values obtained for the estimation sample.

[10] Consider a simpler random utility setting in which there are three mutually exclusive discrete alternatives: work, welfare, and home (no welfare). Given a reduction in welfare benefits, if the increase in the proportion who work exceeds the decline in the proportion who are on welfare, then the proportion taking leisure must decline. However, it is not possible in this setting for a reduction in

behavior that the more flexible logit does not, produced plausible forecasts. Hence, it seems to be the preferable model for analyzing large policy interventions.

The next section describes the structure of the DP model. Section 3 describes the data, Section 4 the estimation method, and Section 5 the results. The final section concludes.

2. MODEL

In this section, we provide an outline of our model.[11] We consider a woman who makes joint decisions at each age "a" of her life about the following discrete alternatives: whether or not to attend school, s_a, work part-time, h_a^p, or full-time, h_a^f, in the labor market (if an offer is received), be married (if an offer is received), m_a, become pregnant (if she is of a fecund age), p_a, and receive government welfare (if she is eligible), g_a. Thus, a woman chooses from as many as 36 mutually exclusive alternatives at each age during her fecund life cycle stage, and 18 during her infecund stage.[12] The fecund stage is assumed to begin at age 14 and to end at age 45; the decision period extends to age 62. Decisions are made at discrete six-month intervals, i.e., semiannually. A woman who becomes pregnant at age a has a birth at age $a + 1$, with n_{a+1} representing the discrete birth outcome.[13] Consumption, C_a, is determined uniquely by the alternative chosen.

The woman receives a utility flow at each age that depends on her current choices and consumption, and on state variables that reflect past choices, for example, the number of children already born, N_a, and their current ages (which affect child-rearing time costs), and the current level of completed schooling, S_a (which affects utility from attendance). We also allow preferences to evolve with age. The five choices (school, work, marriage, pregnancy, welfare) are subject to a vector of five age-varying serially independent preference shocks ε_a. And, we allow for permanent heterogeneity in tastes across individuals by birth cohort, race, and U.S. state of residence, and in a permanent unobservable characteristic we refer to as a woman's "type."[14]

Conditional on current choices, the utility of an individual at age a of type k can be written

$$(1) \qquad U_a^k = U_a\big(C_a, s_a, m_a, p_a, g_a, h_a^p, h_a^f; \varepsilon_a, I(\text{type} = j), \Omega_a^u\big),$$

welfare benefits, which reduces only the value of the welfare alternative, to reduce the prevalence of either of the other two alternatives.

[11] A complete description of the model with exact functional forms is provided in our companion paper, Keane and Wolpin (2006).

[12] Being married and receiving welfare is not an option. Although the AFDC-Unemployed Parent (AFDC-UP) program provided benefits for a family with an unemployed father, it accounts for only a small proportion of total spending on AFDC.

[13] In keeping with the assumption that pregnancies are perfectly timed, we only consider pregnancies that result in a live birth, i.e., we ignore pregnancies that result in miscarriages or abortions. We assume a woman cannot become pregnant in two consecutive six-month periods.

[14] In the model, we assume women do not change their state of residence, and we restrict our estimation to a sample with that characteristic.

where Ω_a^u represents the subset of the observed state variables that affects utility.[15,16]

The budget constraint, assumed to be satisfied each period, is given by

$$(2) \qquad C_a = y_a^o(1 - m_a)(1 - z_a) + [y_a^o + y_a^m]m_a\tau_a^m + [y_a^o + y_a^z\tau_a^z]z_a$$
$$+ \beta_1 g_a b_a - [\beta_3 I(S_a \geq 12) - \beta_4 I(S_a \geq 16)]s_a,$$

where y_a^o is the woman's own earnings at age a, y_a^m is the spouse's earnings if the woman is married, τ_a^m is the share of household income the woman receives if she is married, y_a^z is her parents' income, a share, τ_a^z, of which she receives if she coresides with her parents, b_a is the amount of welfare benefits the woman is eligible to receive. β_1 is a fraction that converts welfare dollars into a monetary equivalent consumption value.[17] β_3 is the tuition cost of college and β_4 the cost of graduate school. S_a is the completed level of schooling at age a. By assumption, income is pooled when married, but not when co-residing with parents.

Living with parents and being married are taken to be mutually exclusive states. In particular, if a woman receives a marriage offer (see below) and chooses to be married she cannot live with parents. A single woman lives with her parents according to a draw from an exogenous probability rule, π_a^z. We assume that the probability of co-residing with parents, given the woman is unmarried, depends on her age and lagged co-residence status. The woman's share of her parents' income, when co-resident, depends on her age, her parents' schooling and whether she is attending post-secondary school (the latter captures parental transfers to help finance college).

In each period a woman receives a part-time job offer with probability π^{wp} and a full-time job offer with probability π^{wf}. Each of these offer rates depends on the woman's previous-period work status. If an offer is received and accepted, the woman's earnings is the product of the offered hourly wage rate and the number of hours she works, $y_a^o = 500 \bullet w_a^p h_a^p + 1000 \bullet w_a^p h_a^f$. The hourly wage rate is the product of the woman's human capital stock, Ψ_a, and its per unit rental price, which is allowed to differ between part- and full-time jobs, r^j for $j = p, f$. Specifically, her ln hourly wage offer is

$$(3) \qquad \ln w_a^j = r^j + \Psi(\bullet) + \varepsilon_a^w, \quad j = p, f.$$

The woman's human capital stock is modeled as a function of completed schooling, accumulated work hours up to age a, H_a, whether or not the woman worked part-

---

[15] $I(\bullet)$ is the indicator function equal to one when the argument is true and zero otherwise.

[16] Monetary costs, when unmeasured, are not generally distinguishable from psychic costs. It is thus somewhat arbitrary what to include in the utility function or the the budget constraint. For example, we include in Equation (1) (i) a fixed cost of working; (ii) a time cost of rearing children that varies by their ages; (iii) a time cost of collecting welfare (waiting at the welfare office); (iv) a school reentry cost; and (v) costs of switching welfare and employment states.

[17] β_1 reflects the fact that welfare recipients are restricted in what they may purchase with welfare benefits, e.g., food stamps cannot be used to purchase alcohol.

or full-time in the previous period, her current age, and her skill endowment at age 14. As with permanent preference heterogeneity, the skill endowment differs by race, state of residence, and unobserved type. Random shocks to a woman's human capital stock, ε_a^w, are assumed to be serially independent.

There is stochastic assortative mating. In each period a single woman draws an offer to marry with probability π_a^m, that depends on her age and welfare status. If the woman is currently married, with some probability that depends on her age and duration of marriage, she receives an offer to continue the marriage. If she declines to continue, the woman must be single for one period (six months) before receiving a new marriage offer.

The husband's earnings depend on his human capital stock, Ψ_a^m. If a woman receives a marriage offer, the potential husband's human capital is drawn from a distribution that depends on a subset of the woman's characteristics: her schooling, age, race/ethnicity, state of residence, and unobserved (to us) type. In addition, there is an i.i.d. random component to the husband human capital draw that reflects a permanent characteristic unknown to the woman prior to meeting, μ^m. Thus, a woman can profitably search for husbands with more human capital and can also directly affect the quality of her potential husbands by her choice of her schooling. There is a fixed utility cost of getting married, which augments a woman's incentive to wait for a good husband draw before choosing marriage (we allow for a cohort effect in this fixed cost). After marriage, the woman receives a utility flow from marriage and a share of husband income. His earnings evolve with a fixed trend subject to a serially independent random shock, ε_a^m. Specifically,

$$(4) \qquad\qquad \ln y_a^m = \mu^m + \Psi_{0a}^m(\bullet) + \varepsilon_a^m,$$

where Ψ_{0a}^m is the deterministic component of the husband's human capital stock.

Welfare eligibility and the benefit amount for a woman residing in state s at calendar time t depends on her number of minor children and her household income. For any given number of children under the age of 18 residing in the household, N_a^{18}, the schedule of benefits can be accurately approximated by two line segments. The first corresponds to the guarantee level; it is assumed to be (approximately) linearly increasing in the number of minor children and, in the case of a woman co-residing with her parents, linearly declining in parents' income, y_a^z. The second line segment is negatively sloped as a function of the woman's own earnings, y_a^o, plus parents' income if she is co-resident, and also linearly increasing in the number of minor children. The negative slopes reflect the benefit reduction (or tax) applied to income.

In general, benefits are equal to the guarantee level until the woman's earnings reach some positive amount, as the rules provide a child care/work expense allowance for working mothers. Denoting this (state-specific) "disregard" level of earnings as $y_{at}^{s1}(N_a^{18})$, and the level of earnings at which benefits become zero (where the second line segment intersects the x-axis) as $y_{at}^{s2}(N_a^{18})$, the benefit schedule for a woman with $N_a^{18} > 0$ children is given by

(5)

$$b_t^s(N_{at}^{18}, y_{at}^o, y_{at}^z)$$

$$
\begin{aligned}
&= b_{0t}^s + b_{1t}^s N_{at}^{18} - b_{3t}^s \beta_2 y_{at}^z z_{at} && \text{for } y_{at}^o < y_{at}^{s1}(N_a^{18}), \\
&= b_{2t}^s + b_{4t}^s N_{at}^{18} - b_{3t}^s[(y_{at}^o - y_{at}^{s1}) + \beta_2 y_{at}^z z_{at}] && \text{for } y_{at}^{s1}(N_a^{18}) < y_{at}^o < y_{at}^{s2}(N_a^{18}) \\
&= 0 && \text{otherwise.}
\end{aligned}
$$

We refer to $b_t^s(N_{at}^{18}, y_{at}^o, y_{at}^z)$ as the benefit rule, and the b_{kt}^s's as the state/time specific benefit rule parameters. We exclude β_2 from this set because it is treated as a fixed parameter in our model.[18]

As the benefit rule parameters, and thus benefits themselves, change over time, women who are at all forward-looking should incorporate forecasts of future values of the rule parameters into their decision rules. We assume that benefit rule parameters evolve according to the following general vector autoregression (VAR), and that women use the VAR to form their forecasts of future benefit rules:

(6)
$$b_t^s = \lambda^s + \Lambda^s b_{t-1}^s + u_t^s$$

where b_t^s and b_{t-1}^s are 5×1 column vectors of the benefit rule parameters λ^s is a 5×1 column vector of regression constants, Λ^s is a 5×1 matrix of autoregressive parameters, and u_t^s is a 5×1 column vector of i.i.d. innovations drawn from a stationary distribution with variance–covariance matrix Ξ^s. We call Equation (6) the evolutionary rule (ER) and λ^s, Λ^s, Ξ^s the parameters of the ER. Evolutionary rules are specific to the woman's state of residence.[19]

The woman is assumed to maximize her expected present discounted value of remaining lifetime utility at each age. The maximized value (the value function) is given by

(7)
$$V_a(\Omega_a) = \max E\left[\sum_{\tau=a}^{62} \delta^{\tau-a} U_\tau(\bullet) \,\middle|\, \Omega_a\right],$$

where the expectation is taken over the distribution of future preference shocks, labor market, marriage, and parental co-residence opportunities, and the distribution of the future innovations of the benefit ER. The decision period is six months

---

[18] β_2 represents the fraction of parent's income that is included when calculating a woman's benefits if she lives with her parents. The exact treatment of parents' income is quite complicated and varies even within states. Thus, rather than attempting to model this explicitly, as an approximation we chose to estimate β_2 as a fixed parameter.

[19] As noted earlier, it is assumed that a woman remains in the same location from age 14 on. Clearly, introducing the possibility of moving among states in a forward-looking model such as this would greatly complicate the decision problem.

until age 45, the assumed age at which the women becomes infecund, but one year thereafter.[20] In (7), the state space Ω_a denotes the relevant factors known at age a that affect current or future utility or that affect the distributions of the future shocks and opportunities.

The solution to the optimization problem is a set of age-specific decision rules that give the optimal choice at any age, conditional on the elements of the state space at that age. Recasting the problem in a dynamic programming framework, the value function, $V_a(\Omega_a)$, can be written as the maximum over alternative-specific value functions, denoted $V_a^j(\Omega_a)$, i.e., the expected discounted value of choice $j \in J$, that satisfy the Bellman equation, namely

$$V_a(\Omega_a) = \max_{j \in J} \left[V_a^J(\Omega_a) \right]$$

(8) $$V_a^j(\Omega_a) = U_a^j + \delta E(V_{a+1}(\Omega_{a+1}) \mid j \in J, \Omega_a) \quad \text{for } a < A,$$

$$= U_A^j \qquad\qquad\qquad\qquad\qquad \text{for } a = A.$$

A woman at each age a chooses the option j that gives the greatest expected present discounted value of lifetime utility. The value of each option depends on the current state Ω_a, which depends on the state of residence and the ER for that state (6), as well as the current realizations of the benefit rule parameters, preference shocks, own and husband's earnings shocks, parental income shocks, and labor market, marriage, and parental co-residence opportunities.

The solution of the optimization problem is in general not analytic. In solving the model numerically, one can regard its solution as consisting of the values of $EV_{a+1}(\Omega_{a+1} \mid j \in J, \Omega_a)$ for all j and elements of Ω_a. We refer to this function as *Emax* for convenience. As seen in Equation (8), treating these functions as known scalars for each value of the state space transforms the dynamic optimization problem into the more familiar static multinomial choice structure. The solution method proceeds by backwards recursion beginning with the last decision period.[21]

3. DATA

The 1979 youth cohort of the National Longitudinal Surveys of Labor Market Experience (NLSY79) contains extensive information about schooling, employment, fertility, marriage, household composition, geographic location, and welfare participation for a sample of over 6000 women who were age 14–21 as of January 1, 1979. In addition to a nationally representative core sample, the NLSY79 contains oversamples of blacks and Hispanics. We use the annual interviews from

---

[20] Allowing for a longer decision period after age 45 reduces the computational burden of the model (see Wolpin, 1992).

[21] Because the size of the state space is large, we adopt an approximation method to solve for the Emax functions. The Emax functions are calculated at a limited set of state points and their values are used to fit a polynomial approximation in the state variables consisting of linear, quadratic, and interaction terms. See Keane and Wolpin (1994, 1997) for details. As a further approximation, we let the Emax functions depend on the expected values of the next period benefit parameters, rather than integrating over the benefit rule shocks.

1979 to 1991 for women from the core sample and from the black and Hispanic oversamples.

The NLSY79 collects much of the relevant information on births, marriages and divorces, periods of school attendance, job spells, and welfare receipt as dated events. We adopt a decision period of six-months. Periods are defined on a calendar year basis, beginning either on January 1 or on July 1 of any given year. The first decision period is the first six-month calender period that the woman turns age 14. The last period we observe is the second six-month calendar period in 1990 (or, if the woman attrited before then, the last six-month period in which the data are available). The first calendar period observation, corresponding to that of the oldest NLSY79 sample members, occurs in the second half of 1971. There are 15 other birth cohorts who turned age 14 in each six-month period through January 1979.

We restrict the sample to the six states in the U.S. that have the largest representations of NLSY79 respondents: California, Michigan, New York, North Carolina, Ohio, and Texas. The estimation is performed using only the first five states. Texas is used as a holdout or validation sample on which to perform out-of-sample validation tests of the model. The reason for this choice is that Texas is by far the least generous state in terms of welfare benefits and thus requires a fairly extreme out-of-sample extrapolation.

As noted, we consider the following choices: whether or not to (i) attend school, (ii) work (part- or full-time), (iii) be married, (iv) become pregnant, and (v) receive welfare (AFDC). The variables are defined as follows:

School Attendance: The NLSY79 collects a monthly attendance record for each women beginning as of January 1979. A woman was defined to be attending school if she reported being in school each month between January and April in the first six-month calendar period and each month between October and December in the second calendar period. Given the sample design of the NLSY79, school attendance records that begin at age 14 exist only for the cohort that turned 14 in January 1979.

Employment Status: Using employment event history data, we calculated the number of hours worked in each six-month period. A woman was considered working part-time in the period (500 hours) if she worked between 260 and 779 hours and full-time (1000 hours) if she worked at least 780 hours. As with school attendance, employment data do not extend back to age 14 for many of the cohorts. We assume that initial work experience, that is, at age 14, is zero.

Marital Status: The NLSY79 provides a complete event-dated marital history that is updated each interview. However, dates of separation are not reported. Therefore, for the years between 1979 and 1990, data on household composition were used to determine whether the woman was living with a spouse. But, because these data are collected only at the time of the interview, marital status is treated as missing during the noninterview periods, in most cases for one six-month period per year. Marital event histories were used for the periods prior

TABLE 1

CHOICE DISTRIBUTIONS BY AGE: ESTIMATION SAMPLE OF THE COMBINED FIVE STATES

Age	Attending School			Working (PT or FT)			Married			Becomes Pregnant			Receives AFDC		
	W	B	H	W	B	H	W	B	H	W	B	H	W	B	H
14	100	93.3	100	14.3	10.5	12.5	0.0	0.0	0.0	0.0	0.0	0.0	0.0	0.0	0.0
15	97.7	100	100	11.4	9.9	5.2	0.0	0.0	0.0	1.0	3.4	1.0	1.0	1.3	0.0
16	88.3	87.5	90.3	30.0	14.5	19.3	3.0	1.0	2.9	3.1	3.8	2.1	1.0	1.0	1.0
17	84.6	80.7	79.2	50.0	26.9	32.4	8.7	1.4	6.4	5.6	5.3	2.5	1.3	2.5	2.3
18	42.8	50.9	41.5	63.0	32.6	50.7	16.4	3.7	11.9	3.7	4.5	6.7	2.6	9.0	3.3
19	32.5	32.1	27.1	65.6	43.4	51.2	24.9	7.1	19.9	4.5	8.6	5.6	3.6	15.6	6.8
20	23.8	22.2	18.8	67.5	46.4	52.2	31.5	11.7	27.1	4.3	6.0	4.9	5.4	17.3	10.3
21	19.4	12.3	12.2	69.6	49.2	58.3	37.1	14.4	34.2	6.0	7.9	6.3	5.1	21.2	13.7
22	10.8	8.3	7.7	70.0	52.5	60.6	37.5	20.3	35.9	4.5	5.3	5.7	6.1	25.6	15.1
23	4.2	6.2	3.9	72.0	54.2	58.5	49.1	22.3	39.7	5.9	6.1	5.3	6.2	27.2	15.3
24	3.8	5.4	4.6	72.7	55.4	57.7	54.1	22.8	45.7	6.6	6.9	7.9	7.0	27.8	17.2
25	4.0	5.9	2.9	73.8	62.8	55.6	58.5	20.9	47.2	7.6	7.0	7.2	6.4	26.8	16.0
26–29	3.2	3.6	2.2	71.5	61.1	56.7	63.6	25.6	52.1	5.8	4.4	5.8	5.0	25.7	15.4
30–33	4.5	2.3	2.6	72.6	63.3	64.9	72.8	32.0	56.7	4.3	2.3	5.3	2.6	22.3	14.5

to 1979 even though it is uncertain from that data whether the spouse was present in the household.

Pregnancy Status: Although pregnancy rosters are collected at each interview, conception dates are noisy and miscarriages and abortions are underreported. We ignore pregnancies that do not lead to a live birth, dating the month of the conception as occurring nine months prior to the month of birth. Except for misreporting of births, there is no missing information on pregnancies back to age 14 for any of the cohort.

Welfare Receipt: AFDC receipt is reported for each month within the calendar year preceding the interview year, i.e., from January 1978. We define a woman as receiving welfare in a period if she reported receiving an AFDC payment in at least three of the six months of the period.[22] As with school attendance and employment, data are missing back to age 14 for most of the cohorts. It is assumed that none of the women received welfare prior to age 14, as is consistent with the fact that none had borne a child by that time.

Descriptive Statistics: Table 1 provides (marginals of) the sample choice distribution by full-year ages and by race aggregated over the five states used in the estimation. Notice that school attendance is essentially universal until age 16, drops about in half at age 18, the normal high school graduation age, and falls to

---

[22] The use of almost any cutoff in establishing welfare participation would have only a small effect on the classification; most women who report receiving welfare in any one month during a six-month period report receiving it in all six months.

around 10% at age 22. About 3% of the sample attends school at ages after 25. The implied school completion levels that result from these attendance patterns are, at age 24, 12.9 for whites, 12.7 for blacks, and 12.2 for Hispanics. Employment rates for white and Hispanic women (working either part- or full-time) increase rapidly through age 18 but only slowly thereafter. They are higher for whites throughout by about 10–20 percentage points. In contrast, employment rates for black females rise more continuously, roughly doubling between age 18 and 25, and are comparable to that of Hispanics at ages after 25.

Marriage rates rise continuously for whites and Hispanics, reaching about 60% by age 25 for whites and 50% for Hispanics. However, for blacks, marriage rates more or less reach a plateau at about age 22, at between 20% and 25%. With respect to fertility, by age 20, white, black, and Hispanic females had, on average, 0.28, 0.47, and 0.40 live births, respectively. By age 27, these figures are 1.06, 1.36, and 1.39, respectively, and by age 30, they are 1.54, 1.61, and 1.76, respectively. Welfare participation increases with age, at least through age 24. Race differences are large; participation peaks at 7% for whites, 28% for blacks, and 17% for Hispanics. Teenage pregnancies that lead to a live birth are higher by 68% for blacks than for whites and by 43% for Hispanics than for whites.

There are large differences between women in the five states used in estimation (the estimation sample) and Texas (the validation sample). The largest differences are for AFDC take-up and for full-time employment. For example, among black women, welfare receipt peaked at about 30% in the estimation sample, whereas it peaked at only about 10% in the validation sample. Full-time employment is much higher in Texas. For example, at age 25, the difference in the proportion engaged in full-time work is 14.3 percentage points for whites, 18.9 percentage points for blacks, and 19.6 percentage points for Hispanics.[23]

Benefit Rules: In order to estimate the benefit schedules (5), and the evolutionary rules governing changes in benefit parameters (6), we collected information on the rules governing AFDC and Food Stamp eligibility and benefits in each of the 50 states for the period 1967–90. We then simulated a large sample of hypothetical women, with different numbers of children and different labor and nonlabor income, and calculated their benefits according to the exact rules in each state and each year. We took the sum of monthly AFDC and Food Stamp benefits and expressed them in 1987 New York equivalent dollars. This data set was used to estimate the (approximate) benefit rule parameters, b_{t0}^s, b_{t1}^s, b_{t2}^s, b_{t3}^s, b_{t4}^s, for each state s and year t.[24] Given the estimates of the benefit rule parameters, we then estimated (6), the evolutionary rule, for each state s.

Table 2 transforms the benefit parameters obtained from the estimates of (5) into a more convenient set of benefit measures, namely the total monthly income

---

[23] See the working paper version, Keane and Wolpin (2005), for further details.

[24] The approximation given by Equation (5) fits the monthly benefit data quite well, with R^2 statistics for the first line segment mostly above 0.99 and for the second, mostly about 0.95. See Keane and Wolpin (2005) for the regression estimates.

TABLE 2

SUMMARY STATISTICS OF TOTAL MONTHLY BENEFITS BY NUMBERS OF CHILDREN AND EARNINGS BY STATE: 1967–90

		Monthly Earnings					
		Zero		$500		$1000	
		One Child	Two Children	One Child	Two Children	One Child	Two Children
CA							
	μ	589	724	351	517	87	196
	σ	60	67	85	91	89	151
	1970	459	568	416	560	297	440
	1975	652	794	441	620	132	311
	1980	617	757	405	560	156	311
	1985	596	730	260	414	0	46
	1990	594	728	303	476	0	110
MI							
	μ	654	809	429	621	150	304
	σ	92	106	161	179	158	215
	1970	671	830	585	799	302	516
	1975	735	912	551	762	273	483
	1980	660	808	424	602	152	330
	1985	561	705	235	405	0	58
	1990	551	694	293	484	0	156
NY							
	μ	574	718	334	514	92	204
	σ	52	71	126	152	98	189
	1970	562	726	469	685	189	406
	1975	635	798	443	643	172	372
	1980	552	679	322	473	61	211
	1985	524	644	189	334	0	0
	1990	528	649	230	393	0	31
NC							
	μ	480	566	274	384	35	132
	σ	48	58	68	82	40	66
	1970	455	513	348	432	143	227
	1975	570	679	356	502	50	197
	1980	462	553	260	364	31	134
	1985	454	543	199	295	0	69
	1990	438	530	249	367	13	131
OH							
	μ	489	607	270	414	87	128
	σ	34	43	69	88	36	87
	1970	460	565	361	511	106	256
	1975	552	688	339	514	27	202
	1980	499	619	284	423	11	151
	1985	459	570	185	305	0	0
	1990	455	566	218	346	0	0
TX							
	μ	377	476	217	329	69	106
	σ	50	60	51	73	21	43
	1970	417	514	297	429	169	201
	1975	445	561	253	398	0	117
	1980	334	436	198	295	0	96
	1985	375	474	170	264	0	52
	1990	343	442	181	287	0	101

of nonworking women (with zero nonearned income) who have either one or two children, and the total monthly income of women with one or two children who have part-time monthly earnings of 500 dollars or full-time earnings of 1000 dollars.[25] Referring to Table 2, among the six states, NY, CA, and MI are considerably more generous than NC, OH, and TX. Among the first group Michigan is the most generous, with average benefits over the 24 years for a woman with one child being 654 (1987 NY) dollars per month. Among the second group Texas is the least generous, with the same average benefits figure only 377 dollars. CA and NY were about equally generous on average (589 and 574 dollars) over the period as were NC and OH (480 and 489 dollars).[26]

As Table 2 reveals, there was a steep decline in benefit amounts between the early 1970s and the mid-1980s, and relative constancy thereafter. For example, in Michigan monthly benefits fell from 735 dollars for a woman with no earnings and two children in 1975 to 561 dollars in 1985. For the same woman with 500 dollars in monthly earnings, benefits fell from 762 dollars in 1975 to 405 dollars in 1985, and then rose slightly to 484 dollars in 1990.

4.   ESTIMATION METHOD

Numerical solution to the agents' maximization problem provides (approximations to) the Emax functions appearing on the right hand side of (8). The alternative-specific value functions, V_t^j for $j = 1, \ldots, J$, are known to the agents. But, in general, the econometrician does not observe the random preference shocks, full- and part-time wage offer shocks, the earnings shock of the husband, and the income of parents. Also, the choice set depends on shocks governing whether a marriage offers, job offers, and parental co-residence offers are received.

Thus, conditional on the deterministic part of the state space, the probability an agent is observed to choose option j is an integral over the region of the several-dimensional error space such that k is the preferred option. The order of integration needed to form the likelihood contribution depends on the observed choice. For example, if the agent chooses a work option, then the wage offer is observed, and we need not integrate over the wage shock. In that case, the likelihood of the observation includes the density of the wage error.

As the choice set contains up to 36 elements, evaluation of the choice probabilities is computationally burdensome. Efficient smooth unbiased probability simulators, such as the GHK method (see, e.g., Keane, 1993, 1994), are often useful in such situations. Unfortunately, smooth unbiased simulators like GHK generally rely on a structure in which the value of each alternative is a strictly monotonic function of a single stochastic term, and where $(J-1) \bullet (J-1)$ variance matrix of the error terms has full rank. Also, as discussed in Keane and Moffitt

---

[25] See Keane and Wolpin (2005) for summary statistics on the benefit parameters.

[26] Benefit reduction rates for AFDC and for Food Stamps are federally set. They differ across states in our approximation due to the fact that AFDC payments terminate at different income levels among the states while food stamp payments are still nonzero and the two programs have different benefit reduction rates. There is thus a kink in the schedule of total welfare payments with income that our approximation smooths over.

(1998), when the number of choices exceeds the number of errors, boundaries of the regions of integration for the choice probabilities are often intractably complex. Thus, given our model, the most practical method to simulate the choice probabilities would be to use a kernel smoothed frequency simulator. These were proposed in McFadden (1989), and have been successfully applied to models with large choice sets in Keane and Moffitt (1998) and Keane and Wolpin (1997).[27]

In the present context, however, standard simulated maximum likelihood methods are not feasible because of severe problems created by unobserved state variables. As noted, we do not generally have complete histories of employment, schooling, or welfare take-up back to age 14, so the state variables for work experience, schooling, and welfare dependence cannot be constructed. Parental co-residence and marital status are also only observed once a year.

A further complication is that a youth's initial schooling level at age 14 is observed only for 1 of the 16 cohorts. Unobserved initial conditions (see Heckman, 1981), and unobserved state variables in general, pose formidable computational problems for estimation of dynamic discrete choice models. If some elements of the state space are unobserved, one must integrate over their distributions to construct the conditional choice probabilities. Even in much simpler dynamic models than ours, such distributions are typically computationally intractable.

Keane and Wolpin (2001b) develop a simulation algorithm that deals in a practical way with unobserved state variables. The idea is based on simulating complete outcome histories (age 14 to the terminal age) for a set of artificial agents. A history consists of initial schooling, S_0, parental schooling, $\mathbf{S}^Z$, and simulated values in all subsequent periods for all of the outcome variables in the model (i.e., school attendance, part- or full-time work, etc.). Denote by $\tilde{O}^n$ the simulated outcome history for the nth such person, $\tilde{O}^n = (S_{14}^n, S^z, \tilde{O}_{a=1}^n, \ldots, \tilde{O}_{a=A}^n)$, for $n = 1, \ldots, N$.

To motivate the algorithm, it is useful to ignore for now the complication that some outcomes are continuous. Let O^i denote the observed outcome history for person i, which may include missing elements. An unbiased frequency simulator of the probability of the observed outcome history for person i, $P(O^i)$, is just the fraction of the N simulated histories that are consistent with O^i. In this construction, missing elements of O^i are counted as consistent with any entry in the corresponding element of $\tilde{O}^n$. The construction of this simulator relies only on unconditional simulations: It does not require evaluation of choice probabilities conditional on state variables. Thus, unobserved state variables create no problem for this procedure.

Unfortunately, because the number of possible outcome histories is huge, consistency of a simulated history with an actual history is an extremely low probability event. Hence, simulated probabilities will typically be 0, as will be the simulated likelihood, unless an impractically large simulation size is used (see Lerman and Manski, 1981). In addition, the method breaks down if any outcome is continuous, e.g., the woman's wage offer, regardless of simulation size, because agreement of observed with simulated wages is a measure zero event.

---

[27] Kernel smoothed frequency simulators are biased for positive values of the smoothing parameter, so consistency requires it to approach zero as sample size increases.

We solve this problem by assuming, as is apt, that all observed quantities are measured with error. With measurement error there is a nonzero probability that any observed outcome history might be generated by any simulated outcome history. Denote by $P(O^i \mid \tilde{O}^n)$ the probability that observed outcome history O^i is generated by simulated outcome history $\tilde{O}^n$. Then $P(O^i \mid \tilde{O}^n)$ is the product of classification error rates on discrete outcomes and measurement error densities for wages that are needed to make O^i and $\tilde{O}^n$ consistent. Observe that $P(O^i \mid \tilde{O}^n) > 0$ for any $\tilde{O}^n$, given suitable choice of error processes. The specific measurement error processes that we assume are described below. The key point here is that $P(O^i \mid \tilde{O}^n)$ does not depend on the state variables at any age a, but only depends on the outcomes.

Using N simulated outcome histories we obtain the unbiased simulator

$$(9) \qquad \hat{P}_N(O^i) = \frac{1}{N} \sum_{n=1}^{N} P(O^i \mid \tilde{O}^n).$$

This simulator is analogous to a kernel-smoothed frequency simulator, in that $I(O^i = \tilde{O}^n)$ is replaced with an object that is strictly positive, but that is greater if $\tilde{O}^n$ is "closer" to O^i. However, (9) is unbiased, as measurement error is assumed to be present in the true model.

It is straightforward to extend the estimation method to allow for unobserved heterogeneity. Assume that there are K types of women who differ in their permanent preference parameters and skill endowments.[28] Let $\pi_{k,0}$ and π_k denote the frequency of type k according to the simulation and the model, respectively, and let $\tilde{O}_k^n$ indicate that artificial agent n is of type k. Then, we obtain

$$(10) \qquad \hat{P}_N(O^i) = \frac{1}{N} \sum_{n=1}^{N} P(O^i \mid \tilde{O}_k^n) \frac{\pi_k}{\pi_{k0}}.$$

Observe that in Equation (10), the conditional probabilities $P(O^i \mid \tilde{O}^n)$ are weighted by the ratio of the proportion of type k according to the model to the proportion of type k in the simulation.

This simulator is not smooth because $P(O^i \mid \tilde{O}^n)$ will "jump" at points where changes in model parameters cause a simulated outcome history $\tilde{O}^n$ to change discretely. But Equation (10) can be smoothed by applying an importance sampling procedure: Hold simulated outcome histories fixed and reweight them as parameters are varied. Given an initial parameter vector θ_0 and updated vector θ', the appropriate weight for sequence $\tilde{O}^n$ is the ratio of the likelihood of simulated history n under θ' to that under θ_0. This importance sampling weight (i.e., ratio of densities under the target and source distributions) is a smooth function of model parameters. Note it is straightforward to simulate the likelihood of an artificial history $\tilde{O}^n$ using conventional methods because the state vector is fully observed

---

[28] Initial schooling, parents schooling, and the latent type are drawn from a joint distribution that we estimate. In Equation (10), type refers to this vector of three initial conditions.

at all points along the history. Choice probabilities along a path $\tilde{O}^n$ are simulated using a kernel smoothed frequence simulator. As $P(O^i \mid \tilde{O}^n)$ is now smooth in the model parameters, standard errors can be obtained by the BHHH algorithm.

For the measurement error processes, we assume discrete outcomes are subject to a simple form of classification error: There is some probability the reported response category is the truth and some probability that it is not.[29] For continuous variables, we assume that the woman's wage error and the husband's income error are multiplicative and the parents' income error is additive. Measurement errors are assumed to be serially and mutually independent.

5. RESULTS

Both to provide a metric for assessing the fit of the dynamic programming (DP) model and as possible alternatives to it, we also estimated a multinomial logit (MNL) that relates four of the five choice variables, welfare take-up, school attendance, work, and pregnancy, to the state variables of the model at each age. We estimated four different specifications of the MNL, but present the results for now of only the one that best fit the estimation and validation samples.[30]

The variables included in the MNL are the benefit amount for a woman with one child and no earnings, state dummies, age, age squared, parents schooling, whether the woman was on welfare, worked, or was pregnant in the previous period, whether she was pregnant two periods before, the number of children already born, the woman's years of schooling and its square, whether the woman was living in a nuclear family at age 14, and race dummies. There are 13 mutually exclusive choices (3 were combined because of small cell size) and 240 parameters.

In comparison, the DP model is more comprehensive, including also a marriage decision and a distinction between full- or part-time work. It also embeds additional structural relationships (functions describing the probability of living with a parent, husband's income if married and parent's income if co-resident, and full- and part-time wage offers). Nevertheless, that DP model has a similar number of parameters (202).

Table 3 shows the fit to the estimation sample for the MNL and the DP models by four age groups (15–17.5, 18–21.5, 22–25.5, 26–29.5) for each race separately. Although there are clear differences in the fit of the two models, neither seems to be uniformly better. For example, the MNL fits welfare take-up better for blacks than does the DP model, but fits Hispanics worse and whites about the same. Similarly, the MNL model seems to fit the work alternative better for Hispanics at earlier ages, but the DP model fits better at later ages. Both models capture well age trends and quantitative differences by race. The table also compares the fit to two of the state variables, the mean number of children ever born before ages 20,

---

[29] To ensure that the measurement error is unbiased, the probability that the reported value is the true value must be a linear function of the predicted sample proportion (see Keane and Wolpin, 2005 for details). Keane and Sauer (2005) have applied this algorithm successfully with more general classification error processes.

[30] These regressions are available on request.

TABLE 3

ACTUAL AND PREDICTED CHOICE PROBABILITIES BY AGE FOR THE ESTIMATION SAMPLE: MNL AND DP MODELS

	White			Black			Hispanic		
	Actual	MNL	DP	Actual	MNL	DP	Actual	MNL	DP
Percent Receiving Welfare									
Age 15–17.5	0.9	0.5	1.3	1.9	2.3	4.8	1.3	0.6	4.4
Age 18–21.5	4.3	3.4	4.7	16.9	16.6	15.5	9.2	5.4	11.2
Age 22–25.5	6.4	5.0	7.1	26.9	23.9	24.6	15.0	10.3	15.1
Age 26–29.5	4.7	4.5	7.1	21.6	21.6	28.0	15.2	10.2	15.8
Percent in School									
Age 15–17.5	86.4	81.4	85.3	86.3	82.0	84.2	84.6	84.2	79.2
Age 18–21.5	27.3	28.9	29.8	26.1	25.2	29.5	22.0	29.2	21.4
Age 22–25.5	5.2	5.4	8.3	6.3	6.3	8.0	5.0	5.2	6.0
Age 26–29.5	3.1	2.2	3.5	3.5	2.5	3.5	2.0	2.1	2.8
Percent Working									
Age 15–17.5	35.2	29.7	28.4	19.2	17.6	18.3	22.2	20.1	26.6
Age 18–21.5	66.7	66.3	63.8	44.1	47.9	53.8	52.8	53.0	58.5
Age 22–25.5	72.4	74.9	70.4	56.8	56.0	59.4	58.7	62.2	57.8
Age 26–29.5	71.1	78.7	69.8	61.1	62.1	57.7	56.1	66.8	55.4
Percent Pregnant									
Age 15–17.5	2.5	2.1	1.9	4.6	2.9	3.0	3.2	3.8	3.2
Age 18–21.5	4.4	5.3	4.7	6.7	5.9	6.5	6.9	7.0	6.5
Age 22–25.5	5.5	6.0	5.1	5.8	6.2	7.3	6.7	7.1	7.7
Age 26–29.5	5.5	5.1	4.8	4.2	5.0	6.6	5.9	5.9	6.6
Children Born Before									
Age 20	0.32	0.32	0.31	0.53	0.39	0.47	0.40	0.43	0.48
Age 24	0.72	0.81	0.72	1.05	0.90	1.02	1.00	1.00	1.03
Age 28	1.26	1.24	1.13	1.41	1.20	1.62	1.60	1.49	1.61
Highest Grade Completed									
By Age 24	12.87	13.03	13.08	12.68	12.90	12.97	12.20	12.83	12.38

24, and 28, and the mean highest grade completed by age 24. The performance is similar with respect to these measures, except for the severe overstatement of schooling for Hispanics by the MNL model.

Table 4 presents the same comparison for the validation sample. The MNL clearly does better than the DP model in terms of welfare participation, especially for blacks in the last two age groups. Other comparisons also seem to favor the MNL, although differences seem to be small. As with the estimation sample, age trends and racial differences are captured well. Neither model is very far off in forecasting children ever born or schooling.[31]

---

[31] We also considered the fit of the DP model to all of the other variables for both the estimation sample and the validation sample (see Keane and Wolpin, 2005). The fit with respect to the estimation sample is uniformly good, capturing well age trends and racial differences. In some cases, the fit is remarkably close. For example, because of selection, fitting accepted wages when working percentages are low is challenging. Nevertheless, the DP model predictions are quite close to the actual data. For example, predicted mean accepted wage rates are often within 5% of the actual wage rates.

TABLE 4

ACTUAL AND PREDICTED CHOICE PROBABILITIES FOR VALIDATION SAMPLE BY AGE: MNL AND DP MODELS

	White			Black			Hispanic		
	Actual	MNL	DP	Actual	MNL	DP	Actual	MNL	DP
Percent Receiving Welfare									
Age 15–17.5	0.0	0.1	0.1	0.6	0.8	1.3	1.3	0.4	0.5
Age 18–21.5	0.0	0.3	0.7	7.3	7.3	6.4	4.2	3.8	2.3
Age 22–25.5	0.8	0.5	1.6	7.8	9.1	13.0	5.0	4.8	4.9
Age 26–29.5	0.7	0.3	1.9	7.3	8.5	17.7	4.7	4.6	5.9
Percent in School									
Age 15–17.5	93.6	88.5	87.0	87.8	82.0	85.4	80.3	81.0	82.0
Age 18–21.5	36.5	38.4	31.1	27.9	25.2	29.1	29.8	31.4	22.5
Age 22–25.5	6.9	7.7	9.4	3.5	6.3	8.5	4.4	5.7	6.5
Age 26–29.5	4.4	3.7	4.0	1.9	2.5	3.8	4.5	3.4	3.0
Percent Working									
Age 15–17.5	39.3	37.3	38.2	24.7	18.6	24.2	24.1	21.6	33.3
Age 18–21.5	68.9	72.8	75.8	60.5	57.4	64.9	55.0	54.4	64.1
Age 22–25.5	80.0	84.2	82.0	73.1	71.5	70.7	68.1	68.5	64.5
Age 26–29.5	79.6	83.5	82.5	72.8	72.3	69.1	64.9	69.5	63.9
Percent Pregnant									
Age 15–17.5	1.3	2.1	1.7	4.5	2.1	2.9	3.8	4.2	3.3
Age 18–21.5	3.7	5.3	4.8	6.9	4.9	6.7	6.7	6.6	7.1
Age 22–25.5	4.5	6.0	4.9	5.8	5.0	7.4	6.4	6.2	7.5
Age 26–29.5	4.2	5.1	4.8	3.5	3.9	6.6	4.9	5.2	7.0
Children Born Before									
Age 20	0.22	0.18	0.29	0.65	0.58	0.46	0.50	0.50	0.52
Age 24	0.49	0.56	0.68	1.12	0.99	1.03	1.06	1.06	1.11
Age 28	0.86	0.92	1.09	1.71	1.45	1.63	1.54	1.54	1.72
Highest Grade Completed									
By Age 24	13.27	13.47	13.24	12.81	12.71	13.02	12.21	12.41	12.49

To summarize the overall fit to the estimation and validation samples, Table 5 reports the RMSE, calculated from deviations between actual and forecasted age-specific means, for the DP model and the four alternative MNL models. The MNL model that we discussed above is labeled MNL1-FE, where FE indicates it includes state fixed-effects, and "1" indicates welfare rules are summarized by a single variable (the benefit level for a woman with one child). MNL1-No FE drops the fixed effects, but instead includes the mean one-child benefit for the state over the period 1967–90. In model MNL2-FE, the "2" indicates that the five state-specific benefit parameters from Equation (5) are included in the specification separately, instead of just of the one-child benefit. MNL2-No FE drops the state fixed-effects, and instead includes the means of those five benefit parameters over the 1967–90 period.

With respect to the estimation sample, all of the MNL models and the DP model appear about equally good. Notable exceptions are the better fit of the DP model to school attendance among whites (0.028 vs. 0.044 for MNL1-No FE), the worse fit of the DP model to work (0.066 vs. 0.030 for MNL1-No FE) for blacks, and the

TABLE 5

ROOT MEAN SQUARED ERROR FOR ALTERNATIVE MNL SPECIFICATIONS AND FOR DP MODEL: SELECTED CHOICE VARIABLES

	Estimation Sample					Validation Sample				
	MNL1 FE	MNL1 No FE	MNL2 FE	MNL2 No FE	DP	MNL1 FE	MNL1 No FE	MNL2 FE	MNL2 No FE	DP
					Whites					
Welfare	0.011	0.012	0.012	0.011	0.015	0.010	0.010	0.010	0.815	0.012
(Mean)			(0.043)					(0.004)		
Work	0.054	0.051	0.049	0.048	0.046	0.068	0.093	0.068	0.255	0.077
(Mean)			(0.631)					(0.688)		
Pregnancy	0.012	0.012	0.013	0.012	0.012	0.019	0.022	0.019	0.442	0.021
(Mean)			(0.046)					(0.036)		
In School	0.045	0.044	0.045	0.047	0.027	0.046	0.086	0.045	0.138	0.054
(Mean)			(0.268)					(0.315)		
					Blacks					
Welfare	0.030	0.028	0.027	0.026	0.026	0.021	0.030	0.021	0.844	0.063
(Mean)			(0.189)					(0.061)		
Work	0.035	0.030	0.034	0.032	0.064	0.059	0.054	0.058	0.215	0.065
(Mean)			(0.470)					(0.600)		
Pregnancy	0.015	0.015	0.016	0.016	0.021	0.034	0.037	0.033	0.490	0.036
(Mean)			(0.054)					(0.052)		
In School	0.031	0.031	0.028	0.032	0.034	0.044	0.047	0.046	0.224	0.048
(Mean)			(0.269)					(0.264)		
					Hispanics					
Welfare	0.044	0.052	0.049	0.050	0.024	0.014	0.018	0.014	0.842	0.019
(Mean)			(0.108)					(0.040)		
Work	0.067	0.071	0.059	0.064	0.048	0.050	0.062	0.048	0.169	0.092
(Mean)			(0.491)					(0.550)		
Pregnancy	0.015	0.015	0.015	0.015	0.019	0.022	0.025	0.022	0.487	0.030
(Mean)			(0.059)					(0.056)		
In School	0.050	0.048	0.049	0.050	0.047	0.034	0.059	0.034	0.177	0.058
(Mean)			(0.246)					(0.264)		

better fit of the DP model to welfare (0.024 vs. 0.044 for MNL1-FE), to work (0.048 vs. 0.059 for MNL2-FE), and to school attendance (0.033 vs. 0.048 for MNL1-No FE) for Hispanics.

On the other hand, large differences in fit emerge for the validation sample.[32] Among the MNL models, the two that include state dummies (MNL1-FE and MNL2-FE) have the lowest RMSEs. Although using the five benefit parameters to capture welfare rules (MNL2-FE) provides a statistically significant improvement in the estimation-sample fit, there is no discernible impact on the RMSE for the validation sample.[33]

[32] To forecast Texas for the MNL models with state dummies, we reestimated the model on Texas data with Texas state dummies, constraining all other parameters to be the same as in the estimation sample.

[33] The chi-square statistic for the joint test that all of the additional benefit parameters are zero has a p-value of 0.000.

Replacing the state dummies with the mean one-child benefit does adversely affect the RMSE. For example, comparing the MNL1-FE versus MNL1- No FE models, the largest increases in RMSE are from 0.068 to 0.093 for work and from 0.046 to 0.086 for school attendance for whites, from 0.021 to 0.030 for welfare for blacks, and from 0.050 to 0.062 for work and from 0.034 to 0.059 for school attendance for Hispanics.

But, the deterioration in fit is much greater for the MNL2 models. Dropping the state dummies, and instead including the five state-specific means of the five benefit parameters in (5), increased the RMSE enormously. The fit to welfare was particularly adversely affected, rising from 0.010 (MNL2-FE) to 0.815 (MNL2-No FE) for whites, from 0.021 to 0.844 for blacks and from 0.014 to 0.842 for Hispanics. Thus, in specifications that include only the one-child benefit (MNL1) instead of the five benefit rule parameters (MNL2), dropping the state fixed-effects does not lead to such a serious deterioration of the fit to Texas. We take this result as evidence that the validation sample is capable of identifying overfitting in a way that the estimation sample was not.

The DP model uniformly does not fit as well as MNL1-FE and overall fits about the same as MNL1-No FE; fitting better for whites, but worse for blacks and Hispanics. Based on the evidence from this validation exercise, it would therefore appear that MNL1-FE would be the best model to use for counterfactual experiments.

Given that expectation, Table 6 reports on the results from a counterfactual experiment where the estimation sample states are given Texas' welfare benefits. We report on the effects for both MNL1 specifications and for the DP model. The predicted effects from the MNL1-FE specification are seemingly perverse. Welfare receipt and fertility are predicted to increase substantially, and there is a similarly large decline in work. The predictions from the MNL1-No FE specification are exactly the opposite, a large reduction in welfare receipt, a large increase in work, and a relatively small reduction in fertility.

Keane and Wolpin (2001a) noted an important distinction between specifications with and without state-specific effects. If women are forward looking, the effect of a change in welfare benefit rules on behavior depends critically on how that change affects expectations about future benefit rules. Changes in welfare benefits can have very different effects depending on whether they are perceived as being permanent or transitory. Estimates that use different sources of variation in benefits, variation across states versus variation within states over time, may result in different estimates simply because they identify responses to benefit changes that may be perceived as having different degrees of permanence.

For example, if benefits are change from year to year, the effect of a change in the current year's benefits on fertility will depend on the degree to which the change is viewed as permanent. This, in turn, depends on the process by which benefits evolve and how potential welfare recipients form expectations. If the perceived benefit process is such that an increase in benefits in one year is anticipated to be followed by declines in subsequent years, then it is possible that fertility may actually respond negatively to the transitory increase.

TABLE 6

COUNTERFACTUAL OF OTHER STATES WITH TEXAS WELFARE BENEFITS: MNL AND DP COMPARISON

	Actual	MNL1 FE		MNL1 No FE		DP	
		Baseline	With Texas	Baseline	With Texas	Baseline	With Texas
Whites							
Percent Receiving Welfare							
Age 15–17.5	0.9	0.5	3.0	0.6	0.2	1.3	0.4
Age 18–21.5	4.3	3.4	19.4	3.6	1.1	4.7	3.0
Age 22–25.5	6.4	5.0	25.9	4.8	1.1	7.1	5.5
Age 26–29.5	4.7	4.5	17.1	4.5	0.7	7.1	5.8
Percent In School							
Age 15–17.5	86.4	81.4	82.6	80.4	78.2	85.3	85.4
Age 18–21.5	27.3	28.9	26.5	27.7	21.1	29.8	29.9
Age 22–25.5	5.2	5.4	4.6	5.3	2.8	8.3	8.3
Age 26–29.5	3.1	2.2	2.0	2.4	1.3	3.5	3.5
Percent Working							
Age 15–17.5	35.2	29.7	15.6	29.8	32.9	28.4	27.8
Age 18–21.5	66.7	66.3	37.0	66.5	77.6	63.8	64.1
Age 22–25.5	72.4	74.9	40.4	74.5	87.1	70.4	71.8
Age 26–29.5	71.1	78.7	48.7	77.9	90.1	69.8	71.1
Percent Pregnant							
Age 15–17.5	2.5	2.1	3.6	2.2	1.5	1.9	1.9
Age 18–21.5	4.4	5.3	15.4	5.4	4.7	4.7	4.8
Age 22–25.5	5.5	6.0	16.9	6.0	5.2	5.1	5.1
Age 26–29.5	5.5	5.1	10.8	5.1	4.6	4.8	4.8
Children Ever Born Before							
Age 20	0.32	0.32	0.67	0.34	0.30	0.31	0.31
Age 24	0.72	0.81	1.85	0.82	0.74	0.72	0.71
Age 28	1.26	1.25	2.76	1.27	1.14	1.13	1.13
Highest Grade Completed							
By Age 25	12.87	13.03	12.93	12.97	12.68	13.08	13.09
Blacks							
Percent Receiving Welfare							
Age 15–17.5	1.9	2.3	7.3	2.5	1.1	4.8	3.1
Age 18–21.5	16.9	16.6	42.3	17.5	8.2	15.5	12.2
Age 22–25.5	26.9	23.9	57.9	24.9	9.6	24.6	20.4
Age 26–29.5	21.6	21.6	53.0	22.1	7.1	28.0	24.3
Percent In School							
Age 15–17.5	86.3	82.0	78.8	81.6	80.6	84.2	84.6
Age 18–21.5	26.1	25.2	18.0	25.7	19.5	29.5	29.9
Age 22–25.5	6.3	6.3	3.0	6.6	3.0	8.0	8.2
Age 26–29.5	3.5	2.5	1.0	2.7	1.3	3.5	3.6
Percent Working							
Age 15–17.5	19.2	17.6	9.6	17.6	20.1	18.3	18.1
Age 18–21.5	44.1	47.9	22.5	46.4	62.3	53.8	54.9
Age 22–25.5	56.8	56.0	23.3	55.3	75.1	59.4	62.9
Age 26–29.5	61.1	62.1	27.2	61.6	80.7	57.7	61.6
Percent Pregnant							
Age 15–17.5	4.6	2.9	5.4	2.9	1.5	3.0	3.0
Age 18-21.5	6.7	5.9	21.4	5.9	5.1	6.5	6.5
Age 22–25.5	5.8	6.2	22.5	6.1	5.7	7.3	7.3
Age 26-29.5	4.2	5.0	14.4	5.0	4.9	6.6	6.6
Children Ever Born Before							
Age 20	0.53	0.39	0.96	0.40	0.34	0.47	0.47
Age 24	1.05	0.90	2.52	0.91	0.82	1.02	1.02
Age 28	1.41	1.30	3.90	1.33	1.21	1.62	1.62
Highest Grade Completed							
By Age 25	12.68	12.90	12.56	12.92	12.62	12.97	13.00

(Continued)

TABLE 6
(CONTINUED)

	Actual	MNL1 FE Baseline	MNL1 FE With Texas	MNL1 No FE Baseline	MNL1 No FE With Texas	DP Baseline	DP With Texas
				Hispanics			
Percent Receiving Welfare							
Age 15–17.5	1.3	0.6	8.7	0.6	0.1	4.4	1.7
Age 18–21.5	9.2	5.4	49.0	5.1	0.8	11.2	7.0
Age 22–25.5	15.0	10.3	57.5	8.9	1.2	15.1	10.2
Age 26–29.5	15.2	10.2	34.5	9.1	0.9	15.8	11.6
Percent In School							
Age 15–17.5	84.6	84.2	80.9	84.4	82.6	79.2	79.4
Age 18–21.5	22.0	29.2	20.5	28.8	23.3	21.4	21.6
Age 22–25.5	5.0	5.2	4.2	4.9	2.7	6.0	6.1
Age 26–29.5	2.0	2.1	1.3	2.0	1.2	2.8	2.9
Percent Working							
Age 15–17.5	22.2	20.1	8.7	20.2	24.0	26.6	26.4
Age 18-21.5	52.8	53.0	14.6	54.4	70.9	58.5	59.7
Age 22–25.5	58.7	62.2	15.6	63.8	83.6	57.8	61.2
Age 26-29.5	56.1	66.8	31.9	67.2	86.7	55.4	58.9
Percent Pregnant							
Age 15–17.5	3.2	3.8	7.6	3.8	1.5	3.2	3.1
Age 18–21.5	6.9	7.0	30.0	6.9	5.2	6.5	6.6
Age 22–25.5	6.7	7.1	30.2	7.6	6.1	7.1	7.1
Age 26–29.5	5.9	5.9	17.5	5.9	5.4	6.6	6.6
Children Ever Born Before							
Age 20	0.40	0.43	1.29	0.43	0.30	0.48	0.48
Age 24	1.00	1.00	3.35	0.96	0.78	1.03	1.02
Age 28	1.60	1.49	5.06	1.44	1.23	1.61	1.61
Highest Grade Completed							
By Age 25	12.20	12.80	12.50	12.94	12.53	12.38	12.40

Thus, the counterfactual using MNL1-FE is not, under this interpretation, identifying the effect of replacing the estimation sample states' welfare systems with
Texas' system. Recall that in performing the external validation exercise, we estimated Texas state dummies, which has the effect of rescaling the means. The
counterfactual, however, uses the state dummies obtained from the estimation
sample. Given these results, the superior performance of the MNL1-FE in forecasting Texas is an artifact of the treatment of the state dummies.

Unlike MNL1-FE, MNL1-No FE replaces not only benefit realizations but also
the mean, or permanent benefit level as well. However, the effects predicted by
MNL1-No FE appear to be implausible as well. For example, although welfare
participation among whites falls by 3.8 percentage points (from 4.5% to 0.7%)
at ages 26–29.5, employment increases by 12.2 percentage points. Indeed, for all
three race groups, the reduction in welfare participation is usually considerably
less than the increase in employment at all ages. The prediction that employment
rates would reach close to 90% (for whites) with the adoption of Texas' welfare
benefits is also not credible.

The counterfactual based on the DP model, which accounts for the entire set
of welfare parameters, replaces each of the estimation sample state's benefit

realizations as well as its evolutionary rule (6) with that of Texas' realizations and rule. The resulting effects are more modest than in the MNL1-No FE specification. The largest effects are for Hispanics, where welfare participation falls by as much as 5 percentage points (from 15.3% to 10.2%) at ages 22–22.5 and employment increases by 3 percentage points at those ages. For all races, within each age group, the increase in employment is no larger than the fall in welfare participation. In addition, for each race, mean schooling by age 25 increases, though very slightly. Overall, the results from the DP model appear more reasonable than the MNL-No FE specification.[34]

6. CONCLUSIONS

In this article, we presented and structurally estimated a dynamic programming (DP) model of life-cycle decisions of young women. The model significantly extends earlier work on female labor supply, fertility, marriage, education, and welfare participation by treating all five of these important decisions as being made jointly and sequentially within a life-cycle framework. Needless to say, the resulting model is quite complex, and many behavioral and statistical assumptions were needed to make its solution and estimation feasible. Of course, the model is literally false, as our assumptions are designed to abstract from and simplify the full complexity of how people really make life-cycle decisions. Thus, the model is simultaneously both mathematically complex, yet highly stylized as a depiction of actual behavior. Nevertheless, we believe that such models, tightly specified on the basis of very specific theoretical and statistical assumptions, are potentially quite useful for policy analysis. The issue addressed in this article is how to develop faith, or validate, that such a model is indeed useful.

To that end, we pursued a range of approaches to model validation. First, we examined the within-sample fit of the DP model across a number of dimensions of interest and compared its fit to a group of "flexible" models, specified as four alternative multinomial logits estimated on a subset of the choice data. Using a RMSE criterion (the number of parameters are similar), there seemed to be no clear winner in this cross-model competition. Based on these results, our view was that the DP model fit the data well enough to continue to consider it as potentially useful for prediction.

Second, we performed an external validation using data from a nonrandom holdout sample, specifically data from the state of Texas, which had a very different welfare policy regime from the five states that were used in estimation. In terms of the same RMSE criterion, one of the models (MNL2-No FE) produced predictions for Texas that were terribly inaccurate by any standard, leaving us with no faith in its usefulness. Further, the models with state fixed-effects (MNL1-FE, MNL2-FE) fit the data from Texas better than both the DP model and the remaining logit (MNL1-No FE), although there was no clear ranking of these latter two models.

---

[34] Effects of the counterfactual experiment for the DP model on additional variables, considered in Keane and Wolpin (2005), are predicted to be quite small. For example, by ages 26–29.5, the marriage rate is predicted to increase from 65.6% to 65.9% for whites, from 28.2% to 28.8% for blacks, and from 55.7% to 56.9% for Hispanics.

However, we were surprised that the state fixed-effect specification, which identifies the behavioral effects of only transitory changes in welfare benefits, could best predict the effect of Texas' permanently different welfare rules. This result led us to a third method of validation. We used the models to predict the effect of a policy intervention that has no analogue in the historical data, but where basic economic theory provides tight priors, in a qualitative sense, on certain aspects of what might possibly happen.

The counterfactual experiment was to give the five estimation states the same welfare rules as Texas. Our strong priors were (i) that welfare participation should drop, since the Texas benefits are less generous, and (ii) that work should increase, but that the decline in welfare places an upper bound on the increase in work. The specifications with state fixed effects violated the first, most basic, theoretical prediction that welfare participation be increasing in welfare generosity. The only reason that the state fixed-effects specification had performed better in the external validation was because, in that exercise, we had estimated Texas state dummies. Moreover, the specification without state fixed-effects, whose performance in terms of the fit to the estimation sample and to the Texas hold-out sample was satisfactory, violated the second prior. Thus, we came to view all four MNL models as unreliable for policy prediction. In contrast, the predictions of the DP model were consistent with both priors.

In summary, the DP model, in our judgment, performed well on three different tests of validity. In light of this evidence, we updated our priors about the potential usefulness of the model (for policy prediction) in a favorable direction. Our research strategy is to continue to look for opportunities to further validate the model, and as these opportunities arise they will either increase or reduce our confidence in the model's usefulness.

One opportunity is presented by the important changes in welfare rules that occurred beginning in the mid-1990s, after our sample period ended. This included EITC expansion, imposition of work requirements for receipt of benefits, and benefit receipt time limits. As discussed in Fang and Keane (2004), there was substantially heterogeneity across states in terms of how exactly these policy changes were structured, and we can use our model to simulate the impact of these changes on a state-by-state basis.[35]

As a final observation, we conjecture that most economists would have professed a greater a priori faith in the ability of the MNL models to forecast behavior than in the DP model. That is, they would be concerned that, because the many assumptions invoked in setting up the DP model could all be questioned, it is unlikely such a model could forecast accurately. In contrast, they would view the MNL models, which simply model the value of each alternative as a flexible function of the state variables, as being much less "restrictive." Thus, the poor predictions that the MNL models produced should serve as a cautionary tale, from which we draw two morals.

---

[35] Of course, this experiment provides only an imperfect validation tool because other aspects of the economic and social environment may have changed.

First, economists should be concerned with model validation regardless of the estimation approach; one needs to hold all models to the same standard. Second, our experience illustrates well the potential strengths of DP models for making policy predictions. It is precisely the economic structure of the model that constrains it to make predictions that are reasonable in a qualitative sense. The MNL models' failure is, at least in part, attributable to the fact that they lack sufficient economic structure to impose such reasonable constraints on their predictions. Economics is indeed valuable in econometrics.

REFERENCES

BAJARI, P., AND A. HORTACSU, "Are Structural Estimates from Auction Models Reasonable? Evidence from Experimental Data," *Journal of Political Economy* 113 (2005), 703–41.

BUSEMEYER, J. R., AND Y.-M. WANG, "Model Comparisons and Model Selections Based on Generalization Criterion Methodology," *Journal of Mathematical Psychology* 44 (2000), 171–89.

FANG, H., AND M. P. KEANE, "Assessing the Impact of Welfare Reform on Single Mothers," *Brookings Papers on Economic Activity* 2004 (2004), 1–116.

HECKMAN, J. J., "The Incidental Parameters Problem and the Problem of Initial Conditions in Estimating a Discrete Time-Discrete Data Stochastic Process and Some Monte Carlo Evidence," in C. F. Manski and D. McFadden, eds., *Structural Analysis of Discrete Data with Econometric Applications* (Cambridge, MA: MIT Press, 1981), 179–95.

KEANE, M. P., "Simulation Estimation for Panel Data Models with Limited Dependent Variables," in G. S. Maddala, C. R. Rao, and H. D. Vinod, eds., *Handbook of Statistics 11* (Amsterdam: Elsevier Science Publishers, 1993), 545–72.

——, "A Computationally Practical Simulation Estimator for Panel Data," *Econometrica* 62 (1994), 95–116.

——, "A New Idea for Welfare Reform," *Federal Reserve Bank of Minneapolis Quarterly Review* 19 (1995), 2–28.

——, AND R. MOFFITT, "A Structural Model of Multiple Welfare Program Participation and Labor Supply," *International Economic Review* 39 (1998), 553–90.

——, AND R. SAUER, "A Computationally Pratical Simulation Estimation Algorithm for Dynamic Panel Data Models with Unobserved Endogenous State Variables," Mimeo, Yale University, 2005.

——, AND K. I. WOLPIN, "The Solution and Estimation of Discrete Choice Dynamic Programming Models by Simulation and Interpolation: Monte Carlo Evidence," *Review of Economics and Statistics* 76 (1994), 684–72.

——, AND ——, "The Career Decisions of Young Men," *Journal of Political Economy* 105 (1997), 473–522.

——, AND ——, "Estimating Welfare Effects Consistent with Forward-Looking Behavior, Part I: Lessons From a Simulation Exercise," *Journal of Human Resources* 37 (2001a), 600–22.

——, AND ——, "The Effect of Parental Transfers and Borrowing Constraints on Educational Attainment," *International Economic Review* 42 (2001b), 1051–103.

——, AND ——, "Exploring the Usefulness of a Non-Random Holdout Sample for Model Validation: Welfare Effects on Female Behavior," Mimeo, University of Pennsylvania, 2005.

——, AND ——, "The Role of Labor and Marriage Markets, Preference Heterogeneity and the Welfare System on the Life Cycle Decisions of Black, Hispanic and White Women," Mimeo, University of Pennsylvania, 2006.

LERMAN, S. R., AND C. F. MANSKI, "On the Use of Simulated Frequencies to Approximate Choice Probabilities," in C. F. Manski and D. McFadden, eds., *Structural Analysis of Discrete Data with Econometric Applications* (Cambridge, MA: MIT Press, 1981), 305–19.

LISE, J., J. SMITH, AND S. SEITZ, "Equilibrium Policy Experiments and the Evaluation of Social Programs," Mimeo, Queens University, 2005.

LUMSDAINE, R., J. STOCK, AND D. WISE, "Three Models of Retirement: Computational Complexity vs. Predictive Validity," in D. Wise, ed., *Topics in the Economics of Aging* (Chicago: University of Chicago Press, 1992).

MCFADDEN, D., *Urban Travel Demand Forecasting Project Final Report*, Volume 5 (Berkeley: Institute of Transportation Studies, University of California, 1977).

——, "A Method of Simulated Moments for Estimation of Discrete Response Models without Numerical Integration," *Econometrica* 57 (1989), 995–1026.

MOFFITT, R., "Incentive Effects of the U.S. Welfare System: A Review," *Journal of Economic Literature* 30 (1992), 1–61.

MOSIER, C. I., "Problems and Designs of Cross-Validation," *Educational and Psychological Measurement* 11 (1951), 5–11.

SANDERS, S., "A Dynamic Model of Welfare and Work," Mimeo, Carnegie Mellon University, 1993.

SWANN, C. A., "Welfare Reform When Recipients Are Forward Looking," *Journal of Human Resources* 40 (2005), 31–56.

TODD, P., AND K. I. WOLPIN, "Assessing the Impact of a School Subsidy Program in Mexico: Using a Social Experiment to Validate a Dynamic Behavioral Model of Child Schooling and Fertility," *American Economic Review* 96 (2006), 1384–417.

WISE, D., "A Behavioral Model Versus Experimentation: The Effects of Housing Subsidies on Rent," in P. Brucker and R. Pauly, eds., *Methods of Operations Research*, Volume 50 (Berlin: Verlag Anton Hain, 1985), 441–89.

WOLPIN, K. I., "The Determinants of Black-White Differences in Early Employment Careers: Search, Layoffs, Quits and Endogenous Wage Growth," *Journal of Political Economy* 100 (1992), 535–60.

INTERNATIONAL ECONOMIC REVIEW
Vol. 48, No. 4, November 2007

COHERENCY AND COMPLETENESS OF STRUCTURAL MODELS CONTAINING A DUMMY ENDOGENOUS VARIABLE*

By Arthur Lewbel[1]

Boston College, U.S.A.

Let y be a vector of endogenous variables and let w be a vector of covariates, parameters, and errors or unobservables that together are assumed to determine y. A structural model $y = H(y, w)$ is complete and coherent if it has a well-defined reduced form, meaning that for any value of w there exists a unique value for y. Coherence and completeness simplifies identification and is required for many estimators and many model applications. Incoherency or incompleteness can arise in models with multiple decision makers, such as games, or when the decision making of individuals is either incorrectly or incompletely specified. This article provides necessary and sufficient conditions for the coherence and completeness of simultaneous equation systems where one equation is a binomial response. Examples are dummy endogenous regressor models, regime switching regressions, treatment response models, sample selection models, endogenous choice systems, and determining if a pair of binary choices are substitutes or complements.

1. INTRODUCTION

Let y be a vector of endogenous variables, and let $w \in \Omega$ be a vector of observables and unobservables that determine y. Here w could contain unknown parameters, exogenous observed covariates, and error terms. Consider a proposed structural model of the form $y = H(y, w)$. Gourieroux et al. (1980) define the model to be *coherent* if for each $w \in \Omega$ there exists a unique value for y, which we may denote by the reduced form equation $y = G(w)$, such that $G(w) = H[G(w), w]$. Heckman (1978) refers to this condition as the *principal assumption* and as *conditions for existence of the model*. Other authors who consider coherency of various model specifications include Blundell and Smith (1994) and Dagenais (1997). More recently, Tamer (2003) uses the term *coherency* to only refer to existence of a y that solves $y = H(y, w)$, and calling the model *complete* if the solution is unique. I will adopt this newer terminology. Coherency and completeness of a structural model together imply existence and uniqueness of a reduced form.

Incoherent or incomplete models with dummy endogenous regressors arise in some simultaneous games, e.g., the industry entry game of Bresnahan and Reiss

---

* Manuscript received September 2005; revised April 2006.

[1] The author wishes to thank Jim Heckman, Chuck Manski, Elie Tamer, Andrew Chesher, Richard Blundell, participants of the Festshrift for Daniel McFadden, and anonymous referees for many helpful comments. Any errors are my own. Please address correspondence to: Arthur Lewbel, Department of Economics, Boston College, 140 Commonwealth Ave., Chestnut Hill, MA 02467, USA. Phone: (781) 862-3678. E-mail: *lewbel@bc.edu*.

(1991) yields a system of two binary choice equations, each of which depends on the outcome of the other. Tamer (2003) observes that incoherency corresponds to the case where the game has no Nash equilibrium and incompleteness to the case of multiple equilibria. Aradillas-Lopez (2005) removes the incompleteness in these games by showing that a unique Nash equilibrium exists when the player's information sets are incomplete.

Incoherence can be interpreted as a form of model misspecification, since it implies that for some feasible values of w there does not exist a corresponding value of y, whereas in reality some value of y would be observed. We may think of incompleteness as a model that is not fully specified, since for some feasible values of w, the model does not deliver a corresponding unique value for y. Parameters of incoherent or incomplete models can sometimes be point identified and estimated (Tamer, 2003 provides examples), however, such models cannot be used to make predictions about y over the space of all values of w, and they cannot be used with any parameter identification scheme or estimator that depends on the existence of a well-defined reduced form. Incompleteness may often give rise to models with parameters that are set rather than point identified. See, e.g., Manski and Tamer (2002). Nevertheless, coherency and completeness are certainly desirable and commonly assumed properties of econometric models. If nothing else, it is important to know when a model may or may not be coherent or complete for estimation and interpretation of the model.

Incompleteness or incoherency can arise in models with multiple decision makers, with one example being strategically interacting players. Models of a single optimizing agent will typically be coherent though sometimes incomplete (if, e.g., the same utility or profit level can be attained in more than one way), though more general incoherency or incompleteness can arise in such models when the decision making process is either incorrectly or incompletely specified or is not characterized by optimizing behavior. Ad hoc equilibrium selection mechanisms or rules for tie breaking in optimization models can be interpreted as techniques for resolving this type of incompleteness. These are relatively harmless when incompleteness, such as ties, can only occur with probability zero. This article will be concerned with more fundamental incompleteness or incoherence, where no solutions or multiple solutions exist on a positive measure subset of relevant variables' supports.

Let $y = (y_1, y_2)$, where y_1 is a dummy endogenous variable. This article provides necessary and sufficient conditions for coherence and completeness of

(1) $$y_1 = H_1(y_1, y_2, w)$$

(2) $$y_2 = H_2(y_1, y_2, w)$$

for arbitrary functions H_1 and H_2, where H_1 can only equal zero or one. Structural models of this type are very common in econometrics. Examples include discrete endogenous regressor models, regime shift models, treatment response models, sample selection models, joint continuous-discrete demand models, and simultaneous choice models (in which both y_1 and y_2 are discrete). Heckman (1978),

Blundell and Smith (1994), and Dagenais (1997) each provide conditions required for coherence and completeness of different special cases of this class of models, whereas Gourieroux et al. (1980) analyze coherency and completeness for closely related piecewise linear models.

The system of Equations (1) and (2) is defined to be triangular, or recursive, if either H_1 does not depend on y_2 or H_2 does not depend on y_1. See, e.g., Maddala and Lee (1976). Triangular systems are generally coherent and complete if the individual equations are separately coherent and complete.

To illustrate the completeness and coherency problems in simultaneous systems, consider the simple model

$$y_1 = I(y_2 + e_1 \geq 0)$$
$$y_2 = \alpha y_1 + e_2,$$

where $w = (\alpha, e_1, e_2)$ and I is the indicator function that equals one if its argument is true and zero otherwise. These equations could be the reaction functions of two players in some game, where player one makes a discrete choice y_1 (such as whether to enter a market), and player two makes some continuous decision y_2 (such as the quantity to produce of a good). Then $y_1 = I(\alpha y_1 + e_1 + e_2 \geq 0)$ so $y_1 = 0$, $y_2 = e_2$ if $0 = I(e_1 + e_2 \geq 0)$, that is, $e_1 + e_2 < 0$, and $y_1 = 1$, $y_2 = a + e_2$ if $1 = I(\alpha + e_1 + e_2 \geq 0)$, meaning $\alpha + e_1 + e_2 \geq 0$. Therefore, the model implies both $y_1 = 0$ and $y_1 = 1$, and so is incomplete, if $-a \leq e_1 + e_2 < 0$. Neither $y_1 = 0$ nor $y_1 = 1$ satisfies the model if $0 \leq e_1 + e_2 < -a$, so in that region the model is incoherent. This model is both coherent and complete only if $a = 0$ or if $e_1 + e_2$ is constrained to not lie between zero and $-a$.

The next section provides general characterizations of conditions for completeness and coherence. This is then followed by examples including endogenous selection and treatment models, dummy endogenous regressor models, and regime switching models. Next, simultaneous systems of binary choice equations are considered in depth. For these models completeness and coherency are obtained both by applying the general characterization theorems and by replacing the simultaneous system with a model of optimizing behavior, and examples of likelihood functions for such models are provided. Application of these models for determining if a pair of binary choices are substitutes or complements is described.

2. NECESSARY AND SUFFICIENT CONDITIONS FOR COHERENCE AND COMPLETENESS

THEOREM 1. *Assume* $y_1 \in \{0, 1\}$, $y_2 \in \Psi$, *and* $w \in \Omega$ *for some support sets* Ψ *and* Ω. *The system of Equations (1) and (2) is coherent and complete if and only if there exists a function* $g : \{0, 1\} \times \Omega \to \Psi$ *such that, for all* $w \in \Omega$, *the following equations hold*

(3) $$H_1[1, g(1, w), w] = H_1[0, g(0, w), w]$$

(4) $$y_2 = g(y_1, w).$$

Theorem 1 demonstrates the severity of the completeness and coherency conditions with a dummy endogenous variable. Equation (3) shows that, after substituting out y_2 into the equation for y_1, the right side of the resulting expression must be independent of y_1.

As an example, consider the general selection model in which y_1 indexes whether y_2 is observed.

COROLLARY 1. *The general endogenous selection model*

$$y_1 = R(y_2, w)$$
$$y_2 = r(w)y_1$$

is coherent and complete if and only if R is independent of y_2.

Corollary 1 illustrates the strength of Theorem 1, by showing that no complete, coherent selection model can be endogenous, where endogeneity is defined as having the selection criterion y_1 depend on the observed outcome y_2. Note, however, that completeness is possible using some other notion of endogeneity, such as having y_1 depend on the latent outcome $r(w)$.

Next consider a typical binary choice specification for y_1, with a latent additive error. Replace Equation (1) with

(5) $$y_1 = I[h(y_1, y_2, w) + e_1 \geq 0]$$

for some function h, where $e_1 \in w$. If Equation (4) holds, define functions s_0 and s_1 by

$$s_0(w) = h[0, g(0, w), w]$$
$$s_1(w) = h[1, g(1, w), w].$$

THEOREM 2. *The system of Equations (5) and (2) is coherent and complete if and only if there exists a function g such that Equation (4) holds and, for every $w \in \Omega$, either $s_0(w) = s_1(w)$ or e_1 does not lie in the interval bounded by $-s_0(w)$ and $-s_1(w)$. The equality $s_0(w) = s_1(w)$ holds if and only if there exists a function f such that*

(6) $$y_1 = I[f[y_2 + [g(0, w) - g(1, w)]y_1, w] + e_1 \geq 0]$$

Alternatively, $s_0(w) = s_1(w)$ holds if and only if there exists a function ϕ and a dummy function d that only takes on the values zero and one, such that

(7) $$y_1 = I[\phi[(1 - d(w))y_2, w] + e_1 \geq 0]$$

(8) $$y_2 = g[d(w)y_1, w]$$

Theorem 2 shows there are only two methods to obtain coherence and completeness in the presence of a binary choice equation. One method is to restrict the support of the errors to rule out regions of incoherency or incompleteness. Dagenais (1997) is a special case of this method. It is, however, difficult to motivate such data-dependent restrictions on the values that the error can take on.

The only other way to obtain coherence is to restrict attention to the class of models that can be represented by Equations (4) and (6) or equivalently by (7) and (8). The usefulness of one of these representations over the other will depend on context, e.g., taking f to be linear in (6) yields a different coherent system than taking ϕ to be linear in (7). The next section provides examples.

Theorem 2 shows that, unless one peculiarly restricts the support e_1, by Equations (7) and (8) completeness requires a model that is equivalent to a triangular system, though the direction of dependence (whether y_1 depends on y_2 or y_2 depends on y_1), which is indexed by the binary dummy variable $d(w)$, may vary across observations. It is perhaps surprising that the simple introduction of d to generalize triangular systems has not been proposed before. In contrast, the representation given by Equations (4) and (6) can be interpreted as the nonlinear generalization of Blundell and Smith (1994).

Equations (7) and (8) readily extend to provide coherent, complete specifications for endogenous y having any support. The system

$$y_1 = g_1[(1 - d(w))y_2, w]$$
$$y_2 = g_2[d(w)y_1, w]$$

is coherent for any functions g_1 and g_2, since it has the well-defined reduced form

$$y_1 = g_1[(1 - d(w))g_2(0, w), w]$$
$$y_2 = g_2[d(w)g_1(0, w), w].$$

3. EXAMPLES

Let $d = d(w)$ be a dummy variable that only takes the values zero and one. Here d can either be observed or it can be a known function of errors, covariates, and parameters. Let x be a vector of regressors, which can include both d and a constant term. For integers j let each e_j be an unobserved error that may have conditional support equal to the real line, let each β_j be a parameter vector, and let each α_j and γ_j be scalar parameters.

3.1. Nonparametric Dummy Endogenous Regressor and Treatment Models.
Consider a model of y_2 where y_1 is a dummy endogenous regressor. For some functions G_1 and G_2 let

$$y_1 = G_1(y_2, x, e_1)$$
$$y_2 = G_2(y_1, x) + e_2,$$

where e_1 is independent of x and $E(e_2 \mid x) = 0$. Das (2004) proposes a nonparametric estimator for the function G_2, leaving G_1 unspecified. The function G_2 can be interpreted as the conditional average outcome of an endogenous treatment y_1.

Theorem 1 shows that coherency and completeness of this model requires that $G_1[G_2(y_1, x) + e_2, x, e_1]$ be independent of y_1. Analogous to Equation (6), a complete, coherent alternative model is

$$y_1 = G_1[y_2 + [G_2(0, x) - G_2(1, x)]y_1, x, e_1]$$
$$y_2 = G_2(y_1, x) + e_2,$$

which would permit application of the Das estimator to G_2.

Another complete coherent alternative is

$$y_1 = G_1[(1 - d)y_2, x, e_1)$$
$$y_2 = G_2(dy_1, x) + e_2,$$

which for $d = 1$ equals a standard treatment effects specification.

3.2. *Linear Dummy Endogenous Regressor Models.*   Consider the linear dummy endogenous regressor system

$$y_1 = I[x'\beta_1 + y_2\alpha_1 + e_1 \geq 0]$$
$$y_2 = x'\beta_2 + y_1\alpha_2 + e_2.$$

Without restricting the support of the errors, Heckman (1978) found that coherency and completeness of this model requires either $\alpha_1 = 0$ or $\alpha_2 = 0$, which are triangular systems. A recent semiparametric estimator for this model is Klein and Vella (2001). Blundell and Smith (1994) proposed the generalization

$$y_1 = I[x'\beta_1 + y_2\alpha_1 + y_1\gamma_1 + e_1 \geq 0]$$
$$y_2 = x'\beta_2 + y_1\alpha_2 + e_2,$$

which they found to be complete and coherent if $\gamma_1 = -\alpha_1\alpha_2$. This model equals the special case of Equations (4) and (6) in which the functions f and g are linear.

A new complete coherent system may be obtained by taking the functions ϕ and g in Equations (7) and (8) to be linear. This yields the model

$$y_1 = I[x'\beta_1 + (1 - d)y_2\alpha_1 + e_1 \geq 0]$$
$$y_2 = x'\beta_2 + dy_1\alpha_2 + e_2,$$

which is complete and coherent without restriction on the coefficients. We could also add $y_2\alpha_3 + dy_1\gamma_1$ to the latent variable determining y_1 and maintain completeness by imposing $\gamma_1 = -\alpha_2\alpha_3$.

3.3. *Endogenous Regime Switching Models.*   The linear regime switching regression specification

$$y_1 = I[x'\beta_1 + y_2\alpha_1 + e_1 \geq 0]$$
$$y_2 = x'\beta_2 + e_2 + (x'\beta_3 + e_3)y_1$$

will not be coherent except under severe restrictions such as $\alpha_1 = 0$. Paralleling the previous section, Theorem 2 suggests two alternatives. One is

$$y_1 = I[(x'\beta_1 + y_2\alpha_1 + y_1x'\beta_4 + e_4 \geq 0]$$
$$y_2 = x'\beta_2 + e_2 + (x'\beta_3 + e_3)y_1,$$

which is coherent and complete if $\beta_4 = -\alpha_1\beta_3$ and $e_4 = -\alpha_1 y_1 e_3 + e_1$ for some e_1. Another is

$$y_1 = I[x'\beta_1 + (1 - d)y_2\alpha_1 + e_1 \geq 0]$$
$$y_2 = x'\beta_2 + e_2 + (x'\beta_3 + e_3)dy_1,$$

(where d is again a binary dummy variable), which is coherent and complete without restrictions on the coefficients.

4.   SIMULTANEOUS SYSTEMS OF BINARY CHOICES

Consider the simultaneous system of binomial responses

$$y_1 = I[h_1(y_1, y_2, w) + e_1 \geq 0]$$
$$y_2 = I[h_2(y_1, y_2, w) + e_2 \geq 0].$$

A practical application of models like this is to determine whether interrelated binary choices are substitutes or complements, e.g., finding out if selecting $y_1 = 1$ increases or decreases the probability of choosing $y_2 = 1$. Dagenais (1997) obtains coherence and completeness in this model by imposing linearity on h_1 and h_2 and restricting the support of (e_1, e_2) to rule out regions of values that result in either no solutions or multiple solutions for y_1 and y_2.

Based on Theorem 2, a coherent and complete simultaneous system of binary choices that does not restrict the error supports is

$$y_1 = I[f_1[y_2 - r(w)y_1, w] + e_1 \geq 0]$$
$$y_2 = I[f_2(y_1, w) + e_2 \geq 0]$$

for arbitrary choices of the functions f_1 and f_2, where the function r is defined by

$$r(w) = I[f_2(1, w) + e_2 \geq 0] - I[f_2(0, w) + e_2 \geq 0].$$

Alternatively, Equations (7) and (8) in Theorem 2 suggest a simpler, more symmetric system

$$y_1 = I[\phi_1[(1 - d)y_2, w] + e_1 \geq 0]$$
$$y_2 = I[\phi_2[dy_1, w] + e_2 \geq 0],$$

which will be coherent and complete for any choice of the functions ϕ_1, ϕ_2, and binary dummy d. In particular, a nearly linear complete system of binary choice equations is

(9) $$y_1 = I[x'\beta_1 + (1 - d)y_2\alpha_1 + e_1 \geq 0]$$

(10) $$y_2 = I[x'\beta_2 + dy_1\alpha_2 + e_2 \geq 0],$$

which can be readily estimated with, e.g., jointly normal errors. Here d may be included in the list of regressors x. An example of d is to let $d = 1$ for individuals that make decision y_1 first, otherwise let $d = 0$.

Given a completely specified model, estimation can proceed using maximum likelihood by parameterizing the error distributions and evaluating the probability or density of each value the endogenous variables can take on. For example, in the model of Equations (9) and (10), the probability that $y_1 = 1$ and $y_2 = 1$ is the probability that $x'\beta_1 + (1 - d)\alpha_1 + e_1 \geq 0$ and $x'\beta_2 + d\alpha_2 + e_2 \geq 0$, and the probability that $y_1 = 0$ and $y_2 = 1$ is the probability that $x'\beta_1 + (1 - d)\alpha_1 + e_1 < 0$ and $x'\beta_2 + e_2 \geq 0$ (note the absence of $d\alpha_2$ in this last equation, because $y_1 = 0$). Let $f(e_1, e_2, \lambda)$ denote the joint probability density functions of e_1 and e_2, parameterized by a vector λ, assumed independent of x. Then, conditioning on x, the probability of choosing $y_1 = 1$ and $y_2 = 1$ is

$$P_{11}(\theta \mid x) = \int_{-x'\beta_2 - d\alpha_2}^{\infty} \left(\int_{-x'\beta_1 - (1-d)\alpha_1}^{\infty} f(e_1, e_2, \lambda) \, de_1 \right) de_2,$$

where θ denotes the set of parameters $\beta_1, \beta_2, \alpha_1, \alpha_2, \lambda$. Similarly, the probabilities of choosing other values for y, denoted P_{y_1, y_2}, are

$$P_{01}(\theta \mid x) = \int_{-x'\beta_2}^{\infty} \left(\int_{-\infty}^{-x'\beta_1 - (1-d)\alpha_1} f(e_1, e_2, \lambda) \, de_1 \right) de_2$$

$$P_{10}(\theta \mid x) = \int_{-\infty}^{-x'\beta_2 - d\alpha_2} \left(\int_{-x'\beta_1}^{\infty} f(e_1, e_2, \lambda) \, de_1 \right) de_2$$

$$P_{00}(\theta \mid x) = \int_{-\infty}^{-x'\beta_2} \left(\int_{-\infty}^{-x'\beta_1} f(e_1, e_2, \lambda) \, de_1 \right) de_2.$$

If e_1 and e_2 are independent standard normals, then these expression simplify to

$$P_{11}(\theta \mid x) = [1 - \Phi(-x'\beta_1 - (1-d)\alpha_1)][1 - \Phi(-x'\beta_2 - d\alpha_2)]$$
$$P_{01}(\theta \mid x) = \Phi(-x'\beta_1 - (1-d)\alpha_1)[1 - \Phi(-x'\beta_2)]$$
$$P_{10}(\theta \mid x) = [1 - \Phi(-x'\beta_1)]\Phi(-x'\beta_2 - d\alpha_2)$$
$$P_{00}(\theta \mid x) = \Phi(-x'\beta_2)\Phi(-x'\beta_1).$$

Using either expression for the P functions, assuming n draws with independent errors, the log likelihood function for this model is then

$$\sum_{i=1}^{n} y_{1i} y_{2i} \ln P_{11}(\theta \mid x_i) + (1 - y_{1i}) y_{2i} \ln P_{01}(\theta \mid x_i)$$

$$+ y_{1i}(1 - y_{2i}) \ln P_{10}(\theta \mid x_i) + (1 - y_{1i})(1 - y_{2i}) \ln P_{00}(\theta \mid x_i),$$

which may be maximized with respect to θ to yield estimates of $\beta_1, \beta_2, a_1, a_2$.

If the temporal order of the decisions is not observed, one might let $d = I(|x'\beta_1 + e_1| > |x'\beta_2 + e_2|)$, so the choice that an individual feels most strongly about (as evidenced by the magnitude of the latent variable) is the decision that is made first. In this case estimation might be facilitated by using simulated moments as in McFadden (1989), though this would also introduce the difficulty of a nondifferentiable objective function.

4.1. Binary Choice Systems Based on Maximizing Behavior.

Many of the example models provided so far are somewhat ad hoc, that is, they apply Theorems 1 or 2 to obtain coherency and completeness, but no underlying economic argument is provided to motivate the resulting models. One set of economically rationalizable models arising from Theorem 2 is those that use the dummy regressor d, which can be motivated as a model of sequential decision making, with d being the indicator of which decision an individual makes first, or which player in a sequential game moves first. This generalizes the usual triangular systems that are known to be coherent and complete, by permitting the direction of triangularity to vary across individuals.

In some applications, incompleteness may be eliminated by more fully modeling the behavior of agents, e.g., incompleteness resulting from games having multiple equilibria may be resolved by modeling how agents choose among the equilibria.

Consider an individual who makes two simultaneous binary decisions. The naive model in which each decision depends upon the other as a regressor,

(11) $$y_1 = I[x'\beta_1 + y_2\alpha_1 + e_1 \geq 0]$$

(12) $$y_2 = I[x'\beta_2 + y_1\alpha_2 + e_2 \geq 0],$$

is incoherent and incomplete without some restrictions on the parameters, the supports of the errors, or both. One way to resolve both incoherency and incompleteness is by sequential decision making, using Equations (9) and (10).

Another possibility is to avoid incoherence by restricting the parameters and augmenting the model to resolve incompleteness. For example, suppose the individual acts as if this were a game, choosing a Nash equilibrium that allows for randomness (essentially, flipping weighted coins to construct mixed strategies). If $\alpha_1\alpha_2 \leq 0$, then a unique mixed strategy equilibrium exists, resulting in a coherent and complete model. In this case the coin tosses and Nash behavior complete an otherwise incomplete model. See Bresnahan and Reiss (1991), Tamer (2003), and Aradillas-Lopez (2005) for a more detailed analysis of treating (11) and (12) as a two-person game.

Yet another way to avoid incoherence and incompleteness is to consider a random utility model, as in McFadden (1973). Equation (11) arises from assuming that the difference in utility U_1 between choosing $y_1 = 1$ versus $y_1 = 0$ is $x'\beta_1 + y_2\alpha_1 + e_1$, and so the individual chooses y_1 to maximize U_1. Similarly, the individual chooses y_2 using Equation (12) to maximize the utility U_2 associated with that decision. To eliminate incoherency and incompleteness, we may assume the consumer chooses both y_1 and y_2 to maximize an overall utility function $U(U_1, U_2)$ that depends upon the utilities associated with each choice. Equivalently, if y_1 and y_2 are the actions of two players in a game, this would correspond to removing incoherency and incompleteness by collusion.

Generally, maximizing $U(U_1, U_2)$ results in the structure of a multinomial choice problem, maximizing the overall utility associated with each of the four values that $y = (y_1, y_2)$ can take on. However, specific forms for $U(U_1, U_2)$ will give rise to restricted versions of this model. Suppose

(13) $$U(U_1, U_2) = U_1 + U_2,$$

where

(14) $$U_1 = (x'\beta_1 + y_2\alpha_1 + e_1)y_1$$

(15) $$U_2 = (x'\beta_2 + y_1\alpha_2 + e_2)y_2.$$

For example, if the individual is a firm, $x'\beta_1 + y_2\alpha_1 + e_1$ could be the difference in profit resulting from choosing $y_1 = 1$ versus $y_1 = 0$ holding y_2 fixed, and similarly $x'\beta_2 + y_1\alpha_2 + e_2$ could be the difference in profit resulting from choosing $y_2 = 1$ versus $y_2 = 0$ holding y_1 fixed. Then profit is maximized by choosing the value of

$y = (y_1, y_2)$ that maximizes $U_1 + U_2$ with U_1 and U_2 given by Equations (14) and (15).

This model has the feature that, conditioning on y_2, the utility maximizing choice for y_1 is given by Equation (11), and that conditioning on y_1, the utility maximizing choice for y_2 is given by Equation (12). This model is therefore consistent with the logic that gives rise to ordinary binary choice models such as probit or logit for each of the choices considered separately, while avoiding the incoherency or incompleteness of Equations (11) and (12) as a system. The potential incoherency or incompleteness is eliminated by simultaneously considering the utilities of both choices. Letting $a = a_1 + a_2$, and letting $V(y)$ denote the utility associated with choice y, the result is

$$V(0, 0) = 0$$
$$V(1, 0) = x'\beta_1 + e_1$$
$$V(0, 1) = x'\beta_2 + e_2$$
$$V(1, 1) = x'(\beta_1 + \beta_2) + a + e_1 + e_2,$$

where one chooses whichever value of y yields the maximum of these four values of V. This is a special case of ordinary multinomial choice where the utility associated with the last value y is $x'(\beta_1 + \beta_2) + a + e_1 + e_2$, instead of $x'\beta_3 + e_3$.

The above model is coherent and complete (or more formally only has a harmless, probability zero chance of incompleteness) as long as e_1 and e_2 are continuously distributed, which ensures that ties in utility, which make the choice of y indeterminate, happen with probability zero.

Let $f(e_1, e_2, \lambda)$ denote the joint probability density functions of e_1 and e_2, parameterized by a vector λ, assumed independent of x. For example, if e_1 and e_2 are independent normals, then $f(e_1, e_2, \lambda) = \phi\,(e_1/\sigma_1)\phi\,(e_2/\sigma_2)/(\sigma_1\sigma_2)$ where $\lambda = (\sigma_1, \sigma_2)$ and ϕ is the standard normal probability density function. Conditioning on x, the probability of choosing $y = (1, 1)$ is the probability that $V(1, 1)$ is larger than the other values of V, which is

$$P_{11}(\theta \mid x) = \int_{-x'\beta_2-a}^{\infty} \left(\int_{\max[-x'\beta_1-a,\,-x'(\beta_1+\beta_2)-a-e_2]}^{\infty} f(e_1, e_2)\,de_1 \right) de_2,$$

where θ denotes the set of parameters $\beta_1, \beta_2, a, \lambda$. Similarly, the probabilities of choosing other values for y, denoted P_{y_1, y_2}, are

$$P_{01}(\theta \mid x) = \int_{-\infty}^{-x'\beta_2} \left(\int_{-\infty}^{\min(-x'\beta_1-a,\,x'(\beta_2-\beta_1)+e_2)} f(e_1, e_2)\,de_1 \right) de_2$$

$$P_{10}(\theta \mid x) = \int_{-\infty}^{-x'\beta_2-a} \left(\int_{\max[-x'\beta_1, x'(\beta_2-\beta_1)+e_2]}^{\infty} f(e_1, e_2)\, de_1 \right) de_2$$

$$P_{00}(\theta \mid x) = \int_{-\infty}^{-x'\beta_2} \left(\int_{-\infty}^{\min(-x'\beta_1, -x'(\beta_1+\beta_2)-a-e_2)} f(e_1, e_2)\, de_1 \right) de_2.$$

Assuming n draws with independent errors, the log likelihood function for this model is then, as before,

$$\sum_{i=1}^{n} y_{1i} y_{2i} \ln P_{11}(\theta \mid x_i) + (1 - y_{1i}) y_{2i} \ln P_{01}(\theta \mid x_i)$$

$$+ y_{1i}(1 - y_{2i}) \ln P_{10}(\theta \mid x_i) + (1 - y_{1i})(1 - y_{2i}) \ln P_{00}(\theta \mid x_i).$$

4.2. *Are Binary Choices Substitutes or Complements?*   Does engaging in one risky behavior like speeding or smoking make one more or less likely to engage in other risky behaviors like not wearing seat belts or gambling? Does adopting a poison pill make firms more or less likely to adopt other antitakeover measures? Let y_1 and y_2 denote two binary choices, such as the decision to smoke and the decision to drink, respectively. If we wanted to know whether drinking makes one more or less likely to smoke, then a standard model is Equation (11), where $\alpha_1 > 0$, means that drinking increases the probability of smoking, making it a complement; otherwise it is a substitute. Similarly, the sign of α_2 in Equation (12) would show whether smoking increases or decreases the probability of drinking, but both equations together can be incoherent.

One complete, coherent solution is to estimate the system of Equations (9) and (10). In this model the signs of α_1 and α_2 still indicate whether each choice is a substitute or a complement for the other. They can have opposite signs, e.g., if $\alpha_1 > 0$ and $\alpha_2 < 0$, then individuals that decide y_1 first, or more generally have $d = 1$, view the choices as substitutes, whereas for individuals that have $d = 0$, the choices are complements.

Another complete, coherent solution, one that does not require ordering the decisions, is Equations (13)–(15) described in the previous section. In that model a_1 and a_2 are not separately identified, since the chosen outcome only depends on their sum a. If a_1 and a_2 are known to have the same sign, then identification of a tells whether the choices are substitutes or complements. Even if a_1 and a_2 have opposite signs, it is still reasonable to say that the choices are complements if the sum a is positive and substitutes if a is negative, because having $a > 0$ in this model increases the utility of (and hence the probability of choosing) $y_1 = y_2 = 1$, relative to other choices

5. CONCLUSIONS

Necessary and sufficient conditions for coherency and completeness of simultaneous systems containing a binary choice equation were provided. One interpretation of the results is that coherency and completeness usually requires the model to be triangular or recursive, similar to Heckman's (1978) linear model result,

except that nonlinearity permits the direction of causality to vary across observations. Alternatively, coherency and completeness can be obtained by nesting
the behavioral models that generate each equation separately into a single larger
behavioral model that determines both.

APPENDIX

PROOF OF THEOREM 1.   Assume first that the system is coherent and complete.
Suppose for a given w that $y_1 = 1$. Then for that w the equation $y_2 = H_2(1, y_2, w)$ must be complete, which requires the existence of a uniquely valued function
g_{21} such that $g_{21}(w) = H_2[1, g_{21}(w), w]$. Similarly, if for the given w we have
$y_1 = 0$, then there exists g_{20} such that $g_{20}(w) = H_2[0, g_{20}(w), w]$. We may then
define the function g in Equation (4) by $g(y_1, w) = g_{20}(w)(1 - y_1) + g_{21}(w)y_1$.
Substituting (4) into (1) gives $y_1 = H_1[y_1, g(y_1, w), w]$. Let $I_1(w) = H_1[1, g(1, w), w]$ and $I_0(w) = H_1[0, g(0, w), w]$. If $I_1(w) = 1$ and $I_0(w) = 0$, then Equation (1)
is satisfied for both $y_1 = 1$ and $y_1 = 0$, which contradicts completeness. If $I_1(w) = 0$ and $I_0(w) = 1$, then Equation (1) is not satisfied by either $y_1 = 1$ or $y_1 = 0$,
which also contradicts coherence. We therefore require $I_1(w) = I_0(w)$, which is
Equation (3). It has now been shown that completeness and coherency implies (3)
and (4). To show the converse, we have that given (3) and (4) the reduced form
model is given by $y_1 = I_1(w) = I_0(w)$ and $y_2 = g[I_1(w), w]$. It can then be verified
by the definitions of I_1, I_0, and g that this reduced form defines unique values for
y_1 and y_2 that satisfy Equations (1) and (2).   ∎

PROOF OF COROLLARY 1.   Applying Equation (3) in Theorem 1 shows that completeness requires $R[r(w), w] = R(0, w)$, and hence that $R(y_2, w) = R(0, w)$ for
every value y_2 may take on.   ∎

PROOF OF THEOREM 2.   Applying Theorem 1 implies completeness of (2) and
(5) if and only if (4) holds and $I[s_0(w) + e_1 \geq 0] = I[s_1(w) + e_1 \geq 0]$. If $s_0(w) \neq s_1(w)$, then this completeness requirement will be violated if and only if e_1 equals
the negative of any value between $s_0(w)$ and $s_1(w)$.
   Now consider $s_0(w) = s_1(w)$. Define the functions r and $\tilde{f}$ by $r(w) = g(1, w) - g(0, w)$ and $\tilde{f}[\psi_1, \psi_2 - r(w)\psi_1, w] = h(\psi_1, \psi_2, w)$. Given Equations (3) and (4),
we have that $s_0(w) = s_1(w)$ implies $\tilde{f}[0, g(0, w), w] = \tilde{f}[1, g(0, w), w]$, so we may
define the function f by $f[\psi_2 - r(w)\psi_1, w] = \tilde{f}[0, \psi_2 - r(w)\psi_1, w]$. This shows
that completeness implies existence of a function f satisfying Equation (6). To
show the converse, observe that for any functions f and g, the system (4) and (6)
has the reduced form $y_1 = I[f[g(0, w), w] + e_1 \geq 0]$ and $y_2 = g[I[f[g(0, w), w] + e_1 \geq 0], w]$.
   Next, starting from Equations (4) and (6) let $d(w) = I[r(w) \neq 0]$, and $\phi[\psi, w] = f[\psi + d(w)g(0, w), w]$. With these definitions, the equivalence of (4) with (8)
follows from both being equivalent to $y_2 = g(0, w) + r(w)y_1$. For the equivalence
of (6) with (7) observe that $y_2 - r(w)y_1 = [1 - d(w)]y_2 + d(w)[y_2 - r(w)y_1]$
$= [1 - d(w)]y_2 + d(w)g(0, w)$. Substituting this expression for $y_2 - r(w)y_1$ into
Equation (6) gives Equation (7). It has now been shown that given completeness,

and hence an f and g, we may construct corresponding functions ϕ and d. To show the converse, observe that the system (7) and (8) has the reduced form $y_1 = I[\phi[(1 - d(w))g(0, w), w] + e_1 \geq 0]$ and $y_2 = g[d(w)I[\phi[(1 - d(w))g(0, w), w] + e_1 \geq 0], w]$. ∎

REFERENCES

ARADILLAS-LOPEZ, A., "Semiparametric Estimation of a Simultaneous Game with Incomplete Information," Unpublished manuscript, 2005.

BLUNDELL, R., AND R. J. SMITH, "Coherency and Estimation in Simultaneous Models with Censored or Qualitative Dependent Variables," *Journal of Econometrics* 64 (1994), 355–73.

BRESNAHAN, T. F., AND P. C. REISS, "Empirical Models of Discrete Games," *Journal of Econometrics* 48 (1991), 57–81.

DAGENAIS, M., "A Simultaneous Probit Model," Unpublished manuscript, 1997.

DAS, M., "Instrumental Variables Estimators of Nonparametric Models with Discrete Endogenous Regressors," *Journal of Econometrics* 124 (2004), 335–61.

GOURIEROUX, C., J. J. LAFFONT, AND A. MONFORT, "Coherency Conditions in Simultaneous Linear Equations Models with Endogenous Switching Regimes," *Econometrica* 48 (1980), 675–95.

HECKMAN, J. J., "Dummy Endogenous Variables in Simultaneous Equation Systems," *Econometrica* 46 (1978), 931–60.

KLEIN, R., AND F. VELLA, "The Semiparametric Binary Treatment Model under Heteroscedasticity," Unpublished manuscript, 2001.

MADDALA, G. S., AND L.-F. LEE, "Recursive Models with Qualitative Endogenous Variables," *Annals of Economic and Social Measurement* 5 (1976), 525–45.

MANSKI, C. F., AND E. TAMER, "Inference on Regressions with Interval Data on a Regressor or Outcome," *Econometrica* 70 (2002), 519–46.

McFADDEN, D. L., "Conditional Logit Analysis of Qualitative Choice Behavior," in P. Zarembka, ed., *Frontiers in Econometrics* (New York: Academic Press, 1973).

——, "A Method of Simulated Moments for Estimation of Discrete Response Models without Numerical Integration," *Econometrica* 57 (1989), 995–1026.

TAMER, E., "Incomplete Simultaneous Discrete Response Model with Multiple Equilibria," *Review of Economics Studies* 70 (2003), 147–65.

INTERNATIONAL ECONOMIC REVIEW
Vol. 48, No. 4, November 2007

PARTIAL IDENTIFICATION OF COUNTERFACTUAL CHOICE PROBABILITIES*

By Charles F. Manski[1]

Northwestern University, U.S.A.

This article shows how to predict counterfactual discrete choice behavior when the presumed behavioral model partially identifies choice probabilities. The simple, general approach uses observable choice probabilities to partially infer the distribution of types in the population and then applies the results to predict behavior in unrealized choice settings. Two illustrative applications are given. One assumes only that persons have strict preferences. The other assumes strict preferences and utility functions that are linear in attribute bundles, with no restrictions on the shape of the distribution of preference parameters.

1. INTRODUCTION

From the early 1970s on, applied economists have used parametric random utility models (RUMs) to interpret observed discrete-choice behavior and to predict the choices that persons would make in counterfactual choice settings. McFadden (1974) initiated what has become the standard econometric implementation of discrete choice analysis. One poses an RUM that characterizes alternatives as attribute bundles and that specifies the population distribution of preferences over attribute bundles up to a point-identified parameter vector. One uses data on observed choices to estimate the parameters of the preference distribution. One then applies the estimated RUM to infer the choice probabilities that would occur in counterfactual settings of interest.

McFadden originally embodied this vision of discrete choice analysis in the remarkably tractable conditional logit model, which has remained prominent in applications through the present day. The severe preference assumptions of the logit model were apparent from the outset, and econometricians have mainly responded by studying more flexible parametric RUMs that point-identify counterfactual choice probabilities. Advances in computing technology and development of new estimation methods have steadily expanded the menu of tractable models. Thus, we now have multinomial probit models (e.g., Daganzo et al., 1977; Hausman and Wise, 1978; Lerman and Manski, 1981; Berry et al., 1994), nested logit and

* Manuscript received September 2005.

[1] This research was supported in part by National Science Foundation grant SES-0549544. I am grateful to Ben Handel for able research assistance and to Guido Imbens and Alex Tetenov for comments. I have benefitted from the opportunity to present this work in seminars at the California Institute of Technology, Northwestern University, the Tinbergen Institute, and University College London. Please address correspondence to: Charles F. Manski, Department of Economics, Northwestern University, 2001 Sheridan Road, Evanston, IL 60208-2600, U.S.A. Phone: 847-491-8223. Fax: 847-491-7001. E-mail: *cfmanski@northwestern.edu*.

generalized extreme value models (McFadden, 1978, 1981), and mixed logit models (McFadden and Train, 2000). A separate stream of research has studied semiparametric and nonparametric RUMs that point-identify choice probabilities when the population is observed to face a sufficiently rich variety of choice sets. See, for example, Cosslett (1983) and Matzkin (1992).

However hard econometricians may work to develop new specifications for RUMs, strong predictive power inevitably requires strong assumptions. And there is no escaping what I have called *the Law of Decreasing Credibility*: The credibility of inference decreases with the strength of the assumptions maintained (Manski, 2003). Researchers concerned with the credibility of discrete choice analysis need to understand the tension between predictive power and strength of assumptions. And they should be willing, to some degree, to give up predictive power in return for enhanced credibility. These considerations lead naturally to the study of behavioral models that partially identify counterfactual choice probabilities, the subject of this article.

In the econometric literature on discrete choice analysis, the closest precedent for methodological research of the type to be presented here is my own early investigation of a semiparametric RUM that reveals the ordering of choice probabilities across alternatives, but not their magnitudes (Manski, 1975, 1988). Although the associated body of work on maximum score estimation mainly studies point-identification and estimation of the parametric part of these models, Manski (1988, Section 3) considered counterfactual prediction in binary choice settings and did not presume that the parametric part of the model is point identified. Less direct precedents, but still relevant, are some recent papers that study partial identification of RUM parameters in certain observational settings; see Manski and Tamer (2002), Honoré and Tamer (2006), and Magnac and Maurin (2007). These papers do not study counterfactual prediction, but their findings can be applied to that purpose.

A distinct precedent is a body of research on RUMs stemming from Marschak (1960). Marschak asked what restrictions on binary choice probabilities are implied by the elementary RUM assumptions that persons behave rationally and have strict preference orderings over alternatives. Considering a setting with a universe of three alternatives, say (c, d, e), Marschak showed that the three binary-preference probabilities $P(c \succ d), P(d \succ e)$, and $P(c \succ e)$ satisfy the *triangular condition* $P(c \succ e) \leq P(c \succ d) + P(d \succ e)$. He proposed use of this inequality to test the hypothesis that the population obeys an RUM with strict preferences. Marschak did not study counterfactual prediction, but his finding can be applied to that purpose. I explain how in Section 3.2.

The contribution of this article is achieved by first going back to basics and then moving forward to develop a simple new approach to counterfactual prediction. To go back to basics, Section 2 frames prediction of choice behavior as a problem of predicting treatment response, the treatment being a choice set and the response being the chosen alternative. The language and notation of analysis of treatment response make clear how choice data, assumptions about the process generating observed choice sets, and behavioral models combine to enable counterfactual prediction.

The new approach to prediction is presented in Section 3. I consider situations with a finite universe of alternatives. In these situations, there exists a finite set of logically possible *types*, each type having a distinct choice function. Behavioral models and choice data place restrictions on the distribution of types within the population. These restrictions enable partial prediction of population behavior in counterfactual settings. I show that when a behavioral model places linear equality or inequality restrictions on the distribution of types, the identification region for a counterfactual choice probability is an interval whose lower and upper bounds solve two linear programming problems.

Aside from the finiteness of the universe of alternatives, the prediction approach is entirely general. I present two illustrative cases. In the first, the behavioral model assumes that all members of the population have strict preference orderings over the universe of alternatives. This is the setup in Marschak (1960) and I re-derive his triangular condition. In the second case, the behavioral model characterizes alternatives as attribute bundles and assumes that each member of the population has a utility function that is linear in parameters. I show that partial prediction of counterfactual behavior is possible whenever the distribution of preference parameters is continuous—one need not assume anything about the shape of this distribution.

Section 4 considers statistical inference when one observes the choices made by a random sample of the population. Here I develop finite-sample confidence sets for partially identified counterfactual choice probabilities. Section 5 concludes.

2. CHOICE AS TREATMENT RESPONSE

Research on discrete choice has not previously used the language and notation of the analysis of treatment response, but it is easy to define concepts in those terms and helpful to do so.[2] I show how here and introduce the type of counterfactual prediction problem studied in this article.

The standard treatment-response setting begins with a population J and a set of potential treatments T. Each person $j \in J$ has a response function $y_j(\cdot) : T \to Y$ mapping treatments $t \in T$ into outcomes $y_j(t) \in Y$. Persons may also have observable covariates, but I suppress them to simplify notation.

The population is a "large" probability space (J, Ω, P), in the sense that J is uncountable and $P(j) = 0$, $j \in J$. The probability distribution $P[y(\cdot)]$ of the random function $y(\cdot) : T \to Y$ describes treatment response across the population.

Person j actually receives some treatment $z_j \in T$ and realizes the outcome $y_j \equiv y_j(z_j)$. The outcomes $[y_j(t), t \neq z_j]$ that would have been experienced under other treatments are counterfactual. Observation of the population reveals the population distribution $P(z, y)$ of realized treatments and outcomes. The problem is to predict the counterfactual outcomes that would occur if members of the population were to receive unrealized treatments.

---

[2] The language and notation of analysis of treatment response has previously been used to describe classical demand settings, where the problem is to choose the quantity of a homogeneous commodity. There the treatment is the price of the commodity, which indexes the budget set, and the response is the quantity demanded at that price. See Manski (1995, Chapter 6, 1997) and Angrist et al. (2000).

In the case of discrete choice, one begins with a population J and a universe of distinct alternatives A. Distinct alternatives need not be qualitatively different, as in the proverbial "apples and oranges." They may carry the same common-language name but differ quantitatively in their attributes. For example, they may be eggs that vary in size and price.

The set of potential treatments T is the set of all nonempty finite subsets of A, each of which is a possible choice set. The response function $y_j(\cdot)$ is a *choice function* specifying the alternative that person j would choose when facing any choice set. Thus, $y_j(C)$ is the alternative that person j would choose if he were to face set C. The realized choice made by person j is $y_j \equiv y_j(z_j)$, where z_j is the choice set that this person actually faces. The problem is to predict the counterfactual choices that would occur if members of the population were to face unrealized choice sets.[3]

This article considers prediction of behavior in a counterfactual scenario where all persons face the same choice set, again denoted C. The objective is to predict the fraction of the population who would choose a specified alternative $c \in C$. Thus, the problem is to learn the counterfactual choice probability $P[y(C)=c]$. Scenarios where counterfactual choice sets vary across the population are notationally more complex, but the approach to be developed applies to them as well.

As a prelude, consider the prediction problem using choice data alone. The Law of Total Probability and the definition $y \equiv y(z)$ give

$$(1) \quad P[y(C) = c] = P[y(C)=c \mid z=C]P(z=C) + P[y(C)=c \mid z \neq C]P(z \neq C)$$
$$= P(y=c \mid z=C)P(z=C) + P[y(C)=c \mid z \neq C]P(z \neq C).$$

Realized choice sets and choices are observable, so choice data can reveal $P(y = c \mid z = C)$ and $P(z)$ but not $P[y(C) = c \mid z \neq C]$. Hence, one may conclude that

$$(2) \quad P[y(C)=c] \in [P(y=c \mid z=C)P(z=C), P(y=c \mid z=C)P(z=C)+P(z \neq C)].$$

This is the standard result for prediction of treatment response using empirical evidence alone (Manski, 1990, 2003, Chapter 7), applied here to prediction of choice behavior.

The above shows that if a positive fraction of the population actually faces choice set C, the counterfactual choice probability $P[y(C) = c]$ is partially identified using choice data alone. However, it is common in discrete choice analysis to want to predict behavior when C differs from all realized choice sets. Then $P(z = C) = 0$ and Equation (2) becomes the uninformative statement that $P[y(C) = c] \in [0,1]$. This formalizes the obvious fact that data on observed choices alone reveal nothing about behavior in an entirely counterfactual choice setting. Prediction is possible only when the choice data are combined with assumptions that have identifying power. This article studies prediction with such assumptions.

---

[3] The assumption that each person actually faces one choice set is standard in econometric analysis of discrete choice. It is also standard in analysis of treatment response more broadly, as treatments are defined to be mutually exclusive. This assumption is not maintained in Samuelson's version of revealed preference analysis, which supposes that one can observe how a person with fixed preferences would behave in multiple choice settings (Samuelson, 1948; Afriat, 1967).

It is useful to distinguish assumptions about the process generating observed choice sets from ones on the decision rules that persons use when facing specified choice sets. This article maintains the usual "exogenous choice set" assumption that realized choice sets z and choice functions $y(\cdot)$ are statistically independent. That is,

$$(3) \qquad\qquad P[y(\cdot)] = P[y(\cdot) \mid z].$$

When considering assumptions about the decision rules that persons use, it is useful to distinguish assumptions restricting the set of types found within the population from assumptions on the shape of the distribution of types. A type is defined by a choice function. All persons who share the same choice function are of the same type.

In the econometric literature on discrete choice, assumptions restricting the set of types appear through the basic RUM assumption that all members of the population behave rationally and the common additional assumption that utility functions are linear in person-specific parameters. Assumptions on the shape of the distribution of types appear when researchers suppose that the distribution of preference parameters is, say, Type I extreme value or multivariate normal.

To keep attention focused on the identification problem at the heart of counterfactual prediction, I suppose in Section 3 that the observable distribution $P(z, y)$ of realized treatments and outcomes is known. Section 4 addresses statistical inference when $P(z, y)$ must be inferred from sample data.

3. PREDICTION WITH A FINITE UNIVERSE OF ALTERNATIVES

3.1. *Anatomy of the Problem.* The relevant universe of alternatives for counterfactual prediction comprises all alternatives that appear in a realized choice set or the counterfactual choice set. Let $(D_m, m \in M)$ denote the collection of realized choice sets in the population of interest. The objective is to predict choice from a counterfactual choice set C. Hence, the relevant universe is $A = C \cup (D_m, m \in M)$.

The basic maintained assumption of the present analysis is that M, hence A, is finite.[4] Finiteness of A implies that there are finitely many possible choice sets, specifically $2^{|A|} - 1$ many. Hence, there are finitely many distinct choice functions. Let $y_k(\cdot)$ be the choice function for persons of type k. Let K denote the set of logically possible types. Let π_k denote the fraction of the population who are of type k. Then $\pi \equiv (\pi_k, k \in K)$ is the multinomial distribution of types. A behavioral model is an assumption that π lies in some specified set of distributions, say Π.

The objective is to learn about a counterfactual choice probability $P[y(C) = c]$, where $c \in C$. This probability is related to π by the linear equation

$$(4) \qquad\qquad P[y(C) = c] = \sum_{k \in K} 1[y_k(C) = c] \cdot \pi_k.$$

---

[4] It is natural to want to extend the present analysis to settings with infinite universes of alternatives. I am tempted to assert that such extensions should be possible with sufficient attention to regularity conditions and technical details. However, I think it more prudent to simply say that the question is open.

What is known about π? Members of the population face the realized choice sets $(D_m, m \in M)$. Under the maintained statistical independence Assumption 3, choice data reveal the choice probabilities $P[y(D_m) = d], d \in D_m, m \in M$.[5] These probabilities are related to π through the equations[6]

$$(5) \qquad P[y(D_m) = d] = \sum_{k \in K} 1[y_k(D_m) = d] \cdot \pi_k, d \in D_m, m \in M.$$

Distribution π necessarily solves the logical adding-up and nonnegativity conditions

$$(6) \qquad \sum_{k \in K} \pi_k = 1; \pi_k \geq 0, k \in K.$$

Finally, the behavioral model assumes that

$$(7) \qquad \pi \in \Pi.$$

The identification region for π is the set $H(\pi)$ of values of π that solve (5), (6), and (7). If the behavioral model is correct, then $H(\pi)$ is nonempty. If $H(\pi)$ is empty, the behavioral model is incorrect. Supposing the model to be correct, π is point identified if $H(\pi)$ is a singleton. It is partially identified if $H(\pi)$ is not a singleton but is a proper subset of the space of all multinomial distributions on the set of logically possible types.

The identification region for $P[y(C) = c]$ follows immediately from $H(\pi)$. It is the set

$$(8) \qquad H\{P[y(C) = c]\} = \left\{ \sum_{k \in K} 1[y_k(C) = c] \cdot \lambda_k, \lambda \in H(\pi) \right\}$$

obtained by applying Equation (4) with all feasible values of π.

---

[5] In econometric analysis of discrete choice, realized choice sets often vary systematically across subpopulations of persons with different covariates. For example, choice sets may vary geographically, or persons with higher income may face larger choice sets than persons with lower income. Assumption 3 supposes that choice-set variation is statistically independent of preferences. For example, if choice sets vary geographically, it supposes that the residents of different areas have the same distribution of types. This assumption is maintained in most econometric analysis of discrete choice, implicitly if not explicitly.

Inference on π is much more difficult without Assumption 3. Then Equation (5) below does not hold because choice data reveal only $P[y(D_m) = d \mid z = D_m], d \in D_m, m \in M$. These conditional choice probabilities are related to π through the equations

$$P[y(D_m) = d \mid z = D_m] = \sum_{k \in K} 1[y_k(D_m) = d] \cdot \pi_{km}, d \in D_m, m \in M,$$

where π_{km} is the fraction of type k within the subpopulation of persons who face choice set D_m.

[6] For each $m \in M$, the choice probabilities $P[y(D_m) = d], d \in D_m$ sum to one. Hence, the collection of equations in (5) contains redundancies. These are harmless, so I do not remove them here. However, I will do so in Section 4 when constructing confidence sets.

3.1.1. *Linear behavioral models.*   I shall say that a behavioral model is *linear* if Π is a set of multinomial distributions that satisfies specified linear equalities or inequalities. Particularly common in applications are models assuming that the population does not contain some types K_0. These are linear models that set $\pi_k = 0, k \in K_0$.

The identification regions resulting from linear models have simple structures. Set $H(\pi)$ is convex. Convexity of $H(\pi)$ and linearity of Equation (4) in π imply that the set $H\{P[y(C) = c]\}$ is an interval. The lower and upper bounds of this interval solve two linear programming problems. The lower bound solves

(9)
$$\min_{\lambda} \sum_{k \in K} 1[y_k(C) = c] \cdot \lambda_k$$

subject to

$$P[y(D_m) = d] = \sum_{k \in K} 1[y_k(D_m) = d] \cdot \lambda_k, \quad d \in D_m, m \in M,$$

$$\sum_{k \in K} \lambda_k = 1; \lambda_k \geq 0, k \in K; \lambda \in \Pi.$$

The upper bound solves the analogous problem, with a max replacing the min in (9).

When the behavioral model is not linear, minimization problem (9) still gives the sharp lower bound on $P[y(C) = c]$, and the corresponding maximization problem gives the sharp upper bound. However, the identification region may or may not be the entire interval connecting these bounds, depending on the structure of Π.

3.2. *Random Utility Models with Strict Preferences.*   As a first application of Section 3.1, assume that all members of the population have strict preference orderings on A. This is a linear behavioral model that excludes all types whose choice functions are not consistent with a strict preference ordering. There are $|A|!$ strict preference orderings on A, hence this many feasible types.[7]

The simplest nontrivial case occurs when A has three elements, say (c, d, e). Then there are six feasible types, with preference orderings $(c \succ d \succ e)$, $(c \succ e \succ d)$, $(d \succ c \succ e)$, $(d \succ e \succ c)$, $(e \succ c \succ d)$, and $(e \succ d \succ c)$. There are four nontrivial choice sets, these being (c, d, e), (c, d), (c, e), and (d, e). The relationship between choice probabilities and the distribution of preferences is as follows:

(10a) $P[y(c, d, e) = c] = P(c \succ d \succ e) + P(c \succ e \succ d),$

----

[7] The assumption that all persons have strict preference orderings can be weakened. However, when considering prediction with RUMs, it is essential that at least some positive fraction of preference orderings be strict rather than weak. The concept of rationality makes no prediction about choice among equally ranked alternatives. An RUM that permits an unknown fraction of the population to be indifferent among all elements of A is vacuous.

(10b) $P[y(c, d, e) = d] = P(d \succ c \succ e) + P(d \succ e \succ c),$

(10c) $P[y(c, d, e) = e] = P(e \succ c \succ d) + P(e \succ d \succ c),$

(11a) $P[y(c, d) = c] = P(c \succ d \succ e) + P(c \succ e \succ d) + P(e \succ c \succ d),$

(11b) $P[y(c, d) = d] = P(d \succ c \succ e) + P(d \succ e \succ c) + P(e \succ d \succ c),$

(12a) $P[y(c, e) = c] = P(c \succ d \succ e) + P(c \succ e \succ d) + P(d \succ c \succ e),$

(12b) $P[y(c, e) = e] = P(e \succ d \succ c) + P(e \succ c \succ d) + P(d \succ e \succ c),$

(13a) $P[y(d, e) = d] = P(c \succ d \succ e) + P(d \succ e \succ c) + P(d \succ c \succ e),$

(13b) $P[y(d, e) = e] = P(c \succ e \succ d) + P(e \succ d \succ c) + P(e \succ c \succ d).$

With this as background, we can study counterfactual prediction given observation of choice behavior from different choice sets. Here are two examples.

3.2.1. *All persons face (c, d, e) and the objective is to predict choice from (c, d).*
The empirical evidence reveals $P[y(c, d, e)]$. Hence, Equation (5) takes the form
(10). Combining (10a) and (11a) gives

(14) $P[y(c, d) = c] = P[y(c, d, e) = c] + P(e \succ c \succ d).$

Equation (10c) shows that $0 \le P(e \succ c \succ d) \le P[y(c, d, e) = e]$. This bound is
sharp. Hence,

(15) $P[y(c, d, e) = c] \le P[y(c, d) = c] \le P[y(c, d, e) = c] + P[y(c, d, e) = e].$

In words, if alternative e were eliminated from choice set (c, d, e), the persons
who chose c or d would not change their behavior. The persons who chose e now
must choose either c or d. The lower bound on $P[y(c, d) = c]$ occurs if they would
all choose d and the upper bound if they would all choose c.

3.2.2. *Some persons face (c, d), some face (d, e), and the objective is to predict
choice from (c, e).*   Given statistical independence Assumption 3, the empirical
evidence reveals $P[y(c, d)]$ and $P[y(d, e)]$. Hence, Equation (5) takes the form
(11) and (13). Combining (11a) and (12a) gives

(16) $P[y(c, e) = c] = P[y(c, d) = c] - P(e \succ c \succ d) + P(d \succ c \succ e).$

Equations (11b) and (13a) shows that $0 \le P(d \succ c \succ e) \le \min\{P[y(c, d) = d], P[y(d, e) = d]\}$. Equations (11a) and (13b) show that $0 \le P(e \succ c \succ d) \le \min\{P[y(c, d) = c], P[y(d, e) = e]\}$. Hence,

(17) $\max\{0, P[y(c, d) = c] - P[y(d, e) = e]\} \leq P[y(c, e) = c]$

$\leq \min\{1, P[y(c, d) = c] + P[y(d, e) = d]\}.$

Letting $S \equiv P[y(c, d) = c] + P[y(d, e) = d]$, bound (17) can be written more concisely as

(17′) $\max(0, S - 1) \leq P[y(c, e) = c] \leq \min(1, S).$

Thus, the lower bound is informative when $S > 1$ and converges to one as $S \rightarrow 2$. The upper bound is informative when $S < 1$ and converges to zero as $S \rightarrow 0$.

It remains to show that the bound is sharp. This is so if there exist distributions of types that solve (11) and (13) and that make $P[y(c, e) = c]$ equal the lower and upper bounds. It suffices to consider the lower bound, as the upper bound on $P[y(c, e) = c]$ equals one minus the lower bound on $P[y(c, e) = e]$. There are two cases to consider. If $P[y(c, d) = c] \geq P[y(d, e) = e]$, the lower bound is achieved when

$P(c \succ d \succ e) = P[y(c, d) = c] - P[y(d, e) = e], \quad P(c \succ e \succ d) = 0,$

$P(d \succ c \succ e) = 0, \qquad\qquad\qquad\qquad P(d \succ e \succ c) = P[y(c, d) = d],$

$P(e \succ c \succ d) = P[y(d, e) = e], \qquad\qquad\quad P(e \succ d \succ c) = 0.$

If $P[y(c, d) = c] \leq P[y(d, e) = e]$, it is achieved when

$P(c \succ d \succ e) = 0, \qquad\qquad\qquad P(c \succ e \succ d) = 0,$

$P(d \succ c \succ e) = 0, \qquad\qquad\qquad P(d \succ e \succ c) = P[y(d, e) = d],$

$P(e \succ c \succ d) = P[y(c, d) = c], \quad P(e \succ d \succ c) = P[y(d, e) = e] - P[y(c, d) = c].$

Bound (17) is the triangular condition of Marschak (1960). Marschak's use of the bound presumed that one observes all the binary choice probabilities $P[y(c, d) = c]$, $P[y(d, e) = d]$, and $P[y(c, e) = c]$. His objective was to test the consistency of these choice probabilities with a strict-preference RUM. They are consistent with such an RUM if and only if $P[y(c, e) = c]$ lies within the bound. A subsequent body of research extends Marschak's work to settings in which the universe A contains more than three alternatives and one observes the choice probabilities for all binary subsets of A. Fishburn (1992) and McFadden (2005) review this literature.[8]

---

[8] The triangular condition clearly holds when A contains more than three alternatives. That is, given any three-element subset of A, say (c, d, e), the binary choice probabilities $P[y(c, d) = c]$, $P[y(d, e) = d]$, and $P[y(c, e) = c]$ are consistent with a strict-preference RUM only if bound (17) holds. The question addressed in the literature is the sufficiency of the triangular condition when A contains more than three alternatives. That is, if the triangular condition holds for all three-element subsets of A, does this imply consistency of the choice data with a strict-preference RUM? This question turns out to be subtle, the answer being positive if A contains fewer than six alternatives but not otherwise.

3.3. *Linear Utility Models with Random Coefficients.*   The strict preference assumption per se has no power to identify the choice probability for an alternative that appears in no realized choice set. Suppose, for example, that the only realized choice set is (d, e) and that the objective is to predict behavior when the choice set is (c, d, e). The quantity $P[y(c, d, e) = c]$ can lie anywhere in the interval $[0, 1]$.

To enable prediction of behavior when choice sets contain new alternatives, econometricians have often characterized alternatives as observable attribute bundles, presumed that persons maximize utility functions defined on attribute bundles, and assumed that the distribution of utility functions has specified properties. Leading cases were cited in Section 1.

As a second application of Section 3.1, I now characterize alternatives as attribute bundles and assume that almost all members of the population have linear utility functions.[9] Thus, each alternative d now is characterized by a distinct observable attribute vector w_d and the utility of d to person j is $u_j(d) = w_d \theta_j$, where θ_j is the person's vector of preference parameters. For example, in a study of choice among travel modes, the attributes characterizing an alternative may be (travel time, travel cost, vehicle class), where vehicle class distinguishes car from bus.

In contrast to prevailing econometric practice, I assume nothing about the shape of the population distribution of θ. I only assume that almost all members of the population have strict preference orderings. A sufficient but not necessary condition for almost-everywhere strict preferences is continuity of the distribution of utility, as has routinely been assumed in the literature. However, it is important to understand that continuity of the distribution of utility does not imply that the population contains a continuum of types. When the universe of alternatives is finite, all persons with sufficiently similar utility functions have the same choice function. Hence, the set of types is finite.

Let A_ℓ, $\ell \in L$, denote the $|A|!$ distinct ordered representations of set A. Let $w_{\ell n}$ be the attribute bundle of the nth element of the ordered set A_ℓ. Let Θ be the space of parameter values that the researcher deems feasible. Let

$$(18) \qquad \Theta_\ell \equiv [\theta \in \Theta : w_{\ell 1}\theta > w_{\ell 2}\theta \cdots > w_{\ell |A|}\theta]$$

be the parameter values that generate preference ordering A_ℓ. All persons with $\theta \in \Theta_\ell$ are of the same type.

When does a linear utility model have identifying power? A model has no power if all of the sets Θ_ℓ, $\ell \in L$ are nonempty. Then every strict preference ordering is representable through a linear utility function. A model may have identifying power if some of the sets Θ_ℓ, $\ell \in L$ are empty. Then some strict preference orderings are not representable through linear utility functions.

When is Θ_ℓ empty? There appears to be no succinct necessary and sufficient condition, as Θ_ℓ depends jointly on the parameter space Θ and the set $(w_d, d \in A)$ of attribute bundles. However, a simple sufficient condition is that A_ℓ contain

---

[9] The reader should not interpret my consideration of linear utility as an endorsement of this functional form. I examine linear utility because it is ubiquitous in applied research and because it enables a simple illustration of general ideas.

an element n such that $w_{\ell n}$ is a convex combination of the attribute bundles that precede it in order ℓ. Suppose that $w_{\ell n} = \sum_{i<n} \alpha_i w_{\ell i}$, where ($\alpha_i \geq 0, i < n$) and $\sum_{i<n} \alpha_i = 1$. Then $\min_{i<n} w_{in}\theta \leq w_{\ell n}\theta \leq \max_{i<n} w_{in}\theta$ for all values of θ. Thus, there exists no value of θ such that all of the alternatives $i < n$ are preferred to n. The same reasoning applies when $w_{\ell n}$ is a convex combination of the attribute bundles that follow it in order ℓ.

With this as background, let $A_\ell, \ell \in L^*$ denote the feasible ordered representations of set A; that is, those such that Θ_ℓ is nonempty. All $\theta \in \Theta_\ell$ yield the same choice function. Hence, without loss of generality, we can select any value $\theta_\ell \in \Theta_\ell$ and proceed as if all persons with $\theta \in \Theta_\ell$ have parameter θ_ℓ. Thus, an assumption that the distribution of θ is continuous is observationally equivalent to the assumption that this distribution has the finite support ($\theta_\ell, \ell \in L^*$).

Now consider the prediction problem. The objective is to learn $P[y(C) = c]$. Equation (4) becomes

$$(19) \qquad P[y(C) = c] = \sum_{\ell \in L^*} 1[w_c\theta_\ell \geq w_d\theta_\ell, d \in C] \cdot \pi_\ell.$$

Equation (5) becomes

$$(20) \quad P[y(D_m) = d] = \sum_{\ell \in L^*} 1[w_d\theta_\ell \geq w_e\theta_\ell, e \in D_m] \cdot \pi_\ell, d \in D_m, m \in M.$$

To perform prediction, one would first determine L^*, next apply (20) to obtain the identification region for π, and then insert the feasible values of π into (19) to determine the feasible values of $P[y(C) = c]$.

3.3.1. *Models with two attributes.* Equations (19) and (20) simplify when there are two attributes and the sign of some element of the coefficient vector is known to be homogeneous across types. For example, the first attribute might measure the quality of a product and the second its price. Then it is reasonable to assume that all persons value the first attribute positively and the second negatively. Thus, $\Theta = [\theta : \theta_1 > 0 \text{ and } \theta_2 < 0]$.

Let $u_\ell(d) = \theta_{\ell 1}w_{d1} + \theta_{\ell 2}w_{d2}$ and normalize the scale of preferences by setting $\theta_{\ell 1} = 1$. Assume that $w_{c2} \neq w_{d2}$ for $d \neq c$. Then (19) becomes

$$(21)$$

$$P[y(C) = c] = \sum_{\ell \in L^*} 1[w_{c1} + \theta_{\ell 2}w_{c2} \geq w_{d1} + \theta_{\ell 2}w_{d2}, d \in C] \cdot \pi_\ell$$

$$= P[\theta_2 \geq (w_{d1} - w_{c1})/(w_{c2} - w_{d2})] \text{ if } w_{c2} - w_{d2} > 0,$$

$$\leq (w_{d1} - w_{c1})/(w_{c2} - w_{d2}) \text{ if } w_{c2} - w_{d2} < 0; d \in C, d \neq c]$$

$$= P[r(c, C) \leq \theta_2 \leq s(c, C)],$$

where

$$r(c, C) \equiv \max_{d \in C:(w_{c2}-w_{d2})>0} (w_{d1} - w_{c1})/(w_{c2} - w_{d2}) \text{ and}$$

$$s(c, C) \equiv \min_{d \in C:(w_{c2}-w_{d2})<0} (w_{d1} - w_{c1})/(w_{c2} - w_{d2}).$$

Similarly, (20) becomes

$$(22) \qquad P[y(D_m) = d] = P[r(d, D_m) \leq \theta_2 \leq s(d, D_m)], \quad d \in D_m, m \in M.$$

Thus, the counterfactual $P[y(C) = c]$ is the probability that θ_2 lies in the interval $[r(c, C), s(c, C)]$. Choice data reveal the probability that θ_2 lies in each of the intervals $[r(d, D_m), s(d, D_m)], d \in D_m, m \in M$. Knowledge of the latter probabilities may imply restrictions on the former one.

3.3.2. *Numerical examples.*   Here are some examples that illustrate prediction with two attributes, the first being quality and the second being price. Normalize the scale of preferences by setting $\theta_{j1} = 1$ for all $j \in J$. Let θ_2 be distributed uniform on the interval $[-4, -0.25]$. Let $A = (a, b, c, d, e)$, with $w_a = (0, 0)$, $w_b = (1, 1)$, $w_c = (0.25, 0.5)$, $w_d = (0.75, 1.25)$, and $w_e = (1.5, 2)$.

First suppose that choice probabilities are observed for choice sets (a, b), (a, c), (a, d), and (b, c). Let the counterfactual choice set be (a, e). The assumed uniform distribution of price preferences implies that the observed choice probabilities are

$$P[y(a, b) = a] = 0.8, \quad P[y(a, c) = a] = 0.93,$$
$$P[y(a, d) = a] = 0.91, \quad P[y(b, c) = b] = 0.33.$$

The counterfactual choice probability is $P[y(a, e) = a] = 0.87$. Its identification region, which is computed using only knowledge of the observed choice probabilities, is $P[y(a, e) = a] \in [0.8, 0.91]$.

Next consider the same observed choice sets and let the counterfactual choice set be (c, d, e). The counterfactual choice probabilities are

$$P[y(c, d, e) = c] = 0.84, \quad P[y(c, d, e) = d] = 0, \quad P[y(c, d, e) = e] = 0.16.$$

Their identification regions are

$$P[y(c, d, e) = c] \in [0.8, 0.91], \quad P[y(c, d, e) = d] = 0,$$
$$P[y(c, d, e) = e] \in [0.09, 0.2].$$

The choice probability for d must be zero because no value of θ_2 makes this alternative preferred to both c and e. Alternative d is preferred to c if $\theta_2 > -2/3$, and it is preferred to e if $\theta_2 < -1$.

Finally suppose that choice probabilities are observed for choice sets (a, b, c), (a, c, d), and (b, c, d). Let the counterfactual choice set be (a, b, e). The assumed distribution of preferences implies that the observed choice probabilities are

$$P[y(a, b, c) = a] = 0.8, \quad P[y(a, b, c) = b] = 0.2, \quad P[y(a, b, c) = c] = 0.$$

$$P[y(a, c, d) = a] = 0.91, \quad P[y(a, c, d) = c] = 0, \quad P[y(a, c, d) = d] = 0.09.$$

$$P[y(b, c, d) = b] = 0.33, \quad P[y(b, c, d) = c] = 0.67, \quad P[y(b, c, d) = d] = 0.$$

The counterfactual choice probabilities are

$$P[y(a, b, e) = a] = 0.8, \quad P[y(a, b, e) = b] = 0.13, \quad P[y(a, b, e) = e] = 0.07.$$

Their identification regions are

$$P[y(a, b, e) = a] = 0.8, \; P[y(a, b, e) = b] \in [0.11, 0.2], \; P[y(a, b, e) = e] \in [0, 0.09].$$

4. FINITE-SAMPLE CONFIDENCE SETS

Suppose that one does not observe the choice probabilities $P[y(D_m) = d]$, $d \in D_m$, $m \in M$. Instead one observes the choices made by a random sample of the population. Then the counterfactual prediction problem involves statistical inference.

A growing literature develops asymptotically valid confidence sets for partially identified parameters; see Beresteanu and Molinari (2006), Chernozukhov et al. (2007), Horowitz and Manski (2000), Imbens and Manski (2004), and Rosen (2006), among others. Some of the approaches proposed in this literature apply to the present counterfactual prediction problem. However, the structure of the present problem is so simple that one does not need to resort to asymptotics. I show here how to develop confidence sets that are valid for all sample sizes.

4.1. Observed Binary Choice Sets.

I first consider settings where all observed choice sets have two alternatives. Consider Equation (5). For each $m \in M$, let (d_m, e_m) denote the two elements of D_m. Then (5) takes the form

$$(23) \qquad P[y(D_m) = d_m] = \sum_{k \in K} 1[y_k(D_m) = d_m] \cdot \pi_k, \quad m \in M.$$

We need not consider the analogous equation for $P[y(D_m) = e_m]$ because it is redundant, the choice probabilities for d_m and e_m necessarily summing to one.

Let $p_m \equiv P[y(D_m) = d_m]$ and $p \equiv (p_m, m \in M)$. Let N_m be the number of sample members facing choice set D_m and $\bar{y}_m$ be the empirical frequency of choice of alternative d_m. The problem is to use knowledge of $[(\bar{y}_m, N_m), m \in M]$ to construct a confidence set for the vector p of choice probabilities. Conditional on the sample sizes, the components of $(\bar{y}_m, m \in M)$ are statistically independent of one another.

Hence, it suffices to consider each value of m separately and use knowledge of $(\bar{y}_m, N_m)$ to construct a confidence set for p_m. The coverage probability for p of the Cartesian product of these sets then equals the product of their separate coverage probabilities.

Use of random-sample data to construct a confidence set for the probability of an event is among the most basic problems of statistical inference, and the literature offers many alternative procedures. Let $\alpha_m \in (0, 1)$ be a desired coverage probability for p_m. To enable finite-sample inference, we want a procedure whose *confidence coefficient* (infimum of the coverage probabilities across all feasible values of p_m) is known to be at least α_m. Clopper and Pearson (1934) first proposed a confidence interval with this property, and statisticians have studied others since then. The aim has been to tighten or otherwise refine the Clopper–Pearson interval while still achieving a confidence coefficient at least equal to α_m. See Blyth and Still (1983), Casella (1986), Agresti and Min (2001), and Brown et al. (2001), among other sources.

Let $Q(\bar{y}_m, N_m, \alpha_m)$ be any confidence interval for p_m that has confidence coefficient α_m or greater. Consider the $|M|$-dimensional rectangle

$$(24) \qquad Q = \underset{m \in M}{\times} Q(\bar{y}_m, N_m, \alpha_m).$$

Conditional on $(N_m, m \in M)$, the coverage probability for p of set Q is at least $\alpha \equiv \prod_{m \in M} \alpha_m$.

Having obtained Q as a confidence set for p, let $q \in Q$ and let $H_q(\pi)$ be the set of type distributions that satisfy the conditions

$$(25) \qquad q_m = \sum_{k \in K} 1[y_k(D_m) = d_m] \cdot \pi_k, \quad m \in M.$$

$$\sum_{k \in K} \pi_k = 1; \quad \pi_k \geq 0, \quad k \in K; \quad \pi \in \Pi.$$

Then $H_Q(\pi) \equiv \cup_{q \in Q} H_q(\pi)$ is a confidence set for π with coverage probability at least α. Finally,

$$(26) \qquad H_Q\{P[y(C) = c]\} = \left\{ \sum_{k \in K} 1[y_k(C) = c] \cdot \lambda_k, \lambda \in H_Q(\pi) \right\}$$

is a confidence set for $P[y(C) = c]$ with coverage probability at least α.

Construction of $H_Q\{P[y(C) = c]\}$ is particularly simple when the behavioral model is linear. Let $Q(\bar{y}_m, N_m, \alpha_m)$ be the interval $[q_0(\bar{y}_m, N_m, \alpha_m), q_1(\bar{y}_m, N_m, \alpha_m)]$. Then $H_Q\{P[y(C) = c]\}$ is an interval whose lower bound solves the linear programming problem

$$(27) \qquad \min_{\lambda} \sum_{k \in K} 1[y_k(C) = c] \cdot \lambda_k$$

subject to

$$q_0(\bar{y}_m, \alpha_m) \leq \sum_{k \in K} 1[y_k(D_m) = d] \cdot \lambda_k \leq q_1(\bar{y}_m, N_m, \alpha_m), \ m \in M,$$

$$\sum_{k \in K} \lambda_k = 1; \quad \lambda_k \geq 0, \quad k \in K; \quad \lambda \in \Pi.$$

The upper bound solves the analogous problem, with a max replacing the min in (27).

4.2. *Observed Multinomial Choice Sets.* Construction of confidence sets when observed choice sets have three or more alternatives is conceptually similar to the case with binary choice sets, but differs in an important detail.

Generalizing the notation introduced above, let $p_{md} \equiv P[y(D_m) = d]$, $p_m \equiv \{P[y(D_m) = d], d \in D_m\}$, and $p \equiv (p_m, m \in M)$. Again let N_m be the number of sample members facing choice set D_m. Let $\bar{y}_{md}$ be the empirical frequency of choice of alternative d, and let $\bar{y}_m = (\bar{y}_{md}, d \in D_m)$. The problem is again to use knowledge of $[(\bar{y}_m, N_m), m \in M]$ to construct a confidence set for the choice probabilities p. As above, the components of $(\bar{y}_m, m \in M)$ are statistically independent of one another conditional on the sample sizes, so it suffices to consider each value of m separately and use knowledge of $(\bar{y}_m, N_m)$ to construct a confidence set for p_m. Again, the coverage probability for p of the Cartesian product of these sets equals the product of their separate coverage probabilities.

The important difference in detail concerns construction of the confidence set for p_m. When a choice set is binary, p_m has one nonredundant element and the statistical literature provides confidence intervals with known finite-sample coverage. When a choice set is multinomial, p_m has multiple nonredundant elements and one faces the problem of joint inference on a vector of multinomial probabilities. Research on this subject has a long history but, as far as I am aware, proposed procedures have been studied solely from an asymptotic perspective. See, for example, Goodman (1965), Fitzpatrick and Scott (1987), and Sison and Glaz (1995).

In the apparent absence of a literature on multinomial confidence sets with known finite-sample coverage, I will suffice here with a conservative suggestion. Again let e_m be the redundant element of D_m. The problem is to use knowledge of $(\bar{y}_m, N_m)$ to construct a set $Q(\bar{y}_m, N_m, \alpha_m)$ that covers $(p_{md}, d \in D_m/e_m)$ with probability α_m or greater. For each $d \in D_m/e_m$ and $\gamma_{md} \in (0, 1)$, one can use the Clopper–Pearson or another procedure to construct a confidence interval $Q_d(\bar{y}_m, N_m, \gamma_{md})$ that covers p_{md} with probability γ_{md} or greater. Now let $Q(\bar{y}_m, N_m, \alpha_m)$ be the $\{|D_m| - 1\}$-dimensional rectangle

(28) $$Q(\bar{y}_m, N_m, \alpha_m) = \underset{d \in D_m/e_m}{\times} Q_d(\bar{y}_m, N_m, \gamma_{md}).$$

The Bonferroni inequality shows that this confidence set for $(p_{md}, d \in D_m/e_m)$ has coverage probability at least equal to

$$(29) \qquad \gamma_m = 1 - \sum_{d \in D_m/e_m} (1 - \gamma_{md}).$$

Hence, coverage of at least α_m is achieved by choosing $(\gamma_{md}, d \in D_m/e_m)$ so that $\gamma_m \geq \alpha_m$.

5. CONCLUSION

This article has used the basic structure of discrete choice analysis to develop a simple approach to counterfactual prediction of population choice behavior. The first step of the derivation in Section 3.1 recognized that discrete choice analysis is a problem of decomposition of probability mixtures, where one uses observable choice probabilities to infer the distribution of types in the population. The second step used the inferred restrictions on the distribution of types to predict behavior in unrealized choice settings. Section 4 showed how the approach may be implemented when one observes random-sample data on choices rather than population choice probabilities.

Sections 3.2 and 3.3 gave two illustrative applications. Both restricted the set of types appearing in the population. Section 3.2 considered prediction under the sole assumption that all persons have strict preferences. Section 3.3 studied prediction when almost all persons have strict preferences and utility functions that are linear in attribute bundles. In contrast to prevailing econometric practice, nothing was assumed about the shape of the distribution of preference parameters.

Looking beyond these applications, I foresee enormous scope for research that uses the general approach of Section 3.1 to make predictions with other behavioral models. Researchers who are comfortable with the assumption of strict preferences but who are uncomfortable with linear utility functions on attribute bundles may want to pose other assumptions on preference orderings. Those who are uncomfortable with the assumption of rational behavior may want to consider types who are nonrational in various ways.

Although this article has focused on prediction, the derivation of Section 3.1 also enables the testing of behavioral models. Suppose that one hypothesizes a model and finds that the implied identification region for the distribution of types is empty. Then one should conclude that the hypothesized model is incorrect.

REFERENCES

AFRIAT, S., "The Construction of Utility Functions from Expenditure Data," *International Economic Review* 8 (1967), 67–77.

AGRESTI, A., AND Y. MIN, "On Small-Sample Confidence Intervals for Parameters in Discrete Distributions," *Biometrics* 57 (2001), 963–71.

ANGRIST, J., K. GRADDY, AND G. IMBENS, "The Interpretation of Instrumental Variables Estimators in Simultaneous Equations Models with an Application to the Demand for Fish," *Review of Economic Studies* 67 (2000), 499–527.

BERESTEANU, A., AND F. MOLINARI, "Asymptotic Properties for a Class of Partially Identified Models," Mimeo, Department of Economics, Cornell University, 2006.

BERRY, S., J. LEVINSOHN, AND A. PAKES, "Automobile Prices in Market Equilibrium," *Econometrica* 63 (1994), 841–90.

BLYTH, C., AND H. STILL, "Binomial Confidence Intervals," *Journal of the American Statistical Association* 78 (1983), 108–16.

BROWN, L., T. CAL, AND A. DASGUPTA, "Interval Estimation for a Binomial Proportion," *Statistical Science* 16 (2001), 101–33.

CASELLA, G., "Refining Binomial Confidence Intervals," *The Canadian Journal of Statistics* 14 (1986), 113–29.

CHERNOZHUKOV, V., H. HONG, AND E. TAMER, "Estimation and Confidence Regions for Parameter Sets in Econometric Models," *Econometrica* 75 (2007), 1243–84.

CLOPPER, C., AND E. PEARSON, "The Use of Confidence or Fiducial Limits Illustrated in the Case of the Binomial," *Biometrika* 26 (1934), 404–13.

COSSLETT, S., "Distribution-Free Maximum Likelihood Estimation of the Binary Choice Model," *Econometrica* 51 (1983), 765–82.

DAGANZO, C., F. BOUTHELIER, AND Y. SHEFFI, "Multinomial Probit and Qualitative Choice: A Computationally Efficient Algorithm" *Transportation Science* 11 (1977), 338–58.

FISHBURN, P., "Induced Binary Probabilities and the Linear Ordering Polytope: A Status Report," *Mathematical Social Sciences* 23 (1992), 67–80.

FITZPATRICK, S., AND A. SCOTT, "Quick Simultaneous Confidence Intervals for Multinomial Proportions," *Journal of the American Statistical Association* 82 (1987), 875–78.

GOODMAN, L., "On Simultaneous Confidence Intervals for Multinomial Proportions," *Technometrics* 7 (1965), 247–54.

HAUSMAN, J., AND D. WISE, "A Conditional Probit Model for Qualitative Choice: Discrete Decisions Recognizing Interdependence and Heterogeneous Preferences," *Econometrica* 46 (1978), 403–26.

HONORÉ, B., AND E. TAMER, "Bounds on Parameters in Panel Dynamic Discrete Choice Models," *Econometrica* 74 (2006), 611–29.

HOROWITZ, J., AND C. MANSKI, "Nonparametric Analysis of Randomized Experiments with Missing Covariate and Outcome Data," *Journal of the American Statistical Association* 95 (2000), 77–84.

IMBENS, G., AND C. MANSKI, "Confidence Intervals for Partially Identified Parameters," *Econometrica* 72 (2004), 1845–57.

LERMAN, S., AND C. MANSKI, "On the Use of Simulated Frequencies to Approximate Choice Probabilities," in C. Manski and D. McFadden, eds., *Structural Analysis of Discrete Data with Econometric Applications* (Cambridge, MA: M.I.T. Press, 1981).

MAGNAC, T., AND E. MAURIN, "Identification and Information in Monotone Binary Models," *Journal of Econometrics* 139 (2007), 76–104.

MANSKI, C., "Maximum Score Estimation of the Stochastic Utility Model of Choice," *Journal of Econometrics* 3 (1975), 205–28.

——, "Identification of Binary Response Models," *Journal of the American Statistical Association* 83 (1988), 729–38.

——, "Nonparametric Bounds on Treatment Effects," *American Economic Review Papers and Proceedings* 80 (1990), 319–23.

——, *Identification Problems in the Social Sciences* (Cambridge, MA: Harvard University Press, 1995).

——, "Monotone Treatment Response," *Econometrica* 65 (1997), 1311–34.

——, *Partial Identification of Probability Distributions* (New York: Springer-Verlag, 2003).

——, AND E. TAMER, "Inference on Regressions with Interval Data on a Regressor or Outcome," *Econometrica* 70 (2002), 519–46.

MARSCHAK, J., "Binary Choice Constraints on Random Utility Indicators," in K. Arrow, ed., *Stanford Symposium on Mathematical Methods in the Social Sciences* (Stanford: Stanford University Press, 1960).

MATZKIN, R. "Nonparametric and Distribution-Free Estimation of the Binary Threshold-Crossing and the Binary Choice Models," *Econometrica* 60 (1992), 239–70.

McFADDEN, D., "Conditional Logit Analysis of Qualitative Choice Behavior," in P. Zarembka, ed., *Frontiers in Econometrics* (New York: Academic Press, 1974).

——, "Modelling the Choice of Residential Location," in A. Karlqvist, L. Lundqvist, F. Snickars, and J. Weibull, eds., *Spatial Interaction Theory and Planning Models* (Amsterdam: North-Holland, 1978).

——, "Econometric Models of Probabilistic Choice," in C. Manski and D. McFadden, eds., *Structural Analysis of Discrete Data with Econometric Applications* (Cambridge, MA: M.I.T. Press, 1981).

——, "Revealed Stochastic Preference: A Synthesis," *Economic Theory* 26 (2005), 245–64.

——, AND K. TRAIN, "Mixed MNL Models for Discrete Response," *Journal of Applied Econometrics* 15 (2000), 447–70.

ROSEN, A., "Confidence Sets for Partially Identified Parameters that Satisfy a Finite Number of Moment Inequalities," Mimeo, Department of Economics, University College London, 2006.

SAMUELSON, P., "Consumption Theory in Terms of Revealed Preferences," *Economica* 15 (1948), 243–53.

SISON, C., AND J. GLAZ, "Simultaneous Confidence Intervals and Sample Size Determination for Multinomial Proportions," *Journal of the American Statistical Association* 90 (1995), 366–69.

INTERNATIONAL ECONOMIC REVIEW
Vol. 48, No. 4, November 2007

NONPARAMETRIC SURVEY RESPONSE ERRORS*

By   Rosa L. Matzkin[1]

University of California, Los Angeles, U.S.A.

I present nonparametric methods to identify and estimate the biases associated with response errors. When applied to survey data, these methods can be used to analyze how observable and unobservable characteristics of the respondent, and characteristics of the design of the survey, affect errors in the responses. This provides a method to correct the biases that those errors generate, by using the estimated response errors to "undo" those biases. The results are useful also to design better surveys, since they point at characteristics of the design and of subpopulations of respondents that can provide identification of response errors. Several models are considered.

1.   INTRODUCTION

Surveys have been extensively used in economics, marketing, sociology, and political science, among other fields. They provide a quick and relatively inexpensive method for gathering data on individuals. Some of this data might be very difficult to get through any other way. In surveys, a representative sample of individuals is asked, either verbally or in written form, to respond to a series of questions. These may include questions about factual aspects of the respondent's life, such as age, gender, and marital status; hypothetical questions, such as what the respondent would do in a future situation; or opinions such as approval or disapproval of some government action.

As with any other method, surveys have their own drawbacks. Survey responses are typically plagued by response errors. (Battistin, 2003; Bound and Krueger, 1991; McFadden et al., 2003; Philipson, 1997, 2001; Poterba and Summers, 1986; Schwarz et al., 1985; Tourangeau et al., 2000; and the references in Bound et al., 2001 are some of the works that provide strong evidence for the existence of

---

* Manuscript received October 2005; revised July 2007.

[1] The support of the National Institute of Aging through grant F014613//AG012846-12S1 and of NSF through grants BCS-0433990 and SES-0551272 is gratefully acknowledged. This article was written while I was a Professor of Economics at Northwestern University. I am also grateful for the hospitality of the University of California, Berkeley, while I was a Visiting Scholar (October 2005) and of the California Institute of Technology, while I was a Visiting Professor of Economics (August 2006–June 2007). This article has greatly benefited from the input of Daniel McFadden and Joaquim Winter. I am also grateful for the comments and suggestions of Whitney Newey, Stefan Hoderlein, two anonymous referees, the research assistance of Gabriel Katz, and the comments of participants at the joint UC Berkeley/RAND Workshop on Response Errors in Surveys of the Elderly and Internet Interviewing (January 2004), the UC Berkeley Conference in Honor of Daniel McFadden (May 2005), and the University College London Conference on Microeconometrics: Measurement Matters (June 2007). Please address correspondence to: Rosa L. Matzkin, Department of Economics, UCLA, Los Angeles, CA 90095, U.S.A. Phone: (310) 825-7371. Fax: (310) 825-9528. E-mail: matzkin@econ.ucla.edu.

response errors.) Survey errors may be affected by the length of the recall period (Neter and Waksberg, 1964; Cannell et al., 1965; Gems et al., 1982), the salience or importance of the behavior to be retrieved (Waksberg and Valliant, 1978; Chase and Harada, 1984), the social desirability or acceptability of their correct answers (Loftus, 1975), aspects of the design of the survey, such as whether it is face-to-face or telephonic or characteristics of the interviewer (Groves, 1989). Unless biases in the responses are dealt with, the conclusions obtained from survey data might be far from the valid ones. (See McFadden, 2007, for a discussion of statistical issues about surveys.)

In this article, we develop several nonparametric methods to deal with the identification and estimation of survey response errors. The methods will allow one to identify the form of and to measure the noise generated from different sources. Hence, these methods can then be used to (i) predict biases, due to response errors, in new surveys for either the same or a new population of respondents, (ii) "undo" the biases due to response errors, by using the measured errors, and (iii) design surveys that either minimize survey response errors or that allow one to identify and estimate the response errors.

One of the methodologies that is commonly used as a first step when analyzing response errors uses descriptive tools to analyze the relationship between responses and a few observable variables. This analysis may look at how the average response to some question varies as the value of some observable characteristics, either of the respondents or of the survey, change. Many results in experimental psychology, some of which are described in Tourangeau et al. (2000), are presented in this way. Schwarz et al. (1991) is one such example. These authors provided evidence that the category range offered in the answer to a survey question affects reported behavior. In their study, they asked respondents for their daily use of television. Two different scales for the answers were used, one ranging from "up to half an hour" to "more than two and a half hours," and the other ranging from "up to two and a half hours" to "more than four and a half hours." The analysis of the responses concluded that respondents faced with the former range reported less use of television than those faced with the latter. Similarly, in economics, response errors often are analyzed as a function of observable variables. For example, Bollinger (1998), following Bound and Krueger (1991), estimated a nonparametric regression of the error in reported income as a function of true income, using data from the Social Security Administration to match data from the Current Population Survey.

The above type of studies are extremely useful to provide evidence about the existence of a particular response error, uncover relationships among a few observable variables, and to make simple response error predictions. However, these studies can seldom be used to predict quantitatively what will happen in a new situation, such as when data from a different survey are used. A more structural model is typically needed if one wants to measure the relationships, incorporate unobservable variables, model the interaction among different errors, and analyze and measure the effect of different characteristics of the survey design.

A more structural method proceeds by specifying a set of functions and distributions as known up to a few parameters and by modeling the dependence among the variables. For example, in a yes or no answer, this approach would proceed by first specifying that a particular individual will answer yes if the value of an unobservable variable is above some threshold, where the value of this variable is a linear function of some observable and unobservable characteristics of the respondent. Using data on each individual's responses and observable characteristics, this method provides numbers for the coefficients of the linear function, which could then be used to analyze, predict, and correct errors in the response of individuals. This analysis has been typically used to measure the effect of a variable in a certain response, while controlling for other variables that may also affect this response, and to uncover the distributions of relevant unobservable variables. The analysis of survey response biases in Hurd et al. (1998) and McFadden et al. (2003) are representatives of such type of analysis.

The methodology that we present in this article provides a way of incorporating elements of both approaches of analysis described above. As with the latter method, it allows one to estimate underlying functions and distributions of key unobservable variables, in different stages of the response process. As with the former method, it does not require specifying a priori parametric structures for the underlying functions and distributions. The new methods can possess as few or as many levels of complexity as one may be interested in analyzing.

As an example of how one can use the new methods to add a minimal amount of structure to a descriptive model of the former type described, suppose that one is interested in understanding the variation in the response of individuals that are otherwise equal in their relevant observable characteristics. For example, in a situation closely related to one analyzed in McFadden et al. (2003), suppose that individuals are asked their perceived probability of an end-of-life health hazard, such as needing nursing home care. Health status and family status will typically be the observable characteristics that one may plot this answer against. However, another important variable, which is unobservable but can explain the variation in the response of individuals within a common health and family status, is the attitude of the respondent toward living in a nursing home. Being able to identify and estimate the distribution of attitudes toward living in a nursing home, and the variables that affect this taste distribution, is very important to predict future demand for nursing homes and to measure the well-being of nursing home users. Moreover, this distribution of attitudes toward living in a nursing home will also influence the variation in the response to other related questions, such as "Have you purchased insurance for nursing home care?" The response to the latter question may depend on a larger set of observable and unobservable characteristics than the former question, which may include the income and the unobservable attitude toward risk of the respondent. Identifying the distribution of attitudes toward living in a nursing home, from the response to the first question, will make it feasible to identify the distribution of the unobservable attitude toward risk, from the responses to the second question. Analyzing the latter distribution will have important implications to predict demand for various types of insurance, and its identification will allow us to pursue the identification of other important unobservable variables as well as other further studies in which knowing this distribution is important.

The nonparametric, structural approach provides many benefits. First, it provides a bridge among the two different methods described above, which have been used to analyze behavior in survey response. Second, it provides more "trusted" predictions than the parametric analysis, because its conclusions do not depend on ad hoc parametric specifications for the underlying functions and distributions. Third, it provides a method to test particular parametric assumptions, by evaluating how close the nonparametric estimates are to the parametric ones. Fourth, it allows us to infer all types of shapes for the structural anomalies, because the underlying functions will be estimated without imposing on them particular shapes. And, fifth, it allows one to infer the unobserved heterogeneity across otherwise observable equal individuals, which has implications toward their heterogeneous responses in other questions and toward predicted behavior by these individuals.

When used in estimation, reported values of variables will suffer from measurement error, due to survey response errors. A large literature exists on measurement errors. Aigner et al. (1984), Fuller (1987), Carroll et al. (1995), Wansbeek and Meijer (2000), Bound et al. (2001), Hausman (2001), Moffit and Ridder (2007), and Chen et al. (2007) provide excellent surveys of the topic. This article contributes to this literature by specifying structures that could be useful in the design of surveys and the analysis of data. Other recent papers within this realm, which also consider nonparametric methods, but make use of different structures, are McFadden (2006) and Hoderlein and Winter (2007). As in Philipson (1997, 2001), these papers incorporate a decision model for the respondent. McFadden (2006) applies incentive theory to the design and administration of economic surveys. Hoderlein and Winter (2007) analyze models of boundedly rational survey response behavior.

The outline of the article is as follows. In the next section, we motivate our results making use of a well-known empirical model. Section 3 deals with cases where the distribution of an unobservable variable of interest is known. Section 4 deals with cases where the distribution of the unobservable variable of interest is unknown. Section 5 provides conclusions, and describes extensions of the methods presented in the main sections. All the proofs are presented in the Appendix.

2.   A MOTIVATING MODEL

To provide motivation for our methods through a well-known empirical problem, consider a model similar to that used in Bound (1991) and in Bound et al. (2001) to analyze the effect of health on the retirement decision of the elderly. Bound (1991) and Bound et al. (2001) discuss the different biases that may arise as a result of using various measures of health. Self-reported health may generate biases not only because it is a subjective measure, but also because older workers may use poor health to justify decreasing the amount of hours worked, when their true reasons for decreasing hours of work are less sociably acceptable. In fact, Ettner (1997) provides evidence that women report health less frequently than men as a reason for retirement, which is consistent with the fact that it is more socially acceptable for women to retire due to reasons other than health.

One of the models analyzed by Bound (1991) and Bound et al. (2001) is (after changing the notation to one that is more suitable for this article)

$$H = \beta_1 X_1 + \lambda_1 Y^* + \varepsilon_1,$$

where H denotes the choice of hours of work, X_1 denotes the relative benefit of working, Y^* denotes unobserved health status, and ε_1 denotes the effect of other random components. Letting Y denote self-reported health, these authors consider the equation

$$Y = \beta_2 X_1 + \lambda_2 Y^* + \varepsilon_2.$$

They assumed that Y^* and X_1 are orthogonal to ε_1 and ε_2. In addition, the correlation between benefits from work (X_1) and health (Y^*) is specified by

$$X_1 = \lambda_4 Y^* + \zeta.$$

The models that we present is this article can be used to estimate the function that determines self-reported health, either as a function of X_1 or as a function of H, nonparametrically. This can then be used to identify the effect of health on hours of work. We consider different situations, starting from the simplest ones, and ending with the simultaneous model where the effect of desired hours of work on reported health is identified.

As above, let Y^* denote the true value of an unobservable variable, and let Y denote the response when asked the value of Y^*. Let $X = (X_1, X_2)$ denote a vector of observable characteristics of the respondent, let W denote observable characteristics of the survey, and let Z denote other observable external variables. In the next section, we first consider the identification of the nonparametric response function m, specified as

$$Y = m(Y^*, X, W),$$

where m is assumed to be strictly increasing in Y^* and the distribution of Y^* (health) conditional on X_1 (work benefits) is known. We then extend this model to include a response error, which depends on X_1 (work benefits, gender), directly added to Y^*, of the form

$$Y = m(Y^* + \eta, X_2, W_2)$$
$$\eta = v(X_1, W_1, \delta),$$

where δ is an unobservable random term that is distributed independently of (X, W, Y^*), and where v is an unknown function that is strictly increasing in δ. We then show that adding an error ε_2, can be done in a similar fashion. Hence, we consider

$$Y = m(Y^* + \eta, X_2, W_2) + \varepsilon_2,$$

where now

$$\varepsilon_2 = s(Z, \omega).$$

In Section 4.1, we deal with the situation where the distribution of Y^* conditional on X_1 is unknown. We show how one may use the knowledge about an exogenous change in relative work benefits (e.g., a change in social security benefits) to identify this distribution. We also show how observable determinants of Y^* can be used to identify this distribution.

In Section 4.2, we deal with the simultaneous model where desired hours of work enter directly into the response function. We consider the model

$$H = m_1(Y^*, X_1) + \varepsilon_1$$

$$Y = Y^* + m_2(H, X_2) + \mu_2$$

and describe what results can be used to identify and estimate the unknown functions and distributions in this model.

3.   KNOWN DISTRIBUTION OF THE TRUE VALUE Y^*

In many situations, one may be able to know the distribution of some variable of interest but not be able to know the particular value of such variable for any particular individual. For example, when Y^* denotes true income, the distribution of Y^* may be obtained from the Social Security Administration records. In the model in Section 2, one may be able to know the distribution of health status, Y^*, conditional on work benefits, X_1, using medical records. Following the notation in Section 2, let Y denote the response when asked about Y^*, $X = (X_1, X_2)$ denote the observable characteristics of the worker, and W denote the vector of characteristics of the survey. Assume that Y^* is independent of (X_2, W) conditional on X_1, and that the model is given by

$$(1) \qquad\qquad\qquad Y = m(Y^*, X, W).$$

Let $F_{Y|X,W}$ denote the joint distribution of the observable variables (Y, X, W). Let $F_{Y^*|X_1}$ denote the distribution of Y^* conditional on X_1. The following result follows by Matzkin (2003):

THEOREM 1 (Matzkin, 2003). *Suppose that, conditional on $X_1 = x_1$, Y^* is distributed independently of (X_2, W) with an everywhere positive, known density. Suppose also that for each (X, W), the function m is strictly increasing in Y^*. Then, for all y^*, x, w for which the values of $F_{Y^*|X_1=x_1}(y^*)$ and of $F_{Y|X=x,W=w}^{-1}(F_{Y^*|X_1=x_1}(y^*))$ exist,*

$$(2) \qquad\qquad m(y^*, x, w) = F_{Y|X_1=x_1, X_2=x_2, W=w}^{-1}\left(F_{Y^*|X_1=x_1}(y^*)\right).$$

Hence, the function m is identified nonparametrically from the joint distribution of (Y, X, W).

Equivalently, we can state that, under the assumptions of Theorem 1, an individual for which $X_1 = x_1$ and who answers $Y = y$ when faced with $(X_2, W) = (x_2, w)$ has a value of the latent variable Y^* equal to

$$y^* = F^{-1}_{Y^*|X_1=x_1}(F_{Y|X_1=x_1, X_2=x_2, W=w}(y)).$$

Replacing $F_{Y|X,W,Z=z}$ (and $F_{Y^*|Z=z}$) by a nonparametric estimator, one can obtain from the above equations estimators for the response function, $m(y^*, x, w)$, and for the value of the latent variable of any individual, given his response, y.

The assumptions in the above model are such that there is a 1 to 1 relationship between the true value, Y^*, of the response and the response, Y. The distributions of Y^* and of Y conditional on (X, W) allow one to determine uniquely such a 1 to 1 relationship. From this, one can map any response with its true corresponding value, without any error. In some cases, this situation may be unrealistic. The same value of the true latent variable Y^* may generate different responses even from individuals that possess the same observable characteristics, X, and are asked the same question, characterized by W. In the model considered in Bound (1991), an unobservable variable, μ_1, added to the response model allowed this effect. Another alternative is to model an added response error to Y^*. In the model in Section 2, we may specify that the response error is

(3) $$\eta = v(X_1, W_1, \delta),$$

where X_1 denotes work benefits and gender, δ is an unobservable random term that is distributed independently of (X, W, Y^*), and where v is an unknown function that is strictly increasing in δ. The inclusion of W_1 allows for this response error to be affected by characteristics of the survey. The model that determines the response Y as a function of Y^*, η, X and W may then be given by

(4) $$Y = m(Y^* + \eta, X_2, W_2).$$

An added term, μ_1, as in the model in Bound (1991), can be handled similarly, by specifying that for some unknown function s, a vector of observable variables, Z, and an unobservable ω

(5) $$\mu_1 = s(Z, \omega),$$

where s is strictly increasing in ω, and ω has an everywhere positive density. The models above then become

(6) $$Y = m(Y^*, X_2, W_2) + \mu_1$$

and

(7) $$Y = m(Y^* + \eta, X_2, W_2) + \mu_1,$$

where

(8) $$\mu_1 = s(Z, \omega).$$

The critical assumptions we make to deal with the multiple unobservables are that for at least one value, $\tilde{z}$, of Z, $s(\tilde{z}, \omega) = 0$ for all ω, and for at least one value $(\tilde{x}_1, \tilde{w}_1)$ of (X_1, W_1), $v(\tilde{x}_1, \tilde{w}_1, \delta) = 0$ for all δ, in addition to assuming that δ is independent of (X, W, Z, ω, Y^*) and ω is independent of (X, W, Z, δ, Y^*). In the model of Section 2, X_1 may denote work benefits from working and gender. Since there exists evidence that women's self-reported health is much less influenced by work benefits than that of men, one may assume that $(\tilde{x}_1, \tilde{w}_1)$ denotes the value of a vector for which a coordinate of X_1 corresponds to women. Another obvious example is where η denotes recall error, on a question that refers to an event in the past, and W_1 denotes how long ago the event refers to. When $W_1 = 0$, one may assume that the value of v is zero for all values of X_1 and δ.

Since the analysis is similar in either case, with η and μ_1 or with only η, we next consider the case with η only. Hence, the model we consider is (4) with (3). In such a model, the following theorem establishes the identification of the functions v and m and of the distributions of δ and η, under some assumptions.

THEOREM 2. *Suppose that (Y^*, δ) is distributed independently of (X_2, W) conditional on X_1, with an everywhere positive density, δ is distributed independently of (X, W, Y^*) with an everywhere positive unknown density, the function m is strictly increasing in $Y^* + \eta$, the function v is strictly increasing in δ, the distribution of Y^* conditional on X_1 is known, and its characteristic function is everywhere different from zero. Restrict the function v to satisfy at one point $(\tilde{x}_1, \tilde{w}_1)$ of (X_1, W_1) the condition: $v(\tilde{x}_1, \tilde{w}_1, \delta) = 0$ for all δ, and at another point $(\tilde{x}_1, \tilde{w}_1)$ of (X_1, W_1) the condition: $v(\tilde{x}_1, \tilde{w}_1, \delta) = \delta$. Then, the function m, the function v, and the distributions of δ and of η conditional on (X_1, W_1) are identified nonparametrically from the joint distribution of (Y, X, W).*

Theorem 2 establishes the nonparametric identification of the response error, $v(x_1, w_1, \delta)$, and the response function m, when the distribution of the variable of interest Y^* is known. Since the proof is constructive, one can use the proof to derive nonparametric estimators for these functions. Note that if the function v were specified as $v(x_1, w_1, \delta) = \delta x_1 + \delta w_1$, then the restrictions on the function v would be satisfied for $\tilde{x}_1 = \tilde{w}_1 = 0$ and for $(\tilde{x}_1, \tilde{w}_1) = (1, 0)$ or $(\tilde{x}_1, \tilde{w}_1) = (0, 1)$.

4. UNKNOWN DISTRIBUTION OF THE TRUE VALUE Y^*

4.1. *Y^* Conditionally Independent of the Explanatory Variables.* The analysis in Section 3 rested on the assumption that the distribution of Y^* conditional on X_1 was either known or could be estimated. Often, one may need to impose additional restrictions or to augment the data to be able to identify, and therefore estimate, this distribution. We next analyze how this can be done by augmenting the data. Consider again the model in Section 2. Suppose that in some period there was a change in the laws regarding work benefits. Let Z_1 denote work benefits for a worker before the change and X_1 denote the work benefits after the change. The exogeneity of the law change may allow one to assume that for some unknown function s,

$$X_1 = s(Z_1, \delta),$$

where δ is independent of the vector of all the observable and other unobservable variables in the model and s is strictly increasing in δ. Using the results in Matzkin (2004), one can then show that, under some monotonicity and support conditions, one can identify the distribution of Y^* conditional on X_1.

Alternatively, we may have information about some of the determinants of Y^*. Consider, for example, the model where

$$Y = m(Y^* + \eta, X_2, W_2), \quad \text{and}$$
$$\eta = v(X_1, W_1, \delta).$$

Suppose that for some unknown function s, some vector, Z, of observable variables, and an unobservable variable, ξ,

$$Y^* = s(Z, \xi).$$

Under assumptions similar to those made in Theorem 2, and some additional assumptions on s and ξ, one can show that the functions m, v, and s are identified. The later set of assumptions may be imposed on the function s, similarly to those imposed in Theorem 2 on the function v and δ, or on the distribution of ξ. We consider the former.

THEOREM 3. *Suppose that (ξ, δ) is distributed independently of (X, W, Z) with an everywhere positive unknown density, δ is distributed independently of (X, W, Z, ξ) with an everywhere positive unknown density, the function m is strictly increasing in $Y^* + \eta$, the function v is strictly increasing in δ, the function s is strictly increasing in ξ, and the characteristic function of ξ is everywhere different from 0. Restrict the function v to satisfy at one point $(\bar{x}_1, \bar{w}_1)$ of (X_1, W_1) the condition: $v(\bar{x}_1, \bar{w}_1, \delta) = 0$ and at another point $(\tilde{x}_1, \tilde{w}_1)$ of (X_1, W_1) the condition: $v(\tilde{x}_1, \tilde{w}_1, \delta) = \delta$. Restrict the function s to satisfy at one point $\bar{z}$ of Z the condition: $s(\bar{z}, \xi) = \xi$. Restrict the function m to satisfy at one point $(\bar{x}_2, \bar{w}_2)$ of (X_2, W_2) the condition: $m(t, \bar{x}_2, \bar{w}_2) = t$. Then, the functions m, v, and s as well as the distributions of δ, η, ξ, and Y^* conditional on (X, W, Z) are identified nonparametrically from the joint distribution of (Y, X, W, Z).*

4.2. *Y^* Not Conditionally Independent of the Explanatory Variables.* The model where work benefits are included directly in the response function does not allow one to infer directly the effect of the desired hours of work on self-reported health. A more structural model would be

$$H = m_1(Y^*, X_1) + \varepsilon_1$$
$$Y = m_2(Y^*, H, X_2, W) + \mu_2.$$

The identification and estimation of the unknown functions and distributions in this model can be analyzed using the results in Matzkin (2007) (see also Matzkin, 2005). In particular, suppose that for unknown functions m_1, m_2, s_1, s_2,

$$H = m_1(Y^*, X_1) + \varepsilon_1,$$

$$Y = Y^* + m_2(H, X_2) + \mu_2,$$

$$X_1 = s_1(Z_1, \delta),$$

and

$$\mu_2 = s_2(Z_2, \omega_2),$$

where X_2 may denote here a characteristic of either the respondent or the survey. Let $f_{\varepsilon_1, y^*}(\varepsilon_1, y^*)$ denote the joint density of (ε_1, y^*), conditional on $Z_1 = \bar{z}_1, Z_2 = \bar{z}_2$ where $\bar{z}_1$ and $\bar{z}_2$ denote particular given values of Z_1 and Z_2. Let $\tilde{x}_1$ denote a given value of X_1. Matzkin (2007) makes use of the following assumptions to show that the derivatives of m_1 and m_2 are identified:

   (i) m_1 is strictly increasing in Y^*, s_1 is strictly increasing in δ, and s_2 is strictly increasing in ω_2,
  (ii) the vector (X, W, Z, H, Y) and the vector $(X, W, Z, \varepsilon_1, \omega_2, \delta, Y^*)$ have full support,
 (iii) ω_2 is independent of $(Y^*, \varepsilon_1, X_1, X_2, \delta)$ conditional on $Z_1 = \bar{z}_1, Z_2 = \bar{z}_2$;
  (iv) δ is independent of $(Y^*, \varepsilon_1, X_2, w)$ conditional on $Z_1 = \bar{z}_1, Z_2 = \bar{z}_2$,
  (iv) for all $\omega_2, s_2(\bar{z}_2, \omega_2) = 0$
   (v) at $X_1 = \tilde{x}_1, m_1(y^*, \tilde{x}_1) = y^*$;
  (vi) (ε_1, Y^*) is independent of (X_1, X_2), conditional on $Z_1 = \bar{z}_1, Z_2 = \bar{z}_2$ and
 (vii) for all values of y^*, there exists a value of ε_1 such that

$$\frac{\partial \log f_{\varepsilon_1, y^*}(\varepsilon_1, y^*)}{\partial \varepsilon_1} = 0 \quad \text{and} \quad \frac{\partial \log f_{\varepsilon_1, y^*}(\varepsilon_1, y^*)}{\partial y^*} \neq 0.$$

In Matzkin (2007) a method to directly calculate, from the density of the observable variables, the derivatives of m_1 and m_2 is presented.

5.   EXTENSIONS

The results that have been presented in the previous sections can be extended to analyze models with nested response errors and models where the responses are discrete.

Answering a survey question involves the stage of comprehension of the question, the stage of retrieving and assembling relevant information, the stage of filtering the information, and the stage of actually responding to the question with an answer that may or may not be the one that the respondent have come up with prior to responding (see Tourangeau et al., 2000). Each of these stages adds a level of noise to the response, which will typically be different across respondents. Variation in the noise may depend on observable characteristics, but, it will typically also depend on unobservable characteristics. The design of the survey and of the particular question being asked add additional layers of possible noise, which interact and affect the magnitudes of the processing noise. A model that allows for all these errors at the different stages may take, for example, the form

$$Y = m(s((v(\delta_3, X_3, W_3) + \delta_2), X_2, W_2) + \delta_1, X_1, W_1)$$

or the form

$$Y = m(s(X_2, W_2, \delta_2) + v(X_3, W_3, \delta_3) + \delta_1, X_1, W_1).$$

The identification and estimation of the unknown functions and distributions in these models can be achieved by following a similar analysis to that described in the previous sections.

Discrete responses are also very common. Some questions ask for a 0 or 1 answer. Some respondents prefer not to answer some questions. The identification and estimation of such models can be performed also by extending the above results. Consider for example a situation where an individual is asked whether he thinks that the probability that he will ever need a nursing home is above or below 0.5. The individual may decide jointly the answer to the question and whether or not to answer. Let $R = 1$ if he answers and $R = 0$ otherwise. Let $Z = 1$ if the response is that the probability is above 0.5; $Z = 0$ otherwise. Some of the variables affecting the respondent's behavior may be observable and some may be unobservable. Suppose, in particular, that $R = 1$ if $W_1 + v(X, W_2, \eta) \geq \varepsilon_R$, where $W_1, W_2,$ and X are observable and η and ε_R are unobservable, and the value of v is known at one point. (This setup generalizes a model of discrete response to survey treatments W_1 analyzed by McFadden, 1994.) Suppose that $Z = 1$ if $\tilde{W}_1 + r(\tilde{X}, \tilde{W}_2, \eta) \geq \varepsilon_Z$, where $\tilde{W}_1, \tilde{W}_2,$ and $\tilde{X}$ are observable, ε_Z is unobservable, and the function r is known at one point. Then

$$\Pr(R = 1, Z = 1 \mid X, W, \tilde{X}, \tilde{W}, \eta) = F_{\varepsilon_R, \varepsilon_Z}(W_1 + v(X, W_2, \eta), W_1 + r(\tilde{X}, \tilde{W}_2, \eta)).$$

Under strong independence and support conditions, and some normalizations on the functions v and r, one can identify the nonparametric distribution of $(\varepsilon_R, \varepsilon_Z, \eta)$ and the nonparametric functions v and r (see Matzkin, 1993, 1994, 2005, 2006; Briesch et al., 1997, 2007; Lewbel, 2000).

APPENDIX

PROOF OF THEOREM 1. By conditional independence between Y^* and (X_2, W) given X_1, and strict monotonicity, it follows that for all (x, w)

$$F_{Y^* \mid X_1 = x_1}(y^*) = \Pr(Y^* \leq y^* \mid X_1 = x_1) = \Pr(Y^* \leq y^* \mid X = x, W = w)$$
$$= \Pr(m(Y^*, X, W) \leq m(y^*, x, w) \mid X = x, W = w)$$
$$= F_{Y \mid (X, W) = (x, w)}(m(y^*, x, w)).$$

Since the assumptions imply that $F_{Y \mid (X, W) = (x, w)}$ is strictly increasing, it follows that

$$m(y^*, x, w) = F^{-1}_{Y \mid X = x, W = w}\left(F_{Y^* \mid X_1 = x_1}(y^*)\right).$$

Hence, m is identified. ∎

PROOF OF THEOREM 2. Since (Y^*, δ) is distributed independently of (X_2, W), conditional on X_1, Y^* is distributed independently of (X_2, W_2) conditional on any values of (X_1, W_1), $Y^* + \delta$ is distributed independently of (X_2, W_2) conditional on any values of (X_1, W_1), and $Y^* + \eta = Y^* + v(X_1, W_1, \delta)$ is distributed independently of (X_2, W_2) conditional on any values of (X_1, W_1). Moreover, when $(X_1, W_1) = (\tilde{x}_1, \tilde{w}_1)$, $\eta = v(\tilde{x}_1, \tilde{w}_1, \delta) = 0$ and $Y^* + \eta = Y^*$; and when $(X_1, W_1) = (\check{x}_1, \check{w}_1)$, $\eta = v(\check{x}_1, \check{w}_1, \delta) = \delta$ and $Y^* + \eta = Y^* + \delta$. Hence, for any (x_2, w_2)

(A.1) $F_{Y^* \mid X_1 = \tilde{x}_1}(y^*)$

$$= F_{Y^* + \eta \mid (X_1, W_1) = (\tilde{x}_1, \tilde{w}_1)}(y^*)$$
$$= F_{Y^* + \eta}(y^* \mid (X_1, W_1) = (\tilde{x}_1, \tilde{w}_1), (X_2, W_2) = (x_2, w_2))$$
$$= \Pr(Y^* + \eta \leq y^* \mid (X_1, W_1) = (\tilde{x}_1, \tilde{w}_1), (X_2, W_2) = (x_2, w_2))$$
$$= \Pr(m(Y^* + \eta, X_2, W_2) \leq m(y^*; x_2, w_2) \mid (X_1, W_1) = (\tilde{x}_1, \tilde{w}_1),$$
$$(X_2, W_2) = (x_2, w_2))$$
$$= F_{Y \mid X = (\tilde{x}_1, x_2), W = (\tilde{w}_1, w_2)}(m(y^*, x_2, w_2)).$$

Since our assumptions imply that $F_{Y \mid X = (\tilde{x}_1, x_2), W = (\tilde{w}_1, w_2)}$ is invertible, this implies that for any t and any (x_2, w_2)

(A.2) $$m(t, x_2, w_2) = F^{-1}_{Y \mid X = (\tilde{x}_1, x_2), W = (\tilde{w}_1, w_2)}\left(F_{Y^* \mid (X_1, W_1) = (\tilde{x}_1, \tilde{w}_1)}(t)\right).$$

Hence, m is identified nonparametrically.

Using a similar reasoning as above, we get that for any (x_2, w_2)

(A.3) $F_{Y^*+\delta|X_1=\tilde{x}_1}(y^* + \delta)$

$= F_{Y^*+\eta}(y^* + \delta \,|\, (X_1, W_1) = (\tilde{x}_1, \tilde{w}_1))$

$= F_{Y^*+\eta}(y^* + \delta \,|\, (X_1, W_1) = (\tilde{x}_1, \tilde{w}_1), (X_2, W_2) = (x_2, w_2))$

$= \Pr(Y^* + \eta \leq y^* + \delta \,|\, (X_1, W_1) = (\tilde{x}_1, \tilde{w}_1), (X_2, W_2) = (x_2, w_2))$

$= \Pr(m(Y^* + \eta, X_2, W_2) \leq m(y^* + \delta, x_2, w_2) \,|\, (X_1, W_1) = (\tilde{x}_1, \tilde{w}_1),$

$\qquad (X_2, W_2) = (x_2, w_2))$

$= F_{Y|X=(\tilde{x}_1,x_2), W=(\tilde{w}_1,w_2)}(m(y^* + \delta, x_2, w_2)).$

Using (A.1), this implies that

$$F_{Y^*+\delta|X_1=\tilde{x}_1}(y^* + \delta) = F_{Y|X=(\tilde{x}_1,x_2), W=(\tilde{w}_1,w_2)}\big(F^{-1}_{Y|X=(\tilde{x}_1,x_2), W=(\tilde{w}_1,w_2)}\big(F_{Y^*|X_1=\tilde{x}_1}(y^* + \delta)\big)\big).$$

Hence, for any t

(A.4) $$F_{Y^*+\delta||X_1=\tilde{x}_1}(t) = F_{Y|X=(\tilde{x}_1,x_2), W=(\tilde{w}_1,w_2)}\big(F^{-1}_{Y|X=(\tilde{x}_1,x_2), W=(\tilde{w}_1,w_2)}\big(F_{Y^*|X_1=\tilde{x}_1}(t)\big)\big).$$

This implies that the distribution of $Y^* + \delta$ conditional on $X_1 = \tilde{x}_1$, is identified. Since, by assumption, the distribution of Y^* conditional on $X_1 = \tilde{x}_1$ is known, and δ is independent of X_1, one can obtain the distribution of δ by deconvolution. Hence, the distribution of δ is identified.

Next, we derive an expression for the distribution of $Y^* + \eta$ conditional on any (X_1, W_1). Similarly to above,

(A.5) $F_{Y^*+\eta|(X_1,W_1)=(x_1,w_1)}(y^* + \eta)$

$= F_{Y^*+\eta}(y^* + \eta \,|\, (X_1, W_1) = (x_1, w_1), (X_2, W_2) = (x_2, w_2))$

$= \Pr(Y^* + \eta \leq y^* + \eta \,|\, (X_1, W_1) = (x_1, w_1), (X_2, W_2) = (x_2, w_2))$

$= \Pr(m(Y^* + \eta, X_2, W_2) \leq m(y^* + \eta, x_2, w_2) \,|\, (X_1, W_1) = (x_1, w_1),$

$\qquad (X_2, W_2) = (x_2, w_2))$

$= F_{Y|X=(x_1,x_2), W=(w_1,w_2)}(m(y^* + \eta, x_2, w_2))$

$= F_{Y|X=(x_1,x_2), W=(w_1,w_2)}\big(F^{-1}_{Y|X=(\tilde{x}_1,x_2), W=(\tilde{w}_1,w_2)}\big(F_{Y^*|X_1=\tilde{x}_1}(y^* + \eta)\big)\big),$

where the last equality follows by (A.2). Hence, for any t and any (x_1, w_1),

(A.6)

$$F_{Y^*+\eta|(X_1,W_1)=(x_1,w_1)}(t) = F_{Y|X=(x_1,x_2), W=(w_1,w_2)}\big(F^{-1}_{Y|X=(\tilde{x}_1,x_2), W=(\tilde{w}_1,w_2)}\big(F_{Y^*|X_1=\tilde{x}_1}(t)\big)\big).$$

This implies that the distribution of $Y^* + \eta$ conditional on $(X_1, W_1) = (x_1, w_1)$ is identified. Since, by our assumptions, Y^* is distributed independently of η conditional on (X_1, W_1), Y^* is distributed independently of W_1, conditional on X_1, and the distribution of Y^* conditional on X_1 is known, we can get from the distribution of $Y^* + \eta$ conditional on (X_1, W_1) the distribution of η conditional on (X_1, W_1), by deconvolution. Hence, the distribution of η conditional on (X_1, W_1) is identified.

Last, to show that the function v is identified, we use the strictly monotonicity of v in δ and the independence between δ and (X_1, W_1), to establish as in the proof of Theorem 1 that for any t and any (x_1, w_1)

$$F_\delta(t) = F_{\eta|(X_1, W_1)=(x_1, w_1)}(v(x_1, w_1, t)).$$

This implies that

(A.7) $$v(x_1, w_1, t) = F^{-1}_{\eta|(X_1, W_1)=(x_1, w_1)}(F_\delta(t)).$$

Since F_δ and $F_{\eta|(X_1, W_1)=(x_1, w_1)}$ are identified, v is identified. This completes the proof. ∎

PROOF OF THEOREM 3.   Following arguments as in the proof of Theorem 2, we have that since (ξ, δ) is distributed independently of (X, W, Z), ξ is distributed independently of (X_2, W_2, Z) conditional on any values of (X_1, W_1), $\xi + \delta$ is distributed independently of (X_2, W_2, Z) conditional on any values of (X_1, W_1), and $Y^* + \eta = s(Z, \xi) + v(X_1, W_1, \delta)$ is distributed independently of (X_2, W_2) conditional on any values of (X_1, W_1, Z). Moreover, when $(X_1, W_1, Z) = (\bar{x}_1, \bar{w}_1, \bar{z})$, $Y^* + \eta = \xi$; and when $(X_1, W_1) = (\tilde{x}_1, \tilde{w}_1)$, $\eta = v(\tilde{x}_1, \tilde{w}_1, \delta) = \delta$ and $Y^* + \eta = Y^* + \delta$. Hence, for any e and (x_2, w_2)

(A.8) $F_\xi(e)$

$$= F_{\xi|X=(x_1, x_2), W=(w_1, w_2), Z=z}(e)$$

$$= F_{Y^*+\eta|X=(\bar{x}_1, x_2), W=(\bar{w}_1, w_2), Z=\bar{z}}(e)$$

$$= \Pr\left(Y^* + \eta \le e \mid (X_1, W_1, Z) = (\bar{x}_1, \bar{w}_1, \bar{z}), (X_2, W_2) = (x_2, w_2)\right)$$

$$= \Pr\left(m(Y^* + \eta, X_2, W_2) \le m(e, x_2, w_2) \mid (X_1, W_1, Z) = (\bar{x}_1, \bar{w}_1, \bar{z}),\right.$$
$$\left.(X_2, W_2) = (x_2, w_2)\right)$$

$$= F_{Y|X=(\bar{x}_1, x_2), W=(\bar{w}_1, w_2), Z=\bar{z}}(m(e, x_2, w_2)).$$

Since for all t, $m(t, \bar{x}_2, \bar{w}_2) = t$

(A.9) $$F_\xi(e) = F_{Y|X=(\bar{x}_1, \bar{x}_2), W=(\bar{w}_1, \bar{w}_2), Z=\bar{z}}(e)$$

Hence, F_ξ is identified. Using this in (A.8), we get that

$$F_{Y|X=(\bar{x}_1, \bar{x}_2), W=(\bar{w}_1, \bar{w}_2), Z=\bar{z}}(e) = F_{Y|X=(\bar{x}_1, x_2), W=(\bar{w}_1, w_2), Z=\bar{z}}(m(e, x_2, w_2)).$$

Since our assumption imply that $F_{Y|X=(\bar{x}_1,x_2),W=(\bar{w}_1,w_2),Z=\bar{z}}$ is invertible, this implies that for any t and any (x_2, w_2)

$$(A.10) \qquad m(t, x_2, w_2) = F^{-1}_{Y|X=(\bar{x}_1,x_2),W=(\bar{w}_1,w_2),Z=\bar{z}}(F_{Y|X=(\bar{x}_1,\bar{x}_2),W=(\bar{w}_1,\bar{w}_2),Z=\bar{z}}(t)).$$

Hence, m is identified nonparametrically.

Using a similar reasoning as in (A.8), we get that for any (x_2, w_2) and any z

$$(A.11) \qquad F_\xi(e) = F_{\xi|X=(x_1,x_2),W=(w_1,w_2),Z=z}(e)$$
$$= F_{Y|X=(\bar{x}_1,x_2),W=(\bar{w}_1,w_2),Z=z}(s(z,e)).$$

Equation (A.9) together with the strict monotonicity of $F_{Y^*|X=(\bar{x}_1,x_2),W=(\bar{w}_1,w_2),Z=z}$ imply then that

$$(A.12) \qquad s(z, e) = F^{-1}_{Y|X=(\bar{x}_1,x_2),W=(\bar{w}_1,w_2),Z=z}(F_{Y|X=(\bar{x}_1,\bar{x}_2),W=(\bar{w}_1,\bar{w}_2),Z=\bar{z}}(e)).$$

Hence, the function s is identified. Since the distribution of ξ is also identified, this implies that the distribution of Y^* conditional on Z is also identified.

The distribution of δ is identified because for any t

$$F_{\xi+\delta}(t) = F_{Y|(X_1,W_1)=(\bar{x}_1,\bar{w}_1),(X_2,W_2)=(x_2,w_2),Z=\bar{z}}(m(t, x_2, w_2)),$$

and, using (A.10), it follows that for any x_2, w_2

$$m(t, x_2, w_2) = \big(F^{-1}_{Y|X=(\bar{x}_1,x_2),W=(\bar{w}_1,w_2),Z=\bar{z}}(F_{Y|X=(\bar{x}_1,\bar{x}_2),W=(\bar{w}_1,\bar{w}_2),Z=\bar{z}}(t))\big).$$

This implies that the distribution of $\xi + \delta$ is identified. Hence, by deconvolution, we can obtain the distribution of δ, using the already identified distribution of ξ.

The distribution of η conditional on (X_1, W_1) is identified because for any t, x_2, w_2

$$F_{\xi+\eta|(X_1,W_1)=(x_1,w_1)}(t) = F_{Y|(X_1,W_1)=(x_1,w_1),(X_2,W_2)=(x_2,w_2),Z=\bar{z}}(m(t, x_2, w_2))$$

and

$$m(t, x_2, w_2) = \big(F^{-1}_{Y|X=(\bar{x}_1,x_2),W=(\bar{w}_1,w_2),Z=\bar{z}}(F_{Y|X=(\bar{x}_1,\bar{x}_2),W=(\bar{w}_1,\bar{w}_2),Z=\bar{z}}(t))\big).$$

Hence, since the distribution of ξ is known, and ξ is distributed independently of (X_1, W_1), the distribution of η conditional on (X_1, W_1) is identified. From this conditional distribution and the distribution of δ, we can identify $v(x_1, w_1, \delta)$, by the arguments in Theorem 1, as

$$v(x_1, w_1, \delta) = F^{-1}_{\eta|(X_1, W_1)=(x_1, w_1)}(F_\delta(\delta)).$$

This completes the proof.   ■

REFERENCES

AIGNER, D. J., C. HSIAO, A. KAPTEYN, AND T. WANSBEEK, "Latent Variable Models in Econometrics," in Z. Griliches and M. D. Intriligator, eds., *Handbook of Econometrics* Vol. 2 (North Holland, Amsterdam, 1985), 1323–1393.

BATTISTIN, E., "Errors in Survey Reports of Consumption Expenditures," Working Paper 0307, Institute for Fiscal Studies (2003), London.

BOLLINGER, C. R., "Measurement Error in the Current Population Survey: A Nonparametric Look," *Journal of Labor Economics* 16 (1998), 576–94.

BOUND, J., "Self-reported vs. Objective Measures of Health in Retirement Models," *Journal of Human Resources* 26 (1991), 106–138.

BOUND, J., AND A. KRUEGER, "The Extent of Measurement Error in Longitudinal Earning Data: Do Two Wrongs Make a Right?" *Journal of Labor Economics* 16 (1991), 576–94.

——, C. BROWN, AND N. MATHIOWETZ, "Measurement Error in Survey Data," in J. J. Heckman and E. Leamer, eds., *Handbook of Econometrics*, Volume 5 (Amsterdam: Elsevier, 2001), 3705–843.

BRIESCH, R., P. CHINTAGUNTA, AND R. L. MATZKIN, "Nonparametric Discrete Choice Models with Unobserved Heterogeneity," Mimeo, Northwestern University, presented at the Far-Eastern Meeting of the Econometric Society, 1997.

——, "Nonparametric Discrete Choice Models with Unobserved Heterogeneity," mimeo, Northwestern University, 2007.

CANNELL, C., G. FISHER, AND T. BAKKER, "Reporting of Hospitalizations in the Health Interview Survey," *Vital and Health Statitics,* Series 2, Number 6 (Washington: Public Health Service, 1965).

CARROLL, R. J., D. RUPPERT, AND D. STEFANSKI, *Measurement Error in Nonlinear Models* (New York: Chapman and Hall, 1995).

CHASE, D. R., AND M. HARADA, "Response Error in Self-Reported Recreation Participation," *Journal of Leisure Research* 16 (1984), 322–29.

CHEN, X., H. HONG, AND D. NEKIPELOV, "Measurement Error Models," Mimeo, NYU, 2007.

ETTNER, S., "Is Working Good for You? Evidence on the Endogeneity of Mental and Physical Health to Female Employment," Unpublished paper, Harvard School of Public Health, 1997.

FULLER, W., *Measurement Error Models* (New York: Wiley, 1987).

GEMS, B., D. GHAOSH, AND R. HITLIN, "A Recall Experiment: Impact of Time on Recall of Recreational Fishing Trips," *Proceedings of the Section on Survey Research Methods* (Alexandria, VA: American Statistical Association, 1982), 168–73.

GROVES, R. M., *Survey Errors and Survey Costs* (New York: Wiley, 1989).

HAUSMAN, J., "Mismeasured Variables in Econometric Analysis: Problems from the Right and Problems from the Left," *The Journal of Economic Perspectives* 15 (2001), 57–67.

HODERLEIN, S., AND J. WINTER, "Recall Errors in Surveys," Mimeo, Mannheim University, 2007.

HURD, M. D., D. McFADDEN, H. CHAND, L. GAN, A. RMERRILLL, AND M. ROBERTS, "Consumption and Saving Balances of the Elderly: Experimental Evidence on Survey Response Bias," in D. Wise, ed., *Frontiers in the Economics of Aging* (Chicago, IL: University of Chicago Press, 1998), 353–87.

LEWBEL, A., "Semiparametric Qualitative Response Model Estimation with Unknown Heteroskedasticity and Instrumental Variables," *Journal of Econometrics* 97 (2000), 145–77.

LOFTUS, E. F., "Leading Questions and the Eyewitness Report," *Cognitive Psychology* 7 (1975), 560–72.

MATZKIN, R. L., "Nonparametric Identification and Estimation of Polychotomous Choice Models," *Journal of Econometrics* 58 (1993).

——, "Restrictions of Economic Theory in Nonparametric Methods," in R. F. Engel and D. McFadden, eds., *Handbook of Econometrics*, Volume 4 (Amsterdam: North Holland, 1994).

——, "Nonparametric Estimation of Nonadditive Random Functions," *Econometrica* 71 (2003), 1339–75.

——, "Unobservable Instruments," Mimeo, Northwestern University, 2004.

——, "Identification in Nonparametric Simultaneous Equations," Mimeo, Northwestern University, 2005.

——, "Heterogeneous Choice," in R. Blundell, W. Newey, and T. Persson, eds., *Advances in Economics and Econometrics, Theory and Applications, Ninth World Congress* (New York: Cambridge University Press, 2006).

——, "Estimation in Nonparametric Simultaneous Equations," Mimeo, Northwestern University, 2007.

McFADDEN, D. L., "Contingent Valuation and Social Choice," *American Journal of Agricultural Economics* 76 (1994), 689–708.

——, "How Consumers Respond to Incentives," Jean-Jacques Laffont Lecture, Mimeo, University of California at Berkeley, 2006.

——, *Foundations of Economic Survey Research* (Princeton, N.J.: Princeton University Press, 2007), forthcoming.

——, A. C. Bemmaor, F. G. Caro, J. Dominitz, B.-H. Jun, A. Lewbel, R. L. Matzkin, F. Molinari, N. Schwarz, R. J. Willis, and J. Winter, "Statistical Analysis of Choice Experiments and Surveys," *Marketing Letters* 16 (2005).

——, N. SCHWARZ, AND J. WINTER, "Measuring Perceptions and Behavior in Household Surveys," Mimeo, Mannheim Research Institute for the Economics of Aging, 2003.

MOFFIT, R., AND G. RIDDER, "The Econometrics of Data Combination," in J. J. Heckman and E. E. Leamer, eds., *Handbook of Econometrics*, Volume 6 (Amsterdam: Elsevier, 2007).

NETER, J., AND J. WAKSBERG, "A Study of Response Errors in Expenditures Data from Household Interviews," *Journal of the American Statistical Association* 5 (1964), 17–55.

PHILIPSON, T., "Data Markets and the Production of Surveys," *Review of Economic Studies* 64 (1997), 47–72.

——, "Data Markets, Missing Data, and Incentive Pay," *Econometrica* 69 (2001), 1099–111.

POTERBA, J., AND L. SUMMERS, "Reporting Errors and Labor Market Dynamics," *Econometrica* 54 (1986), 1319–38.

SCHWARZ, N., H. J. HIPPPLER, B. DEUTSCH, AND F. STRACK, "Response Categories: Effects on Behavioral Reports and Comparative Judgements," *Public Opinion Quarterly* 49 (1985), 388–95.

——, B. KNAUPER, H. J. HIPPLER, E. NOELLE-NEUMANN, AND F. CLARK, "Rating Scales: Numeric Values May Change the Meaning of Scale Labels," *Public Opinion Quarterly* 55 (1991), 618–30.

TOURANGEAU, R., L. J. RIPS, AND K. RASINSKI, *The Psychology of Survey Response* (New York and Cambridge, UK: Cambridge University Press, 2000).

WAKSBERG, J., AND R. VALLIANT, "Final Report on the Evaluation and Calibration of NEISS" (Westat, Inc., for Consumer Products Safety Commission), 1978.

WANSBEEK, T., AND E. MEIJER, *Measurement Error and Latent Variables in Econometrics* (New York: North Holland, 2000).

INTERNATIONAL ECONOMIC REVIEW
Vol. 48, No. 4, November 2007

NONPARAMETRIC CONTINUOUS/DISCRETE CHOICE MODELS*

BY WHITNEY K. NEWEY[1]

M.I.T., U.S.A.

Modeling choices that are both discrete and continuous is important in several settings. The purpose of this article is to explore formulation and identification of such models when indirect utility functions are specified nonparametrically. Here we consider general nonseparable disturbances. We give identification results for nonseparable sample selection models and use these to analyze identification of discrete/continuous choice models.

1. INTRODUCTION

Modeling choices that are both discrete and continuous is important in several settings. Dubin and McFadden (1984) analyze appliance choice and the demand for electricity. Others have used such models for housing demand. The purpose of this article is to explore formulation and identification of such models when indirect utility functions are specified nonparametrically. Such models can help avoid functional form misspecification.

In these models it is essential to allow disturbances that are not additively separable. Since the demand function depends on derivatives, additively separable disturbances will not lead to unobserved heterogeneity in demands. Dubin and McFadden (1984) specified a model with a multiplicative disturbance. Here we consider general nonseparable disturbances.

As is well known, estimation of demand functions generally requires accounting for sample selection from the discrete choices. In order to do this we develop results for identification of nonseparable models with sample selection. We use these results to consider identification of the discrete/continuous choice models.

Section 2 of the article describes the model. Section 3 of the article gives identification results for a nonseparable sample selection model. Section 4 applies these results to identification of the discrete/continuous choice model.

2. THE MODEL

The model we consider is a nonparametric generalization of the model of Dubin and McFadden (1984). In that model there is a good that is demanded, such as electricity, where the demand depends on a choice among several discrete outcomes,

---

* Manuscript received July 2007.

[1] The NSF provided support via SES 0136869. An early version of this article was presented at the CEME conference at Berkeley in honor of Daniel McFadden. Please address correspondence to: Whitney K. Newey, Department of Economics, M.I.T. Cambridge, MA 02139, U.S.A. Phone: 617-253-6420. Fax: 617-253-1330. E-mail: *wnewey@mit.edu*.

such as heating systems. To describe the model let q denote the consumption of the good, p_1 its price, p_2 the price of outside goods, and y income. Let $j \in \{1, \ldots, J\}$ index the discrete choice and r_j denote the price of choice j. Also let ε be a disturbance vector representing individual heterogeneity. Suppose also that the agent chooses j and q to maximize utility in a two stage optimization, with q being chosen to maximize utility for each given j and j being chosen to maximize utility. Let $V_j(p_1, p_2, y, \varepsilon)$ denote the indirect utility function for choice j for the agent indexed by ε. For simplicity we do not allow for other observable variables to enter the indirect utility function, although it would be straightforward to allow for this.

As is customary, we describe the agents' optimal discrete choice by a vector of dummy variables $(d_1, \ldots, d_J)$ with

$$d_j = 1(V_j(p_1, p_2, y - r_j, \varepsilon) \geq V_k(p_1, p_2, y - r_k, \varepsilon), k \neq j).$$

By Roys identity the consumption q_j of the good when j is chosen is

$$q_j = -\frac{\partial V_j(p_1, p_2, y - r_j, \varepsilon)/\partial p_1}{\partial V_j(p_1, p_2, y - r_j, \varepsilon)/\partial y}.$$

Together these equations describe the discrete choices d_j and the continuous demand q_j.

This models is a version of the model of Dubin and McFadden (1984) that allows for the disturbances ε to enter in a general nonseparable way. It would be good to undertake a general analysis of identification of this model. Such an analysis would be difficult. Little is known about identification of demand in the case where there is no discrete choice. Some progress has been made, see Matzkin (2007), etc., but we are still some distance from full results. In keeping with this state of the literature we take a more modest goal of deriving identification results when the discrete choices have an index structure. This still represents a nonparametric generalization of Dubin and McFadden (1984) and is based on new identification results for nonseparable sample selection models that are given here.

The model we focus on restricts the indirect utility function to take the form

$$V_j(p_1, p_2, y, \varepsilon) = T(v_j(p_1, p_2, y) + \eta_j; p_2, p_1, \varepsilon),$$

where η_j is a scalar element of ε and for each p_1, p_2, and ε, $T(v; p_2, p_1, \varepsilon)$ is a strictly increasing function of v. In this model the discrete outcome will be given by

$$d_j = 1(v_j(p_1, p_2, y - r_j) + \eta_j \geq v_k(p_1, p_2, y - r_k) + \eta_k, k \neq j).$$

This is the familiar multinomial choice model with additive disturbances. Let $X = (p_1, p_2, y - r_1, \ldots, y - r_J)$ denote the vector of prices and income net of purchase prices for the alternatives and let $X_j = (p_1, p_2, y - r_j)$. Given choice j the demand is obtained from Roy's identity as

$$h_j(X_j.\varepsilon) = -\left[\frac{\partial T(v_j + \eta_j; p_2, p_1, \varepsilon)}{\partial v} \frac{\partial v_j(p_1, p_2, y - r_j)}{\partial y}\right]^{-1}$$

$$\times \left[\frac{\partial T(v_j + \eta_j; p_2, p_1, \varepsilon)}{\partial v} \frac{\partial v_j(p_1, p_2, y - r_j)}{\partial p_1}\right.$$

$$\left. + \frac{\partial T(v_j + \eta_j; p_2, p_1, \varepsilon)}{\partial p_1}\right],$$

where $v_j = v_j(p_1, p_2, y - r_j)$.

The above model generalizes the model that Dubin and McFadden (1984) considered in their application. That model was specified with $\varepsilon_j = \eta_j, (j = 1, \ldots, J)$, and

$$V_j(p_1, p_2, y, \varepsilon)$$

$$= \left(\alpha_0^j + \frac{\alpha_1^j}{\beta} + \alpha_1^j p_1 + \alpha_2^j p_2 + \beta(y - r_j) + \varepsilon_{J+1}\right) e^{-\beta p_1} - \alpha_5 \ln p_2 + \eta_j.$$

This model is a special case of the above model where

$$v_j = \left(\alpha_0^j + \frac{\alpha_1^j}{\beta} + \alpha_1^j p_1 + \alpha_2^j p_2 + \beta(y - r_j)\right) e^{-\beta p_1},$$

$$T(v; p_1, p_2, \varepsilon) = v + \varepsilon_{J+1} e^{-\beta p_1} - \alpha_5 \ln p_2.$$

The above model does not include the most general model mentioned by Dubin and McFadden (1984), which takes the form

$$V_j(p_1, p_2, y, \varepsilon) = \psi\left([M^j(p_1, p_2) + y + \eta_j/\beta_j]e^{-\beta_j p_1}, p_2, \varepsilon_j\right).$$

This model does not give choice utilities that are additively separable in disturbances and so does not fit in our framework. Also, Dubin and McFadden did not use this model in their estimation. For this model the choice probabilities would not have the linear index form that is most common in applications.

The choice and demand equations can be thought of as a nonseparable sample selection model where the selection and outcome equations are related to each other. The specification of the demand function $h_j(X_j, \varepsilon)$ depends on the choice j. This demand function may depend on disturbances that are correlated with the disturbances $v_1, \ldots, v_J$ of the choice equation. Consequently, it is important to account for the choices in identifying the demand equations. In the next section, we consider identification of such a nonseparable sample selection model.

3. THE NONSEPARABLE SAMPLE SELECTION MODEL

To obtain identification results for the discrete/continuous choice model it is helpful to consider a nonseparable sample selection model. This model may also be of interest in its own right, in view of the many potential applications of sample selection models. Here, we will let Y denote the outcome variable, X observable variables affecting the outcome, and ε disturbances affecting the outcome, and assume that

$$Y = g(X, \varepsilon).$$

The sample selection problem is that Y is only observed on a subset of the sample and that the event that Y is observed may be related to ε. Let S be a selection indicator that is equal to 1 when Y is observed and zero otherwise. If the event $S = 1$ is not independent of ε conditional on X, then ignoring the sample selection is an error.

In the discrete/continuous choice model demand based on one choice, say choice j, can be considered a sample selection model. There the selection indicator S is an indicator for j being chosen. There X is X_j and the outcome equation $g(X, \varepsilon) = h_j(X_j, \varepsilon)$ is the demand equation for the jth choice.

We will begin by considering the case where there is a single index that governs selection. Below we will extend the results to the multiple index cases needed for discrete/continuous choice models. In addition to X we will assume that there is a (possibly vector valued) variable Z that affects the probability of selection.

Our single index assumption is:

ASSUMPTION 1. *For observed Z and unobserved u and $F_u(t)$ the CDF of u,*

$$S = 1(u \leq \Pi(X, Z)), (\varepsilon, u) \text{ and } (X, Z) \text{ independent,}$$

and $F_u(t)$ is strictly monotonic.

Under this condition the selection probability will be

$$P = \Pr(S = 1 \mid X, Z) = F_u(\Pi(X, Z)).$$

This selection probability is often referred to as the "propensity score."

Here the variable Z is one that is excluded from X but included in the selection equation. This kind of exclusion restriction, which is necessary for identification of many objects of interest, is available in discrete/continuous choice models. If Y is demand when the jth choice is made, then $y - r_k$ for some k not equal to j will be such an excluded variable. In other sample selection models, where the model is not motivated so closely by economics, it may be more difficult to justify this kind of exclusion restriction.

Because of the index form of selection, X and ε will be independent conditional on the propensity score P, in the selected data. Thus, the propensity score is a control function for the selected data. Consequently, known results on identification of nonseparable models with control functions can be applied here to identify structural effects in the selected sample, i.e., conditional on the event $S = 1$. In the sample selection model identification of such conditional effects seems all one can hope for, because Y is not even observed if $S = 0$.

The following result demonstrates the conditional independence.

THEOREM 1. *If Assumption 1 is satisfied, then ε and X are independent conditional on P.*

PROOF. By monotonicity of $F_u(t)$

$$S \stackrel{def}{=} \{S = 1\} = \{u \leq F_u^{-1}(P)\}.$$

Then for any bounded function $a(\varepsilon)$, by iterated expectations

$E[a(\varepsilon) \mid X, P, S]$

$\quad = E\big[E[a(\varepsilon) \mid u, X, Z] \mid X, P, u \leq F_u^{-1}(P)\big] = E\big[E[a(\varepsilon) \mid u] \mid X, P, u \leq F_u^{-1}(P)\big]$

$\quad = E\big[E[a(\varepsilon) \mid u] \mid P, u \leq F_u^{-1}(P)\big] = E\big[E[a(\varepsilon) \mid u, P] \mid P, S\big] = E[a(\varepsilon) \mid P, S].$

Since this holds for any function $a(\varepsilon)$ it follows that X and ε are independent conditional on P and S. ∎

In models where $g(X, \varepsilon)$ is additive in ε, mean independence of ε and X conditional on P and $S = 1$ has often been used to identify sample selection models. The pioneering result was given by Heckman (1979). Ahn and Powell (1993), and Newey (1988) used this approach to develop semiparametric estimators. Das et al. (2003) gave results for a nonparametric model with additive disturbances. Theorem 1 extends the conditional mean independence result for additive models to conditional independence for nonseparable models with disturbances of arbitrary dimension. This allows us to apply results of Chamberlain (1984), Altonji and Matzkin (2005), Wooldridge (2002), Blundell and Powell (2003), Chesher (2003), and Imbens and Newey (2006) to identify structural effects in nonseparable sample selection models.

Identification of some structural effects will use the following condition:

ASSUMPTION 2 (Common Support). *For all $X \in \mathcal{X}$, the support of P conditional on X and S equals the support of P conditional on S.*

For example, suppose that the support of $P = \Pr(S = 1 \mid X, Z)$ is $[0, 1]$. Then conditional on X fixed at some value, P varies only with Z. Common support means that (conditional on X), the variable Z must move the propensity score over all of $[0, 1]$.

An example of a structural effect that would be identified under Assumptions 1 and 2 is the average structural function of Blundell and Powell (2003), that is also known in the treatment effects literature at the average treatment effect, conditional on selection. This object is given by

$$\mu^S(x) = \int g(x, \varepsilon)\, F(d\varepsilon \mid S),$$

where $F(\varepsilon \mid S)$ is the marginal distribution of ε conditional on selection. It is identified from the fact that for all $x \in \mathcal{X}$,

$$\mu^S(x) = \int g(x, \varepsilon) F(d\varepsilon \mid P, S) F(dP \mid S) = \int g(x, \varepsilon) F(d\varepsilon \mid X = x, P, S) F(dP \mid S)$$

$$= \int E[Y \mid X = x, P, S] F(dP \mid S),$$

where the first equality follows by iterated expectations, the second equality uses Assumption 1 and the integral is well defined by Assumption 2, and the third equality uses $Y = g(X, \varepsilon)$. This equation means that $\mu^S(x)$ is the integral over the conditional distribution of P given selection of the expectation $E[Y \mid X = x, P, S]$ of Y given X, P, and selection. This argument varies from previous results in being conditional on selection.

Despite the conditioning on selection the average structural function is an object of interest. For instance, note that as long as integration and differentiation can be interchanged,

$$\frac{\partial \mu^S(x)}{\partial x} = E\left[\frac{\partial g(x, \varepsilon)}{\partial x} \,\middle|\, S\right].$$

That is, the derivative of the average structural function is the average of the partial derivative of $g(x, \varepsilon)$ with respect to x, a structural object, over the conditional distribution of ε given selection. In effect, the fact that we only observe Y in the selected sample means that we can only estimate the average effect over values of ε from the selected sample.

Another effect that can be identified under Assumption 2 is the quantile structural function (QSF) for the selected sample. This is given by

$q_Y^S(\tau, x)$ equal to the τth quantile of $g(x, \varepsilon)$ for the distribution of ε given S.

In this definition x is fixed and ε is what makes $g(x, \varepsilon)$ random. In treatment effects models, $q_Y^S(\tau, x'') - q_Y^S(\tau, x')$ is the quantile treatment effect of a change in x from x' to x'' in the selected sample. When ε is a scalar and $g(x, \varepsilon)$ in monotonic increasing in ε, then $q_Y^S(\tau, x) = g(x, q_\varepsilon^S(\tau))$, where $q_\varepsilon^S(\tau)$ is the τth quantile of ε conditional on selection. The QSF is one generalization of the value of $g(x, \varepsilon)$ at a particular ε to the case where ε is a vector, e.g., where there are multiple sources of heterogeneity.

The identification proof for the QSF is the same as in Imbens and Newey (2007) conditional on selection. By Assumption 1,

$$(1) \qquad F_{Y|X,P,S}(y\,|\,x,p) = \int 1(g(x,e) \le y) F_{\varepsilon\,|\,X,P,S}(de\,|\,x,p)$$

$$= \int 1(g(x,e) \le y) F_{\varepsilon\,|\,P,S}(de\,|\,p).$$

Then under Assumption 2, we can integrate over the marginal distribution of P in the selected data and apply iterated expectations to obtain

$$(2) \qquad \int F_{Y|X,P,S}(y\,|\,x,p) F_{P,S}(dP)$$

$$= \int 1(g(x,e) \le y) F_{\varepsilon,S}(de) = \Pr(g(x,\varepsilon) \le y\,|\,S) \overset{\text{def}}{=} G^S(y,x).$$

Then by the definition of the QSF we have

$$(3) \qquad q_Y^S(\tau,x) = G^{S,-1}(\tau,x).$$

Thus the QSF is the inverse of the integral over the marginal distribution of υ of the conditional CDF of Y given X and υ. The role of Assumption 2 is to ensure that $F_{Y|X,\upsilon}(y\,|\,x,\upsilon)$ is identified over the entire support of the marginal distribution of υ.

Given the strength of common support condition it is interesting to consider effects that can be identified without this condition. One of these is the average derivative. Using similar arguments as for the average structural function we find that

$$E\left[\frac{\partial g(X,\varepsilon)}{\partial x}\,\bigg|\,S\right] = E\left[E\left[\frac{\partial g(X,\varepsilon)}{\partial x}\,\bigg|\,X,P,S\right]\,\bigg|\,S\right]$$

$$= E\left[\int \frac{\partial g(X,\varepsilon)}{\partial x} F(d\varepsilon\,|\,X,P,S)\,\bigg|\,S\right]$$

$$= E\left[\int \frac{\partial g(X,\varepsilon)}{\partial x} F(d\varepsilon\,|\,P,S)\,\bigg|\,S\right]$$

$$= E\left[\frac{\partial}{\partial x} \int g(X,\varepsilon) F(d\varepsilon\,|\,P,S)\,\bigg|\,S\right]$$

Thus we find that the average derivative in the selected sample is identified without the common support assumption. This would be useful for evaluating the average effect of X on the outcome.

As discussed in Imbens and Newey (2007), without Assumption 2 it is possible to identify other structural objects and to bound the quantile structural function.

For brevity we do not apply that discussion here, except to note that as above, those objects and bounds will be conditional on the selected sample.

4. IDENTIFICATION OF DISCRETE/CONTINUOUS CHOICE

There are several different objects that might be useful to identify in these discrete/continuous choice models. One is the prediction of the demand for the commodity, i.e., the conditional expectation of the commodity conditional on prices and income. For welfare analysis it may be important to identify the utility function. In this section, we consider these two objects and give conditions under which they are identified.

In estimating the demand one could, in principle, get a prediction from a nonparametric regression of q on $X = (p_1, p_2, y - r_1, \ldots, y - r_J)$ (where we now return to the notation of Section 2). However, the discrete choice model has structure that may be useful for estimation. In particular, the demand for each alternative depends only on $X_j = (p_1, p_2, y - r_j)$. Also, the choice probabilities are given by

$$P_j(X) = \Pr(d_j = 1 \mid X) = \Pr(\{v_j + \eta_j \geq v_k + \eta_k; k \neq j\})$$
$$= P_j(v_2 - v_1, \ldots, v_J - v_1);$$

these also have structure, being a $J - 1$ dimensional function of three-dimensional functions. This structure reduces the curse of dimensionality.

The demand also has a recursive structure that may be helpful in estimation. Assume that the choice probabilities are one-to-one functions of $v_2 - v_1, \ldots, v_J - v_1$, a common assumption in applied industrial organization. Then for each j there is a function $\bar{h}_j(X_j, P_2, \ldots, P_J)$ such that

$$E[q \mid X, d_j = 1] = \bar{h}_j(X_j, P_2, \ldots, P_J).$$

Then we have

$$E[q \mid X] = \sum_{j=1}^{J} \bar{h}_j(X_j, P_2, \ldots, P_J) P_j(v_2 - v_1, \ldots, v_J - v_1).$$

This approach is essentially a two-step method of identifying the sequential demand. The first step is identification of the choice probabilities. The second step is identification of the conditional means given each choice, where the choice probabilities enter as regressors. In practice, the corresponding two-step estimation method could be important. Dubin and McFadden find in their application that most of the impact on demand of changing X is the effect on the choice probabilities. This two-step identification approach could help allow for such impacts.

Identifying the indirect utility function is more challenging. For simplicity we consider a two-choice example and suppress the p_2 argument and let $p = p_1$. We also assume that $\varepsilon = (\eta_1, \eta_2, u)$ is three dimensional and that the indirect utility function takes the form

$$V_j(p, y, \varepsilon) = v_j(p, y) + \eta_j + T(p, u), (j = 1, 2).$$

In this case the choice probability for alternative 2 is

$$\Pr(\eta_1 - \eta_2 \leq v_2(p, y - r_2) - v_1(p, y - r_1)) = G(v_2(p, y - r_2) - v_1(p, y - r_1)),$$

where $G(u)$ is the CDF of $\eta_1 - \eta_2$. The demands conditional on each choice are

$$h_1(p, y - r_1, u) = -\frac{\partial v_1(p, y - r_1)/\partial p + \partial T(p, u)/\partial p}{\partial v_1(p, y - r_1)/\partial y},$$

$$h_2(p, y - r_2, \tilde{u}) = -\frac{\partial v_2(p, y - r_2)/\partial p + \partial T(p, \tilde{u})/\partial p}{\partial v_2(p, y - r_2)/\partial y}.$$

where we distinguish u and $\tilde{u}$ so that it is better understood that they can be evaluated at different points. For notational simplicity we will suppress the arguments of the functions and let subscripts denote partial derivatives, so that the choice probability is

$$\pi(X) = \Pr(d_2 = 1 \mid X) = G(v_2 - v_1).$$

The demands are then

$$h_1 = -\frac{v_{1p} + T_p}{v_{1y}}, \quad h_2 = -\frac{v_{2p} + T_p}{v_{2y}}.$$

The identification question is what characteristics of the utility function are identified from the data on demands on different outcomes and from the binary choice.

For simplicity we assume that the CDF G of $\eta_1 - \eta_2$ is known. Then $r = v_2 - v_1$ is identified and hence so is its partial derivative with respect to p and y. Assume that the common support condition (Assumption 2) is identified. Then the quantile structural function conditional on each choice is known. Further, assume that $T_p(p, u)$ is strictly monotonically decreasing in u, so that each h_j is strictly monotonic increasing in u. Then by the identification result for the quantile structural function in the selected sample both h_1 and h_2 are identified up to different monotonic transformations of u. Also, multiplying through by the denominators in the demand equations gives

$$v_{1y}h_1 + v_{1p} + T_p = 0, \quad v_{2y}h_2 + v_{2p} + T_p = 0.$$

Assume that we can evaluate at two values for u where T_p are equal in both cases. Subtracting the second equation from the first then gives

$$0 = v_{1y}h_1 - v_{2y}h_2 - r_p = (r_y - v_{2y})h_1 - v_{2y}h_2.$$

Solving gives

$$v_{2y} = \frac{r_y h_1}{h_1 + h_2}.$$

We also have

$$v_{1y} = r_y - v_{2y}.$$

This identifies v_{1y} and v_{2y}. Substituting this formula back in to the first equation give

$$\frac{r_y h_2 h_1}{h_1 + h_2} + v_{1p} + T_p = 0.$$

Differentiating this equation with respect to the u that appears in h_1 then gives

$$T_{pu} = -\frac{\partial}{\partial u} \frac{r_y h_2 h_1}{h_1 + h_2}.$$

This identifies T_{pu}. Similarly, differentiating with respect to y gives

$$v_{1py} = -\frac{\partial}{\partial y} \frac{r_y h_2 h_1}{h_1 + h_2}.$$

This then identifies T_p and v_{1p} up to an additive function of p.

This analysis provides an example showing how features of the utility function can be identified from discrete/continuous choices. It would be useful to extend this approach to the case where there are many discrete choices.

REFERENCES

AHN, H. AND J. L. POWELL, "Semiparametric Estimation of Censored Selection Models with a Nonparametric Selection Mechanism," *Journal of Econometrics* 58(1993), 3–29.

ALTONJI, J., AND R. MATZKIN, "Cross Section and Panel Data Estimators for Nonseparable Models with Endogenous Regressors," *Econometrica* 73 (2005), 1053–102.

BLUNDELL, R., AND J. L. POWELL, "Endogeneity in Nonparametric and Semiparametric Regression Models," in M. Dewatripont, L. Hansen, and S. Turnovsky, eds., *Advances in Economics and Econometrics* Chapter 8 (Cambridge: Cambridge University Press, 2003), 312–57.

——, AND ——, "Endogeneity in Semiparametric Binary Response Models," *Review of Economic Studies* 71 (2004), 581–913.

CHAMBERLAIN, G., "Panel Data," in Z. Griliches and M. Intriligator, eds., *Handbook of Econometrics, Vol. 2.* (Amsterdam: North-Holland, 1984).

CHESHER, A., "Identification in Nonseparable Models," *Econometrica* 71 (2003), 1405–41.

DAS, M., W. K. NEWEY, AND F. VELLA, "Nonparametric Estimation of Sample Selection Models," *Review of Economic Studies* 70 (2003), 33–58.

DUBIN, J., AND D. McFADDEN, "An Econometric Analysis of Residential Electric Appliance Holdings and Consumption," *Econometrica* 50 (1984), 345–62.

HECKMAN, J. J., "Shadow Prices, Market Wages, and Labor Supply," *Econometrica* 42 (1974), 679–93.

——, "Sample Selection Bias as a Specification Error," *Econometrica* 47 (1979), 153–61.

——, "Varieties of Selection Bias," *American Economic Review, Papers and Proceedings* 80 (1990), 313–18.

——, AND R. ROBB, "Alternative Methods for Evaluating the Impact of Interventions," in O. Ashenfelter and R. Lalonde, eds., *The Economics of Training* (VT: Elgar, 1996).

IMBENS, G., AND W. NEWEY, "Identification and Estimation of Triangular Simultaneous Equations Models without Additivity," MIT Working Paper, 2006.

MANSKI, C., "Nonparametric Bounds on Treatment Effects," *American Economic Review* 80 (1990), 319–23.

——, *Identification Problems in the Social Sciences* (Cambridge, MA: Harvard University Press, 1995), 138–66.

MATZKIN, R., "Identification of Nonparametric Models," *Handbook of Econometrics* (Amsterdam: North Holland, 2007).

NEWEY, W. K., "Two Step Series Estimation of Sample Selection Models," MIT Department of Economics Working Paper, 1988.

——, AND D. McFADDEN, "Large Sample Estimation and Hypothesis Testing," *Handbook of Econometrics Volume 4* (Amsterdam: North Holland, 1994).

STOCK, J., "Nonparametric Policy Analysis: An Application to Estimating Hazardous Waste Cleanup Benefits," in W. Barnett, J. Powell, and G. Tauchen, eds., *Nonparametric and Semiparametric Methods in Econometrics*, Chapter 3 (Cambridge University Press, 1988), 77–98.

WOOLDRIDGE, J., *Econometric Analysis of Cross Section and Panel Data* (Cambridge, MA: MIT Press, 2002).

INTERNATIONAL ECONOMIC REVIEW
Vol. 48, No. 4, November 2007

ESTIMATION WITH CENSORED REGRESSORS: BASIC ISSUES*

By Roberto Rigobon and Thomas M. Stoker[1]

MIT, U.S.A.

We study issues that arise for estimation of a linear model when a regressor is censored. We discuss the efficiency losses from dropping censored observations, and illustrate the losses for bound censoring. We show that the common practice of introducing a dummy variable to "correct for" censoring does not correct bias or improve estimation. We show how censored observations generally have zero semiparametric information, and we discuss implications for estimation. We derive the likelihood function for a parametric model of mixed bound-independent censoring, and apply that model to the estimation of wealth effects on consumption.

1. INTRODUCTION

It is easy to argue that the development of models of discrete elements in economic data is the most important evolution in econometrics in the latter part of the 20th century. Many decisions by consumers and producers are inherently discrete; what brand to buy, what mode of transportation to take, what house to choose, etc. More subtle but no less important is how discrete criterion can affect the selected nature of data samples: Only women who choose to work have measured market wages, only consumers who choose to redeem a coupon get the discount, etc. The modeling of discrete elements had the further consequence of requiring substantial understanding of nonlinear models in econometrics, as discrete actions or choices are not well represented by standard linear regression models. This began with a thorough development of the econometrics of parametric discrete choice and selection models and continued with development of more flexible semiparametric and nonparametric econometric models. There is no more important name in this development than Daniel McFadden. His work has had an enormous impact on the work of several generations of econometricians, both on the theoretical side and the practical side. No one else comes close.

In this article, we look at an aspect of discreteness in econometrics that has been largely overlooked, where regressors in an economic model are discretely censored. The well-known problem covered in the literature is when a dependent

* Manuscript received September 2005; revised January 2007.

[1] We thank Jonathan Parker for his generosity in sharing with us not only his data but all the programs used to reproduce the results in his NBER Macro Annual paper. We have received valuable comments from James Heckman, Vincent Hogan, Dale Jorgenson, Richard Blundell, Charles Manski, Orazio Attanasio, James Banks, Costas Meghir, Alberto Abadie, Jerry Hausman, Gary Chamberlain, Peter Bickel, Jin Hahn, Elie Tamer, and especially Whitney Newey. Please address correspondence to: Thomas M. Stoker, Sloan School of Management, MIT, 50 Memorial Drive, Cambridge, MA 02142, U.S.A. Phone: 617-253-2625. Fax: 617-258-6855. E-mail: *tstoker@mit.edu.*

variable is censored or selected. That problem has the impact of altering the effective sample for estimation and, for instance, causes biases in OLS estimates of linear model coefficients. This has stimulated a great deal of work on consistent estimators of coefficients when there is a censored dependent variable.

As such, it seems surprising that very little attention has been paid to the implication of having a censored regressor, or independent variable, in the estimation of a linear model. Indeed, it would seem that researchers encounter censored regressors as often or even more often than situations of censored dependent variables. Consider how often variables are observed in ranges, including unlimited top and bottom categories. For instance, observed household income is often recorded in increments of $1000 or $5000, but would have a top-coded response of, say, "$100,000 and above." Another example is where imperfect measurement has the impact of censoring; for instance, in measuring components of household wealth, there may be many zero values, some of which are genuine zeros but many represent nonreporting or other mismeasurement. These are just a couple examples of where censoring appears, but it seems clear that censored regressors are a common phenomena in empirical work.

If one ignores the censored nature of a regressor, one can induce a particularly insidious practical problem, namely estimates that are too large. This phenomenon, which we term *expansion bias*,[2] can give a spurious impression of the importance of a regressor. To see how this can arise, Figure 1 shows a scatterplot where a regressor is top- and bottom-coded, or double bound censored. The small circles are the resulting data points when the regressor is censored at upper and lower bounds. The estimated regression using the censored regressor clearly has a steeper slope that the one using the uncensored regressor. Expansion bias arises because of the "pile-up" of observations at each limit. Obviously, expansion bias would arise if there was either top- or bottom-coding alone.

One approach would be to just view any observation with censoring as bad and drop them for estimation. This is called *complete case* analysis. However, this has the potential to introduce further bias from selecting the sample in an endogenous way. This is not a problem under *exogenous censoring* as we define below; in that situation, complete case analysis provides consistent parameter estimates.

We consider several aspects of model estimation with a censored regressor. We assume exogenous censoring, which reflects censoring that is not connected to the dependent variable under study. Our interest is in issues of estimation with the full data sample. We illustrate the efficiency loss due to censoring, highlighting nonindependent censoring such as top-coding. We show that the common practice of including a dummy variable for censored observations is not advisable—the procedure eliminates bias only under strong restrictions, and otherwise, no useful information is gained from including the censored observations in this way. We show that there is zero semiparametric information for the parameters of interest in the censored data, when there are no restrictions on the distribution of the censored observations. We discuss general estimation under the assumption that

---

[2] Expansion bias is the opposite of *attenuation bias*, familiar from problems such as errors-in-variables or censored dependent variable models.

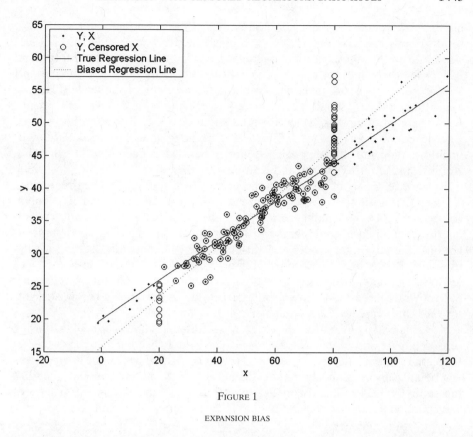

FIGURE 1

EXPANSION BIAS

a proxy equation is appropriate for the censored regressor. For our empirical application, we specify a parametric model of mixed independent and bound censoring. We derive the likelihood function to facilitate maximum likelihood estimation of our mixed censoring model.[3]

We discuss how censored regressors arise in the estimation of wealth effects on consumption. We show how extensive censoring can be, when components of wealth are taken into consideration. We apply our mixed censoring model to analyze household consumption and wealth data and compare the estimation results to those obtained from linear regression that ignores the censoring. We show how expansion bias manifests in simple regression models and how the the size and precision of wealth and income effects is changed when wealth censoring is taken into account. Our discussion is intended to give concrete illustration to the ideas, and we plan to carry out further applications as part of future research.

As mentioned above, there is relatively little literature on censored regressors in econometrics. An exception is Manski and Tamer (2002), who study identification and consistent estimation with interval data. The statistical literature on

---

[3] Our discussion focuses on exogenous censoring, but the derivation of the likelihood function includes the situation where the censored regressor is endogenous and instruments are observed.

missing data problems covers some situations of censored regressors, with most
results applicable to data missing at random. See the surveys by Little (1992)
and Little and Rubin (2002) for coverage of this large literature and Moffitt and
Ridder (forthcoming) for survey of the related literature on data combination.[4]
Top- and bottom-coding are nonignorable data coarsenings in the sense of Heitjan
and Rubin (1990, 1991).[5] Also related is recent work on partially identified econometric models, which includes situations of censored regressors; see
Chernozhukov et al. (2004) and Shaik (2005), among others. Related discussions
on information and efficiency can be found in Horowitz and Manski (1998, 2000),
Robins and Rotnitzky (1995), and Rotnitzky et al. (1998).

This article is part of a series on the problems raised by censored regressors.
The bias that arises from censored regressors is studied in great detail in Rigobon
and Stoker (2006a), including results for bias in OLS estimators, bias in IV estimators when the censored regressor is endogenous, and bias transmission in situations of multiple regressors and with extreme 0–1 censoring. Testing for the
presence of bias from censored regressors is covered in Rigobon and Stoker
(2006b). This amounts to testing whether potentially censored values are, in fact,
correctly measured.[6] Under exogenous censoring as introduced below, straightforward chi square tests are available.

The article is organized as follows: Section 2 discusses the basic results of using
censored regressors in the estimation of linear models. Section 3 discusses consistent estimation with the full data sample, presents our model of mixed independent
and bound censoring, and derives the likelihood function for that model. Section 4
illustrates the biases that arise in an application where the marginal propensity of
consumption out of wealth is estimated. Finally, Section 5 concludes.

2. BASIC ISSUES OF ESTIMATION WITH CENSORED REGRESSORS

2.1. *Framework: Linear Model and Censoring.* We consider the impact of
censoring in a linear regression framework. We assume that the true model is an
equation of the form

$$(1) \qquad\qquad y_i = \alpha + \beta x_i + \phi' w_i + \varepsilon_i \quad i = 1, \dots, n,$$

where x_i is a single regressor of interest, and w_i is a k-vector of other regressors.
We assume that the distribution of $(x_i, w_i', \varepsilon_i)$ is nonsingular and has finite second
moments. We assume that the model is a properly specified regression model, with
$E(\varepsilon_i \mid x_i, w_i) = 0$.

---

[4] A valuable early contribution is Ai (1997). Recent contributions include Chen et al. (2004, 2005),
Liang et al. (2004), Tripathi (2003, 2004), Mahajan (2004), and Ichimura and Martinez-Sanchis (2005).

[5] Some recent work has shown how data heaping in duration data (censoring or rounding due to
memory effects) can be accomodated in estimation of survival models. See Torelli and Trivellato (1993)
and Petoussis et al. (2004), among others.

[6] For instance, suppose a variable is bounded below by 0. The question is whether the observed 0
values are correct observations or censored values.

We do not observe x_i for all observations, but rather a censored version of it. Suppose that the indicator d_i describes the censoring process, with $d_i = 0$ denoting an uncensored observation and $d_i = 1$ a censored one, for which we observe the value ξ. That is, we observe

$$(2) \qquad\qquad x_i^{\text{cen}} = (1 - d_i)x_i + d_i\xi,$$

where x_i^{cen} is the censored version of x_i. The probability of censoring is denoted as $p = \Pr\{d = 1\}$, and we assume that $0 < p < 1$.

Our model of censoring includes most of the common types of censoring found in practice. The process for d_i can be quite general, but we assume $p < 1$, so that some correct (uncensored) values of x_i are observed. Another restriction is censoring to a single value ξ. This is a convenience, and many of the points we make will apply to censoring to two or more different values.

Our framework includes single value *bound censoring*. For instance, *top-coding* involves observing x_i only when it is less than a bound ξ, namely,

$$(3) \qquad\qquad d_i = 1[x_i > \xi],$$

and the bound ξ is the censoring value. *Bottom-coding* involves observing x_i only when it is above a bound ξ, with

$$(4) \qquad\qquad d_i = 1[x_i < \xi].$$

Double bounding, where there is both top- and bottom-coding is two-value censoring. This case would not change our analysis meaningfully.

The processes (3) and (4) have d_i determined by x_i, and our framework includes cases where d_i is a stochastic censoring process or a more complicated deterministic censoring process. For instance, independent censoring refers to where d_i is statistically independent of x_i, w_i and ε_i. Random processes that involve dependence of virtually any kind can be included.[7] One important omission from our discussion is 0–1 censoring. This refers to where a dummy variable is observed in place of x_i, for instance

$$(5) \qquad\qquad x_i^{\text{cen}} = 1[x_i \geq \xi],$$

where x_i^{cen} indicates whether x_i is above the threshold ξ. This is two-value censoring, but the problem is that no true values of x_i are observed. Every observation is censored, which is a violation of $p < 1$. Estimation in this case will involve some different considerations that those we discuss here.[8]

---

[7] In the parlance of the missing data literature (cf. Little and Rubin, 2002), our notion of independent censoring is analogous to "missing completely at random," or MCAR. Top- and bottom-coding involve censoring determined by the value of the regressor, so that they are analogous to "not missing at random" processes, or NMAR, where in addition, the censoring threshold is given by the censoring value ξ.

[8] See Rigobon and Stoker (2006a) for a discussion of OLS bias with 0–1 censoring.

It is worth mentioning that, in linear regression analysis, the main problem that censoring causes is bias. Namely, if we ignore that x_i^{cen} is not x_i and estimate the model

$$(6) \qquad\qquad y_i = a + b x_i^{\text{cen}} + f' w_i + u_i \quad i = 1, \ldots, n,$$

then the estimates $\hat{a}, \hat{b}, \hat{f}$ are asymptotically biased estimators of α, β, ϕ.[9] The bias can easily be seen to depend on the censoring process as well as the censoring value ξ.

2.2. *Selection and Exogenous Censoring.* Since we observe x_i for a fraction of the sample, why not just estimate with those complete observations? To consider this, suppose that the sample is ordered with the $n_0 = \sum_{i=1}^{n}(1 - d_i)$ uncensored observations first, $i = 1, \ldots, n_0$, followed by the $n_1 = \sum_{i=1}^{n} d_i$ censored observations, $i = n_0 + 1, \ldots, n_0 + n_1$. Consider estimating the equation

$$(7) \qquad\qquad y_i = \alpha + \beta x_i + \phi' w_i + \varepsilon_i \quad i = 1, \ldots, n_0.$$

This is referred to as *Complete Case (CC)* regression analysis.

This raises issues that are familiar to students of selection problems. The question is how the distribution of ε_i is altered by restricting attention to observations with $d_i = 0$. When the mean of ε_i varies with d_i, then CC analysis induces biases from truncation. This is the same problem as with traditional models of (bound) censored dependent variables, where $d_i = 1[y_i < \zeta]$, and a CC regression must be adjusted for the truncated nature of the CC data.[10] That is, in full generality, a censored regressor can induce problems similar to those caused by censoring of the dependent variable.

For our discussion of basic issues raised by censored regressors, we assume *exogenous censoring*, namely,

$$(8) \qquad\qquad E(\varepsilon_i \mid d_i, x_i, w_i) = 0.$$

This assumes away the standard problems of censoring or truncating the dependent variable. Under exogenous censoring, the CC model (7) is a well-specified regression model. CC regression analysis gives consistent estimators of α, β, and ϕ. For part of our discussion, we will need a stronger version of exogeneity. In particular, we define *strict exogenous censoring* as statistical independence of ε_i

---

[9] Zero asymptotic bias occurs only in very unusual situations. One case arises with three conditions holding simultaneously: (a) d_i is independent of x_i, w_i, and ε_i, (b) censoring is to the mean $\xi = E(x)$, and (c) x_i is independent of w_i.

[10] That is, one adds

$$E(\varepsilon_i \mid d_i = 0, x_i, w_i) = E(\varepsilon_i \mid \varepsilon_i \geq \zeta - \alpha - \beta x_i - \phi' w_i)$$

to the regression. When ε_i is normally distributed, this expectation is the inverse Mill's ratio, which is added to the regression equation to facilitate consistent estimation.

from d_i conditional on x_i and w_i. Thus the distribution of ε_i conditional on x_i and w_i is the same when further conditioned by $d_i = 0$, which clearly includes (8).

Under exogenous censoring, the basic estimation issues concern how best to employ the censored observations to improve estimation. We now turn to those issues. In passing, it is worth mentioning that exogenous censoring also provides the foundation for straightforward Hausman tests of the absence of bias from censored regressors. Under exogenous censoring, estimation of (7) with complete cases gives consistent estimates of α, β, and ϕ, and under the null hypothesis of no bias, estimation of (6) with the full sample gives efficient estimates. Chi-square tests based on the difference of these estimators are developed and illustrated in Rigobon and Stoker (2006b).

2.3. Efficiency Loss from Censored Regressors.   Recall that the model is

$$(9) \qquad y_i = \alpha + \beta x_i + \phi' w_i + \varepsilon_i \quad i = 1, \dots, n$$

applying to the full sample, and for simplicity, we now assume homoskedasticity of ε_i,

$$(10) \qquad \operatorname{Var}(\varepsilon_i \mid x_i, w_i) = \sigma^2.$$

We assume strict exogenous censoring. Therefore, CC analysis is consistent; the OLS estimates $\hat{\alpha}_0$, $\hat{\beta}_0$, $\hat{\phi}_0$, and $\hat{\sigma}_0^2$ of

$$(11) \qquad y_i = \alpha + \beta x_i + \phi' w_i + \varepsilon_i \quad i = 1, \dots, n_0$$

are consistent for α, β, ϕ, and σ^2, respectively.

We are interested in how valuable the censored observations are to estimation. The regression model appropriate for the censored observations is

$$(12) \qquad y_i = \alpha + \beta g_1(w_i) + \phi' w_i + u_i \quad i = n_0 + 1, \dots, n_0 + n_1,$$

where

$$(13) \qquad g_1(w_i) = E(x_i \mid w_i, d_i = 1).$$

The disturbance

$$(14) \qquad u_i = \beta(x_i - g_1(w_i)) + \varepsilon_i$$

has $E(u_i \mid w_i, d_i = 1) = 0$ and $\sigma_u^2(w_i) = \operatorname{Var}(u_i \mid w_i, d_i = 1) = \beta^2 \operatorname{Var}(x_i \mid w_i, d_i = 1) + \sigma^2$. In essence, since x_i is not available, the best possible situation is where you know the value $g_1(w_i)$ of the conditional expectation for each i, and $\sigma_u^2(w_i)$ for each i. Then you could do an efficient pooled estimation of (11)–(12), estimating with the whole sample. For the ith observation of the censored data, this amounts to using $g_1(w_i)$ in place of x_i^{cen}, and weighting by $1/\sqrt{\sigma_u^2(w_i)}$. Clearly, this is the

TABLE 1

EFFICIENCY RELATIVE TO COMPLETE SAMPLE

| | | | One Additional Regressor | | | |
| | Bivariate | | Correlation 0.5 | | Correlation 0.9 | |
Truncation	Procedure	Eff $\hat{\beta}$	Eff $\hat{\beta}$	Eff ϕ	Eff $\hat{\beta}$	Eff ϕ
20%	CC	47%	52%	80%	71%	80%
	Known mean	88%	62%	86%	76%	83%
40%	CC	25%	30%	60%	48%	60%
	Known mean	78%	46%	71%	58%	65%
60%	CC	13%	15%	40%	28%	40%
	Known mean	66%	36%	56%	42%	45%

best regression procedure given that $x_i - g_1(w_i)$ is not observed. This leads us to two efficiency comparisons to gauge the loss from censoring. First is the relative efficiency of CC analysis with estimation with the full uncensored sample (with x_i observed). Second is the efficiency of the pooled estimation of (11)–(12) described above with $g_1(\cdot)$ known, relative to estimation with the full uncensored sample.

For interpretation, consider the case of where d_i is independent of x_i and w_i. Censoring of $p = 20\%$ of the observations coincides with efficiency of $1 - p = 80\%$ of CC analysis relative to estimation with the full uncensored sample, since the censoring alters nothing but the sample size. If $g_1(w_i)$ is known, there are more efficiency gains the more highly correlated x_i is with w_i, as the unobserved term $x_i - g_1(w_i)$ will have smaller variance.

With independence, the censored observations have the same distribution as uncensored observations. Alternatively, consider bound censoring, or top-coding in particular. Top-coding does not resemble independent censoring; it involves censoring the upper tail, which contains some of the most influential observations for estimating the regression parameters.[11] CC analysis with 20% top-coding will involve a lower efficiency than 80%.

How much lower? Table 1 presents efficiencies for normally distributed regressors for different amounts of censoring from top-coding.[12] The bivariate column uses a model with no w_i, so that the conditional mean is a constant $g_1 = E(x_i \mid d_i = 1)$ and $\sigma_u^2 = \beta^2 \text{Var}(x_i \mid d_i = 1) + \sigma^2$. With one additional regressor w_i, the mean $g_1(w_i)$ and variance $\sigma_u^2(w_i)$ are computed for the bivariate normal regressors. We see that for the bivariate model, the relative efficiency of CC analysis is much lower than it would be with random sampling: 47% efficiency with 20% top-coding, 25% efficiency with 40% top-coding, etc. Table 1 also addresses how valuable it is to know the mean of the top-coded data. Notice how a great deal of the efficiency loss can be eliminated when $g_1(w_i)$ is known.

---

[11] "Influential" is used here in the same sense as in the literature on regression diagnostics or experimental design: see Belsley et al. (1980) among many others.

[12] We set $\alpha = 1$, $\beta = 1$, and $\phi = 1$, and took the variances of x and z to be the same and equal to half the value of the variance of ε.

When there is an additional regressor, the efficiency loss in estimating β is less than in the bivariate case, and improves with higher correlation between x and w. When the conditional mean of the top-coded data is known, the efficiency improves for each coefficient, but not to the same extent as with the bivariate model. Finally, we notice that the improvements in efficiency for β and ϕ (from knowing the mean) are more balanced with higher correlation.[13]

As such, it appears that with substantial censoring, the efficiency losses from CC analysis can be large, depending on the nature of the censoring. Even with top coding, these losses could be recovered to a large degree if the conditional means and variances for the censored observations are known.

2.4. *Ineffectiveness of Dummy Variable Methods.* We now take a slight detour to discuss an empirical technique that will, eventually, lead us back to our discussion of efficiency. A common practice in empirical work is to regress y_i on a constant, x_i^{cen}, w_i and the censoring dummy d_i. Here we discuss the practice of including d_i to empirically "correct" for the censoring.

The true model (1) written with the censored regressor is

$$(15) \qquad y_i = \alpha + \beta x_i^{\text{cen}} + \phi w_i + \beta(g_1(w_i) - \xi) \cdot d_i + u_i \quad i = 1, \ldots, n,$$

where $u_i = \beta(x_i - g_1(w_i)) d_i + \varepsilon_i$, and we take $g_1(\cdot)$ as unknown. Thus, the true "coefficient" of d_i varies with w_i, which is a potentially very serious misspecification. Unless $g_1(\cdot)$ is constant, $g_1(w_i) = g_1$, or approximately so,[14] all the coefficient estimates will be biased. It is not clear whether they will be more or less biased than the coefficients obtained from regressing y_i on a constant, x_i^{cen} and w_i—or ignoring the original censoring. In general, the inclusion of the censoring dummy is not advisable.

Consider where the constancy assumption is valid by construction, namely in the bivariate model where there is no additional variable w_i. Now the true model is

$$(16) \qquad y_i = \alpha + \beta x_i^{\text{cen}} + \beta(g_{1_i} - \xi) \cdot d_i + u_i \quad i = 1, \ldots, n,$$

where $g_1 = E(x \mid d = 1)$. This is a well-specified regression model including the intercept, x_i^{cen} and censoring indicator d_i. However, there is another issue. For the complete cases $(i = 1, \ldots, n_0)$, the model is linear with intercept α and slope β. For the censored data, the model is a constant, with value $\alpha + \beta g_1$. If g_1 is not known, then there is no parameter restriction between the complete cases and the censored data.[15] Therefore, the estimate of β from model (16) is exactly the same as the estimate from CC analysis, or estimating with complete cases only, and it has the same variance. There is no gain from including the censored observations together with the censoring indicator.

---

[13] These calculations are done with optimal (GLS) weighting, but we did not find that the results were very sensitive to whether weighting was done or not.

[14] For example, if x were income and z a demographic variable, then constancy implies that the mean of top-coded income is the same for all demographic groups indicated by z.

[15] This includes the variances as well.

The same remarks apply to the related procedure of including interactions with d_i. That is, from (15), one might consider approximating $g_1(w_i)$ by a general linear function in w_i. For this, one would regress y_i on an intercept, x_i^{cen}, w_i, d_i, and $d_i w_i$. It is easy to see that if $g_1(w_i)$ were linear, then this would be a well-specified model. But this parametrization has the same effect as discussed for (16); namely there is no parameter restriction between the complete cases and the censored data. As before, with the mean $g_1(w_i)$ unknown, this procedure yields no gain over CC analysis.

Similar issues arise for the practice of imputing tail means with bound censoring. For instance, if observed income is top-coded at \$100,000, the practice is to replace all top-coded values with an imputed mean of incomes over \$100,000. In view of (16), this practice will adjust for censoring bias in bivariate regression.[16] But when there are additional regressors w_i, this practice is only correct when $g_1(w_i)$ is constant; namely when x_i is mean-independent of w_i given $d_i = 1$. That is, the appropriate imputation would be to replace top-coded values by their conditional expectation on all other regressors, $g_1(w_i)$; doing that correctly could bring the efficiency gains for available when $g_1(\cdot)$ is known.

2.5. *The Semiparametric Information in Censored Observations.*   The fact that dummy variable methods fail to uncover new information about the parameters is ominous, and indicative of a more general issue for flexible approaches to estimation. How much information about the parameters of interest—α, β, ϕ and σ^2—is available in the censored data? We now answer this question by appealing to the concept of semiparametric information.[17].

The structure we seek is clear from the following example:

EXAMPLE 1.   For the model (12)–(14) for censored data, assume

$$\varepsilon \sim \mathcal{N}(0, \sigma^2) \quad \text{and} \quad \beta(x_i - g_1(w_i)) \sim \mathcal{N}(0, \sigma_{\beta x}^2).$$

Suppose that η is a vector of nuisance parameters, parameterizing the conditional expectation $g^\eta(w) = E(x \mid w, d = 1, \eta)$, where by construction $\eta = 0$ coincides with the true function $g_1(w) = g^0(w)$. Under these assumptions, the density of y for the censored data is

$$(17) \qquad \ln f(y \mid w, \alpha, \beta, \phi, \eta) = -\ln \sqrt{2\pi} - (1/2)\ln \left(\sigma_{\beta x}^2 + \sigma^2\right)$$

$$- (1/2)\frac{(y - \alpha - \beta g^\eta(w) - \phi w)^2}{\left(\sigma_{\beta x}^2 + \sigma^2\right)}.$$

---

[16] For bivariate regression, censoring bias is given as plim $\hat{b} = \beta(1 + \Lambda)$, where

$$\Lambda = .p(1-p) \cdot \frac{(E(x \mid d = 1) - \xi)(\xi - E(x \mid d = 0))}{\text{Var}(x^{\text{cen}})}.$$

Imputation sets $\xi = E(x \mid d = 1)$, which zeros the bias.

[17] See Newey (1990) for the definition of semiparametric information and the semiparametric variance bound.

Denoting $\varepsilon = y - \alpha - \beta g^\eta(w) - \phi w$, the scores of the parameters of interest are

$$
(18) \qquad \ell_\alpha = \frac{\partial \ln f}{\partial \alpha} = \frac{\varepsilon}{\left(\sigma_{\beta x}^2 + \sigma^2\right)},
$$

$$
(19) \qquad \ell_\beta = \frac{\partial \ln f}{\partial \beta} = \frac{\varepsilon}{\left(\sigma_{\beta x}^2 + \sigma^2\right)} \cdot g_1(w)
$$

$$
(20) \qquad \ell_\phi = \frac{\partial \ln f}{\partial \phi} = \frac{\varepsilon}{\left(\sigma_{\beta x}^2 + \sigma^2\right)} \cdot w
$$

and

$$
(21) \qquad \ell_{\sigma^2} = \frac{\partial \ln f}{\partial \sigma^2} = -\frac{1}{2\left(\sigma_{\beta x}^2 + \sigma^2\right)} + \left(\frac{1}{2}\right) \cdot \frac{\varepsilon^2}{\left(\sigma_{\beta x}^2 + \sigma^2\right)^2}.
$$

The scores of the nuisance parameters are

$$
(22) \qquad \ell_\eta = \frac{\partial \ln f}{\partial \eta} = \frac{\varepsilon}{\left(\sigma_{\beta x}^2 + \sigma^2\right)} \cdot \frac{\partial g^\eta(w)}{\partial \eta}
$$

$$
(23) \qquad \ell_{\sigma_{\beta x}^2} = \frac{\partial \ln f}{\partial \sigma_{\beta x}^2} = -\frac{1}{2\left(\sigma_{\beta x}^2 + \sigma^2\right)} + \left(\frac{1}{2}\right) \cdot \frac{\varepsilon^2}{\left(\sigma_{\beta x}^2 + \sigma^2\right)^2}.
$$

The semiparametric information on α, β, ϕ, and σ^2 is the variance of their scores, after projection onto subspace orthogonal to that spanned by the scores of the nuisance parameters. When $g_1(w)$ is unrestricted, then a sufficiently rich parameterization $g^\eta(w)$ can be found such that linear combinations of $\{\partial g^\eta(w)/\partial \eta_j\}$ will approximate a constant, w and $g_1(w)$ arbitrarily well. Therefore, the projection of ℓ_α, ℓ_β, ℓ_ϕ, ℓ_{σ^2} onto the subspace orthogonal to the span of ℓ_η, $\ell_{\sigma_{\beta x}^2}$ will be arbitrarily small. Consequently, the semiparametric information on α, β, ϕ, and σ^2 is zero.

It is clear that for more general settings—in particular, general densities of ε and of x given w—we have the same conclusion[18]

PROPOSITION 1. *If there are no restrictions on the conditional expectation $g_1(w) = E(x \mid w, d = 1)$, then the semiparametric information on α, β, ϕ, and σ^2 from the censored data is zero. The semiparametric variance bound for the estimation of α, β, ϕ, and σ^2 using complete cases only is the same as the semiparametric variance bound using the complete cases together with the censored data.*

Thus, the phenomena discussed with regard to dummy variable methods above applies more generally. There is no gain in estimation from using the censored

---

[18] The semiparametric variance bound is the inverse of the semiparametric information.

data, unless restrictions can be applied to the conditional expectation $g_1(w)$.[19] We now discuss estimation with this in mind.

3.   ESTIMATION WITH THE FULL DATA SAMPLE

There are a number of approaches for estimation that include the censored observations, but all must add information beyond the basic regression model.[20] We now discuss these issues in the context of (corrected) regression estimators.

3.1.   *Use of a Proxy Equation.*   We consider pooled estimation using the complete cases, with model

$$(24) \qquad y_i = \alpha + \beta x_i + \phi' w_i + \varepsilon_i \quad i = 1, \ldots, n_0,$$

together with the censored observations. As noted above, a correctly specified regression model for the censored observations is

$$(25) \qquad y_i = \alpha + \beta g_1(w_i) + \phi' w_i + u_i \quad i = n_0 + 1, \ldots, n_0 + n_1,$$

where $E(u_i \mid w_i) = 0$, since

$$(26) \qquad g_1(w_i) = E(x_i \mid w_i, d_i = 1)$$

is the appropriate proxy for x_i, for the censored observations. The question is how to estimate $g_1(w_i)$, in a way that will be valuable for the estimation of α, β, ϕ, and σ^2.

With the uncensored observations, we can identify and estimate the conditional expectation of x_i given w_i, namely,

$$(27) \qquad g_0(w_i) = E(x_i \mid w_i, d_i = 0).$$

This raises one immediate approach to identifying $g_1(w_i)$ that has received much attention in the econometrics literature, namely, independent censoring. If d_i is independent of x_i and w_i, then

$$(28) \qquad g_1(w_i) = g_0(w_i).$$

Estimation with the full sample can proceed as follows: Form the estimate $\hat{g}_0(\cdot)$ with the complete cases and then use $\hat{g}_0(w_i)$ in place of x_i^{cen} for the censored observations.[21]

---

[19] Similar structure is discussed in Horowitz and Manski (1998, 2000). See also Robins and Rotnitzky (1995).

[20] There are also likely to be approaches based on partial information and bounds. We do not pursue this here, but note it as a potentially fruitful area of future research.

[21] For instance, Arellano and Meghir (1992) propose using the best linear predictor of x on w as a proxy, which can be estimated using the complete cases only when the censoring is independent or does not introduce bias. Much recent methodological work relies on the "censoring at random" or "missing at random" structure—see Chen et al. (2004, 2005) and Liang et al. (2004), among others.

When (28) is not valid, we need some other structure that bridges the censored and uncensored observations. Perhaps the most natural is to assume the existence of a proxy equation for x_i that applies in the full sample. A regression proxy is based on the model

$$(29) \qquad\qquad x_i = G(w_i) + v_i,$$

where $E(v_i \mid w_i) = 0$; namely, $G(w_i) = E(x_i \mid w_i)$ is the regression applicable to the full sample. When the proxy $G(w_i)$ can be estimated, then we have a method of estimating $g_1(w_i)$. Namely, we estimate $g_0(\cdot)$ with the complete cases, and with the full data sample, we estimate the conditional probability of censoring

$$(30) \qquad\qquad p(w_i) = E(d_i \mid w_i).$$

Therefore, we can estimate $g_1(w_i)$ by plugging those estimates into the identity

$$(31) \qquad\qquad g_1(w_i) = \frac{G(w_i) - (1 - p(w_i))g_0(w_i)}{p(w_i)}.$$

The most flexible versions of this approach will require significant regularity conditions; for instance, if a nonparametric estimator of $p(\cdot)$ is used in the denominator of (31), then trimming or some other method will be needed.[22]

The model (29) often will permit estimation of $G(\cdot)$ with the complete cases. If d_i represents bound censoring, say with $d = 1[x > \xi]$, then (29) restricted to complete cases is a truncated regression model.[23] If $G(w)$ is linear, then a variety of semiparametric procedures can be applied to estimate the coefficients. Depending upon the structure assumed, index model estimators, or quantile estimators would be applicable. Here, we implement a fully parametric model of censoring, in part because we are interested in the structure of censoring in our empirical application. However, there is no reason to use that much structure, in principle.

3.2. A Normal Mixed-Censoring Model.

3.2. *A Normal Mixed-Censoring Model.* Our application focuses on the wealth effects on consumption. Log wealth is bounded below and censored to 0, but it is not obvious that the censoring follows a natural pattern for censoring

---

[22] It is useful to note that there are other estimation approaches based on $G(\cdot)$. For instance, one could discard x_i in the complete cases and estimate using the proxy G for the entire sample, fitting

$$y_i = \alpha + \beta \cdot G(w_i) + \phi' w_i + U_i; \quad i = 1, \ldots, n_0 + n_1.$$

This idea would seem valuable only in unlikely settings, such as where the complete cases were a tiny fraction of the full data sample, but for some reason $G(w_i)$ is a terrific proxy, capturing almost all of the variation in x_i. Then the loss of $x_i - G(w_i)$ for the complete cases would involve a small loss in estimation efficiency.

[23] One might consider estimating (24) as a reverse regression, but that will not work in our framework. Although the reverse regression has a censored dependent variable (x_i^{cen}), it is not well specified, because the regressor (y_i) is correlated with the error term, and part of that correlation is due to the censoring of x_i that we are studying here. An instrument or other additional information would be required.

from bottom-coding alone. That is, it is not obvious that low wealth values are more likely to be censored than high wealth values. We now propose a parametric censoring model that allows us to examine this issue together with the impact on the estimation of wealth effects. We retain our notation above, where later x_i will be log wealth and $\xi = 0$.

We add to the basic Equation (1) by assuming that the proxy $G(w_i) = E(x_i \mid w_i)$ of x_i is linear

$$(32) \qquad G(w_i) = \delta_0 + \delta_1' w_i,$$

and we assume that v_i of (29) is normally distributed and homoskedastic

$$(33) \qquad v_i \sim \mathcal{N}(0, \sigma_v^2).$$

This assumption facilitates modeling bottom-coding with formulae familiar from censored normal regression models.[24]

In our application, we implement a more general censoring model, that allows a mixture of independent censoring and bottom-coding. The approach is to model bottom-coding together with (conditionally independent) censoring of probability $R(w_i)$ for observations that are not bottom-coded. Let

$$(34) \qquad d_{1i} = 1[v_i < \xi - (\delta_0 + \delta_1' w_i)]$$

and

$$(35) \qquad d_{2i} = 1[s_i < -(\eta_0 + \eta_1' w_i)]$$

represent the two sources of censoring. We assume $v_i \sim \mathcal{N}(0, \sigma_v^2)$ and $s_i \sim \mathcal{N}(0, 1)$, and that v_i and s_i are conditionally independent given w_i.

The overall censoring indicator d is now defined as

$$(36) \qquad d_i = d_{1i} + d_{2i} - d_{1i} d_{2i}.$$

This reflects bottom-coding, plus a probability of

$$(37) \qquad R(w_i) = \Phi(-(\eta_0 + \eta_1' w_i))$$

of (nonbottom-coded) observations being randomly censored to the same value ξ, with Φ the normal c.d.f. To simplify the formulae that follow, denote the probability of bottom-coding as

$$(38) \qquad P(w_i) \equiv \Phi\left(\frac{\xi - (\delta_0 + \delta_1' w_i)}{\sigma_v}\right).$$

---

[24] See, for instance, Ruud (2000), Green (2003), or Davidson and McKinnon (2004). Analogous formulae are available for top-coding.

To compute the required regression formulae, note first that $d = 0$ if and only if $d_1 = 0$ and $d_2 = 0$. Therefore, by conditional independence,

$$(39) \qquad \Pr\{d = 0 \mid w_i\} = [1 - P(w_i)][1 - R(w_i)]$$

so that the overall probability of censoring is

$$(40) \qquad p(w_i) = \Pr\{d = 1 \mid w_i\} = P(w_i) + R(w_i) - P(w_i) \cdot R(w_i).$$

For the regression of x on w in the complete cases, we have

(41)
$$
\begin{aligned}
g_0(w_i) &= E(x_i \mid w_i, d = 0) \\
&= E(x_i \mid w_i, d_{1i} = 0 \text{ and } d_{2i} = 0) \\
&= \delta_0 + \delta_1' w_i + E(v_i \mid w_i, \, v_i < \xi - (\delta_0 + \delta_1' w_i) \text{ and } s_i < -(\eta_0 + \eta_1' w_i)) \\
&= \delta_0 + \delta_1' w_i + E(v_i \mid w_i, v_i < \xi - (\delta_0 + \delta_1' w_i)),
\end{aligned}
$$

where the last equality follows from the conditional independence of v_i and s_i given w_i. Therefore, $g_0(\cdot)$ is given by the following formula (which is also appropriate for bottom-coding only)

$$(42) \qquad g_0(w_i) = \delta_0 + \delta_1' w_i + \sigma_v \cdot \lambda_0 \left(\frac{\xi - (\delta_0 + \delta_1' w_i)}{\sigma_v} \right).$$

Here $\lambda_0(\cdot) \equiv \phi(\cdot)/[1 - \Phi(\cdot)]$, with ϕ the normal density function.

The regression of x_i on w_i for the censored data is found by applying (31) using (40) and (41). The result is

$$(43) \qquad g_1(w_i) = \delta_0 + \delta_1' w_i - \Psi(w_i) \cdot \sigma_v \cdot \lambda_1 \left(\frac{\xi - (\delta_0 + \delta_1' w_i)}{\sigma_v} \right),$$

where $\lambda_1(\cdot) \equiv \phi(\cdot)/\Phi(\cdot)$ and

$$(44) \qquad \Psi(w_i) = \frac{P(w_i)[1 - R(w_i)]}{R(w_i) + P(w_i)[1 - R(w_i)]}.$$

The correction term Ψ is easily seen to be $\Psi(w_i) = (p(w_i) - R(w_i))/p(w_i)$, the relative probability of bottom-coding in the mixed censoring.

It is worth pointing out that all the parameters of the model are identified. In brief, the linear regression (1) applied to the complete cases identifies α, β, ϕ, and σ_ε, and the normal truncated regression (41) applied to the complete cases identifies δ_0, δ_1, and σ_v. Finally, with δ_0, δ_1, and σ_v, the (scaled) probit model (39) applied to the full sample identifies η_0 and η_1. We could consider various estimation approaches using the moment restrictions implied by the various regressions above, but instead we derive the likelihood function for consistent and efficient estimation.

3.3. *The Likelihood Function for the Normal Mixed Censoring Model.* We derive the likelihood function for a slightly more general model than above, allowing for the possibility of separate instruments for the (uncensored) regressor. In brief, the model is

$$y_i = \beta x_i + W_i' \gamma + \varepsilon_i$$
$$x_i = Z_i' \theta + v_i$$
$$x_i^{\text{cen}} = 1(x_i \geq 0) \cdot 1(Z_i' \eta + s_i \geq 0) \cdot x_i,$$

where W_i, Z_i need not coincide, and each may contain a constant. We assume the normal parametric specification

$$\begin{pmatrix} \varepsilon_i \\ v_i \\ s_i \end{pmatrix} \sim \mathcal{N} \left(\begin{pmatrix} 0 \\ 0 \\ 0 \end{pmatrix}, \begin{bmatrix} \sigma_\varepsilon^2 & 0 & 0 \\ 0 & \sigma_v^2 & 0 \\ 0 & 0 & 1 \end{bmatrix} \right).$$

We use a censoring value of $\xi = 0$ in the following, without loss of generality.

We construct the likelihood function following Ruud (2000, Chapter 18), by first deriving the joint c.d.f. of (y, x^{cen}) conditional on W and Z, namely,[25]

$$(45) \qquad F(c_1, c_2) = \Pr\{y \leq c_1, x^{\text{cen}} \leq c_2\}.$$

We then derive the likelihood by differentiating with respect to c_1, c_2 where possible, and differencing where not. First, for the case where $c_2 < 0$, we have

$$(46) \qquad F(c_1, c_2) = 0, \quad c_2 < 0.$$

For $c_2 > 0$, we have that

$$y \leq c_1 \Leftrightarrow \varepsilon \leq c_1 - \beta x^{\text{cen}} - W' \gamma$$

and

$$x^{\text{cen}} \leq c_2 \Leftrightarrow v \leq c_2 - Z' \theta,$$

where this condition is sufficient regardless of the value of s. Therefore,

$$(47) \qquad F(c_1, c_2) = \Phi \left(\frac{c_1 - \beta x^{\text{cen}} - W' \gamma}{\sigma_\varepsilon} \right) \cdot \Phi \left(\frac{c_2 - Z' \theta}{\sigma_v} \right), \quad c_2 > 0.$$

---

[25] We suppress the dependence of F on W and Z in the notation, which hopefully will not cause any confusion.

The final case, $c_2 = 0$, requires some calculation. Begin by writing y in terms of the errors as

$$y = \beta Z'\theta + W'\gamma + \beta v + \varepsilon.$$

Therefore, $F(c_1, 0) = \Pr\{y \le c_1, x^{\text{cen}} \le 0\}$ is the probability that

$$I: \qquad \beta v + \varepsilon \le c_1 - \beta Z'\theta - W'\gamma$$

and that either

$$II: \qquad v \le -Z'\theta \quad \text{or} \quad III: \qquad s \le -Z'\eta$$

holds. Denoting II' and III' as the opposite condition to II and III, respectively, we have

$$
\begin{aligned}
(48) \qquad F(c_1, 0) &= \Pr\{I \text{ and } (II \text{ or } III)\} \\
&= \Pr\{I\} - \Pr\{I \text{ and } II' \text{ and } III'\} \\
&= \Pr\{I\} - \Pr\{I \text{ and } II'\}\Pr\{III'\} \\
&= \Pr\{I\} - [\Pr(I) - \Pr\{I \text{ and } II\}]\Pr\{III'\} \\
&= \Pr\{I\}\Pr\{III\} + (1 - \Pr\{III\})\Pr\{I \text{ and } II\},
\end{aligned}
$$

where the third equality is by independence of s and ε, v. Clearly, we have that

$$\Pr\{I\} = \Phi\left(\frac{c_1 - \beta Z'\theta - W'\gamma}{\sqrt{\beta^2\sigma_v^2 + \sigma_\varepsilon^2}}\right)$$

and

$$\Pr\{III\} = \Phi(-Z'\eta) = 1 - \Phi(Z'\eta).$$

We complete the ingredients of (48) by noting that

$$\Pr\{I \text{ and } II\} = \int_{-\infty}^{-Z'\theta} \int_{-\infty}^{c_1 - \beta Z'\theta - W'\gamma} \phi_{\text{biv}}\left(\begin{pmatrix} \beta v + \varepsilon \\ v \end{pmatrix}, \Sigma\right) d(\beta v + \varepsilon)\, dv,$$

where ϕ_{biv} is the bivariate normal density, with covariance matrix

$$\Sigma = \begin{bmatrix} \beta^2\sigma_v^2 + \sigma_\varepsilon^2 & \beta\sigma_v^2 \\ \beta\sigma_v^2 & \sigma_v^2 \end{bmatrix}.$$

In summary

(49)
$$F(c_1, 0) = (1 - \Phi(Z'\eta)) \cdot \Phi\left(\frac{c_1 - \beta Z'\theta - W'\gamma}{\sqrt{\beta^2 \sigma_v^2 + \sigma_\varepsilon^2}}\right)$$

$$+ \Phi(Z'\eta) \cdot \int_{-\infty}^{-Z'\theta} \int_{-\infty}^{c_1 - \beta Z'\theta - W'\gamma} \phi_{\text{biv}}\left(\begin{pmatrix} \beta v + \varepsilon \\ v \end{pmatrix}, \Sigma\right) d(\beta v + \varepsilon) \, dv.$$

Now, to compute the components of the likelihood function, we differentiate/difference the c.d.f. For $c_2 < 0$, we have that

(50)
$$\frac{\partial F(c_1, c_2)}{\partial c_1 \partial c_2} = 0.$$

For $c_2 > 0$, we have that

(51)
$$\frac{\partial F(c_1, c_2)}{\partial c_1 \partial c_2} = \frac{1}{\sigma_\varepsilon} \phi\left(\frac{c_1 - \beta x^{\text{cen}} - W'\gamma}{\sigma_\varepsilon}\right) \cdot \frac{1}{\sigma_v} \phi\left(\frac{c_2 - Z'\theta}{\sigma_v}\right).$$

For $c_2 = 0$, we differentiate w.r.t. c_1 as

$$\frac{\partial F(c_1, 0)}{\partial c_1} = (1 - \Phi(Z'\eta)) \cdot \frac{1}{\sqrt{\beta^2 \sigma_v^2 + \sigma_\varepsilon^2}} \phi\left(\frac{c_1 - \beta Z'\theta - W'\gamma}{\sqrt{\beta^2 \sigma_v^2 + \sigma_\varepsilon^2}}\right)$$

$$+ \Phi(Z'\eta) \frac{\partial}{\partial c_1}\left(\int_{-\infty}^{-Z'\theta} \int_{-\infty}^{c_1 - \beta Z'\theta - W'\gamma} \phi_{\text{biv}}\left(\begin{pmatrix} \beta v + \varepsilon \\ v \end{pmatrix}; \Sigma\right) d(\beta v + \varepsilon) \, dv\right).$$

The final derivative is solved for explicitly using the fact that if $u \equiv v - \rho(\beta v + \varepsilon)$ is independent of $\beta v + \varepsilon$, where

$$\rho = \frac{\beta \sigma_v^2}{\beta^2 \sigma_v^2 + \sigma_\varepsilon^2},$$

and that the variance of u is

$$\sigma_u^2 = \sigma_v^2\left(1 - \frac{\beta^2 \sigma_v^2}{\beta^2 \sigma_v^2 + \sigma_\varepsilon^2}\right).$$

Now, we have

$$
\frac{\partial}{\partial c_1}\left(\int_{-\infty}^{-Z'\theta}\int_{-\infty}^{c_1 - \beta Z'\theta - W'\gamma} \phi_{\text{biv}}\left(\begin{pmatrix}\beta v + \varepsilon \\ v\end{pmatrix};\Sigma\right) d(\beta v + \varepsilon)\, dv\right)
$$

$$
= \int_{-\infty}^{-Z'\theta} \phi_{\text{biv}}\left(\begin{pmatrix}c_1 - \beta Z'\theta - W'\gamma \\ v\end{pmatrix};\Sigma\right) dv
$$

$$
= \phi\left(c_1 - \beta Z'\theta - W'\gamma;\beta^2\sigma_v^2 + \sigma_\varepsilon^2\right) \cdot \int_{-\infty}^{-Z'\theta} \phi\left(v - \rho(c_1 - \beta Z'\theta - W'\gamma);\sigma_u^2\right) dv
$$

$$
= \frac{1}{\sqrt{\beta^2\sigma_v^2 + \sigma_\varepsilon^2}}\phi\left(\frac{c_1 - \beta Z'\theta - W'\gamma}{\sqrt{\beta^2\sigma_v^2 + \sigma_\varepsilon^2}}\right) \cdot \Phi\left(\frac{-Z'\theta - \rho(c_1 - \beta Z'\theta - W'\gamma)}{\sigma_u}\right)
$$

$$
= \frac{1}{\sqrt{\beta^2\sigma_v^2 + \sigma_\varepsilon^2}}\phi\left(\frac{c_1 - \beta Z'\theta - W'\gamma}{\sqrt{\beta^2\sigma_v^2 + \sigma_\varepsilon^2}}\right)
$$

$$
\cdot \Phi\left(-\frac{\sqrt{\beta^2\sigma_v^2 + \sigma_\varepsilon^2}}{\sigma_v\sigma_\varepsilon}Z'\theta - \frac{\beta\sigma_v}{\sqrt{\beta^2\sigma_v^2 + \sigma_\varepsilon^2}\sigma_\varepsilon}(c_1 - \beta Z'\theta - W'\gamma)\right).
$$

In summary, we have

(52)
$$
\frac{\partial F(c_1,0)}{\partial c_1} = \frac{1}{\sqrt{\beta^2\sigma_v^2 + \sigma_\varepsilon^2}}\phi\left(\frac{c_1 - \beta Z'\theta - W'\gamma}{\sqrt{\beta^2\sigma_v^2 + \sigma_\varepsilon^2}}\right)
$$
$$
\cdot \left(1 + \Phi(Z'\eta)\left[\Phi\left(-\frac{\sqrt{\beta^2\sigma_v^2 + \sigma_\varepsilon^2}}{\sigma_v\sigma_\varepsilon}Z'\theta \right.\right.\right.
$$
$$
\left.\left.\left. - \frac{\beta\sigma_v}{\sqrt{\beta^2\sigma_v^2 + \sigma_\varepsilon^2}\sigma_\varepsilon}(c_1 - \beta Z'\theta - W'\gamma)\right) - 1\right]\right).
$$

These calculations allow us to write the log-likelihood function directly. Recall that $d_i = 1[x_i^{\text{cen}} = 0]$ indicates an observation with a censored regressor. We have

(53)
$$
\ln\mathcal{L} = C + \sum_{i=1}^{n}(1 - d_i)\left(-\ln\sigma_\varepsilon - \frac{1}{2}\frac{(y_i - \beta x_i^{\text{cen}} - W_i'\gamma)^2}{\sigma_\varepsilon^2}\right)
$$
$$
+ \sum_{i=1}^{n}(1 - d_i)\left(-\ln\sigma_v - \frac{1}{2}\frac{(x_i^{\text{cen}} - Z_i'\theta)^2}{\sigma_v^2}\right)
$$
$$
+ \sum_{i=1}^{n}d_i\left(-\frac{1}{2}\ln(\beta^2\sigma_v^2 + \sigma_\varepsilon^2) - \frac{1}{2}\frac{(y_i - \beta Z_i'\theta - W_i'\gamma)^2}{\beta^2\sigma_v^2 + \sigma_\varepsilon^2}\right)
$$
$$
+ \sum_{i=1}^{n}d_i\ln\left(1 + \Phi(Z_i'\eta)\left[\Phi\left(-\frac{\sqrt{\beta^2\sigma_v^2 + \sigma_\varepsilon^2}}{\sigma_v\sigma_\varepsilon}Z_i'\theta \right.\right.\right.
$$
$$
\left.\left.\left. - \frac{\beta\sigma_v}{\sqrt{\beta^2\sigma_v^2 + \sigma_\varepsilon^2}\sigma_\varepsilon}(y_i - \beta Z_i'\theta - W_i'\gamma)\right) - 1\right]\right).
$$

The terms are easy to interpret; the first three are normal log-likelihoods for regressing y on x^{cen} and W in the complete cases, for regressing x^{cen} on Z in the complete cases, and for regressing y on $Z'\theta$ and W in the censored data, respectively. This final term corrects for selection on y induced by the censoring of x. As such, this log-likelihood has natural similarity to the log-likelihood for normal selection models.

It is not difficult to establish the conditions for consistency and asymptotic normality of maximum likelihood, as laid out in Newey and McFadden (1994). For consistency—Newey and McFadden Theorem 2.5—we create a compact parameter space by bounding all parameters. We assume variances have a small positive lower bound and a large upper bound, and other parameters have (large) negative lower bounds and positive upper bounds. Continuity is apparent, and the bounding condition is clear for all four terms above (for instance, the last term is bounded above by $\ln(1) = 0$). For asymptotic normality—Newey and McFadden Theorem 3.3—the log-likelihood is clearly twice continuously differentiable, and the remaining regularity conditions follow for the first three terms from standard normal linear regression and for the last term from the linear forms within the normal c.d.f. (as with a probit model).

It is worth remarking that the authors have failed to discover general conditions under which this log-likelihood displays gobal concavity. However, since the first three components are very well behaved (and globally concave themselves), it is natural to suspect that some situations exist where overall global concavity can be shown. Then, maximum likelihood estimation would be as well behaved as for some other censoring problems, such as a normal regression model with a censored dependent variable.

4.   THE EFFECTS OF WEALTH ON CONSUMPTION

4.1.   *General Discussion.*   In recent years, many developed countries have witnessed tremendous expansion in consumption expenditures at the same time as substantial increases in household wealth levels.[26] This has fueled great interest in the measurement of the effects of wealth on consumption decisions.

One encounters many types of censoring when studying consumption at the household level. Income is typically top-coded, by survey design. Wealth is nonnegative, in part because of survey bounding but more because of a failure to observe negative wealth components such as household debt. Thus, our analysis of log wealth as censored may be incomplete, as we will take positive wealth observations as correct. That is, there may be further mismeasurement issues applicable to our "complete cases."

Published estimates of the elasticity of consumption with regard to financial wealth seem unusually large. With aggregate data, estimates in the range of 4%

---

[26] During the 1990s there were multiyear expansions in consumption in the United States and the United Kingdom (among others). During the same time, the total wealth of Americans grew more than 15 trillion dollars, with a 262% increase in corporate equity and a 14% increase in housing and other tangible assets (see Poterba, 2000, for an excellent survey). Housing prices increased in both countries as well.

but up to 10% can be found, varying with the type of asset included and the time period under consideration.[27] With individual data, estimates tend to be larger,[28] such as 8%. We are interested in whether the censored character of income and wealth can help account for the magnitude of these estimates[29]

It is worth mentioning that estimates of wealth effects are of substantial interest to economic policy. A key issue of monetary policy is how much aggregate demand is affected by changes in interest rates. Interest rates affect consumption directly, but also housing wealth as well as financial wealth. A substantial impact of wealth on consumption, either through enhanced borrowing or cashing out of capital gains, will be a big part of whether interest rates have a real impact or not, and thus are relevant for the design of effective monetary policy.[30]

4.2. Application to Consumption Data.

We now study the impact of censored regressors in an application to household consumption and wealth.[31] The data includes consumption, current income and a computed permanent component of consumption that depends on the cohort in which the household belongs, characteristics of the household (such as retirement status, family size, etc.), and financial information. By construction, the income variables are *not* censored—the observations with top-coded income variables of the original survey have been dropped. That is, our data is already a set of "complete cases" in terms of income. The only censored variables are the financial wealth variables. There are three sorts of wealth variables that interest us: total wealth, housing wealth, and stock market wealth.

In Table 2, we show the proportion of the variables that are at the censoring bound in the data. There is a moderate proportion of total wealth observations at the bound (27%) but this increases to 43% for housing, to 76% for stock market wealth, and to 81% when one or more wealth variables is at the bound.[32] This raises substantial concerns for the estimation of consumption impacts from different types of wealth.[33]

---

[27] Lawrence Meyer and Associates (1994) find an elasticity of 4.2%, Brayton and Tinsley (1996) find 3%, Ludvigson and Steindel (1999) estimate an overall elasticity of 4% (as well as some estimates as high as 10%).

[28] See Parker (1999), Juster et al. (1999), and Starr-McCluer (1999).

[29] Similarly, large effects of housing wealth on consumption are estimated by Aoki et al. (2002) and Attanasio et al. (2003), among others. Somewhat smaller estimates are given in Engelhardt (1996) and Skinner (1996).

[30] See Muellbauer and Murphy (1990), King (1990), Pagano (1990) Attanasio and Weber (1994), and Attanasio et al. (2003), for various arguments on the connection between consumption and housing prices. In terms of whether assets prices should be targeted as part of monetary policy, see Bernanke and Gertler (1999, 2001), Cecchetti et al. (2000), and Rigobon and Sack (2003).

[31] We thank Jonathan Parker for his tremendous help and support in providing us not only with the data but with valuable suggestions.

[32] For consistency among the components, total wealth is censored when it is less than $5,000, housing wealth when it is less than $4,000 and stock market wealth when it is less than $1,000. This gives slightly higher censoring than when all levels are censored at zero, but facilitates taking logarithms.

[33] An issue we have not highlighted here is that for some of the wealth observations, a value at the bound may be the correct wealth value. That is, zero wealth may be zero wealth, as opposed to a censored nonzero wealth. In our estimates, this is partly accomodated for by allowing for random

TABLE 2

PROPORTION OF CENSORING IN TOTAL WEALTH, HOUSING, AND STOCK MARKET WEALTH

	Percentage Censored	Total Observations	Not Censored
Total Wealth	26.6%	11,903	8,735
Housing	43.4%	11,903	6,737
Stock Market	76.5%	11,903	2,797
One or More Censored	80.9%	11,903	2,272

TABLE 3

LOG CONSUMPTION RESULTS, SIMPLE MODELS

	OLS			
	All Data	CC	All Data	CC
Sample Size	11,903	8,735	11,903	2,272
Total Wealth	0.181	0.140	0.149	0.055
	(0.0029)	(0.0038)	(0.0054)	(0.0135)
Housing Wealth			0.020	0.069
			(0.0053)	(0.0132)
Stock Market Wealth			0.033	0.012
			(0.0032)	(0.0069)

To see a coarse impact of censoring, Table 3 gives estimates of linear regressions of log consumption on log wealth and wealth components, without any additional regressors.[34] If only total wealth is included, there are 8,735 complete (uncensored) cases, and when all three wealth variables are included, there are 2,272 complete cases. With the bivariate regression of log consumption on log wealth, there is an expansion bias of 29%, namely $(0.181/0.140) - 1$. With the components included, using all data gives a total wealth elasticity of 0.202, whereas the complete cases give a total elasticity of 0.136, which reflects a 48% expansion bias. There are some huge relative shifts; in particular a much larger housing wealth effect in the complete case data.

To apply our model of wealth censoring, we focus on the total wealth effect, using a log-form regression equation similar to that estimated by Parker (1999):

$$(54) \quad \ln C_{it} = \alpha + \beta \cdot \ln W_{it} + \phi_1 \ln PINC_{it} + \phi_2 \ln INC_{it} + \phi_3' Controls_{it} + \varepsilon_{it},$$

where $C_{i,t}$ is consumption of household i at time t. W_{it} is total wealth, which is censored.[35] There are two income variables; $PINC_{it}$ is a constructed permanent component of income and $INC_{i,t}$ is the current income, which are uncensored

---

censoring. By a fuller treatment, this possibility could be more fully modeled. We did carry out the test of Rigobon and Stoker (2006b), and rejected that censoring bias was zero.

[34] Heteroskedasticity consistent (White) standard errors are presented in parentheses.

[35] To include housing and stock market wealth, we would need to model the joint censoring process of all wealth components. We focus on total wealth only just to keep things simple here.

TABLE 4

LOG CONSUMPTION RESULTS

	OLS		Maximum Likelihood with Censoring	
	All data	CC	No Controls	All Controls
Sample size	11,903	8,735	11,903	11,903
Total wealth	0.052	0.054	0.064	0.062
	(0.0045)	(0.0062)	(0.0035)	(0.0040)
Current income	0.180	0.165	0.202	0.179
	(0.0117)	(0.0137)	(0.0049)	(0.0048)
Permanent income	0.175	0.177	0.214	0.180
	(0.0160)	(0.0208)	(0.0065)	(0.0068)

regressors in our data. *Controls$_{it}$* are variables accounting for retirement status, family size, cohorts, time, etc. For a detailed description of the data and the definition of the variables, see Parker (1999).

Table 4 presents our estimation results. The first two columns give OLS estimates of wealth and income effects from estimating (54) over the full data and over the complete cases. The third and fourth columns give maximum likelihood estimates of the model with bound censoring and independent random censoring. The third column has only the income variables as additional regressors, setting $\phi_3 = 0$ in (54), and including only the income variables in the equations for wealth bound censoring and for independent random censoring. Finally, the fourth column gives maximum likelihood estimates where all controls are included in (54) and in the equations for bound censoring and for random censoring.

With all controls, there is not a great deal of difference between the OLS estimates for the full sample and those for the complete cases. The maximum likelihood estimates display a larger wealth elasticity than the OLS estimates (roughly 14%). Moreover, the effects of the income variables have much smaller standard errors. The larger wealth elasticity is a bit surprising, but since we had many controls and two types of censoring, it was not clear what type of impact one should expect. Some lowering of the standard errors was expected, since we are now including all of the censored data into the estimation in a consistent fashion.

We did encounter one problem in estimation, that did not seem to impact the estimates presented in Table 4. We estimated a very small independent probability of censoring beyond the bound censoring of wealth. The coefficient estimates for this probability were very imprecise, which makes sense since they appear in the likelihood in the tail of the normal c.d.f. As such, we checked for robustness of the main wealth and income effects by setting different values of the independent censoring probability; this exercise uncovered no substantial differences in the main estimates. In any event, this aspect of the estimation merits further study.[36]

---

[36] All results and estimation details are available from the authors.

5. CONCLUSION

The fact that censoring of regressors can routinely generate expansion bias was a surprise to both authors. We noticed the phenomena for bound censoring in some simulations and were able to understand the source pretty easily. In fact, it is a straightforward point, as Figure 1 can be explained to students with only rudimentary knowledge of econometric methods. Nevertheless, we do not feel that it is a minor problem for practical applications. Quite the contrary, we feel that problems of censored regressors are likely as prevalent or more prevalent than problems of censored dependent variables in typical econometric applications. Some evidence of this is the development of the faulty empirical practice of including a dummy variable for the censored data or that of replacing censored values with imputed tail means.

We feel we have made some progress in understanding the estimation issues posed by censored regressors. The use of a censoring dummy as a "fix" for censoring bias is not advisable, and even the use of tail imputations is only advisable for bound censoring with very simple models. By establishing that there is zero semiparametric information in the censored observations, we have verified that there is no fully nonparametric "fix" for the censoring or the regressor, and that some additional structure (or side information from another data set, etc.) is required. This is true even in the simplest case of exogenous censoring, which has been our focus. We did not address whether there is partial identification from the censored data, for instance, whether top-coded data provides some additional bound information on the parameters. This would be a useful future direction to pursue.

We have illustrated the extent of censoring in an application to household consumption and wealth. We developed a normal parametric model as well as its likelihood function for estimation. Our maximum likelihood estimates had a larger wealth elasticity than OLS estimates, with greater precision of the income effects, because of using the censored data in a consistent fashion with the uncensored data. We found that it was difficult to estimate the exact structure of the normal censoring processes, although that did not have a strong impact on our estimates of the wealth and income effects on consumption. Although this conclusion is dependent on our specific model, we are very optimistic that semiparametric procedures can be developed in future research.

Censoring bias of a similar type arises in instrumental variables estimators when there are censored regressors, although there are some important differences with the case of OLS regression.[37] We cover some results of this kind in Rigobon and Stoker (2006a). Moreover, we have developed specification tests for the presence of censoring bias in Rigobon and Stoker (2006b), which would serve as a useful precursor to a discussion of how to incorporate the censored data in estimation. In any case, our goal is to develop a sufficient set of empirical tools for a researcher to check for bias problems from censored regressors and then appropriately estimate parameters using all available data.

---

[37] For instance, IV estimators with random censoring of an endogenous variable display expansion bias, whereas OLS estimators display attenuation bias.

REFERENCES

AI, C., "An Improved Estimator for Models with Randomly Missing Data," *Nonparametric Statistics* 7 (1997), 331–47.

AOKI, K., J. PROUDMAN, AND G. VLIEGHE, "Houses as Collateral: Has the Link Between House Prices and Consumption in the UK Changed?" *Economic Policy Review* 8 (2002), 163–78.

ARELLANO, M., AND C. MEGHIR, "Female Labor Supply and On-the-Job Search: An Empirical Model Estimated Using Complementary Data Sets," *Review of Economic Studies* 59 (1992), 537–59.

ATTANASIO, O., AND G. WEBER, "The UK Consumption Boom of the late 1980s: Aggregate Implications of Microeconomic Evidence," in *The Economic Journal* 104 (1994), 1269–1302.

——, L. BLOW, R. HAMILTON, AND A. LEICESTER, "Consumption, House Prices, and Expectations," Mimeo, Institute for Fiscal Studies, 2003.

BELSLEY, D. A., E. KUH, AND R. E. WELSCH, *Regression Diagnostics: Identifying Influential Data and Sources of Multicollinearity* (New York: Wiley, 1980).

BERNANKE, B., AND M. GERTLER, "Monetary Policy and Asset Price Volatility," *Federal Reserve Bank of Kansas City Economic Review* LXXXIV (1999), 17–51.

——, AND ——, "Should Central Banks Respond to Movements in Asset Prices," *American Economic Review Papers and Proceedings* XCI (2001), 253–57.

BRAYTON, F., AND P. TINSLEY, "A Guide to the FRB/US: A Macroeconomic Model of the United States." Federal Reserve Board of Governors, Washington DC, Working Paper 1996-42, 1996.

CECCHETTI, S. G., H. GENBERG, J. LIPSKY, AND S. WADHWANI, *Asset Prices and Central Bank Policy* (London: International Center for Monetary and Banking Studies, 2000).

CHEN, X., H. HONG, AND E. TAMER, "Measurement Error Models with Auxiliary Data," *Review of Economic Studies* 72 (2005), 343–66.

——, ——, AND A. TAROZZI, "Semiparametric Efficiency in GMM Models of Nonclassical Measurement Errors, Missing Data and Treatment Effects," Working Paper, November, 2004.

CHERNOZHUKOV, V., H. HONG, AND E. TAMER, "Inference on Parameter Sets in Econometric Models," Working Paper, Duke University, 2004.

DAVIDSON, R., AND J. D. MCKINNON, *Econometric Theory and Methods* (New York: Oxford University Press, 2004).

ENGELHARDT, G., "House Prices and Home Owner Saving Behavior," *Regional Science and Urban Economics* 26 (1996), 313–36.

GREEN, W. H., *Econometric Analysis*, 5th edition (Engelwood Cliff, NJ: Prentice Hall, 2003).

HEITJAN, D. F., AND D. B. RUBIN, "Inference from Coarse Data via Multiple Imputation with Application to Age Heaping," *Journal of the American Statistical Association* 85 (1990), 304–314.

——, AND ——, "Ignorability and Coarse Data," *Annals of Statistics* 19 (1991), 2244–53.

HOROWITZ, J., AND C. F. MANSKI, "Censoring of Outcomes and Regressors Due to Survey Nonresponse: Identification and Estimation Using Weights and Imputations," *Journal of Econometrics* 84 (1998), 37–58.

——, AND ——, "Nonparametric Analysis of Randomized Experiments with Missing Covariate and Outcome Data," *Journal of the American Statistical Association* 95 (2000), 77–84.

ICHIMURA, H., AND E. MARTINEZ-SANCHIS, "Identification and Estimation of GMM Models by Combining Two Data Sets," CEMMAP Working Paper, IFS, London, March, 2005.

JUSTER, F. T., L. JOSEPH, J. P. SMITH, AND F. STAFFORD, "Savings and Wealth: Then and Now," Mimeo, University of Michigan, Institute for Survey Research, 1999.

KING, M., "Discussion," *Economic Policy* 11 (1990), 383–7.

LAWRENCE H. MEYER ET AL., *The WUMM Model Book* (St. Louis: L. H. Meyer and Associates, 1994).

LIANG, H., S. WANG, J. M. ROBINS, AND R. J. CARROLL, "Estimation in Partially Linear Models with Missing Covariates," *Journal of the American Statistical Association* 99 (2004), 357–67.

LITTLE, R. J. A., "Regression with Missing X's: A Review," *Journal of the American Statistical Association* 87 (1992), 1227–37.

——, AND D. B. RUBIN, *Statistical Analysis with Missing Data*, 2nd edition (Hoboken, NJ: John Wiley and Sons, 2002).

LUDVIGSON, S., AND C. STEINDEL, "How Important Is the Stock Market Effect on Consumption," *Federal Reserve Bank of New York Economic Policy Review* 5 (July 1999), 29–52.

MAHAJAN, A., "Identification and Estimation of Single Index Models with Misclassified Regressors," Working Paper, Stanford University, July, 2004.

MANSKI, C. F., AND E. TAMER, "Inference on Regressions with Interval Data on a Regressor or Outcome," *Econometrica* 70 (2002), 519–46.

MOFFITT, R., AND G. RIDDER, "The Econometrics of Data Combination," in J. J. Heckman and E. E. Leamer, eds., *Handbook of Econometrics*, Vol. 6 (Amsterdam: Elsevier, forthcoming).

MUELLBAUER, J., AND A. MURPHY, "Is the UK Balance of Payments Sustainable," *Economic Policy* 11 (1990), 345–83.

NEWEY, W. K., "Semiparametric Efficiency Bounds," *Journal of Applied Econometrics* 5 (1990), 99–135.

——, AND D. L. McFADDEN, "Large Sample Estimation and Hypothesis Testing," Chapter 36 in R.F. Engle and D.L. McFadden, eds., *Handbook of Econometrics*, Volume 4 (Amsterdam: Elsevier, 1994).

PAGANO, C., "Discussion," *Economic Policy* 11 (1990) 387–90.

PARKER, J., "Spendthrift in America? On Two Decades of Decline in the U.S. Saving Rate?" in B. Bernanke and J. Rotemberg, eds., *NBER Macroeconomics Annual 1999* (Cambridge, MA: MIT Press, 1999).

PETOUSSIS, K., R. D., GILL, AND C. ZEELENBERG, "Statistical Analysis of Heaped Duration Data," draft, Department of Psychology, Vrije Universiteit Amsterdam, February 2004.

POTERBA, J. M., "Stock Market Wealth and Consumption," *Journal of Economic Perspectives* (Spring 2000), 99–118.

RIGOBON, R., AND B. SACK, "Measuring the Reaction of Monetary Policy to the Stock Market," *Quarterly Journal of Economics* 118 (2003), 639–69.

——, AND T. M. STOKER, "Bias from Censored Regressors," MIT Working Paper, revised September, 2006a.

——, AND ——, "Testing for Bias from Censored Regressors," MIT Working Paper, revised February, 2006b.

ROBINS, J. M., AND A. ROTNITZKY, "Semiparametric Efficiency in Multivariate Regression Models with Missing Data," *Journal of the American Statistical Association* 90 (1995), 122–9.

ROTNITZKY, A., J. M. ROBINS, AND D. O. SCHARFSTEIN, "Semiparametric Regression for Repeated Outcomes with Nonignorable Response," *Journal of the American Statistical Association* 93 (1998), 1321–39.

RUUD, P. A., *An Introduction to Classical Econometric Theory* (Oxford: Oxford University Press, 2000).

SHAIK, A., "Inference for Partially Identified Econometric Models," Working Paper, Stanford University, 2005.

SKINNER, J., "Is Housing Wealth a Sideshow?" in D. Wise, ed., *Advances in the Economics of Aging* (Chicago: University of Chicago Press, 1996), 241–68.

STARR-MCCLUER, M., "Stock Market Wealth and Consumer Spending," Mimeo, Federal Reserve Board of Governors, 1999.

TRIPATHI, G., "GMM and Empirical Likelihood with Imcomplete Data," Working Paper, December, 2003.

——, "Moment Based Inference with Incomplete Data," Working Paper, June, 2004.

TORELLI, N., AND U. TRIVELLATO, "Modeling Inaccuracies in Job-Search Duration Data," *Journal of Econometrics* 59 (1993), 185–211.

INTERNATIONAL ECONOMIC REVIEW
Vol. 48, No. 4, November 2007

VEHICLE CHOICE BEHAVIOR AND THE DECLINING MARKET SHARE OF U.S. AUTOMAKERS*

By   Kenneth E. Train and Clifford Winston[1]

*University of California, Berkeley,
U.S.A.; Brookings Institution, U.S.A.*

We develop a consumer-level model of vehicle choice to shed light on the erosion of the U.S. automobile manufacturers' market share during the past decade. We examine the influence of vehicle attributes, brand loyalty, product line characteristics, and dealerships. We find that nearly all of the loss in market share for U.S. manufacturers can be explained by changes in basic vehicle attributes, namely: price, size, power, operating cost, transmission type, reliability, and body type. U.S. manufacturers have improved their vehicles' attributes but not as much as Japanese and European manufacturers have improved the attributes of their vehicles.

1. INTRODUCTION

Until the energy shocks of the 1970s opened the U.S. market to foreign automakers by spurring consumer interest in small fuel-efficient cars, General Motors, Ford, and Chrysler sold nearly 9 out of every 10 new vehicles on the American road. After gaining a toehold in the U.S. market, Japanese automakers, in particular, have taken significant share from what was once justifiably called the Big Three (Table 1). Today, about 40% of the nation's new cars and 70% of its light trucks are sold by U.S. producers.[2] And new competitive pressures portend additional losses in share, especially in the light truck market—a traditional stronghold for U.S. firms partly because of a 25% tariff on light trucks built outside of North America and the historical absence of European automakers from this market. Japanese automakers are building light trucks in the United States to avoid the tariff and introducing new minivans, SUVs, and pickups, and European automakers are starting to offer SUVs.

The domestic industry's loss in market share is not attributable to the problems experienced by any one automaker (Table 2). Indeed, GM, Ford, and Chrysler are all losing market share at the same time. Toyota has recently surpassed Ford as

* Manuscript received July 2005; revised February 2006.

[1] We are grateful to S. Berry, F. Mannering, C. Manski, D. McFadden, A. Pakes, P. Reiss, J. Rust, M. Trajtenberg, F. Wolak, and seminar participants at Berkeley, Maryland, Stanford, UC Irvine, and Yale for helpful comments. A. Langer provided valuable research assistance. Please address correspondence to: Kenneth E. Train, Department of Economics, 549 Evans Hall #3880, University of California, Berkeley, CA 94720-3880, U.S.A. Phone: 415-291-1023. Fax: 415-291-1020. E-mail: *train@econ.berkeley.edu*.

[2] Ford and General Motors have partial ownership of some foreign automakers. However, the industry and manufacturer shares reported here would not be affected very much if Ford's and GM's sales included, on the basis of their ownership shares, the sales of these automakers.

TABLE 1

U.S. AND FOREIGN AUTOMAKERS' MARKET SHARE OF VEHICLE SALES IN THE UNITED STATES*

Year	Manufacturer by Geographic Origin		
	U.S.	Japan	Europe
Market share of cars (%)			
1970	86	3	8
1975	82	9	7
1980	74	20	6
1985	75	20	5
1990	67	30	5
1995	61	31	5
2000	53	32	11
2005	42	40	11
Market share of light trucks (%)**			
1970	91	4	4
1975	93	6	1
1980	87	11	2
1985	81	18	0
1990	84	16	0
1995	87	13	0
2000	77	19	1
2005	70	25	3
Market share of cars and light trucks (%)			
1970	87	4	7
1975	85	8	6
1980	77	18	6
1985	77	19	4
1990	72	24	3
1995	72	23	3
2000	66	26	6
2005	57	32	7

NOTES: *Shares generally do not sum to 100 because of rounding, the omission of Korean manufacturers, and imports that Automotive News does not assign to any manufacturer or country of origin.
**Light trucks include SUVs, minivans, and pickups weighing over 6000 pounds.
SOURCE: Automotive News Market Data Book (1980–2006).

the second largest seller of new cars in the United States and Honda has surpassed Chrysler (notwithstanding Chrysler's merger with Daimler-Benz in 1998) and is within reach of Ford. Both companies as well as Nissan (not shown) are also likely to increase their share of the light truck market as their new offerings become available. On the other hand, General Motors' share of new car and light truck sales has not been so low since the 1920s.

It may be believed that the industry's losses in share are confined to certain geographical regions of the country such as parts of the East and West Coasts and some affluent areas in the Southwest. However, Japanese and European automakers have built manufacturing plants and research and development facilities in the mid-West and mid-South that have spurred local employment and helped increase market share in these areas because American consumers no longer view auto "imports" as costing themselves or their friends a job. In addition, during the

TABLE 2

"BIG THREE" AND SELECTED FOREIGN AUTOMAKERS' MARKET SHARE OF VEHICLE SALES IN THE U.S.

| Year | Manufacturer | | | | |
	General Motors	Ford	Chrysler (Domestic)	Toyota	Honda
Market share of cars (%)					
1970	40	26	16	2	0
1975	44	23	11	3	1
1980	46	17	9	6	4
1985	43	19	11	5	5
1990	36	21	9	8	9
1995	31	21	9	9	9
2000	28	17	8	11	10
2005	22	13	9	16	11
Market share of light trucks (%)*					
1970	38	38	9	1	0
1975	42	31	15	2	0
1980	39	33	11	6	0
1985	36	27	14	7	0
1990	35	30	14	6	0
1995	31	33	16	5	1
2000	28	28	15	8	3
2005	30	23	18	11	6
Market share of cars and light trucks (%)					
1970	40	28	15	2	0
1975	43	25	12	3	1
1980	45	20	9	6	3
1985	41	21	12	6	4
1990	35	24	11	8	6
1995	31	26	12	7	5
2000	28	23	12	9	7
2005	26	19	14	13	9

NOTES: *Light trucks include SUVs, minivans, and pickups weighing over 6000 pounds. AMC/Jeep was acquired by Chrysler in 1987, but is not included in Chrysler's share to maintain consistency over time.
SOURCE: Automotive News Market Data Book (1980–2006).

past decade Japanese automakers in particular have significantly expanded their dealer network in interior regions of the country.

The forces that cause a tight oligopoly to lose its market dominance are central to our understanding of competition and industry performance. Academic researchers, industry analysts, and even industry executives have offered various supply-side and demand-side explanations for the U.S. automakers' decline. Aizcorbe et al. (1987) found that Japanese automakers were able to build an additional small car during the 1970s and early 1980s for $1,300 to $2,000 less than it cost the U.S. automakers to build the same car. This cost advantage translated into greater market share for the Japanese firms. However, recent evidence compiled by Harbour and Associates suggests that the U.S.–Japanese cost differential has narrowed.[3] For example, an average GM vehicle now requires 24 hours of

[3] A summary is contained in *Automotive News* email alert June 2, 2005.

assembly time whereas an average Honda North American vehicle requires 22.3 hours. Compared with Japanese transplants, American plants have also significantly reduced the labor that they require to build a car.

Recently, industry executives such as Bill Ford of Ford and Rick Wagoner of General Motors have argued that their competitive position has been eroded by rising health care and pension costs and an undervalued yen. They have called on the federal government to provide the industry with various subsidies and tax breaks and to pressure Japan to raise the value of its currency. However, the U.S. industry's market share was declining long before it began to incur the costs of an aging workforce and has continued to decline during times when the dollar/yen exchange rate was quite favorable for U.S. automakers.

From a consumer's perspective, Japanese automakers have developed a reputation for building high-quality products that suggests that their technology in cars represents better value than American technology in cars. Indeed, using various measures of quality and reliability, widely cited publications such as *Consumer Reports* and the *J.D. Power Report* have generally given their highest ratings in the past few decades to cars made by Japanese and European manufacturers instead of American manufacturers. Changes in market share since the 1970s could therefore be explained by the relative value of the technology in domestic and foreign producers' vehicles as captured in basic vehicle attributes such as price, fuel economy, power, and so on.

Consumers' preferences may also be affected by more subtle attributes of a vehicle such as the feel of a stereo knob and the shine of plastics used in interiors. Robert Lutz, General Motors' vice chairman for product development, claims that attention to these subtle attributes sends a powerful message to consumers that an automaker cares about its products.[4] An even more subtle consideration is consumers' unobserved tastes that are expressed, as John DeLorean colorfully put it, in whether their eyes light up when they walk through an automaker's showroom and whether they buy a car that they are in love with.[5] U.S. automakers may have lost market share because of the poor workmanship of their products or factors that although difficult to quantify have adversely influenced consumers' tastes toward domestic vehicles.

Brand loyalty is inextricably related to developing, maintaining, and protecting market share. Mannering and Winston (1991) found that a significant fraction of GM's loss in market share during the 1980s could be explained by the stronger brand loyalty that American consumers developed toward Japanese producers' vehicles compared with the loyalty that they had for American producers' vehicles. Ford and Chrysler were able to retain their share during that period, but the American firms' subsequent losses in share may be partly attributable to the intensity of consumer loyalty toward Japanese and European automakers.

Economic theory suggests that product line rivalry may be an important feature of competition in the passenger-vehicle market because consumers have strongly

---

[4] Danny Hakim, "G.M. Executive Preaches: Sweat the Smallest Details," *New York Times*, January 5, 2004.

[5] Danny Hakim, "Detroit's New Crisis Could Be its Worst," *New York Times*, March 27, 2005.

varying preferences. Industry analysts stress that it is important for automakers to develop attractive product lines that anticipate and respond quickly to changes in consumer preferences. General Motors, for example, has offered an assortment of vehicles that missed major trends such as the growth in the small-car market in the late 1970s and early 1980s, the interest in more aerodynamic midsize cars in the late 1980s, and the rise of sport utility vehicles based on pickup truck designs in the 1990s. Two key features of an automaker's product line are the range of vehicles that are offered and whether any particular vehicle generates "buzz" that spurs sales of all of the automaker's vehicles. Finally, the competitiveness of a product line is also affected by an automaker's network of dealers. Changes in market share since the 1970s could therefore reflect the relative strengths of domestic and foreign manufacturers' product lines and distribution systems.

Given the myriad of hypotheses that have been offered, it is useful to empirically assess as many of them as possible. This article develops a model of consumer vehicle choice to investigate the major potential causes of the domestic industry's shrinking market share. A long line of research beginning with Lave and Train (1979), Manski and Sherman (1980), Mannering and Winston (1985), and Train (1986) indicates that such models are a natural way to quantify a variety of influences on consumers' behavior, some of which may prove useful for understanding the industry's decline. However, these models have accumulated several specification and estimation concerns including the independence of irrelevant alternatives (IIA) assumption maintained by the multinomial logit model that is often used to analyze choices, the possibility that vehicle price is endogenous because it is related to unobserved vehicle attributes, the importance of accounting for heterogeneity among vehicle consumers, and the appropriate treatment of dynamic influences on choice such as brand loyalty.

We explore these concerns in the process of estimating the choices of U.S. consumers who acquired new vehicles in 2000. Although we do not claim to provide definitive solutions to all of the methodological issues that we confront, we do obtain plausible evidence that choices are strongly influenced by vehicle attributes, brand loyalty, and automobile dealerships but surprisingly they are not affected by product line characteristics. We use the choice model to simulate market shares under alternative scenarios to explore the reasons for the loss in market share by U.S. manufacturers.

We find that the U.S. industry's loss in share during the past decade can be explained almost entirely by relative changes in the most basic attributes of new vehicles, namely, price, size, power, operating cost, transmission type, reliability, and body type. The result is surprising in its simplicity, implying that it is not necessary to resort to the plethora of explanations just described. Arguments based on subtle attributes such as the design of interior features, unobserved responses by consumers to vehicle offerings, or even measurable attributes beyond those listed above do not play a measurable role in the industry's competitive problems. Similarly, changes in loyalty patterns, whether an automaker's product line is broad or narrow or includes a hot car, and changes in dealership networks do not contribute much to the industry's decline. Our finding suggests that U.S. automobile executives should focus more attention on understanding why their companies seem unable to improve the basic attributes of their vehicles as rapidly as their foreign competitors are able to improve their vehicles' basic attributes, and try to remedy the situation.

2. CHOICE OF MODEL AND ITS FORMULATION

Our objective is to investigate the most likely determinants of market share changes in the new vehicle market during the past decade. The approach we take is to estimate the *conditional* choice of buying a new car. In a complete vehicle choice model, consumers can choose to buy a new car, buy any used car, continue using their current vehicles, or not own any vehicle and presumably rely on pubic transportation. Our model, which accounts for unobserved taste variation and is conditional on a subset of the vehicle choice alternatives (i.e., new car purchases), could yield inconsistent estimates if tastes that affect which new car the consumer chooses also affect whether the consumer chooses one of these cars instead of another alternative. It is thus useful to discuss the advantages and drawbacks of different approaches to analyzing new vehicle choices before formulating our model.

2.1. *Controlling for Related Choices.* One approach to the problem of related choices that is taken, for example, by Berry et al. (2004), is to aggregate all the other alternatives into one alternative—which is often called an outside good. The weakness of this approach is that it is difficult to specify attributes that meaningfully represent this alternative. Thus, including an outside good is still likely to yield inconsistent estimates because unobserved tastes that affect a consumer's assessment of new cars can also affect a consumer's assessment of other alternatives through the *attributes* of those alternatives. For example, the value that consumers place on vehicle price affects their evaluation of each used car based on a used car's price, not just on the existence of an unspecified outside good.[6]

A further difficulty with using an outside good is that the sample of new car buyers needs to be weighted to be consistent with the general population. These weights differ greatly over observations, because the subpopulation of new car buyers is quite different from the general population. Thus, the density of tastes among the subpopulation of new vehicle buyers is derived as being proportional to the population density times the probability of a buying a new car. But this probability is influenced by the attributes of other alternatives including but not limited to all used and currently owned vehicles. However, as noted, an outside good does not control for these attributes; hence, the conditional density is likely to be incorrectly inferred from the population density.

In our view, the distribution of preferences among new car buyers can be estimated more accurately by estimating it directly on a sample of new car buyers

---

[6] The utility of the outside good is usually specified as a function of demographic characteristics and random terms. Although these elements tend to have significant effects, indicating that they are capturing differences between people who buy the good and those who do not, the utility of the outside good is not structural because it does not relate to the attributes of the alternatives that are subsumed into the aggregate "outside good."

and by conducting extensive tests of error components that capture vehicle attributes and socioeconomic variables that are likely to affect consumers' new vehicle choices as well as their related choices. Our approach also has the practical advantage that it can include explanatory variables whose distributions are not known for the general population. In contrast, the outside good approach restricts the set of explanatory variables to those whose distributions in the U.S. population are known, because the population distribution is used to weight the sample. Thus, we would be precluded from exploring, among other influences, the impact of brand loyalty and an automaker's network on vehicle choice because measures of these effects are very difficult to obtain for the general population.[7]

Of course, the issues raised here could potentially be avoided by analyzing a complete model of vehicle ownership. The problems posed by this approach are cost and empirical tractability. As noted later, we must conduct a customized survey of households to collect information on such variables as past vehicle purchases, vehicles seriously considered when selecting a new vehicle, and so on. This information is not included in publicly available surveys. Customized surveys are expensive—in our case, the cost was roughly $50 per household. Households that actually acquire a new vehicle represent roughly 12% of the general population of households. Thus, the cost of assembling a sample of all households in the population, which would be necessary to analyze the choice of whether a consumer decides to acquire a vehicle, would run into the hundreds of thousands of dollars. For those households who actually purchase a vehicle, we would have to analyze whether they selected a new or used vehicle, which would result in an enormous choice set that could not be reduced because our model does not invoke the IIA assumption. Finally, even a complete model of vehicle ownership is open to the criticism that it is conditional on other related decisions such as mode choice to work and residential location. Using our approach as a starting point, future research can consider the trade-off between additional modeling and costly data collection and possible improvements in the accuracy of parameter estimates.

2.2. *Model Formulation.*   Our analysis is based on a random utility function that characterizes consumers' choices of new vehicles by make (e.g., Toyota) and model (e.g., Camry). A mixed logit model relates this choice to the average utility of each make and model (i.e., average over consumers), the variation in utility that relates to consumers' observed characteristics, and the variation in utility that is purely random and does not relate to observed consumer characteristics. In an auxiliary regression equation, the average utility of each make and model is related to the observed attributes of the vehicle, using an estimation procedure that accounts for the possible endogeneity of vehicle prices.

---

[7] By conditioning choices on the purchase of a new vehicle, we are precluded from analyzing or forecasting changes in market size. However, we are interested in decomposing potential influences on changes in market shares, especially the decline in the U.S. manufacturers' share. We can conduct this analysis without having to control for changes in market size.

We index consumers by $n = 1, \ldots, N$, and the available makes and models of new vehicles by $j = 1, \ldots, J$. The utility, U_{nj}, that consumer n derives from vehicle j is given by

$$(1) \qquad\qquad U_{nj} = \delta_j + \beta' x_{nj} + \mu'_n w_{nj} + \varepsilon_{nj},$$

where δ_j is "average" utility (or, more precisely, the portion of utility that is the same for all consumers[8]), x_{nj} is a vector of consumer characteristics interacted with vehicle attributes, product line and distribution variables, and brand loyalties (capturing observed heterogeneity); β represents the mean coefficient for each of these variables in the population; w_{nj} is a vector of vehicle attributes that may be interacted with consumer characteristics (capturing unobserved heterogeneity); μ_n is a vector of random terms with zero mean that corresponds to vector elements in w_{nj}; and ε_{nj} is a random scalar that captures all remaining elements of utility provided by vehicle j to consumer n.

Brownstone and Train (1999) point out that the terms $\mu'_n w_{nj}$ represent random coefficients and/or error components. Each term in $\mu'_n w_{nj}$ is an unobserved component of utility that induces correlation and nonproportional substitution between vehicles, thus overcoming the IIA restriction imposed by the standard logit model. Note that elements of w_{nj} can correspond to an element of x_{nj}, in which case the corresponding element of β represents the average coefficient and the corresponding element of μ_n captures random variation around this average. Elements of w_{nj} that do not correspond to elements of x_{nj} can be interpreted as capturing a random coefficient with zero mean.

Denote the density of μ_n as $f(\mu \mid \sigma)$, which depends on parameters σ that represent, for example, the covariance of μ_n. Note that f is the density conditional on a new vehicle purchase and may therefore depend on observed variables in the model that arise from a consumer's optimizing behavior that leads to a new vehicle purchase. We explore the empirical form of f and its dependence on observed variables as part of our estimation.

We assume that ε_{nj} is i.i.d. extreme value. Note that the average utility associated with omitted attributes, which varies over vehicles, is absorbed into δ_j. Given the distributional assumption on ε_{nj}, the probability that consumer n chooses alternative i is given by the mixed logit model (see, e.g., Revelt and Train, 1998; McFadden and Train, 2000): [9]

$$(2) \qquad\qquad P_{ni} = \int \frac{e^{\delta_i + \beta' x_{ni} + \mu' w_{ni}}}{\sum_j e^{\delta_j + \beta' x_{nj} + \mu' w_{nj}}} f(\mu \mid \sigma) \, d\mu.$$

---

[8] The explanatory variables x_{nj} have nonzero mean in general, thus average utility is actually δ_j plus the mean of $\beta' x_{nj}$. We use the term "average utility" to refer to δ_j because other terms, such as "common utility" or "fixed portion of utility," seem less intuitive. The main point is that δ_j does not vary over consumers whereas the other portions of utility do.

[9] These references are for mixed logits on consumer-level choice data. Mixed logits on market share data have been estimated by Boyd and Mellman (1980), Cardell et al. (1980), and more recently revived by Berry et al. (1995).

McFadden and Train (2000) demonstrate that by making an appropriate choice of variables and mixing distribution, a model taking this form can approximate any random utility model—and pattern of vehicle substitution—to any level of accuracy.

Market (or aggregate) demand is the sum of individual consumers' demand. The true (observed) share of consumers buying vehicle i is S_i. As in Berry et al. (2004) and Goolsbee and Petrin (2004), we use market shares instead of sample shares to avoid the sampling variance associated with the latter shares. The predicted share, denoted $\hat{S}_i(\theta, \delta)$, is obtained by calculating P_{ni} with parameters $\theta = \{\beta, \sigma\}$ and $\delta = \{\delta_1, \ldots, \delta_J\}$ and averaging P_{ni} over the N consumers in the sample. Berry (1994) has shown that for any value of θ, a unique δ exists such that the predicted market shares equal the actual market shares. This fact allows δ to be expressed as a function of θ, thereby reducing the number of parameters that enter the likelihood function. We denote $\delta(\theta, S)$, where $S = \{S_1, \ldots, S_J\}$, as satisfying the relation

$$(3) \qquad S_i = \hat{S}_i(\theta, \delta(\theta, S)) = \sum_n P_{ni}(\theta, \delta(\theta, S))/N \quad i = 1, \ldots, J.$$

The parameters of the choice model θ are estimated by maximum likelihood procedures described below, and δ is calculated such that predicted market shares match observed market shares at θ.

The alternative-specific constant for each vehicle, $\delta_j(\theta, S)$, captures the average utility associated with observed as well as unobserved attributes, whereas the variables that enter the random utility model capture the variation of utility among consumers. To complete the model, we specify average utility as a function of vehicle attributes, z, with parameters, α, that do not vary over consumers:

$$(4) \qquad \delta_j(\theta, S) = \alpha' z_j + \xi_j,$$

where ξ_j captures the average utility associated with omitted vehicle attributes. Note that elements of w_{nj} in the random utility function given in Equation (1) can correspond to an element of z_j.

Vehicle price, an element of z_j, is likely to be affected by unobserved attributes, so that ξ_j does not have a zero mean conditional on z_j. To address this problem, let y_j be a vector of instruments that includes the nonprice elements of z_j plus other exogenous variables that we discuss below. The assumption that $E(\xi_j \mid y_j) = 0$ for all j is sufficient for the instrumental variables estimator of α to be consistent and asymptotically normal, given θ.

3. ESTIMATION PROCEDURES

Estimation of the random utility function presented here is complicated by our efforts to capture preference heterogeneity (i.e., σ), the average utility for each make and model (i.e., δ), and the effect of brand loyalty on vehicle choice. We discuss each of these issues in turn.

3.1. *Preference Heterogeneity and Vehicles Considered.* The set of vehicles that consumers consider before making a purchase provides additional information on their tastes that may be useful in identifying preference heterogeneity. We therefore asked consumers in our sample to list the vehicles that they seriously considered in addition to the vehicle that they purchased. Most consumers indicated that they considered only one vehicle besides their chosen vehicle; no consumer listed more than five vehicles.

We included this information in estimating the choice model by treating the chosen vehicle and the vehicles that were seriously considered as constituting a ranking. Consumers who indicated only one "considered" vehicle generated a utility ranking of $U_{ni} > U_{nh} > U_{nj}$ for all $j \neq i, h$ for chosen vehicle i and considered vehicle h. Consumers who indicated more than one considered vehicle generated a utility ranking in the order that they listed the vehicles.

Luce and Suppes (1965) demonstrated that when the unobserved component of utility is i.i.d. extreme value, the probability of a utility ranking, starting with the first-ranked alternative, is a product of logit formulas. Therefore, conditional on μ_n, the probability, $L_n(\mu_n)$, that a consumer buys vehicle i and also considered vehicle h is

$$(5) \qquad L_n(\mu_n) = \left(\frac{e^{\delta_i(\theta,S)+\beta'x_{ni}+\mu'_n w_{ni}}}{\sum_{j=1}^{J} e^{\delta_j(\theta,S)+\beta'x_{nj}+\mu'_n w_{nj}}} \right) \left(\frac{e^{\delta_h(\theta,S)+\beta'x_{nh}+\mu'_n w_{nh}}}{\sum_{j=1,j\neq i}^{J} e^{\delta_j(\theta,S)+\beta'x_{nj}+\mu'_n w_{nj}}} \right),$$

where the sum in the second logit formula is over all vehicles except i. The probability of the consumer's ranking conditional on μ_n is defined analogously for consumers who listed more than one considered vehicle. The unconditional probability of the consumer's ranking is then

$$(6) \qquad R_n = \int L_n(\mu) f(\mu \mid \sigma) d\mu.$$

We found in preliminary estimations that it was essential to include the vehicles that consumers considered to estimate the distribution of their tastes. When we included only the choice of the vehicle that consumers purchased, the parameters of the systematic part of the model were hardly affected but we were unable to obtain any statistically significant error components. In contrast, the standard deviations for several elements of μ_n were found to be significant when we included the vehicles that consumers seriously considered. Berry et al. (2004) also reported that they were unable to estimate unobserved taste variation without including consumers' rankings.

3.2. *Average Preferences.* We included dummy variables for all the makes and models in our sample to estimate consumers' average value of utility from each vehicle. In the numerical search for the maximum of the likelihood function (see below), δ is calculated for each trial value of θ. We use the contraction procedure developed by Berry et al. (1995) where at any given value of θ, the following formula is applied iteratively until predicted shares equal observed market shares (within a given tolerance):

$$(7) \qquad \delta_j^t(\theta, S) = \delta_j^{t-1}(\theta, S) + \ln(S_j) - \ln(\hat{S}_j(\theta, \delta^{t-1}(\theta, S))) \qquad j = 1, \ldots, J.$$

As in previous applications of this procedure, we found that the algorithm attains convergence quickly.

3.3. *Brand Loyalty.* Brand loyalty has been a crucial consideration in automobile demand analysis beginning with Manski and Sherman (1980), who included a transactions dummy variable in their vehicle choice model, Mannering and Winston (1985), who included lagged utilization variables, and Mannering and Winston (1991), who included "brand loyalty" variables defined as the number of previous consecutive purchases from the same manufacturer. We use the last measure of brand loyalty here. The notion of brand loyalty suggests that households may behave myopically with respect to their vehicle ownership decisions—that is, they do not take full account of the impact of their present consumption of automobiles on future tastes. Indeed, households do appear to behave myopically as indicated by high implicit discount rates based on vehicle purchase decisions (Mannering and Winston, 1985) and by frequent breaks in loyalty. Accordingly, researchers have not modeled consumers' vehicle choices as arising from the maximization of an intertemporal utility function subject to an intertemporal budget constraint.

We specify separate brand loyalty variables in our model for GM, Ford, Chrysler, Japanese manufacturers as a group, European manufacturers as a group, and Korean manufacturers as a group. However, care must be taken when interpreting these coefficients (Mannering and Winston, 1991). One interpretation, which is based on the idea of state dependence that we are attempting to capture, posits that a consumer's ownership experience with a manufacturer's products builds confidence in that manufacturer (e.g., reduces perceived risk) thereby producing a greater likelihood that a consumer will buy the manufacturer's products in the future. Consumers' actual experiences with a manufacturer's vehicles determine the intensity of their loyalty—positive experiences are reflected in a large coefficient for the manufacturer's loyalty variable. An alternative interpretation is that the loyalty variable captures unobserved taste heterogeneity among consumers that is not controlled for elsewhere in the model: Previous purchases reflect consumers' tastes that influence their current purchase.

As Heckman (1991) pointed out, state dependence and consumer heterogeneity are fundamentally indistinguishable unless one imposes some structure on the way observed and unobserved variables interact. In our case, we contend that it is more likely that brand loyalty is capturing state dependence instead of heterogeneity because it is defined for manufacturers that produce a wide range of vehicles, especially when Japanese and European vehicles are each considered as a group. Unobserved heterogeneity is more likely to be associated with makes and models than with manufacturers. For example, if a middle-aged male bought a Honda

S2000 in the past because it best matched his tastes, then, based on his revealed tastes, it is reasonable to expect that he would be more likely to buy a Porsche Boxer or a Mercedes SLK in his current choice than to buy a Honda Accord or Toyota Camry.

Our brand loyalty variables could nevertheless be subject to endogeneity bias to the extent that they relate to unobserved tastes for vehicle attributes; that is, the distribution of random terms in the choice model may be different conditional on different values of the brand loyalty variables. Heckman (1981a, 1981b) pioneered the development of dynamic discrete choice models with lagged dependent variables and serially correlated errors, recognizing the critical role of initial conditions. However, applying his methods to address the possible bias of brand loyalty coefficients is thwarted by formidable data and computational requirements. First, we would have to obtain data for all sampled consumers indicating their vehicle choices and the attributes of the vehicles that were available at the time of each previous purchase *beginning with the first vehicle that they ever purchased*. Second, we would have to simultaneously estimate previous and current vehicle choice probabilities incorporating these data and a plausible specification of how consumers' tastes are likely to change over time.

We therefore take a simpler and more tractable approach that, although not necessarily leading to a consistent stochastic structure, can be expected to capture the primary differences in the error distribution of the random utility function conditional on our brand loyalty variables. As reported later, we also estimate the model without any loyalty variables and find that the estimates for all other parameters are nearly the same with and without the loyalty variables. Hence, any inconsistency that is induced by the loyalty variables and our treatment of the conditional error distribution is confined to the loyalty parameters themselves and does not affect other parameters.

We represent the information contained in the loyalty variables about consumers' preferences across manufacturers by denoting each consumer's manufacturer preference as η_{nm}, with $m = 1, \ldots, 6$ indexing the six manufacturer groups (GM, Ford, Chrysler, Japanese, European, and Korean.) These preferences result from the manufacturers' offerings and consumers' tastes for the vehicles' attributes. In the past, consumer n chose the manufacturer with the highest value of η_{nm}. The unconditional distribution of $\eta_n = \{\eta_{n1}, \ldots, \eta_{n6}\}$ is $g(\eta_n)$. The distribution of η_n conditional on the consumer having chosen manufacturer m is

$$(8) \qquad h(\eta_n \mid \eta_{nm} > \eta_{ns} \forall s \neq m) = \frac{I(\eta_{nm} > \eta_{ns} \forall s \neq m)g(\eta_n)}{\int I(\eta_{nm} > \eta_{ns} \forall s \neq m)g(\eta_n)d\eta_n},$$

where $I(\cdot)$ is a 0–1 indicator of whether the statement in parentheses is true.

For the current choice, the utility of vehicle j, which is produced by manufacturer $s(j)$, is as previously specified plus a term $\lambda\eta_{ns}$, where λ is the coefficient of the additional element of utility. Conditional on the past choice of manufacturer, the choice probability is then the logit formula with this term added to its argument, integrated over the conditional density of η_n. Formally, the probability that consumer n chooses vehicle i produced by manufacturer $s(i)$, given that the consumer chose a vehicle by manufacturer m in the past (where m may equal $s(i)$) is:

$$P_{ni} = \iint \frac{e^{\delta_i + \beta' x_{ni} + \mu'_n w_{ni} + \lambda \eta_{ns(i)}}}{\sum_{j=1}^{J} e^{\delta_j + \beta' x_{nj} + \mu'_n w_{nj} + \lambda \eta_{ns(j)}}}$$

$$(9) \qquad \times f(\mu \mid \sigma) h(\eta_n \mid \eta_{nm} > \eta_{ns} \forall s \neq m) \, d\mu \, d\eta_n.$$

This choice probability is a mixed logit with an extra error component whose distribution is conditioned on the consumer's past choice of manufacturer. Similarly, the probability for the observed choices of consumer n, who for instance bought vehicle i and ranked vehicle h as second, is the same as Equation (5) but expanded to include the extra error component

$$R_n = \iint \frac{e^{\delta_i + \beta' x_{ni} + \mu'_n w_{ni} + \lambda \eta_{ns(i)}}}{\sum_{j=1}^{J} e^{\delta_j + \beta' x_{nj} + \mu' w_{nj} + \lambda \eta_{ns(j)}}}$$

$$\times \frac{e^{\delta_h + \beta' x_{nh} + \mu'_n w_{nh} + \lambda \eta_{ns(h)}}}{\sum_{j \neq i, j=1}^{J} e^{\delta_j + \beta' x_{nj} + \mu' w_{nj} + \lambda \eta_{ns(j)}}} f(\mu \mid \sigma) h(\eta_n \mid \eta_{nm} > \eta_{ns} \forall s \neq m) \, d\mu \, d\eta_n.$$

$$(10)$$

Note we also account for additional ranked choices as appropriate.

3.4. *Estimators.* The choice probabilities, P_{ni}, in Equation (9) and the ranking probabilities, R_n, in Equation (10), are integrals with no closed form solution. We use simulation to approximate the integrals. The simulated choice probability is

$$(11) \qquad \tilde{P}_{ni} = \frac{1}{D} \sum_{d=1}^{D} \frac{e^{\delta_i(\theta, S) + \beta' x_{ni} + \mu'_d w_{ni} + \lambda \eta_{rdns(i)}}}{\sum_j e^{\delta_j(\theta, S) + \beta' x_{nj} + \mu'_d w_{nj} + \lambda \eta_{rdns(j)}}},$$

for draws $\mu_d, d = 1, \ldots, D$ from density $f(\mu \mid \sigma)$ and draws from the conditional distribution h. The probability of consumer n's purchased and ranked vehicles are simulated similarly, giving $\tilde{R}_n$.

The simulated log-likelihood function for the observed first and ranked choices in the sample is $LL = \sum_n \ln \tilde{R}_n$, which is maximized with respect to parameters $\theta = \{\beta, \sigma\}$ and λ. As described above, estimates of $\delta = \{\delta_1, \ldots, \delta_J\}$ are obtained using the iteration formula in Equation (7) to ensure that predicted shares equal observed market shares.[10] Goolsbee and Petrin (2004) also use maximum likelihood procedures to estimate choice probabilities. Petrin (2002) and Berry et al.

---

[10] Our sample size is small relative to the number of available makes and models, and thus relative to the number of elements in δ. However, this is not problematic because observed market shares rather than sample shares are used to determine δ. Note that the sample of new vehicle buyers is large relative to the number of elements in θ that reflect differences in preferences among households, and it is this sample that is used to estimate θ.

(2004) used a generalized method of moments estimator with moments based on consumer-level choices.

We use 200 Halton draws for simulation.[11] Halton draws are a type of low-discrepancy sequence that, as R rises, has coverage properties that are superior to pseudo-random draws. For example, Bhat (2001) and Train (2000) found that 100 Halton draws achieved greater accuracy in mixed logit estimations than 1,000 pseudo-random draws.[12] To estimate the impact of different numbers of draws on parameter estimates, we estimated the model using 100, 150, and 200 draws. The estimates differed an average of 8% when we increased the number of draws from 100 to 150 and differed an average of 4% when we increased the number of draws from 150 to 200. The differences are well within the confidence intervals for the parameters and indicate that simulation noise and bias are sufficiently small to not warrant further increases in the number of draws. In addition, we evaluated the log-likelihood function, gradient, and Hessian using 400 draws at the parameter estimates obtained with 200 draws. The average log-likehood changed only very slightly, from –6.5163 to –6.5141. The test statistic $g'H^{-1}g$, where g is the gradient vector and H is the Hessian, took the value 0.00351. Under the null hypothesis that the gradient is zero, this test statistic is distributed chi-squared with degrees of freedom equal to the number of parameters. The extremely low value indicates that we cannot reject the hypothesis that the gradient using 400 draws is zero at the estimates using 200 draws at any meaningful level of significance. For these reasons, we concluded that using 200 Halton draws for simulation was sufficient. We report robust standard errors that take into account simulation noise, as suggested by McFadden and Train (2000).

After estimating the ranked choice probabilities, we estimate the regression given by Equation (4), which relates the alternative-specific constants that capture average utilities to vehicle attributes. As noted, we use instrumental variables because price is likely to be correlated with omitted attributes. Nash equilibrium in prices implies that the price of each vehicle depends on the attributes of all the other vehicles, which indicates that appropriate instruments can be constructed from these attributes because they are unlikely to be correlated with a given vehicle's omitted attributes. Letting d_{ji} be the difference in an attribute, say fuel economy, between vehicle j and i, we calculate four instruments for vehicle i for each attribute: the sum of d_{ji} over all j made by the same manufacturer, the sum of

---

[11] Draws from the conditional distribution h were obtained by an accept/reject procedure: draw values of η_n from $g(\eta_n)$ and retain those for which $\eta_{nm} > \eta_{ns}$ for all $s \neq m$. We assume $g(\eta_n)$ is a product of standard normal variables and use 200 accepted draws in the simulation of the integral over η_n.

[12] Other forms of quasi-random draws have been investigated for use in maximum simulated likelihood estimation of choice models. Sándor and Train (2004) explore (t,m,s)-nets, which include Sobol, Faure, Niederreiter, and other sequences. They find that Halton draws performed marginally better than two types of nets and marginally worse than two others, and that all the quasi-random methods vastly outperformed pseudo-random draws. In high dimensions, when Halton draws tend to be highly correlated over dimensions, Bhat (2003) has investigated the use of scrambled Halton draws, and Hess et al. (2006) propose modified Latin hypercube sampling procedures. The dimension of integration in our model is not sufficiently high to require these procedures.

d_{ji} over all j made by competing manufacturers, the sum of d_{ji}^2 over all j made by the same manufacturer, and the sum of d_{ji}^2 over all j by competing manufacturers.

The four measures are the instruments obtained from the exchangeable basis developed by Pakes (1994). The first two have been used by Berry et al. (1995) and Petrin (2002). The latter two measures, which have not been used before, capture the extent to which other vehicles' nonprice attributes differ from vehicle i's nonprice attributes. We found them to be quite useful in our estimations because without them parameter estimates tended to be less stable across alternative specifications.

Estimation of the first stage regressions for price and retained value (the two endogenous variables described further below) obtained R^2 of 0.82 and 0.83, respectively. Based on F-tests, the hypotheses that all instruments have zero coefficients and that the extra instruments that do not also enter as explanatory variables in the second stage have zero coefficients, can be rejected at the 99% confidence level. We should point out, however, that use of the instruments assumes that unobserved attributes, although correlated with price, are independent of the observed nonprice attributes of vehicles. This assumption, previously maintained by Berry et al. (1995, 2004) and Petrin (2002), is justified to some extent by pragmatic considerations. In future work, it would be useful to explore the possibility of and remedies to any endogeneity in observed nonprice attributes.

4. MODEL SPECIFICATION, DATA, AND ESTIMATION RESULTS

The random utility function in Equation (1) posits that consumers' vehicle choices and their ranking of vehicles that they seriously considered are determined by vehicle attributes, their socioeconomic characteristics and brand loyalty, and an automaker's product line and distribution network. The regression model specifies the average utility of a given make and model as a function of vehicle attributes.

In addition to a vehicle's purchase price, the attributes that we include in the models are fuel economy, horsepower, curb weight, length, wheelbase, reliability, transmission type, and size classifications. These attributes encompass those used in previous research. Other safety-related variables such as airbags and antilock brakes were not included because most vehicles in our sample were equipped with them. Because automobiles are a capital good, consumers' choices may also be influenced by their expectations of how much a vehicle's value will depreciate. We therefore include as a separate variable the percentage of a vehicle's purchase price in 2000 (consistent with the sample discussed below) that it is expected to retain after two years of ownership. Calculating the retained value based on three years of ownership produced a slightly worse fit than using two years of ownership, whereas calculating the value based on four years of ownership produced a noticeably worse fit. We expect that consumers are more likely to select a vehicle that retains its value (i.e., the coefficient should have a positive sign) because it could be sold or traded in for a higher price than a vehicle that retains little of its value. As noted, we measure brand loyalty by a consumer's consecutive purchases of the same brand of vehicle. The socioeconomic characteristics that we include are sex, age, income, residential location, and family size.

Our specification extends previous vehicle demand models by exploring the effect of automakers' product line and distribution network on choice. Researchers have typically used brand preference dummy variables to capture these influences. Economic theory suggests that broad product lines can create first mover advantages to a firm and overcome limited information in a market; thus, we specify the number of distinct models (i.e., nameplates) offered by an automaker to capture these possible effects. During the past decade, GM in particular has been criticized for offering too many models that are essentially the same vehicle, suggesting that the sign of this variable may vary by automaker. Industry analysts stress that automakers benefit from having a "hot car" in their product line because it may draw attention to other vehicles that they produce. For many decades, a well-known axiom among the Big Three was: "bring them into the showroom with a convertible, and sell them a station wagon." Recently, GM tried to get buzz for the Pontiac G6 sedan that it hoped would spillover to its other products by giving away 276 of these vehicles on Oprah Winfrey's television show. We constructed a dummy variable that indicated whether a manufacturer produced a hot car, where a hot car was defined as having sales equal to the mean sales of its subclass plus twice the standard deviation of sales. (We also explored other definitions.) An automaker's network of dealers distributes its products to potential customers; thus, we also include the number of each manufacturing division's dealerships.

We performed estimations based on a random sample of 458 consumers who acquired—that is, paid cash, financed, or leased—a new 2000 model year vehicle.[13] Although these consumers differed in how they financed a vehicle, we found that their choice model parameters were not statistically different and thus combined them to estimate a single model. The sample was drawn from a panel of 250,000 nationally representative U.S. households that is aligned with demographic data from the Current Population Survey of the U.S. Bureau of the Census. The panel is administered by National Family Opinion, Inc., and managed by Allison-Fisher, Inc. The response rate for our sample exceeded 70%. The data consist of consumers' new vehicle choices by make and model, their ranking of the vehicles they seriously considered acquiring, vehicle ownership histories, which are used to construct the brand loyalty variables, and socioeconomic characteristics. Vehicle attributes and product line variables are from issues of *Consumer Reports*, the *Market Data Book* published by Automotive News, and *Wards' Automotive Yearbook*. We follow previous research and use the manufacturer suggested retail price, MSRP, for the purchase price. Although manufacturers discount these prices with various incentives, such as cash rebates and interest free loans, during our sample period the difference between the incentives offered by American, Japanese, and European manufacturers as a percentage of the retail prices of their

---

[13] The sample size is limited by our requiring data for each consumer on the number of dealers within 50 miles that sell each make/model of vehicle and consumers' vehicle ownership histories and rankings of vehicles they considered in their 2000 choice. This information is not available from standard surveys such as the CES. Our survey enabled us to obtain the information, but at a high cost per respondent.

TABLE 3

DESCRIPTION OF THE SAMPLE (CONSUMERS WHO ACQUIRED A NEW VEHICLE IN THE YEAR 2000)

Socioeconomic Characteristics Variable	Sample Value
Average household income	$67,767
Average age	54.2
Percent male	54
Percent with child aged 1–16	19
Percent who live in rural location*	45

Market Share of Cars and Light Trucks by Manufacturer's Geographic Origin:	
Manufacturer	Share (percent)
U.S.	64
Japanese	28
European	5
Other	3

NOTE: *A rural location is defined as being outside of an MSA of 1 million people or more.

vehicles was quite small. Vehicles' expected retained values were obtained from the *Kelley Blue Book: Residual Value Guide*. The number of division dealerships within 50 miles of a respondent's zip code was obtained from the automakers' websites. A 50-mile radius seems appropriate for our analysis because CNW Marketing Research found that consumers travel 22 miles, on average, to acquire a new vehicle. In addition, some automakers' web pages only display dealerships within 50 miles of the inputted zip code.

Table 3 provides some descriptive information about the sample. It is difficult to obtain population data to assess the sample because it is conditional on a consumer acquiring a new 2000 model year vehicle. However, as noted, the sample is derived from a panel of U.S. households whose demographics are consistent with national figures; accordingly, the sample values of the socioeconomic characteristics appear to be representative. Moreover, the sample market shares of the manufacturers by geographic origin are well aligned with the national market shares reported in Table 1.

Each consumer's choice set consisted of the 200 makes and models of new 2000 vehicles. We treated a number of manufacturers that merged in the late 1990s, for example, Daimler-Benz and Chrysler, as offering distinct makes because it was likely that consumers had not yet perceived that their vehicles were made by the same manufacturer. Indeed, we obtained more satisfactory statistical fits under this assumption than using the merged entity as a unit of analysis. Given this choice set, we estimated a mixed logit model that included brand loyalty, product line and distribution variables, and vehicle attributes interacted with consumer characteristics, error components, and an alternative specific constant for each vehicle make and model. The estimated constants, which capture average utility, were then regressed against vehicle attributes using instrumental variables.

Table 4 presents estimation results for all parts of the model because each part contributes to consumers' utility. The first panel gives coefficients for two

TABLE 4

VEHICLE DEMAND MODEL PARAMETER ESTIMATES[*]

Average Utility: Elements of $\alpha'z_j$	Coefficient (Standard Error)	
Constant	−7.0318	−6.8520
	(1.4884)	(1.5274)
Manufacturer's suggested retail price *(in thousands of 2000 dollars)*	−0.0733	−0.1063
	(0.0192)	(0.0635)
Expected retained value after 2 years *(in thousands of 2000 dollars)*	–	0.0550
		(0.1011)
Horsepower divided by weight *(in tons)*	0.0328	0.0312
	(0.0117)	(0.0120)
Automatic transmission dummy *(1 if automatic transmission is standard equipment; 0 otherwise)*	0.6523	0.6787
	(0.2807)	(0.2853)
Wheelbase *(inches)*	0.0516	0.0509
	(0.0127)	(0.0128)
Length minus wheelbase *(inches)*	0.0278	0.0279
	(0.0069)	(0.0069)
Fuel consumption *(in gallons per mile, times 10^4 for scaling)*	−0.0032	−0.0032
	(0.0023)	(0.0023)
Luxury or sports car dummy *(1 if vehicle is a luxury or sports car, 0 otherwise)*	−0.0686	−0.0558
	(0.2711)	(0.2726)
SUV or station wagon dummy *(1 if vehicle is a SUV or wagon, 0 otherwise)*	0.7535	0.7231
	(0.4253)	(0.4298)
Minivan and full-sized van dummy *(1 if vehicle is a minivan or full-sized van, 0 otherwise)*	−1.1230	−1.1288
	(0.3748)	(0.3757)
Pickup truck dummy *(1 if the vehicle is a pickup truck, 0 otherwise)*	0.0747	0.0661
	(0.4745)	(0.4756)
Chrysler manufacturer dummy	0.0228	0.0654
	(0.2794)	(0.2906)
Ford manufacturer dummy	0.1941	0.2696
	(0.2808)	(0.3060)
General Motors manufacturer dummy	0.3169	0.3715
	(0.2292)	(0.2507)
European manufacturer dummy	2.4643	2.4008
	(0.3424)	(0.3624)
Korean manufacturer dummy	0.7340	0.8017
	(0.3910)	(0.4111)

Utility that Varies over Consumers Related to Observed Characteristics: Elements of $\beta'x_{nj}$	Coefficient (Standard Error)
Manufacturers' suggested retail price divided by respondent's income	−1.6025
	(0.4260)
Vehicle reliability based on the *Consumer Reports'* repair index for women aged 30 or over *(0 otherwise)*[a]	0.3949
	(0.0588)
Luxury or sports car dummy for lessors *(1 if the vehicle is a luxury or sports car and the respondent leased, 0 otherwise)*	0.6778
	(0.4803)
Minivan and full-sized van dummy for households with an adolescent *(1 if the vehicle is a van and the respondent's household has children aged 7 to 16, 0 otherwise)*	3.2337
	(0.5018)
SUV or station wagon dummy for households with an adolescent *(1 if vehicle is a SUV or Wagon and the respondent's household includes a child aged 7 to 16, 0 otherwise)*	2.0420
	(0.4765)

(Continued)

TABLE 4

CONTINUED

	Coefficient (Standard Error)
ln(1+Number of dealerships within 50 miles of the center of a respondent's zip code)[b]	1.4307 (0.2714)
Number of previous consecutive GM purchases	0.3724 (0.1471)
Number of previous consecutive GM purchases for respondents who live in a rural location[c]	0.3304 (0.2221)
Number of previous consecutive Ford purchases	1.1822 (0.1498)
Number of previous consecutive Chrysler purchases	0.9652 (0.2010)
Number of previous consecutive Japanese manufacturer purchases	0.7560 (0.2255)
Number of previous consecutive European manufacturer purchases	1.7252 (0.4657)

Utility that Varies over Consumers Unrelated to Observed Characteristics (Error Components): Elements of $\mu'_n w_{nj} + \lambda \eta_{ns}$	Coefficient (Standard Error)
Manufacturer's suggested retail price divided by respondent's income times a random standard normal	0.8602 (0.4143)
Horsepower times a random standard normal *(divided by 10^4 for scaling)*	45.06 (72.34)
Fuel consumption *(gallons of gasoline per mile, times 10^4 for scaling)* times a random standard normal	−0.0102 (0.0020)
Light truck, van, or pickup dummy *(1 if vehicle is a light truck, van, or pickup truck; 0 otherwise)* times a random standard normal	6.8505 (2.5572)
Manufacturer loyalty: conditional standard normal as described in text.	0.3453 (0.1712)

NOTES: *Estimated coefficients for vehicle make and model dummies not shown.
Number of observations: 458.
Log-likelihood at convergence for choice model: −1994.93.
R^2 for regression model: 0.394 without retained value, 0.395 with retained value.
[a] The *Consumer Reports'* repair index is a measure of reliability that uses integer values from 1 to 5. A measure of 1 indicates the vehicle has a "much below average" repair record, 3 is "average," and 5 represents "much better than average" reliability.
[b] A dealership is defined as a retail location capable of selling a vehicle produced by a given division. The dealership variable is equal to 0, 1, 2, or 3 (with 3 representing areas with 3 or more dealerships within a 50-mile radius of the center of the respondent's zip code). This variable is defined for divisions (not manufacturers), because a Chevrolet dealership might sell Chevrolet vehicles without selling Saturn vehicles (GM manufactures both Chevrolet and Saturn).
[c] A respondent is classified as living in a rural location if he or she does not live in a Metropolitan Statistical Area or lives in a Metropolitan Statistical Area with less than 1 million people.

specifications of average utility; for reasons explained below, one specification does not include the retained value and the other does. The second panel contains the estimated coefficients for the variation in utility that relates to consumers' observed characteristics; and the third, coefficients for the error components, assumed to be normally distributed, that capture variation in utility that is not related to observed characteristics. Alternative distributions for the error components such as the lognormal did not produce fits as satisfactory as the normal.

TABLE 5

ESTIMATED PRICE COEFFICIENTS AND ELASTICITIES FOR MODELS WITH AND WITHOUT THE RETAINED VALUE

	Model without Retained Value		Model with Retained Value	
	OLS	IV	OLS	IV
Purchase price	−0.043	−0.073	−0.122	−0.106
	(0.0094)	(0.0192)	(0.0362)	(0.0635)
Retained value	–	–	0.130	0.055
			(0.0577)	(0.1011)
Average price elasticity	−1.7	−2.3	−3.2	−2.9

4.1. *Price Coefficients.* Consumers' response to a change in the price of a given vehicle is captured by an average effect, an effect that varies with income, and an effect that varies over consumers with the same income. That is, for the model without retained value, the estimate of the derivative of utility with respect to price is

$$-0.073 - 1.60/\text{consumer income} + 0.86\eta/\text{consumer income},$$

where η is distributed standard normal. As previously indicated, the first term is estimated using instrumental variables (IV); when ordinary least squares (OLS) is used the coefficient falls to −0.043 indicating that omitted attributes are correlated with price and that it is important to correct for endogeneity in estimation. Based on these coefficients, the average price elasticity for all vehicles is −2.32, which is consistent with estimates obtained by Berry et al. (2004).[14]

When a vehicle's expected retained value is specified as an additional explanatory variable, it appears to play an important role in controlling for the endogeneity of price. We isolate this effect in Table 5, which reports the coefficients for the purchase price and the retained value estimated by OLS and IV. Given that the retained value is derived from the purchase price, it is likely to be correlated with unobserved attributes of the vehicle and should therefore be estimated by IV. As noted, when we include price but not the retained value in the specification, the difference between the OLS and IV estimates indicated a considerable degree of endogeneity. But when we also include the retained value, it appears to absorb most of the endogeneity bias whereas the OLS and IV estimates of the purchase price are very similar. This finding suggests that unobserved attributes are correlated with a vehicle's retained value but not with the *difference* between its price and retained value (i.e., expected vehicle depreciation).

Note that the retained value represents about 60%, on average, of the purchase price (as measured by the MSRP) of a vehicle; thus, the combined effect, regardless of whether it is estimated by OLS or IV, of the retained value and price on

[14] The elasticities are calculated as the percent change in predicted market share that results from a 1% change in price, where predicted market shares are obtained by integrating over both observed and unobserved consumer attributes. A separate elasticity is calculated for each make and model of vehicle. The average given in the text is over all makes and models.

average utility is roughly the same as the effect of price when it is entered by itself. This relationship suggests that the model with the retained value effectively decomposes the two components of price to which a consumer responds. Moreover, holding retained value constant, Table 5 shows that consumers' response to price (i.e., the average price elasticity) is clearly higher than when the retained value is allowed to vary. The reason is that the retained value is determined by competitive used-vehicle markets; hence, if a manufacturer raises the price of a new vehicle without improving its attributes, the retained value will not rise proportionately and may not rise at all.

As expected, the separate price effects are estimated with less precision than the combined effect. Indeed, the estimated coefficient of retained value obtains a *t*-statistic of only 0.5, which suggests that the hypothesis that consumers do not differentiate between the two components of price cannot be rejected. Nonetheless, the pattern of estimates is consistent with rational behavior and a plausible form of endogeneity, and may have important implications for estimating the price elasticity that is actually relevant to firms' behavior. It therefore seems reasonable to maintain the concept of retained value as a potential influence among the set of vehicle attributes affecting consumer choice and subject it to further exploration in future research.[15]

4.2. *Other Coefficients.* The nonprice vehicle attributes in Table 4 enter utility with plausible signs and are nearly always statistically significant. Vehicle reliability, horsepower divided by curb weight, automatic transmission included as standard equipment, wheelbase, and vehicle length beyond the wheelbase have a positive effect on the likelihood of choosing a given vehicle, while fuel consumption per mile (the inverse of miles per gallon) has a negative effect. Note that wheelbase tends to reflect the size of the passenger compartment and therefore, as expected, has a larger coefficient than vehicle length beyond the wheelbase. Other measures of vehicle size, such as width and a proxy for interior volume, did not have statistically significant effects. We also performed estimations that included engine size (in liters), but it had a statistically insignificant effect.

Our findings that the (dis)utility of price is inversely related to income and that reliability has a positive and statistically significant effect on utility for women over 30 years of age but has an insignificant effect for men and for women under 30 exemplify observed heterogeneity in consumer preferences. Other examples

---

[15] The inclusion of retained value may alternatively be interpreted as an application of Matzkin's (2004) method of correcting for endogeneity. Retained value would qualify as the extra variable needed for Matzkin's approach if it is related to the price only through exogenous perturbations, but is correlated with the unobserved attributes of a vehicle. Under these conditions, the original error term may be expressed as a function of the retained value and a new error term that is independent of all explanatory variables including price, which would permit OLS estimation of the regression to yield consistent parameter estimates. As expected from an endogeneity correction, the OLS estimate of the price coefficient rises when the retained value is included in the model (compare the OLS estimate in the third column of Table 5 with the OLS estimate in the first column) and is similar to the IV estimate of the price coefficient (in the second column). We also estimated the function of retained value nonparametrically and obtained essentially the same results as when we specified retained value linearly.

are that consumers who lease a vehicle are more likely to engage in upgrade behavior by choosing a luxury or sports car than consumers who purchase a vehicle (Mannering et al., 2002, discuss this phenomenon), and that households with adolescents are more likely than other households to choose a van or SUV presumably to use for work and nonwork trips.

Unobserved preference heterogeneity is captured in error components related to vehicle price, horsepower, fuel consumption, and consumers' preferences for cars versus trucks (including light trucks, vans, and SUVs).[16] The last coefficient reflects greater substitution among cars and among trucks than across these categories, which is confirmed by our estimates of vehicle cross-elasticities. For example, we find that the cross-elasticity of demand with respect to the price of a given make and model of a van is, on average, 0.038 for other makes and models of vans, 0.026 for makes and models of SUVs, 0.018 for makes and models of pickup trucks, 0.0025 for makes and models of regular cars, and 0.0021 for makes and models of sports and luxury vehicles.[17] As expected, cross-elasticities are higher for more similar types of vehicles. We also found reasonable cross-elasticity patterns for the prices of other vehicle types. In contrast, a model that maintained the IIA property would restrict the cross-elasticity of demand with respect to a given vehicle's price to be the same for all vehicles; that is, IIA implies that the elasticity of vehicle j's demand with respect to a change in vehicle i's price is the same for all $j \neq i$.

Surprisingly, we found that, all else constant, consumers were not more likely to purchase a vehicle from automakers that offered a large (or small) number of models or that produced a "hot car." We explored various definitions of a hot car to construct its dummy variable, based on deviations from mean sales and sales growth, but they were all statistically insignificant. We also specified hot car dummies based on vehicle size classifications but they were also statistically insignificant. Although automakers cannot rely on product line "externalities" to improve their sales, we found that their dealer network does have a statistically significant effect on choice. We constructed the dealership variable by division as the natural log of one plus the actual number of dealers within 50 miles of the consumer up to a maximum of three. Thus, the variable takes on a value of zero if no dealers within the circumscribed area sell the vehicle. In addition, the functional form assumes that the impact of having one dealer instead of none is greater than the extra impact of having a second dealer instead of one, and so on, with the impact of additional dealers negligible beyond three. This specification

---

[16] These components were determined after extensive testing of a variety of specifications, including models that allowed the densities to depend on income and other variables. We were not able to identify any other statistically significant influences on the components beyond those captured in the fixed portion of utility (i.e., the mean of the error components). Recall that we could not identify significant error components without including data on considered vehicles, which suggests that the data contain limited information on the distribution of unobserved taste variation.

[17] To put the magnitude of the cross-elasticities in perspective, if a vehicle had a market share of 0.005 (i.e., the average share because there are 200 makes and models of vehicles) and had an own-price elasticity of –3.0, then the cross-price elasticity for each other vehicle, assuming it did not vary, would be 0.0151.

fit the data better than a linear specification, indicating that it is important for automakers to have a dealer within reasonable proximity to potential customers but that additional dealers will have a diminishing impact on sales.

Finally, we included separate brand loyalty variables for GM, Ford, and Chrysler as well as for the Japanese and European automakers as distinct groups. Preliminary estimations indicated that it was statistically justifiable to aggregate the Japanese and European automakers into single loyalty variables. We could not estimate a brand loyalty parameter for Korean automakers because only one consumer in the sample chose a Korean vehicle in his or her most recent previous purchase. The estimated coefficients are positive, statistically significant, and fairly large and the error component for brand (manufacturer) loyalty is statistically significant. We found that the likelihood function increased when we used the conditional distribution of η_n instead of its unconditional distribution, which indicates that conditioning provides useful information about consumers' choices.

When our estimates are assessed in the context of previous findings that use the same measure of brand loyalty as used here, it becomes clear that loyalties have undergone considerable shifts as consumers have gained experience with and adjusted to new information about automakers' products. Mannering and Winston (1991) found that during the 1970s, American consumers had the greatest brand loyalty toward Chrysler, had comparable loyalty toward GM and Japanese automakers, and the least loyalty for Ford. During the 1980s, after American consumers developed greater experience with Japanese vehicles, Mannering and Winston found that loyalty toward Japanese automakers exceeded loyalty toward any American automaker. But during the mid-1990s, as American consumers gained experience with certain automakers by leasing their vehicles and purchasing a greater share of light trucks, Mannering et al. (2002) found that American consumers developed strong brand loyalty toward European automakers and revived some of their loyalty toward American firms.

Our brand loyalty estimates indicate that this recent shift is intact because consumers have the strongest loyalty toward European automakers and loyalty for Ford and Chrysler now exceeds loyalty toward Japanese automakers. Of course, Ford's and Chrysler's loyalty coefficients may indicate that as their market shares have fallen, they have retained a smaller but more loyal group of customers. GM has the least loyalty and, in contrast to Ford and Chrysler, appears to be retaining only loyal rural customers as its share falls.

We stress that our interpretations should be qualified on theoretical grounds because the loyalty coefficients could also be capturing heterogeneity in tastes. We cannot resolve the theoretical debate, but we did explore additional empirical treatments of brand loyalty to shed light on the validity of our interpretation. In particular, if the phenomenon we are capturing were unobserved tastes for vehicle types, then it is likely that such tastes would be correlated with at least some of the vehicle attributes in the model. But, as noted earlier, when we performed estimations without a manufacturer error component and without including the brand loyalty variables, the other (nonbrand loyalty) parameters were nearly the same as those presented in Table 4. Of course, this exploration does not rule out the possibility that the loyalty variables themselves are subject to endogeneity bias;

but at a minimum it indicates that such bias does not affect the other parameters of the model, which is an important consideration when we assess the sources of changes in market shares.

5. ASSESSING THE U.S. AUTOMAKERS' DECLINE

The main purpose of the vehicle choice model is to guide an exploratory assessment of the ongoing decline in U.S. automakers' market share. As discussed in the introduction, several hypotheses that explain the decline could be derived from the academic literature and the views of industry observers and participants including changes in basic vehicle attributes, subtle vehicle attributes, unobserved tastes, brand loyalty, product line characteristics, and distribution outlets.

The findings obtained from the vehicle choice model narrow the range of possible explanations to vehicle attributes and unobserved tastes. The statistically insignificant parameter estimates for the product line variables and the apparent relative improvement in brand loyalty for Ford and Chrysler suggest that these factors are unlikely to have been a major source of the industry's loss in market share. Foreign automakers have improved their distribution networks over time, but U.S. automakers compete effectively in this dimension. Thus, we first focus on the impact of changes in basic vehicle attributes during the past decade on U.S. automakers' market shares and if necessary turn to less observable factors.

We use data on the vehicles offered in 1990 and their attributes to forecast the change in U.S. automakers' market share attributable to changes in vehicle attributes given consumers' tastes in 2000. Data for vehicle offerings and attributes in 1990 were obtained from *Consumer Reports*, Automotive News' *Market Data Book*, and *Wards' Automotive Yearbook*. Prices for vehicles in 1990 were expressed in 2000 dollars. By construction, forecasted shares equal actual shares in 2000 when the forecasts are obtained with the choice probabilities P_{ni} estimated in Table 4. These forecasts rely on δ_j for all j, including its unobserved component ξ_j. The values of the ξ_j's are not known for vehicles in any year other than that used in estimation. To forecast what market shares would have been in 2000 given 1990 basic vehicle attributes and offerings, we adopted an approach that is similar to that implemented by Berry et al. (2004). For any 1990 vehicle that was still offered under the same model name in 2000, we used the estimated value of ξ_j for that vehicle in 2000. For 1990 vehicles that did not continue into 2000, we used the average of ξ_j over 2000 vehicles of the same type (i.e., SUV, van, pickup, sports, and other) by the same manufacturer (with Japanese, European, and other manufacturers each grouped.)[18] By utilizing this procedure for the ξ_j's, our forecasts (and changes in shares) represent the impact of changes in the observed basic attributes of vehicles between 1990 and 2000 but not changes in

---

[18] We obtained an indication of the impact of this type of averaging of the ξ_j's by applying the procedure in forecasts for 2000, using the estimated ξ_j for 2000 vehicles that also existed in 1990 and using the manufacturer/type averages for 2000 vehicles that did not also exist in 1990. The forecasted share of U.S. manufacturers based on this procedure was 0.65625 compared with the actual share of 0.65650, indicating that averaging has little impact on forecasts of U.S. manufacturers' share.

unobserved attributes. As noted below, we explored two other procedures for treating the ξ_j's in our forecasts.

Market shares are forecasted for the 1990 vehicle offerings and attributes, thereby allowing us to compare consumers' 2000 choices with a prediction of what vehicles they would have purchased in 2000 had they been offered the vehicles (and attributes) that were available in 1990. A simple consumer surplus calculation based on the familiar "log sum" expression for the logit model indicated that all of the automakers (by geographical origin) improved the attributes of their vehicles over the decade. Thus, the change in U.S. automakers' market share predicted by the model reflects the *relative* improvement in their vehicles.

We find that the relative change in American manufacturers' offerings and attributes was responsible for the industry losing 6.34 percentage points of market share, which accounts for almost all of the 6.80 percentage points of market share that the U.S. industry actually lost during the past decade.[19] Our sample is not large enough to provide reliable breakdowns by automaker and vehicle classification; however, we can report that virtually all segments of the American manufacturers' products experienced some loss in market share. This important but disturbing finding suggests that although the American industry has received various kinds of trade protection for more than two decades ostensibly to help it "retool" and has benefited from robust macroeconomic expansions during the 1980s and 1990s, it continues to lag behind foreign competitors when it comes to producing a vehicle with desirable attributes. It is particularly noteworthy that the loss of the American industry's market share can be explained by changes in the basic attributes—price, fuel consumption, horsepower, and so on—that are included in our model, instead of subtle attributes such as styling and various options or unobserved tastes.[20]

We performed a simulation to determine how much U.S. manufacturers would have to reduce their prices in 2000 to attain the same market share in 2000 that they had in 1990 and found that prices would have to fall more than 50%. This large price reduction is reasonable because U.S. manufacturers' market share in 2000 is roughly two-thirds and the price elasticity with respect to a simultaneous change in all U.S. vehicle prices is small. (The price elasticities between −2.0 and −3.0 that we reported previously refer to the change in the price of an *individual* make and model of a vehicle.) Although it would not be profit maximizing for U.S.

---

[19] We also forecasted the changes in market shares using two other ways of handling the unobserved attributes of vehicles, ξ_j. In one procedure, we integrated the choice probabilities over the empirical distribution of the unobserved attributes. That is, for each vehicle we randomly chose a value of ξ_j from the values estimated for the year 2000 vehicles; we repeated the forecasts numerous times and averaged the results. The estimated change in market share for U.S. manufacturers was 6.71, which is even closer to the 6.80 change that actually occurred. Second, following a suggestion of Steven Berry, we used a variant on this integration procedure in which the correlation between price and unobserved attributes is incorporated. The estimated change was essentially the same as in the first procedure.

[20] We also forecast the impact of the changes in dealership networks that occurred from 1990 to 2000 and found that the change in dealership networks resulted in a loss of 0.5 percentage points for U.S. manufacturers. This predicted loss is very small, indicating that the relative improvement in foreign automakers' networks is not an important factor in the decline of U.S. manufacturers' share. However, combining this loss in share with the loss due to changes in basic vehicle attributes enables us to account for the entire loss of 6.8 percentage points that actually occurred.

firms to contemplate such a strategy, they have recently attempted to retain and possibly recover some of their market share by offering much larger incentives than foreign automakers offer. However, even this short-term fix has had little effect on their sales; as suggested by our simulation, the price reductions that would be needed to affect their share are considerably larger than those that have been offered. Indeed, despite offering incentives in 2005 that were as much as $3,000 per vehicle greater than the incentives offered by Japanese manufacturers, U.S. automakers' market share of cars and light trucks in that year fell 2 percentage points from its share in the previous year.

In contrast to the U.S. automakers, European firms' market share increased some 5 percentage points over the decade, partly because they intensified competitive pressure on the U.S. automakers by offering attractive entry-level luxury vehicles such as the restyled BMW 3-series. Indeed, European automakers achieved a net gain of 12 new vehicle models over the decade, whereas U.S. and Japanese automakers' net change was negligible. Japanese automakers gained roughly a percentage point of share as they expanded their presence in the higher (and more profitable) end of the market with various new offerings from Lexus, Infiniti, and Acura.

6. CONCLUSION

Concerns about the competitiveness of the U.S. automobile industry developed in the early 1980s when Chrysler needed a bailout from the federal government to avoid financial collapse and Ford and General Motors suffered large losses. Since then, the profitability of the domestic industry has fluctuated and its market share has steadily declined. Investors in the stock market, who are the most experienced and credible soothsayers of an industry's future, envision that difficult times lie ahead for Ford, General Motors, and Daimler-Chrysler as the sum of their current market capitalization is less than half the combined market capitalization of Honda, Toyota, and Nissan and less than Toyota's market capitalization alone. Toyota's consistent profitability has allowed it to invest in fuel-efficient hybrid engine systems for compact and luxury cars, and to take risks, like starting a youth-focused brand, Scion, thereby increasing pressure on other automakers.

We have attempted to shed light on the U.S. industry's current predicament by applying recent econometric advances to analyze the vehicle choices of American consumers. Notwithstanding these advances, we have been confronted with some formidable methodological challenges that necessitated some compromises. We have identified the advantages and limitations of our approach while setting the stage for future research.

We have found that the U.S. automakers' loss in market share during the past decade can be explained almost entirely by the difference in the basic attributes that measure the quality and value of their vehicles. Recent efforts by U.S. firms to offset this disadvantage by offering much larger incentives than foreign automakers offer have not met with much success. In contrast to the numerous hypotheses that have been proffered to explain the industry's problems, our findings lead to the conclusion that the only way for the U.S. industry to stop its decline is to improve the basic attributes of their vehicles as rapidly as foreign competitors have been able to improve the basic attributes of theirs. The failure of U.S. automobile firms to address this fundamental deficiency suggests that these organizations may be saddled with constraints that researchers and industry analysts have yet to identify.

REFERENCES

AIZCORBE, A., C. WINSTON, AND A. FRIEDLAENDER, "Cost Competitiveness of the U.S. Automobile Industry," in Clifford Winston and Associates, eds., *Blind Intersection? Policy and the Automobile Industry* (Washington, DC: Brookings, 1987).

BERRY, S., "Estimating Discrete-Choice Models of Product Differentiation," *RAND Journal of Economics* 25 (1994), 242–62.

——, J. LEVINSOHN, AND A. PAKES, "Automobile Prices in Equilibrium," *Econometrica* 63 (1995), 841–90.

——,——, AND ——, "Differentiated Products Demand Systems from a Combination of Micro and Macro Data: The New Vehicle Market," *Journal of Political Economy* 112 (2004), 68–105.

BHAT, C., "Quasi-Random Maximum Simulated Likelihood Estimation of the Mixed Multinomial Logit Model," *Transportation Research Part B* 35 (2001), 677–93.

——, "Simulation Estimation of Mixed Discrete Choice Models Using Randomized and Scrambled Halton Sequences," *Transportation Research Part B* 37 (2003), 837–55.

BOYD, J., AND R. MELLMAN, "The Effect of Fuel Economy Standards on the U.S. Automotive Market: A Hedonic Demand Analysis," *Transportation Research Part A* 14 (1980), 367–78.

BROWNSTONE, D., AND K. TRAIN, "Forecasting New Product Penetration with Flexible Substitution Patterns," *Journal of Econometrics* 89 (1999), 109–29.

CARDELL, S., N. SCOTT, AND F. DUNBAR, Measuring the Societal Impacts of Automobile Downsizing," *Transportation Research Part A* 14 (1980), 423–34.

GOOLSBEE, A., AND A. PETRIN, "The Consumer Gains from Direct Broadcast Satellites and the Competition with Cable TV," *Econometrica* 72 (2004), 351–81.

HECKMAN, J., "Statistical Models for the Analysis of Discrete Panel Data," in C. Manski and D. McFadden, eds., *Structural Analysis of Discrete Data* (Cambridge, MA: MIT Press, 1981a).

——, "The Incidental Parameters Problem and the Problem of Initial Conditions in Estimating a Discrete Stochastic Process and Some Monte Carlo Evidence on Their Practical Importance," in C. Manski and D. McFadden, eds., *Structural Analysis of Discrete Data* (Cambridge, MA: MIT Press, 1981b).

——, "Identifying the Hand of the Past: Distinguishing State Dependence from Heterogeneity," *American Economic Review* 81 (1991), 75–9.

HESS, S., K. TRAIN, AND J. POLAK, "On the Use of a Modified Latin Hypercube Sampling (MLHS) Method in the Estimation of a Mixed Logit Model for Vehicle Choice," *Transportation Research Part B* 40 (2006), 147–67.

LAVE, C., AND K. TRAIN, "A Disaggregate Model of Auto-Type Choice," *Transportation Research Part A* 13 (1979), 1–9.

LUCE, R., AND P. SUPPES, "Preference, Utility, and Subjective Probability," in R. Luce, R. Bush, and E. Galanter, eds., *Handbook of Mathematical Psychology, III* (New York: Wiley, 1965).

MANNERING, F., AND C. WINSTON, "A Dynamic Empirical Analysis of Household Vehicle Ownership and Utilization," *RAND Journal of Economics* 16 (1985), 215–36.

——, AND ——, "Brand Loyalty and the Decline of American Automobile Firms," *Brookings Papers on Economic Activity: Microeconomics* (1991), 67–114.

——, ——, AND W. STARKEY, "An Exploratory Analysis of Automobile Leasing by U.S. Households," *Journal of Urban Economics* 52 (2002), 154–76.

MANSKI, C., AND L. SHERMAN, "An Empirical Analysis of Household Choice among Motor Vehicles," *Transportation Research Part A* 14 (1980), 349–66.

MATZKIN, R., "Unobservable Instruments," Working Paper, Department of Economics, Northwestern University, 2004.

MCFADDEN, D., AND K. TRAIN, "Mixed MNL Models for Discrete Response," *Journal of Applied Econometrics* 15 (2000), 447–70.

PAKES, A., "Dynamic Structural Models, Problems and Prospects: Mixed Continuous/Discrete Controls and Market Interactions," in J.-J. Laffont and C. Sims, eds., *Advances in Econometrics: The Sixth World Congress of the Econometric Society* Volume II (New York: Cambridge University Press, 1994).

PETRIN, A., "Quantifying the Benefits of New Products: The Case of the Minivan," *Journal of Political Economy* 110 (2002), 705–29.

REVELT, D., AND K. TRAIN, "Mixed Logit with Repeated Choices: Households' Choice of Appliance Efficiency Level," *Review of Economics and Statistics* 80 (1998), 647–57.

SÁNDOR, Z., AND K. TRAIN, "Quasi-random Simulation of Discrete Choice Models," *Transportation Research Part B* 38 (2004), 313–27.

TRAIN, K., *Qualitative Choice Analysis: Theory, Econometrics, and an Application to Automobile Demand* (Cambridge, MA: MIT Press, 1986).

——, "Halton Sequences for Mixed Logit," Working Paper, Department of Economics, University of California, Berkeley, 2000.